Fighting Words

The BCSIA Studies in International Security book series is edited at the Belfer Center for Science and International Affairs at Harvard University's John F. Kennedy School of Government and published by The MIT Press. The series publishes books on contemporary issues in international security policy, as well as their conceptual and historical foundations. Topics of particular interest to the series include the spread of weapons of mass destruction, internal conflict, the international effects of democracy and democratization, and U.S. defense policy.

A complete list of BCSIA Studies in International Security appears at the back of this volume.

Fighting Words

Language Policy and Ethnic Relations in Asia

Editors
Michael E. Brown
Šumit Ganguly

BCSIA Studies in International Security

in cooperation with the
Center for Peace and Security Studies   **Pacific Basin Research Center**

CENTER FOR PEACE
AND SECURITY STUDIES
School of Foreign Service
Georgetown University

The MIT Press
Cambridge, Massachusetts
London, England

This book was typeset in Palatino by Wellington Graphics and was
printed and bound in the United States of America.

Library of Congress Cataloging-in-Publication Data

Fighting words : language policy and ethnic relations in Asia / editors, Michael E.
Brown, Sumit Ganguly.
p. cm.—(BCSIA studies in international security)
Project sponsored by the BCSIA Studies in International Security in cooperation with
the Center for Peace and Security Studies, and the Pacific Basin Research Center.
Includes bibliographical references and index.
ISBN 0-262-02535-3 (alk. paper)—ISBN 0-262-52333-7 (pbk.: alk. paper)
1. Language policy—Asia. 2. Asia—Ethnic relations. I. Brown, Michael E. (Michael
Edward), 1954. II. Ganguly, Sumit, III. Belfer Center for Science and International
Affairs, IV. Georgetown University Center for Peace and Security Studies. V. Pacific
Basin Research Center. VI. Series.

P119.32.A78 P54 2003
306.44′95—dc21   2002032162

On the cover: Two Uygur men have a discussion in a market in Turfan, China.

Contents

Preface

Ethnic problems are widespread, and their effects can range from merely debilitating to truly catastrophic. Although ethnic problems are influenced by numerous factors, they are shaped to a significant degree by the decisions and actions of political leaders and governments. Government policies must be taken into account if we are to understand the dynamics of ethnic problems and if we are to develop effective strategies for conflict prevention, conflict management, and conflict resolution.

With these considerations in mind, we ran a multiperson research project from 1995 to 1997 that analyzed the effects of a wide range of government policies on ethnic relations in sixteen countries in Asia and the Pacific. This effort led to the production of a large edited volume, *Government Policies and Ethnic Relations in Asia and the Pacific* (MIT Press, 1997). In 1999 we launched a follow-on project that took a more detailed look at government policies in one critical area—language policy. This book is the result.

This study analyzes language policies in fifteen key countries in South Asia (Bangladesh, India, Pakistan, and Sri Lanka), Southeast Asia (Burma, Indonesia, Laos, Malaysia, Papua New Guinea, the Philippines, Singapore, Thailand, and Vietnam), and East Asia (China and Taiwan). These country studies trace the evolution of government policies with respect to language issues, and they analyze the impact of these policies on ethnic relations over time. The book as a whole generates new ideas for thinking about language issues as well as policy guidelines and recommendations for the future.

A study that examines the complex forces that influence ethnic relations in fifteen disparate countries could not be written by one or two scholars working on their own in any reasonable time frame. We were able to produce this book relatively quickly because twelve distinguished scholars—Alyssa Ayres, Jacques Bertrand, Mary Callahan, Jyotirindra Dasgupta, Neil DeVotta, June Teufel Dreyer, Caroline Hau, Charles Keyes, Ron May, Amena Mohsin, Victoria Tinio, and Thaveeporn Vasavakul—drew on their wealth of substantive expertise and wrote country studies focused specifically on the issues this study seeks to illuminate. Their willingness to commit precious time and energy to the project's substantive agenda was critical to the success of this joint venture. We are profoundly grateful to these scholars for their participation in this project.

Four leading authorities on Asian affairs—Alasdair Bowie, Robert Hardgrave, Minxin Pei, and David Steinberg—took time out of their busy schedules and helped us review first drafts of the country studies over the course of a three-day workshop. Speaking for the entire group, we would like to thank these eminent individuals for graciously sharing their expertise and providing intellectual guidance at a critical juncture.

Even the most accomplished scholars need help turning their insights into compelling arguments and pristine prose, and orchestrating the production of a large volume is a truly monumental task. We were extremely fortunate because these pivotal editorial and production responsibilities were handled by Diane McCree. Diane worked on this project for more than a year—editing chapters, working with authors, generating proofs, and coordinating with more than a dozen people scattered across at least three continents. More than any other person, she is responsible for transforming a stack of draft chapters into a tightly constructed, reader-friendly book. This volume will have more of an impact on important real-world questions and it will reach a wider audience because of Diane's work on it and her contributions to it.

On the production front, Tom D'Espinosa and his staff at Wellington Graphics handled a massive typesetting job with great skill, and Celeste Newbrough produced a first-rate index in record-setting time. We would also like to acknowledge Maps.com, which produced the map templates that we utilized herein.

This project was conducted under the aegis of the Center for Peace and Security Studies (CPASS) of the Edmund A. Walsh School of Foreign Service, Georgetown University, and we would like to thank the many people at CPASS who contributed to this effort. Erin Roussin managed the budget and handled financial matters over the duration of the project. Jim Ludes and Mackenzie Eaglen handled the logistics for the three-day workshop at which draft chapters were reviewed. Alissa Elliott, Shubha Sastry, and Abha Shankar provided valuable research assistance. Christina Zechman Brown discovered Maps.com for us and, drawing on their templates, produced the maps herein. She also provided important administrative help in the project's final stages. We are grateful to one and all. Bernard Finel and Elizabeth Stanley-Mitchell provided institutional leadership for CPASS and organizational support for this project.

Another strong source of institutional support for this project came from the Belfer Center for Science and International Affairs (BCSIA) at the John F. Kennedy School of Government, Harvard University, and we are grateful to our colleagues there as well. Karen Motley, the executive editor of BCSIA Studies in International Security, the series in which this volume appears, helped us with many technical matters, large and small, as the book moved into production. Sean Lynn-Jones, the series editor of BCSIA Studies, supported this venture from the beginning and gave us good advice along the way. Steven Miller, the director of the International Security Program at BCSIA and the founder of the BCSIA Studies series, was one of the guiding lights behind our earlier book project (*Government Policies and Ethnic Relations in Asia and the Pacific*), and he has been a strong supporter of this project as well. His encouragement helped to get us started and keep us going.

For its generous financial support of this project, we would like to thank the Pacific Basin Research Center (PBRC) of Soka University of America. PBRC provided the core funding for our earlier project, and it provided the lion's share of the funding for this endeavor. We are deeply grateful to John Montgomery, the director of PBRC, for his inspiration, his enthusiasm, and his sustained support of these projects over many years. We would also like to thank Virginia Kosmo, the project coordinator at PBRC, for her assistance and patience.

Finally, we would like to acknowledge the United States Institute of Peace for its support of Šumit Ganguly's research trip to Malaysia.

Multiperson projects are elaborate, expensive undertakings, but they can bring exceptional intellectual resources to bear on critical problems. We hope that this project sheds some light on how ethnic conflicts start, how they evolve over time, and what well-meaning people can do to prevent, manage, and resolve them.

Michael E. Brown
Washington, D.C.

Šumit Ganguly
Austin, Texas

Introduction

Michael E. Brown and Šumit Ganguly

This book is based on three premises. First, ethnic problems are important policy problems. Very few countries are ethnically homogeneous, which means that most countries have to contend with ethnic problems of one kind or another.[1] These problems often have tremendous political, economic, social, and military consequences. They can disrupt political and economic development in countries that are struggling to advance. When ethnic problems turn violent, countries can be ripped apart, entire regions can be destabilized, and the humanitarian consequences can be staggering.

Second, language is an important issue in many ethnic settings. Language is a critical marker for many groups—defining the boundaries of the group and determining membership in the group. In multiethnic set-

---

1. One scholar estimates that at least 160 of the more than 180 states in the world today—roughly 90 percent—are ethnically heterogeneous in the sense that minorities constitute more than five percent of the total population. See David Welsh, "Domestic Politics and Ethnic Conflict," in Michael E. Brown, ed., *Ethnic Conflict and International Security* (Princeton, N.J.: Princeton University Press, 1993), pp. 43–60. Another scholar finds that almost 75 percent of the world's largest 127 states have politically salient minorities, even though he excludes groups that have fewer than 100,000 members or that constitute less than 1 percent of the total population of the country in question. See Ted Robert Gurr, *Minorities at Risk: A Global View of Ethnopolitical Conflicts* (Washington, D.C.: United States Institute of Peace Press, 1993), pp. 10–11. Still another estimates that approximately half of the states in the internationally system have to contend with self-determination movements. For details on 210 self-determination movements in 91 states, see James Minahan, *Nations without States: A Historical Dictionary of Contemporary National Movements* (Westport, Conn.: Greenwood, 1996), pp. 651–688.

tings, language policies have far-reaching effects in the educational, economic, and political arenas. Languages policies are therefore contentious issues in multiethnic countries.

Third, although ethnic problems and conflicts are influenced by a wide range of factors, they are shaped to a significant degree by the decisions and policies of political leaders and governments. Government policies must be taken into account if we are to understand the dynamics of ethnic problems and if we are to develop effective responses to these problems.

This book seeks to advance our understanding of these issues by analyzing language policies in fifteen key countries in South Asia (Bangladesh, India, Pakistan, and Sri Lanka), Southeast Asia (Burma, Indonesia, Laos, Malaysia, Papua New Guinea, the Philippines, Singapore, Thailand, and Vietnam), and East Asia (China and Taiwan). Each chapter examines the origins of different language policies, traces how these policies have evolved over time, and assesses their impact on ethnic relations on the country in question. The goal is to identify the various problems that language policies have encountered and the conditions under which such policies have successfully promoted ethnic harmony and ethnic justice. This leads to the development of policy lessons and policy recommendations for the countries in question as well as for policymakers who have to contend with these problems in other countries around the.

The comparative advantage of this study is comparative analysis. Books that focus on a single country, a single ethnic group, or a single ethnic problem will naturally be able to provide more historical and descriptive detail. Although depth has important analytic virtues, breadth does as well. By focusing on a common set of issues in a wide range of countries, this book has a strong empirical foundation for the development of analytic generalizations and policy recommendations.

Unfortunately, very little work in the area of ethnic studies has focused squarely on government policies.[2] Studies of language policy have tended to focus on single policy problems, rather than language policy as a whole.[3] Countless studies have examined language problems in single

---

2. One exception is Michael E. Brown and Šumit Ganguly, eds., *Government Policies and Ethnic Relations in Asia and the Pacific* (Cambridge, Mass.: MIT Press, 1997).

3. Leading studies include Joshua A. Fishman, Charles A. Ferguson, and Jyotirindra Das Gupta, eds., *Language Problems of Developing Nations* (New York: Wiley and Sons, 1968); Joan Rubin and Bjorn H. Jernudd, ed., *Can Language Be Planned? Sociolinguistic Theory and Practice for Developing Nations* (Honolulu: University of Hawaii Press, 1971); William O'Barr and Jean F. O'Barr, eds., *Language and Politics* (The Hague: Mouton, 1976); Trevor Conner, ed., *Education in Multicultural Societies* (New York: St. Martin's, 1984); Chris Kennedy, ed., *Language Planning and Language Education* (London: Allen

countries. What is missing is work that analyzes policy problems in an expansive, comparative, and prescriptive manner. We hope that this book will help to fill that gap in the scholarly literature, thereby making a contribution to the understanding of these important issues.

The Importance of Language Issues

Language is an important issue in many ethnic settings. Along with religion, it is one of the most common and most powerful ethnic markers.[4] Language often determines membership in ethnic groups, and it demarcates group boundaries. Language issues are often among the most contentious issues in intergroup relations because the stakes are high. To be more specific, language is important to ethnic groups for three main reasons: survival, success, and symbolism.

First, language is an existential issue for many ethnic groups because a lot of communities define themselves in linguistic terms. For these groups, language is not just *a* marker, it is *the* marker: It determines who is and is not a member of the group, and what the boundaries of the group are. It is the wellspring of group identity because it makes the group unique. In these cases, challenges to the continued viability of group languages are challenges to the survival of these groups as peoples. Challenges to group survival usually lead to political mobilization, and they can result in violent confrontation.[5]

Second, language is important because language policies have far-reaching educational, economic, and political effects. In multiethnic

and Unwin, 1984); William A. Beer and James E. Jacob, eds., *Language Policy and National Unity* (Totowa, N.J.: Rowman and Allanheld, 1985); Brian Weinstein, ed., *Language Policy and Political Development* (Norwood, N.J.: Ablex, 1990); Tove Skutnabb-Kangas and Robert Phillipson with Mart Rannut, eds., *Linguistic Human Rights: Overcoming Linguistic Discrimination* (Berlin: Mouton de Gruyter, 1995); and Harold F. Schiffman, *Linguistic Culture and Language Policy* (London: Routledge, 1996).

4.   Estimates of the number of ethnolinguistic groups in the world vary widely—from 3,000 to 9,000—depending on how researchers define ethnicity and language. See Minahan, *Nations Without States*, p. xvi; and Bernard Nietschmann, "The Third Word War," *Cultural Survival Quarterly*, Vol. 11, No. 3 (September 1987), pp. 1–16. For a discussion of the difficulties associated with the usage of terms such as "language" and "dialect," see "Introduction," Barbara F. Grimes, ed., *Ethnologue: Languages of the World*, 14th ed. (Dallas, Tex.: Summer Institute of Linguistics, 2000), especially pp. vii–ix.

5.   For different assessments of the prospects for violence, see William W. Bostock, "Language Grief: A 'Raw Material' of Ethnic Conflict," *Nationalism and Ethnic Politics*, Vol. 3, No. 4 (Winter 1997), pp. 94–112; and David D. Laitin, "Language Conflict and Violence: The Straw That Strengthens the Camel's Back," *Archives Européennes de Sociologie*, Vol. 41, No. 1 (2000), pp. 97–137.

countries, language policies can determine who has access to schools, who has opportunities for economic advancement, who participates in political decisions, who has access to governmental services, and who gets treated fairly by governmental agencies (including the police and the courts). Language policies can determine who gets ahead and who gets left behind. Language policies affect the prospects for ethnic success—for ethnic groups and for individuals in these groups.

Finally, language issues are important because people attach great symbolic value to their languages and how these languages are treated by other members of society. In multiethnic societies, languages are often situated in hierarchies: Some are informal social hierarchies; others are formal policy hierarchies. In some countries, some languages are elevated to the status of national languages while others have more modest stations. These hierarchies have practical ramifications, as discussed above, and they have symbolic ramifications as well. People want to be treated fairly by their government. When they are not, they are generally quick to mobilize. Language issues are often the driving forces behind ethnic mobilizations.

Five sets of language policy issues emerge in the country studies that follow. First, political leaders and governments have to grapple with contentious *national language* questions: Should a national language be established? If so, which language or languages should be elevated to national language status? What roles and functions should the national-language play in the political, economic, and social life of the country?

Second, political leaders and governments have to deal with thorny *minority-language* questions: What roles should minority languages play in the political, economic, and social affairs of a country? Should minority languages be phased out (through forced or induced assimilation), or should they be tolerated? Should minority languages be protected, nurtured, or even promoted? If so, how?

Third, political leaders and governments must make decisions on a broad range of difficult language and *education* questions: What languages should be used in schools? Which ones should be taught in schools? Should minority, local, or vernacular languages be used in primary schools and then phased out at higher levels? Will bilingual or multilingual programs be introduced and implemented? How should resources be allocated to minority-language education programs?

Fourth, political leaders and governments have to grapple with complex *regional* questions: Is it advisable to institute federal or quasi-federal frameworks that give political autonomy to different regions of the country? If so, should these regions be defined in linguistic terms? What kinds of language policies should these regions adopt? If regions are defined along linguistic lines, what kinds of language policies should these regions adopt toward their own linguistic minorities?

Finally, political leaders and governments must grapple with the advantages and disadvantages of *democracy*. Democratic processes often work to the advantage of minority languages because politicians have electoral incentives to use them in political campaigns; it is an effective way to win votes. Unfortunately, democratic processes also give incentives to politicians to pander to ethnic groups. This can lead to "ethnic outbidding" and the adoption of extremist positions.[6] What, if anything, can political leaders and governments do to structure these electoral incentives in benign ways?

The Importance of Government Policies

Scholars and analysts in the field of ethnic studies should pay attention to government policies for both academic and practical reasons.[7] First, although ethnic problems are influenced by a wide range of factors, they are often shaped by the decisions and actions of political leaders and governments. If we are to develop a comprehensive understanding of the origins and dynamics of ethnic problems, we must take government policies into account. They constitute an important part of the analytic equation. Second, if one hopes that the study of the dynamics of ethnic problems will ultimately lead to the development of strategies for conflict prevention, conflict management, and conflict resolution, then it makes sense to pay particular attention to government policies: Governmental decisions and actions are comparatively manipulable; they are easier to change than factors such as group histories and economic modernization processes, for example. Government policies are not infinitely flexible, but they are relatively elastic. This is an area where academic research could generate considerable leverage over important real-world problems.

Because the focus of this book is on government policies in the ethnic arena, we need to define several key terms: "government policies," "ethnic groups," and "policy success."

We define "government policies" broadly to include federal (national), provincial (state), and local policies. In addition to examining the

---

6. See the chapter by Neil DeVotta in this volume.

7. This discussion draws on Michael E. Brown and Šumit Ganguly, "Introduction," in Brown and Ganguly, *Government Policies and Ethnic Relations in Asia and the Pacific*, pp. 11–14.

formal decisions and actions of duly constituted governing bodies, we consider informal practices as well as patterns of neglect: Nondecisions and inaction can also influence ethnic problems, and they therefore merit attention. We limit our focus, however, to the decisions and actions (along with the nondecisions and inaction) of governments constituted in the countries in question. The activities of corporations (local, national, and multinational), nongovernmental organizations, regional and international powers, and international organizations are also significant, but they are beyond the scope of this book.

Because we think that there is value in looking at a wide range of intercommunal relations, we employ a broad definition of ethnicity. For our purposes, an "ethnic group" is a human population that has a name and thinks of itself as a group; a common ancestry, common historical ties, and shared historical memories; and a shared culture, which can be based on a combination of race, language, religion, laws, customs, institutions, dress, music, crafts, and food.[8] In this book, ethnic groups include both majority and minority communities, groups based on both linguistic and religious identifications, indigenous peoples, settlers, and in some cases, immigrants and migrant workers. We do not examine groups defined primarily by shared ideological agendas (political parties, for example) or economic agendas (labor unions). Obviously, ethnic markers vary from country to country, so groups are categorized on a country-by-country basis.[9]

Because we seek to distinguish successful policies from their less successful counterparts, we need to have a clear sense of what we mean by policy "success" and "failure." For the purposes of this book, policy success is defined in terms of two criteria: the promotion of ethnic peace, order, and stability; *and* the promotion of political, economic, and social justice.[10] The challenge for governments, of course, is to promote stability and justice at the same time. Authoritarian governments are often effective at maintaining political order (at least in the short term), but their methods leave much to be desired and they often do not get good grades on the "justice" dimension.

---

8. This definition is derived from Anthony D. Smith, "The Ethnic Sources of Nationalism," in Brown, *Ethnic Conflict and International Security*, pp. 27–41.

9. There is no simple solution to the problem of defining ethnicity and categorizing specific groups and individuals. Many people have mixed ethnic backgrounds and multiple ethnic identities.

10. Peace, order, and stability are relatively easy to measure. Political, economic, and social justice is not—and it is highly subjective. One benchmark is whether groups receive fair treatment under the law. Another is whether they have equal access to the political, economic, and social levers of power in the country in question.

Case Selection

To be comprehensive, a study of ethnic issues in Asia would have to examine approximately fifty countries. Such a study would be cumbersome at best and confused at worst. To make this study both more manageable and more incisive, we narrowed our focus to fifteen countries.

First, we excluded the countries of West Asia (the Middle East) because they deserve a focused, comparative study of their own. The same is true for the Russian Federation and the states of the Caucasus and Central Asia that emerged out of the collapse of the former Soviet Union in 1991. These post-Soviet entities became independent states only recently, and they face unique political, economic, social, and ethnic challenges. Afghanistan, which was occupied by the Soviet Union for most of the 1980s and in chaos for most of the 1990s, does not have a fully functioning national government at the present time. The situation there is too unsettled for this kind of investigation. Our focus in regional terms, therefore, is South Asia, Southeast Asia, and East Asia.

Second, we excluded countries with minuscule ethnic minorities. Our rationale for doing so is simple but compelling: Countries with demographically and politically marginal minorities have highly unusual ethnic settings and highly unusual ethnic problems. Studies of these countries are unlikely to generate lessons that would be applicable to countries with more complex—and more typical—ethnographic pictures. Japan, North Korea, and South Korea were not included for this reason.[11]

Third, we excluded countries that have idiosyncratic political systems or that are operating under highly unusual political circumstances. The rationale here as well is that it is difficult to draw generalizations that will have wide applicability from cases that are extraordinary. Bhutan and Brunei, two very small countries that are ruled by monarchies, were consequently left out of this study. Mongolia was under Moscow's thumb until the Soviet Union began to collapse. East Timor was a Portuguese colony and then was occupied by Indonesia in 1975; it became an independent state only in May 2002. Both were left out of this study as well.

Although this book does not cover the entirety of Asia, it does examine South, Southeast, and East Asia in a fairly thorough and systematic manner.[12] More important, the case studies in this volume examine a

---

11.   For more details on the ethnolinguistic composition of these countries, see Grimes, *Ethnologue,* pp. 538–540, 542.

12.   This is a fairly comprehensive set of cases, but it is not exhaustive. Good arguments could be made for including Cambodia and Nepal in this study. In the end,

wide range of ethnic settings, language policies, and political outcomes. This provides the study as a whole with a good empirical foundation for developing generalizations about these issues. Moreover, because these kinds of settings, policies, and outcomes are found in many countries in many other regions, we believe that this study generates lessons and recommendations that are applicable, not just across Asia but around the world.

Organization of the Book

This book has four main parts. The first three parts contain the case studies that comprise the heart of this volume. They are organized along regional lines, examining South Asia, Southeast Asia, and East Asia in turn. Most of these case studies focus on developments that have taken place since 1900 or, as appropriate, since the attainment of political independence. The fourth part of the book draws on these case studies to consider government policies on language issues from a broad comparative perspective and to develop some analytical generalizations, policy lessons, and policy recommendations.

SOUTH ASIA

The first part of the book focuses on South Asia, analyzing developments in India, Pakistan, Bangladesh, and Sri Lanka.

INDIA. Jyotirindra Dasgupta begins with the important observation that it is often difficult to describe the ethnic and linguistic settings in complex societies with a high degree of precision. Head counts and censuses are rarely simple, and they are often far from perfect. This is not just an academic matter: If policymakers are unsure about basic facts, it follows that they will have difficulty devising effective policies. India's ethnic setting is extraordinarily complex, and this makes India's policy successes in this area all the more remarkable. Dasgupta notes that the national-language issue has been handled with considerable sensitivity in India, although the track record is not unblemished. The process of creating linguistically defined states has unfolded in starts and stops over India's postindependence history. Fortunately, as Dasgupta explains, the policy crises that did develop were spread out over time and space; they did not converge into a nationwide emergency. Although the creation of linguistically defined states has helped to defuse some ethnic problems in

---

difficult decisions had to be made about case selection, given the practical constraints under which these kinds of studies operate.

India, it has generated others. The regional leaders who campaigned for the creation of new regional states have often treated minorities badly. The creation of linguistically defined states has on the whole been positive, but it has not been a panacea. In looking back at India's postindependence history, Dasgupta concludes that it is misleading to think of ethnic problems as inherently intractable and destructive. Ethnic problems can be dealt with effectively if conciliative, inclusive, constructive policies are implemented. India's encouraging track record suggests that well-intentioned leaders can make progress even in the face of formidable policy challenges.

PAKISTAN. The state of Pakistan was created when the British colony in South Asia was partitioned in 1947 along Hindu-Muslim lines. From the beginning, as Alyssa Ayres relates, Pakistan's leaders faced formidable challenges in their campaign to forge a functioning state. The most obvious problem was the country's territorial division into two separate wings, East Pakistan and West Pakistan, with the vast mass of India in between. Unfortunately, Ayres argues, Pakistan's leaders have mishandled the country's political and ethnic problems, making a bad situation far worse. The heart of the problem is that Pakistan's leaders have had an idealized image of a homogeneous Pakistan that has always been at odds with the country's ethnic heterogeneity. The decision made at independence to enshrine Urdu as the national language of Pakistan, even though it was spoken by only 7 percent of the population, set the stage for decades of ethnic trouble. Those who did not speak Urdu—including the Bengalis (who constituted 56 percent of Pakistan's total population and the vast majority of those living in East Pakistan) and the Sindhis (12–13 percent of the population of West Pakistan)—understood that this was not just a language issue: This policy would privilege some groups over others. Indeed, Pakistan has been run for most of its history by *mohajirs* (settlers who came to Pakistan after the partition), many of whom spoke Urdu, and Punjabi. Political and economic disenfranchisement, galvanized by the language issue, was the driving force behind East Pakistan's secession and the creation of the independent state of Bangladesh in 1971. Remarkably, Pakistan's leaders failed to learn from this catastrophic policy failure, and they have not made significant changes in ethnic and language policies in subsequent decades. As a result, Pakistan has continued to experience high levels of ethnic strife, particularly in Sind. One important lesson, Ayres concludes, is that ethnic problems should not be neglected; they will not solve themselves and go away on their own. Political leaders must make sustained efforts over time to address ethnic injustices and to ensure that government policies are not creating new problems along the way. In Pakistan, ethnic and language policies have been deeply flawed, and the country's ethnic divisions have intensified over time.

BANGLADESH. It is ironic that Bangladesh has also instituted and implemented hegemonic and chauvinistic language policies. Amena Mohsin contends that Bangladesh's leaders have been both hypocritical and shortsighted in their handling of ethnic and language issues. The country's leaders have been hypocritical, she says, because they have not stood by the principles they once championed. Throughout the 1950s and 1960s, Bengali leaders argued that Pakistan should be ethnically inclusive, that Urdu should not be Pakistan's sole national language, and that other languages (Bengali, in particular) had important roles to play in the life of the country. Since Bangladesh became independent in 1971, however, the country's leadership has pursued a staunchly nationalistic platform based on the promotion of the Bengali language and designed to create a homogeneous nation. The constitution declares Bengali to be the country's sole official language. Bengali is the language of instruction in government-sponsored schools. The government has made no effort to promote or even protect minority languages. Although Bangladesh's minorities are small—generally estimated to be 1–2 percent of the total population—Mohsin argues that the government's policies are shortsighted in addition to being hypocritical and unjust. They are shortsighted, she maintains, because people who experience ethnic discrimination and political marginalization are more likely to develop militant movements. Indeed, the country's non-Bengali peoples have rejected the government's conception of nationhood and the government's hegemonic policies toward minorities. An armed insurrection was carried out in the minority strongholds of the Chittagong Hill Tracts from the early 1970s until 1997, when a peace accord was signed. The tragedy, Mohsin observes, is that Bangladesh's leaders should have learned these lessons from their own unhappy experiences as second-class citizens in Pakistan. Instead, the formerly oppressed have now become the oppressors.

SRI LANKA. Language issues are important parts of the ethnic equation in many settings, but nowhere has this been more acute than in Sri Lanka. As Neil DeVotta explains, Sri Lanka's main ethnic groups—the Sinhalese and the Tamils—had cordial relations for more than 2,000 years. Unfortunately, this harmonious situation was disrupted first by British colonial rule, which favored the minority Tamils over the majority Sinhalese, and then by the divisive linguistic policies that Sinhalese leaders have pursued since independence in 1948. Motivated by a desire to win Sinhalese votes in a competitive electoral environment, Sinhalese politicians pandered to Sinhalese nationalism and embraced the view that Sinhala (the language of the Sinhalese) should be the country's sole official language. The passage of the Sinhala-Only Act of 1956 was a turning point in Sinhalese-Tamil relations. Tamil grievances subsequently grew because, in Sri Lanka as elsewhere, language policies had wide-ranging implications for educational and economic opportunities. By the 1970s many Tamil youth had become both radicalized and militarized: They favored the creation of an independent Tamil state, and they were willing to use force to attain their goal. An armed insurgency developed, exploding into open civil war in 1983. The war outlasted the twentieth century, killing more than 50,000 to date. DeVotta points to the important role that electoral temptations played in this process: Politicians had powerful electoral incentives to engage in "ethnic outbidding" and adopt extremist ethnic positions. Short-term electoral advantages were more important to these individuals than the long-term political health of the country. Political expediency triumphed over statesmanship. Sri Lanka's sad postindependence history shows how volatile language issues can be and how these problems can become more intractable over time. Perhaps the greatest tragedy of the Sri Lankan case is that the accommodative policies that one now finds at the core of most peace proposals would have prevented the outbreak of civil war if they had been implemented earlier on.

SOUTHEAST ASIA

The second part of the book analyzes the evolution of language policies and ethnic relations in nine Southeast Asian countries: Burma, Thailand, Laos, Vietnam, Malaysia, Singapore, Indonesia, Papua New Guinea, and the Philippines.

BURMA. Mary Callahan argues that, to understand ethnic and language issues in Burma, one must begin by distinguishing between "insider politics"—the struggle for power at the center of the country—and "outsider politics"—struggles between the center and the minority groups who reside along the country's periphery. She contends that, from the time of British colonial rule and continuing through the postindependence era, "insider politics" has dominated the country's political agenda. The country's elites have paid little attention to minority issues as a general rule, taking it for granted that the ongoing effort to promote the Burmese language as a national language and create a common national identity would succeed. They have taken it as a given that minority problems in the periphery would eventually evaporate. Minority groups, however, have not viewed the Burmanization campaign in benign terms, and some have engaged in sustained, armed insurrections. Against this backdrop, ethnic relations in Burma entered a new phase starting in the late 1980s. According to Callahan, the military junta that ruled the country for decades, fearing that pro-democracy activists at the center might forge an alliance with rebel minority groups in the periphery, signed cease-fire agreements with most of the latter. At the same time, the junta launched an intense campaign to assimilate and co-opt the country's minorities, initiating an array of educational and economic development programs in the periphery. It renamed the country "Myanmar," concocting an elaborate fantasy about the historical and cultural unity of the "Myanmar" people. Callahan observes that the junta may have unwittingly strengthened the hands of those who challenge its rule: By propagating the Burmese language in the periphery and facilitating contact between the periphery and the center, it will be easier for rebel minorities in the periphery to communicate with pro-democracy activists at the center.

THAILAND AND LAOS. Charles Keyes analyzes the very different paths that Thailand and Laos have taken in the development of national languages. In Thailand, a program to forge a national identity was launched in the late 1800s in response to European colonial encroachment in Southeast Asia; a strong state supported by a strong national identity was needed to resist European advances. The development of a national language—Thai—was one of the main pillars of that effort. According to Keyes, the case of Thailand shows how a strong central government can establish a national language if it engages in a sustained effort over several generations. Although many languages are still spoken in Thailand today, more than 90 percent of the country's population is familiar with Thai. Keyes argues that, with a national language now fully established, the country's leaders should make a more energetic effort to preserve the country's linguistic diversity. He notes that the advent of democratic political processes in Thailand may help to preserve local languages: Politicians find it expedient to use local languages in election campaigns.

The process of developing a national language in Laos has been more tumultuous. Keyes explains that, although the rudiments of a program to promote Lao as a national language were developed during French colonial rule in the 1930s, the implementation of this program was stymied by the civil war that wracked the country from 1954 until 1975. As Keyes notes, language policy was not a pressing issue while hostilities were under way. Although the war has ended, the government of Laos has been hampered by a weak transportation and communication infrastructure as well as a lack of resources. In addition, some minorities have resisted the institution of a national language. As a result, the government has had limited success in promoting Lao as a national language.

VIETNAM. Thaveeporn Vasavakul shows that, in addition to decades of war, Vietnam experienced tumultuous developments on the linguistic front in the twentieth century. Chinese and French, which had been used extensively, were pushed to the side. The Vietnamese language was transformed from a secondary vernacular language into a national language with a romanized writing system and a growing array of educational and social functions. Economic development, internal migration, and an increase in the number of ethnically mixed communities led the government to decree in 1980 that Vietnamese would be the country's common language, the study of Vietnamese would be compulsory, and bilingualism would be further encouraged. According to Vasavakul, a hierarchy of languages has emerged in Vietnam, with Vietnamese becoming the main medium of communication in the country and prominent minority languages being used as regional languages. Although the government has made an effort to preserve the languages of major minority groups (developing romanized writing systems for many minority languages), Vasavakul argues that this preservation policy is inadequate. She contends that passive preservation efforts need to be superceded by more active policies to promote minority languages.

MALAYSIA AND SINGAPORE. Malaysia and Singapore had common colonial experiences under British rule, but they have subsequently embraced fundamentally different conceptions of nationhood, which in turn has led to the implementation of strikingly different policies with respect to ethnic minority and language issues. Šumit Ganguly explains that Malaysia has adopted a conception of ethnic nationalism that has elevated and enshrined Malay privileges, with Bahasa Malaysia instituted as the national language. The country's Chinese and Indian communities have not directly challenged this policy, which has strong support among the majority Malay population. Even so, Malaysia faces a new, indirect challenge to its language policies as the twenty-first century unfolds: If Malaysia is to fulfill the leadership's stated goal of becoming a developed country, more Malaysians must become proficient in the English language. Changes in the country's language policies have to be considered.

Ganguly observes that Singapore's policies on ethnic and language issues provide a fascinating contrast to those of Malaysia. Following the country's split from Malaysia in 1965, Singapore's leadership has embraced civic nationalism and a vision of a multiracial, multicultural society. Even though speakers of Chinese dialects constitute more than 75 percent of the population, the country's leadership has accepted the Malay language (as Bahasa Malaysia is known in Singapore) as the national language and English as the de facto official language of the state. Every child in Singapore is expected to learn English as well as his or her mother tongue. These unusual policy choices were based on the leadership's recognition of the country's unusual geographic location in a predominantly Malay cultural region, its historic ties to Malaysia, and its strategy of economic development. Ganguly concludes that, on the whole, language policy in Singapore has been successful. The country's leadership has, against formidable odds, forged a common Singaporean identity in a predominantly Chinese city-state.

INDONESIA. Although Indonesia is one of the most ethnically diverse countries in the world, with more than 400 languages spoken across an archipelago of hundreds of islands, language issues have not been contentious in the country's postindependence history. Jacques Bertrand observes that, contrary to what one might have expected, language issues in Indonesia have not been politicized, they have not been a major source of intergroup tension, and the country has consequently not experienced much violent conflict over language problems. Bertrand argues that the policy of promoting Bahasa Indonesia as the country's national language has been the key to this policy success. Bahasa Indonesia has been accepted as the national language because it was used as a lingua franca by many people in the archipelago prior to independence and because it was seen as ethnically neutral. In addition, the government has implemented this policy incrementally, and it has extended official protection to local languages. Bertrand contends that the use of Bahasa Indonesia has been encouraged but not forced. It has been widely accepted, he says, because it has been seen as the language of both national unity and economic opportunity. Although Indonesia's overall track record in language policy is positive, Bertrand observes that there is nonetheless room for improvement. In particular, declaratory commitments to local languages have to be backed up by more resources; small ethnic groups need more support if they are to preserve their languages. Bertrand concludes that, if political leaders elsewhere adopt neutral linguistic positions, proceed incrementally, and eschew harsh, assimilationist policies, they might be able to duplicate Indonesia's policy successes.

PAPUA NEW GUINEA. R.J. May analyzes language policy in Papua New Guinea, the most linguistically diverse country in the world. The 4 million people of Papua New Guinea speak more than 850 languages, and the country has experienced considerable intergroup fighting since independence in 1975, but none of this conflict has centered on language issues. According to May, there are two reasons for this. First, Papua New Guinea's extreme linguistic fragmentation has dissipated the potential for conflict along linguistic lines. The country's ethnolinguistic groups generally do not seek to expand their linguistic domains, and none is large enough to imagine that its language could become the national language. Second, Papua New Guinea's leadership has decided against the adoption of a national language, recognizing that conflict would probably ensue if one lingua franca were chosen over another. The country's constitution says very little about language issues. English is widely used in government, business, and schools, and local languages are used in schools as well. May argues that, in sharp contrast to most governments in most countries, postindependence governments in Papua New Guinea have not developed a coherent language policy. It would be more accurate, he says, to refer to Papua New Guinea's "nonpolicy" on language issues. He contends that this "nonpolicy" has been a notable success: It has not placed added stress on intergroup relations, and it has provided a space for the natural development of Tokpisin, the most widely used lingua franca. May concludes that political leaders in other countries should draw an important lesson from Papua New Guinea's experience: A nonpolicy is preferable to a flawed policy.

THE PHILIPPINES. Caroline Hau and Victoria Tinio examine language policy issues in the Philippines, focusing in particular on the national-language project that has unfolded since 1935. They relate how the initial campaign to develop "Pilipino" as a national language was problematic because Pilipino was based on Tagalog, the language of a single ethnic group; non-Tagalog speakers objected to giving Tagalog such a privileged position. This campaign was modified in 1973, the new goal being the development of "Filipino" as a more inclusive national language. The 1987 constitution designated Filipino as the country's national language. Although Filipino's use has spread due to internal migration and its growing role in the mass media, Hau and Tinio contend that more could and should be done. The problem, they argue, is that English is still seen as the most prestigious language in the country's linguistic hierarchy; it is still perceived to be the language of power, and it is widely used in government and business. This problem is compounded, they say, by the government's bilingual education policy, which devotes resources to both English and Filipino. Unfortunately, the government's resources are limited, and the result is not bilingualism but "semilingualism" in which neither English nor Filipino is spoken with facility by a majority of the population. Hau and Tinio believe that the government should abandon this bilingual effort, teach English strictly as a second language, and devote more resources to the development of Filipino as a national language. This, they argue, would constitute the foundation of a more effective language policy for the Philippines.

EAST ASIA

The third part of the book examines East Asia. June Teufel Dreyer provides detailed studies of the evolution of language policies in both China and Taiwan.

CHINA. Language policies in the People's Republic of China have gone through several distinct phases since the communist takeover in 1949, with periods of ethnic accommodation alternating with ideologically driven crackdowns. Dreyer explains that the communist government's policies toward minorities were comparatively benign at first. The communist leadership had to consolidate control over a vast territory, and minorities resided in many strategic areas along the country's periphery. Accommodation was therefore politically expedient in the early years of the regime, and language policies were fairly tolerant of ethnic minorities and minority languages, at least on paper. The government's ethnic and language policies reversed course in 1958, when the Great Leap Forward placed a premium on ideological purity; Beijing's capacity for tolerating ethnic diversity diminished drastically as a result. The government's assimilationist initiatives generated a backlash and even rebellion in some minority areas. The leadership in Beijing consequently adopted a somewhat more moderate stance on ethnic and linguistic issues in the early to mid-1960s. This period of relative tranquility came to an end in 1966, when the Cultural Revolution launched a harsh attack on ethnic minorities and the use of minority languages. After a sustained, brutal crackdown, the official position toward minorities and minority languages began to ease in the early 1970s. Since the late 1970s, Beijing's desire for economic development has led it to embrace more liberal economic policies as well as relatively liberal policies on ethnic issues, including the use of minority languages. The rationale for the latter is that greater toleration toward minorities and their languages will stimulate economic production. The ideologically driven assimilationist campaigns of earlier decades were replaced by an economically driven agenda. Although this policy shift has helped to improve relations between Beijing and some minority groups, problems remain. Education levels are still low in minority areas, the use of minority languages in schools is still limited, and social instability in some minority areas has intensified. Dreyer concludes that Beijing faces a difficult policy challenge as the twenty-first century begins: It has to meet its now-established commitments to minorities and the use of minority languages while maintaining national unity and political stability.

TAIWAN. The island of Taiwan has been buffeted by intense colonial experiences and regional developments that have shaped the island's ethnolinguistic composition. Dreyer observes that, although European colonial rulers were mainly interested in trade, the period of Japanese colonial rule (1895–1945) was marked by a fierce and ultimately successful campaign to educate the inhabitants of Taiwan in the Japanese language. After Japan was defeated in World War II, Taiwan was administered by the Kuomintang (KMT, or Chinese Nationalist) government. When the KMT lost control of mainland China to the communists, the autocratic KMT leadership and 2 million followers fled to Taiwan, substantially altering both the ethnic composition and the political administration of the island. Dreyer relates that the KMT regime subsequently launched an ambitious nation-building campaign, forcing Taiwan's inhabitants to study, speak, and write in standard Mandarin. In contrast to the mainland, where policies toward minorities and their languages swung between harsh assimilationist and relatively accommodative alternatives, policies toward minorities and their languages in Taiwan unfolded in a more linear fashion. Dreyer argues that internal pressures for democratization combined with external pressures from the mainland led to a gradual "Taiwanization" of the island. As the country's political system moved away from the "hard authoritarianism" of the early postwar years, gradually becoming more democratic, the country's politicians found it increasingly expedient to embrace policies that favored linguistic diversity. Pressures from Beijing for reunification also led Taiwan's leaders to favor the development of a distinct national identity in Taiwan. The net effect of these pressures was that government policies increasingly encouraged the use of native languages. Dreyer believes that the worst of Taiwan's "culture wars" has past, but the country's ethnic problems have not been eliminated. The process of "Taiwanization" has created tensions between the island's ethnic groups; these tensions are most acute during election campaigns, when candidates make ethnic appeals in the hope of winning votes. Now that Taiwan has become fully democratic, the island's leaders will have to face up to the continuing challenge of managing ethnic tensions in a dynamic democratic setting.

GENERALIZATIONS AND RECOMMENDATIONS

In the book's concluding chapter, Michael Brown draws on these case studies, develops a series of generalizations about language policy and ethnic relations, and outlines a set of policy recommendations for political leaders who seek to prevent, manage, and resolve ethnolinguistic problems.

Part I
South Asia

Chapter 1

Language Policy and National Development in India

Jyotirindra Dasgupta

Language differences in complex multicultural societies raise a number of intriguing questions regarding the role of public policy in ensuring fair treatment of cultural claims and group rights. The fairness problem is particularly complicated in developing democracies due to challenges associated with the formative stages of authoritative institutions and political consolidation. The history of language policy in India is illustrative in this regard, offering important insights into the process of multicultural national construction in a democratic setting.

The purpose of this chapter is to analyze the role of India's public policy in dealing with the claims of different language communities in terms of their implications for national as well as regional development. The efficacy of language policy in developing countries is usually judged by its impact on national unity.[1] This is an unfortunate reflection of the centralist bias that drives theories of homogenizing nationalism to deprecate differentiated community claims.[2] This study, however, seeks to ex-

---

1.   Different perspectives on the relation between language and national development are presented in, for example, J.A. Fishman, C.A. Ferguson, and J. Dasgupta, eds., *Language Problems of Developing Nations* (New York: John Wiley, 1968); W.R. Beer and J.E. Jacob, eds., *Language Policy and National Unity* (Totowa, N.J.: Rowman and Allanheld, 1985); and B. Weinstein, ed., *Language Policy and Political Development* (Norwood, N.J.: Ablex, 1990). Several chapters in these comparative volumes deal with India.

2.   The homogenizing bias is discussed in C. Taylor, "Nationalism and Modernity," in J.A. Hall, ed., *The State of the Nation* (Cambridge: Cambridge University Press, 1998), pp. 191–218; and B. Parekh, "The Incoherence of Nationalism," in R. Beiner, ed., *Theorizing Nationalism* (Albany: State University of New York Press, 1999), pp. 295–325.

plore the connections and complementarities between differentiated cultural rights and democratic national development.[3] Its evaluation of the relative efficacy of India's language policy is based on judgments at both the national and subnational levels. This multilevel approach is particularly warranted in India's case because its constitutional design weaves together democracy and federalism in a complex institutional system that promotes national development as well as cultural rights and regional autonomy.

Independent India began with a nationalist agreement on the importance of reconciling the language sentiments of the country's major regional communities. At the same time, the importance of replacing the colonial language of administration—English—with an indigenous language was also generally recognized. The constitutional provision for the choice of Hindi as India's official language was carefully balanced by an allowance to keep English as an official language until non-Hindi speakers were willing to remove it. India's "official" language issues were complex. The Hindi-English controversy unfolded mainly at the federal level. Every state in the federation had the right to select its own official state language. Because many languages were spoken in most of India's regions, the constitution's framers wisely made special language provisions for large concentrations of minority-language speakers within regions.

These efforts, however, did not prevent the eruption of dramatic episodes of contention and even occasional violence over language issues. At the federal level, the issue of ending English's status as an official language was explosive during the mid-1960s. Hindi leaders' haste in attempting to make their language the sole official language enraged many non-Hindi leaders. The situation in Tamil Nadu turned violent for a brief period in 1965. The opposition was repressed in less dramatic ways in other non-Hindi states. By 1967 it was agreed that the dual-language policy would continue for federal business. The issue of regional language autonomy—expressed in terms of demands to redraw state boundaries along language lines—also took some dramatic turns beginning in the 1950s. Fortunately, these policy crises were temporally and territorially staggered, and these disquieting episodes never added up to a national crisis.

The creation of linguistically defined states in India was not a panacea, however. The rules of autonomy and group rights were frequently

---

3. For a case for differentiated rights, see W. Kymlicka, *Multicultural Citizenship* (Oxford: Clarendon, 1966), especially p. 26ff.; and a critical essay by B. Walker, "Modernity and Cultural Vulnerability: Should Ethnicity Be Privileged?" in Beiner, *Theorizing Nationalism*, pp. 141–165.

violated by the leaders of regional movements when they came to power. These same leaders often cared much less about language use—in schools, for example—than their dramatized devotion to community and culture appeared to suggest. Yet there is also an interesting story of strengthened democracy and increasing political mobility in class terms that is rarely captured by studies that stress the disruptive aspects of ethnolinguistic contention. These are some of the aspects of the Indian case that this study seeks to consider and clarify.

To limit the scope of this study, I focus on the following themes. Some basic features of the language situation in India are discussed to frame the landscape of communities, loyalties, and identities as well as realignments over time. Problems of analyzing the relevant connections and political transitions between language loyalty and organized demands are explored at the national, regional, and subregional levels. The objective is to examine the interactive relations between the associations and movements engaged in representing language communities or coalitions, on the one hand, and government authorities, on the other. A look at a series of episodes reveals the degree of institutionalization gradually attained by the policy system and its capacity to serve a multicultural society.

The domains of language policy can extend widely in a country as large and diverse as India. In this chapter, I concentrate first on the policy problems concerning the relative official status of contending languages at the national level.[4] This is followed by an analysis of language demands at the regional level and their connection with collective autonomy issues ranging from regional self-governance within the federation to separatism and secessionism. Another important dimension of language policy is the mode of collaboration among federal, state, and substate authorities directed toward the systematic development of language resources for generating communicative capabilities within and across language communities. This aspect highlights the special importance of minority language rights within regional state boundaries.[5] If the list of topics is long, its gains become apparent when we study these aspects as important elements of the interactive policy system involving changing authorities and publics over time. The linkages in the system

---

4. Various types of "judicial status" of speech communities are discussed in H. Kloss, "Notes Concerning a Language-Nation Typology," in Fishman, Ferguson, and Dasgupta, *Language Problems of Developing Nations*, p. 79ff.

5. See T. Skutnabb-Kangas, "Linguistic Diversity, Human Rights, and the 'Free' Market," in M. Kontra, R. Phillipson, T. Skutnabb, and T. Várady, *Language: A Right and a Resource* (Budapest: Central European University Press, 1999), pp. 187–222.

emerge from the constitutionally warranted processes of democratic federalism that determine the procedures of pursuing language rights and their policy treatment.[6]

This overview provides a useful context for understanding the role of language politics in the Indian policy system. It may be instructive to treat language politics largely as one mode of democratic representation of cases for recognition, mobility, reduction of group disadvantage, and inclusion. The advantage of a long view is that most of the movement's leaders, including many of the secessionists, have progressively become part of the government. Political opportunities for change, adjustment, and negotiation, as well as incorporation, have progressively legitimized the relevant policy system.

Finally, this account seeks to demonstrate that there is more to language policy than merely processing demands as they come along. Deliberate and anticipatory public action to develop language resources, and their planned use to promote social capability and the cultural status of relevant communities, may deserve special notice in a policy setting that has apparently inherited the political culture of the Indian nationalist movement.[7]

The Linguistic Setting

It is not easy to define the language situation of any multicultural society marked by a complex multiplicity of languages, dialects, sociolects, and other variations associated with speech communities.[8] Even a simple head count of mother-tongue speakers may not be easy because the definition of "mother tongue," as in the case of Indian census data, may vary from one enumeration to another. Other decisions, such as the choice of criteria of enumeration, may significantly affect the data on language of identification. India's 1961 census mentioned 1,642 languages;

---

6. These are discussed by E. Annamalai, "Language and the Indian Constitution," in R.S. Gupta, A. Abbi, and K.S. Aggarwal, eds., *Language and the State* (Delhi: Creative Books, 1995), pp. 24–27.

7. See J. Dasgupta and C.A. Ferguson, "Problems of Language Planning," in J. Rubin and R. Jernudd, eds., *Language Planning Processes* (The Hague: Walter de Gruyter, 1977), pp. 3–7.

8. Problems of describing the "language situation" are discussed in, for example, C.A. Ferguson, "National Sociolinguistic Profile Formulas," in W. Bright, ed., *Sociolinguistics* (The Hague: Walter de Gruyter, 1966), pp. 309–324. See also J.J. Gumperz, *Language in Social Groups*, papers selected by A.S. Dil (Stanford, Calif.: Stanford University Press, 1971), pp. 1–76.

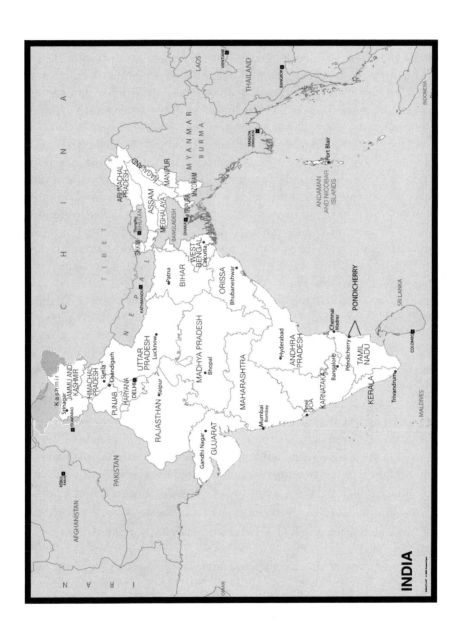

INDIA

in 1971 the figure reported was 221, and in 1981 it dropped to 106.[9] The numerically based distinction between major and minor languages can also be arbitrary in most countries, including India. However, most accounts of language situations use these categories along with one called "special languages," implying some hierarchy. India accords a special status called "scheduled languages" to 18 languages, including 12 that also qualify for the label "major." The other 6 scheduled languages account for less than 1 percent each of the total population.[10] Sanskrit as a classical language of prestige was included in the latter group, although it represented a negligible number of users.

Among all the languages in India, Hindi enjoys the highest numerical advantage.[11] Although it accounts for nearly 40 percent of the total population (1991 census), Hindi apparently needs wider support from other language communities to assume a leading position in national communication. No other language comes close to its numerical standing. (See Table 1.1.) Bengali (8.2 percent), Telugu (7.8), Marathi (7.4), Tamil (6.3), and other languages follow rather remotely in numerical strength. But a combination of some of these languages could hope to successfully challenge any unwarranted move for Hindi domination. Their countervailing strength offers a valuable assurance in favor of multicultural balance.[12] Relative proportions, however, need to be placed in proper contexts to yield reliable information about the meaning of language difference for policy purposes. Hindi itself is a composite name that covers a wide linguistic area, including hundreds of communities whose members are historically accustomed to reporting their linguistic identity by other names.[13] How these names are socially and politically recognized depends on factors that go beyond intellectual debates on the choice of labels such as "language," "varieties of language," or "dialects."

Decisions made by the federal census authorities in India can make a big difference in determining the definitions, boundaries, and strength of a language such as Hindi. Thus where the 1961 census, using a narrow

---

9. See L.M. Khubchandani, "The Eighth Schedule as a Device of Language Engineering," in Gupta, Abbi, and Aggarwal, *Language and the State*, especially pp. 34–35.

10. For detailed discussions of the scheduled languages, see the collection of papers in ibid., especially B. Mallikarjun, "The Eighth Schedule Languages," pp. 61–83.

11. Hindi, with nearly 500 million speakers in India and abroad, is the third largest language in the world.

12. See J. Dasgupta, *Language Conflict and National Development* (Berkeley: University of California Press, 1970), p. 33ff.

13. See H.R. Dua, "Hindi-Urdu as Pluricentric Language," in M. Clyne, ed., *Pluricentric Languages* (Berlin: Walter de Gruyter, 1992), pp. 381–400.

Table 1.1. Language Distribution in India.

Language	Percentage	Main Concentration
Hindi	39.85	Uttar Pradesh, Bihar, Rajasthan Madhya Pradesh, Haryana, Himachal Pradesh
Bengali	8.22	West Bengal, Tripura
Telugu	7.80	Andhra Pradesh
Marathi	7.38	Maharashtra
Tamil	6.26	Tamil Nadu
Urdu	5.13	Uttar Pradesh, Bihar, Maharashtra, Andhra Pradesh
Gujarati	4.81	Gujarat
Kannada	3.87	Karnataka
Malayalam	3.59	Kerala
Oriya	3.32	Orissa
Punjabi	2.76	Punjab
Assamese	1.55	Assam
Kashmiri	0.46[a]	Jammu and Kashmir
Nepali	0.25	West Bengal, Sikkim
Sindhi	0.25	[b]
Konkani	0.21	Goa
Manipuri	0.13	Manipur
Sanskrit	0.01	[b]

SOURCE: Center for Monitoring Indian Economy, *India's Social Sectors* (Bombay: CMIE, February 1996), pp. 101–105. For Hindi through Sindhi, see Government of India, *India, 1999* (Delhi: Government of India, 1999), p. 17.
[a]Approximate.
[b]Stateless.

definition, arrived at a figure of 30 percent of the total population for Hindi, a much broader concept pushed the figure to nearly 38, 39, and 40 percent in the 1971, 1981, and 1991 censuses respectively. (See Table 1.1.) At the same time, another national organization sponsored by the same federal government recognized some varieties of Hindi as literary languages.[14] The power of policymakers to categorize and enumerate in ways that serve them has had a major impact on the politics of recognizing the differences among Hindi, Hindustani, and Urdu.[15] These three,

14. L.M. Khubchandani refers to the case of Maithili and Rajasthani treated as "varieties" of Hindi for census purposes but recognized by the Sahitya Akademi (Literature Academy) as "literary languages," See Khubchandani, "The Eighth Schedule as a Device of Language Engineering," p. 35.

15. The use of categorization and enumeration as modes of control and domination is discussed in A. Appadurai, "Number in the Colonial Imagination," in C.A.

according to most scholars, are varieties of the same language. Hindi and Urdu are marked by a shared grammar and common core of basic vocabulary, though at the high end of learned use their lexical choices tend to diverge.[16]

Historically, in various uses, the term "Hindustani" came to represent a common area between the two. In the precolonial era, Persianized Urdu enjoyed the support of Muslim rulers. Early British rulers sought to polarize Hindustani along distinctly different lexical lines by making Hindi purge Persian words and pushing Urdu closer to Persian style.[17] Independent India's language policymakers elevated Hindi to be the official language of the federal and several regional governments. Hindustani was ignored.[18] Urdu's status became problematic. The situation was further complicated by political movements that advocated the use of languages and specific styles to serve religious mobilization for political purposes. The active role of political authorities and institutions in influencing the course of language identification, loyalty, differences, and possible contentions should be a reminder that it may be misleading to treat language interests as merely exogenous social or ethnic inputs for public policy.

Political Recognition and National Assurance

Intellectual concerns for language, including sophisticated treatments of phonology and grammar, have long been a part of India's cultural tradition. Literary works dating to about 600 B.C. bear testimony to such sensitivity.[19] The subcontinent became home to a gradual diffusion and interpenetration of many languages belonging to the Dravidian, Indo-Aryan, Aryan, Sino-Tibetan, and Austric speech families. Differences of

---

Breckenridge and P. van der Veer, eds., *Orientalism and the Postcolonial Predicament* (Philadelphia: University of Pennsylvania Press, 1993), pp. 314–339.

16. As H.R. Dua has put it: "Hindi and Urdu are grammatically almost identical . . . and they show some differences in their lexicon and in minor aspects of syntax." Dua, "Hindi-Urdu as Pluricentric Language," p. 390.

17. See M.A. Siddique, *Origins of Modern Hindustani Literature, Source Material: Gilchrist Letters* (Aligarh, Uttar Pradesh: Naya Kitab Ghar, 1963), pp. 17–42.

18. Mahatma Gandhi's strong advocacy of Hindustani appeared to work before 1947, but with the partition of the country his adversaries were victorious. Hindi narrowly won over Hindustani during the Constituent Assembly proceeding dealing with the official language issue. See Dasgupta, *Language Conflict and National Development*, pp. 136–137.

19. S.K. Chatterjee and S.M. Katre, *India: Languages* (New Delhi: Publications Division, Government of India, c. 1970), pp. 208.

language and culture became a normal part of the area's history. More than 2,000 years of interaction also helped to evolve certain significant resemblances.[20] This long passage to similarities has been frequently overlooked by those who tended to confuse difference with distance and insularity. Political observers favoring homogeneity as a nationalist value were too disturbed by the wide variety of languages to undertake any patient examination of common elements. Many perceptive linguists, however, were impressed by the common elements and had little difficulty in defining the subcontinent as a single linguistic area.[21] The historical processes of borrowing, among other things, across the major families of languages (subsuming most people of the area) clearly led to a cumulative emergence of common elements over a long period of time.

The modern emphasis on difference was promoted by the colonial administration in using all manner of diversity to highlight the improbability of overcoming social division. Even more than an aversion to multiplicity, there was also a colonial sense that indigenous languages were associated with poor communication quality; thus English was elevated to the highest rank for official, educational, and other modes of communication. But the colonial rulers never made the mistake of assuming that the regional variety of English gaining currency in India would be anything but substandard.[22] If a desire to dominate made the colonial rulers impose English on India, however, it was a desire to displace that domination that ironically impelled the first-generation leaders of the nationalist movement to demand the introduction of English for higher education and scientific work.

Leaders such as Ram Mohun Roy were persuaded that educated bilingualism (English for Western exposure and Indian languages for general communication) held the best promise for leading the process of national development. Roy, remembered for establishing English schools with his own resources about two decades before the official colonial introduction of English (1839), is also regarded as the father of Bengali prose.[23] Many such leaders were proficient in several languages. They in-

---

20. Ibid., p. 10.

21. For a discussion of South Asia as a linguistic area, see M.C. Shapiro and H.F. Schiffman, *Language and Society in South Asia* (Delhi: Motilal Banarsidass, 1981), pp. 116–149; and M.B. Emeneau, "India as a Linguistic Area," *Language*, Vol. 32, No. 1 (1956), pp. 3–16.

22. For examples of disparaging comments made by English observers, see B.B. Kachru, "English in South Asia," in T.A. Sebeok, *Current Trends in Linguistics*, Vol. 5, *Linguistics in South Asia* (The Hague: Mouton, 1969), especially pp. 627–628.

23. See S. Cromwell Crawford, *Ram Mohan Roy: Social, Political, and Religious Reform in Nineteenth-Century India* (New York: Paragon, 1987), p. 119ff.

creasingly became convinced of the compelling need for multilingual preparation, to enable a wider range of communication to reach larger segments of the multicultural society. Rather than stubborn hindrances, language differences were seen as opportunities to gain communicative competence to serve more regions. Aiding recognition of the plural base of the nationalist project was of course the fact that the leadership of the nationalist associations and their respective constituencies were unmistakably multicultural. Bengali, Marathi, Gujarati, Punjabi, Tamil, and other language-community leaders of the early phase of nationalism evidently needed an accommodative and inclusionary ideology and institutional system as much for their own mutual assurances as for national mobilization.

There was no single community of overwhelming size, and the resulting politics of multicultural accommodation fashioned by liberal nationalists turned out to be a source of strength and durability for the Indian National Congress. Beginning with its founding in 1885, it cautiously cultivated regional language communities and their resources for its sustenance and growth. To the best of such a large organization's ability, it set up codes of institutional conduct that ensured consensual decisions and regional autonomy.[24] The desire of the regional languages communities to manage their affairs was given a practical trial in 1921. The provincial units of the Congress were reorganized along language lines[25]—a bold move for its time. It put a premium on the notion of Indian unity as a democratic process of coordination of nationally nurtured regional sentiments and interregional collaboration.[26] But it also created a certain unease among some modernizing leaders such as Jawaharlal Nehru, who had apprehensions about the divisive implications of regional aspirations.

Language Status and Conciliative Policy

This survey of the long evolution of India's secular nationalist political culture suggests that the makers of language policy in independent India began with a valuable institutional resource. The framing of the Indian

---

24. B. Chandra, *India's Struggle for Independence* (New Delhi: Penguin, 1989), p. 75ff.

25. S. Chitnis, "Towards a New Social Order," in B.N. Pande, ed., *A Centenary History of the Indian National Congress (1885–1985)* (New Delhi: All India Congress Committee, 1990), p. 370. At the same time, the importance of the regional languages in national and provincial communication was recognized by the organization.

26. See C.A. Bayly, *Origins of Nationalism in South Asia* (Delhi: Oxford University Press, 1998), especially p. 116ff.

constitution was crucially aided by the overwhelming majority of the Congress Party in the Constituent Assembly. The partition of the subcontinent strengthened the role of the party in crafting a federal system marked by an absence of profoundly divisive expressions of regional interests.[27] There were disagreements, to be sure, but the flexible opportunities for change appeared to assure the contending advocates of language-based interests that the institutional rules were not arrayed against the differentiated rights of regions or cultural groups. The conciliative tone of the language provisions of the constitution, not surprisingly, reflected an important institutional inheritance that may be significant for an understanding of the conflict over the relative status of languages and the policy outcomes in the formative years of the nation and later.

Given the multiplicity of languages in India, it was not easy to choose a language such as Hindi, with a plurality of 40 percent, as the national language. But the concept of official language at the union (federal) government level was considerably narrower in scope.[28] As a result of sensitivity to the sentiments of the non-Hindi language communities, Hindi was constitutionally allocated the role of federal language only for official and formal communication.[29] English continued to be used as an authorized associated language, subject to periodic renewal by parliament. The proceedings of the Supreme Court and high courts, and bills and acts for either house of parliament, were permitted to be in English.[30] The constitution adopted in 1949 was in English. The Hindi version was authorized, after a long delay, in 1987. In case of any divergence of meaning between the two texts, the Hindi version would be subject to revision.[31]

During the past five decades, there was rarely massive discontent at the federal level from either Hindi or non-Hindi blocs. In 1965 there was a brief moment of grave apprehension, mainly on the part of some southern anti-Hindi organizations, that the use of English as an associate lan-

---

27.   These founding moments of agreement are discussed in G. Austin, *The Indian Constitution: Cornerstone of a Nation* (Oxford: Clarendon, 1966), p. 186ff. Austin has discussed the working of the federal provisions in his *Working a Democratic Constitution: The Indian Experience* (New Delhi: Oxford University Press, 1999), especially p. 565ff.

28.   An official language is for governmental, administrative, or formal state-related communication for the specific level of government (federal or regional). A national language may refer to much wider ranges of national communication.

29.   Article 343. See *Constitution of India*, with selective comments by P.M. Bakshi (Delhi: Universal Law Publishing, 1998), p. 270.

30.   Article 348. See ibid., p. 271.

31.   See D.D. Basu, *Introduction to the Constitution of India* (New Delhi: Prentice Hall of India, 1999), p. 391.

guage was about to be withdrawn. Some inept and hasty moves by the federal government clearly justified these apprehensions.[32] Public agitation and the subsequent response from the federal policy authorities led to stronger legal and political assurances that restored the multicultural balance.[33] The interactive process that brought about the solution involved negotiation among several political parties of different cultural and ideological persuasions at both federal and regional levels. The larger among these parties derived support from a number of language communities. Like the ruling Congress Party at the federal level in 1965, some of the opposition parties, irrespective of their stand on the Hindi dominance issue, were not inclined to take uncompromising positions for fear of losing support from diverse bases.[34] This compulsion to compromise based on the very nature of multicultural support proved to be highly beneficial for maintaining the conciliative and institutional system, even at moments of extreme stress.

Federal language policy, however, should be placed in the wider context of regional policy concerning the official language of states in the union. In India, life for most people takes place in the regional states, with little reference to what goes on at the federal level. Communication among the rural population in West Bengal, for example, hardly calls for any language other than Bengali. Out of twenty-five states in the union, with the exception of six Hindi-speaking states, most states have a similar situation in relation to their regional language. The status of official language for the major regional languages may be of greater importance for the people of all these states, including the Hindi-speaking states.[35]

This offers political assurance to the regional language communities that their languages enjoy a constitutional standing and an autonomous political space of dignity. The official language policy for the states as specified in the constitution is somewhat different from its federal counterpart. The states "may" adopt "any one or more" of the languages in

---

32. These and related developments are discussed in Dasgupta, *Language Conflict and National Development*, p. 236ff.

33. Ibid., p. 255ff.

34. In fact, the most stressful moments for the policy system were contributed mainly by the rigidities of parties that had only a single language-community support base. See ibid., pp. 257ff.

35. Indeed, because the Hindi states, on average, have lower levels of literacy and urbanization, the importance of regional Hindi or even some varieties may be more relevant. In general, for most of the states, the overwhelming importance of agriculture and rural life is likely to call for a greater relevance of regional languages, official or otherwise.

use in the state or Hindi as the official language or languages.[36] (At the federal level, this clause is phrased as an imperative.) But this flexibility may be useful in allowing the political recognition of minority languages within the states. Many states in the federation contain many languages and cultures, so that in different areas of a state there may be a need for special functional recognition of a language's importance for education and administration. This substate recognition, limited in area and function, needs to be distinguished from a statewide status for a second official language in response to the demands of a large minority group.

Some interesting issues of national allocation of status were raised by the framers of the Indian constitution when they included a list of fourteen languages (subsequently expanded to include eighteen [Table 1.1]) that Indian leaders and official documents have treated as "national languages" or "major languages," or otherwise given an honorific national status.[37] The list includes Hindi and other languages of the major speech communities of the country. It also includes a classical language, Sanskrit, which is rarely spoken, and Sindhi, which is not connected with any state in particular. Six of the included languages account for less than 1 percent each of the nation's population. Some unlisted languages such as Bhili and Santali claim more than four times the speakers than Manipuri (a listed language) claimed in the 1991 census.[38] Most of these listed languages are also regarded as official languages of states, though a few are not. The criteria for inclusion or exclusion are confusing; what is clear is that access to the privileged list is influenced more by political support than either numbers of speakers or the literary heritage of a language.

Together the national languages account for more than 96 percent of the population. Inclusion in this recognized category brings a number of benefits besides national prestige to these languages and their speakers. These languages are supposed to be sources from which Hindi might draw elements for its development and broadening, to serve as a composite language for a wider range of communication. In practice, moves in this direction have yielded little.[39] The expectation that a broader ver-

---

36.　Article 345. See *Constitution of India*, p. 271.

37.　The *Report of the Committee on Emotional Integration* concedes these languages the "status of national languages" (Delhi: Manager of Publications, 1962), p. 51.

38.　B.H. Krishnamurti, "Official Language Policies with Special Reference to the Eighth Schedule of the Constitution of India," in Gupta, Abbi, and Aggarwal, *Language and the State*, p. 15.

39.　For a negative appraisal, see D.P. Pattanayak, "The Eighth Schedule: A Linguistic Perspective," in ibid., pp. 49–55.

sion of Hindi would gradually serve as a "link language" has not been realized. The language development programs funded by the federal government have nonetheless been beneficial for all specially recognized languages. In any event, the national recognition seems to reflect multi-cultural sensitivity and access that may be counted as a joint gain for the communities and the policy system.

Language Loyalty, Regional Identity, and Political Autonomy

Language differences or language loyalties are not likely to pose problems for national policymakers unless there are compelling campaigns to use them in public spaces for realizing certain community objectives. Language as a sign of identity enjoys certain advantages in multicultural India. Unlike religion, India's major language groups often have regional distribution that yields an easier negotiating ground for autonomy claims.[40] In India some regional languages extend over a population size or territory that matches that of the larger states of the world.[41] This extension can enable language to play the role of a unifier of smaller subregional groups divided by caste, religion, faction, or location. The idea that language is primarily divisive in a multicultural society often prevents an appreciation of its strategic integrative role within broad regional boundaries.

For example, leaders of the nationalist movement used language as a resource for mass mobilization against colonial rule and discrimination. From the second quarter of the nineteenth century, a network of voluntary associations in different regions of India campaigned for the use of Indian languages for newspapers, general publishing, and instruction in schools.[42] The leaders of these associations had their own political and cultural differences, but they all seemed to agree on the need to promote a sense of pride in regional languages, as opposed to the colonial language. At the same time, many of them were eager to popularize one or another Indian language as a link for interregional communication and national mobilization.

---

40.   Hindu, Muslim, and Christian groups are dispersed across most of the regions and languages of the country. The Sikh community is mainly Punjabi speaking, but Punjabi speakers are distributed over a number of religious groups. In prepartition India, as in contemporary Pakistan, most Punjabi speakers were Muslims. Urdu is spread over a wide variety of regions. Hindi is spoken over six contiguous states.

41.   Uttar Pradesh, one of the Hindi-speaking states, alone claims a population of 139 million (1991 count).

42.   Note the roles of the Brahmo Samaj and Arya Samaj movements in different regions of India.

Contrary to the presumption of the academic literature about what is often dismissively called "linguism," many prominent leaders from non-Hindi regions favored elevating Hindi to a national role.[43] Many Bengali writers and administrators working in Hindi-speaking Bihar were distressed by the colonial mistreatment of Hindi in the area. Their initiative led to the introduction of Hindi in the law courts and schools of Bihar by the closing decades of the nineteenth century.[44] Later, the support of B.G. Tilak (Marathi) and Subhas Chandra Bose (Bengali), and above all the relentless efforts of Mahatma Gandhi (Gujarati), significantly strengthened the case for Hindi's national role.[45] But this multicultural support for Hindi came with the expectation that it would widen itself to reduce the stylistic distance from the Hindustani and Urdu varieties and be receptive to influences from other Indian languages.[46] Whatever the problems of defining Hindi's composition, the promise of breadth allowed the language to become independent India's federal official language.

Equally interesting was the preindependence nationalist movement's recognition of autonomy rights for language communities within a democratic federal constitutional system. As the moment of independence came closer, there was lessened agreement about how to put this recognition into policy practice. Fortunately, the constitutional provisions relevant to autonomy issues were left flexible. The burden of deciding the degree of autonomy that would be acceptable to both regional representatives and national policy authorities was left to an interactive system of negotiation legitimated by the basic design of the federal system. The federal government was supposed to play an important leadership role consistent with the transitional needs of a developing polity. The partition of

---

43.   They included Kashub Chandra Sen of Brahmo Samaj and Dayananda Saraswati of Arya Samaj, who were (mother tongue) Bengali and Gujarati speakers respectively. For different uses of the term "linguism," see G. Myrdal, *Asian Drama*, Vol. 1 (New York: Pantheon, 1968), p. 87; and R.J.L. Breton, *Atlas of the Languages and Ethnic Communities of South Asia* (Walnut Creek, Calif.: Altamira, 1997).

44.   See N.K. Bose, *Modern Bengal* (Calcutta: Vidyo Daya, 1959), p. 81.

45.   See L.K. Verma, ed., *Hindi Andolan* (Allahabad, Uttar Pradesh: Hindi Sahitya Sammelan, 1964) (in Hindi), pp. 23, 32, and passim. See also M.K. Gandhi, *Thoughts on National Language* (Ahmedabad, Gujarat: Navajivan, 1956), pp. 3–4.

46.   In fact, it was more than just an expectation. Article 351 of the constitution makes it "the duty of the Union to promote the spread of the Hindi language, to develop it so that it may serve as a medium of expression for all the elements of the composite culture of India and to secure its enrichment by assimilating . . . the forms, style and expressions used in Hindustani and in the other languages of India specified in the Eighth Schedule." *Constitution of India*, p. 273.

the country and the extensive disorder associated with this traumatic event called for the primacy of order in a new India after 1947. But this stabilizing imperative, fortunately, did not allow the federal government to dictate the time or the terms of reorganization of the constituent states.

Some leaders such as Nehru were more concerned with central administration guidance than the logic of nurturing regional community resources to develop a system of voluntary allegiance to build sustainable unity.[47] The ruling Congress Party, despite its early endorsement of regional autonomy, asked for moderation when reorganization demands were made in the early founding years. But it did not prevent—though it could have—the constitution from giving the parliament enough formal powers to reorganize the states.[48] The colonial legacy of princely states, and the arbitrary organization of major provinces that lumped together language and cultural communities, placed a heavy burden on the postindependence federal system in India. There was widespread recognition of the need for administrative reorganization.

The idea of reorganizing the entire territory into regional communities based on cultural identity and solidarity—mostly expressed in terms of language—seemed to make eminent sense in most parts of India with a territorial concentration of population associated with the major languages. Each of these regional language areas, however, also contained large minorities, some of which were connected with majorities in other states.[49] In some small states, the population was highly fragmented in terms of language identity, but cultural ties or tribal affinity could be expected to offer some sort of base for political unity.[50] In other words, even assuming all the reasonableness of language or cultural ties as a basis for forming autonomous communities, some significant ambiguities persisted. Despite the popularity of cultural autonomy claims, and the justifications advanced by cultural activists, such claims were rarely

47.   Nehru's reservations are discussed in R.D. King, *Nehru and the Language Politics of India* (Delhi: Oxford University Press, 1997), pp. 108–109.

48.   Articles 3 along with 2 and 4 of the constitution read together with the fundamental rights would suggest that the reorganization powers are extensive and that democratic demands for reorganization are legitimate. See J. Bondurant, *Regionalism versus Provincialism: A Study in the Problem of Indian National Unity* (Berkeley, Calif.: Institute of International Studies, 1958), p. 27.

49.   Consider, for example, the connection of Bengali speakers as minorities in Assam with the Bengali majority in the state of West Bengal.

50.   For example, in the case of some smaller northeastern states such as Nagaland, the leading Ao language (in number) accounted for only 13 percent of the population; it was followed by Sema with 12 percent and Konyak with 11 percent (1981 census).

judged in terms of the problems of hegemonic domination and homogenizing propensities of the dominant groups.[51]

Regional Language Communities and State Reorganization

Responding to the demands for the reorganization of states along the lines of language communities was not easy. The ruling Congress Party leaders cautiously attempted to use expert committees to lend a measure of legitimacy to a policy of indefinitely delaying the process of conceding autonomy.[52] Although the party had a comfortable parliamentary majority, it needed to create an impression of conducting policy matters of wide multicultural significance in a nonpartisan manner. At the same time, the domination of leaders such as Nehru within the party was used to keep the regional party units in line and to make sure that dissidents did not form any alliance with the opposition parties that wanted to expedite reorganization. But language loyalties proved to be a grand resource for the opposition parties to use to build popular coalitions for large-scale autonomy movements.

By 1951, for example, a strong movement for the formation of a separate Andhra state for Telugu speakers gained ground. There was so persuasive a case for separating Telugu speakers from Tamil speakers in the massive Madras state that even Nehru had earlier conceded it.[53] The opposition parties that led the successful movement for a new state in 1953 had national as well as socialist credentials. The lapses of the Congress Party and the ruling policy system did not push the movement to exclusivist ethnic separatism or secessionism. Instead, the use of a broad-based movement to correct the policy incompetence and leadership lag at a crucial phase in the development of a federal system contributed to reconstructing the policy system. Moreover, when the new state was enlarged in 1956 to include the Telangana area to form Andhra Pradesh, some interesting socially integrative dimensions to language movements for autonomy were revealed.[54] In this case, the language movement brought

---

51.   A perceptive discussion of these problems is in Walker, "Modernity and Cultural Vulnerability," especially p. 145ff.

52.   For a concise history of the reorganization process, see B. Chandra, *India after Independence* (New Delhi: Viking, 1999), pp. 98–130.

53.   Nehru had stated in late 1947 that the Andhra demand was "perfectly legitimate." Later he changed his mind after some wavering. See King, *Nehru and the Language Politics of India*, p. 108.

54.   A useful account of the pertinent developments is offered in P.R. Rao, "Post-independence Era," in C.S. Rao, ed., *History and Culture of the Andhras* (Hyderabad: Telugu University, 1995), pp. 139–148.

together Telugu speakers of all social levels of Madras and Hyderabad in a large community of cultural and administrative unity.

There was increasing evidence that this movement, based on language loyalty, was able to progressively incorporate lower-status groups in the political process. The mobilization of peasant groups was of course facilitated by radical leaders of communist and socialist groups. Within two years, successive elections (1955 midterm and 1957) helped the Congress Party to return to power. In the course of these electoral battles, the Congress Party was able to cut into the peasant support bases of the communists and their allies and head for a new and broader alignment of forces in favor of the country's largest and oldest national political party. The gains of the language movement thus helped to deepen democratic processes. These inclusionary policy successes and the responses they evoked from public institutions do not reflect the tone of the alarmist literature of ethnopolitics or ethnofederalism.[55]

Andhra's achievement of statehood based on language was followed by a wave of demands for autonomy by other language communities. Once again, the first policy response was to set up a body of experts to "dispassionately" examine reorganization issues. The leaders of the federal government were eager to tame community passions by letting experts remind civic leaders of the virtues of economic and administrative rationality within existing state boundaries. The States Reorganization Commission was appointed in 1953 to make recommendations regarding broad principles used to determine reorganization and also to suggest lines along which particular states were to be reorganized.[56] The commission worked for two years, holding public hearings and considering thousands of memoranda and other evidence to get a fair sense of public opinion. It was an occasion for a massive communication of community sentiments for autonomy and cultural recognition. Although conceding a general recognition of the linguistic principle, the commission's report also stressed administrative and economic efficacy as a rationale for reorganization of the states. The report did not please many groups, but it

---

55. But the indications tend to accord with the definition of policy success offered by M.E. Brown and Š. Ganguly, eds., "Introduction," *Government Policies and Ethnic Relations in Asia and the Pacific* (Cambridge, Mass.: MIT Press, 1997), p. 14. For conventional simplifications, see G. Smith, "Mapping the Federal Condition," Smith, ed., *Federalism: The Multiethnic Challenge* (London: Longman, 1995), pp. 1–28. For the incorporation process in Andhra, see R. Reddi, "The Politics of Accommodation: Caste, Class, and Dominance in Andhra Pradesh," in F.R. Frankel and M.S.A. Rao, eds., *Dominance and State Power in Modern India*, Vol. 1 (Delhi: Oxford University Press, 1989), pp. 280–281.

56. *Report of the States Reorganization Commission* (Delhi: Manager of Publications, Government of India, 1955), pp. i–iv.

gained parliamentary approval for the main recommendations, with some modifications, and was duly implemented. There were fewer problems with the new map in the south and the east. Punjab was unhappy; people in the western part of the country were outraged.

The leaders of the Maharashtra and Gujarat autonomy movements deeply resented the denial of the linguistic principle in reorganizing the Bombay state that contained these large communities. Extensive protest movements supported by opposition parties and some sections of the ruling Congress Party continued for several years. Episodes of violence in 1956 tended to draw attention from the fact that movements enjoyed widespread popular support, including from groups and classes of different ideological persuasions. By 1960 the states of Maharashtra and Gujarat were conceded. Later they turned out to be the most successful industrial states in India. Meanwhile the popularity of the Congress organization was restored. In 1966 Punjab and Haryana joined the list of states. Extensive reorganization in the northeast followed in 1971. The mix of language and culture here was of a different order. Three new states were approved in 2000.[57] The major language-related reorganization of states seems to have been realized, with a map of twenty-five states and seven Union Territories including Delhi, with a special status of capital territory. Twenty-five or even twenty-eight states, however, for 1 billion people may not seem too many, and it may even suggest that the reorganization and the autonomy processes have not yet come to an end.

Privileged Majorities and Minority-Language Rights

Regional language communities using newly acquired rights of self-governance do not always use their autonomy to ensure fairness in treating minority-language groups. Indeed the very term "linguistic" state may have an unsettling effect on the larger minority-language groups. When administrative boundaries become identified with encompassing language communities, the minorities may tend to feel like resident aliens in their own home states. Their differentiated language and cultural rights may become highly vulnerable under the authority of those whose advocacy of their own rights brought them to power. This political privileging of cultural or linguistically defined communities and authorities raises a special set of problems in a country such as India. Minority-language speakers' proportions in the population of states range from

---

57. The case for three new states—Chattisgarh, Uttaranchal, and Jharkhand—was approved in 2000. This time the major criteria were cultural and administrative.

9 percent in Gujarat to 40 percent in Assam or 47 percent in Jammu and Kashmir, or in a small state in Nagaland, as high as 86 percent.[58]

Defining "linguistic minority" for adequate policy sensitivity or responsiveness can be a complex task. Officially in India, the category refers to people whose mother tongue is different from the principal language of the state, and at the substate level different from the principal language of those levels.[59] The nested nature of minority status at various levels in the same state makes policy processes difficult. Several constitutional provisions seek to enunciate safeguards for minority-language groups. These aim to ensure the right to conserve their language, script, and culture; the right to have educational institutions of their choice; a procedure for official recognition of a language when necessary; the provision of facilities for instruction in a mother tongue at the primary stage; and other safeguards.[60] The commissioner for linguistic minorities is charged with keeping track of the policy action in these areas. Reports issued by the commissioner indicate that despite some serious efforts made in most states regarding conservation of languages, recognition for official transactions, and provision of language facilities for instruction, there is still a long way to go to create reasonable minority assurance. Occasionally, judicial decisions have aided the policy process.[61]

The provisions of these decisions are complex and the authorities for implementing them are often confusingly multiple. A successful nationwide minority rights system calls for intricate systems of cooperation among federal, state, local, and interstate institutions such as the state Chief Ministers' Conference or Zonal Councils. Minority input in the policy system is also complicated by the fact that minority languages in one state may enjoy majority status in another. In West Bengal, Hindi is the leading minority language, but it is a majority language in six states. Bengali is spoken by 20 percent of Assam's population, where Assamese is spoken by about 60 percent. The resource advantage of such large and well-connected minority languages may be compared with the smaller and more localized minority languages such as, for example, Tulu in Karnataka.

---

58. For details, see Government of India, *The Twenty-ninth Report of the Commission for Linguistic Minorities in India, 1988–1989* (Allahabad, Uttar Pradesh: Government of India, 1991), p. 109ff.

59. Ibid., p. 3.

60. Ibid., p. 101.

61. See, for example, the Supreme Court case of *D.A.V. College vs. State of Punjab* (1971). See E. Annamalai, "Language and the Indian Constitution," in Gupta, Abbi, and Aggarwal, *Language and the State*, p. 25.

Urdu is a major language, ranked sixth in numerical standing in the country. It is endowed with a rich literary tradition and a historical connection with both the north and the south, but most of its mother-tongue speakers lack commensurate official recognition because they are dispersed as minorities in more than five states. Urdu has the status of second official language in Bihar and some special status in two other states, but the sense of disadvantage is pervasive.[62] On the other hand, Urdu is the official language in Jammu and Kashmir, despite the fact that less than 1 percent of the population in the state reports it as their mother tongue.[63] The major language of the state is Kashmiri, which is spoken by 53 percent of the population. Only a curious mix of religion and politics can explain how, in this case, the concepts of majority and minority can be made to change places.

Collective Alienation and Resistance to Multicultural Union

Political perceptions of minority status may lead language communities to seek a variety of modes of collective action. The range of choice would depend on the definitions of the situation used by community activists and the opportunities provided by the national policy system as well as options offered from abroad. Yet in a country such as India, no one can escape minority standing by mere redefinition.

India's democracy offers a built-in incentive for painting individuals or communities with all kinds of identity colors, some permanent but others mutable. Is Hindi really Hindustani, or is the latter really Urdu? When does the Assamese language movement include Hindus and Muslims, and when does it exclude the latter?[64] The politics of variability of identity depending on community activists' strategic needs may have a lot to do with how community alienation or affection is generated. Language or divisions can serve as negative or positive resources for the federal system, depending on how democratic opportunities are used or abused by combative or cooperative participants.

The Tamil autonomy movement in Sri Lanka has been gradually pushed to a point of violence that now threatens the entire state. India

---

62.   See, for example, I. Farid, "Urdu at the Mercy of Masters," and several other chapters in S. Singh, ed., *Language Problem in India* (New Delhi: Institute of Objective Studies, 1997), especially pp. 84–97.

63.   See Government of India, *The Twenty-ninth Report of the Commission for Linguistic Minorities in India, 1988–1989*, p. 22.

64.   For the changing perception of Muslims and the convenient use of terms designating them as "foreigners," see M. Kar, *Muslims in Assam Politics* (New Delhi: Vikas, 1997), especially p. 370ff.

has the largest Tamil population in the world. In the 1950s, a separatist movement led by some Tamil-language community leaders invoked the symbol of Dravidian regionalism to mobilize a mass movement against the Hindi policy of the federal government. They urged the people to burn the national flag as a symbolic act of resentment.[65] The younger members of the movement, however, were more interested in pursuing their notion of Tamil autonomy through participation in the democratic electoral system.[66] The older authoritarian leaders were unable to prevent the movement from seeking state power to serve the community. At the same time, their aspirations to mobilize all four of the Dravidian language communities to go against the federal system failed. Within a few years, the democratic leaders of the Tamil movement became valuable partners in building national cohesion and development. From the 1960s onward, the regionalist leaders, as successors of the original Dravidian movement, organized the leading political parties in the Tamil area. The history of the DMK and the AIADMK, despite their differences, has been one of lending crucial support for the federal system through four decades.[67] One may look back and wonder if the divergence of the course of Tamil autonomy politics in Sri Lanka and India may have something important to say about India's conciliative federal system.

At this stage, it may be useful to distinguish between the system-resisting and system-supportive expressions and actions of the participants of the language- and region-based movements. The system-resisting actions need not be viewed as alienating in the long run. Their effect may be, in many cases, too localized or of too short or intermittent duration to impair the overall efficacy of the system. Even if not, there is no historical evidence to rule out the possibility of effectively using institutional means of disalienation to restore allegiance to the system. Fortunately for India, language demands or movements by themselves have not been strongly associated with secessionist violence to the extent of seriously disturbing national stability or development.

---

65. See R.L. Hardgrave Jr., *The Dravidian Movement* (Bombay: Popular, 1965), p. 45ff.

66. R. Thandavan and S. Swarnalakshmi, "Dravidian Movement and Participative Democracy," in G. Palanithirai and R. Thandavan, eds., *Ethnic Movement in Transition* (New Delhi: Kanishka, 1998), pp. 52–53.

67. The DMK stands for Dravida Munnetra Kazhagam; its major spinoff organization is known as the All India Anna Dravida Munnetra Kazhagam (AIADMK). In early 1999, the federal coalition government did have problems with the AIADMK, but the reference here is to the federal system as a wider institution. Even those problems were compensated by the important support lent by the DMK to the coalition government following the thirteenth general elections held later in 1999. See S. Dasgupta, "Government Formation," in *India Today* (International Edition), October 18, 1999, pp. 14–16.

Most cases of strong separatism or secessionist violence have been associated with cases where the activists have made use of a convenient assortment of symbols of disaffection, such that the relative salience of each could be manipulated at will. Thus in the northeast in the 1950s and 1960s (Nagaland and Mizoram) or in the north in the 1980s and 1990s (Punjab, and Jammu and Kashmir), there were careful concoctions of elements of disaffection based on ethnicity, religion, territorial affinity, cultural distinctiveness, and language. The strategic virtue of insurgence is that it blurs the borders of specific elements such that policy planners seeking to redress grievances can always be kept guessing.

Separatism and secessionist violence arose in Punjab in the 1980s and Jammu and Kashmir in the 1990s. Factors of region, religion, and language were blended in Punjab in ways that were not always easy to clarify from outside. Before the partition, the Sikh community constituted only 13 percent of undivided Punjab's population. After 1947, with a Hindu majority, Sikhs comprised 33 percent of reconstituted Indian Punjab's population. Muslim separatism leading to partition had already segmented Punjabi ethnicity into two parts. Within a few years, a language movement for Punjabi speakers' autonomy split the state.[68] The new smaller state of Punjab created in 1966, with a 61 percent Sikh and 37 percent Hindu population, provided a new springboard for a religion-based separatist movement. The transitions from Punjabi ethnicity to Punjabi language identity, and further on to exclusive Sikh religious identity, raised the question of how much room was still left for identity shedding or switching. But religious mobilization in favor of separatism did not make much headway so long as political peace served as a context for democratic elections at the state level. Nationally committed Sikh leaders succeeded in winning the highest percentage of votes in all of the five state legislature elections under the secular banner of the Congress Party before 1985.[69] The Akali Dal, the exclusively Sikh political party, had to wait for its day of clear victory.

Politics in a peaceful phase brought out the internal differences of the

---

68. The language issues at this time involved a dispute regarding the status of Hindi and Punjabi for official and educational purposes and the choice of scripts for Punjabi. The Akali Sikhs wanted Gurumukhi script, while the Hindu organizations wanted Devanagri script. The common tradition of writing in Perso-Arabic or Urdu script for Muslims, Sikhs, or Hindus was forgotten. See Chandra, *India after Independence,* pp. 325–328. For a linguistic analysis of the problem of defining Punjabi, see K.C. Bahl, "Punjabi," in Sebeok, *Current Trends,* pp. 153–200.

69. See P. Wallace, "Religious and Ethnic Politics: Political Mobilization in Punjab," in F.R. Frankel and M.S.A. Rao, *Dominance and State Power in Modern India,* Vol. 2 (Delhi: Oxford University Press, 1990), pp. 416–481.

Sikh community. Class, caste, occupation, and other vertical distinctions allowed linkages to be developed across religious lines. But militant separatist forces using purist religious symbols employed sophisticated firepower to beat their opponents with conspicuous violence. This was not, however, a simple battle between regional ethnoreligious forces and secular federal policy authorities of the Congress Party. Instead it was an unfortunate reflection of a three-way contest between moderate Akali forces, armed militant separatists, and Congress Party leaders who were not averse to using the militants to corner non-Congress moderates. This was the case where the federal policy authorities, in effect, undermined the system in Punjab as much as the separatists. Federal military action in 1984 made things worse. For six years, violence claimed thousands of civilian lives. Separatism had little more to offer despite its pipeline of resources based on the remote-control nationalism associated with a segment of the Sikh diaspora. By 1992, however, vertical differences caught up and cut through the horizontal confessional solidarity. Democratic alternation of power among parties and close linkages with the federal system returned.[70] The peaceful processes of regional development and national collaboration that earlier earned the state the reputation of excellence in developmental performance continued. By 2000 the Akali leadership of the state remained a partner of the ruling coalition of the federal government.

The story of separatism and secessionism in Jammu and Kashmir does not seem to belong here, largely because the language component is not a major problem in the secessionist definition of the situation. The external military involvement and imposition of wars and subversion also introduce a different twist to policy analysis. The state leaders' choice of Urdu as the official language and their neglect of Kashmiri, spoken by a majority of the population, says something important about their political and religious logic. This is the only Muslim-majority state of the federation. The non-Muslims' (36 percent) sense of insecurity is such that this is also the state with the largest population exodus.[71]

Minority-language safeguards and protections are not available in Jammu and Kashmir. Even the majority language, Kashmiri, which has a long literary tradition cutting across different religious communities, does not have the rights that minority languages enjoy in most states. The leaders of the state have always been Muslims, and autonomy issues

---

70. For the major episodes, see Chandra, *India after Independence*, pp. 328–338. The authors also note that of the nearly 12,000 killed by the militants in the state during 1981–93, "more than 61 percent were Sikhs." Ibid., p. 338.

71. See T.N. Madan, *Pathways* (Delhi: Oxford University Press, 1994), p. 201.

have generally emphasized the rights of the religious majority. Both the secessionist and the nonsecessionist leadership have either ignored or downplayed the cultural bond of *Kashmiriat* (Kashmiriness) that, for centuries, served as a common source of pride for different language- and religion-based communities.[72] Unlike other states in India, this state has the distinction of having a separate constitution for its administration.[73] This special autonomy of the state apparently facilitates a policy of denial of language rights of nearly half of its population. Regional autonomy, in this case, seriously contravenes the basic principles of multicultural citizenship.

The seamy side of regional autonomy is frequently concealed by the generally valid acceptance of the case for self-governance within the federal system in India. Space does not permit a review of many other cases of regional language communities endangering or suppressing sub-regional autonomy. A large part of the separatist and secessionist episodes of militant alienation and violence in the northeast can be traced, for example, to Assam's language policy. This strengthened the authority of the Assamese speakers in the state in a manner that scared the other language communities. Before independence, Assam was a victim of colonial manipulation of boundaries that changed the demographic pattern of the province several times. Assamese-speaking Hindu leaders of the Brahmaputra valley gained a new sense of confidence in 1947, following the transfer of a large segment of Bengali-speaking Muslims to eastern Pakistan (later renamed Bangladesh). These Assamese leaders always resented the prominence of the Bengali language and people (mostly Hindus after 1947) in education, administration, and employment.[74]

The new Assam, after 1947, witnessed a strong move on the part of these leaders to impose their dominance on all segments of the state's population, including Bengali Hindus and Muslims and the speakers of tribal languages. The numerical majority of Assamese speakers was thin and fragile and made many Assamese leaders nervous.[75] The ruling Con-

---

72. Even a sample of personal names, particularly surnames and nicknames, would show a greater degree of sharing among the major religious communities than in many other parts of India. For a discussion of this aspect, see O.N. Koul, "Personal Names in Kashmiri," in Koul, ed., *Sociolinguistics* (New Delhi: Creative Books, 1995), pp. 145–166, especially p. 166.

73. Article 370 of the Indian constitution includes some special provisions with respect to the state of Jammu and Kashmir. For the history and analysis of the special status of this state, see Basu, *Introduction to the Constitution of India*, pp. 249–258.

74. See Chandra, *India after Independence*, pp. 307–308.

75. In part, this majority was obtained by Muslims of Bengali origin declaring themselves as Assamese speakers for political purposes in the 1951 census. See S. Baruah,

gress Party leaders were less agitated than the young activists who were eager to use a militant mass movement to make Assamese the exclusive official language of the state. The movement used extensive violence. In 1960 the legislative assembly of the state passed the Official Language Act making Assamese the official language "for all or any" purposes of the state.[76] Suddenly, Bengali and tribal-language speakers found themselves at a great disadvantage. Their perception of unilateral imposition disturbed the multicultural unity of the state. The Assamese leaders used the term "foreigners" or "outsiders" to describe any minority group they did not have political use for at any specific moment. The federal government tried to use its influence on the state leaders, but the fears and resentments of the minority-language communities and the militant reactions of the activists only increased. The activists were further aided by a large influx of illegal immigrants from Bangladesh. The 1970s and early 1980s witnessed widespread political disorder and extremist mobilization against democratic institutions.

Fortunately, the federal government was willing to negotiate with the radical activists of the state, many of whom were organized in the Asom Gana Parishad (AGP), and the latter's electoral victory in 1985 restored the institutional system. Another group of activists, however, remained on the radical fringe. Ironically, in recent years it is the ruling AGP that has been a major target of secessionist and separatist terrorism, while it worked in close collaboration with the federal government.[77] Meanwhile the tribal communities of the hills of Assam, with the active assistance of the federal government, have been reorganized as states. Despite some continuing acts of separatist violence in Nagaland, these areas (including Mizoram, Meghalaya, and Arunanchal Pradesh), after gaining recognition as autonomous states, have become important parts of the federal institutional system. The transition of Nagaland and Mizoram from a high incidence of separatism to system-supportive national participation is indicative of the disalienation possibilities of multicultural policy. In these and other states in the northeast, however, cultural sensitivity for their own minorities remains low. Even in Assam, a large-scale movement for the cultural and linguistic autonomy of the Bodo plains tribal community serves as a reminder that the internal politics of cultural recognition and language rights within states need serious attention.

India against Itself: Assam and the Politics of Nationality (Philadelphia: University of Pennsylvania Press, 1999), p. 97.

76. For the relevant sections of the text, see V.R. Trivedi, *Documents on Assam*, Pt. A (New Delhi: Omsons, 1995), pp. 139–142.

77. This was particularly true in the first half of 2000. The AGP lost power in 2001.

Conclusion

This chapter has analyzed language policy in India as an institutional process set in the context of a developing democracy striving to nurture a multicultural sensitivity. It has pointed to continuities in the policy culture that evolved during the secular anticolonial nationalist movement and after. The layering of this system at the federal, regional, and subregional levels has been emphasized to avoid common oversimplifications. Language policy belongs to a special class of policies that deals with cultural recognition, political intervention, and productive coordination for national development. Little prior experience, in India or abroad, was available to guide India's policymakers. Trial and error and interactive learning based on negotiations with policy publics were the best aides to policy planning that the ruling authorities could muster.

Fortunately, even the worst instances of secessionist terror often proved amenable to inclusionary treatment, as for example, in Punjab, Assam, and Mizoram. Policy successes in these areas involving careful processes of disalienation have received considerably less scholarly notice than isolated episodes and transitional phases of violence. My analysis shows how the "seething cauldron" view of destructive conflict stemming from language, culture, or ethnic claims can be highly misleading.[78]

The successful allocation of relative status to different languages for official use at the federal and regional levels indicates conciliative patterns that represented quite an accomplishment for a country of India's complexity. How the interaction between language-based demands for autonomy and the policy authorities at the federal level led to a responsive system of reorganization reveals a constructive policy narrative of vast dimension. It tells us how meeting different demands at different times and dispersed spaces helped policy planners to gradually realize the goal of inclusion. This vast scale of management of autonomy demands reinforced the institutional resilience of the political system. The process was, to be sure, facilitated by the very structure of Indian cleavage patterns: Major social cleavages in India often intersected or crosscut each other.

The simultaneous pursuit of planned investment of resources for nationwide development of economic, cultural, and language-related benefits helped to connect the communities with the federal system in a

---

78. That it can be misleading for many cases in other settings as well is discussed in R. Brubaker, "Myths and Misconceptions in the Study of Nationalism," in Hall, *The State of the Nation*, especially p. 281.

partnership that proved highly productive. Language planning, for example, involved a nationally coordinated project for the development of Hindi and other regional languages along with a selected set of tribal languages. A wide range of material was produced by the federal- and state-level agencies in collaboration with nonofficial organizations in the fields of scientific and technical terminology. Texts in the sciences, arts, and humanities were presented across radio, television, and satellite telecast systems, opening new public access, especially to nonliterates. The social deepening effects of such expanded communication would indicate a productive aspect of language policy and politics rarely captured by studies that concentrate on conflict management.

The sensitivity of language policy to issues of fairness among language communities went far beyond language status and balanced investment in the corpus development of major languages. For example, in the 1960s a three-language formula was adopted by a joint initiative of the Chief Ministers' Conference for use in secondary education for teaching language. The formula included, with some exception allowed, teaching a regional language; Hindi or another Indian language in Hindi areas; and English or any other modern European language. The idea was to ensure equality of language learning among communities. It was not easy to get all states to follow the formula. Gradually, however, resistance to the formula declined, even among most of the southern states. But the Hindi states opted for Sanskrit rather than southern or other regional languages, and Tamil Nadu opted for Tamil and English only. Mizoram also chose Mizo and English. All other states made serious efforts to respect the formula in the interest of using indigenous languages for wider national communication.[79]

Language policy in India, instead of playing the presumed role of weary fire fighting in a country of incendiary language rivalry, has performed an unexpectedly reconstructive function. With every success of conciliative treatment of language demands, identity complementarities have been encouraged. The Andhra movement's successful national incorporation marked the inauguration of inclusionary institutionalism that encouraged, to cite just one example, the complementarity between Telugu, Indian, secular, or other identity labels. It is not surprising that on many occasions when the federal government was in crisis in the late

---

79.   In fact, the Hindi states' reluctance to learn other Indian languages has been a problem for ensuring fairness in other areas. For example, the rate of bilingualism among Hindi speakers has been the lowest in the country. See D.L. Sheth, "The Great Language Debate," in U. Baxi and B. Parekh, eds., *Crisis and Change in Contemporary India* (New Delhi: Sage, 1995), pp. 205–206.

1990s, it was the regional parties—including one from Andhra Pradesh—
that proved to be crucial for national stability.[80] If these were some of the
finest moments of the inclusionary sensitivity of national development in
India, they also called attention to the credit that language policy de-
serves for making regional communities the core of the nation. But the
region-nation relation in a multicultural society reveals only one of the
many levels of operation of language policy. In fact, success in achieving
reasonable coherence between the regions and the national political center would tend to call greater attention to those aspects of language policy that language-community leaders are rarely tempted to talk about.

These issues relate to the development of languages as valued community resources for enabling citizens of a developing country to attain
greater communicative competence. Language politics in India rarely
methodically attends to the problems of language competence, cultivation, and management issues because there is no ready promise of political dividend in these mundane policy areas that lack public attention.[81]
Regional languages, once elevated to official status, may be less often actually used or promoted for new functional roles than one would expect
from the rhetoric of language loyalty. The use of regional language for
graduate education, to take one example, has been sponsored by federal
financial assistance since 1968. Some regional governments produced a
lot more with similar subsidies than others. In terms of original book production for regional language use for graduate study, one of the best records (in terms of number of books for the same grant amount) was
claimed by Kerala for Malayalam-language works. Some of the worst records were seen in the case of the Hindi states.[82] The languages enjoying
the limelight of reorganization politics and autonomy movements, as in
the cases of Marathi and Punjabi, also fared poorly by this measure.

Civic attention needs to be drawn to the productive aspects of language policy. The distributive aspects of language policy—reflected in
the inadequate resources allotted to regional language or minority-
language schools in different states—also need more attention than what

---

80.　For a discussion of the growing importance of coalition politics and its connection with Indian diversity, see B. Arora, "Negotiating Differences: Federal Coalitions
and National Cohesion," in F.R. Frankel, ed., *Transforming India: Social and Political Dynamics of Democracy* (New Delhi: Oxford University Press, 2000), pp. 176–206, especially p. 200.

81.　Some of these aspects are discussed in B. Jernudd, *Lectures on Language Problems*
(Delhi: Bahri, 1991), pp. 14–46, 69–78.

82.　For details, see B. Mallikarjun, "The Eighth Schedule Languages—A Critical Appraisal," in Gupta, Abbi, and Aggarwal, *Language and the State*, pp. 78–79.

the regional or federal policy authorities have given so far. The increasing globalization of the mass media in India and the growing trends of liberalization in television programming, with a special emphasis on the regional markets, may compensate for some of the governmental lapses. Yet even if this trend brings about some change in promoting the production of regional language resources or the use of languages of wider communication (Hindi, for example), it is doubtful that it would aid the distributive process. The autonomy, identity, and allegiance issues of language policy probably still claim too much attention to allow the deeper issues of equity in a poor country to gain the public notice they desperately deserve.

Chapter 2

The Politics of Language Policy in Pakistan

Alyssa Ayres

Since achieving independence in 1947, the state of Pakistan has been unable to formulate and implement policies to address the unabated tensions between the idealized, imagined Pakistan envisaged by the nation's rulers and the reality of its diverse citizenry. Despite the great diversity of languages and ethnicities in Pakistan, the government has paid little attention to language as a policy issue. Seemingly, its leaders continue to believe that ethnic problems can resolve themselves if the proper formulations of political representation are developed.

Questions of national identity and cohesion in Pakistan, even predating the formation of the state itself, have been framed in a way that renders irrelevant (or perhaps unspeakable) the issues of ethnic groups that take language as a significant form of expression and identity. Despite four successive constitutions (1956, 1962, 1973, and 1985), with perhaps another in the offing, Pakistani leaders have proven adept at concocting rules about how the state should function. Since 1985, governments have been dismissed and elections held in a whirlwind of activity that intermittently appears to be democratic. Unfortunately, Pakistan's rulers have not given serious consideration to the implications of language policy for the spread of ethnic conflict. Instead of developing proactive policies, successive governments have in nearly all cases opted for reactive measures. As a result, Pakistan has experienced repeated conflagrations among groups demanding greater ethnic and political accommodation. This approach has been and continues to be deeply flawed.

The Political and Ethnic Setting

Pakistan was created by the partitioning of British India along Hindu-Muslim lines, the first instance in modern history of state formation on the basis of religion alone. The most crucial legacy of partition for contemporary Pakistan is the ideological paradigm behind it—one now thoroughly discredited in academic circles, but a persistent assumption that has determined nearly all of Pakistan's language policy choices. In the years leading up to partition, a primordialist "two nations" theory began to gain momentum in British India. The theory posited that Hindus and Muslims were fundamentally distinct peoples who could not live together. According to this reasoning, territorial partition was needed so that each group could have its own homeland.

Though conceived as a nation of and for Muslims, Pakistan was not homogeneous. Its territory comprised two separate regions, with all of India lodged between the East and West "wings." East Pakistan (East Bengal), a region of relative linguistic and cultural uniformity, contained slightly more than half of Pakistan's total population.[1] West Pakistan was a place of diverse cultures, languages, and special territorial statuses. Despite this cultural and linguistic heterogeneity and the fact no more than 7.3 percent of the Pakistani population claimed Urdu as its first language, the founders of Pakistan insisted that the new state should have one official language, and that language would be Urdu. Since then, Pakistan has not become more homogeneous, the leadership's ideological commitment to the contrary. Linguistic data from censuses conducted in 1951 and in 1981 offer a useful comparison. (See Tables 2.1 and 2.2.) Unfortunately, accurate population data were not made available following Pakistan's last census in 1998.[2] Therefore it is possible only to estimate the sizes of the populations in each of the country's provinces and to hypothesize what this means for language use in Pakistan. (See Table 2.3.)

Conflicts over language identity are not merely about language: They are intertwined with struggles over power and access to it. The vast majority of Pakistan's rulers and policymakers have been Punjabi and *mohajirs* (settlers), while the military has been ruled by a Punjabi-

---

1. According to the 1951 census, the figure was 56 percent. Astute observers would note that Sylhet, Dhaka, and Chittagong, not to mention the Hill Tracts, are hardly uniform. See chapter 3 in this volume.

2. The publication of the 1998 census was suspended to avert potential catastrophe: Political parties and minority communities alike warned that its publication could prompt national disintegration. This points to the enormity of ethnic fissures in contemporary Pakistan.

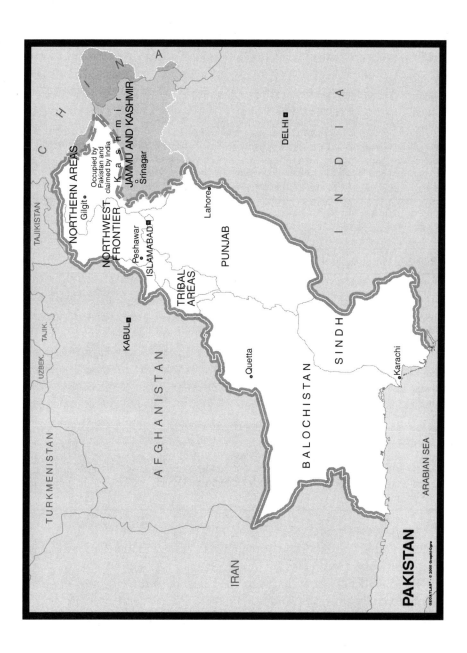

PAKISTAN

Table 2.1. Languages of Pakistan (1951 census).

Language	Percentage (East and West Pakistan)	Percentage (West Pakistan)
Bengali	56.0	0.50
Punjabi	29.0	67.08
Urdu	7.3	7.05
Sindhi	5.9	12.85
Pashto	4.9	8.16
Baluchi	1.5	3.04
Brahvi	—	0.70

SOURCE: Tariq Rahman, "Language Policy in Pakistan," *Ethnic Studies Report*, Vol. 14, No. 1 (January 1996).
NOTE: Siraiki and Hindko are subsumed within the language category "Punjabi" in this census.

Table 2.2. Languages of Pakistan (1981 census).

Language	Percentage (urban)	Percentage (rural)	Percentage (total population)
Punjabi	49.9	47.5	48.2
Urdu	24.4	1.3	7.6
Pashto	8.0	15.1	13.2
Sindhi	6.4	13.8	11.8
Siraiki	4.1	12.0	9.8
Others	3.4	2.6	2.8
Baluchi	1.7	3.5	3.0
Hindko	1.5	2.8	2.4
Brahvi	0.5	1.5	1.2

SOURCE: Jonathan S. Addleton, "The Importance of Regional Languages in Pakistan," in M. Geijbels and Addleton, eds., *The Rise and Development of Urdu and the Importance of Regional Languages in Pakistan* (Murree: Christian Study Center, 198? [year as it appears in the original]).

Mohajir-Pathan nexus. Tariq Rahman has compiled the best available figures on both. (See Tables 2.4 and 2.5.)

These statistics show that some of Pakistan's ethnic groups are disproportionately powerful and advantaged. Punjabi and Mohajir dominance has produced chronic insecurity for other ethnic groups, which justifiably fear that the Punjabis and Mohajirs seek hegemony over the rest of the country. This insecurity has played a crucial role in the rise of regional language movements in Pakistan to protest what these ethnic groups view as incursions of Urdu into their domains.

Table 2.3. Provincial Population Figures (2000 estimates).

Province	Percentage
Punjab	56.1
Sind	22.6
Northwest Frontier Province	13.1
Baluchistan	5.1
Federally Administered Northern Areas	2.6
Federally Administered Tribal Areas and Islamabad	0.6

NOTE: These estimates are based on the (admittedly flawed) assumption that population proportions at the provincial level remained static from 1981 to 2000. Total may not add to 100 percent because of rounding.

Table 2.4. Ethnic Origins of Pakistan's High-Level Bureaucrats.

Ethnicity	Percentage
Punjab	48.89
Pakhtun	8.12
Mohajir	30.29
Sindhi	2.50
Baluchi	0.25
Bengali	9.35

SOURCE: Tariq Rahman, *Language and Politics in Pakistan* (Karachi: Oxford University Press, 1996), p. 121.

The National Language Question

If Urdu was a language spoken by comparatively few in Pakistan—and there were several other languages spoken by many—what led to the decision to make Urdu the national language of the country? What was the justification for choosing a national language with such limited spread?

Mohammad Ali Jinnah's Muslim League was the intellectual inheritance of Sir Sayed Ahmed Khan and the Aligarh movement, which arose in the nineteenth century to educate an elite class of Muslims. This authoritarian movement was dominated by landlords and a professional elite driven by a desire to retain power and aware of their numerical disadvantage in comparison to Hindus.[3] Located in Uttar Pradesh in the

3. See Paul Brass, *Language, Religion, and Politics in North India* (Cambridge: Cambridge University Press, 1974), pp. 119–181; and Khalid bin Sayeed, *Pakistan: The Formative Phase* (Karachi: Pakistan Publishing House, 1960), pp. 191–241.

Table 2.5. Ethnic Origins of Pakistan's High-Level Military Officers.

Ethnicity	Percentage
Punjab	35.4
Pakhtun	39.6
Mohajir	23.0
Sindhi	0.0
Baluchi	0.0
Bengali	2.0

SOURCE: Tariq Rahman, *Language and Politics in Pakistan* (Karachi: Oxford University Press, 1996), p. 121.

heart of what was once Mughal India, the Aligarh movement viewed itself as a training ground for Muslims of privilege who should continue to play leading roles within the British Raj despite their numerical weakness. Scholars have illuminated the extent to which a sense of nobility permeated both the Aligarh movement and the Muslim League, detailing the rise of a Muslim elite convinced that it was needed to maintain and extend the place of Muslims in the subcontinent. These elites romanticized past eras of Muslim glory on the subcontinent—times when Muslim/Mughal rulers spoke Urdu and Persian freely—and they consequently elevated the place of Urdu in their thinking about the future.

At the same time and in reaction to Mughal rule's privileging of Urdu, a Hindi language movement emerged in Uttar Pradesh and Bihar that sought to replace the official use of Urdu with a Devanagari-script Hindi and a Sanskrit-derived vocabulary. The Hindi movement clearly identified itself as a language movement for Hindus, representing a reclamation of a (putative) "Hindu" language to symbolize the reclaiming of India for Hindus. This in turn led the Muslim League to identify Urdu as the "language of the Muslims," despite empirical evidence of language use to the contrary.

The decision that Urdu should be Pakistan's national language was therefore invested with religious significance by decisionmakers in the Muslim League, a significance likely not attached to Urdu by other supporters of the partition.[4] Urdu was not perceived by speakers of other languages to be neutral because it was a startling imposition—particularly for Sind and Bengal—and hence not neutral at all.

4. For a more comprehensive discussion of what Pakistan meant for Bengalis, see Philip Oldenburg, "'A Place Insufficiently Imagined': Language, Belief, and the Pakistan Crisis of 1971," *Journal of Asian Studies,* Vol. 44, No. 4 (August 1985), pp. 711–733.

Linguistic Tensions and Ethnic Conflict

The most significant ethnic problems in Pakistan were the Bengali language movement and ethnic tensions in Sind, both of which were exacerbated by poor government policy. Bangladesh's secession from Pakistan in 1971 marks a moment when the two-nations theory was revealed to be a fiction: Being Muslim was not a sufficient bond for the nation.

Viewed from the lens of language policies and ethnic conflict, however, Pakistan's historical narrative was troubled from the beginning. Less than two months after Pakistan gained independence in 1947, Jinnah suspended the Provincial Assembly of the Northwest Frontier Province (NWFP) in response to what he perceived to be a threat of Pakhtun secessionism in the form of a Pakhtun demand for greater autonomy.[5] Less than six months later, Karachi was relieved of its status as a city of Sind Province and placed under federal control. The Bengali language movement was launched in 1948, and flare-ups involving language issues occurred in East Pakistan in 1951, 1952, 1954, 1956, 1966, and 1970–71. Meanwhile, linguistic movements in southern Punjab under the Siraiki banner were gaining momentum as early as 1956, with demands for the creation of a separate Bhawalpur Province.[6] The idea of a cohesive Muslim Pakistan was a fiction from the earliest days of its existence.

Most of Pakistan's language problems grew out of regional linguistic groups' taking umbrage at the Pakistani state's insistence on making Urdu the national language. The overarching problem in this regard was the government's unaccommodating language policies.

Bengali

The Bengali language movement was at the heart of the best known of Pakistan's internal conflicts. Because the movement's actions resulted in East Pakistan's secession from the rest of the country, it is obvious that the government's policy responses to Bengali demands were inadequate. According to the 1951 census, 56 percent of Pakistan's population counted Bengali as their mother tongue. Thus Bengali should have been declared a national language along with Urdu and English, yet Pakistan's leadership dismissed Bengali demands. This dismissal reflected the tremendous significance that the leadership had invested in Urdu, a

---

5. There is a clear linguistic component here, given that the Pakhtun movement sought the official use of Pashto in the Provincial Assembly as well as in the schools.

6. Tariq Rahman, "The Siraiki Movement in Pakistan," *Language Problems and Language Planning,* Vol. 19, No. 1 (Spring 1995), p. 8.

significance that served to denigrate the role of every other language in Pakistan. The emphasis given to Urdu alienated other language groups throughout the country—Bengalis, in particular.

As early as February 1948, students at Dhaka University questioned the proposition that Urdu should be Pakistan's only national language. Both Jinnah and Liaquat Ali (the governor-general and prime minister, respectively) went on the record with responses that characterized the leadership's narrow vision of Pakistan: "Pakistan is a Muslim state, and it must have its lingua franca, a language of the Muslim nation. The mover [*sic*] should realize that Pakistan has been created because of the demand of a hundred million Muslims in this sub-continent, and the language of a hundred million Muslims is Urdu. It is necessary for a nation to have one language and that language can only be Urdu and no other language."[7]

The 1951 census revealed that only slightly more than 7 percent of the Pakistani population thought of Urdu as their first language. Policymakers could have pointed to Bengali, Sindhi, or Punjabi as the languages of overwhelming numbers of Pakistanis. One scholar notes that Sindhi, for example, has a higher proportion of Arabic words than Urdu, but it was never suggested by Pakistan's national leadership as a potential repository of Muslim identity on the subcontinent.[8]

If the idea was that Urdu was intertwined with Muslim consciousness, the converse seems to have been the case for Bengali, at least as far as West Pakistan was concerned: Bengali, by virtue of its script and vocabulary, was deemed to be inherently un-Islamic. The report of the first Basic Principles Committee (which drafted recommendations for Pakistan's first constitution) recommended that Urdu should be the only state language.[9] The government began Islamicization programs for East Pakistan and Bengali in 1950; the minister of education set up twenty "adult education centers" in East Pakistan to teach Bengali using the Arabic script; and a language committee was established to Islamicize Bengali.[10] The committee's report was never made public, leading one scholar to suggest that its support of state-sponsored policies might have been

---

7.   Quoted in Aijaz Ahmed, *Lineages of the Present: Political Essays* (Delhi: Tulika, 1996 [1993]), p. 203. Liaqat Ali Khan's statement is nearly identical in sentiment and choice of language to Jinnah's remarks of February 24, 1948, in Dhaka. See Oldenburg, "'A Place Insufficiently Imagined,'" p. 716.

8.   Ahmed, *Lineages of the Present*, pp. 203–204.

9.   Rounaq Jahan, *Pakistan: Failure in National Integration* (Dhaka: Oxford University Press, 1973), p. 37.

10.   Tariq Rahman, *Language and Politics in Pakistan* (Karachi: Oxford University Press, 1996), pp. 88–89.

the reason. In the meantime, the idea that Bengali might have its script overhauled sparked strident opposition, and the plan was never implemented.

In September 1950 Prime Minister Ali submitted an interim report (essentially a draft constitution) to the Constituent Assembly. Two key points in the document enraged the Bengalis: First, even in the proposed bicameral system, Bengalis would not have a clear legislative majority despite comprising the majority of Pakistan. Second, the constitution designated Urdu (and only Urdu) as the national language.[11] Bengali opprobrium was so great that Ali withdrew the interim report two months later.

In January 1952 Prime Minister Khwaja Nazimuddin—a Bengali who, by many accounts, had been chosen as governor-general under Prime Minister Ali to appease the Bengalis and had succeeded him as prime minister—proclaimed in Dhaka that Urdu would be the state language of Pakistan.[12] This public declaration ignited student protests, which in turn resulted in the imposition of a curfew on the city. When on February 21 a group of students defied this order, police opened fire, killing four. This event has been memorialized in Bangladesh as Language Day (or Ekushe).[13] Ekushe would have a unifying effect on East Pakistan's demand for government recognition of Bengali as a national language. According to Rounaq Jahan, this episode created "myths, symbols and slogans. . . . It gave [Bengalis] not only a popular common cause but also their first martyrs."[14]

In West Pakistan the Bengali language issue was ignored. Instead Pakistani lawmakers tried to revive the One-Unit policy, which in 1948 had been put forth and then withdrawn for consideration in the draft constitution.[15] The One-Unit policy was presented as a legislative solution to the question of "parity" that troubled both East and West Pakistan—in different ways. Instead of a West Pakistan composed of four provinces, with East Pakistan constituting a fifth province (thus making the Na-

---

11. Allen McGrath, *The Destruction of Pakistan's Democracy* (Karachi: Oxford University Press, 1998), p. 75.

12. Rahman, *Language and Politics in Pakistan*, p. 90.

13. In 1999 the United Nations, after lobbying by Bangladesh, declared February 21 International Mother Language Day. Thus the East Pakistani language riots form the basis for an international day to allow all peoples to recognize the "distinct and enduring value of their languages," according to UN Secretary-General Kofi Annan. Associated Press, February 21, 2000.

14. Jahan, *Pakistan: Failure in National Integration*, p. 44.

15. McGrath, *The Destruction of Pakistan's Democracy*, p. 106.

tional/Constituent Assembly an assembly of five provinces), the One-Unit policy would have united the four provinces of the West into one legislative bloc: The assembly would thus comprise two "wings." This appeared to give a greater voice to East Pakistan, but in practice it eliminated East Pakistan's ability to form alliances with any of the four provinces of West Pakistan—three of which had a shared interest in stemming Punjabi hegemony. Although the One-Unit policy did not directly address the national-language issue, it was part of the policy arsenal that the centralized Pakistani state employed in response to perceived growing provincialism in East Pakistan, a provincialism that was gaining momentum primarily through the Bengali language movement and Ekushe.

By 1953 Sheikh Mujibur Rahman's Awami League, which demanded that Bengali be made a national language, had begun to gain ground in East Pakistan.[16] In elections in March 1954, the United Front, an amalgamation of smaller new parties in East Pakistan (including the Awami League), swept the province. The Muslim League experienced a humiliating defeat. The United Front's Twenty-one Point program contained a litany of demands for autonomy that threatened the Constituent Assembly. When the assembly reconvened, Prime Minister Mohammad Ali Bogra's proposal was passed in May that Bengali be used "along with Urdu" as a national language. This proved to be an empty victory, however. That same month, Bogra dismissed the democratically elected chief minister of East Pakistan, Fazal Huq, along with the provincial cabinet and the Provincial Assembly, on the grounds that Huq had made traitorous remarks. East Pakistan's Provincial Assembly did not reopen until 1956. Bogra then installed Iskander Mirza as governor, and Sheikh Mujibur was arrested.[17] The Bengalis had gained a state language but lost their political voice and thus their ability to pursue any of their policy demands. The new governor, Mirza, was openly hostile toward East Pakistan. He referred to the results of the 1954 provincial elections as "foolish" acts of the "illiterate" and argued that Bengalis needed a "controlled democracy."[18]

Pakistan's 1956 constitution declared Bengali a national language along with Urdu,[19] but this was never implemented. As one scholar has

---

16. Ibid., p. 109. At the same time, the central leadership of Pakistan was in flux. In March 1953, for example, Governor-General Ghulam Mohammad dismissed Prime Minister Khwaja Nazimuddin and appointed Mohammad Ali Bogra to replace him. Also, Pakistan still did not have a constitution.

17. Ibid., p. 120.

18. Ibid., p. 135.

19. Gen. Ayub Khan, not yet the Pakistani head of state, was put in charge of designing the Pakistani constitution by then Governor-General Mohammad, who dis-

observed, "There were complaints from Bengalis that their language was not being treated at par with Urdu. . . . Currency notes, railway and postal signboards, etc. were not in Bengali. . . . The state media gave less time to it than to Urdu."[20]

In October 1958 Gen. Ayub Khan seized power and declared martial law. With his modernist preference for English, he declared in December that every language of Pakistan should adopt a roman script. The declaration rankled almost everyone, including Bengalis, and the plan was never implemented. The Committee on National Education, however, still sought to reduce the "difference" of Bengali by Islamicizing it, and this mandate would be imposed on the Bengali Academy. A new director of the Bengali dictionary project was appointed, someone known for coining new words from Perso-Arabic roots.[21] East Pakistanis were not impressed with the effort to reeducate their language and continued to express their affinity for the Bengali language and the Bengali identity by observing Ekushe with increased vigor.

A report by the drafters of a new Pakistani constitution highlighted a variety of reasons for why parliamentary government had failed in Pakistan. In response, the constitution of 1962 called for the institution of a "Basic Democracies" model of government that would devolve power to the grassroots level: Local representatives of some 80,000 constituencies of no more than 600 people each would vote for the president. With no one else on the ballot, Ayub won the presidential election and remained in power. The 1962 constitution reiterated Bengali's status as a national language along with Urdu, but it did not require Urdu and Bengali to be used by everyone in the country. Bengali's status as a national language was therefore an empty promise. Access to national power and administrative offices, for example, was mainly a function of one's command of English and Urdu—not Bengali.

Further, despite Bengali's new constitutional status, it continued to be viewed as a suspect "Hindu" language, particularly when used in non-Islamic forms of cultural expression. In 1966, for example, the governor of East Pakistan banned popular songs by the well-known Bengali Rabindranath Tagore from Radio Pakistan. He charged that Bengali was a "non-Muslim" language and a carrier of "cultural domination" by Calcutta. These actions took place under a constitution that at least nomi-

---

missed Prime Minister Mohammad Ali Bogra following his visit to the United States in 1956.

20.   Rahman, *Language and Politics in Pakistan*, p. 96.

21.   Ibid., pp. 99–100.

nally designated Bengali a national language. The revival of the attack against the Bengali language, according to one observer, consolidated Bengali opposition to West Pakistan through the "resurgence of linguistic nationalism."[22]

Sheikh Mujibur's Six-Points political program (presented first in 1966) signaled the extent to which the East Pakistanis had moved away from the language issue and toward a political program that emphasized regional autonomy. The program focused instead on issues of representation in the Constituent Assembly and the need for economic equity. Bengali political efforts to achieve linguistic accommodation with West Pakistan had been met with ineffectual language policies that belied the real priorities of West Pakistan's rulers. At this point, it was probably too late for language policy to be employed as a tool of accommodation; that it was not even attempted is even more regrettable. This shift away from cultural accommodation and toward legal and economic equity marked a new, more confrontational East Pakistani policy.

In December 1970 the Awami League swept Pakistan's national elections, which should have allowed it to form the National Assembly. Sheikh Mujibur declared the independence of Bangladesh on March 26, 1971, and was imprisoned for treason the following day. A civil war broke out that would eventually include India. When Pakistan surrendered in December 1971, Bangladesh came into being.

Sindhi

Karachi is a city riven by strife. The primary belligerents are usually characterized as Sindhis and Mohajirs, which implies that the conflict dovetails with ethnic identities that are linked to specific languages. Transnational groups such as the Muttahida Qaumi Movement (the United National Movement, formerly the Mohajir Qaumi Movement or Mohajir National Movement) and the World Sindhi Congress continue to do battle with each other and with Pakistan through mobilized global networks that demand homelands for both Mohajirs and Sindhis. Yet at the same time, the conflict in Sind has become much more complicated than the Sindhi-Urdu dispute. The multiple conflicts in Karachi now include Pathan versus Bihari,[23] Sindhi versus Pathan, Sindhi versus

---

22. Jahan, *Pakistan: Failure of National Integration*, p. 163.

23. The term "Bihari" refers to refugees from East Pakistan who settled in Karachi following the independence of Bangladesh. The term "Mohajirs" refers to settlers who (mainly) moved to Karachi and Hyderabad from the United Provinces (now Uttar Pradesh) in India at the time of partition.

Baluchi, and Sindhi versus Punjabi. Conflict in Sind is generally not limited to disputes over language policies.

The story of Pakistan's Sindhi language movement (and language riots) parallels that of the Bengali language movement from partition in 1947 through Benazir Bhutto's first regime (1988–90). During Bhutto's first term in office, tensions between Karachi's numerous ethnic groups exploded. With the increased availability of small arms left over from the Soviet war in Afghanistan, the conflict grew more violent, fueled by events unrelated to language issues.

Sindhi, like Bengali, enjoyed regional hegemony throughout the time of the British Raj. It has long had a literature and a widespread presence both colloquially and administratively. This was quite different from the situation in other provinces of West Pakistan, where the British had used Urdu.[24] Sind had been a separate province during the Raj. This was due in part to the Sindhi language movement of the 1930s, which had resulted in Sind separating from the Bombay presidency in 1936. This institutionalization of a Sindhi ethnic identity linked directly to language was therefore in place even before partition. Partition would trigger Sindhi ethnic mobilization for two reasons: cultural insensitivity and economic subjugation.

Partition brought massive demographic changes to the subcontinent. Karachi in particular saw an enormous influx of migrants from Uttar Pradesh—the Urdu-speaking Mohajirs—as well as from Punjab, Baluchistan, and the NWFP. At the same time, Hindus, who had comprised 64 percent of the population of Sind prior to partition, fled to India.[25] Homes and possessions left behind in Karachi and other urban centers (as well as agrarian lands in the Sindhi interior) were claimed by Mohajirs. The results were striking: In Karachi, Mohajirs comprised 57.55 percent of the population in 1951; in Hyderabad, 66.08 percent; and in Sukkur, 54.08 percent.[26] These cities were effectively cleaved in half and then populated by strangers.

When Pakistan came into being, Sindhis, like Bengalis, were surprised to find that their language would be subservient to Urdu in the national order. This lower status offended Sindhi cultural pride. The

---

24. Tariq Rahman, "Language Policy in Pakistan," *Ethnic Studies Report*, Vol. 14, No. 1 (January 1996), p. 80.

25. Yu. V. Gankovskiy, "Ethnic Composition of the Population of West Pakistan," in A.M. D'Yakov, ed., *Pakistan: History and Economy* (1961 [1959]), trans. U.S. Joint Publications Research Service, USJPRS 4708 (Washington, D.C.: USJPRS, 1961), p. 22.

26. Tariq Rahman, "The Sindhi Language Movement and the Politics of Sind," *Ethnic Studies Report*, Vol. 14, No. 1 (January 1996), p. 103.

problem was exacerbated by the inherent advantage afforded the new-comer Mohajirs, whose mother tongue was the national language; this gave Mohajirs a considerable advantage in seeking government employment.

A crucial event early in Pakistan's history helped to precipitate Sindhi-Urdu tensions: On July 23, 1948, the provincial government of Sind offered the city of Karachi to the federal government for use as the new capital of Pakistan. The federal government, headed by Jinnah, accepted the offer and then decided to reconstitute the city as a federal territory. When M.A. Khuhro, then chief minister of Sind, objected, he was dismissed by Jinnah on grounds of being both a poor administrator and a corrupt government official.[27] Karachi thus became a federal territory with a heavy Urdu presence. Most important, however, the economic and cultural capital of Sind was perceived as having been hijacked by the Pakistani state. From the Sindhi point of view, these developments created a painful inequity: To obtain government jobs, Sindhis would have to learn a "foreign" language. At the same time, the newly arrived "foreigners" (i.e., Mohajirs) did not have to learn Sindhi to go about their daily lives in urban Sind, where most of them lived. There was no compelling reason for Mohajirs to integrate with Sindhis—a situation that struck the latter as highly discriminatory.[28]

Because Karachi was no longer part of Sind, the University of Sind (established in 1946) was forced to move to Hyderabad; the University of Karachi took its place in 1948–52. Urdu was to be the medium of instruction at the University of Karachi, a displacement of the Sindhi language that deeply offended Sindhis. The cultural arrogance of the Mohajirs exacerbated tensions with the Sindhis, a condition that was compounded by Mohajir contempt for rural Sind.[29] Finally, because Mohajirs had given up so much—including their homes—to help create the Pakistani state, they "saw [themselves] as the standard bearer of the Pakistan 'idea.'"[30] From the Mohajir perspective, it must have seemed unthinkable that Pakistan would not declare Urdu as the national language. Later,

---

27   McGrath, *The Destruction of Pakistan's Democracy*, p. 47.

28.   Gankovskiy, "Ethnic Composition of the Population of West Pakistan," p. 22.

29.   Rahman, "The Sindhi Language Movement and the Politics of Sind," p. 103; Tariq Rahman, "Language, Politics, and Power in Pakistan: The Case of Sindh and Sindhi," *Ethnic Studies Report*, Vol. 17, No. 1 (January 1999), pp. 31–32; and Abbas Rashid and Farida Shaheed, *Pakistan: Ethno-Politics and Contending Elites*, United Nations Research Institute on Social Development Discussion Paper No. 45 (Geneva: UNRISD, 1993), p. 14.

30.   Rashid and Shaheed, *Pakistan: Ethno-Politics and Contending Elites*, p. 14.

Mohajirs would countermobilize against the Sindhi objection to Urdu and Mohajir hegemony in urban Sind.

When the One-Unit proposal was first floated in 1954, Sindhi opposition was intense. The Sindhis perceived the proposal as an effort by the center to take away their identity, though in reality it was created to counter East Pakistani representational influence in the National Assembly. As a result of the One-Unit policy, Sindhi lost its status as a regional language, because the only "region" in West Pakistan was the amalgamated One Unit. The Sindhi Adabi Sangat group demanded that Sindhi be declared "an official language at least for Sind."[31] In an effort to preserve Sindhi culture and language, M.A. Khuhro (who returned to power following Jinnah's death and some deal making with Liaquat Ali) had pressed the Sind legislature to endow a Sind Cultural Advancement Board with funds for a library, gallery, and literature development. The federal government was unmoved.

The One-Unit policy continued after Ayub imposed martial law in 1958. A year later, the Education Commission recommended Urdu and Bengali as Pakistan's national languages. The commission's report, published in 1961, noted that only in some schools in Sind was Sindhi the language of instruction past grade six, and it called for the use of Urdu throughout the country. This was not an unreasonable policy, but the Sindhis viewed it as intrusive and unacceptable. Protests—including the declaration of a "Sindhi Day" on November 9, 1962—went ahead despite the imposition of martial law, and Ayub "finally decided to let Sindhi alone."[32] The laissez-faire approach to Sindhi did not mean, however, that the language would be endorsed by Ayub's regime. To the contrary, "Sindhi was discouraged during this period, and the number of Sindhi-medium schools decreased. This [decrease] was, of course the inevitable consequence of the Mohajirs having become a majority in Karachi but it was seen in the light of a conspiracy by Sindhi nationalists. . . . Sindhi nationalists also complained that in this period Sindhi was replaced by Urdu on official buildings such as railway and bus stations; Sindhi writers were discouraged whereas Urdu ones were patronized; Sindhi publications were denied advertisements and Sindhi broadcasts from the radio were reduced."[33] These steps had demonstrable effects on the use of the Sindhi language in the public sphere—and ethnic Sindhis'

---

31. Rahman, "Language Policy in Pakistan," p. 81.

32. Rahman, "Language, Politics, and Power in Pakistan," p. 34; and Rahman, "The Sindhi Language Movement and the Politics of Sind," p. 105.

33. Rahman, "The Sindhi Language Movement and the Politics of Sind," pp. 105–106.

understanding thereof. Ayub undermined the position of Sindhi without declaring an intention to do so.

When Prime Minister Yahya Khan's education plan was published in 1969, it recommended that Urdu be used in the West wing and Bengali in the East wing. Sindhis saw this as an insult. Sindhi nationalist youth movements, such as the Jeeay Sind Naujawan Mahaz, reacted with a list of demands for retaining Sindhi. Like the Bengali language movement, the Sindhi language movement gained its strength from students.

In August 1970, the University of Sind (based in Hyderabad) declared Sindhi as its language of administration (it had officially implemented Urdu in keeping with national policy only in 1965). Sindhi nationalism had apparently gained in popularity, and more voices—the Sindhi Adabi Sangat and a group of 108 writers, among others—joined the chorus to express support for Sindhi. The Urdu press denounced Sindhi supporters as "leftists, anti-Islamic—anti-Pakistan dissidents."[34] Still, the Hyderabad Board of Intermediate and Secondary Education recommended that Sindhi be adopted as an official language and that it be made a compulsory subject for students who counted Urdu as their first language.[35] It was then that the Mohajirs turned to resistance. Both Mohajir and Sindhi nationalists launched protests against the perceived incursions of the other's language. By this point, both groups had become highly politicized; the protests lasted through January 1971, when the army was called in to restore order.[36]

By 1972 Pakistan had lost its East wing, and Zulfiqar Ali Bhutto—a Sindhi—had taken power of what was left of Pakistan with the help of his Pakistan People's Party. In July 1972 the Sind legislative assembly put forth the Sindhi language bill. The bill made Sindhi and Urdu required subjects from grades four through twelve, and Sindhi a requirement from grade four onward in Urdu-medium schools. It also included a provision for Sindhi to be used in all governmental departments. Mohajirs vehemently opposed the bill, and the language riots that followed were the bloodiest in Pakistan's history. Prime Minister Bhutto responded with a new policy that ensured economic parity for speakers of both languages: "a proclamation to the effect that for twelve years jobs would not be denied for lack of knowledge of Sindhi or Urdu."[37] In practice, however,

---

34. Ibid., p. 107.

35. Ibid., p. 108.

36. Rahman, "Language, Politics, and Power in Pakistan," p. 36.

37. Rahman, "Language Policy in Pakistan," p. 86.

Sindhis remained at a disadvantage because it was impossible for the government to mandate the use of Sindhi by speakers of Urdu.

Bhutto's successor, Mohammad Zia ul-Haq, emphasized Islam as a national unifier and regarded the use of Urdu as a means to achieve that unity. In effect, this represented an implicit endorsement of the Mohajir position. Zia's harsh rule silenced what little opposition there was. But the Movement for the Restoration of Democracy—a panregional alliance whose members were largely from the Left—found support among rural Sindhi nationalists.[38] In the fall of 1983, riots erupted in rural Sind; many targeted public signs and government entities such as post offices and police stations. In a sense, the riots focused on the linguistic symbols of authority.[39] The strength of the Movement for the Restoration of Democracy in rural Sind was a signal to Zia that his policy of appealing to Sindhi feudal landlords was not stemming dissent in the province. As a result, the government may have sought to organize a political movement to neutralize the influence of the Pakistan People's Party in Sind.[40] In 1984 the Mohajir Qaumi Movement, led by Altaf Hussain, may have been assisted by the Inter-Services' Intelligence organization (Pakistan's national intelligence agency), in mobilizing the Mohajirs against the dissenting rural Sindhis.[41]

These explosive movements—once mobilized by linguistic identity—were hijacked for broader political purposes. Indeed the last language policy issue of note was a 1989 Senate Committee declaration that Urdu and Sindhi should be taught and used as official languages.[42] Today radical Sindhi movements call for partition and the creation of a "Sindhu Desh" (Sindhi homeland), while the radicalized Mohajir Qaumi Movement calls for the same in the form of a "Mohajirstan." Lawlessness in Sind has undermined the implementation of any policies, let alone lan-

---

38. According to the 1981 census, Sindhi was spoken by 52.4 percent of households in the province, but if Karachi is removed from the count, Sindhi's share jumps to more than 70 percent. See Jonathan S. Addleton, "The Importance of Regional Languages in Pakistan," in M. Geijbels and Addleton, eds., *The Rise and Development of Urdu and the Importance of Regional Languages in Pakistan* (Murree: Christian Study Centre, 198? [year as it appears in the original]), p. 65.

39. C.G.P. Rakisits, "Centre-Province Relations in Pakistan under President Zia: The Government's and the Opposition's Approaches," *Pacific Affairs*, Vol. 61, No. 1 (Spring 1988), p. 80.

40. Rashid and Shaheed, *Pakistan: Ethno-Politics and Contending Elites*, p. 21.

41. Ibid., p. 29.

42. Rahman, "Language Policy in Pakistan," p. 88.

guage policies, and the proliferation of sectarian violence in addition to ever-increasing ethnic violence has led to a small-scale civil war. Party changes in Islamabad no longer address the crisis in Sind. The situation has continued to deteriorate; there is not much cause for hope; and whatever role language policies might be able to play will have to take a back seat to political negotiations over the terms of a political peace settlement accompanied by measures to reduce drugs and arms trafficking.

Punjabi

Although it is a distinct language with a rich history, Punjabi (here, distinguished from Siraiki) never emerged as a main element in conflict with the Pakistani state itself. Since partition, the relatively low-key Punjabi language movement has raised only minimal policy demands and seems largely focused on organizing cultural celebrations, convening World Punjabi Conferences, and demanding a Punjabi department at the University of the Punjab, a demand that was granted in 1970.

Punjabis have been influential in the Pakistani government, which has caused some ethnic tension. There is, however, no ongoing ethnic fissure in Pakistan with Punjabi at one pole struggling against some other actor. This is mainly because of the overwhelming dominance of the Punjabi elite in state institutions. Another reason is the complementarity of and fuzzy boundary between Punjabi and Urdu from a linguistic and literary perspective.

Punjabi and Urdu have very similar grammars, and the two are mutually intelligible if one learns a few regular sound changes and rules of verb agreement. The closeness of Punjabi to Urdu is notable; this is not the case for Sindhi, Pashto, Siraiki, and Baluchi—all of which have important linguistic markers such as implosive sounds in the case of Sindhi and Siraiki, or distinct grammars in the case of Pashto and Baluchi (which are members of the Iranian language family). Punjabi's numerous dialects (two of which, Siraiki and Hindko, gained language status with the 1981 census) further fragment the picture. Interestingly, the Punjabi language movement has identified the standardization of Punjabi as a main policy goal.[43]

In addition, before the 1947 partition members of Punjabi and Urdu literary circles often intermingled. Many of Urdu's best-known authors were Punjabis, a number of whom (e.g., Manto, Krishan Chander, Rajinder Singh Bedi, Iqbal, Faiz, Munir Niazi, and Hafiz Jallandari)

---

43. Addleton, "The Importance of Regional Languages in Pakistan," p. 68.

sought literary expression through Urdu. They may have spoken Punjabi, but they chose Urdu as their literary voice.

In short, the Punjabi language movement has not been a significant source of ethnic tension in Pakistan. It would not be an exaggeration to characterize it as inert.

Siraiki

Siraiki, grammatically similar to Punjabi but with important phonetic features common to Sindhi, is a language spoken primarily in the area around Bhawalpur and Multan, though there are speakers in Sargodha Division and Dera Ghazi Khan Division as well. A Bhawalpur Province movement—taking Siraiki as important evidence of a separate culture—arose along with the Anti–One Unit Front in 1956. While the Anti–One Unit Front sought redivision of the One Unit along linguistic lines, a Bhawalpur movement began demanding a Siraiki area as compensation for having lost its identity as a separate princely state after it acceded to Pakistan. This almost came to pass in 1957, when the West wing was once again slated for breakup into provinces, but Ayub Khan's declaration of martial law in 1958 ensured that the West wing remained unified until Yahya Khan's decision to restore the provinces eleven years later.[44]

By this time, Bhawalpur Province was headed for amalgamation with Punjab, a position it had never before occupied. Following the province's demand for the creation of a new political party, which would come to be known as the Bhawalpur Mutaheda Mahaz (Bhawalpur United Front), police opened fire on protesters supporting the province's demand. Two marchers were killed, and a number of others wounded.[45] Perhaps because the scope of the violence was limited, the killings did not lead to further escalation; rather they provided the impetus for political action by the Bhawalpur Mutaheda Mahaz. The December 1970 election, which thrust Zulfiqar Ali Bhutto and his Pakistan People's Party into power, saw a sweep of Bhawalpur Mutaheda Mahaz candidates elected to the national and provincial assemblies instead. The Mahaz members apparently did not agitate vigorously for a Bhawalpur province, however, and by 1972 their organization had fragmented.[46]

---

44   Rahman, "The Siraiki Movement in Pakistan," p. 9.

45.   Ibid.

46.   Ibid.

Strangely, the Bhawalpur Mutaheda Mahaz conducted all of its discussions and published its literature in Urdu; implementation of the Siraiki language was not a primary concern. The Mahaz created a mobilized Siraiki identity that flowed naturally into a literary-language movement that began to demand recognition. Twenty-three Siraiki organizations held a Siraiki Literary Conference in Multan in 1975. With government acknowledgment in the 1981 census that Siraiki was a separate language, its stature was temporarily raised. As of 1991, however, the census ceased to include Siraiki.

The Siraiki Lok Sanjh, created in 1985, seeks recognition of Siraiki as a language, calls for the use of Siraiki in official documents of the region, and demands reserved ethnicity-based seats for voting. The Sanjh is not a political party, but it has a clear linguistic and political agenda.[47] Contemporary Siraiki-identity movements (the Siraiki Qaumi Movement, the Sanjh, Siraiki National Party, and the Pakistan Siraiki Party—an offshoot of the Pakistan People's Party) want the federal government to redress a variety of economic grievances, including complaints about the government's allocating land to non-Siraikis from Siraiki areas, the settlement of Biharis on Siraiki land, the reinclusion of Siraiki in the census as a language, and more radio and television programming in the Siraiki language.[48] These demands have thus far not been met. The Siraiki movement is nonetheless unlikely to turn to violence.

Pashto

The government of Pakistan has repeatedly sought to discourage the use of Pashto, fearing that it would contribute to the consolidation of a Pathan identity and strengthen Afghani irredentist claims across the boundaries of the Durrand Line. The Durrand Line, drawn by the British in 1893, separated Pakistan from Afghanistan and has been a focal point of dispute between the two nations since 1947. The line divides Pathan territory, but many Pathans claim allegiance to a broader Pakhtun nation.

One of the first signs that a lack of national unity might be a problem in the newly formed Pakistani state appeared in the NWFP. Khan Abdul Ghaffar Khan, often called the "Frontier Gandhi," had initially chosen not to support Jinnah's Muslim League in the call for partition and the creation of Pakistan. Instead he favored the establishment of "Pakhtun-

---

47. Ibid., p. 12.

48. Ibid., p. 19.

istan"—a free land for the Pathans. In pursuit of this goal, Ghaffar Khan had founded *Pakhtun,* a magazine that promoted the use of Pashto language and literature, in 1928. After 1947 Ghaffar Khan's National Congress Party, which was known to have sympathies with the Indian National Congress, assumed power in the NWFP assembly. The party was led by Ghaffar Khan's brother, Dr. Khan Sahib.[49] Jinnah perceived both brothers as threats to national cohesion and dismissed the assembly less than a week after Pakistan came into existence. He then invited Abdul Qaiyum Khan to establish a government. Qaiyum Khan was not able to secure a majority to form an assembly until January 1948, some five months later, but his allegiance to Jinnah and the idea of Pakistan was apparently preferable to an elected leader of a majority interested in promoting Pashtun identity and an independent Pakhtunistan. This would be just the first of many dismissals to occur in Pakistan.[50]

Pashto, and those who supported the establishment of Pakhtunistan were perceived by the Pakistani government to be antinational elements and, as such, were closely scrutinized. Efforts to promote Pashto (even at the literary level) were apparently monitored by the police. The new legislative assembly of the NWFP, led by Qaiyum Khan, put forward a resolution in 1950 designed to prove Pathan allegiance to the Pakistani nation by making Urdu the language of the courts.[51] The same NWFP government, however, also created a Pashto Academy in Peshawar in 1955, primarily as a sop to the Pathan nationalists.[52]

Ghaffar Khan emerged as a strong opponent of the One-Unit policy and an influential member of the Anti–One Unit Front. The National Awami Party remained a vocal Pashto-language supporter during Ayub's and Yahya Khan's time in office. Because neither was in power, however, they could not legislate on the party's behalf. When the National Awami Party did come to power in 1972 in a coalition with the Jamiat-e-Ulema-i-Islam, they dropped the demand for designating Urdu the official language of the NWFP. One scholar attributes this shift to the party's desire to stay in power and prove its loyalty to the center; this is probably true because Zulfiqar Ali Bhutto had already dismissed the National Awami Party government in Baluchistan and imposed martial law.

---

49. Tariq Rahman, "The Pashto Language and Identity-Formation in Pakistan," *Contemporary South Asia,* Vol. 4, No. 2 (July 1995), pp. 151–170.

50. McGrath, *The Destruction of Pakistan's Democracy,* pp. 45–46; and bin Sayeed, *Pakistan: The Formative Phase,* p. 296.

51. Rahman, "The Pashto Language and Identity-Formation in Pakistan," p. 161.

52. Rahman, "The Sindhi Language Movement and the Politics of Sind," p. 82.

The National Awami Party in the NWFP surely sought to avoid the same fate, though Bhutto ultimately banned the party in 1973.[53]

Political and linguistic agitation subsequently ebbed in the NWFP, with the use of Pashto in the legislative assembly being only slightly contested. Though the official language of the assembly was Urdu, many members of the National Awami Party chose to deliver their remarks in Pashto. During one session in 1972, the debate became so heated that the members of Bhutto's opposition Pakistan People's Party staged a walkout.[54] This represented a significant de-escalation of tensions when compared to Ghaffar Khan's call for a separate Pakhtun nation. Indeed, some observers attribute this reduction in tension to the gradual integration of the NWFP's population "into the state structure and market economy" of Pakistan. Moreover, with the Soviet invasion of Afghanistan in 1979, some 2 million Afghan refugees poured into camps primarily in the NWFP, causing "the nationalist demand for Pakhtunistan, i.e. an autonomous state comprising Pakhtuns on both sides of the Pakistan Afghanistan border" to go unheeded.[55] As a result of the collapse, Zia's regime— one suspicious of regional languages and insistent on the use of Urdu—allowed the introduction of Pashto as a medium of instruction in primary schools in 1984.[56]

The rise of the (primarily Pathan) Taliban in Afghanistan brought about a resurgence of Pathan nationalism in general. The impact of this nationalist surge in the NWFP is unclear, though language and ethnicity issues have begun to resurface. In January 1998 the Pakistani National Assembly rejected the demand of the NWFP's Awami National Party to rename the province "Pakhtunistan." The reemergence of Pathan nationalism in the NWFP bears close watching.

Baluchi

The conflicts in Baluchistan have had few links to issues involving language policy; instead they have been driven by economic deprivation and subjugation to the federal government. Baluchistan is the only province in Pakistan, for example, that has suffered the extended presence of

---

53. The irony of Bhutto, perceived by many to be a "man of the people" who had greater impulses toward regional accommodation, is not lost here. His authoritarian crackdown on NWFP political parties and Baluchistan in particular were unprecedented in Pakistan.

54. Rahman, "The Pashto Language and Identity-Formation in Pakistan," p. 164.

55. Rashid and Shaheed, *Pakistan: Ethno-Politics and Contending Elites,* p. 12.

56. Rahman, "Language Policy in Pakistan," p. 87.

army troops (1973–77). During this period, the shah of Iran actively assisted Pakistan in repressing a Baluchi uprising. The shah apparently feared for Iran's security should Baluchis in Iranian Baluchistan join their movement.

Baluchistan is a large province, comprising 45 percent of Pakistan's territory. It is bounded to the north by Afghanistan and to the west by Iran. Territorial lines of demarcation have partitioned Baluchi tribal areas between Iran and Pakistan. Baluchistan did not acquire equal status with Pakistan's other provinces until the formation of the One Unit in the 1950s; before then it was an amalgamation of princely states with numerous languages spoken among them, the most widely used being Pashto, Baluchi, and Brahui. Once the different peoples in Baluchistan agreed to merge with the One Unit, "Balochistan was soon forgotten and the nation got deeply involved in the war-game of 'parity and disparity' between the two emerging provinces of East Pakistan and West Pakistan."[57]

Conflicts involving Pathans and Baluchs have been prevalent in the province, and extend the reach of the larger Pakhtun conflict with Pakistan. Abdus Samad Khan Achakzai, for example, was "a leading member of the National Awami Party and protagonist of an independent 'Pashtoonistan' . . . [he] demanded a Pathan province on the basis of language by breaking Baluchistan into Baloch and Pathan majority areas." He was arrested by the government of Pakistan in 1958.[58]

Though Baluch–federal government relations have been strained at times, language has not been a source of tension. Bhutto, for example, dismissed the provincial government in 1973 and called in the armed forces. These steps were taken in response to the National Awami Party's leading of the Baluchi Provincial Assembly—a party that opposed Bhutto and participated in a broader call for greater federalism in the nation. But because Baluchistan is so ethnically and linguistically diverse, the Baluchis were already using Urdu as a link language internally. The choice of Urdu as the official language was made by the Baluchi nationalist Ghaus Baksh Bizenjo.[59] Pakistan's national language policy did not cause as much trouble here as elsewhere, though various development policies and the exploitation of Baluchistan's natural gas deposits certainly did.[60]

---

57.   Lt. Col. Syed Iqbal Ahmad, *Balochistan: Its Strategic Importance* (Karachi: Royal Book Co., 1992), p. 154.

58.   Ibid., p. 170.

59.   Some observers suggest that the use of Urdu was intended to hedge against Brahui and Pashto.

60.   Rashid and Shaheed, "The Pashto Language and Identity-Formation in Pakistan," p. 12.

Even so, a Baluchi nationalism is beginning to emerge and is finding some expression through language. During Benazir Bhutto's first term as prime minister, Nawab Akbar Bugti, a well-known Baluchi nationalist, became chief minister. He took up the cause of disseminating the Baluchi language more widely, demanding more radio time and championing Baluch identity through culture and literature—steps that reinforce the role of language in creating a strong sense of ethnic identity. According to one scholar, "Publication of Baluchi manuscripts, radio broadcasts in Baluchi from Karachi and Quetta, and the activities of the Baluch Academy in Quetta have all contributed to the growing sense of Baluchi as an important indigenous language with a distinct literary heritage. Promotion of Baluchi has also been given added impetus with the growth of a Baluchi 'national' movement seeking greater autonomy and, in its most extreme form, independence."[61]

The budding language movement would experience a few years of success after the passage of the Baluchistan Mother Tongue Use Bill (No. 8) in 1990. This bill, a product of Benazir Bhutto's government, mandated the use of Baluchi, Brahvi, and Pashto in governmental nonelite schools. Notably, the bill exempted elite English-medium schools from any such requirement. In 1992, however, with Nawaz Sharif as prime minister and a Pakistan Muslim League chief minister at the helm in Baluchistan, a decision (an amendment of sorts) was passed regarding the Mother Tongue Use Bill: The bill was decreed to be "optional."[62] One scholar reports that in practice, education in mother tongues ceased altogether in Baluchistan; no more textbooks were produced; and teachers were no longer trained in the mother tongues.[63]

In 1996 Baluchi nationalists rejected a Baluchistan assembly resolution that would have given national-language status to Urdu.[64] This could be a harbinger of conflict as Baluchistan begins to deal directly with language as a political issue. Increased violence in Quetta in 2000 suggests that more violent demands for accommodation may emerge from the nationalist Pashtoonkhwa Milli Awami organization and various Baluchi and Brahui tribal interests.[65] Further escalation is possible.

---

61. Addleton, "The Importance of Regional Languages in Pakistan," p. 41.

62. Rahman, "Language Policy in Pakistan," p. 88.

63. Rahman, Language and Politics in Pakistan, pp. 168–109.

64. Lahore University of Management Sciences, "History of Pakistan" (n.d.), http://ravi.lums.edu.pk/PAKISTAN/history.html.

65. Robert Kaplan, "Pakistan's Lawless Frontier," Atlantic Monthly, September 2000, http://www.theatlantic.com/cgi-bin/o/issues/2000/09/kaplan.htm.

English and Urdu

Urdu is a central component of the imagined nation of Pakistan, but English has played a crucial role in the country as well, particularly among the elite. This is a curious hypocrisy for an elite that has insisted that Urdu take the place of other "regional" languages. Anecdotal evidence bears out this hypocrisy: Jinnah's public statements to the effect that Urdu is the sole language of Pakistan were made in English.

Knowledge of English is a sign of privilege in Pakistan: Those who speak it as a first language, or speak it well as a second language, have attended either exclusive English-medium schools or Pakistan's officer or civil service academies. Graduates of these schools often become part of the ruling elite, as do the children who follow in their footsteps.

Early in Pakistan's history, English was viewed as expedient, a language that would eventually be replaced by Urdu. Referring to English during the First Education Conference in Karachi in 1947, however, the chairman, Fazlur Rahman, remarked that Pakistanis "should not throw away a language which give us so easy access to all the secrets of western science and culture."[66] To promote Urdu and Pakistani modernization, institutions were established (primarily in the Punjab) to develop scientific and legal vocabularies in Urdu. One such organization was the Official Language Committee, which was created by Punjab's governor in 1949. Its sole function was to coin new Urdu vocabulary. In addition, schools were ordered to switch from English to Urdu, and the courts, the legislature, and government offices were supposed to conduct business in Urdu. In practice, the only one of these offices to do so was the Language Committee.[67]

In 1948 the Advisory Board of Education agreed that Urdu should be the medium of instruction at the secondary and university levels. The board could not reach a decision, however, regarding the English-medium private schools and civil and military academies. English was still dominant when Ayub ascended to power, and his own emphasis on modernity and progress would only reinforce English at the upper levels. The Hamood ur-Rahman Education report, released in 1966, expressed regret that Karachi and Punjab Universities permitted the bachelor of arts

---

66. Quoted in M. Geijbels, "Urdu and the Pakistani National Language Issue," in Geijbels and Addleton, *The Rise and Development of Urdu and the Importance of Regional Languages in Pakistan*, p. 19.

67. Tariq Rahman, *The History of the Urdu-English Controversy*. Series: *Silsilah-yi matbu'at-I Muqtadirah-yi Qaumi Zaban* (Islamabad: National Language Authority, 1996), p. 54.

examination in Urdu and that the University of Sind allowed the same in Sindhi. The report would have preferred the use of English.

During Yahya Khan's rule, Air Marshall Nur Khan issued *Proposals for a New Educational Policy*, a report recommending that Bengali be the medium of instruction in East Pakistan and Urdu in West Pakistan. The report included a phase-in plan that set 1974 as the target date for these languages to be used by provincial governments and 1975 for the center. The plan would have phased out English for perpetuating a "caste-like distinction between those who feel at ease . . . in English and those who do not."[68] The proposal was hotly contested, and when published a year later as Pakistan's *New Education Policy*, it delegated the issue of phasing out English to a commission to be established in 1972. The nation, however, split before then, and Pakistan's new ruler—Zulfiqar Bhutto—chose not to act on the report.

Zulfiqar Bhutto declared Urdu the national language of Pakistan—a decision already enshrined in Article 251 of the 1973 constitution—but allowed "a period of 15 years . . . for the replacement of English by Urdu."[69] This article has yet to see full implementation.

General Zia's goal of Islamicizing the nation led to his desire for Urdu to predominate in Pakistan. To accomplish this, he "pass[ed] an order that Urdu would be the medium of instruction in all schools from 'class 1 or KG as the case may be from 1979.'" Pressure from the English-medium schools, however, resulted in Zia's withdrawal of the order in 1987. English-medium schools remained—and even proliferated.[70]

Despite the proclamation of every government since 1988 to establish Urdu as Pakistan's official language, with the eventual goal of replacing English, none has taken any actions to achieve this goal. English continues to be the first language of Pakistan's elite.

Arabic

The support for Arabic is an exception to the Pakistani state's generally ineffectual language policies. In Pakistan's search to create a national identity, Islam has been the great unifier and Arabic the religiously sanctioned prestige language. Although Arabic-language policies in Pakistan have their beginnings with Ayub Khan, it is a curious footnote of history

---

68. Quoted in Rahman, *The History of the Urdu-English Controversy*, p. 60.

69. Ibid., p. 62.

70. Rahman, "Language Policy in Pakistan," p. 88; and Geijbels, "Urdu and the Pakistani National Language Issue," p. 21.

that the Aga Khan suggested Arabic as the state language in 1951—as a solution to the contentious Urdu-versus-Bengali debate.[71]

Ayub Khan was the first Pakistani leader to advocate the teaching of Arabic as part of national planning. His Commission on National Education made two recommendations, one that never came to pass and one that represented the first step toward integrating and normalizing private Islamic centers of education, or *madrassa*s. Where his impulse toward modernization caused him to elevate English and Urdu over other languages—his recommendation for romanizing the scripts of Pakistani languages may be recalled here—he sought to affect the curricula of the *madrassa*s as well by proposing "greater integration of English into their teaching. Modern Arabic literature (as opposed to premodern treatises) were [*sic*] additionally advised as a means to 'introduce the ulema to the modern world.'" This proposal, however, was not implemented by the *ulema* (Islamic scholars); one scholar reports that only 2.87 percent of *madrassa*-educated students are taught English. Ayub's educational plan emphasized Urdu and English as the primary languages of Pakistan, but it recommended that Arabic also be a language of instruction. This move was crucial, because it would create a perception that Pakistani development would occur via English and Arabic—thus normalizing the idea of Arabic in state-run schools.[72]

During the regimes of Yahya Khan and Zulfiqar Bhutto, it is not clear if any policies relating to Arabic were proposed, let alone implemented. During Yahya's rule, Air Marshall Nur Khan's ineffectual *New Education Policy* was released. Bhutto's language policy intervention was focused on the ongoing Sindhi-Urdu tensions. The Islamicization programs of Gen. Zia ul-Haq promoted the use of Arabic at the national level. Zia's understanding of national cohesion, based on the two-nations theory, was that Islam was the binding force of the Pakistani state. He thus advocated the promotion of Arabic and Urdu as a means of overcoming forces that threatened to divide the country.

In 1982, faced with a shortage of trained secular teachers of Arabic, Zia conscripted the *ulema* of the *madrassa*s to teach Arabic in state schools. Then in 1984 and 1985, the "Iqra Centres" were established as part of his Literacy and Mass Education Campaign. The centers, whose instructors taught Urdu, were established within local mosques and *madrassa*s.[73]

---

71.   Rahman, "Language Policy in Pakistan," p. 88.

72.   Tariq Rahman, *Language, Education, and Culture* (Islamabad: Oxford University Press and Sustainable Development Policy Institute, 1999), pp. 105, 110.

73.   Ibid., p. 111.

With these two steps, the identification of the Islamic educational system's ideology with state programs began in earnest. Zia additionally instituted the use of state-owned airwaves in 1984 as a powerful medium for his Islamiyat initiatives; also, the state began broadcasting news in Arabic on television.[74] This initiative continues to this day, though it is unclear how many Pakistanis understand these broadcasts, which are supplemented by daytime broadcasts of Arabic instruction and Quranic studies.

The use of conservative eighteenth-century Arabic texts as core teaching materials has ideological implications: Arabic is not taught as a living language; rather it is for textual memorization and recitation only. Students memorize the sounds of Arabic and learn the words' meanings via Urdu, but they never learn to generate their own Arabic sentences.[75]

Zia's reliance on the *madrassas* for teaching Arabic and running literacy programs was based on a loose affiliation of nongovernmental institutions with greater capacity than the state itself to implement education policy. This would free up funds for defense purposes that might have gone to implementing Arabic and Urdu literacy programs. The *madrassa* network is large, self-sustaining via influxes of external capital, and growing: A 1988 government report counted 1,320 *madrassas* of all sects in Punjab, 678 in NWFP, 291 in Sind, and 347 in Baluchistan.[76] Zia's Arabic and Iqra policies contributed to the rising power of the *madrassas* from 1984 to 1994; he left them to their own devices, and in so doing, quietly endorsed whatever they chose to propagate. This is markedly different from, for example, requiring state curricula approvals and reviews of teaching procedures. More detailed research is needed, but it is no leap to suggest a causal link between these early Islamicization programs and today's retrograde radical Islamic movements in Pakistan. Furthermore, it is a commonplace observation that the government of Nawaz Sharif moved the entire nation toward the Wahabi Right, as is the fact that Afghanistan's Taliban traced its origins to *madrassa* education, particularly schools in Quetta (just across the border from Kandahar).

Thus the promotion of Arabic represents Pakistan's most coherent and sustained effort at implementing a new language policy; that it was delegated to ideological radicals is probably the reason it advanced—in sharp contrast to the continual failings of Pakistan's other language pol-

---

74. Rakisits, "Centre-Province Relations in Pakistan under President Zia," p. 80.

75. Rahman, *Language, Education, and Culture,* p. 105.

76. Human Development Centre, *Human Development in South Asia, 1999: The Crisis of Governance* (Karachi: Oxford University Press, 1999), p. 81.

icy efforts, which withered due to indifference and the pull of other priorities. There is a normative dimension implicit in any policy planning. That the Arabic-language policies of the Pakistan government ultimately fostered radical centers of Islamic education that now trouble the government is an alarming sign of a policy gone drastically wrong. Gen. Pervez Musharraf has recently called for a state review of the *madrassas*—a signal that Pakistan has finally grown concerned about this problematic institution built collaboratively by Ayub and Zia.

Conclusion

The call to national consolidation was irretrievably damaged by the founding decision to mandate the use of Urdu throughout Pakistan. Proclamations from the center to the provinces were perceived by the latter as aggressive. Coupled with arbitrary removals of elected leaders beginning in 1948 and continuing to the present, the central government's language policy has undermined every region's sense of identity. Instead of supporting a collaborative project of building a new homeland for Muslims, Pakistan's language policies have reflected the degree to which all but a chosen few were prevented from participating in the process. Rather than drawing the country's provinces into a broad, pluralistic dialogue about language, region, and culture—which might have had a unifying effect—Pakistan's language policies contributed to further divisions. Even when reasonable policy recommendations were developed (e.g., the 1959 Education Commission or the 1969 Nur Khan report), they were either feebly implemented or ignored altogether. Overall, Pakistan's language policies and weak implementation efforts have not facilitated national cohesion.

Pakistan's language policies—limited as they have been—have changed little over the decades. Language-identified movements, deemed antinational by the center, were and still are dealt with primarily through authoritarian crackdowns. Accommodation has been eschewed. Although aware of center-province problems, the Constituent Assembly viewed these not as unmet ethnic needs but as issues that could be addressed through better political frameworks. Compare the crackdown and dismissal of the NWFP government in 1947 with actions in Bengal in 1952 and then 1971. Zulfiqar Ali Bhutto deployed armed forces in Baluchistan from 1973 to 1977 after dismissing a government that, although not agitating primarily on a language-policy issue, sought remedies from the center. In 1998 the National Assembly dismissed the NWFP's Awami Party resolution for the province to be renamed "Pakhtunistan." Time and time again, Pakistan's political leadership has rejected ethnic accommodation and prolonged problems that will not go away on their own.

The central government's chronic mishandling of language policy has contributed significantly to instability and violence in Pakistan. By defining the idea of the nation narrowly, the country's leaders turned the language issue into a zero-sum competition with winners and losers. This exacerbated tensions between different ethnic groups and between most ethnic groups and the central government. There is no simple or easy solution to this complicated problem. Only a massive overhaul of the Pakistani political system—along with a redefinition of Pakistan itself—can undo the damage that has been done and lay the groundwork for a more stable, prosperous future.

Chapter 3

Language, Identity, and the State in Bangladesh

Amena Mohsin

Language is not just a mode of communication, but a way of life. It is steeped in the narratives, histories, cultures, and religions that constitute the crucial markers of a people. Recognizing the importance of language, the United Nations Educational, Scientific, and Social Organization (UNESCO) declared in 1999 that February 21 would henceforth be known as International Mother Language Day. The organization maintained that languages are the most powerful instruments for preserving and developing tangible and intangible heritages. It called on states to "encourage linguistic diversity and multilingual education for the development of fuller awareness of linguistic and cultural traditions throughout the world and to inspire solidarity based on understanding, tolerance and dialogue."[1]

Bangladesh was the driving force behind the UNESCO resolution. The reasons for this are fairly straightforward. The Bangladesh liberation movement was inspired by the ideals of Bengali nationalism, which had its roots in Bengali language and culture. After the formation of the state of Pakistan in 1947, the Bengalis of East Pakistan adopted language as the main pillar of their platform against the hegemony of West Pakistani nationalism, which was primarily based on religion. On February 21, 1952, Pakistani police forces opened fire on Bengali students who were demanding the recognition of Bengali as one of the national languages of Pakistan. Four students lost their lives. February 21 thereafter became a symbol of the Bengalis' quest for independence from Pakistan. The

---

1. *Independent* (Dhaka), February 21, 2000.

UNESCO declaration marked the sacrifice made by Bengalis for this linguistic cause.

Ironically and tragically, the government of Bangladesh has deeply hegemonic and chauvinistic language policies of its own. This is both hypocritical and short-sighted. It is hypocritical because Bengali leaders have not stood by the principles of diversity and autonomy that they once championed. It is short-sighted because their own history tells them that people who experience ethnolinguistic discrimination are prone to develop militant, violent, and even secessionist movements. The government of Bangladesh identifies itself with Bangla (or Bengali) and has imposed its own notions and categories of identification, development, and education on its non-Bengali population.[2] These policies are often out of step with the lives and cultures of the latter. Consequently, these peoples have been marginalized from the Bengali mainstream and have adopted their own constructions of categories of identity. These constructions, whether real or imagined, serve the interests of the communities, at least in the short term, by providing them with tools to fight state hegemony. The non-Bengali Hill people of Chittagong Hill Tracts (CHT), for example, today identify themselves as the Jumma nation to differentiate and distance themselves from the plainland Bengalis. The word "Jumma" has its origins in *jhum*—a slash-and-burn form of cultivation that is the Hill people's traditional mode of agriculture and is not practiced in the plains. The non-Bengali peoples of the plains refer to themselves as Adivashis, meaning indigenous people. Both the Hill people and the Adivashis have demanded constitutional recognition of their cultural uniqueness.

This chapter assesses the role of language in the construction of nationhood in Bangladesh and the impact of state language policies on its non-Bengali population. It argues that language has been used by the state as its most crucial identity marker. Through its adoption of a one-language policy, the government has made a conscious decision to try to create a homogeneous nation. This policy is reflected in Bangladesh's constitution; in political, administrative, and academic institutions; and in the development agendas of the state itself. This policy has profoundly influenced interethnic relations in Bangladesh. The country's non-Bengali peoples have refused to accept the government-sponsored model of nationhood. Indeed they see this policy as the primary cause of their marginalization within Bangladesh. The government has inadvertently politicized minorities who now demand constitutional recognition of their rights and distinctiveness. Bangladesh's non-Bengali population

2. The chapter does not discuss the Bihari community, because the issue of their citizenship is still a disputed matter between Bangladesh and Pakistan.

has become alienated from both the state and the country's Bengali community.

The chapter is divided into four main sections. The first section examines Bangladesh's ethnic setting and relations between the country's Bengali and non-Bengali populations. The second section analyzes the role of language in the construction of nationhood in Bangladesh. It also examines the impact of Bangladesh's language policy on the country's non-Bengali population. The third section assesses the responses of non-Bengali communities to these linguistically hegemonic policies. The chapter concludes with some policy lessons and recommendations.

The Ethnic Setting

No one knows the exact number of non-Bengali communities in Bangladesh. The Bangladesh census of 1991 puts the number at twenty-nine.[3] As one scholar correctly points out, however, the census mistakenly subdivides two groups, which suggests that there are only twenty-seven non-Bengali communities in Bangladesh.[4] Members of these minority communities maintain that there are more than forty-five non-Bengali communities in the country. They contend that, in order to portray Bangladesh as an overwhelmingly Bengali state, the census does not take significant ethnic variations into account.[5]

According to the 1991 census, the non-Bengali population of Bangladesh was 1.2 million, constituting 1.13 percent of the country's total population. Nonofficial estimates differ, however. One scholar notes that, according to the March 1981 *Monthly Statistical Bulletin of Bangladesh*, the non-Bengali population in the five districts in Rajshahi Division was 62,000; Christian missions in private censuses found the number to be twice that.[6] Members of these communities also dispute official figures. They see the census as a government mechanism to characterize them as insignificant minorities.

---

3. Dhaka Bangladesh Bureau of Statistics, *Bangladesh Census Report, 1991*, Vol. 1, *Analytical Report* (Dhaka: Government of Bangladesh, 1994), pp. 195–198.

4. Kibriaul Khaleque, "Ethnic Communities of Bangladesh," in Philip Gain, ed., *Bangladesh Land Forest and Forest People* (Dhaka: Society for Environment and Human Development, 1995), p. 7.

5. Interviews with author, Dhaka University, Bangladesh, April 2000; the students belong to the Garo and Oraon communities.

6. Cited in C.T. Maloney, "Tribes of Bangladesh and Synthesis of Bengali Culture," in M.S. Qureshi, ed., *Tribal Cultures in Bangladesh* (Rajshahi: Institute of Bangladesh Studies, 1984), p. 8.

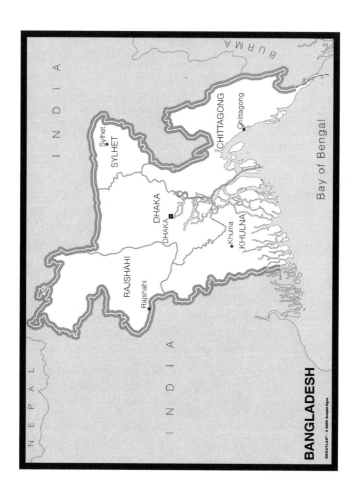

The non-Bengali communities of Bangladesh can be divided into two main groups, based on their geographical habitats: the Plains groups and the Hill groups. The Plains groups live along the borders of the northwest, north, and northeast portions of the country. For instance, non-Bengali communities such as the Koch, Munda, Oraon, Paharia, Rajbongshi, and Saontal have traditionally lived in parts of the Bogra, Dinajpur, Kushtia, Pabna, Rajshahi, and Rangpur Districts in the north. The greater Sylhet District in the north is the traditional home of the Khasi, Manipuri, Pathor, and Tipra communities. The Garo, Koch, and Hajong peoples live in the Mymensingh and Jamalpur Districts in the north and in the Tangail District in the north-central region of the country.[7] Scattered settlements of other non-Bengali peoples are found in the Barisal, Comilla, Dhaka, Faridpur, Khulna, Patuakhali, and other districts.

The non-Bengali Hill people live in the southeastern part of the country known as the Chittagong Hill Tracts. They inhabit two distinct ecological zones: the ridge-top and the valley. The Chakmas, Marmas, and Tripuras are valley-dwelling people, while the Banjogees, Chak, Khamis, Kukis, Lushai, Mro, Riang, and Tanchangya live on the ridges of the Hills. Table 3.1 lists the main linguistic and religious groupings of the country's non-Bengali communities.

BENGALI–NON-BENGALI RELATIONS

The relationship between Bengalis and non-Bengalis in modern-day Bangladesh has been marked by distrust, animosity, and ambiguity. During the colonial period, colonial authorities intervened in favor of indigenous communities and established protective laws such as the Chittagong Hill Tracts Manual of 1900, which restricted the settlement of Bengalis in the CHT and imposed restrictions on land transfers from Hill people to Bengalis. The Adivashis of the plains were similarly protected by the Chota Nagpur Tenancy Act of 1908. Thus, during the colonial period, interactions between Bengalis and non-Bengalis were limited, but mistrust emerged over the land issue.

Since independence in 1971, however, the government of Bangladesh has advanced the interests of Bengalis at the expense of non-Bengalis. For example, the government adopted a policy of Bengali settlement by amending the CHT Manual. Between 1979 and 1984, 40,000 Bengalis were settled in the CHT through a government-sponsored plan.[8] These people were settled by ejecting the Hill people from their traditional

---

7.   Khaleque, "Ethnic Communities of Bangladesh," p. 13.

8.   *Guardian* (London), March 6, 1984.

Table 3.1. Major Minority Groups in Bangladesh.

Group	Language	Religion
Chakma	Indo-Aryan group	Buddhism
Marma	Mixture of Burmese and Rakhaine language, Tibeto-Burman group	Buddhism
Tripura	Cockborok, Bodo group	Hinduism
Tanchangya	Indo-Aryan group	Buddhism
Khami	Kuki-chin group	Buddhism; but has certain rites and beliefs found in animism
Mro	Tibeto-Burman group	Animism
Bawm	Kuki-chin group	Christianity
Kheyang	Kuki-chin group	Buddhism
Pankhoa	Kuki-chin group	Christianity
Chak	Tibeto-Burman group	Buddhism
Lushai	Kuki-chin group	Christianity/animism
Garo	Bodo group	Songsarek/Christianity
Saontal	Offshoot of Kol/Mundari	Animism/Christianity
Khasi	Austroasiatic	Animism
Manipuri	Meithei	Hinduism (Vaisnavite division)
Paharia	Dravidian	Christianity/own religion with Hindu admixtures
Rakhaine	Rakhaine, Bhot-Brahmo group	Buddhism
Rajbongshi	Bodo group (lost), a variation of Bengali	Hinduism/Islam
Koch	Bodo group	
Oraon	Kurukh/Sadri	Animism/Christianity
Hajong	Bodo group	Hinduism
Mahat	Shadri	
Munda	Munda	

SOURCE: This table has been compiled from the following sources: T.H. Lewin, *The Hill Tracts of Chittagong and the Dwellers Therein, with Comparative Vocabularies of the Hill Dialects* (Calcutta: Bengal Printing Co. Ltd., 1869); G.A. Grierson, *Linguistic Survey of India: Bengal (Lower Provinces)* (Calcutta: Office of the Superintendent of Government Printing, 1898); Herbert Risley, *Tribes and Castes of Bengal: Ethnographic Glossary*, Vol. 1 (Calcutta: Bengal Secretariat Press, 1891); W.W. Hunter, *A Statistical Account of Bengal*, Vol. 6, *CHT, Chittagong, Noakhali, Tipperah, Hill Tipperah* (London: Trubner, 1876); E.T. Dalton, *Tribal History of Eastern India* (Calcutta: Office of the Superintendent of Government Printing, 1872); R.H.S. Hutchinson, *Eastern Bengal and Assam District Gazetteers, CHT* (Allahabad: Pioneer Press, 1909); Robert Shafer, *Word: Journal of the Linguistic Circle of New York*, No. 11 (New York: S.F. Vanni, 1955), pp. 94–111; C.T. Maloney, "Tribes of Bangladesh and Synthesis of Bengali Culture," in M.S. Qureshi, ed., *Tribal Cultures in Bangladesh* (Rajshahi: Institute of Bangladesh Studies, 1984), pp. 5–52; Lucien Bernot, "Ethnic Groups of CHT," in Pierre Bessaignet, ed., *Social Research in East Pakistan* (Dhaka: Asiatic Society of Pakistan, 1964); Shugata Chakma, *Parbattya Chattagramer Upajati O Sanskriti* [The tribes and culture of CHT] (Rangamati: Dhira Khisa Chakma, 1993); Abdus Sattar, *In the Sylvan Shadows* (Dhaka: Bangla Academy, 1983); Major Playfair, *The Garos* (Panbazar, Gauhati: United Publishers, 1975); Subhash Jengcham, *Bangladesher Garo Shomprodae* [The Garo community of Bangladesh] (Dhaka: Bangla Academy, 1994); P.R.T. Gordon, *The Khasi* (London: David Nutt, 1907); Qureshi, *Tribal Cultures of Bangladesh*; Fr. Stephen G. Gomes, *The Paharias in Bangladesh: A Case Study of Assimilation and Identification with Policy Implications*, in ibid., pp. 135–157; and Mostafa Mojid, *Patuakhalir Rakhaine Upajati* [The Rakhaine tribes of Patuakhali] (Dhaka: Bangla Academy, 1992).

lands. The government maintains that Bengalis have been settled in *khas* or government-owned land; but to the Hill people, these are communal lands that belong to them, to their ancestors, and to spirits. To the Hill people, land is sacrosanct and not to be commodified. This gap in perception is an obvious indicator of the failure of the government to understand and respect the cultures of its minorities. The Bengalis also control the trade and commerce of the area.

The feelings of animosity between Bengalis and non-Bengalis were exacerbated during the two decades of militant insurgency initiated by the Parbattya Chattagram Jonoshoghoti Samity (PCJSS), a movement formed by Manobendra Narayan Larma in 1972 on behalf of the Hill people; the objective was to attain political, cultural, and economic autonomy. This militancy was a response of the Hill people to the government's denial of their rights and its failure to recognize them as a people distinct from Bengalis. During this period the CHT came under military control, and the region witnessed numerous human rights violations, including rapes of women.

The situation is not much different for other non-Bengali communities. In a survey of 100 Garos and 100 Saontals, 95 percent of Garo respondents felt that they had experienced discrimination, while 80 percent of the Saontals reported that they had.[9] They identified dispossession from their land and forest resources, a dearth of job opportunities, political underrepresentation, and cultural stultification as their main grievances. All respondents in both the Garo and Saontal communities held the government responsible for this situation.

Language and the State

Language is a central component of Bengali nationalism. The government of Bangladesh rests on the linguistic and cultural identity of the Bengali population. "Bangladesh" literally means the land of the Bengali-speaking people.

PREINDEPENDENCE PERIOD

The establishment of the state of Pakistan was based on the two-nation theory of founder Mohammad Ali Jinnah, who argued that the Hindus and Muslims of India constituted two separate nations. The Islamic Republic of Pakistan adopted an assimilative policy in line with its understanding of the meaning of the nation-state. Language—more specifically a common language for the entire population of the state—was consid-

9. Author survey, Dhaka and Rajshahi Divisions, Bangladesh, August 1999.

ered an essential part of nation building. Not surprisingly, this language had to reflect Islamic traditions. Urdu, written in Arabic-Persian script, had become exclusively associated with Muslims and their culture in India. Bengali (spoken in East Pakistan), written in Nagri script (similar to that of Sanskrit), was identified with Hinduism. Accordingly, Jinnah declared in Dhaka in March 1948: "Let me make it very clear to you that the state language of Pakistan is going to be Urdu and no other language. . . . Without one language no nation can remain tied up solidly together and function."[10]

A religious orientation was emphasized by Liaqat Ali Khan, the first prime minister of Pakistan. He stated: "The defence of Bengali language in front of Urdu is against the laws of Islam."[11] In 1949 the central minister for education proposed the introduction of Arabic script for Bengali, arguing that "not only Bengali literature, even the Bengali alphabet is full of idolatry. Each Bengali letter is associated with this or that god or goddess of Hindu pantheon. . . . Pakistan and Devanagari script cannot co-exist. . . . To ensure a bright and great future for the Bengali language it must be linked with the Holy Quran. . . . Hence the necessity and importance of Arabic script."[12]

To resist the imposition of an alien language and cultural identity, the Bengalis countered with a proposal based on secular nationalism, with language and culture as its core. Urdu was seen not only as a language but also as a political tool of hegemony and domination aimed at destroying their cultural identity. On February 21, 1952, the police opened fire in Dhaka on students protesting the imposition of Urdu. The four students who died as a result instantly became Bengali heroes.

To the demands for linguistic and cultural autonomy, the marginalized Bengalis later added appeals for economic and political autonomy. Their demands were voiced through the Twenty-one-Point Formula of the United Front, a group that included the Awami League, the Krishak Sramik Party, the Nizam-i-Islam, and the Ganatantri Dal of East Bengal in 1954. The United Front was formed by the political parties of East Bengal to contest the first general elections of Pakistan. Important among its Twenty-one-Point Formula were Point 1, which demanded the recognition of Bengali as one of the country's national languages; Point 10, which

---

10. Quoted in Jamiluddin Ahmad, ed., *Speeches and Writings of Mr. Jinnah*, Vol. 2 (Lahore: Government of Pakistan, 1964), p. 490.

11. Quoted in Safiqul Islam, "Failure in State-Building: The Case of Pakistan," *Asian Profile*, Vol. 2, No. 6 (1984), p. 585.

12. Quoted in Anisuzzaman, *Creativity, Reality, and Identity* (Dhaka: Institute of Culture and Bengal Studies, 1993), p. 107.

sought the introduction of the vernacular as a medium of instruction; and Point 19, which called for the establishment of full regional autonomy for East Pakistan. In East Bengal, the United Front won a landslide victory over the ruling Muslim League (the party responsible for the independence of Pakistan) and took 301 seats out of 310, with 97.5 percent of the votes cast.[13] The Twenty-one-Point Formula (especially the demand for regional autonomy) was unacceptable to the West Pakistani ruling elite. Within six weeks of its assumption of power, the United Front government was dismissed on the grounds that it was bringing disintegration of the country by working against the interest of the state.

Martial law was declared in Pakistan on October 7, 1958. Gen. Mohammad Ayub Khan, the commander in chief of the Pakistani army, assumed control. All forms of political activity were initially banned. By 1960 Ayub had introduced the Basic Democracy concept, and some political activities were allowed. During his regime, which lasted until 1969, Ayub's perceptions and ideas greatly influenced the course of Pakistan's politics, and more important, West Pakistan's policies toward the East. Ayub's perceptions of the Bengalis are most revealing: "East Bengalis . . . probably belong to the very original Indian races. It would be no exaggeration to say that up to the creation of Pakistan, they had not known any real freedom or sovereignty. They have been in turn ruled either by the caste Hindus, Moghals, Pathans, or the British. In addition they have been and still are under considerable Hindu cultural and linguistic influence. As such they have all the inhibitions of downtrodden races and have not yet found it possible to adjust psychologically to the requirements of newborn freedom."[14]

In an attempt to expunge Hindu influence from Bengali culture, the Ayub regime banned the playing of the songs of Rabindranath Tagore in East Bengal in 1967. By this time, his songs had become an integral part of Bengali culture. This action gave a new impetus to the drive for Bengali autonomy; indeed, in the years that followed, one of Tagore's songs became the symbol of Bengali nationalism and was eventually adopted as the national anthem of Bangladesh.

In 1966 the Awami League, the major political party of East Pakistan, launched its Six-Point Movement, which called for the creation of two autonomous units in Pakistan. It was militant in its emphasis on linguistic and secular nationalism—the basis of Bengali nationalism. The appeal to Bengali nationalism was again revived in the 1969 popular movement

---

13. Islam, "Failure in State-Building," p. 584.

14. Mohammad Ayub Khan, *Friends Not Masters: A Political Autobiography* (London: Oxford University Press, 1967), p. 187.

against Ayub that forced him from office. The Awami League won a landslide victory in the general elections of 1970, gaining all but 2 of the 162 seats in East Bengal.

Throughout this period, Bengalis had charged the West Pakistani regime with economic and political discrimination. East Pakistan remained an economic hinterland for West Pakistan, and the development policies of the central government favored the West. East Pakistan, with 56 percent of the total population of the state and a 60 percent contribution to national revenue, could secure only 25 percent of funds allotted for development projects.

Bengalis, despite being the majority, were also left out of the government's decisionmaking process. In the first decade after independence, although East Bengal had 50 percent representation in the central political elite, its citizens made up a bare 5 percent of the officer corps, only about 30 percent of the civil-bureaucratic elite, and just 10 percent of the entrepreneurial class.[15] During the Ayub era, the Bengalis were again left out of the decisionmaking process; not a single Bengali representative could be found among the ten leading figures in the martial-law administration. In 1969 there was only one Bengali general in the Pakistani army. The 1970 elections, however, brought home to the West Pakistani ruling elite the possibility of having to hand over power to the East Bengalis—a possibility that the leadership deemed unacceptable. Its refusal to transfer power led to the independence of East Bengal, which emerged as independent Bangladesh on December 16, 1971.

Bangladesh's nine-month war of liberation remained identified with the Bengali community. On March 26, 1971, the secretary-general of the Awami League of Chittagong District read aloud the declaration of independence. He called upon the Bengalis—not the people of Bangladesh, who could be non-Bengalis as well as Bengalis—to resist the Pakistani forces. In his opening speech as the first prime minister of Bangladesh, Tajuddin Ahmed declared: "You have shown that a new Bengali nation has been born amidst the ruins of battlefield [sic]. . . . Whilst we remain true to our heritage Bengalis have shown that they are also a warrior people."[16]

But the non-Bengali Garos, Hajongs, Saontals, and Tripuras had also participated in the war of liberation. Despite this, "Amar Sonar Bangla Ami Tomae Bhalobashi" (O My Golden Bengal, I Love Thee), a song by

15. Rounaq Jahan, *Pakistan: Failure in National Integration* (Dhaka: University Press Ltd., 1972), pp. 24–25.

16. Quoted in Ministry of External Affairs, *Bangladesh Documents* (New Delhi: Government of India, 1971), p. 83.

the Bengali Tagore, was adopted as the national anthem of Bangladesh. Bangla was used by the poet in a territorial sense, but Bangla is also a cultural and linguistic identity. The non-Bengali population thereby could not identify with the nationalist movement or the war of liberation, both of which remained overtly Bengali.

POSTINDEPENDENCE PERIOD

The identification with Bengali continued in the independent state of Bangladesh. True to the spirit of the nationalist movement, the new entity predicated itself on the ideals of Bengali nationalism, Bengali language, and Bengali culture. The government took specific constitutional and institutional measures to promote Bengali language and culture. Article 9 of the constitution defined Bengali nationalism as "the unity and solidarity of the Bengali nation, which deriving its identity from its language and culture, attained sovereign and independent Bangladesh through a united and determined struggle in the war of independence, shall be the basis of Bengali nationalism."[17]

Article 3 declared Bengali to be the official language of the republic. According to Article 23, "The state shall adopt measures to conserve the cultural traditions and heritage of the people, and so to foster and improve the national language, literature and the arts that all sections of the people are afforded the opportunity to contribute towards and to participate in the enrichment of the national culture."[18]

The constitution recognizes "the people" as the Bengali people. At the national level, a Bangla Academy was set up to promote the development of Bengali language and culture. The government's refusal to recognize the existence of non-Bengali peoples as distinct cultural communities, combined with its identification and promotion of Bangla, pushed non-Bengali communities toward the periphery. Chakma Chief Raja Devasish has rightly pointed out that Bengali does not need any state protection or promotion; it is the country's other languages that need such help. He has further noted that although the government declared Islam to be the state religion, it also mandated that other religions be allowed to practice in peace; no such protection exists to cover language. He echoes the sentiments of other non-Bengali communities when he describes the constitution as repressive and hegemonic.[19]

17. *Constitution of the People's Republic of Bangladesh* (Dhaka: Government of Bangladesh, 1972), p. 5.

18. *Constitution of the Peoples' Republic of Bangladesh (as amended up to 30 April 1996)* (Dhaka: Government of Bangladesh, 1996), p. 16.

19. Interview with author, Dhaka, Bangladesh, March 9, 2000.

THE ACADEMIC ARENA. Bengali has been adopted as the medium of instruction in all government academic institutions at least until high school. The state universities also provide education in Bengali at the faculties of arts and social sciences, though at this level students can choose between Bengali and English. Bengali is also the medium of official government correspondence. There is no policy for the protection or promotion of other languages, and there have been no official attempts to give instruction to non-Bengali communities in their own languages, even at the primary levels. Making Bengali the medium of instruction obviously puts the non-Bengali population at a disadvantage. Students of these communities say that it is difficult to compete with students whose mother tongue is Bengali. The high dropout rate among students from these communities supports this claim. Interviews of eleven outstanding students from several non-Bengali communities, who were studying in the country's top-ranking academic institutions, revealed that they had all suffered feelings of inferiority during their childhoods because of their different pronunciations and accents. They were teased by fellow students, making them reluctant to speak out in class. They all felt that they could have done much better in school if their primary education had been in their mother tongues.[20] Moreover, teachers expect students to conform to conventional Bengali norms that students from other communities have difficulty adhering to.

The students were also depressed about the state of their own languages (which are often referred to as "dialects" in mainstream discourse). Many also allege that the curricula at all levels of education are heavily biased toward Bengalis. Article 17 of the constitution calls for the establishment of a uniform system of education throughout the country. The histories, cultures, and lives of the non-Bengali communities, however, are absent from this curriculum. The books provided by the national textbooks board narrate the glory of Bengali heroes, stressing their culture and history.

A consequence of this policy is not only a loss of diversity but also, and more dangerous, the silencing of non-Bengali voices and the creation of a high culture within Bangladesh that relegates non-Bengalis to the periphery. The Garos and Saontals fought in Bangladesh's war of liberation, yet their role remains unrecognized—as does that of the Hill people, who also took part in this war. As another example, 400 women from the CHT were raped by soldiers of the Pakistan army and their collaborators, yet

---

20.   Interviews with author, Dhaka, Bangladesh, April 2000; the students belong to the Chakma, Garo, Hajong, Marma, Saontal, Tanchangya, and Tripura communities.

there has been no official acknowledgment of this fact.[21] The discourse on the war of liberation is silent about the sacrifices and contributions of non-Bengali communities.

THE CULTURAL ARENA. As noted, a Bangla Academy was established at the national level to promote the development of Bengali language and culture. Bengali cultural holidays are celebrated with much fanfare. Their special days are observed as national holidays: Pohela Boishakh marks the Bengali New Year, and Eikushey February (February 21) commemorates Martyrs' Day. In fact, the entire month of February features events aimed at the promotion of Bengali language and culture. Book fairs promote publications in Bengali (although English books published in Bangladesh are now also displayed). Cultural programs held throughout the country celebrate the glory of Bengali language, culture, and history. Most of these programs are sponsored and promoted by the government.

The government has established tribal institutes in some districts, but these cater to the promotion of tourism; their publications, for example, are in Bengali. Moreover, no serious attempts have been made to promote local languages and cultures. Rather, the tourist culture is a distortion of the local culture and is strongly resented by most local people.

Radio and television offer programs only in Bengali. Road markers, signs, and license plate numbers are all written in Bengali. A foreign visitor would think that Bangladesh is a land of Bengali-speaking people only. No reflection of its non-Bengali communities is to be found in the streets of Bangladesh, unless one journeys to the CHT or to the interior where non-Bengali people live.

THE ECONOMIC ARENA. Most non-Bengalis in Bangladesh are agriculturists. *Jhum* had been their dominant mode of cultivation. Because of government restrictions on the acquisition of land and forests, however, *jhum* is becoming increasingly difficult to sustain. Many farmers have shifted to wet-rice cultivation.

Language and cultural differences contribute to the economic marginalization of the country's non-Bengali peoples—the critical factor behind their disempowerment. The inability of these peoples to understand or communicate in Bengali hinders economic integration. Further, the unwillingness of the government to understand or accommodate the economic modes associated with cultures that are different from the mainstream undermines their progress.

---

21. This information was acquired in Khagrachari in the CHT during the author's research on Women Victims of 1971, a project sponsored by the Ain 'O Shalish Kendra, Dhaka, Bangladesh, November 1997.

The Garos and Mundas, for example, have lost most of their land to Bengali moneylenders. During lean times, they must borrow money; and because of their inability to communicate in Bengali, they often unwittingly agree to pay exorbitant interest rates—sometimes as high as 400 percent a year, with their land as collateral. Consequently, many of them have become landless. The non-Bengali peoples also allege that they face tremendous language problems in the courts, where they often must go to resolve land disputes. These difficulties discourage them from seeking legal remedies.

Forests constitute an integral component in the lives of the Hill people of CHT and the Garo community. Today, however, these groups have been dispossessed of this vital resource, as the government has appropriated most of the forests as Reserve Forests (RF). Language barriers here have also played a major role in minority groups' alienation from the country's resources. Their inability to understand the Bengali language, combined with the government's refusal to grasp the significance of their connection to the forests, have had extremely damaging effects. The process of converting community forests into RF, for instance, begins with a public notification under Section 4 of the Forest Act of 1927. It identifies the lands involved, and after an inquiry, all or part of these lands are constituted into RF by another notification under Section 20 of the act. A variety of mandated steps are to follow, but such provisions have mostly been neglected; the announcements, for example, are often made improperly. The local people in many instances do not understand Bengali; and more important, they are uninformed about legal procedures, which in any event often do not align with their cultural mores.[22]

In matters of land and forest acquisition, the government has acted without regard for the cultural values of the communities concerned. As mentioned earlier, the government undertook a program of Bengali settlement in the CHT through the acquisition of indigenous lands. The government regards lands that do not have ownership deeds as government owned, but the concept of private ownership is alien to people practicing the *jhum* mode of cultivation. Communal ownership of land forms the basis of their community life and cultural norms. Not only has the government acquired land and forests, but it has also put a ban on *jhum* cultivation. Consequently, many farmers have had to switch to plow cultivation, while others have become landless, a phenomenon previously unknown in the Hills. This situation has changed minority cultures.

---

22. Philip Gain, "Expansion of Reserved Forests Complicate Land Issues in the Chittagong Hill Tracts," *Earth Touch*, No. 5 (Dhaka: Society for Environment and Human Development, October 1999), pp. 26–32.

They have lost their egalitarian foundation and are moving toward stratified relations based on the concept of private ownership of property.

The Garos, who consider themselves to be the "children of the forests," have been similarly affected. Theirs is a matrilineal society, but with their gradual alienation from the land and the introduction of private property, the Garos are moving toward a patrilineal mode of social development. Not only have women lost their traditional status, but in some cases they have become victims of sexual harassment—or worse. Because many women still depend on forest resources to support their families, they continue to seek access to the forests, where they are sometimes confronted by security personnel who pressure them into have sexual relations.[23]

THE POLITICAL ARENA. The government's identification with the Bengali community has had political effects as well, as non-Bengali communities remain underrepresented. The national parliament is a 300-member body elected directly by the people; thirty seats were reserved for women, who were elected by members of parliament. This reservation provision expired in April 2001 and has not been renewed. There is no provision for the reservation of seats for non-Bengali communities. Three seats have been reserved for the CHT, but the seats are for the geographical constituency of the CHT, not for the Hill people per se. Because of a deliberate government policy of Bengali settlement in the CHT, a demographic shift has occurred in the region: Bengalis today constitute almost 50 percent of the total population of the area. It is not surprising that the elected represent- atives from the CHT, even when of non-Bengali origins, have been members of mainstream political parties. And even if three seats were reserved for the Hill people, three members can hardly achieve anything substantial for their constituents in a body of 300 members, particularly if their interests clash with the will of the majority. Members of non-Bengali communities resent the fact that they have no voice at the government's highest decisionmaking levels. In other words, the electoral process as well as the national parliament only reproduces the hegemony of the dominant community—the Bengalis.

Responses of Non-Bengali Communities

Non-Bengali communities have fought back against the government's policies and have begun to reassert their identities. These efforts are occurring at several levels.

In the CHT, the PCJSS has constructed the identity of Jumma nation-

---

23.   *Bangla Bazar* (Dhaka), December 5, 1999.

alism for the Hill people. Taking its seeds from *jhum* cultivation, the PCJSS has claimed that the Hill ecology sets them apart from the Bengalis of the plains and bestows them with a distinct culture and way of life. The Bengalis used the term "Jumma" to disparage the Hill people; the PCJSS has invoked this term to imbue the Hill people with a sense of pride in their own past and present, because *jhum* is not only a mode of cultivation but also a way of life. Language has played an important role in this construction, as certain symbols and traditions in the Hills can be expressed only through native languages. (Although each Hill group has its own language, a pidgin Chittagonian is the lingua franca in the Hills.)

Each group in the Hills is also engaged in the construction of its own identity along linguistic lines. This effort aims to counter the hegemony of the dominant cultures in the Hill Tracts itself; for instance, the Chakmas, Marmas, and Tripuras constitute about 85 percent of the Hill population. The promotion of minority languages also allows them to maintain the cultural diversity of the Hills. The process of cultural exclusiveness is reflected in two major ways. First, rather than giving their children Bengali names (as they once did), the Hill people tend to name newborns in their own language. This distinguishes them both from Bengalis and from other cultural groups in the Hills. Second, the Hill groups are seeking to develop alphabets for their languages. Alphabets have a special significance for the Hill people, because they denote the politics of the region. There is almost a total rejection of Bengali. (See Table 3.2.)[24] These formulations reflect the assertiveness of the identities of the Hill people. An eminent anthropologist from the region has pointed out that only a Hill person who has lived under the dominance of the Bengali language can understand the significance of these alphabets. For the Hill people, the alphabets are symbols of their identity and autonomy and have a life of their own.[25]

Non-Bengali communities in the plains have also protested the government's assimilative policies. Their protests have taken various forms. At the individual level, they see themselves as Garos or Saontals within the state of Bangladesh. Collectively, they see themselves as Adivashis and endeavor to reestablish their special relationship with the land,

24. Fariduddin Ahamed, "Ethnic and Cultural Identity," paper presented at a workshop on Chittagong Hill Tracts, organized by the Bangladesh Rural Advancement Committee, Dhaka, Bangladesh, October 19–23, 1999.

25. Proshanta Tripura, "Bhasha, Horof O Jatiyota: Tripura Jonogoshtir Obhiggota" [Language, alphabets, and nationality: the experience of the Tripura community], *Prothom Alo*, February 21, 2000.

Table 3.2. Development of Alphabets for Minority Languages in Bangladesh.

Group	Form of Alphabets
Chakma	Burmese/Arakanese; has similarities with Marma alphabets
Marma	Burmese/Arakanese (Rakhaine) alphabets
Tanchangya	Has similarities with Chakma alphabets
Bawm	Roman/English alphabets
Lushai	Roman/English alphabets (similar to Bawm alphabets)
Pankhoa	Roman/English alphabets (similar to Bawm alphabets)
Mro	About fifteen years ago, an individual named Menley Mro constructed separate Mro alphabets
Khumi	Mro alphabets
Tripura	Previously Bangla alphabets; now attempts to use Roman/English alphabets
Chak	Attempts to borrow from Burmese/Arakanese/Marma alphabets from Myanmar
Kheyang	Has not yet evolved any alphabets

SOURCE: D.G.A. Khan, *Disintegration of Pakistan (Delhi: Meenakshi Prakashoni, 1985)*, p. 11.

which they feel has been lost because of state encroachment. Their status as Adivashis, they believe, should force the state to recognize their customary rights over land and forests. They resist the ideas of Bengali/Bangladeshi nationalism, because they identify these with Bengali culture, language, and Islam. Nevertheless, they do perceive themselves as Bangladeshi citizens and frequently mention their role in the war of liberation. In their resistance to cultural assimilation and by making a distinction between citizenship and nationality, the Adivashis are taking a conscious political stand. Yet even though they recognize the importance of written language, they have not yet endeavored to form their own written alphabets. Of late, however, the Garos have begun to form their own alphabets using Roman alphabets. There is a strong feeling among the other communities of the need to develop written languages. This they believe is vital for the survival of their languages, which they consider to be the core of their identity.

On February 21, 2000, the students of non-Bengali communities marched at Dhaka University, chanting slogans in their own languages for the first time ever. This was a forceful and creative assertion of their distinctiveness.

Nationalism, Language, and Conflict in Bangladesh

The country's Bengali ruling elite has reached a consensus on the question of Bengali hegemony. Since its emergence as an independent state, Bangladesh has developed two models of nationhood: a Bengali model and a Bangladeshi model. The postindependence period has seen the institutionalization of the Bengali model of nationhood by the Awami League regime. The country's constitution as well as its administrative arrangements cemented Bengali as the official language of communication as well as the medium of instruction in all state academic institutions. Bengali nationalism was imposed on the entire population of Bangladesh. This insensitivity toward Bangladesh's non-Bengali communities has been challenged. Manobendra Narayan Larma, for example, refused to endorse the constitution of 1972, arguing that "you cannot impose your national identity on others. I am a Chakma not a Bengali. I am a citizen of Bangladesh, Bangladeshi. You are also Bangladeshi but your national identity is Bengali. . . . They (Hill People) can never become Bengali."[26]

The Bengali political elite was too arrogant to recognize the logic and implications of Larma's contentions. This elite, which had fought against the hegemony of the Pakistani state using language and culture as tools, themselves became hegemons and attempted to impose their language and culture on other ethnic groups.

The political landscape of Bangladesh changed dramatically on August 15, 1975, when the president, Sheikh Mujibur Rahman, was assassinated by a group of young army officers. During the subsequent military takeover, the country moved from a secular to an Islamic brand of nationalism (i.e., the Bangladeshi model of nationhood). Yet the shift from Bengali to Bangladeshi nationalism did not change government policy toward Bengali language or culture. Bangladeshi nationalism was based on land, language, culture, and religion. In 1988 Islam was declared the state religion of Bangladesh, with the provision that other religions could be practiced in peace.[27] These changes further marginalized the non-Bengali communities, which in the process became religious minorities as well. The Bangladesh Nationalist Party (BNP) and the Jatiyo Party that have subsequently formed governments have held on to the Bangladeshi model of nationhood.

---

26. Quoted in Government of Bangladesh, *Parliament Debates* (Dhaka: Government of Bangladesh, 1972), p. 452.

27. *Constitution of the People's Republic of Bangladesh* (Dhaka: Government of Bangladesh, 1994), p. 6.

No regime in Bangladesh has made any major concessions or given any significant political power to the country's non-Bengali communities. The constitution declares Bangladesh to be a culturally homogeneous state. The BNP regime refused to observe 1993 as the Year of the Indigenous Peoples, as declared by the United Nations. Sheikh Hasina, then the leader of the opposition (and the daughter of Sheikh Mujibur), extended her party's support to the indigenous people's movement by recognizing their rights within Bangladesh. After assuming power in 1996, however, the party changed its position. Sheikh Hasina then maintained that there were some *Nritattik jonogoshti* in Bangladesh. (This is a very ambiguous term, the nearest English equivalent being "ethnographic people.") A consensus has thus emerged among the Bengali political elite on the question of Bengali hegemony in Bangladesh. Occasional variations in this position are ephemeral manifestations of party politics and nothing more.

Government policies created politicized and militant minorities within a year of Bangladesh's independence. By 1972 Manobendra Narayan Larma had formed the PCJSS, the political platform for the Hill people. An armed wing, the Shanti Bahini (Peace Forces), was later added to it. For the next two and a half decades, the country witnessed an armed insurgency in the CHT. In 1975, after changes in the political scene in Bangladesh, Larma crossed over to India. Having grown increasingly favorable toward the PCJSS, the Indian government allowed it to establish a military and political presence in Tripura, India. The Indian military also provided training and assistance to the Shanti Bahini. As a result, the region underwent full-scale militarization. Also during this period, the Bangladeshi military committed numerous human rights violations. Meanwhile, the government undertook a policy of Bengalization and Islamization of the region. With government support Bengalis were settled in the CHT. Bengali men were encouraged to marry local women after they had converted to Islam; local people regarded such intermarriage as "ethnocide." To counter the hegemony of the "Bengali nation," the PCJSS constructed the identity of a "Jumma nation" for the Hill people.[28]

In the mid-1980s, the regime of Hussain Mohammad Ershad opened negotiations with the PCJSS largely as a result of pressure from donor countries, which were becoming increasingly alarmed at reports of human rights violations in the CHT. The negotiations continued during the BNP regime of Khaleda Zia but ultimately failed, largely because of the

---

28. For details, see Amena Mohsin, *The Politics of Nationalism: The Case of the Chittagong Hill Tracts, Bangladesh* (Dhaka: University Press Ltd., 1997), pp. 163–188.

intransigent attitude of the PCJSS. A change of government in 1996, however, brought about a shift. The Awami League, under the leadership of Sheikh Hasina, came to power. With this development, the Indian attitude toward the PCJSS also changed. As a result of the Awami League's good relations with India, the Indian government withdrew its support from the PCJSS. On December 2, 1997, a peace accord was signed between the PCJSS and the government of Bangladesh.

One might have hoped that the signing of the peace accord and UNESCO's 1999 declaration of February 21 as International Mother Language Day would have brought about changes in the government's policies on language as well as minorities. A close examination, however, does not bear this out. The CHT peace accord does provide for the education of local communities in their own languages, at least through primary school. The Regional Council (RC), the institution charged with introducing and promoting these changes in the CHT, was not created until May 1999, however—and it has yet to establish itself as an effective institution. It has been beset by problems involving the government: RC members believe that the government is instead promoting the CHT Affairs Ministry (also set up after the accord), because the minister who heads it is a member of parliament from the ruling party, whereas the RC is headed by the leader of the PCJSS. The PCJSS has established a political party of its own in the region, which the government views as a potential threat to its position in the CHT. The government therefore seeks to undermine the efforts of the RC to project itself and its members as an alternative voice for the Hill people. As a result, the RC has not been able to implement the language provisions of the accord.

Sheikh Hasina, the former prime minister and an ardent champion of Bengali nationalism, had stated her government's intention to establish an International Mother Language Training and Research Center to protect and promote the cultures and languages of ethnic minorities worldwide. Significantly, however, she has made no reference to the existence of non-Bengalis or the status of their languages in Bangladesh. The government has not proposed any changes to the constitution involving the language issue.

Conclusion

Several lessons can be drawn from the Bangladeshis' ethnolinguistic experiences. Attempts to impose homogeneity on diverse peoples, together with refusals to recognize the cultural distinctiveness of ethnic minorities, can create politicized and militant minorities. The construction of true nationhood requires inclusive institutions and, more important, inclusive conceptions of the nation.

In Bangladesh's case, policy changes are needed in the political, cultural, academic, and administrative arenas. The politics and society of Bangladesh must be democratized. The country's elite must accept the fact that a culturally homogeneous population cannot be manufactured in Bangladesh: The country will continue to comprise a variety of culturally heterogeneous communities. Also, Bangladesh must seek unity through common citizenship, while the cultural identities of different ethnic groups are retained.

In addition, the parliament needs to be democratized and decentralized. In its present form, it underrepresents the non-Bengali communities.[29] One idea that has been floated is the creation of at least one parliament for each of the country's divisions. At the central level, there would be a federal parliament with coordinating powers and functions. Under this framework, the divisional parliament would be vested with more power than the federal body.

More generally, the country's constitution must be amended to recognize that Bangladesh is a multicultural, plural state. The constitution should explicitly acknowledge the existence in Bangladesh of languages other than Bengali and make provisions for their development and promotion. In other words, the constitution itself should be democratized.

The country also needs a cultural academy that can conduct research and promote the creative development of all cultures and languages in Bangladesh. The management of the academy ought to be democratic, and its upper echelons should include non-Bengalis. The government's cultural programs ought to reflect the plurality and diversity of Bangladesh's many cultures; only then can everyone in Bangladesh expect to see themselves as part of the cultural fabric of the country. The Bengali majority must be sensitized not only to the need to develop the languages of the other communities but also to the potential consequences of the state's failure to do so. The electronic and print media have a major responsibility in this respect: Non-Bengali communities need to have their own radio and television stations, and these stations must be autonomous.

---

29. See Imtiaz Ahmed, "Electoral Process in Bangladesh: Rationales for Reform," in Devendra R. Pandey, Anand Aditya, and Dev Raj Dahal, eds., *Comparative Electoral Processes in South Asia* (Kathmandu: Nepal South Asia Center, 1999), pp. 28–29. See also Imtiaz Ahmed, *Efficacy of the Nation-State: A Post-Nationalist Critique* (Colombo: International Center for Ethnic Studies, 1999).

Moreover, non-Bengalis should be given the opportunity to pursue an education in their mother tongues through, at a minimum, the primary level. The government should make adequate funds available for both printing books in non-Bengali languages and providing training to non-Bengali teachers. Non-Bengali communities have a major responsibility in this area: They must become strong pressure groups.

The country's academic curriculum ought to be decentralized and democratized. Instead of adhering to a national curriculum, each division should develop its own curriculum suited to the needs of the people in the area. Some subjects and textbooks should be common to all of the divisions, so that students can learn about other groups as well as their own. The curriculum must reflect the different cultures, histories, and experiences that make up Bangladesh's diverse minority communities. A judicious balance ought to be struck so that children grow up learning about and respecting other cultures. Universities should establish departments of cultural studies. The Institute of Modern Languages at Dhaka University should be renamed the Institute of Languages, given the loaded nature of the word modern. This body ought to carry out research and work for the creative development of as many languages as possible.

Finally, the government's administrative apparatus must be democratized. Ministries—especially those dealing with land, forest, law and parliamentary affairs, cultural affairs, and defense—ought to have representation from minority communities. There should also be a separate ministry for Adivashi affairs led by members of that community. Its head should have the rank and status of full minister, which the minister for CHT affairs already has.

In addition, administrative powers and responsibilities should be decentralized. Local governmental institutions must be strengthened and must include representation from across the ethnic spectrum. These institutions should be capable of generating their own financial resources and should have control over them. Local governments must take full responsibility for the judicial and administrative affairs of their communities. They should also be able to establish commissions to deal with disputes involving land issues as well as other problems created by differences involving ethnic identification.

These changes will not be easy to implement. Nonetheless, the current state of affairs in Bangladesh is highly problematic, and fundamental changes must be made across the board. This will require a major shift in the thinking and functioning of the Bangladeshi state. Encouraging in this regard is the emergence of a nascent civil society in Bangladesh. This civil society exhibits greater sensitivity to issues such as human rights, minority rights, and democratization. Perhaps this force can compel those in Bangladesh's political sphere to acknowledge the need to create a society where language is used to promote communication and understanding, not build barriers. To succeed in this endeavor, the country's Bengali and non-Bengali communities will need to work together.

Chapter 4

Ethnolinguistic Nationalism and Ethnic Conflict in Sri Lanka

Neil DeVotta

In 1972 Isaiah Berlin observed that nationalism "seems to be caused by wounds, some form of collective humiliation."[1] Sri Lanka's ethnic conflict between the majority Sinhalese and minority Tamils is rooted in such wounds and feelings of mutual humiliation. If Britain's divide-and-rule colonial practices deliberately marginalized the country's majority, the Sinhalese Buddhists, the latter's postindependence language policies methodically marginalized the minority Tamils. Tamil grievances in turn led to extremist reactions and provide the backdrop for the island's ongoing civil war.

Both groups, in the main, enjoyed cordial relations for more than 2,000 years. Then, in the 1950s the Sinhalese abandoned the movement to make both Sinhala and Tamil the country's official languages and instead instituted Sinhala as its sole official language.[2] The Sinhala-Only Act of 1956 led to ethnic riots in that year and in 1958, marking the beginning of acute Sinhalese-Tamil animosity. The manner in which the Sinhala-Only Act and Sinhalese linguistic nationalism facilitated violent conflict, however, has not been fully appreciated. Scholars have tended to overemphasize disputes over internal colonization and resource allocation as the driving forces behind the downturn in Sinhalese-Tamil relations.[3]

---

1. Isaiah Berlin, "The Bent Twig: A Note on Nationalism," *Foreign Affairs*, Vol. 51, No. 1 (October 1972), p. 17.

2. Many authors alternate between "Sinhalese" and "Sinhala" when referring to the majority community and their language. I use "Sinhalese" and "Sinhala" specifically to refer to the community and its language, respectively. "Tamil," on the other hand, refers to both the predominant minority and its language.

3. David Laitin argues that the Sinhala-only policy was not the most salient reason

Comprising nearly 74 percent of the population and controlling 80 percent of the electorate, the Sinhalese have determined which party has governed the country since independence in 1948. Although the 1978 constitution mandated proportional representation, Sri Lanka's ethnic composition ensured that the Sinhalese would continue to dominate both the government and politics. Thus, for Sinhalese elites and their political parties, acceding to the majority community's preferences has been viewed as the key to power. With the Tamils voting primarily for Tamil regional parties, the two major Sinhalese parties and their "ethnic entrepreneurs" sought to corral the Sinhalese vote by appealing to Sinhalese ethnonationalism.[4] In the postindependence period, this process of "ethnic outbidding" has centered on the language issue.[5] The significant impact of pro-Sinhala language policies on state-sector employment and education ensured that the Sinhalese achieved socioeconomic upward mobility while the Tamils, initially overrepresented in the bureaucracy and university systems, subsequently experienced relative deprivation and marginalization.

This chapter examines Sri Lanka's postindependence language policies and argues that the Sinhala-Only Movement and the Sinhala-Only Act of 1956 were the catalysts for most of the antiminority policies that followed. The discrimination that stemmed from language-related policies led to extremist reactions that eventually led to the civil war.

Asia's rich religious heritage has enabled religion, language, and their attendant myths and symbols to be fused for nationalist purposes. This is especially true in South Asia. Indeed, the fusing of religious and linguistic identities is especially likely when religious texts and rituals are used in the language in question. Therefore, to understand Sinhalese nationalism and its relationship to Sri Lanka's civil war, one must appreciate how the Sinhalese have merged religion and language for nationalist purposes even while emphasizing language for specific political and economic gains.

The first section of this chapter provides an overview of Sri Lanka's polyethnic society, briefly contrasts the historical antecedents of today's

for Sri Lanka's ethnic conflict. See Laitin, "Language Conflict and Violence: The Straw That Strengthens the Camel's Back," *European Journal of Sociology*, Vol. 41, No. 1 (April 2000), pp. 97–137.

4. "Ethnic entrepreneurs" are political (but often also business and religious) elites who promote ethnic polarization in attempts to accrue power.

5. "Ethnic outbidding" is an auction-like process wherein politicians create platforms and programs to "outbid" their opponents and win support within the ethnic communities in question.

Sinhalese and Tamils, and maps colonial-era dynamics that led to inter-group rivalry. The second section focuses on Sinhalese linguistic nationalism and the Sinhala-Only Movement. The third section analyzes the consequences of Sri Lanka's postindependence language policies, showing how they contributed to a bloody separatist movement. The final section evaluates the lessons learned from Sri Lanka's linguistic policies and offers some policy prescriptions.

The Ethnic and Historical Setting

With 25,332 square miles, Sri Lanka (called Ceylon until 1972) approximates West Virginia in size but has a population of nearly 19 million people. The island was colonized by the Portuguese, Dutch, and British in succession and gained independence in February 1948. The transfer of power was peaceful, mainly due to confraternity among the country's polyethnic elites. The island has enjoyed universal suffrage since 1931 and has conducted elections regularly since 1948. Sri Lanka's two major political parties have alternated in power. Unfortunately, the promulgation of pernicious ethnic policies has resulted in ethnic hostility and civil war.

POLYETHNICITY

According to the 1981 census, Sri Lanka's population was composed of nearly 74 percent Sinhalese; 12.7 percent Ceylon or Sri Lankan Tamils; 5.5 percent Indian Tamils; 7 percent Moors; and 0.6 percent Burghers, Malays, and Veddhas. (See Table 4.1.) Statistics released by Sri Lanka's central bank in 1999 suggest that the country's ethnic composition had changed little since 1981. According to these statistics, Sri Lanka's ethnic breakdown at the end of the twentieth century was 74 percent Sinhalese, 12.6 percent Sri Lankan Tamils, 5.5 percent Indian Tamils, and 7 percent Moors.[6]

The Indian Tamils' nineteenth-century indentured ancestors went to Sri Lanka to work primarily on tea plantations, settling especially in the central hills. Most were denied citizenship by laws passed in 1948–49. Their numbers dropped drastically when, in the mid-1960s, the government of India agreed to the deportation of some Indian Tamils to India. As a result, Sri Lanka's Indian Tamil population declined from 11.7 per-

6. See V.S. Sambandan, "A Tough Presidential Race," *Frontline*, Vol. 16, No. 26 (December 11–24, 1999). More than 500,000 Tamils—some estimates place the figure close to 850,000—have fled to India and numerous Western countries since the 1983 anti-Tamil riots. The statistics presented here do not appear to take this exodus into account. Indeed recent estimates suggest that 15,000–18,000 Tamils leave Sri Lanka every year. See "Blood and Money," *Economist*, August 8, 1998, p. 38.

Table 4.1. Ethnic Composition in Sri Lanka, 1946, 1971, and 1981.

Group	Number (1946)	Percentage	Number (1971)	Percentage	Number (1981)	Percentage
Sinhalese	4,621,000	69.41	9,131,000	71.96	10,980,000	73.95
Sri Lankan Tamils	734,000	11.01	1,424,000	11.22	1,887,000	12.70
Indian Tamils	781,000	11.73	1,175,000	9.26	819,000	5.52
Sri Lankan Moors	374,000	6.52	828,000	6.52	1,047,000	7.05
Indian Moors[a]	36,000	0.53	27,000	0.21	—	—
Europeans[b]	5,000	0.08	—	—	—	—
Burghers and Eurasians	42,000	0.63	45,000	0.35	39,000	0.26
Malays	23,000	0.34	43,000	0.34	47,000	0.32
Veddhas[b]	2,000	0.04	—	—	—	—
Others	41,000	0.62	16,000	0.13	28,000	0.19

SOURCE: *Statistical Pocket Book of the Democratic Socialist Republic of Sri Lanka* (Colombo: Department of Census and Statistics, 1996), pp. 15–16.
[a]Included under "Others" for 1981.
[b]Included under "Others" starting in 1963.

Table 4.2. Population by Religion in Sri Lanka, 1971 and 1981.

Religion	Number (1971)	Percentage	Number (1981)	Percentage
Buddhist	8,536,900	67.27	10,288,300	69.30
Hindu	2,238,700	17.64	2,297,800	15.48
Christian	1,004,300	7.91	1,130,600	7.61
Muslim	901,800	7.11	1,121,700	7.55
Other	8,300	0.07	8,300	0.06

SOURCE: *Statistical Pocket Book of the Democratic Socialist Republic of Sri Lanka* (Colombo: Department of Census and Statistics, 1996), p. 14.

cent in 1946 to 5.5 percent in 1981. The 1978 constitution enfranchised many Indian Tamils, although it is thought that nearly 200,000 are still considered stateless. Although the group's overall economic position improved markedly in the 1980s and 1990s, these Tamils, who continue to sustain the island's crucial tea industry, remain the least educated and most socioeconomically marginalized group in Sri Lanka's class- and caste-conscious society. The island's separatist violence nonetheless does not involve the Indian Tamils.[7]

The Moors—Muslims—primarily migrated as traders from Malabar, India, and the rest of the Coromandel Coast beginning in the tenth century. Although they concentrated along the country's littoral, their significant numbers in Eastern Province, which the Sri Lankan Tamils claim as part of their traditional homeland, have led to tensions between the two groups. Although the Moors speak the Tamil language, their ethnic identity is tied to their Islamic faith. With Moor numbers added to the linguistic equation, Tamil is spoken by more than 25 percent of Sri Lanka's population.

The Sinhalese are primarily Buddhists, and the Tamils are primarily Hindus. Although the country's Christian population includes both Sinhalese and Tamils, one rarely encounters a Sinhalese who is Hindu or a Tamil who is Buddhist. As indicated in Table 4.2, the 1981 census estimated the country's religious composition to be 69.3 percent Buddhist, 15.5 percent Hindu, 7.6 percent Christian, and 7.5 percent Muslim.

DISPUTACIOUS LEGACIES

Given that claims to a historical homeland help to solidify nationalist aspirations, it is not surprising that both the Sinhalese and the Tamils de-

---

7. Unless indicated otherwise, the term "Tamils" is used in this chapter to refer to the Sri Lankan Tamils.

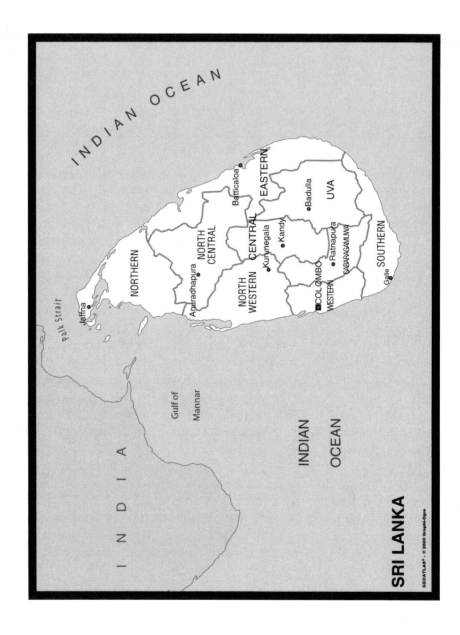

clare themselves to be the island's original settlers. The Sinhalese point to a mythical account in the *Mahavamsa*—a historical chronicle apparently written to legitimate Buddhism's prominence in the island—and claim that their North Indian/Aryan ancestors were the first to reach Sri Lanka's shores almost 2,500 years ago. According to this colonization myth's most popular account, the founder of the Sinhalese race, Prince Vijaya, arrived on the island with 700 followers after being exiled by his father.

The Tamils claim that their Dravidian South Indian ancestors were the first to land on the island. Common sense suggests that if aborigines reached the island continent of Australia almost 40,000 years ago, and determined settlers crossed the Pacific Ocean to reach America's western coast at least 13,000 years ago, then it is highly unlikely that South Indians were unaware of an island situated only twenty-two miles across the shallow Palk Strait. A.L. Basham argued that "Dravidian infiltration into Ceylon must have been going on from the earliest historical times and probably before."[8] Some claim that only Dravidians settled the island, but Buddhism and its Pali scriptures created an "ascriptive cleavage" to divide the Dravidians into Sinhalese and Tamils. According to Satchi Ponnambalam, "The Sinhalese, then, in terms of their origin, are not an Aryan people as popularly claimed, but Tamil people who adopted a language which developed from Pali, an Aryan dialect."[9] Such assertions infuriate the Sinhalese.

These claims and counterclaims aside, there is little doubt that contemporary Sri Lankans are of mixed ethnic background. From Sri Lanka's ruling elite to its lowliest classes, miscegenation, conversion, and acculturation appear to have been common over the centuries. As a result, contemporary "Sinhalese and Tamil labels are porous sieves through which diverse groups and categories of Indian peoples, intermixed with non-Indians . . . , have passed through."[10]

The account of the Buddhist warrior king Dutthagamani (second century B.C.) in the *Mahavamsa*, likely extrapolated from a historical event but certainly embellished thereafter, describes how the king, his army, and 500 Buddhist monks battled and defeated the Chola king Elara, who had usurped the power of the Anuradhapura kingdom. Nineteenth- and

---

8.   A.L. Basham, "Prince Vijaya and the Aryanization of Ceylon," *Ceylon Historical Journal*, Vol. 1, No. 3 (January 1952), p. 167.

9.   Satchi Ponnambalam, *Sri Lanka: The National Question and the Tamil Liberation Struggle* (London: Zed Books, 1983), p. 20.

10.   Stanley J. Tambiah, *Sri Lanka: Ethnic Fratricide and the Dismantling of Democracy* (Chicago: University of Chicago Press, 1986), p. 6.

twentieth-century Sinhalese elites characterized the event as a valiant contest between Sinhalese and Tamils. The activist scholar-monk Walpola Rahula maintained that "the entire Sinhalese race was united under the banner of the young Gamini [Dutthagamani]. This was the beginning of nationalism among the Sinhalese. It was a new race with healthy young blood, organized under the new order of Buddhism. A kind of religio-nationalism, which almost amounted to fanaticism, roused the whole Sinhalese people. A non-Buddhist was not regarded as a human being. Evidently all Sinhalese without exception were Buddhists."[11] Yet as one author has correctly observed, "The facile equating of Sinhalese with Buddhist [sic] for this period is not borne out by the facts, for not all Sinhalese were Buddhist, while on the other hand there were many Tamil Buddhists."[12]

The Dutthagamani account had a powerful impact on the modern Sinhalese Buddhist psyche, and Sinhalese ethnic entrepreneurs appealed to the account's divisive emotions to portray themselves as defenders of Buddhism and the Sinhalese race. These elites blended folklore and religion to fashion a nationalist ideology that promoted the belief that Sri Lanka was *Sihidipa* (the island of the Sinhalese) and *Dhammadipa* (the island chosen to preserve and propagate Buddhism). This led to the claim that "for more than two millennia the Sinhalese have been inspired by the ideal that they were a nation brought into being for the definite purpose of carrying the torch lit by the Buddha."[13] Walter Schwarz has astutely observed that "the most important effect of the early history on the minority problem of today is not in the facts but in the myths that surround them, particularly on the Sinhalese side."[14]

COLONIALISM AND SINHALESE NATIONALISM

There is no doubt that Buddhism in Sri Lanka suffered greatly under the Portuguese, Dutch, and British. The Portuguese, energetic in proselytizing Catholicism, committed atrocities against Buddhist institutions and other local religions. The Dutch in turn promoted the Dutch Reformed Church. The Portuguese and Dutch, however, controlled only some coastal areas. Buddhism's marginalization was more profound under the

11.   Walpola Rahula, *History of Buddhism in Ceylon: The Anuradhapura Period, 3rd Century B.C.–10th Century A.C.* (Colombo: M.D. Gunasena and Co., 1956), p. 79.

12.   K.M. de Silva, *A History of Sri Lanka* (Delhi: Oxford University Press, 1981), p. 15.

13.   D.C. Vijayavardhana, *The Revolt in the Temple* (Colombo: Sinha Publications, 1953), p. 3.

14.   Walter Schwarz, *The Tamils of Sri Lanka*, 4th ed., Minority Rights Group Report No. 25 (London: Minority Rights Group, 1988), p. 5.

British, who were the first to control the entire island. Although the British eschewed oppressing local religions, they nevertheless made it policy to provide economic and civil benefits to Christians while neglecting Buddhist needs, in particular.

The marginalization of the Sinhalese Buddhists was consistent with Britain's divide-and-rule policies. Under British colonial domination, non-Buddhists and ethnic minorities became disproportionately overrepresented in the bureaucracy, civil service, and primary and secondary educational institutions. Northern Sri Lanka's arid, inhospitable terrain coupled with a restrictive caste-based society spurred many Tamils to seek governmental and other careers throughout the island. Thanks to American missionary and educational efforts in the north, a large number of Tamils became conversant in English. Indeed by 1930, English literacy in Northern Province was second only to that in Colombo.[15] This led Tamils to become the most overrepresented minority within the colonial government's educational system. Tamil success was bolstered by British discriminatory policies toward the majority Sinhalese Buddhists, which outraged the latter. This anger was reflected in anti-British and anti-Tamil rhetoric promulgated by Sinhalese Buddhist nationalists such as Anagarika Dharmapala.[16]

It was Sri Lanka's polyethnic English-speaking elites who articulated and, with their liberal credentials, legitimated the need for independence. The Sinhalese in their midst did not initially embrace the extremist positions espoused by Sinhalese Buddhist nationalists. This was partly due to the belief that the liberal culture espoused by the elites and their interethnic confraternity would hold sway over the communalists' exclusionary positions. The possibility that Sri Lanka's elites could become ethnic entrepreneurs was disregarded. This was exemplified by the 1946 Soulbury Constitution, which merely stipulated that the government should not favor one religion or community over another.

This idealism was shattered by Sinhalese nationalists less than a decade into the postindependence era. The nationalist vehicle was the Sinhala language.[17] The "Sinhala only" policy promoted educational and economic disparities among Sri Lanka's ethnic groups, demonstrated that

---

15.   Jane Russell, "The Dance of the Turkey Cock—The Jaffna Boycott of 1931," *Ceylon Journal of Historical and Social Studies*, Vol. 8, No. 1 (1982), p. 50.

16.   See Neil DeVotta, "The Utilisation of Religio-Linguistic Identities by the Sinhalese and Bengalis: Toward a General Explanation," *Journal of Commonwealth and Comparative Politics*, Vol. 39, No. 1 (March 2001), pp. 66–95.

17.   Robert Kearney provides a concise and useful account of Sri Lanka's language issue. Kearney, *Communalism and Language in the Politics of Ceylon* (Durham, N.C.:

the Tamil minority's poor integration into the national polity was officially sanctioned, and ultimately, in many Tamil minds, justified the establishment of *eelam* (a separate Tamil state).

Linguistic Nationalism

With the *Theravada* Buddhist scriptures written in Pali and with the Sinhala language related to Pali, language and religion coalesce to form the Sinhalese Buddhist identity. Significantly, however, although the movement to make Sinhala Sri Lanka's official language preceded independence, it was not used to polarize ethnic relations in the country until after independence.

THE SWABASHA MOVEMENT

Preindependence agitation surrounding the language issue was fomented by lower-class leaders outside the mainstream of the political spectrum. This movement included both Sinhalese and Tamils who campaigned for their languages to replace English, although English served as an important link between the ethnic communities. The Education Ordinance of 1939 instituted a free education system and raised the island's literacy rate from 17 percent in 1881 to 65 percent in 1953,[18] yet only about 14 percent of this literate population was conversant in English.[19]

Those with an education were eager to free themselves from "rural life, from manual toil, from work which they [considered] . . . degrading."[20] Full emancipation, however, required not just an education but also viable employment, and the vernacular schools that educated nearly 85 percent of the school-going population were not equipped to promote upward mobility. According to S.W.R.D. Bandaranaike, who eventually played a pivotal role in developing the country's language policies, "Over ninety per cent of the [state-sector] jobs . . . are restricted to ten per cent of the people who know English. In this land of ours, those ignorant

---

Duke University Press, 1967). The issue is also described in K.M. de Silva, "Coming Full Circle: The Politics of Language in Sri Lanka, 1943–1996," *Ethnic Studies Report*, Vol. 14, No. 1 (January 1996), pp. 11–48.

18. Ceylon Department of Census and Statistics, *Ceylon Year Book, 1958* (Colombo: Government Press, 1959), p. 33.

19. Percentages are based on figures obtained from Ceylon Department of Census and Statistics, *Census of Ceylon, 1953*, Vol. 1 (Colombo: Government Press, 1957), pp. 192, 196.

20. See E.B. Denham, *Ceylon at the Census of 1911* (Colombo: Government Printer, 1912), p. 399.

of English are capable of obtaining much less than 10 per cent of the Government jobs!"[21] A select committee of the State Council reported in 1946 that "the present Government of this country is . . . a Government of the Sinhalese- or Tamil-speaking 6,200,000, by the English-speaking 20,000 Government servants, for the 400,000 English-speaking public."[22]

Indeed a vernacular education proved insufficient for conducting even routine interactions. For example, telegrams could not be sent in the vernacular languages until 1956.[23] Banking transactions in these languages were deemed illegal as late as 1953. Even parliamentary debates were conducted in English, and permission was required to use Sinhala and Tamil.[24] The *Swabasha* (self-language) Movement thus recognized that the dominant status of English in the educational and governmental arenas was largely responsible for marginalizing the burgeoning middle classes who spoke only Sinhala or Tamil. Consequently, it was not surprising that non-English-speaking Sinhalese and Tamils who favored *swabasha* made education reform their foremost goal.

The excellent English education system instituted by American missionaries in the country's northern regions enabled Sri Lankan Tamils to become disproportionately represented in the elite Ceylon civil service, the judicial service, and the higher educational arena. For example, although they constituted only 11 percent of the country's population, Tamils comprised 33 percent of the civil service and 40 percent of the judicial service just two years prior to independence.[25] They further accounted for 31 percent of students in the university system. In the medical and engineering fields, Tamil representation numerically equaled that of the Sinhalese. This overrepresentation made the Swabasha Movement unattractive to upper-class and upper-caste Tamils. Thus the

21.   From a talk given in parliament on September 1, 1953, in S.W.R.D. Bandaranaike, *Towards a New Era* (Colombo: Department of Information, 1961), p. 927.

22.   *Sinhalese and Tamil as Official Languages,* Sessional Paper 22 (Colombo: Government Press 1946), p. 10.

23.   The first "*swabasha* telegram" was sent to the prime minister, Sir John Kotelawala, and its message did not augur well for polyethnic coexistence. Dictated by the minister of posts and broadcasting, the message stated: "Today is an auspicious day for our mother tongue. May Sinhalese prosper till the end of time. May you, our nation and our language be victorious." See "Swabasha 'Wires' Were Popular in a Few Hours," *Ceylon Daily News* (*CDN*), March 15, 1956, p. 1.

24.   James Manor, *The Expedient Utopian: Bandaranaike and Ceylon* (Cambridge: Cambridge University Press, 1989), pp. 229, 219.

25.   C.R. de Silva, "Sinhala-Tamil Ethnic Rivalry: The Background," in Robert B. Goldmann and A. Jeyaratnam Wilson, eds., *From Independence to Statehood: Managing Ethnic Conflict in Five African and Asian States* (New York: St. Martin's, 1984), p. 116.

movement to replace English with vernacular languages was mainly Sinhalese-led, though some Tamils did mobilize to encourage *swabasha* reforms. Indeed the Tamil Jaffna Youth Congress and Teachers' Association energetically supported *swabasha*. This support fizzled out when Sinhalese nationalists, apparently agitated by the overrepresentation of Tamils in the coveted civil service, began to adopt a communalist posture and demanded that *swabasha* favor Sinhala only. As Ceylonese Governor Andrew Caldecott noted when writing to the secretary of state for the colonies, "I have no doubt whatever that a great deal of the communalism that is so unfortunately rampant derives directly from competition and jealousy about Government appointments."[26]

The Tamils recognized that, given the existence of a Sinhalese majority, Sinhala would eventually dominate the country's bureaucratic and educational arenas. Consequently, by the late 1930s the Hindu board of education decided to introduce Sinhala as a compulsory subject in northern schools, and the Jaffna Youth Congress called for Sinhala and Tamil to be made required subjects throughout the island. The latter's anti-English position, coupled with the clamor for independence from the British, even led to the boycott of the 1931 State Council elections in Jaffna.

At the same time, the Sinhalese realized that speaking Tamil was not essential for achieving upward mobility, and they displayed no enthusiasm for acquiring another vernacular language. Sinhalese disregard for Tamil was revealed by future Prime Minister and President J.R. Jayewardene when he introduced a resolution in June 1943 calling for Sinhala to "be made the medium of instruction in all schools" and "a compulsory subject in all public examinations" so that it could become the "official language of Ceylon."[27] The motion was later amended to include both Sinhala and Tamil. This was possible because the ruling Sinhalese elites at first preferred to implement the *swabasha* transition gradually.

In adopting this gradualist approach, however, Sinhalese elites misgauged the frustrations of the Sinhalese lower and middle classes. The Ceylon National Congress, a polyethnic, elitist body that was fast becoming a Sinhalese and Buddhist body, called in 1939 for both Sinhala and Tamil to be declared official languages. Moreover, a 1944 State Council resolution stipulated that the island's vernacular languages should replace English within a reasonable period of time. Likewise, the Select Committee on Official Language Policy, appointed in September 1945,

---

26. Colonial Office, Great Britain, *Correspondence Relating to the Constitution of Ceylon*, Cmd. 5910 (London: His Majesty's Stationery Office, 1938), p. 20.

27. The resolution is reproduced in State Council, *Debates*, May 24, 1944, col. 745.

recommended that both Sinhala and Tamil be made administrative languages by January 1957. Yet in October 1953, the chairman of the Official Languages Commission, E.A.L. Wijeyewardene, added a rider to the commission's final report suggesting that "the replacement of English by Swabhasha would have been very much easier if instead of two Swabhasha Languages as Official Languages one alone had been accepted."[28] Wijeyewardene, like many Sinhala-only proponents, appears to have held that linguistic parity was nonessential, given that the Sinhalese comprised more than 70 percent of the country's population. It was only a matter of time before opportunistic politicians adopted the language issue for electoral gain.

The emotional power of the Sinhala-Only Movement caught the country's elites off guard, but some, such as S.W.R.D. Bandaranaike, recognized that intensifying pro-Sinhala sentiments could be manipulated for political gain. Bandaranaike was a cabinet member in the ruling United National Party (UNP) when he realized that he would not succeed the country's first prime minister, D.S. Senanayake. He consequently left the UNP in July 1951 and joined the opposition. Bandaranaike sincerely believed that he was the best qualified candidate to replace Senanayake. He undoubtedly was among the most intelligent and eloquent leaders of his generation and one who placed great faith in liberal democracy. But he was also vain and opportunistic. His wealthy, aristocratic forebears had converted from Hinduism to Buddhism to Roman Catholicism to the Dutch Reformed Church to Anglicanism to gain favor with the ruling powers of the day.[29] Bandaranaike, who himself became disenchanted with Christianity and converted to Buddhism, soon sought to become the standard bearer of the Sinhala-Only Movement. Senanayake, on the other hand, staunchly opposed recognizing the vernacular languages because he believed that this step would complicate Sinhalese-Tamil relations.

In the mid-1930s Bandaranaike organized the Sinhala Maha Sabha (Great Sinhalese League), a communalist body that he would subsequently use at opportune moments. The Sinhala Maha Sabha was an element within the UNP until Bandaranaike merged it into the Sri Lanka Freedom Party (SLFP), which he formed two months after crossing over to the opposition in 1951. Though it claimed to be a centrist party, the SLFP was a leftward-leaning, pro-Buddhist entity. In organizing the

28. *The Final Report of the Official Languages Commission,* Sessional Paper 22 (Colombo: Government Press, 1953), p. 26.

29. See Yasmine Gooneratne, *Relative Merits: A Personal Memoir of the Bandaranaike Family of Sri Lanka* (London: C. Hurst, 1986), pp. 3–6.

party's grassroots base, Bandaranaike appealed to the *sangha* (Buddhist clergy) and the Sinhalese masses. His efforts paid few dividends in the 1952 election, but they did help to catapult him to power four years later.

THE 1956 GENERAL ELECTION

Bandaranaike cared sincerely for Sri Lanka's disadvantaged and believed that the country's potential was realizable only if the marginalized were integrated into its socioeconomic processes. The Swabasha Movement was seen as a step in that direction, and even after leaving the UNP, Bandaranaike maintained the need for both Sinhala and Tamil to replace English. His position was not unique in the early 1950s: The leftist parties, the UNP, and "even *bhikkhus* [Buddhist monks], Sinhala writers, and teachers—people who might have been expected to seek preferment for Sinhala alone—tended to appeal on behalf of Tamil as well."[30] By late 1954, however, anti-Tamil and anti-Christian sentiments had coalesced to invigorate the Sinhala-Only Movement. Thus when UNP Prime Minister Sir John Kotelawala visited Jaffna in 1955 and agreed with former Youth Congress leader Handy Perinbanayagam that both Sinhala and Tamil should be made official languages, he was castigated. This incident was used by extremists in the *sangha* and by Sinhalese nationalists to galvanize support for a Sinhala-only policy.

The Mahajana Eksath Peramuna (People's United Front)—the coalition that Bandaranaike cobbled together for the 1956 election—was plagued with jingoists. Moreover, its opportunistic leader reversed positions and became a vociferous champion of a Sinhala-only policy. In May 1944, when the State Council debated Jayewardene's motion to make Sinhala the official language of the country, Bandaranaike argued that it "would be ungenerous on our part as Sinhalese not to give due recognition to the Tamil language." He further noted that "if the object[ion] is that it is rather awkward to have more than one official language, I would like to point out that other countries are putting up with more than two official languages and are carrying on reasonably satisfactorily."[31] Continuing to promote linguistic parity, Bandaranaike observed, "It is necessary to bring about that amity, that confidence among the various communities which we are all striving to achieve within reasonable limits. Therefore, . . . I have no personal objection to both these languages being considered official languages; nor do I see any particular harm or

---

30. Manor, *The Expedient Utopian*, p. 231.

31. Quoted in State Council, *Debates*, May 25, 1944, pp. 810–811.

danger or real difficulty arising from it."[32] Ten years later, when a newspaper mistakenly reported that he was against making Sinhala the official language, Bandaranaike responded in a letter by saying, "It is stated that I said that I would never make Sinhalese the State language. The word 'only' has been omitted. What I said was that neither I nor my Party [the SLFP] are in favour of Sinhalese only being made the official language of the country but that both Sinhalese and Tamil be made official languages."[33]

By 1956, however, Bandaranaike was determined to become prime minister. He manipulated the Sinhalese community's grievances and repeatedly portrayed the language issue as a "life and death struggle."[34] He claimed that UNP leaders supported parity only because they were traitors to both their race and their language, and he argued that parity would spell disaster for the Sinhalese because it would enable the Tamils to use "their books and culture and the will and strength characteristic of their race . . . [and] exert their dominant power over us."[35] Though such communalist rhetoric was antithetical to his core liberal proclivities, Bandaranaike believed that the chauvinists he was manipulating could be tamed after he came to power. His naïve expectation was that the Sinhala-only furor would dissipate once the Sinhala-only bill was passed, and then he could sponsor legislation to accommodate the Tamils. Bandaranaike appears to have believed that because the Tamils' options were limited, he could eventually convince their leadership to accept a language policy short of parity. The SLFP manifesto issued in September 1955 consequently endorsed a Sinhala-only position, but it also noted the need for Tamil to be used for administrative and educational purposes in Northern and Eastern Provinces.

In promulgating chauvinist rhetoric, Bandaranaike was assisted by numerous lay Buddhists and activist *bhikkhus* who demanded a Sinhala-only policy. Indeed the Sinhala-Only Movement gave prominence to the controversial political *bhikkhus*, who characterized the Tamils as "parasites," argued that linguistic parity was undemocratic and unjust, and claimed that the failure to institute a Sinhala-only policy "would be the death-knell of the Sinhalese."[36] The political *bhikkhu*

32.   Quoted in ibid.

33.   Quoted in Senate, *Debates,* Vol. 10, July 5, 1956, col. 593.

34.   See "Press for a 'Sinhalese Only' Pronouncement—SWRD," *CDN,* November 28, 1955, p. 6.

35.   Quoted in "Parity Means Disaster to Sinhalese—SWRD," *CDN,* November 24, 1955, p. 7.

36.   See "Leftist Leader Assailed at Language Meeting," *CDN,* November 28, 1955,

Walpola Rahula argued that the separation of church and state was a calculated Western construct designed to disempower the masses and that "from the earliest days the Sinhala monks, while leading the lives of *bhikkhus*, were in the forefront of movements for the progress of their nation, their country, and their religion."[37] Rahula argued that by using the Dutthagamani account and linking the *sangha*'s activism to patriotism, "both *bhikkhus* and laymen considered that even killing people in order to liberate the religion and country was not a heinous crime."[38] In campaigning for the Sinhala-only policy, the *bhikkhus* operated primarily under the Eksath Bhikkhu Peramuna (United Buddhist Front), which became an umbrella political organization for a *sangha* divided along caste lines, though many also became active through the numerous *sangha sabhas* (*bhikkhu* associations). They were joined by other powerful groups such as the Young Men's Buddhist Association, the Theosophical Society, the Ayurveda Sangamaya (Congress of Indigenous Medical Practitioners), the Bhasa Peramuna (Language Front), and the Lanka Jatika Guru Sangamaya (Sinhalese Teachers' Association)—the latter two uniting Sinhala-language teachers, educators, poets, and writers.

The 1956 election coincided with the *Buddha Jayanthi*, the 2,500th anniversary of Buddha's death. The Sinhala-only forces co-opted the enthusiasm surrounding this event, emphasizing the unique Sinhalese religiolinguistic identity and promoting the belief that, as legatees of *Sihadipa* and *Dhammadipa*, the Sinhalese were entitled to make Sinhala the island's sole national language. The year 1956 also saw the All Ceylon Buddhist Congress publish *The Betrayal of Buddhism*, which highlighted Buddhism's decline under colonialism and indicted the postindependence UNP governments for failing to halt this decline. This Sinhalese Buddhist upswell forced the UNP, whose governments favored linguistic parity, to adopt a Sinhala-only position in February 1956. The UNP's

---

p. 5; "'Parity Will Be Undemocratic,' Says Bhikkhu," *CDN*, October 12, 1955, p. 5; "Sinhalese 'Death-Knell' If Language Solution Failed," *CDN*, November 23, 1955, p. 6; and "Parity 'Disgraceful, Unjust,'" *CDN*, November 25, 1955, p. 6.

37.   Walpola Rahula, *The Heritage of the Bhikkhu: A Short History of the Bhikkhu in Educational, Cultural, Social, and Political Life* (New York: Grove, 1974), p. 132.

38.   Ibid., p. 21. With the chief monks of the three Buddhist sects demanding a military (as opposed to a political) solution to the ethnic conflict, even the government-owned *Sunday Observer* could recently note that "it is frightening to observe the insouciance with which the most revered prelates of the Maha Sangha talk of a recourse to arms." See "The Maha Sangha and the Nation," *Sunday Observer*, March 19, 2000, http://www.lanka.net/lakehouse/2000/03/19.edito.htm (accessed March 19, 2000).

about-face marked the beginning of ethnic outbidding in Sri Lankan politics—a phenomenon that persists today.

The 1956 election represented the triumph of linguistic nationalism in Sri Lanka. The way that the *sangha* and the nationalists manipulated the *Buddha Jayanthi* proved that religion was never absent from rhetoric promoting the Sinhala-Only Movement. Nevertheless, "the dominant issue that drove it [the election] forward was that of language. Religion—which is to say Buddhism—ran in a close second."[39] This is because "linguistic nationalism had an appeal which cut across [even] class interests, and . . . evoked as deep a response from the Sinhalese working class as it did among the peasantry and the Sinhalese educated elite."[40] The emphasis on language dampened intra-Sinhalese divisions. The emphasis on Buddhism in the preindependence era had, conversely, led to Sinhalese Christians being vilified and marginalized. Indeed, ethnic differentiation along linguistic lines subsequently became so ingrained in the country that commonalities among Tamil and Sinhalese Christians, for example, are now disregarded while Sinhalese Buddhists and Christians, their religious differences aside, coalesce as a common sociopolitical unit. Finally, the surge in ethnolinguistic nationalism in postindependence Sri Lanka coincided with increased centralization, bureaucratization, and modernization efforts and, in particular, with state-sponsored educational opportunities afforded to thousands of youth.

THE NEXUS BETWEEN LINGUISTIC NATIONALISM AND DEVELOPMENT

Although religious nationalism in Sri Lanka extends back at least to the sixteenth century, linguistic nationalism is a post-1870 phenomenon.[41] As numerous scholars have observed, this is essentially related to the different political and economic possibilities inherent in traditional communities and modern societies.[42] Unlike traditional communities (which were

---

39. Manor, *The Expedient Utopian*, p. 231. Some, however, saw Buddhism playing the more important role. For example, G.P. Malalasekera's letter to the *New York Times* claimed that "the Ceylon [1956] elections were decided on a few very clear-cut issues. The chief of these was the Buddhist issue." See "Voting in Ceylon," *New York Times*, May 6, 1956, p. E8.

40. De Silva, *A History of Sri Lanka*, p. 518.

41. Eric Hobsbawm, *Nations and Nationalism since 1780: Programme, Myth, Reality*, 2d ed. (Cambridge: Cambridge University Press, 1990), pp. 105–106.

42. See, for example, Karl W. Deutsch, *Nationalism and Social Communication: An Inquiry into the Foundations of Nationality*, 2d ed. (Cambridge, Mass.: MIT Press, 1966); Jyotirindra Dasgupta, *Language Conflict and National Development* (Berkeley: University

primarily agrarian and decentralized), modern societies (which are bu-
reaucratized, centralized, and relatively industrialized) facilitate resource
accrual—that is, employment, education, welfare benefits, and government contracts—and increased interactions with official and unofficial
institutions. Thus the proliferation of such institutions, coupled with increased literacy, made language an important mechanism for negotiating
interactions and amassing resources. This was the case in postindependence Sri Lanka. A brief discussion of some salient features in the pre-
and postindependence eras highlights this point.

The preindependence presence of the Portuguese and the Dutch in
Sri Lanka had little effect on domestic economic relations: Most of the
country's people continued to rely on subsistence agriculture. The British
introduced an export-dependent plantation economy centered primarily
on the cultivation of tea, rubber, and coconut; industrialization did not
begin until the late 1950s. The country's literacy rate in 1921 was 39.9 percent,[43] though most of those considered literate had attended vernacular
schools and received only "basic instruction for living in a community
with very limited horizons."[44] The best secondary institutions, which ca-
tered primarily to the elites and the upper-middle-class strata, were
Christian. Graduates from these Christian schools staffed the low- and
midlevel ranks of the civil service. A university college was not created
until 1921, and there were no technological institutes in the country until
"well into the twentieth century."[45] The island's "gainfully occupied"
population in 1921 was 62.4 percent, of which the majority engaged in agriculture and fishing.[46] The caste system circumscribed societal relations,
and intra-Sinhalese divisions along caste and religious lines were more
acute than the ethnic divisions beginning to take shape. This socioeconomic milieu was not conducive to making language a mechanism for
mobilization. The anti-British movement in the preindependence era consequently focused on religion as a mobilizing issue.[47]

---

of California Press, 1970); and Ernest Gellner, *Nations and Nationalism* (Oxford: Basil
Blackwell, 1983).

43. *Census of Ceylon, 1946,* Vol. 1, Pt. 1 (Colombo: Department of Census and Statistics, 1950), p. 186.

44. Unattributed quote in de Silva, *A History of Sri Lanka,* p. 413.

45. Michael Roberts, "Elite Formation and Elites, 1832–1931," in K.M. de Silva, ed.,
University of Ceylon History of Ceylon, Vol. 3 (Colombo: Department of Census and Statistics, 1950), p. 273.

46. *Census of Ceylon, 1946,* Vol. 1, Pt. 1, p. 225.

47. This is not to trivialize the efforts headed by Munidasa Cumaratunge, who
sought to resuscitate a form of "pure" Sinhala, and some secondary English school

By the 1950s Sri Lanka was developing and modernizing. Free education was raising expectations at a time when the state was the most significant employer in the country. Nearly twenty-five years of experience with suffrage had led to the formation of numerous grassroots movements that sought to manipulate elections to channel scarce resources to neglected communities. At the same time, politicians and parties were becoming cognizant of how pork-barrel politics and patron-client ties could be used to garner electoral support. Moreover, a vibrant labor movement was demanding labor reform and increased representation in governmental institutions. The social and welfare programs instituted by the British and Sri Lankan elites in the 1930s had been designed to neutralize the threat posed by leftist/Marxist elements represented by the labor movement. One such program was the so-called rice subsidy. The public's dependence on this subsidy was so acute that when the UNP government under Dudley Senanayake increased the price of rice, it led to a Marxist-inspired *hartal* (shop closures and work stoppages as forms of protest) and the prime minister's resignation in October 1953. Thus by 1956, the overwhelmingly rural Sri Lankan electorate was also politically sophisticated and demanded attention from the state's institutions.

The April 1956 election enabled the Sinhalese to coalesce around their linguistic identity. The result was a landslide victory for Bandaranaike's Mahajana Eksath Peramuna. Bandaranaike had campaigned on the slogan "Sinhala only, and in twenty-four hours." Once he was elected, there was no reneging on this promise. As L.H. Mettananda, a leading educator who was also among the most notorious pro-Sinhalese and pro-Buddhists chauvinists, proclaimed, "Not even hydrogen bombs can prevent Sinhalese becoming the official language of Ceylon."[48] Consequently, despite vociferous opposition from leftist/Marxist parties and the Tamils, the Official Language Act of 1956, making Sinhala the "one official language of Ceylon," was passed in June. The bill's passage marked the turning point in ethnic relations in Sri Lanka. In a parliamentary debate, Colvin de Silva of the Lanka Sama Samaja Party (LSSP, or Lanka Equal Society Party) noted that unless the government changed course, the act's passage meant that "two torn little bleeding states may yet arise out of one little state."[49] The Communist's Party's Pieter

teachers, who sought to mobilize politically by using the Sinhala language, in the 1930s. Both, however, were strongly opposed by the liberal and pro-English political elites.

48. "Mettananda Says He Is Sure of Sinhala Bill," *CDN*, May 5, 1956, p. 5.

49. Quoted in House of Representatives, *Parliamentary Debates*, June 14, 1956, col. 1917.

Keuneman claimed that although the Sinhala-Only Act had already led to communal riots, "Ten years from now it will be several times worse. This Bill is heading straight for the division of the country. . . . Every order and regulation under it will be a cause for further strife."[50] These observations proved prescient.

The Sinhala-Only Act of 1956 and Its Aftermath

The Tamil protests that accompanied the passage of the Sinhala-Only Act were unprecedented. When the bill was introduced on June 5, 1956, the Tamil Federal Party organized a *satyagraha* (peaceful protest) outside the parliament building. The Tamil protest was met by a counterprotest organized by the Eksath Bhikkhu Peramuna. A mob representing the latter attacked the Tamil protesters and was responsible for unleashing riots that killed nearly 150 Tamils. Rioting broke out in Colombo, Batticaloa, Trincomalee, and Gal Oya, the latter a Sinhalese colonization settlement in Eastern Province. Tamils flew black flags at their businesses and homes in Northern and Eastern Provinces. In addition, "shops and schools were closed, lawyers stayed away from the courts, and bus services were stopped and a day of mourning was observed."[51] Tamil leaders characterized the Sinhala-Only Act as a form of "apartheid," and their followers mobilized throughout the island to counter this discriminatory legislation.[52]

When the bill was debated in parliament, Tamil politicians defended their language passionately while railing against the act, heightened their demand for a federal arrangement based on ethnolinguistic demarcations, and threatened to form a separatist movement. Tamil, it was observed, was "a living and virile language spoken by over 40 million people in Sri Lanka and southern India."[53] Chellappah Suntharalingam, the representative for Vavuniya and one of the earliest and most vociferous advocates of *eelam*, claimed that "we were . . . under the dominion of the Portuguese, Dutch and the English, and we shall not tolerate any foreign domination by the Sinhalese. We shall resist to the bitter end."[54] G.G. Ponnambalam, founder of the All Ceylon Tamil Congress, noted that "the imposition of Sinhalese as the sole official language of this country must

---

50. Quoted in ibid., col. 1711.

51. See "Day of Mourning in North," *CDN*, June 7, 1956, p. 1.

52. "Sinhala Bill Called 'Policy of Apartheid,'" *CDN*, July 2, 1956, p. 5.

53. Quoted in House, *Debates*, May 3, 1956, col. 214.

54. Quoted in House, *Debates*, May 2, 1956, col. 142.

inevitably and inexorably put an end, even if that is not your real objective today, to the Tamil nation and the Tamil people as such."[55] Many Tamils saw their future in such terms. The belief among some Sinhalese that a Sinhala-only policy would lead to a homogeneous nation merely heightened Tamil concerns.[56] One way to avoid this outcome was to ensure that Tamils attained greater political autonomy within Sri Lanka. It was not coincidental that the Tamil Federal Party, formed in 1951, gained increased prominence after the Sinhala-Only Movement gathered momentum.

A Federal Party convention held in August 1956 called for a federal constitution that provided autonomy for Northern and Eastern Provinces and equal status for the Sinhala and Tamil languages.[57] The Sinhalese, however, feared that this would constitute a first step toward the island's dismemberment. Given that millions of Tamils lived in India's Tamil Nadu state, this fear was understandable, though it was exaggerated by Sinhalese radicals. Thus between 1956 and 1958, Tamil fears for their future under a Sinhala-only regime, coupled with the determination of Sinhalese extremists to prevent any compromise over the language issue, inflamed communalist passions. As one parliamentarian noted, "People who have never been communalists have become communalists and those who have been moderates have become extremists while extremists have become incorrigible fanatics."[58]

The 1956 Federal Party convention threatened to launch a nonviolent protest if the government did not accede to the party's demands within a year. This led to discussions between Bandaranaike and Federal Party leader S.J.V. Chelvanayakam, and resulted in the Bandaranaike-Chelvanayakam (B-C) Pact of July 1957. According to the terms of the pact, Tamils agreed to drop their demands for linguistic parity and their plans for another *satyagraha*, while the Sinhalese agreed to recognize Tamil as a minority language. This would have allowed Tamil to be used for administrative purposes in Northern and Eastern Provinces. Further-

---

55. Quoted in House, *Debates*, June 7, 1956, col. 939.

56. It was even proposed that providing state employment "on a linguistic . . . basis" would expedite such homogenization.

57. The convention also demanded that Sinhalese colonization in traditional Tamil homeland areas be halted and that Indian Tamils who were denied citizenship under statutes passed by the UNP government in 1948–49 be made citizens. The irony in this second demand was that many Northern Province Tamil representatives, submitting to their casteist and communalist proclivities, had joined their Sinhalese counterparts to deny citizenship to many Indian Tamils born and bred in Sri Lanka.

58. Quoted in House, *Debates*, November 20, 1958, col. 1747.

more, it was agreed that regional councils would be created to deal with education, agriculture, and Sinhalese colonization of Tamil areas.

The B-C Pact was a commendable compromise, but it prompted the opposition UNP, supported by the omnipresent *sangha* and Sinhalese nationalists, to engage in ethnic outbidding. The militant Eksath Bhikkhu Peramuna and other Sinhalese groups demanded that the pact be abrogated and threatened to conduct their own *satyagraha*. UNP leader Senanayake claimed that the pact would ensure that the "majority race is going to be reduced to a minority" whereby "Ceylon would in no time be a state of India." He proclaimed, "I am prepared to sacrifice my life to prevent the implementation of the Bandaranaike-Chelvanayakam Agreement, which is a racial division of Ceylon under the guise of the regional council system and is an act of treachery on the part of the Prime Minister."[59] He was assisted by supposed moderates within the UNP who also sought political gain by resorting to ethnic outbidding. For example, two days before the Sinhala-only legislation was introduced in parliament, UNP politician J.R. Jayewardene argued that "no Government should and could make Sinhalese the official language by trampling down the language rights of over a million of the permanent residents of the country. It cannot thrust to the wilderness the cherished languages of these people. The doors of the public services should not be closed to the thousands of youth who did not know Sinhalese for no fault of their own. Surely that was the way to sow the seeds of a civil war."[60] This view was renounced a year later when Jayewardene, eager to become the UNP's leader, organized a protest march against the B-C Pact from Colombo to Kandy and showed that the ethnic card could be utilized for both inter- and intraparty machinations. Sinhalese jingoists and extremist *bhikkhus* ably assisted these ethnic entrepreneurs. For example, F.R. Jayasuriya, a prominent Sinhala-only ideologue, claimed that the island would become "part of Madras in six months" if linguistic parity was introduced.[61] He vilified the B-C Pact and argued that "the Prime Minister has performed the last act of treachery against the Sinhalese people. The bitterest enemy of the Sinhalese would not have done any worse."[62] A leading *bhikkhu* likewise claimed that Bandaranaike was "trying to ruin our race."[63] Such

59. Quoted in "Pact a Racial Division of Ceylon, Says Dudley," *CDN*, August 12, 1957, p. 7.

60. Quoted in "J.R. Jayewardene on Sinhale [sic] Bill," *CDN*, June 4, 1956, p. 5.

61. Quoted in "Death-Fast Lecturer Issues Two Statements," *CDN*, May 25, 1956, p. 3.

62. Quoted in "Mixed Reception," *CDN*, July 27, 1957, p. 1.

63. Quoted in "Sinhalese Told: Be Watchful," *CDN*, September 17, 1957, p. 3.

rhetoric catalyzed Sinhalese opinion against the B-C Pact. Tamils were used "as whipping horses for contending Sinhala political factions,"[64] with political, social, and religious groups coalescing to undermine Tamil confidence in the country's governmental and nongovernmental institutions.

Tamils who clamored for linguistic parity and therefore opposed the B-C Pact added fuel to the communalist flames. For example, Tamil Congress President G.G. Ponnambalam claimed that the Federal Party had "stabbed the trusting Tamils on [sic] the back."[65] Other Tamils branded the pact "ignominious" because it relegated their "community to a very subordinate and inferior position in an apparently free country."[66] Ponnambalam argued that the pact was "an agreement with the Federal party leaders and not with the Tamil people."[67]

In late March 1958, buses owned and operated by the state were transferred north with the Sinhala letter "sri" marked on their license plates. Its use on all vehicles was based on a new directive from the minister of transport and works. At a time when linguistic nationalism was raging in both communities, the Tamils viewed this as another Sinhalese attempt to dominate them. The Federal Party consequently began a campaign to efface the Sinhala letter "sri" and substitute it with Tamil lettering. The Sinhalese retaliated by smearing tar over Tamil street signs, commercial boards, and vehicles with English lettering. Even the prime minister's Cadillac, displaying a "Left Hand Drive" sign in Sinhala, Tamil, and English, was tarred.[68] When a band of bhikkhus parked themselves outside the prime minister's residence and refused to budge until the B-C Pact was abrogated, Bandaranaike used the bus controversy in Jaffna as an excuse to accede to their demands. The B-C Pact's death knell was sounded when Bandaranaike "tore up a copy of the pact in front of the assembled monks who clapped in joy."[69] Ironically, despite caving in

---

64. Quoted in Sinnappah Arasaratnam, *Sri Lanka after Independence: Nationalism, Communalism, and Nation Building* (Madras, Tamil Nadu, India: University of Madras, 1986), p. 32.

65. Quoted in "Political Leaders Comment on PM's Statement No. 1," *CDN*, August 14, 1957, p. 7.

66. Quoted in "F.P. Acceptance of Sinhala Act Ignominious," *CDN*, September 4, 1957, p. 11.

67. "Tamils Duped, Says Ponnambalam," *CDN*, September 23, 1957, p. 7.

68. "It Went On Till Late at Night," *CDN*, April 2, 1958, p. 1.

69. M.R. Narayan Swamy, *Tigers of Lanka: From Boys to Guerrillas* (Columbia, Mo.: South Asia Books, 1995), p. 12.

to the demands of the Sinhalese extremists, Bandaranaike was assassinated by a *bhikkhu* in September 1959.

Soon after the B-C Pact was abrogated in April 1958, a train carrying delegates to a Federal Party convention was derailed and its Tamil occupants beaten. The accompanying anti-Tamil riots in Colombo and other areas left hundreds dead and thousands displaced. Sinhalese living in the north were also attacked and forced to relocate to the south.[70] These developments should have made the authorities wary of alienating the Tamils. Instead the language issue was utilized to fashion policies that marginalized the Tamils while benefiting the Sinhalese. The rabi anti-Tamil rhetoric that preceded the March 1960 and July 1960 elections also suggested that Sinhalese politicians had no qualms about vilifying the Tamils. This was especially true of Bandaranaike's widow, Sirimavo.

TOWARD SINHALESE DOMINANCE AND TAMIL SEPARATISM

According to a Bandaranaike relative, "In Solla's [Bandaranaike's] time Sirima[vo] presided over nothing fiercer than the kitchen fire."[71] Yet, supported by party leaders, this political ingenue was catapulted to the premiership of the Sri Lankan government, becoming the world's first woman prime minister in July 1960. Although her husband vacillated on ethnic questions, Sirimavo Bandaranaike—whether out of inexperience or deliberate disregard for Tamil concerns—consistently eschewed ethnic compromise and instead pursued an agenda that further poisoned relations between the Sinhalese and the Tamils. For example, in the 1960s and early 1970s, Mrs. Bandaranaike banned Sri Lanka's Dravida Munnetra Kazhagam (Dravidian Progressive Front—DMK), an insignificant group named after the influential Tamil Nadu political party. She also banned the import of Tamil films, magazines, and newspapers and denied entrance visas to Tamil movie stars and Tamil Nadu's chief minister.[72] Although the DMK in Tamil Nadu certainly sympathized with and supported Sri Lanka's Tamils, prompting legitimate concern among Sri Lanka's leaders, such actions displayed a blatant disregard for Tamil cultural preferences. These actions were benign, however, when compared to Mrs. Bandaranaike's other anti-Tamil policies.

In August 1958 the S.W.R.D. Bandaranaike government had approved the Tamil Language (Special Provisions) Act No. 28. This legisla-

---

70. The 1958 race riots are best described in Tarzie Vittachi, *Emergency '58: The Story of the Ceylon Race Riots* (London: A. Deutsch, 1958).

71. Quoted in Gooneratne, *Relative Merits*, p. 160.

72. Ponnambalam, *Sri Lanka: The National Question*, p. 142.

tion empowered the prime minister to allow the "reasonable use of Tamil" to ensure correspondence with government departments, administer northern and eastern areas, conduct civil service entrance examinations, and support educational programs. The requisite regulations to implement the bill, however, were not approved in the political flux following Bandaranaike's assassination. When the SLFP hinted during the July 1960 elections that it was amenable to accommodating the Tamil language, the Federal Party encouraged Tamils in the south to vote for Mrs. Bandaranaike. Once attaining power, however, Mrs. Bandaranaike's government sought to rigorously implement the Sinhala-only policy, which was due to take effect on January 1, 1961.

Government officials who did not have proficiency in Sinhala were subsequently denied bonuses and salary increases; public servants hired after 1956 were given three years to learn Sinhala or forfeit their jobs; and, most chafing to northern Tamils, Sinhalese civil servants were transplanted north to ensure that government agencies in Tamil areas operated in the Sinhala language. The Language of the Courts Act No. 3 of 1961 further called for Sinhala to gradually replace English in all courts, including those in Tamil areas. No effort was made to implement the Tamil Language Act. Rather, a government policy was instituted to hire Sinhalese into government service. The effects of these policies were dramatic: In 1956, 30 percent of the Ceylon administrative service, 50 percent of the clerical service, 60 percent of engineers and doctors, and 40 percent of the armed forces were Tamil. By 1970 those numbers had plummeted to 5 percent, 5 percent, 10 percent, and 1 percent, respectively.[73]

When the Federal Party protested by resorting to *satyagraha* campaigns and blocking access to district administrative buildings in Northern and Eastern Provinces, the government declared a state of emergency and deployed military troops. The Sinhalese-dominated military was soon viewed by Tamils in these regions as an occupation force.

Regulations for implementing the Tamil Language Act were finally approved in January 1966 under a UNP-led coalition that included support from the Federal Party and the Tamil Congress. Approval of the Tamil Language (Special Provisions) Regulations of 1966, however, was bitterly opposed by the SLFP and Sri Lanka's two Marxist parties—the Lanka Sama Samaja Party and the Communist Party. As late as 1963, the LSSP proudly proclaimed itself to be the only party favoring linguistic parity. Averse to becoming politically marginalized, the LSSP and other Marxist parties reversed their positions and joined the ethnic outbidding bandwagon in time for the March 1965 general election. The SLFP, which

---

73. Ibid., p. 174.

from its inception was a pro-Sinhalese Buddhist party and under Mrs. Bandaranaike treated the Tamils with arrogance, was defeated and thereafter resorted to chauvinistic propaganda to put the UNP-led coalition on the defensive on language and ethnic issues. In particular, it opposed the Senanayake-Chelvanayakam Pact of 1965—which, if implemented, would have (1) recognized Northern and Eastern Provinces as Tamil speaking, (2) amended the Language of the Courts Act of 1961 so that both Sinhalese and Tamil could be used in all courts, and (3) given Tamils first preference when colonizing Tamil areas.

The SLFP claimed that the UNP had promised the Tamil leadership to undo the Sinhala-only policy. The fact that the Federal Party and the Tamil Congress supported the UNP and that M. Tiruchelvam, a leading Federal Party member, was a cabinet member only underscored the SLFP claims. Thus, when the UNP under Senanayake sought to approve a devolutionary scheme through the District Councils Bill of 1968, it was vehemently opposed by the SLFP, which was ably assisted by the *sangha*, Sinhalese Buddhist nationalists, and Marxists. The Muslims, who had come to fear Tamil dominance over their Eastern Province settlements, also joined the opposition. The UNP was ultimately forced to abandon the bill.

The sad irony was that the UNP, which opposed Bandaranaike's plans for devolution, had tried to implement something akin to the B-C Pact only to be opposed by the SLFP and Bandaranaike's widow, who purported to champion the "Bandaranaike revolution." When combined with the Marxists' reversal on the language issue, the effort to approve the bill highlighted the high degree to which Sri Lanka's politicians and parties had embraced ethnic outbidding. The only consistent actors in Sri Lankan politics were the extremist *bhikkhus* and the Sinhalese nationalists who clamored for a Sinhala-speaking, Sinhalese Buddhist Sri Lanka where minorities would live under the majority community's rule.

EDUCATION POLICY

Under the British, the country's Christian mission schools, which Buddhist leaders had long viewed as proselytizing centers, had benefited immensely. These schools continued to rely on government finances in the postindependence era, even though they admitted few non-Christians. Mrs. Bandaranaike acceded to the demands of Buddhist organizations and nationalized these schools in 1961. Except for thirty-eight (mostly Roman Catholic) schools that chose to stay private, all others were brought under government control. Every school—both private and government controlled—was forced to phase out English-language instruction so that by the mid-1970s, English was taught only as a second language.

Until 1969 university entrance was based on merit, and Tamil students were constantly overrepresented, especially in science-based disciplines. The Sinhala-only policy, coupled with a "youth bulge,"[74] led to large numbers of Sinhala-educated students clamoring for a university education. The second Sirimavo Bandaranaike government (1970–77) sought to accommodate these students by introducing discrepant requirements for university entrance. Under this new system, Tamil students in many fields had to score twenty points higher on exams than their Sinhalese counterparts to gain university admittance.[75] Though the system was "standardized" in 1974 and various district-level quota schemes were introduced thereafter, Tamil enrollment in universities plummeted as a result of these policies. Although Tamils were still disproportionately overrepresented in Sri Lanka's universities in 1975, the way Mrs. Bandaranaike's government curtailed Tamil enrollment reaffirmed Tamil fears that Sinhalese authorities were determined to marginalize them.

OTHER PROVOCATIVE POLICIES

Other government policies reinforced Tamil concerns about marginalization. For example, successive governments allocated insufficient resources to Tamil areas and even shelved internationally sponsored development projects in these areas. When development projects were commissioned in the north and northeast, they were designed to benefit Sinhalese colonizers.[76] The government also refused to discipline policemen who attacked attendees of the Fourth International Tamil Conference in January 1974, even though an independent commission condemned the police for killing nine Tamils.

Most significantly, the constitution of the First Republic of Sri Lanka, enacted by the SLFP-led United Front government in May 1972, declared Sri Lanka "a Unitary State," gave "Buddhism the foremost place," made it the state's duty "to protect and foster Buddhism," instituted Sinhala as

74. The term, made in reference to Sri Lanka, is from Gary Fuller, "The Demographic Backdrop to Ethnic Conflict: A Geographic Overview," in Central Intelligence Agency, *The Challenge of Ethnic Conflict to National and International Order in the 1990s: Geographic Perspective*, RTT 95-10039 (Washington, D.C.: Central Intelligence Agency, October 1995), p. 154.

75. C.R. de Silva, "Sinhala-Tamil Relations and Education in Sri Lanka: The University Admissions Issue—The First Phase, 1971–77," in Goldmann and Jeyaratnam, *From Independence to Statehood*, p. 137.

76. See Neelan Tiruchelvam, "Ethnicity and Resource Allocation," in ibid., pp. 185–195; and Bruce Matthews, "Radical Conflict and the Rationalization of Violence in Sri Lanka," *Pacific Affairs*, Vol. 59, No. 2 (Spring 1986), p. 33.

the "Official Language of Sri Lanka," and mandated that the regulations drafted under the Tamil Language Act of 1958 were "subordinate legislation." The new constitution also disbanded the Soulbury Constitution's minority safeguards. Many Sinhalese were dissatisfied that the country had never developed an anticolonial nationalism and therefore viewed the Soulbury Constitution, through which the British monarch continued to operate as the nominal head of state, as a colonial artifact. They thus embraced the new constitution as both a nationalist and autochthonous document. Tamil leaders, however, protested that the constitution denied Tamils basic rights and called for an amendment that would provide linguistic parity. They further threatened to conduct a nonviolent struggle and promised to boycott the State Assembly, though by now it had become clear that the Tamils were unlikely to attain any gains through the political process. With minority rights undermined and majority preferences constitutionalized, Sri Lanka became increasingly polarized.

THE TAMIL TURN TO RADICALISM

Reacting to decreases in Tamil university enrollment and in state-sector employment, the dearth of private-sector opportunities for upward mobility, and the military's heavy-handed practices in the north, Tamil youth became increasingly radicalized. When Tamil leaders reversed course and decided to participate in the State Assembly, hundreds of Tamil youth invaded an All Ceylon Tamil Congress meeting and demanded that Tamil politicians boycott parliament. As the *Ceylon Daily News* recognized, Tamil politicians may have threatened to boycott parliament for propagandist reasons, but a "movement of militant youth rooted in the soil of Jaffna and nourished by material frustration, a feeling of humiliation and bitterness, could be another kettle of fish."[77]

Tamil mobilization initially took the form of strikes and boycotts, which led to arrests and detentions that only further exacerbated Tamil grievances. The pressure imposed on Tamil politicians forced the moderate Tamil United Liberation Front—formed after the Federal Party, the Tamil Congress, and the Ceylon Workers' Congress (which represented the Indian Tamils) joined forces—to issue the May 1976 Vaddukkodai resolution. The resolution emphasized that the Tamils were "a nation distinct and apart from the Sinhalese" and claimed that because successive Sinhalese governments had deprived the "Tamil nation of its territory, language, citizenship, economic life, opportunities of employment and education," the Tamils were resolved to establishing "the Free, Sovereign, Secular, Socialist State of Tamil Eelam based on the right of self-

---

77. "What's Up in the North?" *CDN,* July 10, 1972, p. 6.

determination inherent in every nation." It is plausible that the call for *eelam* was a tactical maneuver to marginalize the burgeoning Tamil militant youth movement. Alternatively, it might have been a gesture designed to force the Sri Lankan government to compromise and grant the Tamils increased autonomy. Whatever the case, *eelam* galvanized many extremist and young Tamils. By 1977, when the UNP attained power under J.R. Jayewardene, Tamil youth had begun to target progovernment politicians, assassinate police constables, and rob banks to fund their incipient rebellion.

POST-1977 LINGUISTIC ACCOMMODATION: TOO LITTLE, TOO LATE
The landslide UNP victory in July 1977 ushered in a new political and economic era in Sri Lanka. Drawing on aid from Western countries, the International Monetary Fund, and the World Bank, the new government jettisoned the previous regime's autarkic policies and adopted large-scale infrastructure development and structural adjustment reforms. The healthy parliamentary majority that it garnered also enabled the UNP to replace the 1972 constitution with a new constitution in August 1978. The new constitution introduced a presidential system, mandated proportional representation, and explicitly provided for some minority rights. It reiterated that the "official Language of Sri Lanka shall be Sinhala" and that "the official language shall be the language of administration throughout Sri Lanka," even while recognizing Tamil as a national language that could be used for any transaction in Northern and Eastern Provinces. It also gave "Buddhism the foremost place" in the country and stated that "it shall be the duty of the state to protect and foster the Buddha *Sasana* [Buddhist institutions and religion]."

The 1978 constitution declared that "no citizen shall suffer any disability by reason of language" and guaranteed the use of Tamil in courthouses throughout the island. It further incorporated the Tamil Language Act. The thirteenth amendment to the constitution made Tamil an official language in November 1987, while the sixteenth amendment solidified this position by declaring both Sinhala and Tamil as national languages for administrative purposes. To compensate for the desultory status of the Department of Official Languages that was created under the ministry of finance in 1955, the UNP government re-created an Official Language Department in 1978. Under the Official Language Commission Act No. 18 of 1991, another UNP government further created the Official Languages Commission to implement language policy. Yet more than a decade later, the commission has hardly succeeded in fulfilling its mandate. Some government institutions demand interactions in Sinhala only; certain courts conduct proceedings in Sinhala to prosecute Tamils not conversant in Sinhala; destination boards on buses and signs at hospitals, police stations, and post offices rarely include Tamil; Tamil students in rural areas are deprived of equal educational opportunities (mainly because thousands of Tamil teaching positions go unfilled) government-produced Tamil textbooks are replete with mistakes; and Sinhalese and Buddhist history dominates schoolbooks while the minority's religious and cultural heritage is disregarded.[78] In sum, the 1978 constitution did not address long-standing Tamil claims for autonomy, and the Tamil language was afforded equal status only after Tamil youth mobilized militarily and embraced the goal of *eelam*. The government's accommodative policies were too little, too late.

In 1994 the People's Alliance government, headed by the Bandaranaikes' daughter Chandrika Kumaratunga, came to power and soon proposed constitutional reform. Chapter 4 of the draft constitution proclaims that "the Official languages of Sri Lanka shall be Sinhala and Tamil." Although Sinhala, Tamil, and English shall be considered national languages, both "Sinhala and Tamil shall be the languages of administration throughout Sri Lanka," and minority groups shall have access to public records in their language wherever it "exceeds one-fifth of the total population." A new constitution, however, has still not been enacted. These moves have not alleviated Tamil-language grievances because widespread anti-Tamil practices contradict these constitutional promises.

POST-1977 ANTI-TAMIL VIOLENCE

In August 1977, one month after the UNP was elected, anti-Tamil riots spread across Sri Lanka. The riots were influenced by antigovernment actions perpetrated by disgruntled northern Tamil youth and by UNP nationalists eager to prove their Sinhalese credentials. UNP officials such as cabinet minister Cyril Matthew voiced chauvinist rhetoric in parliament even while their party tried to introduce linguistic parity. The following May, the government proscribed the Liberation Tigers of Tamil Eelam (LTTE) and other rebel groups. The Prevention of Terrorism Act, passed in 1979, enabled security forces to arrest and imprison suspected Tamil subversives without trial for eighteen months. Many young Tamils were subsequently abused and tortured, which merely strengthened their determination to secede. Violence perpetrated by Tamil rebels and govern-

---

78. Tamil complaints along such lines often appear in the Tamil press. For a good account, see A. Theva Rajan, *Tamil as Official Language: Retrospect and Prospect* (Colombo: International Center for Ethnic Studies, 1995), pp. 82–123.

ment forces during the June 1981 District Development Councils' elections in Jaffna led the latter to burn down the Jaffna Municipal Library.[79] The fire destroyed nearly 100,000 ancient and rare documents and convinced Tamils that some Sinhalese were determined to annihilate their culture. This was followed by intermittent anti-Tamil riots throughout July and August of 1981, with the government's supporters playing a major role in the mayhem. The worst anti-Tamil riots, however, ensued in July 1983 after the LTTE ambushed and killed thirteen soldiers in the north.

The government's post-1977 economic policies marginalized many Sinhalese entrepreneurs, who had until then relied on government quotas and licenses to maintain their monopolistic practices. This Sinhalese lumpen bourgeoisie, together with some politicians, the ruling party's *goondas* (hoodlums), Sinhalese nationalists, and extremist elements within the *sangha*—all of whom were aided by the government's security forces—wrecked havoc during the 1983 riots. Tamil businesses and homes were looted and burned, thousands became refugees, and between 400 and 2,000 Tamils were murdered. As the *Economist* reported, "The majority Sinhalese observed that more than half of 'their' new industries were Tamil-owned—and, cutting the nose to spite the face, burnt down the Tamil factories."[80] President Jayewardene failed to impose a curfew or address the nation until three days after the riots. When he did face the country, he evinced "not a syllable of sympathy for the Tamil people or any explicit rejection of the spirit of vengeance," again according to the *Economist*.[81] The president's dilatory, mild response to the anti-Tamil violence and the numerous official and nonofficial institutions that coalesced to attack Tamils ultimately drove thousands to fight for Tamil *eelam*.

At the same time, the government's pro-Western foreign policy tilt, influenced by the government's economic reforms, alienated India. New Delhi subsequently destabilized Sri Lanka by arming and training Tamil youth who joined rebel groups following the riots.[82] This marked the beginning of Sri Lanka's most savage ethnic conflict to date. Yet although checkered economic fortunes and petty ethnic jealousies influenced the

79. This was a scheme designed to promote limited devolution throughout the country.

80. "Ergophobia," *Economist*, August 13, 1983, p. 29.

81. "Sri Lanka Puts a Torch to Its Future," *Economist*, August 6, 1983, p. 25.

82. See Neil DeVotta, "Sri Lanka's Structural Adjustment Program and Its Impact on Indo-Lanka Relations," *Asian Survey*, Vol. 38, No. 5 (May 1998), pp. 457–473.

1983 riots, this spasm of violence was only the proximate cause of the war that followed. The underlying causes of the war were the Sinhala-only language policy, the culture of ethnic outbidding, and the institutional decay that the language issue initiated.

THE SINHALA-ONLY POLICY AND ETHNIC CONFLICT

Although the Sinhala-only policy was implemented gradually, successive Sri Lankan governments, especially under Mrs. Bandaranaike, worked hard to ensure a Sinhala-only and Sinhalese-dominated regime. Paradoxically, Tamils faced little immediate discrimination from Sinhala-only legislation because the bureaucracy was reluctant to follow the new directives and the government lacked the resources to forcefully implement the Sinhala-Only Act of 1956.[83] Indeed, soon after the Sinhala-only legislation was enacted, Bandaranaike issued Gazette Notification No. 10,949 declaring that any languages that had "hitherto been used for official purpose . . . may be . . . so used until the necessary change is effected."[84] The Gazette Notification ensured that there would be no immediate implementation of Sinhala-only policies. Even so, the Sinhala-Only Act affected state employment and educational policies at a time when the state was the country's largest employer and when university education was viewed as a key to socioeconomic progress. Equally important, the act led to ethnic outbidding, and it legitimated Sinhalese jingoism, which only radicalized an otherwise culturally and politically conservative Tamil community. The Sirimavo Bandaranaike governments were so successful in favoring the Sinhalese that the majority community became disproportionately overrepresented, especially in the bureaucracy.

Although other factors—such as the government's internal colonization policies—played a significant role in Sri Lanka's ethnic relations, the language issue was the most important item on the agenda for both Sinhalese and Tamils. Indeed it permeated the public policy agenda. As has been correctly observed, "Up to the early 1950s the Tamils' concept of nationalism lacked coherence and cohesion despite all their talk of a linguistic, religious and cultural separateness from the Sinhalese. As with the Sinhalese, it was language that provided the sharp cutting edge of a new national self-consciousness. Indeed the Federal Party's crucial contribu-

---

83. See the two chapters by R.G.G. Olcott Gunasekera and S.G. Samarasinghe, in K.N.O. Dharmadasa, ed., *National Language Policy in Sri Lanka, 1956–1996: Three Studies in Its Implementation,* Occasional Papers 6 (Kandy: International Center for Ethnic Studies, 1996), pp. 17–111.

84. "UNP on the Sinhala Bill," *CDN,* July 18, 1956, p. 3.

tion to Tamil politics was its emphasis on the role of language as the determinant of nationhood."[85] This determination to attain Tamil nationhood was exemplified by a Tamil parliamentarian who prophetically claimed that "if the Sinhalese will not agree to federation the Tamils will have a fully autonomous Tamil linguistic State by whatever means they can get it, by all the methods of history—rebellion, guerilla warfare or anything you please."[86] The emergence of the Tamil language as an ethnic, nationalistic mobilizer, however, was Sinhalese induced. As one scholar has observed, the Sinhala-only policy promoted a climate "for the subversion of democratic institutions . . . [that then led to] terror, anomie, and the violent call for a separate state."[87] The Sinhala-Only Movement and the Sinhala-Only Act were driving forces behind Sri Lanka's ethnic conflict.

Conclusion

Sri Lanka's ethnolinguistic nationalism and its subsequent civil war offer numerous lessons. First, they indicate how communalism is easily stoked when discriminatory language policies are introduced. In hindsight, it appears that Sri Lanka's political elites could have reconfigured the socioeconomic opportunity structure so that depressed classes from any ethnic background would be provided with avenues for upward mobility even while the Sinhalese Buddhists, being both the majority community and the community most marginalized under British colonial rule, were disproportionately overaccommodated. This would have eventually reduced upper-class Sinhalese and Tamil overrepresentation in the bureaucracy and the university system. Such a policy might have dampened ethnolinguistic nationalism and thereby suppressed the ethnic outbidding that became the bane of Sinhalese-Tamil relations.

Second, the Sri Lankan case shows how language policies are related to education and thereby to socioeconomic upward mobility. The Sinhala-Only Act blocked the Tamil quest for continued socioeconomic progress and led to Tamil mobilization against the state. When peaceful protests were suppressed, extremist action was legitimized.

Third, the Sri Lankan case suggests that it may be easier to pursue accommodative linguistic policies in multilingual (as opposed to bilingual)

---

85.   De Silva, *A History of Sri Lanka,* p. 513.

86.   House, *Debates,* November 8, 1957, col. 1271.

87.   H.L. Seneviratne, *The Work of Kings: The New Buddhism in Sri Lanka* (Chicago: University of Chicago Press, 1999), p. 204.

societies. Multilingual societies generate more crosscutting cleavages, and they are less likely to face domination by any one ethnic group. This can help to facilitate linguistic accommodation. A dominant community in a bilingual society, however, may assume that it can impose its will on the minority. This in turn can prompt a backlash that can lead to violent conflict.

A fourth lesson from the Sri Lankan case is that, in ethnic conflicts, "escalation is easy" and "de-escalation is hard."[88] This is especially true when ethnic animosities stem from linguistic differences. As Johann Gottfried Herder wondered, "Has a nation anything more precious than the language of its fathers? In it dwells its entire world of tradition, history, religion, principles of existence; its whole heart and soul."[89] In the Sri Lankan case, accommodative policies that may have satisfied the Tamils in the 1950s, the 1960s, and even the 1970s subsequently became inadequate. If the Sinhalese had conceded linguistic parity in the 1950s, it is unlikely that the Tamils would have clamored for federalism and devolution. If devolution had been incorporated into the 1978 constitution, Sri Lanka might have avoided ethnic warfare in the 1980s. Thus Sri Lanka's leaders failed to take advantage of numerous windows of opportunity in the 1950s, 1960s, and 1970s. This testified to both their ineptitude and their quest to place personal and party ambitions above the national interest. Indeed the Sri Lankan case clearly shows the damage done by political leaders when they play the ethnic card.

Finally, the Sri Lankan case demonstrates that regional autonomy arrangements may be better suited than unitary structures in polyethnic societies. Decentralization, whereby a minority group is provided some self-government, may be appropriate when a state harbors territorially based *ethnie*.[90] In retrospect, it is hard to believe that a federal arrangement would not have better served the country. Tragically, the violence that a federal system may have precluded has now hardened the opposition of Sinhalese nationalists to any devolutionary arrangement. Indeed Sinhalese nationalists continue to characterize devolution as a first step toward the island's division. The country's deadly conflict

---

88. Michael E. Brown, "The Impact of Government Policies on Ethnic Relations," in Brown and Šumit Ganguly, eds., *Government Policies and Ethnic Relations in Asia and the Pacific* (Cambridge, Mass.: MIT Press, 1997), pp. 514, 571.

89. Quoted in Isaiah Berlin, *Vico and Herder: Two Studies in the History of Ideas* (New York: Viking, 1976), p. 165.

90. Ted Robert Gurr, "Ethnic Warfare on the Wane," *Foreign Affairs*, Vol. 79, No. 3 (May/June 2000), p. 56.

will not be resolved until a credible power-sharing arrangement is implemented.

Sri Lanka's horrifying ethnic saga is a classic case of how a majority group's ethnolinguistic malpractices can undermine the spirit of accommodation, conciliation, and compromise that is essential to interethnic stability.

Part II
Southeast Asia

Chapter 5

Language Policy in Modern Burma

Mary P. Callahan

The politics of language in Burma, or Myanmar, is highly contentious. Indeed what one calls the country—"Burma" or "Myanmar"—signals a preference for one faction over another in the country's ongoing battle between civilian and military leaders, between democracy and authoritarianism. The military junta's propagandists have constructed a cultural and historical fantasyland called "Myanmar," but few outside the junta have bought into this fantasy. At the same time, the junta has unwittingly unleashed an ethnolinguistic assault that has deepened dissension within the country.

Since the early twentieth century, the geographical focus of politics in Burma—including ethnic politics and language politics—has been central Burma. The main issue on the country's political agenda has been the struggle for power at the center—what I call the arena of "insider politics." Struggles between the center and the minority groups who live in the country's periphery—"outsider politics"—have received much less attention. Rangoon's elites have neglected and virtually forgotten about these minority issues for long stretches of time.

From independence in 1948 until the military coup of 1962, Burma's government barely survived assaults from rebel groups of the central region. From Rangoon's perspective, this intra-elite war represented the country's most pressing crisis. The main priority on the ethnic front was the nationalist struggle to reduce the influence of minorities who had collaborated with the British during the colonial era. This manifested itself in a language policy that promoted Burmese—the language of the ethnic Burman majority—and undercut the status of Hindi, Chinese, and to some extent, English. Burma's elites believed that ethnic problems else-where in the country were much less important and much more manage-able. They also believed that it would be easy to transform the ethnic minorities who lived beyond the central region into loyal citizens of the state once the situation at the center had stabilized. There were few signs that elites in the central region appreciated that linguistic complexities in frontier regions could hinder the had stabilization of the country.

From 1962 to 1988, Burma's socialist governments also focused on "insider politics"—strengthening the power of the central state—although the emergence of separatist movements in border regions elic-ited some attention from Rangoon. Language policy during this period concentrated on the introduction of socialist concepts into the Burmese language and the elimination of the lingering influences of the colonial era—including the use of English and the incorporation of English words into Burmese. Burma's socialist leaders believed that the development of a standardized, ideologically correct Burmese language was one of the keys to turning everyone in the country into good socialists.

After the 1988 pro-democracy uprising and the subsequent reestab-lishment of direct military rule, the junta continued to purify, standard-ize, and censor the Burmese language. It also dramatically expanded the scope of ethnic politics in the country. The junta, worried that the Ran-goon-based opposition (the National League for Democracy, or NLD) and armed minority opposition groups in border regions would form an alliance, sought to keep the opposition divided. With that in mind, gov-ernment bodies "authenticated" the cultures of various minorities, which resulted in local attempts to revive some minority languages. The hope, it appears, was that this would discredit the Burman-dominated NLD and interfere with communication between the NLD and minority opposition groups. Paradoxically, this campaign unfolded in the midst of a cultural homogenization program that was designed to erase differences among the peoples of Burma.

This chapter begins with an overview of Burma' physical, ethnic, and political terrain. It then reviews language policies and ethnic relations in the colonial era; the evolution of these issues from independence in 1948 until the military coup of 1962; the growing attention paid to minorities in border regions between 1962 and 1988; and the dramatic changes that have unfolded in Burma since 1988. The chapter concludes with an as-sessment of how government-sponsored language programs have suc-ceeded in establishing a monolingual public sphere in Burma's central region, while exacerbating minority threat perceptions elsewhere in the country.

The Physical, Ethnic, and Political Terrain

Burma is the largest country in mainland Southeast Asia, sharing land borders with Thailand, Laos, China, India, and Bangladesh. Three north-south chains of mountains make east-west travel and communications difficult, although north-south travel through the valleys of these mountain ranges is relatively accessible via river, road, or railroad.

The largest ethnic group in the country is known in English as the "Burmans," although the military junta that took over the government in 1988 refers to these people as "Bamars." This group resides mainly in the central agricultural valleys of the Irrawaddy and Chindwin Rivers and in the southern coastal and delta regions. The official language of the state is Burmese although other languages are spoken in ethnic-minority regions.

Since 1931 no Rangoon-based government has attempted to conduct a thorough census in minority regions. If data on minority populations were collected in the 1973 and 1983 censuses, they were not made public. Most scholars estimate that the country's dozens of minority groups make up around one-third of the total population of 48 million.[1] (See Table 5.1.)

LINGUISTIC COMPLICATIONS

Ethnologue puts the number of languages spoken in Burma at 111, with 1 extinct language.[2] There is little consensus, however, on this estimate. Data on the numbers of speakers of each language are even less reliable.[3] According to *Ethnologue*, Burma's major languages (those spoken by more than half a million people) are Arakanese, Burmese, Chin, Jingpho, Karen, Mon, Shan, and Wa. (See Table 5.2.)

These numbers overstate the unity and uniformity of Burma's major languages, which in many instances comprise distantly related languages that may not even be uniform enough to be called lingua francas. Neither

---

1. See, for example, Martin J. Smith, *Burma: Insurgency and the Politics of Ethnicity* (London: Zed Books, 1991), pp. 29–32.

2. Barbara F. Grimes, ed., *Ethnologue: Languages of the World*, 12th ed. (Dallas, Tex.: Summer Institute of Linguistics, 1992), pp. 715–723.

3. *Ethnologue* rates the accuracy of statistics on Burma from governmental, United Nations, and other sources as a "C"—its lowest grade: "Needs extensive checking by linguists in the field and more research in published sources." Ibid. G.D. McConnell presents in a catalog format the widely varying estimates of the numbers of speakers of different languages in Burma, compiled from available printed sources. McConnell, *Linguistic Composition of the Nations of the World*, Vol. 6 (Ottawa, Canada: International Center for Research on Language Planning, 1998), pp. 453–489.

Table 5.1. Minority Groups of Burma (population 48 million).

Group	Percentage
Burman	65
Shan	10
Karen	7
Rakhine (Arakanese)	4
Chinese	3
Mon	2
Indian	2
Other	7
Total	100

SOURCE: Based on Martin J. Smith, *Burma: Insurgency and the Politics of Ethnicity* (London: Zed Books, 1991), pp. 29–32.

Table 5.2. Major Languages of Burma.

Language	Number of Speakers
Arakanese	1,875,000
Burmese	21,553,000
Chin	916,000
Jingpho	625,000
Karen	2,600,000
Mon	835,100
Shan	2,920,000
Wa	558,000

SOURCE: Barbara F. Grimes, ed., *Ethnologue: Languages of the World*, 12th ed. (Dallas, Tex.: Summer Institute of Linguistics, 1992).

the British colonial government nor the postindependence Burmese governments ever carried out a formal linguistic survey of the country.[4] These estimates therefore represent some combination of the educated guesses of dedicated linguists and the political fantasies of colonial bureaucrats, postcolonial (ethnic-majority) rulers, and their statisticians in Rangoon.

4. See the autobiographical account of L.F. Taylor, a Rangoon inspector of schools who lost his job, fought the "Fascist decrees" of the colonial government, and ultimately sank his life savings into an ill-fated attempt to carry out such a survey from 1923 into the late 1930s. Taylor, "Account of the Ethnographical and Linguistic Survey of Burma," *Journal of the Burma Research Society*, Vol. 39, No. 2 (December 1956), pp. 159–175.

The last attempt to collect statistics on the numbers of speakers of each language in Burma was in 1931, when the British Census of India attempted to group populations into linguistic categories. One census official noted at the time with great consternation that "some of the races or tribes in Burma change their language almost as often as they change their clothes."[5] Census takers confronting this bewildering and fluid ethnolinguistic pastiche in 1931 created dozens of new racial categories, finally settling on a figure of 135 races.

Postindependence governments minimized group differences. From 1948 to 1988, the central government recognized only seven major "nationalities" (minorities) in the country. The fact that no subsequent government has tried to collect information on languages and their speakers arises from the postindependence political project to downplay the diversity of Burma's population and promote unity-oriented, nation-building programs. As Anna Allott has argued, language-usage statistics "would only draw attention to the size of the different ethnic groups within the country" and would undermine the Rangoon government's fifty-year-old policy of "de-emphasizing the separate interests of the various ethnic minorities in order to encourage national unity."[6]

TWO KINDS OF CONFLICT IN MODERN BURMA

Burma was shaped by two types of political conflict in the twentieth century. The first occurred in the arena of "insider politics"—intra-elite struggles over control of the state. The other occurred in the spatially more diffuse arena of "outsider politics"—the central government's struggles to impose uniformity and authority beyond elite circles. Often conflated in discussions of modern Burmese politics, these two kinds of conflict are usually described in terms of primordial, static "ethnic" characteristics that produce a singular phenomenon called "ethnic conflict." From minority viewpoints, ethnic-majority Burmans are said to be chauvinistic toward and intolerant of other populations inside the country. For example, Kanbawza Win writes: "The crux of all these [ethnic] problems is Myanmar chauvinism. The Burman tribe, better known as Myanmar, are in the majority, and want perpetual domination; and if possible to eradicate the ethnic Shan, Chin, Karen, Kachin, Mon, Arakan

5.   Census Commissioner, Government of India, *Census of India, 1931,* Vol. 11, Pt. 1 (Delhi: Government of India), p. 245.

6.   Anna Allott, "Language Policy and Language Planning in Burma," in David Bradley, ed., *Language Policy: Language Planning and Sociolinguistics in South-East Asia* (Canberra, Australia Capital Territory: Department of Linguistics, Research School of Pacific Studies, Australian National University, 1985), p. 131.

and the Karenni tribes."[7] From the Burman viewpoint, minority populations are backward, untrustworthy, fractious, self-centered, and uncoop-
erative.[8] There has been little discussion of the implications of this
essentialist approach to the study of ethnicity and political conflict in
Burma.[9]

This chapter views ethnicity as well as national identity as the contingent and arbitrary production of common identities. These identities are
not natural or primordial; rather they are fluid, as people continuously
seek to negotiate and redefine them in political, cultural, and economic
arenas. This is not to say that the ethnic identifications of groups in
Burma are not real or meaningful to individuals who claim them, only
that it is important to understand the processes by which identities became meaningful and how they are sustained over time. Ethnic conflict in
twentieth-century Burma should not be characterized as a simple intergroup struggle. Rather it has involved different struggles over identity,
wealth, status, privilege, and power. This chapter focuses on the two
most enduring and territorially bound struggles in Burma that have been
described as "ethnic" in nature: one rooted in a struggle for political and
economic power in the central region of what is now called "Burma" or
"Myanmar," and the other framed by the administrative territorial units
that were created in the colonial era.

Language Politics in the Colonial Era

From its colonial stronghold in India in the nineteenth century, Britain
launched a gradual takeover of the territories of modern-day Burma. This
conquest was completed in 1886, when British and Indian army troops
deposed the last Burman king and Burma became a province of British
India. At that point, Britain divided the colony into two administrative

---

7. Kanbawza Win, *A Burmese Appeal to the UN and U.S.* (Bangkok: CPDSK Publications, 1994), p. 41.

8. See, for example, the Burman-centered analyses of ethnicity and language in
Kyaw Thet, "Burma: The Political Integration of Linguistic and Religious Minority
Groups," in P.W. Thayer, ed., *Nationalism and Progress in Free Asia* (Baltimore, Md.:
Johns Hopkins Press, 1956), pp. 156–168; and Minn Latt Yekhaun, *Modernization of Bur-
mese* (Prague: Oriental Institute in Academia, 1966).

9. Important exceptions include Edmund Leach, "The Frontiers of 'Burma,'" *Comparative Studies in Society and History,* Vol. 3, No. 1 (October 1960), pp. 49–68; Victor
Lieberman, "Ethnic Politics in Eighteenth-Century Burma," *Modern Asian Studies,*
Vol. 12, No. 3 (July 1978), pp. 455–482; Robert H. Taylor, "Perceptions of Ethnicity in
the Politics of Burma," *Southeast Asian Journal of Social Science,* Vol. 10, No. 1 (1982),
pp. 7–22; and Smith, *Burma: Insurgency and the Politics of Ethnicity.*

zones. The central area was called "Ministerial Burma" or sometimes "Burma Proper." This area was the home to most of the ethnic-majority Burmans and smaller numbers of other lowland indigenous peoples as well as immigrant Indians and Chinese. The second zone, called the "Frontier Areas" (later known juridically as the "Excluded Areas" and occasionally called the "Frontier Fringe"), was located in the regions along the colony's newly drawn borders. It was populated by non-Burman indigenous valley and hill peoples. According to Martin Smith, throughout most of the colonial period, "the Frontier Areas remained largely forgotten" by the British, except when local chieftains and princes interfered with British economic interests. They were also largely unknown to those who lived in central Ministerial Burma.[10] Burmese and Western historians of colonial-era politics in Burma write almost exclusively about Ministerial Burma, as if there was no history in the Frontier Areas. The people who lived in these areas were truly "outsiders."

In the central regions, politics was lively and contentious. Groups of lowland peoples whose identities were fluid in precolonial times found themselves locked in competition for the unprecedented wealth, status, and political power generated in the colony.[11] During the colonial era, census takers, tax collectors, land surveyors, police officers, labor recruiters, and moneylenders classified the myriad of lowland and "foreign" contenders into broad ethnic categories, such as "Burmans" or "Burmese" (then used interchangeably), Anglo-Indians, Indians, Chinese, and Karens. Whenever struggles over the distribution of power and wealth reached crisis points—such as during World War I or in the years following the economic depression of 1929—these categories hardened into what were implied to be uniform identities. Ultimately, elite-level politics in central Burma came to be seen as "ethnic conflict" pitting ethnic-majority Burmans against Chinese and Indian merchants as well

---

10. Martin J. Smith, *Ethnic Groups in Burma: Development, Democracy, and Human Rights* (London: Anti-Slavery International, 1994), p. 23. During the colonial period, residents of central Burma, including lowland Burmans and Karens, had no reason or opportunity to visit ethnic-minority, frontier regions. Burmans and Karens in the civil service and the police were posted just in Ministerial Burma; only British and Indian civil servants were deployed to the frontier, and even they were sent only on the rarest occasions. Ethnic-minority residents in the Frontier Areas likewise made few journeys into central Burma. Unlike in central Burma, the British established no government schools in minority regions in the frontier areas, and graduates of indigenous schools from these regions were not admitted to college or university in Burma Proper (although the sons of some Shan princes were educated in England).

11. Leach, "The Frontiers of 'Burma.'"

as Anglo-Burman and Karen police officers and civil servants. Robert Taylor argues that this process transformed "the politically neutral Burmese word, *lu-myo*, literally meaning 'kind of man,' . . . [into] the emotive terms for race or nation."[12]

Ethnic Burmans (along with a small number of centrally based minorities) waged their struggle for the state through the Dobama Asiayone (Our Burma Association), founded in 1930 in the aftermath of four days of anti-Indian rioting in Rangoon. As this group moved to the forefront of the nationalist, anticolonial movement in the 1930s, it targeted a new foe: the indigenous (i.e., not just Indian or Chinese) groups that collaborated with the British imperialists. The Dobama's greatest success in popular mobilization came in its campaign to repudiate foreign influences in language, clothing, and literature and to affirm the traditions of indigenous Burmese language and clothing. Characteristic of this campaign was the Dobama's anthem:

Burma is our country.
Burmese is our literature.
Burmese language is our language.
Love our country.
Praise our literature.
Respect our language.[13]

This campaign supplemented earlier ones against Indians and Chinese who collaborated with the colonizers; it targeted the indigenous people who took English names, wore English clothes, ate English food, and served the interests of the British against those of their fellow natives. As Taylor argues, these campaigns furthered the process in which ethnic categories came to take "on a life of their own, shaping the political thought and behavior of central . . . elites."[14] In postcolonial Burma, Rangoon-based elites continued to fight these battles. For example, in the 1950s ethnic Burmans in the army and civil service discharged Anglo-Burmans and Karens whose historical collaboration with the British made them targets in struggles for postcolonial political power. In the 1960s Gen. Ne Win and his ethnic Burman–dominated Revolutionary Council forced into exile most of the country's Chinese and Indian business owners.

---

12. Taylor, "Perceptions of Ethnicity in the Politics of Burma," p. 8.

13. Khin Kyi, *The Dobama Movement in Burma: Appendix* (Ithaca, N.Y.: Southeast Asia Program, Cornell University, 1988). The Dobama's song became the national anthem during the Japanese occupation and at independence in 1948. The translation of the song is mine.

14. Taylor, "Perceptions of Ethnicity in the Politics of Burma," p. 8.

Explicit language policies during the colonial era were developed in the arena of "insider politics" (i.e., Ministerial Burma). The major point of contention was the government's designation of English as the language of governance and administration. The earliest British plans for education in Burma emphasized that it should be modern in substance and conducted in Burmese so as to reach a wide audience. However, even as the Committee on Vernacular Education prepared to translate textbooks into Burmese in the late nineteenth century, Burmese parents demanded that classes be conducted in English. According to L.E. Bagshawe, "As far as the Burmese were concerned, the reason for paying for their children to attend school . . . was to make money, and English was the key to the world in which money was to be made."[15] Notably, when the first government high school was established in Rangoon in 1874 and later transformed into a constituent college of Calcutta University, there was no instruction in Burmese language or literature.

In 1918 colonial authorities established a committee to plan the curriculum for the new Rangoon University. The committee's actions transformed the language issue from an economic one into a political one. The committee set very high standards for English in university admissions requirements, sparking student opposition and strikes as well as the founding of a grassroots movement to establish "national schools" where Burmese was to be the medium of instruction. Although these vernacular schools were not able to send students on to institutions of higher learning, by the late 1920s, a movement had emerged to give Burmese some kind of status at the university. The politicization of language in the education system led scholar U Pe Maung Tin to write new school readers in Burmese for pre-university students and to establish a small honors course at Rangoon University in Burmese focused largely on the study of inscriptions from the eleventh and twelfth centuries. In the 1930s the earliest graduates of this course founded a new style of writing called *hkit-san* (testing the urge), which emphasized shorter sentences and clear, simple prose; writing in this manner was considered an "act of patriotism" in the anticolonial struggle.[16] The Burmese language campaign be-

15.   L.E. Bagshawe, "A Literature of Schoolbooks," M.Phil. thesis, School of Oriental and African Studies, University of London, 1976, p. 99, quoted in Allott, "Language Policy and Language Planning in Burma," p. 138.

16.   Minn Latt Yekhaun, *Modernization of Burmese*, p. 25. For other analyses of the *hkit-san* movement, see Aung San Suu Kyi, "Socio-political Currents in Burmese Literature, 1919–1940," in Burma Research Group, ed., *Burma and Japan: Basic Studies on Their Cultural and Social Structure* (Tokyo: Tokyo University of Foreign Studies, 1987), pp. 65–83; Anna Allott, Patricia Herbert, and John Okell, "Burma," in Herbert and Anthony Milner, eds., *South-East Asia Languages and Literatures: A Select Guide* (Honolulu:

came a major rallying point for the nationalist movement, for whom the dominance of English was seen to have been "the result of a definite policy formulated by the government rather than the natural end product of the colonial situation."[17]

While this was the main issue of contention regarding language issues, colonial activities in the other arena of ethnic conflict—the Frontier Areas—changed forever the way people and regimes in Burma thought about their languages. With few British or Indian officials, clerks, or soldiers permanently stationed in most of these regions, census takers would visit every ten years to categorize local populations for the state's administrative purposes. They used classification schemes defined by language and mapped enduringly to specific territories. Their assumption was that the "geographical domain of specific languages coincides exactly with specified geopolitical and cultural units."[18] Supported by the work of scholars, scholar bureaucrats, and army recruiters (e.g., Gordon Luce, U Pe Maung Tin, and C.M. Enriquez) who developed genetic taxonomies of "language families," census officials arrived at a tally of 135 different racial groups inhabiting the colony.[19] During World War II, these taxonomies became even more important. At least twelve clandestine Allied units organized anti-Japanese forces in the Frontier Areas. The Allies' propaganda against pro-Japanese Burmans treated each frontier-based ethnolinguistic group as a natural, primordial community long oppressed by the Burmans.[20]

The use of these taxonomies was not a conscious effort to control or subordinate populations, but they nonetheless established hierarchies: Ethnolinguistic categorizations carried with them positions of privilege or backwardness, power or disadvantage. Charles Hirschman's analysis of British census classification schemes in Malaya reveals the presuppositions of the census takers and their project: "Peoples were different not

---

University of Hawaii Press, 1989), pp. 1–22; and Hla Pe, "The Rise of Popular Literature in Burma," *Journal of the Burmese Research Society,* Vol. 51, No. 2 (1968), pp. 123–144.

17. Allott, "Language Policy and Language Planning in Burma," p. 140.

18. Martin Durrell, "Language as Geography," in N.E. Collinge, ed., *An Encyclopaedia of Language* (London: Routledge, 1990), p. 917.

19. Gordon H. Luce, "Burma's Debt to Pagan," *Journal of the Burma Research Society,* Vol. 22, No. 3 (December 1932), pp. 120–127; Pe Maung Tin, "The Dialect of Tavoy," *Journal of the Burma Research Society,* Vol. 23, No. 1 (April 1933), pp. 31–46; and C.M. Enriquez, *Races of Burma* (Delhi: Manager of Publications, Government of India, 1933).

20. Robert H. Taylor, *Marxism and Resistance in Burma, 1942–1945* (Athens: Ohio University Press, 1984); and Andrew Selth, "Race and Resistance in Burma, 1942–1945," *Modern Asian Studies,* Vol. 20, No. 3 (October 1986), pp. 483–507.

only in appearance and culture but also in inherent capacities or potential. . . . Some groups might eventually make it up the ladder of progress, but other peoples were destined to remain 'primitive.'"[21] These assumptions were embraced by both the colonizers and the leaders of the nationalist movement. The leaders of the Dobama Asiayone were fascinated by writings about "master races" and appropriated them to mobilize followers.[22]

The Japanese interregnum (1942–45) hardened the categories of race and territory that emerged under British colonialism. Japan's de facto authority never extended beyond the central regions or former Ministerial Burma, which only deepened the territorial and political segregation of the previous fifty years. At the onset of the Japanese invasion in late 1941, many Burman nationalists of the central and southern regions allied with Japanese forces to oust the British. After the latter's ignominious retreat to India, the British and other Allies operated freely in the former Frontier Areas, recruiting residents into anti-Japanese, anti-Burman guerrilla forces. Some American and British intelligence officers promised minorities postwar autonomy, power, and independence, which they could not deliver. They used anti-Burman propaganda that played on historical grievances but also reminded Chins, Kachins, and Karens that the Burmans were collaborating with the treacherous Japanese. When Burman nationalists turned against the Japanese and allied with the British in late 1944, the former enemies—including Burman nationalists, ethnic-minority guerrilla units, and Allied forces—did not integrate their units, The military campaign was over so quickly that there was no time for conciliation among the parties to this marriage of convenience.[23]

Postcolonial Parliamentary Politics, 1948–62

With independence in 1948 came the incorporation of the former Excluded Areas into a single political entity. These areas comprised 40 percent of the new country's landmass. The 1947 constitution tried to address the difficulty of bringing all of Burma's previously unintegrated, recently warring parties together in a single political unit. It called for the

---

21.   Charles Hirschman, "The Meaning and Measurement of Ethnicity in Malaysia: An Analysis of Census Classifications," *Journal of Asian Studies,* Vol. 45, No. 3 (August 1987), p. 568.

22.   Taylor, "Perceptions of Ethnicity in the Politics of Burma."

23.   Mary P. Callahan, "The Origins of Military Rule in Burma," Ph.D. dissertation, Cornell University, 1996, chaps. 5–6.

formation of a bicameral national legislature, intended to guarantee representation to minority ethnic groups in the Chamber of Nationalities. In practice, however, it did not create any effective mechanisms through which minority concerns could be voiced.

From independence until 1958 and again from 1960 to 1962, the Union of Burma was governed by civilian rulers who operated within a parliamentary form of government. Former nationalist leader U Nu served as prime minister during most of this period. Political life was dominated by one party, the Anti-Fascist People's Freedom League (AFPFL). The early years of independence were characterized by a number of serious threats to the government's survival, including internal ones (communist and separatist ethnic rebellions as well as army mutinies) and external ones (U.S.-backed Kuomintang incursions into Burma, whose participants prepared to stage an assault to retake mainland China from the Chinese communists). As a result of AFPFL infighting, escalating insurgency, and poor economic performance, the military took control as a caretaker government in 1958, and then again more permanently in March 1962.

Characterizations of the political conflict among Burma's ethnic groups during the parliamentary era depended on the vantage point and geographic (less than ethnic) positions of the contenders. In the central region, ongoing "insider" struggles for political and economic power continued to pit ethnic Burman leaders of the AFPFL and their supporters against the Anglo-Burmans, Karens, Indians, and Chinese who were trying to hold on to their wealth, capital, and (mostly for the Indians, Anglo-Burmans, and some Karens) positions of status within the civil service. During this period "insider politics" was dominated by vigorous debates over the crafting of citizenship laws, which ultimately emerged from the ethnic Burman–dominated parliament in a form that greatly disadvantaged Chinese and Indians.[24] Because the constitution established that "the official language of the Union be Burmese," U Nu's government sponsored programs to spread the use of this language. These programs were not really continuations of anticolonial campaigns against English; indeed most of the AFPFL leaders were fluent in English and no doubt considered it to be a more "modern" language. Instead the pro-Burmese campaigns were aimed at undermining the positions of Chinese- and Hindi-speaking merchants in central Burma. The focus of ethnic politics

---

24. Josef Silverstein, "Fifty Years of Failure in Burma," in Michael E. Brown and Šumit Ganguly, eds., *Government Policies and Ethnic Relations in Asia and the Pacific* (Cambridge, Mass.: MIT Press, 1997), pp. 180–181.

on the national level, then, was competing claims for control over the Rangoon-based state, privilege, and wealth;[25] these struggles had little to do with anyone or anything beyond the central region. From the perspective of those in Rangoon, the main threats to the state during the 1950s came from competitors in this struggle within the center—especially from the two communist parties (the Burma Communist Party and the Communist Party of Burma), both of which were in open rebellion after 1948.

Language policy during the parliamentary era grew out of the struggles that gripped "insider politics," and hence emphasized the elevation of Burmese to official status. After independence, former anticolonial activists across the political spectrum affirmed their commitment to make Burmese the medium of instruction in primary and secondary schools as well as in higher education, with English offered as a second language. These affirmations launched a new language "modernization" industry devoted to unification, standardization, and translation. The government supported the founding of the Burma Translation Society (BTS) in 1948. This was followed by the opening of a translation and publications department at the University of Rangoon. The BTS formed committees on history, science, and the publication of a dictionary and an encyclopedia. By 1965 the society had produced more than 5 million copies of books in fields such as science, arts, history, Burmese culture, and education. The Vocabulary Committee's forty terminology subcommittees boasted of translating 65,000 technical terms from sixteen specialized subjects, and assigning them standardized Burmese equivalents in a "vocabulary bank."[26] Commissioned in 1949, the *Burmese Encyclopedia* began appearing volume by volume in the early 1960s.

In central Burma, these language policies did not provoke much resistance. Most Chinese and Indians spoke Burmese as a second language, and they were still able to send their children to private schools where their mother tongues were media of instruction. Moreover, Smith notes that minority presses "thrived" during this era, and at least eleven newspapers published in minority languages in central Burma.[27] Hence, in the center the Burmanization campaign was not particularly contentious.[28] In

---

25. Taylor, "Perceptions of Ethnicity in the Politics of Burma."

26. Howard Hayden, *Higher Education and Development in South-East Asia: Country Profiles*, Vol. 2 (Paris: United Nations Educational, Social, and Cultural Organization, 1967), p. 56.

27. Martin J. Smith, "Unending War," *Index on Censorship*, Vol. 23, No. 3 (July/August 1994), pp. 113–118.

28. There was remarkably little debate about which regional dialect should be designated the "official" language, which is probably a reflection of how few major differ-

fact, a Burmese dictionary, a vocabulary bank, and translated texts constituted the logical pillars of an official language, which was an uncontested element of the nation-building process. Burmanization did not create problems for most elites, so this process was seen as a natural and uncontroversial step in the decolonization process. In the former Frontier Areas, however, many ethnic minorities saw the situation differently. They did not want the country to undergo political, cultural, and linguistic Burmanization.

Two other areas of contention were economic development and religion. In the negotiations that led to the Panglong Agreement of 1947, minority leaders took wartime hero and nationalist leader Aung San's word that the underdeveloped Frontier Areas would be treated equally in Burma's postcolonial development strategy. Aung San promised: "If [central] Burma receives one kyat, you will also get one kyat."[29] The postcolonial government's first two-year and subsequent eight-year economic plans in the 1950s disregarded these promises, however, instead opting for the construction of a Rangoon-centered, social-welfare state, from which minorities were led to believe they would eventually benefit. Prime Minister U Nu's emphasis on Buddhism, which ranged from the huge expenditures laid out for the extravagant Sixth Great Buddhist Council in 1954 to his later campaign to designate Buddhism the state religion, also alienated many non-Buddhist minorities.

For the inheritors of the Burman-dominated anticolonial movement, these programs represented progress. One strident nationalist later wrote: "The declaration of Burmese as the official language of the nation, and as the medium of education, is not a matter of national pride, as some people still tend to see. The dissemination of modern knowledge through a foreign tongue [i.e., English] is abnormal and detrimental to society; only the usage of the mother tongue can really help the nation forward."[30] Minorities, however, saw these programs not as progressive—but threatening.

---

ences exist among the dozen or so dialects of Burmese. Moreover, no one seriously questioned the idea that one dialect should be crowned "official." On regional dialects, see John Okell, *A Reference Grammar of Colloquial Burmese*, Pt. 1 (London: Oxford University Press, 1969); and John Okell "Three Regional Dialects," in David Bradley, ed., *Studies in Burmese Languages*, Papers in Southeast Asian Languages No. 13 (Canberra, NSW: Department of Linguistics, Research School of Pacific Studies, Australian National University, 1995), pp. 1–138; and Minn Latt Yekhaun, *Modernization of Burmese*, pp. 62–63.

29.   Quoted in Martin J. Smith, *Burma: Insurgency and the Politics of Ethnicity*, 2d ed. (London: Zed Press, 1999), p. 78.

30.   Minn Latt Yekhaun, *Modernization of Burmese*, p. 31.

Most people who lived in the former Frontier Areas in the 1950s probably knew little about the government's linguistic standardization projects. Minority threat perceptions nonetheless grew because of the way the military extended the geographical and functional reach of the state beyond central Burma during the parliamentary era. The ethnic Burman–dominated army grew from 2,000 soldiers in 1949 to 100,000 by 1962. The civilian leadership of the government did not hesitate to deploy the army to the former Frontier Areas when there were locally based challenges to the Rangoon regime. This resulted in the army establishing what non- Burman populations came to view as "internal colonialism."[31] Facing army occupation, local populations gradually began to interpret their struggles in ethnic terms, and previously unconnected communities of Shans and Karens began to forge pan-ethnic communities ("the Shans" and "the Karens") to challenge central Burman intrusions on their autonomy. This was particularly stark in the Shan state, where in 1950 the Kuomintang presence prompted Prime Minister U Nu to declare martial law in the Shweli River valley of North Hsenwi state (in the Shan state). He eventually sent the army in to twenty-two of the thirty-three Shan subdivisions to establish military administration.[32] Within a few years, the central government abolished the political and economic autonomy that Shan chieftains had once enjoyed and—in the name of modernization and democratization—established new local political institutions that would permit greater control from Rangoon.

Language was a tool of resistance for Shan groups that were uprooted, conscripted, taxed, and relocated by the military during this period. The soldiers deployed to these regions did not speak local languages and dialects, but they viewed this as merely a temporary and minor inconvenience.[33] For the army and for the government in Rangoon, these "primitive" and "backward" peoples would eventually come around, embrace a national identity, and become full citizens of the Un-

---

31. Inge Sargent, *Twilight over Burma: My Life as a Shan Princess* (Honolulu: University of Hawaii Press, 1994); and Kanbawza Win, *A Burmese Appeal to the UN and U.S.*, p. 42.

32. U Nu initially attempted to bring the Shan state under centralized control so that borders could be defended from further Kuomintang incursions. His great concern was that the presence of U.S.-backed anti–People's Republic of China soldiers in Burmese territory might serve as a pretext for a Chinese invasion or annexation of that territory. The *sawbwas*, however, balked at Nu's proposals for a kind of power sharing that would weaken their authorities while strengthening the Rangoon government's powers in the region. This ultimately led Nu to send in the military.

33. Former Col. Saw Myint, interview, April 27, 1992.

ion of Burma. This optimism was characteristic of the social Darwinism that underlay British colonial rule. By the 1950s the Burmans of central Burma positioned themselves atop the postcolonial civilizational ladder. To them, their identity had natural, historic, and wholly unproblematic roots; other groups had to transcend and leave behind their identities en route to becoming Burmese citizens.

Although this view may have been unproblematic to elites in Rangoon, it was disturbing to ethnic-minority intellectuals and political leaders. The Burman view appeared to Shans, Kachins, and other peoples as a mechanism of domination, similar to what the anticolonial Dobama Asiayone had fought against only a decade or two earlier in the central region. Students and scholars in the Shan state formed new literary societies in the mid-1950s to publish Shan-language books and magazines, such as the *Khitthit Shan Pye* (Modern Shan) journal, and a campaign developed to revive the Shan script and traditional theater. By the early 1960s, most Shan towns had theater companies that reenacted traditional Shan folktales and legends. In the Kachin state, the Kachin Youth Culture Uplift Association mobilized locals in a similar kind of revival.[34]

The Rangoon government's goal to spread education throughout the former Frontier Areas entailed the distribution of some 5 million BTS books—in Burmese—with the message that this was to be the language of power. As Julian Wheatley has argued, Burmese became the language that one had to use in school, in state offices, and in the arenas of authority, while minority languages remained the media of family, market, and informal communication.[35] The government did not force Burmese on frontier peoples, but the official status of the language endowed it with prestige and value that non-Burmese languages could not match. The only other language that "mattered" in the 1950s was English.

The view from the former Frontier Areas was that central government policies were threatening and intrusive. This outlook led to the emergence in the late 1950s of the Federal Movement, which included representatives of several frontier area groups that sought to replace the Burman-dominated "union" constitutional framework with a federal one. The movement's major objective was to devolve political and economic power to minority constituencies. According to F.K. Lehman, "What the minorities wanted, as a minimum common denominator, was

---

34. Smith, *Ethnic Groups in Burma.*

35. Julian Wheatley, "Burmese," in Bernard Comrie, ed., *The World's Major Languages* (New York: Oxford University Press, 1987), p. 834.

more power to distribute central government revenue to and within the non-Burman states."[36]

The Burmese Way to Socialism, 1962–88

From Rangoon's perspective, growing antigovernment sentiment and unruliness in the former Frontier Areas represented problems to be solved rather than serious threats. The solutions to these and other problems were to be developed by Gen. Ne Win, who led the 1962 coup and formed the Revolutionary Council (RC) to replace the elected cabinet and parliament.[37] The army crushed the Federal Movement, killed or jailed its leaders, and silenced voices from the border regions. The army-dominated council suspended the 1947 constitution and proclaimed the "Burmese Way to Socialism," an ideological treatise justifying the institution of a central, command economy and the elimination of foreign control over business in Burma. In 1974 a new constitution was promulgated, providing for a highly centralized, civilian, single-party form of government aimed at expanding the socialist society created under the RC. At the national, state, township, and village levels, government administration was greatly influenced by the Leninist-style Burma Socialist Program Party (BSPP), which stepped up its efforts to build a mass following across the country. Most party and government leadership positions came to be occupied by the same military officers who had held them before 1974, although this time they shed their ranks and uniforms. As chairman of the State Council and party chairman, Ne Win retained his hold on power into the late 1980s.

The Socialist period (1962–88) ushered in a "minority policy" that brought the peoples of the border regions into the spotlight for the first time since World War II. Even so, elite-level politics still focused mainly on control of the state. Socialist governments worried that civilian regimes had tolerated too much disunity in border regions. The RC's "Be-

---

36.   F.K. Lehman, "Ethnic Categories in Burma and the Theory of Social Systems," in Peter Kunstadter, ed., *Southeast Asian Tribes, Minorities, and Nations* (Princeton, N.J.: Princeton University Press, 1967), p. 95.

37.   Most analyses of the 1962 coup d'état accept at face value the military's justification for its intervention: The military intervened to stop the Federalist Movement from breaking up the union. The demands of the Federal Seminar that allegedly precipitated the coup were, however, moderate and not aimed at breaking up the union, which suggests that there were other factors at work. As I have argued elsewhere, intramilitary competition accounts at least in part for the timing and nature of the military's intervention in 1962. See Callahan, "The Origins of Military Rule in Burma," chap. 9.

lief on Nationalities" paper warned that "individual and independent undertakings by nationalities that adversely affect unity, an essential requisite of the Union, should be avoided."[38] Article 21 of the 1974 constitution declared that the BSPP "state shall be responsible for constantly developing and promoting unity, mutual assistance, amity and mutual respect among the national races." National races could pursue their own religious beliefs and develop their languages, traditions, and cultures "provided that the enjoyment of any such freedom does not offend the laws or the public interest." The constitution divided the country into seven divisions in central and southern Burma (largely populated by the Burman majority) and seven states in the Frontier Areas named after the largest groups of ethnic-minority residents.

The Revolutionary Council founded propaganda agencies and programs to promulgate the RC's and later the BSPP's unity theme in the border regions where separatist violence was escalating. Lehman wrote in 1967 that "adherence to a minority cultural tradition is treated as tantamount to subversion of the nation and is branded as a mark of group inferiority within the nation."[39] In 1965 the RC established the Academy for the Development of National Groups at Sagaing, a college for minority students that aimed to produce teachers who would return to their homelands and spread socialist ideology.[40] Political leaders in Rangoon thought that political integration would be easy to accomplish; it was not seen as an issue that would absorb extensive resources. What was necessary, they believed, was to turn everyone—Burman and non-Burman—into socialists first and foremost. Other group identities were tolerated as long as socialism came first. As in the 1950s, problems in the former Frontier Areas were seen to be secondary; the struggle that dominated national-level politics was the struggle over control of the state.

Language policy in this period continued to focus on Burmese and English. Non-Burmese indigenous languages did not receive formal recognition aside from a vague constitutional guarantee that they could be used in unofficial settings. The RC and the BSPP continued the parliamentary-era policy of elevating the status of Burmese and formalizing its usage as the language of state, power, and modernity. In 1964 the RC announced that every university subject would be taught in Burmese as

38.   Quoted in Yebaw Hpyo Aung, "The Nationalities and Patriotism," *Forward*, Vol. 3, No. 13 (February 15, 1965), p. 5.

39.   Lehman, "Ethnic Categories in Burma and the Theory of the Social Systems," p. 104.

40.   A *Forward* staff member, "Academy for Development of National Races," *Forward*, Vol. 3, No. 7 (November 15, 1964), p. 18.

soon as possible and that English would be taught only as a minor foreign language. At the same time, the RC accelerated plans to give Burmese the standing of a national language, including the production of Burma's first monolingual dictionary. In 1963 it appointed thirty scholars to the recently established Literary and Translation Committee charged with "urgent publication of an official standard Burmese Dictionary, a manual of Burmese Composition . . . publication of needed textbooks, reference books, periodicals, etc."[41] In 1972 the government established language committees in every township that would create taxonomies of words and phrases from local usage. The Literary and Translation Committee took these taxonomies into account when deciding on what to include in the dictionary and in grammar and spelling manuals. The five-volume *Myanma abidan akyin-gyok* (Official Burmese Dictionary) was published in 1978–80; a spelling handbook was published in 1978. Work on a Burmese grammar continued, though it did not come to fruition until the 1990s.

This standardization process, unlike that of the 1950s, grew contentious. Perhaps most influential was the campaign by the Upper Burma Writers' Association in Mandalay to simplify the Burmese writing style. The Burmese language is communicated in two very different styles—one is formal, literary, written Burmese; the other is spoken, colloquial Burmese. In general, the literary style is used in formal writing, nonfiction books, newspapers, school readers, comic books, and the narrative portions of serious novels; the colloquial style is used in everyday conversation, classroom lectures, and informal letters, as well as in the dialogue sections of novels. The two styles exhibit "a considerable degree of variation" with respect to usage, grammatical forms, and construction."[42] During the twentieth century, groups of Burmese writers periodically criticized the formal written style, with its more complex particle schemes and syntactic constructions, and for its inaccessibility to much of the population. Following the announcement of the Burmese Way to Socialism, the Mandalay writers' group in 1965 called for replacing the literary style with the colloquial style of Burmese. The writers argued that this would accelerate the social revolution under way in Burma, by making literacy more achievable for uneducated peasants and workers. The RC, backed by the Rangoon-based literati, rejected this proposal, claiming that serious matters could not be expressed in a lowly colloquial language. The latter was said to lack prestige, dignity, and authority. Because

---

41. "Current Affairs: Literature," *Forward*, Vol. 2, No. 3 (September 7, 1963), p. 4.

42. Okell, *A Reference Grammar of Colloquial Burmese*, p. xii.

of the leftist political affiliations of some members of the Upper Burma Writers' Association, anyone who thereafter promoted a simpler language and literary style was called an antigovernment "communist." This style of writing was thereafter deemed subversive.[43]

In 1964, after identifying illiteracy as a major obstacle to the building of socialism, the RC greatly expanded literacy programs in the central regions. During its first fifteen years, the literacy campaign was carried out almost entirely in Burmese-speaking areas. The government's objectives were to inculcate socialist ideology and "correct" thinking and to stimulate increased production and improved living standards.[44]

By the late 1970s, the BSPP's language and literacy policies had begun to shift their focus to areas beyond the central regions. By 1980, literacy teaching programs had been carried out in Tiddim (Chin state), Nyaungshwe (Shan state), Mohnyin (Kachin state), Sandoway (Arakan state), and Hparu-hso (Kayah state). Teachers who spoke Burmese as a first language went to these areas and encountered groups that included only small numbers of second-language Burmese speakers among them. Coming almost entirely from the central regions, these teachers tended to consider anyone who spoke little or no Burmese to be illiterate.

RC and BSPP programs to standardize and elevate the position of Burmese made inroads into the former Frontier Areas through the education system. In government schools, minority languages were not used after the fourth grade; Burmese was the language of instruction. Schoolchildren had to learn and compete in Burmese, which undermined the status of minority languages and inhibited development of minority cultural expression and the arts.[45] In some minority regions, such as the Mon areas, the government dismissed teachers of minority languages and literature. By 1966 the Mon language was no longer taught in schools. Local populations, however, did not abandon their languages, and in the Mon case, "villagers who treasured Mon language and literature hired at their own expense Mon teachers to teach their children."[46]

Press nationalization laws adopted by the RC and sustained under the BSPP made it difficult for minorities anywhere in the country—but

---

43. Allott, "Language Policy and Language Planning in Burma"; Allott, Herbert, and Okell, "Burma"; and Wheatley, "Burmese."

44. Allott, "Language Policy and Language Planning in Burma," pp. 147–149.

45. Smith, "Unending War."

46. Thein Lwin, "The Teaching of Ethnic Language and the Role of Education in the Context of Mon Ethnic Nationality in Burma: Initial Report of the First Phase of the Study on the Thai-Burma Border, November 1999–February 2000," http://www.students.ncl.ac.uk/thein.lwin/ (accessed May 29, 2000).

especially in the border regions—to publish in a language other than Burmese. The works of minority authors had to be translated into Burmese and submitted to a censorship board, which increasingly considered publication of these writings to be against the public interest and the imperatives of national unity. The board even disallowed some translations into minority languages of religious texts such as the Bible. Minority newspapers disappeared altogether. The handful of minority-language publications that continued to be printed were "folksy or domestic magazines" such as the Karen *Leh Su Hyah* (Go Forward).[47]

Even more confrontational was the BSPP's 1982 revision of citizenship laws, which created three categories of citizens: full, associate, and naturalized. This action was probably intended to weaken the legal claims to residence, citizenship, and property rights of the Muslim community on the Bangladesh-Burma border. In practice, these new laws made it very difficult for many indigenous minorities throughout the former Frontier Areas to qualify for anything higher than "associate" citizenship. Full citizenship required presentation of government identification cards, which had never been issued in large parts of rebel-held and even government-held territory. Josef Silverstein has noted that in a large number of cases, minorities "lost their equal standing with other indigenous peoples of Burma and were treated as stateless."[48] Such people were required to hold a foreigners' registration card, which effectively barred them from many occupations and prevented their children from attending university.

The Burmese Way to Socialism ushered in an era of unprecedented concern in Rangoon about the populations who inhabited the former Frontier Areas. This concern, however, was always secondary to intra-elite struggles over state power in the central region. Even literacy campaigns, which could have been used to assimilate minorities, took more than fifteen years to reach minority regions. Even so, those who lived in the former Frontier Areas did not see Rangoon's policies as benign. The fact that these areas were mentioned in the ideological and programmatic statements of the RC and BSPP meant that many in these regions considered themselves to be under political, cultural, and linguistic siege from Rangoon. The socialist government's language policy universalized standards and requirements for language without universalizing access to the policymaking process. As Pierre Bourdieu has put it, this entailed "the imposition of the dominant language and culture as

---

47. Smith, "Unending War," p. 115.
48. Silverstein, "Fifty Years of Failure in Burma," p. 182.

legitimate and . . . the rejection of all other languages into indignity (thus demoted as patois or local dialects). By rising to universality, a particular culture or language causes all others to fall into particularity."[49]

From Socialism to SLORC

In September 1987, following a series of demonetization measures that devastated the economy and wiped out the savings of most Burmese people, student demonstrations erupted in Rangoon and continued sporadically into the following year. This led to the collapse of the BSPP in July 1988, when former Gen. Ne Win and other officials resigned from the party leadership. Antigovernment demonstrations continued until September 18, when the army leadership took power and established the State Law and Order Restoration Council (SLORC) under the chairmanship of the army commander and Ne Win follower, Sr. Gen. Saw Maung. SLORC suspended the 1974 constitution and abolished the presidency, State Council, Council of Ministers, and People's Assembly. Under SLORC's orders, crack military troops put an abrupt end to the popular pro-democracy demonstrations, killing thousands of unarmed civilians. The SLORC also distributed cabinet portfolios to senior military officers.

The political opposition to military rule has been led since 1988 by Daw Aung San Suu Kyi, daughter of martyred national hero Aung San. Since her return to Burma in 1988, she has attracted a broad political following that has at times crossed ethnic, class, and even military lines. Her vision, charisma, and leadership carried her party, the National League for Democracy, to an overwhelming victory in the 1990 parliamentary elections, despite attempts by the military regime to hamper party-building and campaign activities. The junta's subsequent refusal to honor the election results, the arrest or flight of many successful opposition candidates, the five-and-a-half-year (1989–95) and two-year (2000–02) house arrests of Suu Kyi, and the numerous restrictions on party activities since 1990 have all but decimated the loosely organized, populist political organization.

Of all the challenges that the junta has faced since seizing power, it found Suu Kyi's 1989–90 popularity with minority populations, both in rebel-held and government-held territory, to be the most threatening. Her popularity represented a grave threat to the military's power: The junta no doubt calculated that the army did not have the capability to fight battles in border regions and in Rangoon should an alliance develop be-

---

49. Pierre Bourdieu, *Practical Reason: On the Theory of Action*, trans. Randal Johnson (Stanford, Calif.: Stanford University Press, 1998), p. 46.

tween the NLD in central Burma and armed rebels in the former Frontier Areas.

The junta responded to this threat in two ways. First, it initiated an arms modernization program that strengthened it vis-à-vis its internal foes.[50] Second and more important, it sought to drive a wedge between the urban-based NLD and its potential allies in the frontier regions. With this in mind, Lt. Gen. Khin Nyunt launched cease-fire negotiations with ethnic rebel groups in 1989. Since then, seventeen of the twenty-one major antigovernment forces have concluded cease-fire agreements with SLORC. These cease-fires are not signs of a genuine reconciliation between the junta and these groups. Rather they are temporary, ad hoc conveniences.

These cease-fire agreements allowed some groups to keep their arms, to police their own territory, and to use their former rebel armies as private security forces to protect both legal and illegal business operations. This authority, however, is due to run out if and when the junta's hand-picked national convention completes its new constitution. At that point, it is difficult to imagine that the SLORC/SPDC will be able to convince ethnic warlords to turn in their weapons peacefully.[51]

This problem was compounded by former SLORC Chairman Sr. Gen. Saw Maung's ill-conceived ethnic policy— that is, reinvigorating the colonial categorization of indigenous peoples into 135 races. This idea probably appealed to Saw Maung because it aimed to divide the opposition. It derailed progress, however, toward finalizing a new constitution in 1995–96, according to one member of a national convention committee assigned to deal with political arrangements for ethnic minorities. He reported, "We have to accept the 135 races theory, but now all 135 want their own states."[52]

The combination of Saw Maung's 135-race policy and the junta's activities in former war zones near Burma's borders reflected an unprecedented level of regime concern about minority groups. For the first time since the British established two administrative zones in the country, a Rangoon-based regime launched a somewhat coordinated campaign to

---

50. Mary P. Callahan, "Junta Dreams or Nightmares? Observations of Burma's Military since 1988," *Bulletin of Concerned Asian Scholars,* Vol. 31, No. 3 (July–September 1999), pp. 52–58.

51. In November 1997 the SLORC was reorganized and renamed the State Peace and Development Council (SPDC). I refer to the post-reorganization junta as "SLORC/SPDC" to highlight the fact that the change was purely cosmetic. The SPDC has not shown any significant deviation from SLORC policies.

52. Sr. Gen. Saw Maung, interview, September 22, 1997.

deal with the centrifugal impulses of "outsider" ethnic politics. At the heart of this campaign was a policy of cultural homogenization that entailed the most concerted government effort in the country's twentieth-century history to assimilate and disempower Burma's minorities. The campaign began with a number of makeshift solutions to what the military defined as "the national crisis of 1988." It evolved in the 1990s into an unprecedented obsession with the propagation of cultural homogeneity and purity.

The 1988 crisis, in the view of the military, was caused by national disunity. The response was an all-out offensive against any activity or person deemed subversive. The military renamed the country "Myanmar," and some major cities were also renamed, allegedly to eliminate vestiges of imperialism. English-language books were republished with all references to "Burma" whited out and replaced with "Myanmar." After rewriting history to strengthen the case for Burmese socialism, SLORC launched a campaign in 1989 that touted the creation of a sacred and ancient history of a singular national race called the "Myanmar." The junta assigned responsibility to government bodies—such as the Committee for the Compilation of Authentic Data of Myanmar History (later succeeded by the Historical Commission) and the Office of Strategic Studies—for conjuring a highly improbable unilineal, unified, and peaceful history of a single, millennia-old nationality divided only by the trickery and brute force of the British imperialists. Perhaps the most dubious and thus the most representative moment in this campaign was the 1997–98 Pondaung Primate Fossil Exploration archaeological project. With little archaeological expertise, the army-led dig produced specious claims that fossils found in the Pondaung region of the country prove that "human civilization began in our motherland."[53] The government also claims that the fossils "prove" that all ethnic groups in Burma coexisted harmoniously as far back as the Neolithic period.

Similarly, the SLORC/SPDC sponsored numerous large-scale "Myanmafication" performances that revealed the campaign's dual purposes: keeping out foreign influences (thus "purifying" Myanmar culture and undermining the "impure" Aung San Suu Kyi [who had married a British subject]) and papering over differences among indigenous populations. The purification and homogenization purposes were reflected in the regime's founding of new versions of historicized "Myanmar" festivals—including annual regatta, equestrian, and music competitions—

53. May May Aung, "National Museum: The Symbol of Myanmar Pride and Honour," *Myanmar Information Sheet*, December 29, 1997, http://homepages.go.com/myanmarinfosheet/1997/1997.htm (accessed June 11, 1999).

aimed at "strengthening the national pride of being a Myanmar citizen as a unifying bond."[54] At annual Exhibitions to Revitalize and Foster the Spirit of Patriotism, junta Secretary 1, Lt. Gen. Khin Nyunt, enjoined attendees to study "the origins of the Myanmar race, the flowering of Myanmar patriotic spirit during the Bagan, Pinn-Ya, Inn-wa, Taungu, Nyaung-Yan, and Konbaung dynasties, the three Anglo-Myanmar wars."[55] In the 1990s, science, cultural, and national and local history museums sprung up around the country. Built by various ministries, regional commands, and armed forces' directorates, these museums revere the "Myanmar" race as the sacred core of their narratives of national history.

Language issues took center stage in this campaign, but they did so by crashing through the old substantive and territorial boundaries that had limited the reach of the monolingual state in the twentieth century. The regime's earliest moves were typically center focused: It ordered the Myanmasa Ahpwe (Burmese Language Commission) to rewrite the official monolingual Burmese dictionary by stripping out socialist terminology and English loan words where possible. As the regime reassembled the remnants of the socialist state into one under direct military control, it appointed a wave of new committees—all under the direction of military officers—charged with correcting the weaknesses of national unity that caused (in the army's view) the 1988 crisis. One of these committees came directly out of the army's forty years of counterinsurgency combat: the Committee for Writing Slogans for Nationals, established in April 1989. From this committee emerged "Our Three Main National Causes": (1) nondisintegration of the union, (2) nondisintegration of solidarity, and (3) perpetuation of national sovereignty. These slogans and others—such as "Crush all internal and external destructive elements as the common enemy"—appeared in virtually every publication produced in Burma in the 1990s and on red-and-white signs in public places. The slogans all emphasized the urgency of maintaining national unity at any cost. Language was an important tool in the suppression of criticism, rebellion, and sedition.

The unity crusade moved language politics into new arenas, starting with the June 1989 Adaptation of Expressions Law. This law and the renaming campaign that followed had two objectives: (1) to standardize the terms that Burmese-language speakers would use to discuss their public

---

54.   Uta Gartner, "Old Festivals Newly Adorned," Tradition and Modernity in Myanmar conference, Berlin, Germany, Fakultätsinstitut für Asien- und Afrikawissenschaften, 1993, p. 360.

55.   Quoted in *New Light of Myanmar*, October 30, 1998.

identities, and (2) to regulate what non-Burmese speakers—inside and outside the country—would call the country and its public institutions and to create a new romanized orthography for these names. The 1989 law renamed the country "Myanmar," while "Rangoon" was renamed "Yangon" and Maymyo became "Pyin-Oo-Lwin." According to one regime spokesperson, "The term 'Myanmar' has been used as the name of the nation and the people for years countable by the thousands."[56] The junta appeared to be harkening back at least to twelfth-century Burmese inscriptions, wherein "Myanmar" was the written term for the domain of the kings at Pagan, and later at Pegu and Mandalay.

In modern Burmese–language usage, "Mranma/Myanma/Myanmar" has been the formal literary term for the territory of the state since independence in 1948,[57] while "Bama" (from which "Burma" is derived) has been the spoken or colloquial-language equivalent for the sovereign domain of the government (i.e., the name of the country). In modern usage, "Bama" also referred to the ethnic-majority population, known to contemporary English speakers as "Burmans." In 1989 SLORC standardized the romanization of "Bama," opting for "Bamar"; for Burmese speakers, the government redefined the latter term so that it referred in both formal and colloquial language to the ethnic-majority group. Under the SLORC's standardization scheme, citizens of the state—regardless of ethnicity or nationality—were to be called "Myanmars" in both formal and colloquial Burmese; foreign-language speakers were expected to use "Myanmar" as the new standard romanization of the name of the country, its citizens, and its official language. That the language of the "Bamars" was renamed the "Myanmar" language was confusing, given that it was (and is) the first language of only one particular ethnic group and not of the "Myanmars," the newly constructed community of people who inhabit the country.

The SLORC claimed that the name-standardization campaign was aimed at purging imperialist bastardizations of the country's authentic language. It expounded a historically problematic argument that using the term "Myanmar" to refer to citizens throughout the territory would make minority populations feel more included in the nation.[58] In the re-

---

56. Quoted in Tekkatho Myat Thu, "Call Us Myanmar," *New Light of Myanmar*, April 23, 2000.

57. These are common transcriptions, transliterations, and romanizations of the Burmese-language term. No single romanization scheme has gained widespread acceptance, which accounts for this variation.

58. Note that the regime's purification campaign did not extend to purging Burmese Buddhist language of its foreign borrowings from the Indian language Pali.

gime's view, the country should not be called some British pronunciation of a word denoting a single ethnic group. Those who continued to use "Burma" and "Burmese" were said to harbor the "ill intent" of "neo-colonialists [who] are hostile to Myanmar."[59]

In fact, the common usage of "Burma" and "Burmese" prior to the 1989 reforms, the junta's prescriptions for name standardization, and the English versions of these names all refer to slightly different things. In other words, there is no isomorphic mapping of imperialist terms to "authentic" significations, no purging of British corruptions, and no move toward greater ethnic inclusiveness of minorities. Moreover, the SLORC's prescription is linguistically counterintuitive. "Myanmar" and "Bamar" are for the most part adjectives,[60] not nouns, and hence need a noun to follow, such as *pyi* (country), *naing-ngan* (literally, conquered territory, but now refers to the sovereign domain of a state), or *lu-myo* (literally, kind of person, but now used interchangeably with the words "race" and "nationality").

In a sense, the junta's renaming project represented a continuation of the decades-old postcolonial—and inward-focused—project of codifying the Burmese language to enhance its prestige as a language of a nation-state. Whether or not it was intended, however, the renaming project represented one of the more naked assertions of the supremacy of the ethnic-majority Burmans with respect to the country's minorities. As Gustaaf Houtmann has observed, "Neither *Myanma* nor *Bama*, from which Myanmar and Burma are derived, are neutral terms, as both are strongly associated with the Burmese language, the language of the ethnic majority."[61] For speakers of Burmese as a second or third language, the formal, written style—from which almost all the new names derived—was even more inaccessible than the colloquial style, and perhaps most identified with the ethnicity and chauvinism of its mother-tongue speakers. As one critic writes of the renaming project: "[It is] clear proof that the Myanmar [i.e., ethnic-majority group] want to dominate over all other ethnic groups, and is practicing the policy of a great nation of Myanmar, i.e., in the course of time there would be no Shan, Chin,

---

59.   Tekkatho Myat Thu, "Call Us Myanmar."

60.   Okell notes that the Burmese language does not distinguish between nouns and adjectives in the same way English does. Okell, *A Reference Grammar of Colloquial Burmese*. Bama and Myanma/Mranma/Myanmar are almost never used, however, in a way that might look like an English noun.

61.   Gustaaf Houtmann, *Mental Culture in Burmese Crisis Politics: Aung San Suu Kyi and the National League for Democracy* (Tokyo: Institute for the Study of Languages and Cultures of Asia and Africa, 1999), p. 49.

Kachin, Karen, Mon and Arakanese, all would eventually merge into Myanmar. It will be a monolithic whole with one country, Myanmar, instead of the Union of Burma, one religion, Buddhism, and one race, the Myanmarnese [*sic*]."[62]

Beyond the renaming campaign, there is further evidence that Rangoon became increasingly involved in everyday politics, social relations, and language issues in the former Frontier Areas. After decades of neglect, the central government adopted a set of assimilationist policies toward minorities. In the regions where cease-fires had been reached with former insurgent groups, Rangoon deployed the Ministry for the Development of the Border Areas and the National Races (later renamed the Ministry for the Progress of Border Areas and National Races and Development Affairs) to build roads, Burmese-language schools, hospitals, power plants, telecommunications relay stations, and other institutions and facilities aimed at both modernizing and subjugating the inhabitants of the former rebel-held territory. These projects, unprecedented in Burmese history, were carried out by members of the armed forces and local residents conscripted into labor gangs by the military.

The army itself grew from 170,000 soldiers in 1988 to more than 400,000 (mostly Burman) soldiers in 2000, an unprecedented figure in modern Burmese history. It also expanded its matériel holdings at a similarly breakneck pace. The new Burmese military developed a capacity to deploy soldiers, guns, trucks, teachers, doctors, nurses, and other resources in ways the unity-conscious BSPP never could. The BSPP's clumsy attempts to integrate ethnic minority groups into a Union of Burma failed because of the incapacity of the central government to offer compelling incentives to locals to cooperate and negotiate with Rangoon. Although there is little doubt that many local populations still consider the military an occupying force representing Rangoon's continued attempts at internal colonialism, these border-area development activities brought new resources and incentives to bear on insider-outsider relations.

In the realm of education, the Rangoon regime became increasingly intolerant of diversity in former Frontier Areas. For example, in the 1990s the teaching of the Mon language in southern Burma, an area where a former rebel group (the New Mon State Party) concluded a cease-fire agreement in 1995, became a dangerous enterprise. Thein Lwin has written that "the teachers of the Mon language and literature run the risk to be punished by the [Rangoon] government authorities. Some teachers have been arrested." In 1998 the government shut down 120 Mon

---

62.   Kanbawza Win, *A Burmese Appeal to the UN and U.S.*, p. 44.

schools. Subsequent negotiations between the New Mon State Party's education committee and the junta led to the reopening of the schools, but
"the teaching of the Mon language and literature was not officially allowed."[63] In most of the former rebel-held areas where cease-fires were
instituted, non-Burmese languages could be studied only in the first few
years of schooling (but not after the fourth grade) or outside of school
hours.

Religion was also a target of the regime. In 1991 two Mon Buddhist
monks and a Rangoon University lecturer were arrested for trying to
promote usage of the Mon language, a historic language through which
Buddhism was introduced to Burma.

In the 1990s, intra-elite politics in Burma crossed the administra-
tive/territorial divide between the former Ministerial Burma and Frontier Areas when ethnic-Burman opposition in the center courted the
sympathy and support of populations living in the border regions. This
development brought language and cultural politics into dangerous terrain for the first time in the country's history. By launching its cultural
homogenization campaign and its supporting cast of development and
educational initiatives in former Frontier Areas, the SLORC/SPDC demonstrated that it no longer viewed these regions as irrelevant to power
struggles in Rangoon. The regime insisted that the populations of the border areas had to be embraced and remade into "Myanmars." As a regime
spokesperson noted on the subject of education in these regions, "National races residing in the border areas will then be able to think
correctly and work together resolutely for reconsideration of national
races through common awareness and objective and correct belief and
conviction."[64]

Conclusion

Since independence, central governments in Burma have framed their
policies toward ethnic minorities living beyond the central region as programs aimed at teaching backward peoples how to think correctly—that
is, to think with a modern, postcolonial mentality (1950s), as socialists

---

63. Thein Lwin, "The Teaching of Ethnic Language and the Role of Education in the
Context of Mon Ethnic Nationality in Burma."

64. Lt. Col. Thein Han, "Human Resource Development and Nation Building in
Myanmar: Unity in Diversity," in *Human Resource Development and Nation Building in
Myanmar,* proceedings of the Human Resource Development symposium, Yangon,
Myanmar, November 18–20, 1997 (Rangoon: Office of Strategic Studies, 1997), p. 218.

(1962–88), and since 1988 as authentic and pure "Myanmars." During the first two stages of this process, minorities could think, speak, read, and write in any indigenous language of their choosing, as long as the content of one's utterances were pro-Union and later pro-socialist. Since 1988, however, the regime's cultural homogenization programs have demanded that thinking correctly be done in the "Myanmar" language only; diversity has been criminalized. Thinking incorrectly—that is, thinking in a way that does not accord with the junta's Three National Objectives—is dangerous, as is teaching and preaching in non-Burmese indigenous languages.

Language policy in modern Burma has come a long way from its original focus on the creation of a monolingual public sphere in the colonial and postcolonial central regions. Throughout the twentieth century, Rangoon-based regimes promulgated policies aimed explicitly at language usage and standardization in these regions. At issue was how power would be used to favor one elite group over another and to elevate the status of that elite group within the international community. Out of these intra-elite power struggles, various coalitions of ethnic Burmans grasped the reins of government and generated extensive arrays of programs aimed at codifying, empowering, and modernizing their language. These programs were successful in transforming the Burmese language. Indeed Burmese now seems inevitably and naturally the language of this country. No one in central Burma with any serious claims on ruling power would ever question the status of Burmese as the official language of the country's public sphere—a significant change since the colonial era.

During the twentieth century, it was only in this arena of "insider politics" that any explicit language policy materialized in laws, decrees, or other formal policy pronouncements. This does not mean, however, that the policies to modernize Burmese—as well as other outcomes of intra-elite struggles in Rangoon—did not have far-reaching implications for populations living beyond the central regions. From the colonial era onward, the centralization of cultural, symbolic, and political capital in Rangoon led to a hierarchical ordering of territory and populations that placed value, sophistication, civilization, and power in the center. These goods inevitably diminished as one moved from the center. Reinforced by deeply rooted social Darwinist views about the evolution of civilizations, this systematic and tidy ordering of state and society placed at a distinct disadvantage the territorially distant, linguistically distinct populations who lived in the country's periphery. After independence in 1948 and especially after the takeover by the military-socialist regime in 1962, central "insider politics" became increasingly contestable only in Burmese. This turned thinkers, writers, and speakers of other languages into second-class citizens.

From the point of view of those who lived in the former Frontier Areas, postcolonial military, political, and cultural power has been reflected in the Burmese language and narrated according to putative Burman traditions. Minority populations have viewed postcolonial, national-level politics as a series of acts that pitted arrogant, intolerant, expansionist, and often incomprehensible Burmans against increasingly self-identifying, victimized, indigenous minorities. For minorities, little has changed since the 1950s. In areas where the SLORC/SPDC concluded cease-fire agreements in the 1990s, local populations have gained little from integration with Rangoon, although some of their leaders—especially those involved in the production of heroin and meth-amphetamines for the global market—may find easier access to money-laundering services. Few villages and towns view the border-area development programs as anything but a new, more invasive round of Rangoon expansionism; the fact that the army conducts these programs and does so exclusively in the Burmese language reinforces this view. In many of these areas, anything Rangoon does is automatically suspect.

The use of Burmese may nonetheless be spreading. The SLORC/SPDC regime did not promulgate an explicit Burmese- (or "Myanmar"-) only policy, but local and regional commanders handling day-to-day law-and-order affairs have consistently made it difficult for educators, monks, and other public figures to operate in anything but Burmese. Moreover, people living in these remote regions—confronting the pres-ence of tens of thousands of recently arrived Burman soldiers—have new incentives to speak and understand Burmese so as to navigate the new corridors of power in their localities. Fluency in Burmese allows minori-ties to negotiate with the soldiers who commandeer local men, rice, land, and cattle for development or counterinsurgency projects. A generation from now, this bilingualism may lead to what SLORC feared most after 1988: the ability of ethnic minorities to communicate fluently enough in Burmese to team up with the monolingual Burman opposition.

Language politics in twentieth-century Burma was unfailingly one-directional. As elites in the center struggled over national power, they initiated changes in the canon, codes, and standards of the language spoken in the center. Those not privy to the elite's "insider politics" never had an opportunity to steer decisions about language modernization or standardization. At only one point did any grassroots group attempt to sway elite language-makers in a direction that would be more inclusive or more populist; this occurred in 1965 when the Upper Burma Writers'

Association in Mandalay was denounced as communist for suggesting that the formal literary style of writing be scrapped in favor of the more accessible colloquial style. In the 1990s, when the ruling junta's pro-unity, pro-uniformity crusade brought assimilationist programs into minority regions, communications continued to flow in one direction: from Rangoon to the border regions. Rangoon's elites have not sought input into cultural, educational, and social policies from those who have been the targets of these policies.

This single-mindedness is not just an attribute of Burma's military officers. The Rangoon-based opposition has shown few signs of appreciating how assumptions about the primacy of Burmese—and possibly English as well—alienate those who have little access to either of these languages and who have had few if any positive experiences with speakers of the official state language. Nor does there seem to be any recognition of the views of non-Burmese speakers regarding the continued elevation of Burmese as the official language of citizenship and the associated demotion of minority languages. This is reflective of long-held assumptions about the primacy of politics in the central and southern regions of the country. What goes on beyond the central regions is neither seen nor heard. Furthermore, the National League for Democracy's constitutional recommendations appear to be based largely on the 1947 constitution, which considered ethnic minority political, cultural, and social autonomy to be "easy" problems, resolvable by formal (i.e., constitutional) means. The concerns of minorities about the particulars of these solutions have never been a top priority for the NLD, which devotes its meager physical and political resources to bringing down the ruling junta and replacing it with a democratic government. Promises of majority-rule, parliamentary democracy, however, do not necessarily appeal to minorities who would still be subjected to the whims of the ethnic majority in the central regions. Discussing his reservations about the NLD, one ethnic-minority leader has said, "The issue of democracy is often put before the ethnic nationality question, but in our view it [the ethnic question] needs to come first."[65]

---

65. Quoted in Martin J. Smith, "Burma at the Crossroads," *Burma Debate*, Vol. 3, No. 6 (November/December 1996), p. 8.

Chapter 6

The Politics of Language in Thailand and Laos

Charles F. Keyes

In this chapter I examine the relationship between the national languages of Thailand and Laos and the diverse languages that are spoken and written in these two countries. My thesis is that national languages are the products of political processes that privilege one language among the many spoken and read by those who have been subsumed as citizens within the boundaries of a state. Every modern state has included peoples speaking a diversity of languages and dialects and often utilizing a number of different writing systems. The creation of a national language begins with the political choice of a language or dialect as the basis for the language of the state. It next entails the development of a standardized form of this language and then the inculcation of this standard language among the populace. Those who speak, write, and read the national language can ipso facto make a claim to belonging to the nation. Those who do not, or do so at best imperfectly, cannot make this claim.

Literacy is fundamental to establishing a national language. Indeed standardization of a national language is dependent on the existence of texts authorized by the state. As Benedict Anderson has shown, the modern state has supplanted traditional religious authorities as the ultimate arbiter of language standards.[1] The ways in which a national language are spoken can be diverse without undermining the national character of the language, even though such differences may indicate class and other differences within the national community.

---

1. Benedict R.O.G. Anderson, *Imagined Communities: Reflections on the Origin and Spread of Nationalism*, rev. ed. (London: Verso, 1991), chap. 5.

The decisions made at the time a national language is created will shape the politics of language in the state in question for subsequent generations. This politics can take on new forms with migration in and out of the country and as the country orients itself to transnational political-economic forces. Thailand and Laos, like other Asian countries, are often seen as being "old world" countries with their national cultures having deep roots in the past, in contrast to "new world" settler states such as those of the Americas, Australia, and New Zealand. But even in Asia, the flows of peoples, goods, and services across borders have become so significant since the advent of the colonial era that it has been impossible for Asian states to insulate their national languages from external influences.

Thailand and Laos have their origins in the same premodern world, but because of the expansion of European, especially French, colonialism into Southeast Asia, the two became separate states. In both countries the creation of national languages is of recent vintage. In Thailand the process began only in the late 1800s. In Laos the process is even more recent, a consequence of the particular character of French colonial rule imposed on the country between 1893 and 1954 and the political division of the country between 1954 and 1975.

At the outset of the processes leading to the creation of Thai and Lao national languages, a remarkable diversity of languages were spoken and written within the territories that became subsequently legally bounded as "Thailand" and "Laos." In Thailand the politics of language begun in the 1890s led to an accommodation of what William Smalley has termed "linguistic diversity [within] national unity."[2] That is, despite the continued diversity of languages used within the country, for at least a half century more than 90 percent of the citizenry has had sufficient competence in the national language for it to be recognized arguably as the most significant basis for a shared national identity.

In Laos marked linguistic diversity has not been accommodated within a national unity. Although the foundations for a national language were laid down in the late 1930s in the final years of French colonial domination, the civil war that began in the 1950s and lasted until 1975, together with a poor transportation and communications infrastructure, prevented the implementation of policies that would have ensured that the populace would acquire some basic competence in the national language. Even after the Lao People's Revolutionary Party (the Lao Communist Party) succeeded in 1975 in establishing itself as the sole source of

---

2. William A. Smalley, *Linguistic Diversity and National Unity: Language Ecology in Thailand* (Chicago: University of Chicago Press, 1994).

policymaking in the country, the limited resources available to the government, together with the increasing influence of Thai culture, has significantly hindered the ability of the people living in Laos to achieve competence in the national language.

Language Diversity in the Premodern Siamese Empire

In the late eighteenth century, a kingdom was founded in what is today central Thailand with a capital first at Thonburi on the Cao Phraya River and then in 1782 across the river in the city known in English as "Bangkok" and in Thai as "Krungthep," the city of angels. The rulers of this new kingdom succeeded not only in restoring an older kingdom centered on the basin of the Cao Phraya River that had been conquered by Burmese forces in 1767, but in creating a new significantly expanded empire. This empire was known to the external world as "Siam," a term that in various cognates had been used by Europeans since at least the sixteenth century for polities in central Thailand.[3] During the nineteenth century, Bangkok kings sponsored a series of successful military campaigns that brought within the Siamese empire as vassal states (*prathetsarat*) or subordinate feudalities (*huamüang*) all of present-day Laos, what is today northwestern Cambodia, and several Malay states as well as the previously politically independent or autonomous areas that lie in northern and northeastern Thailand.[4] The linguistic complexity of the Siamese empire was extraordinary. (See Tables 6.1 and 6.2.)

Beginning with the core area of old Siam—that is, the area comprising the central plains of Thailand and the northern part of the Malay Peninsula—most people spoke related dialects of the Tai language family that would subsequently become the basis for what today are central

---

3. Henry Yule and Arthur Coke Burnell, *Hobson-Jobson: A Glossary of Colloquial Anglo-Indian Words and Phrases and of Kindred Terms, Etymological, Historical, Geographical, and Discursive*, new ed., ed. William Crooke (London: Routledge and Kegan Paul, 1969 [1886]), pp. 833–834. The term *Sayam*, the Thai equivalent of "Siam," was not used by the rulers of the Siamese empire who, instead, referred to their polity as müang Thai, the country of the "Thai," or by the name of the capital of the kingdom/empire—that is, müang Krunthep (Bangkok). In the late nineteenth century, King Chulalongkorn (1868–1910) and his associates, in connection with launching a series of reforms that would transform the empire into a modern nation-state, adopted *Sayam* as the name for their reconstituted polity. In 1939 a nationalist government would make "Thailand," the literal equivalent in English of the Thai *prathet Thai*, the official name of the country.

4. Siam also competed with Vietnam for control of the rest of Cambodia, but this competition came to an end in 1863 when the king of Cambodia agreed to the establishment of a French protectorate over his country.

Table 6.1. Languages Spoken in the Siamese Empire in the Late Nineteenth Century.

Language	Location	Percentage
Siamese (central Thai) (including the *ratchasap* or royal language register)	Central Siam	15
Lao and Kammüang (northern Thai)	Northeastern Thailand, Laos, northern Thailand	55
Paktai (southern Thai)	Northern Malay Peninsula	4
Khmer, Mon, and Austroasiatic languages	Eastern, northeastern, northern, and western Siamese empire	12
Chinese	Primarily Bangkok	4
Malay and other Austronesian	Southern Thailand	9
Other		1
Total		**100**

SOURCE: Estimates are based primarily on William A. Smalley, *Linguistic Diversity and National Unity: Language Ecology in Thailand* (Chicago: University of Chicago Press, 1994); and Volker Grabowsky, *An Early Thai Census: Translation and Analysis* (Bankok: Institute of Population Studies, Chulalongkorn University, 1993).
NOTE: Percentages are approximate.

Thai (*Thaiklang*) and standard Thai (*Thai mattrathan*), which is the national language.[5] In the nineteenth century, the people speaking these dialects constituted no more than 15 percent of the total population of the Siamese empire.

Even within this core area, there were significant differences in both spoken and written languages. The most striking of these differences was to be found in Bangkok, the capital city. In the court in Bangkok, members of the royal and aristocratic families not only spoke an elite dialect but also used forms of the language that belonged to a distinctive "register" termed *ratchasap* (royal language). Outside the court, this language was known only imperfectly in a few forms used in dramatic productions.

From the middle of the nineteenth century on, the royal and aristocratic residences of Bangkok were increasingly surrounded by shop houses and shantytowns whose inhabitants spoke a variety of Chinese languages—mostly Cantonese, Hainanese, Hokkien, and Teochiu. Speakers of these languages had migrated in huge numbers from south-

---

5. As is conventional in works in English, I use the term "Tai" to refer to peoples speaking related languages who live in China and many parts of mainland Southeast Asia and the term "Thai" to refer to peoples who are citizens of Thailand no matter what their home language might be.

Table 6.2. Major Writing Systems Used in the Siamese Empire in the Nineteenth Century.

Orthographic System	Languages Used with This System	Where and/or Among Whom Used
Sukhodayan Thai (ancestor of the Thai national system)	Siamese (central Thai) and Paktai	Central Siam, northern Malay Peninsula
Tua Wiang (court language; ancestor to the Lao national system)	Lao dialects	Northeastern Thailand, central and southern Laos
Tua Tham/Yuan	Pali, Lao dialects, Tai dialects in northern Thailand, Kengtung (a Burmese Shan state), and Sipsongpanna (southern Yunnan)	Northern and northeastern Thailand, Laos, Kengtung (a Burmese Shan state), Sipsongpanna (southern Yunnan)
Tua Khôm (system derived from old Khmer)	Pali	Central Siam, northern Malay Peninsula, parts of northeastern Thailand and southern Laos
Khmer (post–old Khmer)	Khmer, some other Austroasiatic languages, Pali	Northeastern Thailand and northwestern Cambodia
Chinese	Chinese, Hmong, Mien	Bangkok and other places with Chinese migrant communities; used as a pecialized ritual language among the Mien and some Hmong
Jawi	Malay and Persian/Arabic	Far southern part of the empire

NOTE: On writing systems used for Tai languages, see George Coedès, *Tamnan aksôn Thai* [Accounts of Thai alphabets] (Bangkok: Kurusapha, 1964 [1926]; and Hans Penth, "Thai Scripts: An Outline of Their Origin and Development," in *Yunnan*, comp. Princess Galyani Vadhana (Bangkok: Watthanaphanit, 1986), pp. 246–249.

eastern China to seek work in Bangkok, which had become a dynamic node in the global economy. By the late nineteenth century, visitors to Bangkok had begun to note that the primary languages spoken in the city were ones the new immigrants had brought with them from China. Also in the city were enclaves of speakers of other distinctive languages, while speakers of Tai languages and dialects were in a clear minority.

The dominant written language of the Bangkok court and of central Siam centered on an orthographic system that derived from one first devised in the thirteenth century in the medieval kingdom of Sukhothai—the first state dominated by Tai-speaking people—and was then adopted by the rulers of Ayutthaya, a kingdom that from the mid-fourteenth to mid-eighteenth century was the dominant power in what is now central Thailand. This writing system would become the basis for the orthographic system used for the national language. Prior to the creation of a national language in the late nineteenth century, the Sukhodayan-based system (as I call it) was not the only orthographic system used by the Siamese. Another system, known as *khôm*, which derived from old Khmer, was also widely used by Buddhist monks for texts in Pali, the sacred language of Buddhism. In addition, there were peoples living in central Siam who were literate in other non-Tai languages such as Mon and Chinese.

Although most of the people who lived in the core area of the Siamese empire spoke closely related Tai dialects, there were also speakers of other languages in this area. The biggest number, located in western Siam, were the Mon, a people speaking an Austroasiatic language related to Khmer. Mon had once been dominant in lower Burma, but after the final conquest of this area by Burmans in 1757, thousands had fled and settled in Thailand. They brought not only a distinctive spoken language but also a written one. Because there were close cultural connections between the Mon and the Tai of central Thailand—it was from the Mon that these Tai derived their Buddhist tradition—many Mon had, even in the premodern period, become bilingual and bicultural. The core area of old Siam also included enclaves of peoples who had been resettled after Siamese conquests of what is now Laos.

In sum, in the nineteenth century even in the core area of the Siamese empire there was a marked diversity of spoken and written languages. Beyond the core area, the diversity was even greater.

Closely related dialects of Tai that linguists would label "Lao" constituted the biggest language group in the Siamese empire.[6] One closely related set of Lao dialects (Marvin Brown's "Vientiane Lao") was spoken by the large majority of people living in present-day central and southern Laos and northeastern Thailand, while another set (Brown's "Luang Prabang Lao") was spoken in the northern part of modern-day Laos. There were also in what is today Laos and northeastern Thailand speakers of a number of Tai dialects that were not closely related to the Lao dia-

---

6. I follow J. Marvin Brown's classification of Lao dialects. See Brown, *From Ancient Thai to Modern Dialects* (Bangkok: Social Science Association of Thailand Press, 1965).

lects, of which Phouan, the dominant language of Xieng Khouang principality in Laos was perhaps the largest.

Among the Lao, three distinct writing systems were used. The first, known as "Tua Wiang" (the orthography of the court), is ancestor to the system that would become the official form of written Lao in independent Laos. While also derived from the system devised in Sukhothai in the thirteenth to fourteenth century, it had developed some significant differences from the orthographic system used in central Siam. The second was known as "Tua Tham" (dhammic writing), that is, the orthography used for Buddhist texts. This system was also shared with speakers of other Tai languages living in what is today northern Thailand, the Burmese Shan state of Kengtung (Chiangtung), and the Sipsongpanna area of what is now southern Yunnan. In southern Laos and in parts of northeastern Thailand, a third system, "Tua Khôm," the same system derived from old Khmer used in areas of central Siam, was also used by some for Buddhist texts. There were also at least two other writing systems used among a small number of Tai-speaking people that were different from those used by the Lao.[7]

Although the Siamese used the term "Lao" for most Tai-speaking people living to the north of the core area of Siam, those living in what is today northern Thailand actually spoke dialects distinct from those that linguists consider to be Lao. People speaking Tai dialects of northern Thailand refer to their language as "Kammüang," with *kam* meaning language and *müang*, literally principality, referring to the formerly autonomous principalities that included Chiang Mai, Lampang, and Nan. Dialects spoken in Kengtung in the Burmese Shan states and among the Lue of the Sipsongpanna in southern Yunnan were closely related to the Kammüang dialects. Throughout the area where these dialects were used, a common writing system—sometimes called "Yuan"—very close to the Tua Tham one used among Lao speakers, was used for both religious and secular writings.

Taken together, the speakers of Lao and Kammüang would have constituted at least half of the population of the premodern Siamese empire. Even in the area where Lao and Kammüang dialects were dominant, there were many speakers of other languages. By far the largest number were those who spoke one or another Austroasiatic language. Peoples such as the Lawa (Lua) of northern Thailand and the Khamu of Laos had

---

7.   One of these was the "Black Thai" system used among non-Buddhist Tai in northeastern Laos and northwestern Vietnam; the other was known in Laos as "Tai Neua," or northern Tai, and was the same as that used among a group in Yunnan who are known ethnographically as "Mao Shans" or "Chinese Shans."

extremely close relationships with their Tai-speaking neighbors and were often bilingual. They did not have writing systems for their own languages, at least not until Christian missionaries began working among them, and if any became literate, it was usually in one of the Tai languages.

While many different small groups of Austroasiatic-speaking peoples were found throughout the hilly areas of the northern and eastern parts of the Siamese empire, those who lived on the southern part of the Khorat Plateau (which today is coterminous with northeastern Thailand) and in the northwestern part of modern-day Cambodia recognized their connections with the former Angkorean empire as well as with more recent Khmer kingdoms. In contrast to their preliterate cousins in the hills, Siamese Khmer and closely related Kuy often acquired literacy in written Khmer, a language using an orthographic system different from that of Tua Khôm. Speakers of Khmer and other Austroasiatic languages, together with the much less numerous Mon living in western Siam, probably constituted 15–20 percent of the population of the Siamese empire.

There were also in upland areas of the northern and western parts of the Siamese empire communities of speakers of yet other languages. Among the largest of such upland-dwelling peoples were those living along the border with Burma who spoke Karennic languages. They were related to much larger groups living within the Burman empire. In the northern areas were groups of Tibeto-Burman–speaking peoples, such as the Kô or I-kô—known by ethnographers working in Southeast Asia as Akha and by those working in China as Hani—who were extensions of much larger populations in southern China. In the late nineteenth century, some Hmong and Mien (Yao) migrated from southern China and settled in what would become northern Laos and, to a lesser extent, northern Thailand. Speakers of Karennic, Tibeto-Burman, and Hmong-Mien languages historically did not have distinctive writing systems of their own, but beginning in the nineteenth century, Christian missionaries began to introduce them. Some Hmong and Mien acquired limited knowledge of Chinese, and in the twentieth century, a Hmong millenarian leader would create a totally new system of writing.[8]

In the nineteenth century, Bangkok gained control of the Malay Peninsula down to the northern Malay sultanate of Kedah. In that part of the peninsula, from north of Nakhon Sithammarat to south of Songkhla, most people spoke Tai dialects that were collectively known as "Paktai,"

---

8. See William A. Smalley, Chia Koua Vang, and Gnia Yee Yang, *Mother of Writing: The Origin and Development of a Hmong Messianic Script* (Chicago: University of Chicago Press, 1990).

literally, southern tongue. Paktai dialects were not as different from Siamese dialects as were Lao and Kammüang, and those who were literate in southern Siam used either the Sukhodayan script or Tua Khôm, which was also used in central Siam.

In marked contrast, those living under Siamese rule in Malay sultanates brought under Siamese control—Pattani, Trengannu, Kelantan, and Kedah—together with areas just north of Pattani, spoke distinctive dialects of Malay. Those who were literate in these areas used an orthographic system known as "Jawi," based on Persian/Arabic writing.

During the nineteenth century, Chinese began to migrate in significant numbers to southern Siam where they became engaged in tin mining and the export of tin and, to a lesser extent, in other forms of trade. Like their counterparts in Bangkok, they came mainly from southeastern China and spoke the languages of that area.

The great diversity of languages, both spoken and written, in the Siamese empire of the nineteenth century posed a significant challenge to those seeking to transform parts of this empire into the modern nation-states of Thailand and Laos. Because premodern politics were based on feudal relationships of king and lords and vassals and those of lords and vassals to their followings, there was no pressure to impose linguistic uniformity on the peoples of the empire.[9] The primary impetus for what linguistic standardization there was in the premodern period came from Buddhism, the dominant religion of most of the people of the empire, and Islam, the dominant religion of the Malay-speaking peoples. The situation changed radically at the end of the nineteenth century when a reduced Siamese empire was reconfigured as a state with well-defined boundaries within which there was supposed to be a single people—a single nation.

The Evolution of Thai as the National Language

From 1893 to 1909, the Siamese empire was divided between the colonial domains of British Burma, British Malaya, French Indochina, and a new state that would become Thailand. Although Siam had been compelled to recognize British suzerainty over territories in northern Malaysia from as early as 1796 and French domination of Cambodia in 1863, the rulers of Siam did not perceive a real threat to their empire until the end of the nineteenth century. After France completed its conquest of Vietnam in

---

9.   I use the term "feudal" as a gloss for the Thai term *sakdi na*. For a discussion of this system, see Charles F. Keyes, *Thailand: Buddhist Kingdom as Modern Nation-State* (Boulder, Colo.: Westview, 1987), pp. 29–31.

1883 and Britain its conquest of Burma in 1886, the stage was set for the end of the Siamese empire. The colonial powers did not move to incorporate the whole of this empire within their domains, but they did compel Siam to cede substantial territory. In 1893 French gunboats were sent up the Chao Phraya River to Bangkok to force the Siamese court to agree to a treaty ceding to the French control of all territories east of the Mekong River, most of what is present-day Laos. In subsequent treaties in 1904 and 1907, Siam gave up control to France of northwestern Cambodia and two enclaves on the right bank of the Mekong River. A treaty between Siam and Britain in 1909 gave Britain control of the Malay sultanates of Trengannu, Kelantan, and Kedah (including Perlis), but the sultanate of Pattani remained under Siamese control.

In conjunction with these concessions, Siam was also compelled by the colonial powers to demarcate the boundaries between Siam and the territories that were under colonial rule. The demarcation of these boundaries was one of the major steps in the creation of what Thongchai Winichakul has called a "geobody"—that is, a modern nation-state.[10]

The loss of territories and the continuing threat of colonial expansion motivated King Chulalongkorn (1868–1910) and his advisers to institute reforms in administration, public finance, and the military that were to make Siam a unitary state rather than an empire in which the core kingdom was surrounded by tributary and vassal polities. The Siamese court in the early twentieth century also sought to implement policies relating to religion and education that were aimed at molding the heterogeneous population of the remnants of the Siamese empire into a single nation.

The architect of the reconfiguring of the Siamese empire as a Thai nation was Prince Damrong Rajanubhab (1862–1943), half brother to King Chulalongkorn and founding minister (1892–1915) of the modern ministry of interior. Early in his position as minister, Prince Damrong ordered all provincial officials to cease using the term "Lao" for the people of northeastern and northern parts of the country and to henceforth use terms that identified them according to the regions of the country in which they lived. Reflecting on this action after stepping down as minister, he wrote that "people in Bangkok have long called [the peoples of northern and northeastern Siam] Lao. Today, however, we know they are Thai, not Lao."[11]

---

10. Thongchai Winichakul, *Siam Mapped: A History of the Geo-body of a Nation* (Honolulu: University of Hawaii Press, 1994).

11. Prince Damrong Rajanubhab, *Nithan boran khadi* [Historical anecdotes] (Bangkok: Phrae Phithaya, 1971 [1935]), p. 318.

To transform Lao into Thai required more than an administrative act, however. In the early twentieth century, there were significant religio-political uprisings in both northeastern and northern regions by peoples resistant to the establishment of a unified administration controlled by Bangkok.[12] Although these uprisings failed because the military forces of Bangkok had vastly superior weaponry, the government recognized that to persuade the people in these regions that they were "Thai," much more than military coercion was needed. During the first few decades of the twentieth century, the Bangkok government laid the groundwork for the integration of the Thai nation through co-opting Buddhist monks under a centralized order and employing them to assist in implementing reforms in education.[13]

Prior to the end of the nineteenth century, there had been two systems of education in the core area of Siam. The first was practiced by monks in Buddhist monastic schools. Because nearly every boy attended these schools, there was a high degree of literacy in premodern Siam. Such literacy, however, was oriented primarily to preparing boys to read Buddhist texts and other works kept in temple libraries. Monks who ran these schools did not use a standard curriculum, or even the same system of writing. The differences in monastic education were even more marked in areas beyond the core area of premodern Siam.

The second educational system was that sponsored by the palace with the intent of training a cadre of royal and aristocratic children (mainly, but not exclusively, boys) in the skills needed for administering the country and in literature (always in poetic genres) considered to be the hallmarks of the cultured elite. Often boys who attended these palace-sponsored schools at some point also attended monastic schools.

After Chulalongkorn's accession to the throne in 1868, he and some of his associates—most notably his two half brothers, Prince Damrong and Prince Vajirañña, the latter being a Buddhist monk who headed the reform-oriented order the Thammayut-nikai—began to envision the cre-

---

12.   See Charles F. Keyes, "Millennialism, Theravada Buddhism, and Thai Society," *Journal of Asian Studies*, Vol. 36, No. 2 (1977), pp. 283–302; Chatthip Nartsupha, "The Ideology of 'Holy Men' Revolts in North East Thailand," in Andrew Turton and Shigeharu Tanabe, eds., *Historical and Peasant Consciousness in South East Asia* (Osaka, Japan: National Museum of Ethnology, 1984), pp. 111–134; Ansil Ramsay, "Modernization and Reactionary Rebellions in Northern Siam," *Journal of Asian Studies*, Vol. 38, No. 2 (1979), pp. 283–298; and Shigeharu Tanabe, "Ideological Practice in Peasant Rebellions: Siam at the Turn of the Twentieth Century," in Turton and Tanabe, *Historical and Peasant Consciousness in South East Asia*, pp. 75–110.

13.   Charles F. Keyes, "Buddhism and National Integration in Thailand," *Journal of Asian Studies*, Vol. 30, No. 3 (1971), pp. 551–568.

ation of a type of education that would prepare a somewhat expanded elite to utilize knowledge imported from the West in administering the country in more rationalized and effective ways. By 1870 textbooks were being written for a new curriculum, and by the 1880s palace-sponsored schools had been significantly expanded.[14]

Many surrounding the king felt that there need be no further educational reform beyond the creation of schools to train enough people to fill an expanded, but still small, bureaucracy. Prince Damrong and Prince Vajirañana had a different vision. They proposed instituting a system of compulsory education to replace that offered in monastic schools. They were successful in persuading the king to promulgate a law in 1902 that placed all schools under the authority of a Buddhist ecclesiastical hierarchy headed by a patriarch appointed by the king.

In the initial phase of implementing the radical restructuring of both the Buddhist *sangha* (order of monks) and monastic education, monks were allowed to remain teachers, but they were required to teach according to a curriculum set down by the ministry of public instruction (the predecessor of the ministry of education). The texts used for this curriculum were written in accord with new standards that began to be established for writing Thai.

In 1905 "a prescriptive 'Thai grammar' was prepared by educational authorities. This specified rules for 'correct' Thai and was much revised and expanded during the . . . reign [of] . . . King Rama VI, 1910–25 . . . , culminating in the three-decade (1919–37) masterwork *Principles of the Thai Language* (*lak phasa thai*) of Phaya Upakit-silpasan (Nim Kanchanachiwa)."[15] This volume became the model for all Thai-language textbooks. Phaya Upakit also was responsible for overseeing the production in 1927 of the first "monolingual dictionary for school students" that was published by the textbook department of the ministry of education.[16]

---

14.   This discussion is based on the work of David K. Wyatt, who has written the definitive study on the foundations of modern education in Thailand. See Wyatt, *The Politics of Reform in Thailand: Education in the Reign of King Chulalongkorn* (New Haven, Conn.: Yale University Press, 1969). See also Charles F. Keyes, "The Proposed World of the School: Thai Villagers' Entry into a Bureaucratic State System," in Keyes, ed., *Reshaping Local Worlds: Rural Education and Cultural Change in Southeast Asia* (New Haven, Conn.: Department of Southeast Asian Studies, Yale University, 1991), pp. 87–138.

15.   Anthony Diller, "What Makes Central Thai a National Language?" in Craig J. Reynolds, ed., *National Identity and Its Defenders: Thailand, 1939–1989*, Monash Papers on Southeast Asia No. 25 (Melbourne, Victoria, Australia: Centre of Southeast Asian Studies, Monash University, 1991), p. 102. "Phaya" is a title and "Upakit-silpasan" is a name given in connection with the conferral of the title. Nim Kanchanachiwa is the given name and surname.

16.   Ibid., p. 104.

Although in central Siam educational reform was generally accepted by monks, resistance developed in areas outside of the core of the old empire where very different writing systems were used and different traditions of education thrived. In 1906 a group of officials decided that "in areas where two languages were in use, as in the North and Northeast the 'local language may be taught, but only education in [central] Thai may be supported by the government."[17] In northeastern Thailand, where many senior monks belonged to the Thammayut order headed by Prince Vajirañana, there was little resistance to replacing traditional monastic schooling using the Tua Tham writing system with the new Bangkok- created schooling using standardized Thai. But in northern Thailand there was strong resistance, led by a charismatic monk, *Khruba* (Venerable Teacher) Srivijaya. His campaign would continue until his death in 1939.

This resistance, coupled with problems that began to develop in hybrid schools—ones using a Bangkok-determined secular curriculum but still dependent on monk-teachers—led Prince Vajirañana, who had become patriarch of what had become the Thai national Buddhist *sangha* in 1910, to support the replacement of monks by secular teachers. During the reigns of King Vajiravudh (1910–27) and King Prajadhipok (1927–35), secular teachers began to be trained in sufficient numbers to make possible the conversion of an increasing number of hybrid schools into secular government schools.

King Vajiravudh was concerned not only about the resistance of peoples outside of central Siam to nation-building efforts but also about the large Chinese population living in the capital city. His reign had begun with a major strike by Chinese over taxes.[18] The king was deeply disturbed by this strike. He expressed his strong distrust of the Chinese in an essay written in both English (the king had been educated in England) and Thai entitled "The Jews of the East." The promulgation in 1913–14 of the first Nationality Act was based on the principle that everyone born on Thai soil was a Thai citizen. The act was clearly directed at ensuring that those born of Chinese parents but living in Thailand would become Thai citizens.

CONSOLIDATION OF "THAI-NESS"
In 1932 a group of military officers and ranking civil servants staged a successful coup that compelled King Prajadhipok to accept that national

17.   Wyatt, *The Politics of Reform in Thailand*, p. 333.

18.   G. William Skinner, *Chinese Society in Thailand* (Ithaca, N.Y.: Cornell University Press, 1957), p. 164.

sovereignty derived from a constitution rather than the authority of the monarch. The leaders of the coup did not abolish the monarchy, but after a failed royalist-led counterrevolution in 1933, the king went into exile to England. In 1935 he abdicated, and his young nephew, Ananda Mahidol, was chosen by the privy council to become the next king. Ananda was not be an active monarch, however, because he lived in Switzerland (with the exception of one brief visit to Thailand, between 1935 and 1946). During this period, the rulers of the country sought to promote a sense of national identity that was not dependent on the monarchy. Central to this effort was making standardized Thai the national language.

This effort was intensified after Field Marshal Phibul Songgram became prime minister in 1939. Phibul, with the assistance of an extremely effective ideologue, Wichit Wattakan, undertook to inculcate ultra-nationalism in the populace. In 1939 and 1940, Phibul's government issued a number of edicts, called *Ratthaniyom* (literally, state mandates), aimed at defining the nature of the Thai nation. The first of these changed the name of the country from Siam to Thailand and reaffirmed the principle first laid down at the end of the nineteenth century by Prince Damrong—that the "people" of this country were "Thai."[19] The third *Ratthaniyom* asserted that "the Government is of the opinion that the names *by which the Thais* in some parts of the country have been called do not correspond to the name of the race and the preference of the people so called, and also that the appellation of the Thai people by dividing them into many groups, such as the Northern Thais, the Northeastern Thais, the Southern Thais, Islamic Thais, is not appropriate for Thailand is one and indivisible."[20]

The ninth *Ratthaniyom* concerned the national language: "The Government deems that the continuity and progress of Thailand depends on the usage of the national language and alphabet as important elements." The proclamation went on to emphasize that it was the duty of Thai to gain literacy in the national language: "Thais must not regard the place of birth, domicile, residence or local dialects which varies from locality to locality as marks of differences. . . . Everyone must consider that being born as a Thai means that he has Thai blood and speaks the same Thai language. There is no (inherent) conflict in being born in different localities or speaking the Thai language in different dialects."[21]

19. Thak Chaloetiarana, ed., *Thai Politics: Extracts and Documents, 1932–1957* (Bangkok: Social Science Association of Thailand, 1978), p. 245.

20. Ibid., p. 246 (emphasis added).

21. Ibid., pp. 251–252.

These mandates provided the rationale for the government to move aggressively to ensure that Chinese schools taught only in Thai using the government-determined curriculum,[22] to restrict publication of "foreign" language newspapers to one in each language (aimed primarily at Chinese and English newspapers), and to suppress the use of any writing system for Tai languages other than the national one. The use of Yuan (northern Thai) was singled out for severe attack through the burning of traditional texts in several temple-monasteries because resistance to education using the national language had been the strongest in the north.[23]

By 1939, when Phibul took office, the vast majority of eligible children throughout the country and in the Chinese districts of Bangkok were attending compulsory government schools in which the medium of instruction was Thai. His *Ratthaniyom* made explicit what had effectively already taken place. Although Phibul's first term ended in 1944 when it began to become clear that Japan, with which he had allied, would be defeated in World War II, the establishment of Thai as the national language would never again be questioned. Phibul had not succeeded, however, in eliminating linguistic diversity within the country.

Resurgence of Linguistic Diversity in Thailand

Despite the success of inculcating in the vast majority of people living in Thailand significant competence in both the spoken and written forms of the national language, linguistic diversity has not disappeared. (See Table 6.3.) There was no significant resistance to standard Thai as the national language in the second half of the twentieth century, but there was increasing questioning of the exclusive use of Thai even in many public settings.[24]

Spoken standard Thai has strongly influenced regional Tai languages. So much standard Thai vocabulary has been adopted by Tai-speaking people living in the towns of outlying regions that their languages retain

---

22.   Skinner, *Chinese Society in Thailand*, p. 269.

23.   Harald Hundius, "The Colophons of Thirty Pali Manuscripts from Northern Thailand," *Journal of the Pali Text Society*, Vol. 14 (1990), p. 14. See also Thomas Hudak, "Spelling Reforms of Field Marshal Pibul Sonkram," *Crossroads*, Vol. 3, No. 1 (1986), pp. 123–133.

24.   Nidhi Aeusrivongse, a professor of history at Chiang Mai University and one of the leading public intellectuals in the country, has written the most sustained critiques of the use of standard Thai for a Thai audience in Thailand. See "Phasa Thai matrathan kap kanmüang [Standard Thai language and politics], in Aeusrivongse, *Khon, Kharabao, namnao lae nang Thai* [Masked drama, carabao, pollution, and Thai films] (Bangkok: Matichon, 1995), pp. 126–171.

Table 6.3. Languages Spoken in Contemporary Thailand.

Language Family and Language	Location	Percentage
Tai		**87.0**
Standard Thai	Mainly Bangkok	19.5
Central Thai (Thai Klang)	Central Thailand	27.0
Lao (Isan and northeastern Thai)	Northeastern Thailand	22.9
Kammüang (northern Thai)	Far northern Thailand	9.0
Paktai (southern Thai)	Southern Thailand	8.0
Other Tai languages (Phu Tai, Phuan, So, Shan, Lue, etc.)	Mainly in northeast and north	0.6
Sinitic		**6.8**
Teochiu	Mainly Bangkok	4.1
Hakka	Mainly Bangkok	1.1
Hainanese	Mainly Bangkok	0.7
Cantonese	Mainly Bangkok	0.5
Other Chinese (Hokkien, Taiwanese, and Yunnanese)		0.4
Austroasiatic		**2.7**
Northern Khmer	Southern northeastern Thailand	2.1
Kuy	Southern northeastern Thailand	0.5
Mon	Western Thailand	0.1
Vietnamese	Northeast Thailand and Bangkok	**0.2**
Austronesian		
Pattani Malay	Far southern Thailand	**1.9**
Other		**1.4**
Karennic languages	Northern and western Thailand	0.7
Hmong and Mien	Northern Thailand	0.2
Tibeto-Burman (Lahu, Lisu, and Akha)	Northern Thailand	0.2
Other		0.3
Total		**100**

SOURCE: Data are based primarily on William A. Smalley, *Linguistic Diversity and National Unity: Language Ecology in Thailand* (Chicago: University of Chicago Press, 1994), App. B.
NOTE: Standard Thai refers to those who speak only this language.

distinctiveness primarily in the use of tones and particles.[25] Rural people in the northern, northeastern, and southern regions still continue to speak local languages that are not intelligible to those who speak only standard Thai. Rural children in these regions who enter schools knowing only a local language find themselves disadvantaged because teachers are expected to use only standard Thai in instruction. Serious consideration has never been given to bilingual programs to assist the speakers of languages other than standard Thai in learning their national language.

Those who have grown up speaking standard Thai consider all nonstandard Thai spoken languages to be inferior. This is particularly true of Lao dialects. Not only are Lao dialects officially denigrated, but they are often made the object of public ridicule. (The country bumpkin who speaks a version of a Lao dialect is a stereotype found in many Thai films and television dramas.) Despite such attitudes, many northeastern people, especially those from rural backgrounds, continue to take pride in their language. Not only are Lao dialects used between people for whom these are their mother tongue, but the Lao-medium concerts of traditional northeastern folk opera (*môlam*) held in Bangkok and the major cities of the northeast attract large audiences of northeastern natives. Indeed this musical genre in which singing in Lao is accompanied by the *khaen*, a polyphonic reed instrument often seen as a symbol of Lao culture, serves as a major vehicle for perpetuation of a distinctive Isan or northeastern Thai identity.

The growing strength of democratic institutions in Thailand since the early 1990s has provided a boost to nonstandard Thai languages. Politicians find it expedient, even essential, to make use of local languages in election campaigns. This has been especially true in northeastern Thailand, which accounts for a third of the electorate.

By the start of the twenty-first century, only a few monks and scholars were still able to read Tua Tham, the dhammic script formerly used in northeastern Thailand (and in Laos) for Buddhist texts, and of the Lao writing system also formerly used in northeastern Thailand for secular writings. Knowledge of some of the traditional literature of the region, however, is much more widely held. Since at least the 1950s, some publishers and printers in northeastern Thailand (and some even in Bangkok) have produced sermons, folk opera scripts, books, and pamphlets

---

25. On the decline of knowledge of spoken northern Thai, see Thanet Charoenmuang, "When the Young Cannot Speak Their Own Mother Tongue: Explaining a Legacy of Cultural Domination in Lan Na," in Volker Grabosky, ed., *Regions and National Integration in Thailand, 1892–1992* (Wiesbaden, Germany: Otto Harrassowitz, 1995), pp. 82–93.

using standard Thai orthography that has been adapted for use by speakers of a Lao dialect. The works employ many words and grammatical forms not found in standard Thai. Some faculty at universities and colleges in the region have promoted interest in the folklore, legends, and religious stories as told in the Lao of the region.

In northern Thailand some monks, former monks, and scholars have sought to ensure that some northern Thai continue to acquire competence in reading and writing in the premodern Yuan system. Because fewer and fewer monks have studied Yuan in temple-monasteries, some scholars have begun to look to universities and colleges as places where the northern Thai literary tradition could continue to be taught. It is a sign of the success of the dominance of standard Thai and of the limited success of the revivalist movement that by the start of the twenty-first century the only significant center at which texts in Yuan were studied was in a small master's of arts program at Chiang Mai University. But as in the northeast, knowledge of traditional literature is more widely held because many works originally written in Yuan have also been transliterated into standard Thai. Works in a number of other languages, including those that originally used a Khmer or Mon orthographic system as well as some languages of peoples such as the Karen who were historically alliterate, have also been transliterated or translated into standard Thai.

The only truly successful case of the perpetuation of a nonstandard Thai writing system for use among a significant population has been the Persian/Arabic-derived Jawi, used among Thai-Malay in southern Thailand. Indeed, until the 1990s many Thai-Malay had a strong sense that Malay should be their exclusive written language. Since the adoption of a much more positive policy toward Thai Muslims beginning in the 1980s, however, resistance to education in state schools has markedly declined, and most children are now learning standard Thai.

To date, the position of Thai government agencies responsible for implementing national educational and cultural policies has ranged from ignorance of to outright hostility toward efforts to preserve literatures in languages other than standard Thai or even non-Thai literature in translation. Since the late twentieth century, however, people in Bangkok have expressed growing interest in rediscovering the cultural diversity of the country. This change of attitude may begin to influence public policy.

The ecology of language diversity in Thailand (to echo the title of the influential book by William Smalley) has also undergone a marked change since the late twentieth century because of globalizing influences. Non-Thai languages have proven to be particularly significant because of the success of Thailand in linking its economy to global networks. Most international commercial transactions carried out by Thai citizens are conducted in either English or a Chinese language. Because of the importance of Chinese for intra-Asian trade, there has been a notable upsurge of interest in learning spoken Mandarin, a language that had never been very important in Thailand.[26]

Today there is a hierarchy of language use in Thailand. The economic elite and some of the political elite are highly competent not only in both spoken and written Thai but also in English and/or Chinese. Such multilinguistic competence has also spread significantly among members of the middle class. Many in the political elite also find it useful to have competence both in standard Thai and in the local language spoken by members of their constituencies. At the low end of the hierarchy are those who have effective competence in only a local language or who have, at best, an imperfect understanding of the national language. Even those who are multilingual—as many are—do not have competence, and especially literate competence, in prestige languages.[27]

French Laos and the Foundations of a Lao National Language

The construction of a Lao national language began not with a vision of a Lao nation held by an indigenous elite but with French colonial officials. Between 1893 and 1907, the area that would become Laos was incorporated into the colonial domain that the French called Indochina. Indochina was ruled from Hanoi, and the Vietnamese were the dominant people in this new domain that also included Khmer (Cambodians), Lao, and dozens of minority peoples.

In 1893 the Lao kingdom of Luang Prabang, which had been a vassal of Siam, and areas of central and southern Laos that had been more directly administered by Siam were brought under French rule. Until the 1920s, it was official French policy to promote linkages with the Lao to the Vietnamese and others in Indochina with an ultimate goal of creating a new "Indochina" identity.[28] This vision was never accepted, however, by a number of key French officials, most notably Auguste Pavie, who had been responsible for bringing the Lao under French rule.

---

26. I base this on informal assessments by several Thai scholars. How significant this upsurge has been in the numbers of those learning to speak Mandarin needs to be determined.

27. I am indebted to Viggo Brun for reminding me of the significance of multilingualism among nonelite people. Personal communication, September 1, 2000.

28. See Christopher E. Goscha, *Vietnam or Indochina? Contesting Concepts of Space in Vietnamese Nationalism, 1887–1954* (Copenhagen: Nordic Institute of Asian Studies, 1995).

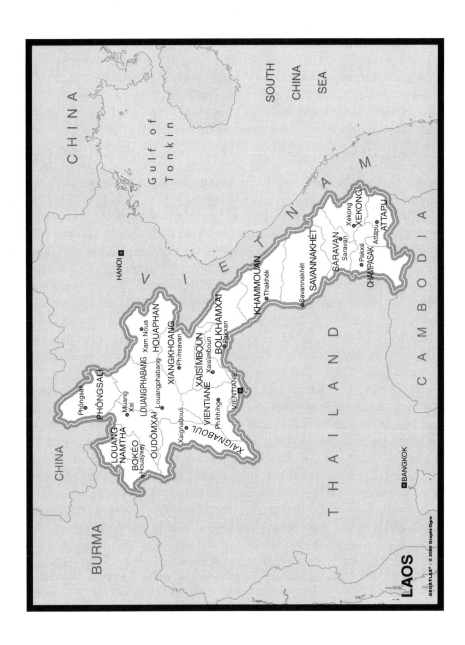

LAOS

GEOATLAS® · © 2000 Graphi-Ogre

The French who worked in Laos in this early period were acutely aware that dialects of Lao belonged to the same language family as the dominant language of Siam and were totally unrelated to Vietnamese. The missionary Marie Joseph Cuaz in his introduction to the first dictionary of Lao published in 1904 saw his "Lao-French dictionary as a 'mere supplement' to his French-Siamese dictionary published earlier."[29] Other French scholars working among the Lao even proposed that the much better established elite form of written Thai—one that would become the basis of the Thai national language—be used as the basis for a standardized Lao language.[30] This was rejected by others who, in the words of Georges Coedès, a member of the Ecole Française d'Extrême-Orient who would subsequently become the foremost Western scholar of both Indochina and Thailand, sought "to defend Laos against Siamese political influence."[31]

The foundations for standardized Lao were laid with the creation in 1917 of a commission charged with preparing textbooks in Laos.[32] Only in the 1930s, however, would significant attention be given to standardization of a literary Lao. The first major step in this effort occurred following the French creation in 1931 of the Buddhist Institute in Phnom Penh with a branch in Vientiane. The institute was intended to reorient Lao and Khmer away from Thai Buddhism. In Vientiane the institute sponsored the publication in 1935 of the first Lao grammar—one that the author, Maha Sila Viravong, a former monk who had been born in northeastern Thailand, based on the study of Buddhist texts in Lao.[33]

There was a fundamental problem, however, with the adoption of the standardized form of Lao as laid out by Maha Sila. Sila's standardization was closely linked to Lao Buddhism in its emphasis on retaining spellings and grammatical forms derived from Pali and Sanskrit, the sacred languages of Lao Buddhism. A Buddhist-based standardized language was not problematic in Thailand where at least 85 percent of the population early in the twentieth century followed one or another version of Theravada Buddhism. The situation was very different, however, in French Laos where more than half of the population were

---

29. Søren Ivarsson, "Bringing Laos Into Existence: Laos between Indochina and Siam, 1860–1945," Ph.D. dissertation, Copenhagen University, 1999, p. 87. Ivarsson is quoting from J. Cuaz, *Lexique Français-Laocien* [French-Laotian lexicon] (Hong Kong: Imprimerie de la Société des Missions étrangères, 1904), p. vi.

30. Ivarsson, "Bring Lao Into Existence," pp. 87–88.

31. Quoted in ibid., pp. 90–91.

32. Ibid., p. 88.

33. Ibid., p. 91.

neither adherents of Buddhism nor native speakers of languages related to Lao.

Those, mainly French officials, who opposed the use of the complex orthographic system and grammatical system first proposed by Maha Sila supported instead the adoption of a simplified system that is easier to learn for those who do not speak Lao dialects or follow Buddhism.[34] In 1938 the French colonial government appointed a commission charged with fixing "official Lao writing and orthography." The commission, in which the discussions were "intense," decided in 1939 to adopt for official purposes (including secular schooling) a simplified orthographic system based on representation of sounds rather than preservation of the spelling of borrowed Pali-Sanskrit words.[35] This decision did not, however, lay the matter to rest. The Maha Sila system was adopted for use in writing Buddhist texts in central and southern Laos, while Buddhist temple-monasteries in the province of Luang Prabang, the site of the royal capital, continued to use an orthographic system (Tua Tham, or dhammic writing) shared with Tai-speaking Buddhists in northern Thailand, southern Yunnan, and the Shan state of Kengtung. The persistence of different writing systems in Laos has continued to complicate national language policy to the present day.

The simplified Lao that was officially backed as the national language continued to compete with other writing systems. Moreover, it was not the language used for official purposes until after the country became independent in 1954. The colonial vision of a new Indochina, which lasted until World War II, endorsed the following linguistic hierarchy: French as the most prestigious language, Vietnamese second, and Lao a distant third.

The marginal place of officially recognized Lao is clearly indicated in educational statistics for the colonial period. Between 1917, when a colonial-sponsored system of primary education was begun, and 1939, few students were taught in government schools. In 1939 the number of students enrolled in government schools was only 6,700.[36] Buddhist

---

34. Viggo Brun has pointed out that the logic of those who opposed that "Buddhist"-based system of orthography was faulty. "A Hmong [or other non-Lao] person who would like to learn Lao would have almost the same problem learning Lao spelling whether it was spelled one way or the other." Personal communication, September 1, 2000.

35. Ibid., p. 92.

36. Frank M. LeBar, Gerald C. Hickey, and John K. Musgrave, comp., *Laos: Its People, Its Society, and Its Culture* (New Haven, Conn.: Human Relations Area Files, 1960), p. 80.

schools (which used the Buddhist system for Lao) educated many more students, but these "were regarded as notorious for poor attendance, low standards, and with low professional quality of the monks as educators."[37] The only secondary school prior to the end of World War II that used a curriculum in French, the Pavie Collège in Vientiane, enrolled few Lao students.[38] Moreover, it did not offer full secondary education until 1947. Only a handful of elite Lao went beyond secondary schooling to higher education, and those who did went primarily to Hanoi.[39]

Geoffrey Gunn has observed that "the stimulus to education in Lao, when it came, was in response to the emergence of Thai irredentist sentiments in the early 1940s."[40] After becoming prime minister of Thailand in 1939, Phibul Songgram promoted an ultranationalist agenda that aimed first at the recovery of territories that Thailand had "lost" to the European colonial powers. In 1941 the Thai undertook a military campaign against French colonial forces and succeeded, after the intervention of the Japanese, in reclaiming two right-bank enclaves that had been ceded to Laos in 1907. Flushed with this "victory," Phibul then launched a movement to unite all "Thai" peoples, intending to include the Lao.

The French colonial government, which operated after late 1941 under the overlordship of the Japanese, instituted a radical change in the administration of Laos to ensure that the people of Laos would see themselves as belonging to a nation distinct from the Thai. They began to promote the king of Luang Prabang as the king of all Lao, and they sought to inculcate in the populace a sense of national consciousness. This was pursued through a marked expansion of the school system in which a distinctive Lao history was taught and the 1939 standardized Lao language was used as the medium of instruction. Between 1939 and 1946, enrollments in government primary schools more than doubled, from 6,700 to 14,700.[41] According to Gunn, "The first schools for the minority population were established in this period, boarding schools and 'mobile' schools for the montagnards . . . opening in 1939–41, and the first government schools for Hmong . . . in 1940–42."[42]

---

37. Geoffrey Gunn, *Political Struggles in Laos (1930–1954): Vietnamese Communist Power and the Lao Struggle for National Independence* (Bangkok: Editions Duang Kamol, 1988), p. 32.

38. LeBar, Hickey, and Musgrave, *Laos*, p. 81.

39. Ibid., p. 80.

40. Gunn, *Political Struggles in Laos (1930–1954)*, p. 33.

41. LeBar, Hickey, and Musgrave, *Laos*, p. 80.

42. Gunn, *Political Struggles in Laos (1930–1954)*, p. 33.

World War II provided the crucible for the beginnings of Lao nationalism. As throughout Indochina, the Japanese initially ruled Laos through the existing French colonial apparatus. With Thai support, a "free Lao" (*Lao seri*) movement was created in 1944, "dedicated to getting rid not only of the Japanese, but also of the French."[43] In March 1945 the Japanese seized control of Indochina from the French colonial authorities and in April sponsored the establishment of an "independent" Lao government under the premiership of Prince Phetsarath, the leader of one nationalist group known as the "Lao Issara," a more formal term also meaning Free Lao.

Independent Laos had but a short existence because, after the Japanese surrender in September 1945, French forces regained control throughout Indochina. The small elite that shared a desire for an independent Laos were deeply divided. Some were strongly oriented toward Vietnam; this was a product both of a French colonial policy that had promoted the incorporation of Laos into a Vietnamese-dominated Indochina and of the recruitment efforts by the Vietnamese-dominated Indochinese Communist Party. Others looked to Thailand as the "elder sibling" of a Laos many of whose people shared a religious, cultural, and even political heritage with the Thai. A few were still loyal to the French.

The French intended to maintain a preeminent role in Laos even after the country was granted nominal independence in 1949. But French intentions met with abysmal failure in 1954 when the Viet Minh defeated the French forces at Dien Bien Phu, a military base in northwestern Vietnam that the French had set up to prevent Viet Minh advances into Laos.

By this time, the Lao elite were divided between two alternative visions of an independent Lao nation-state. On one side were the royalists who envisioned a country similar to Thailand and who received significant support from the Thai military. On the other were the communists, aligned with the Viet Minh, who sought to create a socialist state. The former succeeded in gaining recognition from the French, backed by the Americans, as the dominant element in the post-1954 government of the Kingdom of Laos. This government did not, however, exercise authority over northeastern Laos, where the sparse population comprised non-Lao peoples. This area was controlled by a Viet Minh–backed movement that called itself the "Pathet Lao" (literally, the Lao state).

When Laos became nominally independent in 1949, a royal decree was issued laying the basis for the writing of the national language.[44]

---

43. Martin Stuart-Fox, *A History of Laos* (Cambridge: Cambridge University Press, 1997), p. 57.

44. My information about this ordinance regarding the basis for writing standard

Royal Ordinance No. 10 decreed that words in standardized Lao should be spelled according to the way they sound rather than, as in Tua Tham or Thai, in a way that would show their etymology, especially derivation from Sanskrit or Pali. The functional (sound-based) system for writing Lao was resisted by Buddhist monks and by some laypeople who wanted the language to show the Indic origins of Lao words for religion, art, literature, and government.

In practice, the new standardized system was adopted only for official publications, including those of the Pathet Lao. In royalist areas, an older etymologically based system continued to be used for religious, literary, and some other texts. Language policy was not a pressing issue during the long war, between 1954 and 1975, when royalist forces backed by the Thai and Americans struggled for control of the country, with the Pathet Lao backed by the Vietnamese, Russians, and for a period the Chinese; a small neutral faction sought to mediate between the two sides.

Language Policy and Language Practice in Laos since 1975

In December 1975 the Lao People's Revolutionary Party—the Lao Communist Party—completed its takeover of the government of Laos by eliminating all noncommunist elements from what had been a coalition government and by abolishing the monarchy. This seizure of power prompted tens of thousands of people—mainly from the educated urban Lao and the rural Hmong who had fought against the communists—to flee the country. Approximately 10 percent of the population of this small country of slightly more than 3 million left Laos after 1975 to find homes elsewhere.

The population of Laos that remained under the control of the new government was extremely diverse. (See Table 6.4.) Officially the population was divided between lowland Lao (Lao Loum), hill Lao (Lao Theung), and upland Lao (Lao Soung). In practice, most people in the country related to each other with reference to premodern ethnolinguistic categories such as "Lao," "Lue," and other names for lowland Lao; "Kammu" and other names for hill Lao; and "Hmong" (still often called "Meo") and other names for upland Lao. Census data from 1985 show that ethnic Lao accounted for slightly more than half of the total popula-

Lao comes from the introduction to a Lao dictionary by Russell Marcus (*English-Lao Lao-English Dictionary*, rev. ed. [Rutland, Vt.: Charles E. Tuttle, 1983]) and from personal communication on April 8, 1991, from James Chamberlain, a linguist who has long worked on language issues in Laos.

Table 6.4. Ethnolinguistic Divisions in Laos.

Official Division	Language Family	Ethnic Groups	Percentage
Lao Loum			**53**
(lowland Lao)	Lao		43
		Lao	32
		Lao Phouan	3
		(Lao) Lue	8
	Tai	Tai Khao (White Tai); Tai Dam (Black Tai), Tai Dèng (Red Tai); and other (Yang, Meuiy, Yuan, Yi, Tai Neua, Long, Phong, and Pou Tai)	10
Lao Theung			**34**
(hill Lao)	Austroasiatic (Mon-Khmer)	Khamu (Kammu or Khmu) and other (Lamet, Makong, or Bru, Pounoi, Samtao, Laven, Nyaheun, and 31 other groups)	33
	Tibeto-Burman	Lahu (White Lahu, Black Lahu, and Lahu Bakeo)	<1
Lao Soung			**12**
(upland Lao)	Tibeto-Burman	Akha (11 subgroups)	1
	Miao-Yao	Hmong (White Hmong, Striped Hmong, and Blue [or Green] Hmong); Yao (Iu-Mien); and Lanten (lowland Yao)	11
Immigrant groups	Chinese (Cantonese and Yunnanese/Haw), Vietnamese, Indians, and Europeans		**1**
Total			**100**

SOURCE: Donald P. Whitaker, Helen A. Barth, Sylvan M. Berman, Judith M. Heimann, John E. MacDonald, and Kenneth W. Martindale, *Area Handbook for Laos,* Foreign Area Studies DA PAM 550-58 (Washington, D.C.: Superintendent of Documents, U.S. Government Printing Office, 1972).

tion.[45] The government that asserted control over the whole of the territory within the boundaries of Laos faced the daunting problem of promoting a shared national identity among the peoples of the country. Central to the effort to achieve this goal was the establishment of a national language.

After the founding of the Lao People's Democratic Republic in 1975, a national system of writing was instituted throughout the country. This system was the functional (sound-based) system adopted in 1949.

Lao as a national language is taught in schools throughout the country and is supposed to be learned by students no matter what language or dialect of Lao they speak at home or even if another language or dialect is spoken in the classroom. Although the school system has been very weak, it has still left most who pass through it "with general impressions . . . [that] are enough for them to clearly identify themselves as Lao."[46] The school system has not succeeded, however, in creating a sense of national unity that subsumes the ethnolinguistic diversity of Laos.

Lao as a written language in its national form has almost totally supplanted other written languages that were historically employed by various peoples in Laos. Few monks have a knowledge of Tua Tham, the system traditionally used for Buddhist texts. Of the other systems used for various Tai languages—for example, Lue (which is closely related to Tua Tham), Tai Dam, and Tai Neua—only Lue is taught in a few monasteries.[47] Romanized orthographies of several different non-Lao languages devised by missionaries have also all but disappeared because the communist-led government has continued the policy of the previous royalist government in refusing permission for texts to be produced

---

45. This figure is based on estimates of ethnic divisions of the country in the 1985 census obtained from the Committee for Social Science, Institute for Ethnology, Lao People's Democratic Republic.

46. Grant Evans, *The Politics of Ritual and Remembrance: Laos since 1975* (Chiang Mai, Thailand: Silkworm Books, 1998), p. 76.

47. In the Muang Sing District in northern Laos, I observed (on a field trip in April 1991) that Lue was being taught in all of the monasteries. I was told that nearly all boys in lowland villages in the district spend long enough time as novices to learn this system. On the other hand, I was also told by a Tai Dam researcher that few people in Laos today learn the written form of this language. He said that the only publications he knew of in the Tai Dam writing system were produced by refugees in the United States. Knowledge of the Tai Neua writing system, a system distinctive from any of the other Tai orthographies found in Laos, has always been limited to a few men in Tai Neua villages in northwestern Laos. I found in Muang Sing that a few older men still knew the system, but that younger men and boys were not learning it.

in these writing systems.[48] A unique writing system for Hmong developed by a messianic leader seems to have disappeared from use among Hmong in Laos,[49] although it continues to be used by some Hmong refugees.

Although spoken standard Lao has become a lingua franca for most people when interacting with peoples of different ethnic groups in Laos, it is only in Vientiane and surrounding areas of central Laos along the Mekong River that it has become the language of everyday use. At marketplaces in northern Laos, one hears a cacophony of languages and dialects; officials often communicate with other officials using a distinctive mother tongue rather than standard Lao;[50] and Lao-speaking people in the old royal capital of Luang Prabang take pride in their distinctive dialect.

In 1990 a national seminar was convened to reconsider language policy in Laos. The conference was attended by scholars, the minister of justice, a member of the Supreme National Assembly, officials of the ministries of education and sports and information and culture, and representatives of Buddhist organizations.[51] Those attending the seminar were asked to consider (1) the relationship between the official writing system and the literary and cultural heritage of the Lao people and (2) the relationship between Lao as a national language and the languages of non-Lao peoples. Although the seminar legitimated the value of religious and other cultural texts written in nonstandard Lao, it did not give serious attention to how non-Lao languages might be accorded greater value. The government in power in Laos since 1975 has thus made no real place for the languages spoken by nearly half the population.

Although Lao is the country's only "national" language, some foreign languages are officially sanctioned for use within Laos. French has not totally disappeared. It has been designated, together with English, as an official foreign language for use in transactions between Lao and for-

---

48. James Chamberlain reported that the ban on the use of missionary-developed romanized orthographies dates to 1967. Personal communication, April 8, 1991.

49. Smalley, Vang, and Yang, *Mother of Writing*.

50. I observed this among a group of officials traveling from Oudomsai to Luang Nam Tha in northern Laos. These officials, including a deputy governor, a provincial health officer, and a foreign ministry official returning for a holiday, all spoke Hmong (their mother tongue) rather than Lao except when talking with me and my Black Tai assistant.

51. I was able to obtain the papers presented at this conference and to discuss them with several participants while I was engaged in fieldwork in Laos in 1991.

eigners. The teaching of French in schools has increased significantly since the mid-1980s. English became popular when the United States was heavily involved in Laos in the 1960s and early 1970s. Although the use of English was not proscribed after 1975, it had a very limited role until the mid-1980s. Since then English has again become popular and is used for many official purposes. After 1975 Russian and Vietnamese became the most favored foreign languages, and both were taught in schools. Since the late 1980s, Vietnamese has dropped from favor, and interest in Russian declined precipitously after the Soviet Union began to downgrade its aid program in Laos in the late 1980s.[52]

Although officially disapproved, Thai is probably the most widely known foreign language in Laos. Publications in Thai were legally prohibited from being sold in Laos until the early 1990s, and since then only a few works have been legally sold. Many Thai-language publications are nonetheless in circulation in the country, and many employees of government agencies make use of technical manuals, research reports, and textbooks written in Thai. Thai television, which is watched widely throughout the areas bordering Thailand, has contributed to literacy in Thai.[53]

In Laos as in Vietnam,[54] the Communist Party sought to promote egalitarianism through proscription of sacred terms and substitution of "comrade" (*sahai*) for kin terms. In actuality, the term "comrade" became restricted primarily, if not exclusively, to those belonging to the party. Thus its use signaled a difference between those with power and those without. Since the late 1980s, there has been a marked decline in the use of "comrade" in Laos, although it remains a term used in official dis-

---

52. It is important to point out, however, that large numbers of Lao who today occupy most of the mid- and upper-mid levels of the government were trained in the Soviet Union, Vietnam, or Eastern Europe. For these people, Russian and Vietnamese continue to be important foreign languages.

53. Kongdeuane Mettavong, the head of the National Library of Laos, reported in an interview in April 1991 that her staff had discovered the role of Thai television in communicating literacy in Thai when they introduced a few Thai children's stories in portable library units taken to schools in Vientiane Province. When Lao children were shown these books, they not only could read them but could do so with a Thai accent. It was discovered that this was a direct result of exposure to Thai television. It is ironic that a medium typically seen as antithetical to literacy in the West has proven to be a tool of literacy in Laos. The extensive use of written texts on Thai television is a reflection of the high degree of literacy within Thailand itself.

54. See Hy Van Luong, "Discursive Practices and Power Structure: Person-Referring Forms and Sociopolitical Struggles in Colonial Vietnam," *American Ethnologist*, Vol. 15, No. 2 (1988), pp. 239–253.

course within party circles. In contrast to the decline of "socialist" language, there has been a significant reemergence in spoken Lao of terms indicating hierarchical relationships derived from Buddhist and royal language.

Although the socialist government of post-1975 Laos has had some progress in promoting Lao as a national language, it has commanded too few resources to give the language salience for many in the country. Laos has a poorly developed system of communications that makes it difficult for the government to assert a presence in many areas. In addition, the government lacks resources to ensure that education following an officially approved curriculum is implemented in many areas. Ironically, the communist-led government continues to use Buddhist monks as teachers because of the severe lack of trained secular teachers. The lack of resources also puts the government at a significant disadvantage in promoting Lao language in areas in the Mekong Valley where influences from the Thai side, especially in the form of television programs, are extremely strong.

In addition to these economic constraints, there is significant resistance among some minorities—especially Hmong—and even many ethnic Lao to the national language as promoted by the state. This resistance also finds support among refugees and descendants of refugees living outside of Laos. Young people from these overseas communities also demonstrate the value of knowing English or French.

Paradoxically, there is strong support for a Lao national language among some members of the cultural elite of Thailand. They see the maintenance of a distinct Lao literary tradition as key to promoting recognition for many of the other distinctive linguistic and literary heritages of the country and of Tai peoples more generally. Princess Sirindhorn, the popular daughter of King Bhumipol of Thailand, has taken leadership in promoting positive valuation by Thai of Lao.[55] Such interest from the Thai side points to the critical conclusion that language policy in Laos cannot be independent of influences from Thailand.

Conclusion

In the premodern world of the Siamese empire, Lao in various dialects was the most prevalent language spoken. Yet in the postcolonial world, Lao has not only been unequivocally subordinated to Thai in Thailand,

---

55. See Charles F. Keyes, "A Princess in a People's Republic: A New Phase in the Construction of the Lao Nation," in Andrew Turton, ed., *Civility and Savagery: Social Identity in Tai States* (Richmond, Surrey, U.K.: Curzon, 2000), pp. 206–226.

but it is still only tenuously the national language of the state that became Laos. The national language policy of Laos, therefore, can only be understood with reference to developments in Thailand.

The case of Thailand demonstrates that a strong country—in which a central government exercises a monopoly over education and controls all significant technologies of power—can over several generations impose a minority language as a national language on most of the populace of a country. At the same time, this policy's success has generated new tensions. The case of Laos, on the other hand, shows that a weak country with a diverse population can have difficulty promoting a dominant language as the national language.

I would like to conclude with some reflections on possible policy changes that would reduce linguistic tensions in both countries. The literary and cultural traditions associated with a national language do not constitute the totality of the "heritage" of any nation. If the linguistic and literary heritage of peoples living within a state are not given a space in a national heritage, they can feel alienated or marginalized. A strong state such as Thailand can afford to provide official support for at least the major linguistic and literary traditions of the country. This can be achieved in a number of ways, some of which are now being tried in Thailand.

Support can be provided for the conservation of alternative writing systems through academic study and other modes of valorization. This is being done in Thailand in a limited way for the rich literary tradition of northern Thailand through grants that support the preservation and study of traditional texts and through the teaching of the Yuan system of writing at a few academic institutions. Much less positive official attention, though, has been given to the Lao traditions of northeastern Thailand. There has been some support from Thailand, however, primarily from a small number of academics, for efforts in Laos to promote Lao linguistic and literary traditions. Nevertheless, much more could be done.

Related to this is the transliteration of works in other systems of writing using the orthography of the national language. Such works can be useful for promoting literacy in the national language because they can instill familiarity with a national writing system while giving people access to works in their own languages. Although some transliterations have been done in Thailand, there has never been an effort to standardize transliteration systems for any of the country's various languages.[56]

---

56. In this connection, see William A. Smalley, ed., *Phonemes and Orthography: Language Planning in Ten Minority Languages of Thailand*, Pacific Linguistics, Series C–No. 43 (Canberra, Australian Capital Territory: Department of Linguistics, Research School of Pacific Studies, Australian National University, 1976).

Literary works, including works of folk literature, in languages other than the national language can be translated or adapted and taught in schools along with the core texts of the national language. Some literary works from northern and northeastern Thailand have been translated into Thai, and there is precedent from experiments in the 1970s for production of supplementary school texts in Thai that use stories from the cultural traditions of minority peoples. I have seen texts prepared in this period for use among Malay-speaking Muslims in southern Thailand, tribal Karen in northern Thailand, and Khmer-speaking people in northeastern Thailand. Only the latter seems to have led to a continuing effort to bring local traditions into the national curriculum.

Bilingual education programs have been shown in other countries to be very effective in preparing students to move from home situations in which a language other than the national language is used to situations in which the national language is used exclusively. Bilingual education has never been officially approved in Thailand, and although some teachers have occasionally used local languages in instruction, this has always been ad hoc. Bilingual education would not threaten the preeminent position of the national language and could reinforce it by reducing conflicts between local and national languages.

English and Mandarin Chinese are special cases. Many of the Thai who are most successful in contributing to the economic growth of their country are fluent in English and/or Chinese as well as Thai. The long-standing prohibition against Thai citizens attending schools in which instruction is in other than Thai, except for foreign language classes, has been relaxed for some members of the elite who can afford to send their children to English-medium international schools. It would be extremely beneficial if this privilege could be extended to a larger percentage of the population.

Fundamental problems of infrastructure and politics overshadow language policy issues in Laos. Much more needs to be invested in government-sponsored education to increase both competence in standardized Lao and identification with the Lao nation. If more investment could be made, it would be strongly preferable to include bilingual education programs as basic components of the curriculum. This, however, is unlikely to happen. The government cannot obtain sufficient monies from tax revenues and, for political reasons, it is unwilling to seek more than modest amounts of foreign assistance for education.

If the Lao government would recognize officially that because there are strong connections between Lao and Thai national languages and that Thai has a unique place as a "foreign" language in Laos, it might be possible for the Lao government to promote improved technical education using Thai textbooks. This might also encourage the forging of alliances between Laos and groups in Thailand that are supportive of Laos being primarily responsible for the preservation of distinctive components of the heritage of Tai-speaking peoples.

Finally, the government in Laos needs to allow more dissent from rigid one-party control. Because the government is strongly resistant to opening the political system, members of the Hmong minority, Lao who retain an attachment to the former royal family, and others who advocate a more democratic system for Laos's multiethnic society have resorted to violence. Political violence in Laos has increased since the late 1990s.

At the outset of the twenty-first century, there is a growing recognition that the compelling drive to promote linguistic unity among peoples whose ancestors spoke, read, and wrote many different languages has had significant negative consequences as well as positive benefits. While Laos remains a country in which this drive has faltered because of serious infrastructural and political impediments, Thailand is one in which the drive has been highly successful. One would hope that, before much of the linguistic and literary heritage of the peoples of the country is relegated to memory at best, new efforts will be undertaken to ensure that some of this heritage can be preserved.

Chapter 7

Language Policy and Ethnic Relations in Vietnam

Thaveeporn Vasavakul

Language policy in Vietnam since independence in 1945 has been based on a two-pronged strategy of promotion and preservation. The policy of promotion has focused on the development of the Vietnamese language, the propagation of a romanized writing system (*quoc ngu*) for it, and the expansion of its social functions. The promotion of the Vietnamese language has been complemented by efforts to preserve the languages of major minority groups. Minority languages are said to be the cultural property of the entire nation, and the government has recognized the right of ethnic minorities to use their spoken and written languages. This acknowledgment has been translated into policies to develop romanized writing systems for many minority languages. By the end of the twentieth century, the Vietnamese language and its romanized script had developed from a patois into a national language. Chinese and French, both used extensively in the past as spoken and written languages, were relegated to the status of foreign languages. A hierarchy of languages emerged in Vietnam, with Vietnamese becoming the main medium of communication and major minority languages being used regionally.

This chapter examines the language policy of the Democratic Republic of Vietnam, or DRV (1945–76), and the Socialist Republic of Vietnam (1976–present). It contains four main sections. The first section focuses on the ethnic setting in Vietnam, outlining the ethnic composition and the historical and cultural positions of the country's major ethnic groups. The second section discusses the linguistic setting in Vietnam and the country's changing linguistic landscape prior to 1945. The third section focuses on the Vietnamese government's language policy from 1945 to the present. The final section evaluates the impact of language policies on ethnic relations in Vietnam and develops some policy recommendations.

I argue that bilingualism and multilingualism have long coexisted in Vietnam, especially among minorities. This can be attributed to intermingled settlement patterns as well as to the government's policy since 1945 to promote both the Vietnamese language and major minority languages.

The Ethnic Setting

Vietnam comprises fifty-four ethnic groups. In the 1990s the Viet, also known as the Kinh, made up the majority of the population, 86.8 percent, while the other fifty-three ethnic groups made up the remaining 13.2 percent.[1] This classification is based on the official academic definition of "ethnicity" as "a stable community, formed over a historical period and involving the relationship of identity in regard to language, habitat range, socioeconomic activities, and cultural characteristics—a community whose members are conscious of their shared ethnic identity, on the basis of the foregoing relations."[2]

Most of Vietnam's ethnic groups are small. Of the country's fifty-three ethnic minorities, only two groups, the Tay and the Thai, have more than 1 million people each. Ten ethnic groups have between 100,000 and 990,000 people. Twenty-two ethnic groups have between 10,000 and 99,000 people. Fourteen ethnic groups have between 1,000 and 9,900 people. Five ethnic groups have fewer than 1,000 people.[3] According to the 1994 census, the ten largest ethnic groups in Vietnam are, in descending order, the Tay, Thai, Muong, Hoa, Khmer, Nung, Hmong, Yao, Gia-rai, and E-de. The five smallest groups are the Si La, Pu Peo, Brau, Ro-man,

---

1.   Vietnamese ethnologists needed almost two decades to classify ethnic groups living in Vietnam. Dang Nghiem Van points out that it was Ho Chi Minh who first asked local authorities in northern mountainous provinces about the number of ethnic groups residing within their territories. Local authorities provided conflicting answers, relying on different sets of criteria in classifying ethnic groups. Research on the question began in 1958 but was not concluded until 1979. See Dang Nghiem Van, "Ethnic Identification in Vietnam: Principles and Process," in Dang Nghiem Van, *Ethnological and Religious Problems in Vietnam* (Hanoi: Social Sciences Publishing House, 1998), pp. 10–11.

2.   Ibid., p. 14.

3.   Khong Dien, "Ve van de chu viet cua cac dan toc thieu so" [Problems with writing systems for minorities], in Vien Ngon Ngu Hoc, ed., *Nhung van de chinh sach ngon ngu o Viet Nam* [Issues on language policy in Vietnam] (Hanoi: Khoa Hoc Xa Hoi, 1993), pp. 115–122.

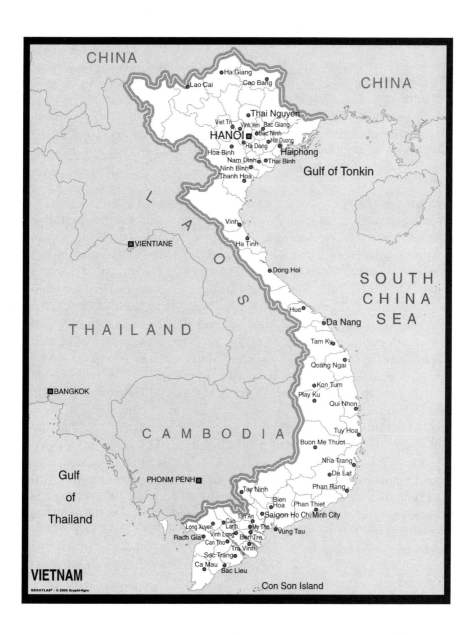

VIETNAM

and O-du.[4] (See Table 7.1.) The Ro-man are found only in a village in Sa Thay District, Kon Tum Province (in the central highlands), while the O-du consist of six families living in the village of Xop Pot in Kim Da Commune, Tuong Duong District, in Nghe An Province. They are considered to be ethnic groups by ethnologists because they have identified themselves as Ro-man and O-du and have maintained cultural traits that are distinct from those of other ethnic groups around them.[5]

Although this classification system is useful as a starting point, it only partially reflects the complexity of the ethnic landscape in Vietnam. To understand ethnic relations in this country, one must also consider the existence of local groups, the role of migration and demographic distribution, and the cultural dimensions of its many ethnic groups.

ETHNIC COMPOSITION: GROUPS AND LOCAL GROUPS

Within each ethnic group in Vietnam, there are small local groups (called *nhom dia phuong* in Vietnamese). The Tay, for example, consist of four local groups: the Ngan, Phen, Thu Lao, and Pa Di. The Thai are composed of the White Thai, Black Thai, Tay Muong, Tay Thanh, Tay Muoi, Phu Thay, Tho Da Bac, and Moc Chau Thai. The Chinese, or Hoa, are composed of nine local groups: Trieu Chau, Phuc Kien, Quang Dong, Quang Tay, Hai Nam, Xa Phang, Thoong, Nan, and He. The same is true even of very small ethnic groups. The Co Lao, for example, consist of White Co Lao, Green Co Lao, and Red Co Lao.[6] Vietnam's fifty-four main ethnic groups are composed of 195 distinct local groups.

The concept of "local groups" was developed by Vietnamese ethnologists when they attempted to classify the country's ethnic groups. First, they found that there were ethnic groups whose members spoke different but related languages. Second, they discovered very small groups that lived in isolation from larger communities with whom they shared common linguistic and cultural features. Third, they discovered groups that had migrated far from the original group and adopted cultural and linguistic practices derived from their new neighbors. A good example of the latter is the Thai groups in Nghe An Province that emigrated from the northwest of Vietnam in the fifteenth century. They lived with the Viet and Viet-Muong peoples in Nghe An and, in the process, transformed their speech patterns and some cultural practices. They were often

---

4. Dang Nghiem Van, Chu Thai Son, and Luu Hung, *Ethnic Minorities in Vietnam* (Hanoi: The Gioi, 2000), pp. 266–275.

5. Dang Nghiem Van, "Ethnic Identification in Vietnam," pp. 20–21.

6. *Vietnam: The Land and the People* (Hanoi: The Gioi, 2000), pp. 53–62; and Dang Nghiem Van, "Ethnic Identification in Vietnam," pp. 25–26.

Table 7.1. Ethnic Composition of Vietnam (as of 1994).

Ethnic Group	Population Size	Local Groups
Kinh (Viet)	55,900,000	—
Tay	1,190,000	4
Thai	1,040,000	8
Muong	914,000	2
Hoa	900,000	8
Khmer	895,000	6
Nung	705,000	11
Hmong	558,000	6
Yao	474,000	8
Gia-rai	242,000	3
E-de	195,000	23
Ba-na	137,000	5
San Chay	114,000	2
Cham	99,000	4
Xo-dang	97,000	6
San Diu	94,630	—
Hre	94,000	—
Co-ho	92,000	6
Ra-glai	72,000	2
Mnong	67,000	12
Tho	51,000	7
Xtieng	50,000	—
Kho-mu	43,000	1
Bru-Van Kieu	40,000	5
Giay	38,000	1
Co-tu	37,000	2
Gie Trieng	27,000	4
Ta-oi	26,000	2
Ma	25,000	3
Co	23,000	—
Cho-ro	15,000	—
Ha Nhi	12,500	4
Chu-ru	11,000	—
Xinh-mun	11,000	2
Lao	10,000	—
La Chi	8,000	—
Phu La	6,500	8
La Hu	5,400	4
Khang	4,000	7
Lu	3,700	—
Pa Then	3,700	2
Lo Lo	3,200	2
Chut	2,400	7

Table 7.1. (*continued*)

Ethnic Group	Population Size	Local Groups
Mang	2,300	2
Co Lao	1,500	3
Bo Y	1,450	2
La Ha	1,400	2
Cong	1,300	4
Ngai	1,200	5
Si La	600	—
Pu Peo	400	—
Brau	250	—
Ro-mam	250	—
O-du	100	—

SOURCE: *Vietnam: The Land and the People* (Hanoi: The Gioi, 2000), pp. 53–62.

classified as "Muong," when in fact they still considered themselves Thai. Thus the concept of the local group was introduced to refer to a group that is part of a given ethnicity and that possesses historical, linguistic, and cultural links with that parent group and has a clear consciousness of belonging to that parent group; yet it also has a distinct, discrete identity as a group, an identity that it seeks to maintain.[7]

DEMOGRAPHIC DISTRIBUTION AND SETTLEMENT PATTERNS

Ethnic groups in Vietnam are both indigenous and the product of migration. The mountainous areas of the north were the homelands of the ancestors of the Tay. The upper waters of the Red River and the Lo River and perhaps the northwest region were the land of the ancestors of the Kadai-speaking groups. The delta areas of north and north-central Vietnam were the homelands of the Viet-Muong. The central highlands were the homelands of the ancestors of the Mon-Khmer. Over the centuries, waves of immigrants traveled across these regions. Between the eleventh and twelfth centuries and the fourteenth and fifteenth centuries, the Thai who had lived in northwest Vietnam moved throughout the northwest, fundamentally transforming the demographic and ethnic composition of the area.

From the eleventh to the eighteenth centuries, the Viet in the Red River Delta began moving south and, in the process, took control of areas once occupied by the kingdoms of Champa and Cambodia. The Cham

7. Dang Nghiem Van, "Ethnic Identification in Vietnam," p. 26.

now live in the coastal provinces of south-central Vietnam, especially Binh Thuan and Ninh Thuan. They are also found in provinces west of the Mekong Delta, including An Giang, Dong Nai, Tay Ninh, and Ho Chi Minh City. Over the centuries Tay-Thai groups such as the Nung, Giay, San Chay, and Yao migrated to northern Vietnam in small waves—the Yao in the eleventh century and the Nung in the seventeenth and eighteenth centuries.[8] In the sixteenth and seventeenth centuries, Mon-Khmer groups from Laos (e.g., the Ta-oi, Ktu, Bru, and Jeh) left for the central highlands to escape Siamese intrusion into their traditional areas. Also around this time, the Ming Chinese migrated to Vietnam and were allowed to settle in the southern part of the country; the Chinese (Hoa) are now scattered in southern provinces in the Mekong Delta. In the eighteenth and nineteenth centuries, the Hmong migrated to north and north-central Vietnam to escape Chinese expansion.[9] In the mid-nineteenth century, the Khmu migrated to northwest Vietnam and the western part of Nghe An.

Multiple waves of cross-border and internal migration, combined with territorial rivalries and wars in border regions, led to the creation of a checkerboard settlement pattern. In Vietnam, the idea of a territory reserved exclusively for individual ethnic groups did not exist. As of 1945, ethnic minorities occupied around two-thirds of the territory of the country, with the Viet settled mainly in the plain areas along the coast.

The northeastern highlands, extending from the coast along the common border with China to the Red River, are the home of the Tay, Nung, Hmong, and Yao peoples, as well as other less numerous groups. The Tay, the country's most populous minority group, according to the 1994 census, comprise about 22 percent of North Vietnam's minority population and 1.6 percent of the country's total population. They live mainly in the provinces of Bac Can, Thai Nguyen, Ha Giang, Tuyen Quang, Cao Bang, and Lang Son, where they represent up to 70 percent of the total provincial population. The Nung live side by side with the Tay.

The northwest highlands, from the western bank of the Red River along the border with China to the common border with Laos, are the home of the Thai and the Muong. The Black Thai live in Son La Province, Dien Bien and Tuan Giao Districts in Lai Chau Province and some dis-

---

8. Le Si Giao, "A Glimpse of the Thai-Tay Speaking Groups in Vietnam," *Vietnamese Studies*, No. 4 (1999), pp. 21–31. Nguyen Van Loi of the Institute of Linguistics has argued, however, that the Nung Din were the first Nung to arrive in Vietnam between the eighth and tenth centuries. Interview with author, Hanoi, November 2000.

9. During the colonial period, they were called "Meo." The term "Hmong" gained general acceptance only in the 1980s.

tricts of Yen Bai Province. The White Thai live mainly in Lai Chau Province; Quynh Nhai, Bac Yen, and Phu Yen Districts of Son La Province; and Da Bac District of Hoa Binh. The Muong live in the area extending from Yen Bai Province to Thanh Hoa, but above all in Hoa Binh Province. The highland and midland regions of Thanh Hoa and Nghe An Provinces are home to 400,000 Thai inhabitants.[10] The Truong Son highlands, extending from Hoa Binh and Thanh Hoa Provinces south to the central highlands, are inhabited by many smaller ethnic groups. The central highlands, comprising the four provinces of Kontum, Gia Lai, Dac Lac, and Lam Dong and having a common border in the west with Laos and Cambodia, are inhabited mainly by the E-de, Ba-na, and Gia-rai peoples. After 1954, when Vietnam was divided in two, these three groups occupied more than 60 percent of South Vietnam's territory even though they made up less than 5 percent of its population.

POLITICAL AND CULTURAL DIMENSIONS OF ETHNIC RELATIONS IN VIETNAM
There are three sets of ethnic relations in Vietnam that deserve special attention: relations between the Viet and the outside world (especially the Chinese and the French, both of whom occupied Vietnam for long periods of time); relations between the Viet and Vietnam's ethnic minorities; and relations among the minorities themselves.

During the Chinese and French occupations, the Viet acculturated and assimilated many foreign attributes, including those involving religious practices, philosophy, language, and education as well as food and dress. These "foreign elements" were integrated into Viet ethnicity and helped to form the Viet national identity. Acculturation was far from the whole story, however. Colonialism also entailed ethnic conflict and even ethnic genocide. Many anticolonial activists in the early twentieth century believed that French colonialism sought to wipe out the Viet people.

During the dynastic period (from the tenth to the early nineteenth century), the Viet court ruled minority areas only indirectly. During the French occupation (1861–1945), the French granted limited autonomy to some minority groups, as they tried to co-opt minorities into the French colonial system. When the Ho Chi Minh government declared independence in 1945, some minority areas were still closely affiliated with the French. This historical context is one of the keys to understanding relations between the Viet and ethnic minorities in Vietnam. Many ethnic groups have histories and cultures distinct from those of the Viet. The

---

10.   Cam Cuong, "Thai Writing as Guarantee of Thai Culture in Vietnam," *Vietnamese Studies*, No. 4 (1999), pp. 32–42.

Thai, for example, are connected with groups in continental Southeast Asia, China, and India. At the same time, the Thai language contributed substantially to the formation of the Viet language. The Muong are descendants of a pre–Viet Muong community from which they split off to form a separate ethnic group around the first centuries of the Christian era. While the present-day Viet moved to the plains and were influenced by Chinese culture, the Muong lived in the mountains. Although they are close to the Viet in origin, they borrowed substantially from the Thai and are now close to the Thai in both social and cultural terms.

Although more research needs to be done on these kinds of ethnic relationships, one can argue that acculturation was encouraged because ethnic communities in Vietnam were intermingled. Many ethnic groups shared cultural traits with their neighbors, because of either cultural borrowing or the need to address common ecological problems. Studies show, however, that small ethnic groups were also willing to adopt the cultural practices of larger groups in order to survive. The smaller groups retained their identities by preserving ethnic myths involving group origins and migrations. In sum, both acculturation and resistance to assimilation have played out in ethnic relations in Vietnam over the long sweep of the country's history.

The Linguistic Setting

Given the country's moderate size, the number of languages spoken and written in Vietnam is large. Experts have placed the languages of the country's fifty-four main ethnic groups into five language families. (See Table 7.2.)

Until 1945, the linguistic landscape of Vietnam was a reflection of the country's complex political and cultural history. Both spoken languages and writing systems were influenced by China and India. Ethnic groups in the orbit of East Asian civilization, including the Viet and the Nung, used Chinese as a spoken language and Chinese characters as the basis for their writing systems. Groups in the orbit of India, including the Thai and Cham, used Sanskrit-based characters to form writing systems for their spoken languages. This situation changed during the French occupation, when the romanized system of writing was introduced to Vietnam. This represented nothing less than a cultural revolution: The abolition of writing systems based on Chinese- and Indian-influenced characters severed the Viet and the country's ethnic minorities from their pasts. Subsequent generations learned the "ancient" writing systems as second languages, and they often learned about their pasts only through translation.

Table 7.2. Language Families, Ethnic Groups, Population Size, and Writing Systems of Vietnam (as of 1994).

Language Family	Ethnic Group	Population Size	Writing System
Austroasiatic			
Viet-Muong Groups			
	Viet	55,900,000	*nom**; romanized
	Muong	914,000	different romanized systems
	Chut	2,400	none
	Tho	1,000	none
Mon-Khmer Groups			
	Khmer	895,000	Sanskrit-based
	Ba-na	137,000	romanized
	Xo-dang	97,000	romanized
	Hre	94,000	romanized
	Co-ho	92,000	romanized
	Mnong	67,000	romanized
	Xtieng	50,000	romanized
	Kho-mu	43,000	none
	Bru-Van Kieu	40,000	romanized
	Co Tu	37,000	romanized
	Gie Trieng	27,000	romanized
	Ta-oi	26,000	romanized
	Ma	25,000	romanized
	Co	23,000	romanized
	Cho-ro	15,000	romanized
	Xinh-mun	11,000	none
	Khang	4,000	none
	Mang	2,300	none
	Brau	250	none
	Ro-mam	250	none
	O-du	100	none
Thai-Kadai			
Thai Groups			
	Tay	1,190,000	*nom;* romanized
	Thai	1,040,000	ancient scripts; proposed romanized system
	San Chay	114,000	*nom*
	Giay	38,000	none
	Lao	10,000	Sanskrit-based
	Nung	5,000	*nom;* romanized
	Lu	3,700	none
	Bo Y	1,450	none

Table 7.2. (*continued*)

Language Family	Ethnic Group	Population Size	Writing System
Kadai Groups			
	La Chi	8,000	none
	Co Lao	1,500	none
	La Ha	1,400	none
	Pu Peo	400	none
Hmong-Yao			
	Hmong	558,000	romanized
	Yao	474,000	*nom;* different romanized systems
	Pa Then	3,700	none
Austronesian			
Malayo-Polynesian			
	Gia-rai	242,000	romanized
	E-de	195,000	romanized
	Cham	99,000	ancient scripts; different proposed romanized systems
	Ra-glai	72,000	romanized
	Chu-ru	11,000	romanized
Sino-Tibetan			
Sinitic Groups	Hoa	900,000	characters
	San Diu	94,630	none
	Ngai	1,200	none
Tibetan-Burman Groups			
	Ha Nhi	12,500	none
	Phu La	6,500	none
	La Hu	5,400	none
	Lo Lo	3,200	ancient scripts
	Cong	1,300	none
	Si La	600	none

SOURCE: Dang Nghiem Van, Chu Thai Son, and Luu Hung, *Ethnic Minorities in Vietnam* (Hanoi: The Gioi, 2000), pp. 266–275. Information on the writing systems comes from Nguyen Van Loi, "Ngon ngu, chu viet cac dan toc thieu so va chinh sach ngon ngu-dan toc o Viet Nam" [Languages and writing systems of minorities, language policy, and ethnic policy in Vietnam], Institute of Linguistics, National Center for Social Sciences and Humanities, Hanoi, May 2000, pp. 63–66.

*Nom is a writing system based on Chinese characters.

THE VIET AND THEIR LANGUAGES

The history of language use in Vietnam has gone through several distinct phases. (See Table 7.3.) During the first Chinese occupation (111 B.C.E. to 939 A.D.), the Viet spoke Vietnamese and Chinese and used one writing system, Chinese. After the Viet gained independence in the tenth century, Viet intellectuals spoke both Vietnamese and Chinese, and the court recorded its proceedings mostly in Chinese. Even major political and literary tracts, such as *Nam Quoc Son Ha* (Land of the Southern Kingdom, written in the eleventh century during the war with the Sung) and *Binh Ngo Dai Cao* (Proclamation of the Pacification of the Ngo, written in the fifteenth century after the victory over the Ming), were written in Chinese. This Sino-Vietnamese culture expanded southward and was incorporated into almost every aspect of the country's life.[11] The use of Chinese continued until the first part of the twentieth century and was sustained by the court's adoption of Confucianism as the state's ideology and the Confucian examination for civil servants.

The Viet, however, also tried to create their own mechanism for linguistic expression. In the thirteenth century, they developed a writing system, *nom*, which is based on Chinese characters. During the dynastic period, Vietnam thus had two languages—Vietnamese and Chinese—and two writing systems—ideographic Vietnamese (*nom*) and Chinese (Sino-Vietnamese).

In the mid-seventeenth century, Catholic missionaries introduced romanized script to Vietnam. Thus there were two languages—Vietnamese and Chinese—and three writing systems—*nom*, romanized Vietnamese (*quoc ngu*), and Chinese. During the French period, Vietnam had three languages—Vietnamese, Chinese, and French—and four writing systems—*nom*, *quoc ngu*, Chinese (Sino-Vietnamese), and French.

For the Vietnamese, the twentieth century was a major turning point in the country's language development. It marked the disappearance of classical spoken and written languages, both Chinese and *nom*, and the beginning of the emergence of *quoc ngu* as the main medium of communication. These two developments were linked closely with French colonial language policy. The French promotion of *quoc ngu* was driven by two considerations. The first was to train Vietnamese collaborators to help administer local affairs. The second motivation was the French desire to sever Vietnam's cultural connections with China and to bring Vietnam into France's cultural orbit. With this in mind, the French opened schools for interpreters and circulated newspapers written in romanized

---

11. For detailed information, see John De Francis, *Colonialism and Language Policy in Vietnam* (New York: Mouton de Gruyter, 1977).

Table 7.3. The History of Language Use in Vietnam.

Period	Language	Writing System
Proto-Vietnam (8th–9th centuries)	Vietnamese and Chinese	Chinese
Archaic Vietnam (10th–12th centuries)	Vietnamese and Chinese	Chinese
Ancient Vietnam (13th–16th centuries)	Vietnamese and Chinese	*nom* and Chinese
Middle Age Vietnam (17th–mid-19th centuries)	Vietnamese and Chinese	*nom*, Chinese, and *quoc ngu*
Contemporary Vietnam (French colonial rule, 1861–1945)	Vietnamese, Chinese, and French	*nom, quoc ngu*, Chinese, and French
Present-day Vietnam (since 1945)	Vietnamese	*quoc ngu*

SOURCE: Nguyen Tai Can, "Twelfth-Century History of the Vietnamese Language: Essay on the Delimitation of Periods," *Vietnamese Studies*, No. 3 (1999), p. 7.

script. They also abolished the old examination system, first in Cochin China and then in Tonkin in 1915 and in Annam in 1918. The French colonial government set up a Franco-Vietnamese school system in 1917, patterned after the French metropolitan school system. The French had no intention, however, of developing *quoc ngu* into an official language; they wanted it to function only as a bridge that would enable Vietnamese to study French. *Quoc ngu* was taught only in the first three years of primary school; thereafter French became the primary medium of instruction.

The development of *quoc ngu* took place in the context of the anticolonial struggle, and it spread primarily through the mass media and literary channels. Promoters of *quoc ngu* were Vietnamese intellectuals who were either collaborators or anticolonial revolutionaries. A turning point in the use of the Vietnamese language in the news media occurred with the publication of *Thanh Nien* (Youth), the mouthpiece of the Revolutionary Youth League founded by Nguyen Ai Quoc/Ho Chi Minh in 1926. Nguyen Ai Quoc hoped that, through reading and thinking about their plight, the people of Vietnam would unite in revolution.

Quoc ngu was further consolidated in the 1930s when it was used by a literary group known as the Tu Luc Van Doan (Self-Strengthening Literary Group). Writers belonging to this group used *quoc ngu* to pen popular short stories and novels. Also in the 1930s, Vietnamese intellectuals and activists began to propagate *quoc ngu* among the illiterate through the Association for the Propagation of Quoc Ngu.[12] In 1943 the Viet Minh, under the leadership of Ho Chi Minh, issued its Cultural Thesis, which also called for the teaching and study of Vietnamese romanized script.[13]

With the Japanese coup d'état of March 1945 came the founding of a Vietnamese-staffed government led by Tran Trong Kim. Hoang Xuan Han, the minister of education, launched a reform effort to transform the country's Franco-Vietnamese schools. One of his initiatives was to replace French with Vietnamese as the language of instruction at every level of schooling. Given that Vietnamese had never been seen as a major "academic" language in the education system, this new policy was an innovation. Although the use of Vietnamese in primary schools did not create any serious academic problems, its use in upper levels produced some difficulties, at least at first, because of the limitations of Vietnamese scientific vocabulary.

MINORITY LANGUAGES

There is no detailed work that provides a systematic overview of the spoken and written languages of ethnic minorities living in Vietnam. Available materials do indicate, however, that some minorities were able to maintain their spoken languages and continue to develop their writing systems.

The Nung writing system was based on Chinese characters and was widely used in the eighteenth and nineteenth centuries for literary writings, family records, land registration, and traditional medicine recipes. Its popularity diminished in the twentieth century. After 1945 it was estimated that only two to five people per village could read Nung. The ethnic Thai writing system in Vietnam was based on that of the Mon-Khmer and was used by the Thai starting in the eleventh century. The Thai recorded their history in two masterpieces, *Tay Pu Soc* and *Quam To Muong,* that have been preserved in Thai script. Chinese (Han) and Vietnamese (*nom*) ideograms never prevailed over Thai writing in the Thai-inhabited regions of Vietnam. The Cham and the Khmer developed their writing systems based on Sanskrit.

Some minorities were forced to mix with other groups and speak other languages. One example was the O-du, a small ethnic group that

12. Vu Huy Phuc, "Vai net ve phong trao thanh toan nan mu chu o Viet Nam" [Several features of anti-illiteracy campaigns in Vietnam], *Nghien Cuu Lich Su,* No. 30 (September 1961), pp. 33–42.

13. Hoang Trong Phien, "Tieng Viet tren duong phat trien" [Vietnamese in the process of development], 2000.

used Thai, Hmong, or Khmu in everyday conversation. The San Chay originally spoke Yao but abandoned it when they migrated to Vietnam and adopted the Choang language.[14]

In addition to advocating the romanization of Vietnamese, the French also pushed for the romanization of other languages in Vietnam. In 1924 they produced the *French-Nung-Chinese Dictionary*, the first book written in Nung romanized script. In the 1930s and 1940s, many Nung textbooks were published using the writing system adopted in the dictionary. The French also developed romanized writing systems for the E-de, Ba-na, and Gia-rai, and taught these systems in schools, together with French. They also embarked on romanizing the Thai written language, although this effort was poorly received.

THE LINGUISTIC SETTING AT INDEPENDENCE

By 1945 the linguistic landscape of Vietnam had changed in three fundamental ways. First, a number of alternative spoken languages and writing systems for the Viet coexisted. Second, romanized writing systems for Vietnamese and minority languages had been developed and promulgated. Third, French educational and language policies had broadened the cultural gap between the Viet and the country's ethnic minorities.

Prior to 1945 there was no isomorphism between ethnic identity and language in Vietnam. Bilingualism and multilingualism were widespread. This seemed to be the case among the Viet as well as among ethnic minorities. In some cases, the members of a single ethnic group spoke two languages. In other cases, the members of different ethnic groups spoke the same language. Finally, members of some ethnic groups had forgotten their ancestral languages but still considered themselves part of that ethnic heritage.[15] The ethnic picture in Vietnam was complicated because of cultural borrowing, intermingled settlement patterns, and economic ties. Ethnic relations were not always structured along linguistic lines.

Revolutionary Socialism and Language Policy, 1945–80

After independence in 1945, Vietnam began to move toward the adoption of one language (Vietnamese) and one writing system (*quoc ngu*) for the entire nation. At the same time, efforts were made to develop writing systems for prominent minority languages and to promote some minority languages as regional languages.

---

14. Dang Nghiem Van, "Ethnic Identification in Vietnam," p. 16.

15. Ibid., pp. 15–17.

The promotion of the Vietnamese language and *quoc ngu* occurred against the backdrop of the anticolonial struggle. The Democratic Republic of Vietnam, under the leadership of Ho Chi Minh, considered Vietnamese to be an important symbol of national identity and independence. The DRV's language policy was different from that adopted by the Republic of Vietnam, where the promotion of the Vietnamese language was much slower. In 1946 the leadership of the Republic of Vietnam extended the use of Vietnamese only to the last three years of primary education. At the same time, it designated French as the foreign language that would be taught if teachers were available. In 1948 the ministry of education declared that Vietnamese would be used at all levels of instruction; French would henceforth be considered as a second language. Instructors complained, however, that they could not teach mathematics and sciences in Vietnamese because there was no Vietnamese mathematical and scientific vocabulary. Not until the mid-1950s was a hierarchy of Vietnamese and foreign languages established in the Republic of Vietnam.

The DRV's move to develop writing systems for minorities was to some extent a continuation of the French colonial language policy. Another factor, however, was the political importance of minorities. Minorities in northern provinces assisted the League for Vietnam Independence (Viet Minh), a united front organization set up by Ho Chi Minh during the Japanese occupation and the war of resistance with France (1946–54). Prior to 1945 the Viet Minh were based in the northeastern mountainous areas inhabited by the Thay, Nung, and Yao. After war with France broke out, Ho Chi Minh's government moved its political headquarters to a minority-inhabited area north of Hanoi. In 1954 it waged a decisive battle at Dien Bien Phu, a Thai-inhabited area in the country's northwest. At the end of the war, the Vietnamese government established autonomous zones for Thai and Hmong ethnic groups in the northwestern part of the northern region and another zone for the Tay and Nung in the northern part of the same region. In these autonomous zones, minority leaders were allowed to handle their own affairs, including appointing local civil servants and raising militia forces. The Viet from the overpopulated provinces in the Red River Delta were moved into the midlands.

Minorities in the central highlands and the Truong Son mountain range were politically important in the 1950s and later. After Vietnam was partitioned, the central highlands and the Truong Son range became strategically important and therefore contested regions. In the late 1950s, thousands of members of southern mountainous groups went to the north for training before returning to their homelands. By the early 1960s, the North Vietnamese had succeeded in establishing regiments in the central highlands joined by minorities from the Hre, Gia-rai, E-de, and Ba-na ethnic groups. To counter the communist expansion, the government of Ngo Dinh Diem pursued a policy of assimilation, closing down minority schools where classes were taught in native dialects. In addition, the autonomous arrangements for the central highlands that had been set up by the French were replaced, and the regions were put under the direct jurisdiction of the Viet-controlled bureaucracy.

A communist document discovered by American advisers to the South Vietnamese government in 1963 suggested that the government in Hanoi was more respectful than Saigon of minority customs. The document described a number of policies that had been included in the North's Liberation Front program of 1960. It stated that every ethnic group had the right to maintain or change its customs and habits, use its language and script, and develop a culture of its own. Localities where ethnic minorities were concentrated were supposed to be allowed to form autonomous regions, "after the homeland has been liberated and the government has fallen into the people's hands."[16] The DRV's promotion of the romanization of minority scripts was also driven by the fact that U.S. officials had created writing systems for Bru, Hre, Mnong, Chru, Hroi, and Stieng, and had advocated bilingualism in the central highlands. The DRV was therefore pushed to adopt similar policies.[17]

The relationship between the Viet and ethnic minorities turned intermittently sour after 1975. Following the liberation of Saigon, the autonomous zones in North Vietnam were abolished. Between 1975 and 1979, the Socialist Republic of Vietnam imposed a socialist model of development on the entire country. This involved the nationalization of private enterprises in the south, including those owned by the Chinese. This in turn precipitated an exodus of Chinese entrepreneurs, technicians, and skilled workers, all of whom had played an important role in the economy. Problems also developed between the central government and the central highlanders. This period came to a temporary end in 1979, when the Sino-Vietnamese war broke out and minorities in northern mountainous areas were mobilized to fight the Chinese.

PROMOTING THE VIETNAMESE LANGUAGE AND ROMANIZED SCRIPT

After independence, *quoc ngu* became the main medium of communication in Vietnam. The postindependence period witnessed three major moves to spread the use of *quoc ngu:* an anti-illiteracy campaign, the de-

---

16.   Bernard Fall, *The Two Vietnams* (London: Pinter, 1967), p. 445.

17.   Hoang Tue, "53-CP" [Directive 53-CP], *Ngon Ngu*, No. 1 (1981), pp. 1–9.

velopment of a romanized script, and the expansion of its social functions. These moves were collectively carried out by linguistic, literary, and educational experts.

After taking power in the north in August 1945, the Ho Chi Minh government considered illiteracy to be one of the country's worst problems, the other two being famine and foreign aggression. It consequently launched a series of anti-illiteracy campaigns designed to instruct the population in using the romanized script. The campaign continued until 1958, when the government declared that full literacy had been achieved.

Another move was to develop the internal structure of *quoc ngu*. In 1968 the Institute of Linguistics was founded, and its researchers focused on maintaining the purity of the Vietnamese language. Emphasis was placed on the standardization of phonetics,vocabulary, and syntax. Vocabulary developed the most rapidly, as new terms were increasingly added to the lexicon. The institute's vocabulary list grew from around 40,000 terms in use in 1945 to 90,000 terms between 1970 and 1980. Some of these additions were political terms such as democracy (*dan chu*), republic (*cong hoa*), independence (*doc lap*), freedom (*tu do*), equality (*binh dang*), unity (*doan ket*), compatriot (*dong bao*), and comrade (*dong chi*). Another set of terms came from the military domain. A third set included terms associated with social and national relations.[18] Old words were redefined and given new meanings. The grammatical structure of *quoc ngu* became more diversified. After 1945 the complex Confucian/Chinese and Catholic styles of writing gradually disappeared, as a new, argumentative style of writing began to take hold. The social functions of *quoc ngu* were also expanded, and romanized script became increasingly popular in schools and universities.

The Vietnamese language is not monolithic; it consists of regional and local dialects and variations. Several waves of internal migration between 1945 and 1975 helped to dampen these linguistic differences. The first wave occurred during the war with France, when soldiers moved from northern to southern Vietnam, and urban inhabitants moved to rural areas to join the resistance. The second wave took place between 1954 and 1956, when the Geneva conference divided Vietnam into two zones. People moved from one zone to the other, with soldiers and students from the south heading north, and soldiers, officials, and Catholics from the north going south. The third wave occurred during the U.S. war period. In the 1960s and 1970s, soldiers from the north moved south along the Ho Chi Minh trail. During the American bombing period from 1965 to 1975, urban inhabitants were evacuated to rural areas. These waves of

---

18. Hoang Trong Phien, "Tieng Viet tren duong phat trien."

migration helped to propagate the northern dialect among southerners, leading to what one Vietnamese linguist called *pha tieng*, that is, a mixture of dialects. After Vietnam was reunified in 1975, the problem of regional dialects and local variations, although still significant, did not create any acute identity problems.[19]

ENCOURAGING WRITING SYSTEMS FOR MINORITY LANGUAGES

Vietnamese leaders made long-term efforts to promote minority languages and writing systems. Policy documents that reflect concerns over minority languages date back to the political thesis of the First National Party Congress of the Indochinese Communist Party in 1935, the Resolution of the Eighth Plenum of the Indochinese Communist Party in 1941, and the Cultural Thesis of 1943. The Resolution of the Eighth Plenum of the Party in 1941, for example, stated that the cultures and languages of ethnic-minority groups in Vietnam would be allowed to develop freely, be preserved, and be guaranteed. The DRV's 1960 constitution stated that every ethnic group had the right to maintain its customs and use its spoken language and script.

In 1959 the DRV government launched several minority-language projects, including the creation of writing systems for the Hmong and the Tay-Nung languages and the reform of the Sanskrit-based Thai script. Many revolutionaries, for example, had used the *quoc ngu* script to write Tay-Nung, especially when writing petitions and propaganda poems, publishing popular legends, and translating party documents and state decisions.[20] The project was completed in 1961. Also in 1961, the ancient Thai script was reformed.

The romanized and reformed minority writing systems were taught to primary-school students as part of a bilingual language program, and books were also published in these scripts. In Lao Cai, newspapers were printed in the Hmong writing system. In the northwestern region, newspapers were published in the reformed Sanskrit-based Thai script, and in the northeast newspapers appeared in the Tay-Nung script. In the Thai-Meo autonomous zone, primary-level textbooks were written in the Thai language and Thai writing system. Thai philology was made part of secondary-school syllabi in Thai-inhabited regions. During this period,

---

19.   Hoang Thi Chau, "50 nam nhap phuong ngu, tho ngu vao ngon ngu toan dan" [50 years of interpreting local dialects into the national language], *Ngon Ngu*, No. 3 (1995), pp. 8–11.

20.   Luong Ben, "Tinh hinh phat trien cua chu Tay-Nung" [The development of the Tay-Nung writing system], in Vien Ngon Ngu Hoc, *Nhung van de chinh sach ngon ngu o Viet Nam*, pp. 78–90.

linguists published a series of language books and dictionaries: Tay-Nung-Viet (1974), Viet Tay-Nung (1984), and Tay-Nung grammar (1971), as well as school textbooks in Tay-Nung (1963–78) and newspapers.[21]

These policies generated new questions, however. First, which languages should receive priority for romanization? Initially, attention was given to minorities with large populations, such as the Thai, and to those with potential political problems, such as the Hmong. The Yao and the Muong languages, for example, have yet to be romanized.

Second, should ancient scripts be reformed? This question involved the written languages of the Thai, Khmer, and Cham, where discrepancies between ancient and modern pronunciation were evident. Religious figures wanted to retain ancient pronunciation, while many intellectuals called for changes in the scripts to suit modern pronunciation. The government also found that it was difficult to print ancient scripts. Moreover, some languages were not unified. The Thai language, for example, contained local variations because the Thai were divided into different local groups and because they resided under different administrative jurisdictions. There was no consensus on how these local variations should be standardized.

Relatedly, should ancient scipts be romanized? Given the difficulties outlined above, many Vietnamese linguists wondered if ancient scripts even could be romanized, pointing to the fact that both the French and the Americans were unsuccessful in romanizing Cham and Thai scripts. One argument against romanization was that the Thai script was closely linked to Thai culture, and any attempt to romanize it would be inappropriate. One linguist suggested that the question of standardization should be left to the Thai themselves.[22]

Third, how should the internal structures of these languages be developed? The Tay-Nung writing system, for example, turned out to be impractical because it did not reflect local dialects. The Tay-Nung writing system project was predicated on the assumption that the two languages were close. It did not take into consideration, however, the phonetic and lexical particularities of local dialects. The writing system did not have enough diacritics to create tones that reflected common speech.[23] In the 1970s, when Tay-Nung writing was taught in the schools of Viet Bac,

---

21.   Mong Ky Slay, "The Nung Language and Tay-Nung Writing," *Vietnamese Studies*, No. 4 (1999), pp. 66–75.

22.   Cam Cuong, "Nguoi Thai nen hoc va su dung chu Thai nhu the nao o thoi dai ngay nay" [How should the Thai study and use the Thai script?], in Vien Ngon Ngu Hoc, *Nhung van de chinh sach ngon ngu o Viet Nam*, pp. 105–114.

23.   Luong Ben, "Tinh hinh phat trien cua chu Tay-Nung."

many local inhabitants thought that it was intended not for their groups but for groups in other regions. For example, the Nung in Lang Son thought that this writing system was more appropriate for the Tay in Bac Can, while the Tay thought that some of the sounds in the writing system were appropriate for the Nung only. Decades later, when Nung were asked if they had their own writing system, 61 percent answered "no," and only 25 percent answered "yes." When asked whether they thought a script for the Nung should be invented, 49 percent answered "yes" while 46 percent answered "no." Finally, when asked whether they wanted their children to learn the writing system of their ethnic group, some 50 percent of the respondents answered "yes," and 49 percent answered "no."[24]

Fourth, how should minority writing systems be taught? In the 1960s the script of every ethnic group in the DRV was taught in primary school. Local authorities in mountainous provinces in northern Vietnam developed programs for teaching minority writing systems. After Vietnam was reunified in 1975, this policy was applied nationwide. Implementation was uneven, however. As of the early 1990s, only a limited number of communes and districts in 13 of 201 provinces continued to teach minority scripts; every other province had abandoned the project.[25]

Why did this happen? It happened because minority writing systems facilitated the study of *quoc ngu* by ethnic-minority children for whom *quoc ngu* was not their first language. Indeed between 68 percent and 85 percent of primary-school students did not know *quoc ngu*; instructors thus had to rely on minority languages to teach it.[26] This bilingual approach had three consequences. First, the number of children from ethnic-minority schools decreased. According to one survey, only 4.8 percent of Khmer children, 5.6 percent of Hmong children, 6.5 percent of Yao children, and 10.5 percent of Mnong children attended school. Second, the number of students leaving school at an earlier age increased; this was especially true in isolated areas. In Ea Yong in Dac Lac Province, 86 percent of students left primary school. The result was higher adult illiteracy rates. Third, the number of minority students who had to repeat a grade increased; in one case, twenty-six out of twenty-eight students had to repeat their grade.[27]

24. Mong Ky Slay, "The Nung Language and Tay-Nung Writing."

25. Hoang Thi Chau, "Ve viec dat va dua chu viet cac dan toc thieu so vao doi song cu dan mien nui nuoc ta" [On the use of minority writing systems in daily life], in Vien Ngon Ngu Hoc, *Nhung van de chinh sach ngon ngu o Viet Nam*, pp. 91–101.

26. Luong Ben, "Tinh hinh phat trien cua chu Tay-Nung."

27. Nguyen Nhu Y, "Nhung van de chinh sach ngon ngu o Viet Nam" [Problems of

Who, then, should be taught minority-language writing systems, and who should teach them? Some linguists have suggested that adults should be the first to receive instruction, because they need this skill to help maintain their distinctive cultures. It has also been proposed that local cadres should learn minority writing systems so they can write speeches, prepare news bulletins, and record popular culture. Some have suggested that scripts be taught in literacy classes and other adult-education courses. Scripts should be taught to children in secondary school or as upper-level subjects only after they have learned *quoc ngu*. Adults who have learned these scripts are more likely to encourage their children to follow their lead.[28]

Fifth, what social function should minority languages serve? Linguists have suggested that the teaching of ethnic-minority languages and writing systems should continue beyond primary-school level; they should also be used in daily affairs.[29]

These issues continued to receive attention from policymakers and linguists in Vietnam well into the 1980s and 1990s. From 1980 on, however, changing socioeconomic and demographic conditions in minority-inhabited areas generated new issues related to language and identity.

Internal Migration, Economic Development, and Language Policy, 1980–Present

After the war with the United States ended in 1975, minority-dominated areas began to receive more attention in the Vietnamese government's development schemes. The state created new economic zones, moving the Viet (Kinh) from the overcrowded lowlands to the uplands, for example. Most of the increase in the population of the highlands reflected migration by the Viet from overpopulated areas in the deltas. In 1989 the Viet population in the central highland's increased from 5 percent in 1940 to about 66 percent of the total population. In the mountainous provinces of the north, the number of Viet more than tripled, from 640,000 to 2.1 mil-

---

language policy in Vietnam], in Vien Ngon Ngu Hoc, *Nhung van de chinh sach ngon ngu o Viet Nam*, pp. 25–54.

28. Hoang Thi Chau,"Ve viec dat va dua chu viet cac dan toc thieu so vao doi song cu dan mien nui nuoc ta"; and Cam Cuong, "Nguoi Thai nen hoc va su dung chu Thai nhu the nao o thoi dai ngay nay."

29. Nguyen Nhu Y, "Nhung van de chinh sach ngon ngu o Viet Nam"; and Hoang Thi Chau, "Ve viec dat va dua chu viet cac dan toc thieu so vao doi song cu dan mien nui nuoc ta."

lion between 1960 and 1979. By the time of the 1989 census, Viet numbers in these areas had increased 19.3 percent to 2.5 million people.

The number of ethnically mixed communities in minority-inhabited areas grew throughout the country. According to a 1979 survey, 20 of 107 districts in the northern mountainous areas included more than ten ethnic groups living side by side. Only 2.8 percent of communes were composed of a single ethnic group. Most were home to three to four ethnic groups. According to a 1989 survey of Dac Lac Province, only 19 of 177 communes, or 10.7 percent, consisted of a single ethnic group; the remainder had between two and thirteen groups living next to one another. About 50 percent of communes surveyed contained three to five ethnic groups. Most of those surveyed in the central highlands had Viet residents. In Dac Lac Province, 71 percent of the population was Viet; only 2 communes did not have Viet residents.[30]

The rise of ethnically mixed communes necessitated changes in Vietnam's language policy. One major development in this vein was the 1980 Decision 53-CP, which mandated that Vietnamese would be the common language for every ethnic group in the country. It endorsed bilingualism but called for improved proficiency in both Vietnamese and ethnic languages. Decision 53-CP also declared that efforts to teach the Vietnamese language and to continue the romanization of ethnic languages would be expanded; languages with ancient scripts (e.g., Cham, Thai, and Khmer) would be part of this endeavor. The study of Vietnamese was to be compulsory, but the romanization of ancient scripts and spoken languages was voluntary.[31]

Decision 53-CP generated new policy issues and revived old ones. One issue concerned bilingulism generally and involved two different approaches. The first was to encourage the use of Vietnamese as a common language. According to this view, every ethnic group in Vietnam had the right and responsibility to study the Vietnamese language. Moreover, Vietnamese belonged to the large Mon-Khmer family and thus had a close affiliation with at least twenty-three other Mon-Khmer languages found in Vietnam. A second approach urged the use of different common languages for different regions, with the language of the dominant ethnic group becoming the regional language for the area. A second issue involved the romanization of ethnic spoken languages, and a third focused

30. Khong Dien, "Ve van de chu viet cua cac dan toc thieu so"; and Nguyen Van Loi, "Vi the cua tieng Viet o nuoc ta hien nay" [The position of the Vietnamese language], *Ngon Ngu*, No. 4 (1995), pp. 7–14.

31. Hoang Tue, "53-CP."

on where and how individual minority languages could be taught, given the growth of ethnically mixed student bodies.

BILINGUALISM AND LANGUAGE HIERARCHY

Members of ethnic minorities in Vietnam have traditionally been bilingual. They spoke their own languages as well as Vietnamese, the latter being considered of secondary importance. Proficiency in Vietnamese varied from area to area. The Thai in the northwestern region, for example, spoke better Vietnamese than the Hmong, Khmu, and Xinh Mun living in the same area. The Cham in the south-central province of Thuan Hai spoke better Vietnamese than the Thai in the northern provinces.

Decision 53-CP called for the transformation of "natural bilingualism" (*song ngu tu nhien*) into "literary bilingualism" (*song ngu van hoc*).[32] The Viet-minority bilingual language program was not a realistic option, however, for some minorities because Vietnamese was not the only language available as a medium for regional communication. The patterns of the use of various spoken languages and the popularity of a given language were determined by geographical location as well as settlement patterns. Minority groups living in town centers tended to speak Vietnamese and their own ethnic languages, while those living in remote or rural areas tended to use "regional ethnic languages" (*vung ngon ngu dan toc*): Tay-Nung in the northeastern highlands; Thai and Hmong in the northwestern highlands; Muong in Hoa Binh and the western parts of Thanh Hoa; and Nghe An, Ede, and Bana in the central highlands, and Cham in south-central Vietnam. In practice, minorities in many areas had to use three languages. Those who spoke Vietnamese would continue to do so, but they also had to use the regional ethnic language. Those who spoke a regional ethnic language had to study Vietnamese and their own ethnic language. Those who spoke only their own language and resided in remote areas had to study Vietnamese.[33]

The appropriateness of pairing languages in a bilingual language program was a concern for linguists in Vietnam. One classification cast languages into mother tongue (*tieng me de*) and non–mother tongue (*khong phai tieng me de*) categories. The latter did not include "foreign lan-

---

32. "Natural bilingualism" refers to the use of two languages as a result of local settlement patterns. "Literary bilingualism" refers to the study of two languages in school and the ability to use them in written communication.

33. Nguyen Huu Hai, "Mot so quan diem co ban trong chinh sach ngon ngu doi voi cac dan toc thieu so" [Some basic concepts in the language policy toward minorities], in Vien Ngon Ngu Hoc, *Nhung van de chinh sach ngon ngu o Viet Nam*, pp. 135–140.

guages" (*tieng nuoc ngoai*). The Thai, for example, considered the Thai language their mother tongue and those of other nations foreign languages. They considered Tay, spoken by inhabitants of the neighboring region, and Vietnamese to be non–mother tongue languages. They occasionally referred to Hmong, spoken by their neighbors, as their second mother tongue. A question remained as to which should become the second (or third) language of a minority people. One survey showed that members of the Hmong at Co Ma Commune, in the Thuan Chau District of Son La Province, spoke Hmong (which was their mother tongue) as well as Thai (which was both their neighboring language) and the regional ethnic language. They did not speak Vietnamese.[34]

Finally, many linguists questioned the utility of basing language policy on *vung* or "region," because regions have been defined differently throughout Vietnamese history. Regions could be based on geographical features, centering around mountainous and plains areas. Mountainous areas could themselves be divided into lowlands, midlands, and highlands. Regions could also be classified according to sociocultural features: northeastern mountainous region, northwestern mountainous region, northern midland region, northern deltaic region, Truong Son region, central highlands, southern coastal area of Central Vietnam, Mekong Delta, and so on.[35]

ROMANIZATION OF MINORITY LANGUAGES

Another element of the policy promulgated by Decision 53-CP, the romanization of minority languages, raised three questions. First, on what basis should minority scripts be romanized? To date, linguists have used the *quoc ngu* system of writing as the basis for creating minority scripts. Second, should dialects be standardized, and if so, how? Third, should individual languages be romanized or languages belonging to the same language family? For example, the Tay and the Nung are two separate ethnic groups, but they were given the same romanized script system. Linguists justified this move on the grounds that the two languages came from the same language family. In the long run, this would lead to the merger of minority languages, which would result in the abandon-

---

34. Nhu Y, "Suy nghi ve viec day tieng Viet trong chuong trinh thanh toan mu chu cho dong bao thieu so lon tuoi" [Reflection of the teaching of Vietnamese in the anti-illiteracy program for minority adults], *Ngon Ngu*, No. 4 (1991), pp. 27–44.

35. Chu Thai Son, "Tu hien tuong da ngu trong vung xen cu va tieng noi pho bien trong tung khu vuc cua nuoc ta" [From multilingualism in interspersed areas to monolingualism in a region in our country], in Vien Ngon Ngu Hoc, *Nhung van de chinh sach ngon ngu o Viet Nam*, pp. 244–247.

ment of languages spoken by ethnic groups with small populations. Many linguists worried about this, believing that there was an urgent need to preserve the languages of smaller ethnic groups.

It is important to note that the adoption of new languages has been a common practice in Vietnam. For example, as a result of migration and contact with other ethnic groups, the Yao switched to Choang and were later called the Cao Lan or Han Quang Dong people. Similarly, the Tong (Giong Dong Thai) abandoned Tay-Thai to speak Yao. Today the Co Lao and the Tu Di speak Quan Hoa. The Co Lao language is found only in ritual documents that the Co Lao themselves cannot understand. The traditional languages spoken by smaller minority groups were crucial, however, in sociolinguistic terms because they served as links between the major language families. Examples of these languages include La Ha, Pu Peo, Co Lao, and La Chi (known as the Kadai group, which played a role in the development of the Austro-Thai language family).[36]

TEACHING AND LEARNING

Decision 53-CP created difficulties for overburdened primary-school children who had to learn Vietnamese as well as minority scripts. In the 1981–82 academic year, for example, schools in Dac Lac Province instituted an Ede-Vietnamese bilingual program. The program faltered, however, because students found it difficult to study two languages at the same time.[37] Linguists voiced their disapproval, arguing that it was impractical for minority children to study two languages at such an earlier age. They also pointed out that parents wanted their children to study Vietnamese because minority languages were not used outside of school, and thus learning them was not a productive use of their time. Linguists argued that to promote minority languages, the government should target adults first, because they had a cultural need to learn their own language and because they would be the main agents in mobilizing their children to continue the study of minority languages. They also argued that linguistic freedom should not be limited to the educational realm but should be applied more widely—that is, in the mass media, the courts, and local administration. Yet they warned that not all minority languages were suitable for such functions.[38] The government's emphasis

---

36. Pham Duc Duong, "Doi moi tu duy, tim nhung bien phap huu hieu nham phat trien ngon ngu cac dan toc."

37. Y San Enuol, "Tinh Dac Lac va ngon ngu dan toc thieu so ban dia" [Dac Lac and local languages], in Vien Ngon Ngu Hoc, *Nhung van de chinh sach ngon ngu o Viet Nam*, pp. 307–310.

38. Nguyen Nhu Y, "Nhung van de chinh sach ngon ngu o Viet Nam."

on teaching minority languages in school has nevertheless continued. The Education Law of 1991 stated that ethnic minorities have the right to use their spoken and written languages concurrently with the Vietnamese language in order to study at the primary level.[39]

Conclusion

Over the course of the twentieth century, Vietnamese was transformed from a secondary and underdeveloped language into a national language. It has been used as the language of the state apparatus, as a medium for instruction from primary school through university, and as the common language for social and cultural interaction. The twentieth century also witnessed the development of writing systems for Vietnam's ethnic minorities. Of the country's fifty-four main ethnic groups, twenty-six now have written systems. Most of these groups live in southern Vietnam and have benefited from the French, American, and Vietnamese attempts at romanization. These ethnic groups include the Bana, Gia Rai, Ko Ho, Bru, Hre, Mnong, Chu Ru, Gia Lai, Xo Dang, Pa Co, Xtieng, and Cham. Of the thirty-one groups living in northern Vietnam, five—Kinh (Viet), Tay, Thai, Nung, and Hmong—have romanized scripts.[40]

The Vietnamese government has recognized the desires of ethnic groups to use, maintain, and develop their languages. For ethnic minorities, linguistic interaction is allowed in the family, at local schools, and in local communities. Some minority languages are used in the government and local media. In the future, the social functions of minority languages should be expanded to include their use in all primary schools, beyond the local community (e.g., in the workplace), by speakers of the majority language, and in secondary and higher education. This will require action from educators, the mass media, and many others.

More effort is also needed to preserve and promote endangered minority languages. The government's current preservation policy has several shortcomings. First, its classification systems lump different ethnic groups together. For example, the Cao Lan and the San Chi in the northern mountainous provinces have been combined to form the "San Chay." The Gie and Trieng in the central highlands have been grouped as the "Gie Trieng," while the Bru and the Van Kieu in the west of Quang Tri

---

39.   Hoang Van Hanh, "May van de ve giao duc ngon ngu va phat trien van hoa o vung dong bao cac dan toc thieu so cua Viet Nam hien nay" [Several problems on language education and the development of culture in minority areas], *Ngon Ngu*, No. 3 (1994), pp. 1–7.

40.   Nguyen Nhu Y, "Nhung van de chinh sach ngon ngu o Viet Nam."

have become Bru-Van Kieu. Not only has this blurred the identity of some ethnic groups, but it has resulted in some minority languages being neglected or lost entirely.

Vietnam's overarching problem is that the government and many of the country's people do not sufficiently appreciate that minority languages are irreplaceable manifestations of and vehicles for ethnic identity. Minority-language preservation is necessary, but it is not enough: Active promotion of minority languages is needed as well. As Gerald Diffloth has observed, if efforts are not made to promote minority languages, preservation will only slow the degradation of dying languages.[41]

---

41. See Gerard Diffloth, "The Linguistic Treasure of Vietnam," *Vietnamese Studies*, No. 2 (1994), pp. 52–53.

Chapter 8

The Politics of Language Policies in Malaysia and Singapore

Šumit Ganguly

Malaysia and Singapore, though they emerged from a common British colonial tradition, have pursued markedly divergent language policies that have generated significantly different social, political, and economic consequences. In both cases, the politics of language policies have been inextricably linked with the processes of nation building. The pathways to nation building in Malaysia and Singapore, however, were fundamentally different and embodied notably divergent conceptions of nationalism and citizenship. From its emergence as an independent entity following British colonial withdrawal in 1957, Malaysia adopted a vision of ethnic nationalism that enshrined Malay privileges. Singapore, following its split from Malaysia in 1965, professed a commitment to a vision of civic nationalism and accepted, at least in principle, the concept of a multiracial society.[1] These different conceptions, along with political leadership, structural constraints, and the imperatives of economic development, led Malaysia and Singapore to pursue different sets of language policies.

The next section offers ethnolinguistic profiles of Malaysia and Singapore. This is followed by discussions of the language policies of both countries. The conclusion suggests possibilities for improving these policies.

---

1. For a discussion of the different conceptions of ethnic and civic nationalism, see Jack L. Snyder, *From Voting to Violence: Democratization and Nationalist Conflict* (New York: W.W. Norton, 2000). For discussions of the divergent conceptions of nationalism in Malaysia and Singapore, see C.M. Turnbull, *A History of Singapore, 1819–1988*, 2d ed. (Singapore: Oxford University Press, 1989); and William R. Roff, *The Origins of Malay Nationalism*, 2d ed. (Kuala Lumpur: Oxford University Press, 1994).

The Ethnolinguistic Profiles of Malaysia and Singapore

Three major ethnolinguistic groups exist in Malaysia: Malay, Chinese, and Indian. The Malays constitute 60.6 percent of the population, the Chinese 28.1 percent, and the Indians 7.9 percent.[2] The indigenous tribal peoples, referred to as the "Orang Asli," constitute approximately 0.7 percent of the population, and other ethnic groups comprise the remaining 2.7 percent.[3] Important linguistic subgroups exist within the Chinese and Indian communities. The Chinese speak a variety of dialects, whereas Tamil predominates among the Indians. Bahasa Malaysia is the official language of Malaysia.

Singapore is composed of the same major ethnic groups found in Malaysia, though the proportions differ in significant ways. Chinese constitute 76.9 percent of the city-state's population, Malays make up 14 percent, and Indians amount to 7.7 percent. Other ethnic groups comprise the remaining 1.4 percent.[4] The official languages of Singapore are Malay, Chinese (Mandarin), Tamil, and English. Malay is considered the national language, and English is the language of administration. Under governmental pressure since 1979, the Chinese in Singapore have increased their use of Mandarin in place of other Chinese dialects.[5] The Indian community is composed predominantly of Tamil speakers. Segments of this community also speak Malayalam, Punjabi, Telegu, Hindi, and Bengali.

The Politics of Language in Malaysia

Since independence in 1957, language policies in Malaysia have been closely tied to questions of race, ethnicity, and citizenship. In the postindependence era, ascriptive beliefs about race and ethnicity have influenced political choices pertaining to the adoption of language policies.

THE PRIVILEGING OF MALAYS IN THE TRANSFER OF POWER
In the aftermath of World War II, when the British retook Malaya following the defeat of the Japanese in Southeast Asia, a number of Malay

---

2. Department of Statistics, Malaysia, *Census Atlas* (Kuala Lumpur: Department of Statistics, 1996), pp. 16–17.

3. Gordon P. Means, "The Orang Asli: Aboriginal Policies in Malaysia," *Pacific Affairs*, Vol. 58, No. 4 (Winter 1985–1986), pp. 637–652.

4. For these figures, go to http://www.singstat.gov.sg/FACT/SIF/sif3.html.

5. Six major dialects were spoken in Singapore: Cantonese, Foochow, Hainanese, Hakka, Hokkien, and Teochiu. Henceforth "Chinese" when used in the Singaporean context refers to all of these Chinese dialects.

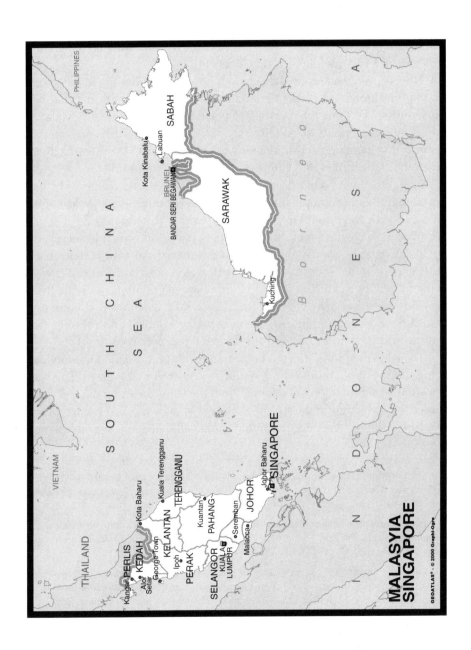

MALAYSIA
SINGAPORE

nationalist groups emerged within the country.[6] These nationalist forces coalesced in the formation of the United Malays National Organization (UMNO) on May 11, 1946. The founder of UMNO was the chief minister of Johore, Dato Onn bin Ja'afar. Despite the explicitly racial basis of UMNO, Dato Onn seemed open to the idea of a multiracial state constructed on the principle of civic citizenship.

His position was not widely shared, however, within the Malay community or among the Malay nationalist elite.[7] The latter argued that because of the economically privileged position of the Chinese in Malaya, the granting of political equality to every ethnic group would significantly disadvantage the Malays in their own land. They feared that, given the opportunity, the Chinese and Indian communities would seek to subjugate them.[8] Significant portions of the Malay community believed that the immigrant Chinese and Indian communities should not be on a par with them following the end of British colonial rule.[9]

Instead of creating a multiracial society based on principles of equality, Malay nationalists sought to cement the special status of Malays in an independent state. They made it clear that as a new political order was being forged, two principles would guide their negotiations with the British and the other two communities. First, Malay cultural dominance would have to be guaranteed. Second, Malay political control over the state would have to be assured for an extended period of time.[10]

The leaders of the Chinese and Indian communities failed to mobilize spirited opposition to this ethnic vision of a postcolonial Malaya. The reasons for this failure were intriguing. First, the Chinese leadership was absorbed in intracommunal struggles, some of which were taking place along class lines.[11] Second, the Indian political leadership was to a large

---

6.   For the standard treatment, see Barbara Watson Andaya and Leonard Y. Andaya, *A History of Malaysia* (London: Macmillan, 1982). The country's name was changed from Malaya to Malaysia by constitutional amendment in 1963.

7.   For a perceptive discussion, see Karl von Vorys, *Democracy without Consensus: Communalism and Political Stability in Malaysia* (Kuala Lumpur: Oxford University Press, 1976), p. 67.

8.   Later the prominent Malay politician and current prime minister of Malaysia, Mahathir bin Mohammed, would echo these sentiments with considerable force in a polemical tract. See Mahathir bin Mohammed, *The Malay Dilemma* (Kuala Lumpur: Federal Publications, 1982).

9.   Much of the Malay attentive public still shares this sentiment. Interview with a senior Malay historian, University of Malaya, Kuala Lumpur, Malaysia, May 17, 2000.

10.   Von Vorys, *Democracy without Consensus*, p. 73.

11.   For a detailed discussion of the divisions within the Chinese and Indian commu-

extent preoccupied with the momentous political changes occurring with British colonial withdrawal from the Indian subcontinent. These distractions created the permissive conditions for the Malay nationalists to negotiate favorable terms for the transfer of political power with the departing British.

The negotiations for the end of British colonial rule in Malaya were vested in a working committee formed in August 1946 and composed of Malays drawn from UMNO and English representatives of the governor-general, Sir Malcolm MacDonald. By July 1947 the committee had published its recommendations. Significantly, it held out the prospect of citizenship for non-Malays but also called for explicit recognition and protection of the special position and rights of Malays.[12] This argument was made on the grounds that the Malays constituted the original inhabitants of the region and that the Chinese and Indian communities had hailed from other parts of Asia. As the report stated, "The Malays live in a country in which they, owing to the influx of *foreign immigrants*, are already numerically inferior. It is important to emphasize that the Malays have no alternative homeland, while the remainder of the population, with few exceptions, retain in varying degrees a connection with their country of origin, and *in a very many cases* regard that country and not Malaya as the primary object of *their* loyalty and affection."[13] The report went on to define the characteristics that would enable one to be considered a Malay. Three criteria were deemed essential: The individual had to be a habitual speaker of Bahasa Malaysia, belong to the Islamic faith, and adhere to Malay customs.[14]

The outbreak of an insurgency led by the Chinese-dominated Malayan Communist Party in 1948 impeded the end of colonial rule.[15] In response, the British declared a state of emergency. Under its provisions, most fundamental rights were suspended, allowing the colonial adminis-

nities, see Timothy Norman Harper, *The End of Empire and the Making of Malaya* (Cambridge: Cambridge University Press, 1999), pp. 88–93.

12. See Federation of Malaya, *Report of the Working Committee Appointed by a Conference of His Excellency the Governor of the Malayan Union, Their Highnesses the Rulers of the Malay States, and the Representatives of the United Malays National Organization* (Kuala Lumpur: Malayan Union Government Press, 1947).

13. Ibid., p. 23 (emphasis in original).

14. In practice, these three criteria have not proven to be as clear-cut in defining "Malayness." According to a well-placed source, the classification of individuals as Malay or non-Malay has been more arbitrary and often subject to bureaucratic whim. Interview with a senior Malaysian social scientist, Nanyang Technological University, Singapore, May 19, 2000.

15. Andaya and Andaya, *A History of Malaysia*, pp. 254–261.

tration to act against the insurgents with impunity. By the mid-1950s the British had largely succeeded in curbing the revolt.

During the late 1940s and 1950s, UMNO's political appeal grew, allowing its leaders to forge two critical alliances that culminated in the creation of a consociational political order.[16] The first alliance was created in 1952 with the Malayan Chinese Association (MCA), a conservative Chinese political organization. The MCA had been founded in 1949 to represent noncommunist Chinese interests.[17] The other alliance was made in 1954 with the Malayan Indian Congress (MIC), which had been formed in 1946 but lacked broad-based support from all sections of the Indian community. The tripartite arrangement between UMNO, the MCA, and the MIC led to the creation of the National Alliance. In July 1955, as the British were moving to grant Malaya independence, federal elections were held. The alliance won 81 percent of the vote and 51 of the 52 contested seats.[18] The Parti Islam Se-Malaysia won the remaining seat. The alliance's overwhelming victory effectively ensured that it would be the governing regime when Britain granted Malaya independence on August 31, 1957. (The country's name was changed from Malaya to Malaysia by constitutional amendment in 1963.)

During the negotiations over the transfer of power, the British made uneven efforts to forge a multiracial society in independent Malaya. Despite Britain's professed commitment to the creation of a multiracial society, some of its actions suggested sympathy for the concerns of the Malays. This bias was evident in a 1951 report by the Barnes commission, headed by L.J. Barnes, an Oxford University official whom the British colonial government appointed in 1950 to formulate an education policy for a postcolonial Malayan state. The commission was composed of nine Malays and five Europeans.[19] To the distress of the Chinese and Indian minorities, the Barnes commission's report stated unequivocally that the primary schooling of all Malaysian citizens should be conducted in Bahasa Malaysia. It based this argument on the belief that such schooling would help to form a common Malayan nationality. Furthermore, the report advised that Chinese- and Indian-language schools should eventu-

---

16. For the classic statement of the concept of consociationalism, see Arendt Lijphart, "A Consociational Democracy," *World Politics*, Vol. 21, No. 2 (January 1969), pp. 207–225.

17. For an excellent account of the origins, growth, and evolution of the MCA, see Heng Pek Koon, *Chinese Politics in Malaysia: A History of the Malaysian Chinese Association* (Singapore: Oxford University Press, 1988).

18. Andaya and Andaya, *A History of Malaysia*, p. 261.

19. Von Vorys, *Democracy without Consensus*, pp. 93–94.

ally be closed and their pupils sent to Bahasa Malaysia–language national schools. The Chinese political leadership in particular greeted the Barnes report with dismay.[20]

In an attempt to assuage the misgivings of Chinese elites, the British felt compelled to invite two other scholars to provide advice on the question of postcolonial education in Malaya. Accordingly, in January 1951 William Fenn, an American who had done work on education in China, and Wu The-yao, a United Nations official, were invited to study the status of Chinese schools in Malaya. Their conclusions, which challenged the findings of the Barnes report, argued that national unity could not be forged through the imposition of Bahasa Malaysia on every community in Malaya. They also contended that a new national culture would emerge only if different languages were allowed to flourish in the educational system. The Chinese-language schools, they concluded, should be eliminated only when the Chinese community itself decided that they were no longer needed.[21]

The British colonial authorities nevertheless chose to support the conclusions of the Barnes report. To this end, they created the Central Advisory Committee on Education, whose findings supported the Barnes report and made only a small concession to minority sentiments: The committee encouraged the government to allow optional instruction in Tamil or Mandarin should the parents of at least fifteen students in a given class so demand.[22]

THE FORMATION OF MALAYSIAN LANGUAGE POLICIES

The Central Advisory Committee's report became the basis of the Education Ordinance of 1952. The importance of this directive cannot be overstated, because it came to form the cornerstone of language policy in postcolonial Malaya. The ordinance gave preference to Bahasa Malaysia over any other language in the educational curriculum. Bahasa Malaysia, in effect, would become the medium of instruction in all government-funded national schools. Also, following the recommendation of the committee's report, the ordinance stated that students could be educated in their mother tongue only if fifteen students or more in a primary-school class made such a request. These provisions applied only to Mandarin and Tamil; the ordinance made no provisions for the

20. Kua Kia Soong, ed., *Mother Tongue Education of Malaysian Ethnic Minorities* (Kajang, Selangor, Malaysia: Dong Jiao Zong Higher Learning Centre, 1998), p. 31.

21. Von Vorys, *Democracy without Consensus*, p. 94.

22. Ibid., p. 95.

indigenous minorities of Malaya, the Orang Asli. The restrictive nature of this ordinance did little to assuage the concerns of the Chinese- and Indian-language communities.

THE RAZAK REPORT AND EARLY LEGISLATION. In the wake of Malaya's first national elections in 1955, and sensing the continuing disquiet in the two largest minority communities, the National Alliance created yet another committee to examine the language question. This committee was headed by a prominent Malay politician (and later prime minister), Dato Tun Abdul Razak. Other members included Too Joon Hing and Im Chong Eu of the MCA and V.T. Sambanthan, the head of the MIC. The committee's recommendations appeared in the 1956 Razak report. The report shared the basic premise that any national education system would necessarily rely on Bahasa Malaysia as the medium of instruction. It aimed, however, to soften some of the more stringent provisions of the Central Advisory Committee report. To this end, the Razak report sought to have mother-tongue education integrated into the national education system.

The Razak report became the foundation of the Education Ordinance of 1957. The ordinance created two types of schools in Malaya: standard primary schools, in which the medium of instruction would be Bahasa Malaysia; and standard-type primary schools, wherein Mandarin or Tamil could be the medium of instruction.[23] The more accommodating features of this ordinance eased the misgivings of the Chinese and Indian communities. Their comfort, however, would be short lived. Malay nationalist agitation intensified after the passage of the ordinance.

Malay opposition arose from two main sources: the legislative bodies and teachers' groups. Agitation in the legislative arena had started before independence, with the release of the report of the Reid commission, chaired by Lord Reid, a British jurist, and charged with the drafting of a constitution for independent Malaya. The Reid commission made three recommendations: (1) Bahasa Malaysia should be the official language of independent Malaya; (2) English should have equivalent standing for the first ten years of independence; and (3) Mandarin and Tamil should be recognized as working languages when dealing with legislative matters.[24]

Malay nationalists charged that the Reid commission was unduly concerned about the rights of the Chinese and Indian communities and not sufficiently sensitive to the needs and expectations of the major-

---

23. Kua, *Mother Tongue Education of Malaysian Ethnic Minorities*, p. 37.

24. Von Vorys, *Democracy without Consensus*, p. 130.

ity community.[25] In their view, the British conceded too much to two "immigrant" communities at the expense of Malays.[26] In the final parliamentary sessions leading up to independence, a number of UMNO legislators, most notably Abdul Ghafar Baba, rebuked members of the opposition for their criticism of the Malay privileges enshrined in the new constitution.[27]

Impatience with what Malays perceived to be the slow implementation of Bahasa Malaysia education also arose from an important UMNO constituency—secondary-school teachers organized under the aegis of the Federation of Malay School Teachers Association (FMSTA). When this powerful body started to agitate for the full implementation of the Razak report, the government explained that the terms of the report could not be implemented speedily because of the lack of trained teachers. This explanation failed the to satisfy FMSTA, however. Faced with the loss of significant political support, the government moved quickly to boost the teaching of Bahasa Malaysia despite the teacher shortage. Chinese educators in particular watched these developments with an increasing sense of foreboding.

Their fears were hardly groundless. Yet another committee was set up in 1960 to implement the recommendations formulated in the Razak report and embodied in the 1957 education ordinance. The committee was chaired by the new minister of education, Abdul Rahman bin Haji Talib, and included four other Malays, three Chinese, and one Indian.[28] The Talib report reversed the few liberal provisions of the 1957 education ordinance, and it reaffirmed the goal of using Bahasa Malaysia and English as the principal media of instruction in all government schools. The report also held that in the interests of promoting national unity, vernacular-language schools should eventually be eliminated. In pursuit of that end, the report suggested that as of January 1, 1962, full governmental assistance should be provided only to vernacular schools that had converted to the national-type system of teaching. It also recommended

---

25. The Reid commission tried to arrive at a balanced treatment of Malay and non-Malay interests because its members believed that singling out Malays for preferential treatment would generate non-Malay hostility and hobble the processes of nation building and national integration. See the discussion in Heng, *Chinese Politics in Malaysia*, pp. 228–231.

26. This sentiment persists among Malay nationalists. It emerged clearly in an interview with a prominent Malay historian, University of Malaya, Kuala Lumpur, Malaysia, May 16, 2000.

27. Von Vorys, *Democracy without Consensus*, p. 138.

28. Ibid., p. 215.

that all public examinations in secondary schools be conducted in English and Bahasa Malaysia—not in vernacular languages.

Despite considerable protests from the Chinese community and segments of the Chinese leadership, the principal recommendations of the Talib report were incorporated into the Education Act of 1961. When the act went into effect, only a handful of Chinese-language schools that could rely on the largesse of the Chinese community refused to convert to the national-type model.

THE NATIONAL LANGUAGE ACT OF 1967. The year 1967 marked a decade of independence for Malaysia. According to Article 152 of the Malaysian constitution, 1967 was also the year in which English would cease to be one of the country's two official languages, making Bahasa Malaysia the sole official language (although the use of English was not prohibited). Some Malay nationalists, however, wanted the government to move more aggressively on the language issue. The leader of the Barisan Bertindak Bahasa Kebangsaan (National Language Action Front) and the first full-time director of the government's Dewan Bahasa dan Pustaka (Language and Literature Department), Tuan Syed Nasir bin Ismail, insisted that according to the constitution, only Bahasa Malaysia could be used in state affairs.[29] Lee San Choon, the MCA Youth president, challenged this view and successfully mobilized Chinese opposition. In an attempt to placate Chinese (and Indian) concern, the National Alliance passed a modified language bill: the National Language Act of 1967. This legislation affirmed Bahasa Malaysia as the country's official language but allowed for the continued use of English at the discretion of state and federal officials as well as for the use of Mandarin and Tamil (and other Indian languages) in all unofficial matters. This compromise failed to meet the expectations of both Malays and non-Malays, and all sides came to resent the new law.

THE CRISIS OF 1969

Parliamentary and state elections in 1969 threatened Malay political dominance, which in turn brought the country to a crisis. During the vigorous and at times bruising campaign, the incumbent and several of his opponents resorted to overt communal appeals. The results of the election in peninsular Malaysia revealed a dramatic loss of support for the ruling party, which won a mere 48.8 percent of the vote and 66 of the 104 parliamentary seats. A substantial number of Malay voters shifted their alle-

---

29.   See William Case, *Elites and Regimes in Malaysia: Revisiting a Consociational Democracy* (Clayton, Victoria, Australia: Monash University Asia Institute, 1996), pp. 104–106.

giance from UMNO to the Parti Islam Se-Malaysia. Within the National Alliance, the MCA proved to be the biggest loser: Twenty of the thirty-three candidates it had put up for election lost.

The non-Malay opposition parties, the Democratic Action Party and the Gerakan Rakyat Malaysia (Malaysian People's Movement), were delighted with the electoral outcome. Although they fell considerably short of victory at the national level, they nevertheless succeeded in denying the National Alliance a two-thirds majority in parliament. Moreover, they were instrumental in toppling the alliance in the key constituencies of Perak and Penang.[30]

The outcome sparked widespread ethnic violence starting on May 13, 1969, three days after the election.[31] In the wake of these riots, both the constitution and the parliament were suspended, a state of national emergency was declared, and the powers of governance were placed in the hands of the newly constituted National Operations Council (NOC). Although the cabinet continued to function under Prime Minister Tunku Abdul Rahman, for all practical purposes the real locus of political power and decisionmaking had shifted to the NOC. The NOC moved to address what it saw as the underlying causes of the ethnic conflagration: the continuing economic (and therefore psychological) backwardness of the Malay community. Accordingly, the NOC recommended the forging of a new social contract to deal with the underlying sources of tension and discord. Herein lay the origin of Malaysia's New Economic Policy (NEP).[32]

The NEP had two clear-cut economic goals and a number of sociopolitical objectives. The economic goals were (1) the elimination of the identification of race with occupation and (2) the eradication of poverty. Although no quantitative targets were set for poverty alleviation, the NOC committed itself to ensuring that as much as 30 percent of the coun-

---

30. This discussion draws on Šumit Ganguly, "Ethnic Politics and Political Quiescence in Malaysia and Singapore," in Michael E. Brown and Ganguly, eds., *Government Policies and Ethnic Relations in Asia and the Pacific* (Cambridge, Mass.: MIT Press, 1997), pp. 233–272.

31. Much has been written about the underlying and proximate causes of the May 13 ethnic riots. For useful discussions and alternative explanations, see Milton J. Esman, *Ethnic Politics* (Ithaca, N.Y.: Cornell University Press, 1994); Just Faaland, J.R. Parkinson, and Rais Saniman, *Growth and Ethnic Inequality: Malaysia's New Economic Policy* (New York: St. Martin's, 1990); and Gordon Means, *Malaysian Politics: The Second Generation* (Singapore: Oxford University Press, 1991).

32. For a detailed discussion of the origins, justifications, and effects of the NEP, see Donald Snodgrass, *Inequality and Economic Development in Malaysia* (Kuala Lumpur: Oxford University Press, 1980).

try's equity would be in Malay hands by 1990. (Malays accounted for a significant segment of the rural poor in Malaysia.) The NOC's new national strategy shrank the terms of political debate within Malaysia and bolstered Malay privileges. Individuals and political parties were thereafter forbidden to question the status of Malay rights, the royalty, and Bahasa Malaysia as the country's national language. These were now considered to be "sensitive issues," and challenging them was deemed to be seditious.

In the arena of language policy, a new assertiveness emerged. The recently appointed education minister, Datuk Abdul Rahman Yaacob, a well-known Malay activist, announced that the Razak and Talib reports would be implemented and the English-medium schools would be converted to Bahasa Malaysia. The government, however, in an attempt to maintain the support of its Chinese and Indian constituents, allowed vernacular-language primary-school systems to remain open with government funding.[33]

LANGUAGE POLICY UNDER THE NEP

During the 1970s the government introduced sweeping changes in educational policy designed to benefit Malays. The conversion of English-language schools to Bahasa Malaysia began to be implemented. In 1970 the first year of primary school was converted to Bahasa Malaysia; each year another grade was converted until the process was completed in 1982. Universities were expected to follow suit by 1983. The National University of Malaysia (Universiti Kebangsaan Malaysia) was established in 1970 with Bahasa Malaysia as the language of instruction.

The Chinese and Indian communities raised few significant challenges to language policy in Malaysia as the NEP unfolded. The ethnic violence that wracked the country in 1969 and its prompt suppression by the government no doubt gave pause to Chinese and Indian activists. In 1974, as part of the NEP program, the government set up the Cabinet Review Committee on Education, chaired by the minister of education, Mahathir bin Mohammed. The committee's tasks were to review the implementation of the existing educational policy and to suggest strategies to promote both discipline and skills. The Mahathir report, submitted in 1979, recommended that private schools be strictly supervised. It also recommended that the government be allowed to shut down schools that failed to conform to governmental expectations. No legislative action followed, however.[34]

---

33. Case, *Elites and Regimes in Malaysia*, p. 110.

34. Kua, *Mother Tongue Education of Malaysian Ethnic Minorities*, p. 45. For further de-

The language issue resurfaced when in 1981 sections of the Chinese community sought to establish a university where Mandarin would be the medium of instruction. This effort, which would become referred to as "the Merdeka University case," was a response to the policy of preference shown toward Malays in university admissions. This policy, embedded in the NEP, significantly limited the prospects of Chinese students seeking to enter university. When the government turned down the request for a new educational institution, it was sued by proponents of the proposal. The Malaysian high court sided with the government in a decision handed down in November 1981. It argued that nothing in the 1961 education act granted a Malaysian citizen the right to be taught in any language other than Bahasa Malaysia. In addition, it held that a university, whether private or public, constituted a "public authority" and as such was under the purview of the Universities and University Colleges Act of 1971. In July 1982 the plaintiffs appealed the decision to a higher court but to no avail: The federal court upheld the high court's decision and dismissed the appeal. The judiciary, in effect, reiterated the government's position on the language issue. In the political arena, however, concessions were made: Under pressure from the MCA, the government allowed the Chinese community to establish Tunku Abdul Rahman College, in which the medium of instruction would be English.

Despite this concession, the language issue remained a potent force in Malaysian politics. Tensions surrounding language policy erupted again in 1987, when the government announced its decision to appoint non-Mandarin-speaking headmasters to Chinese-language schools. The Chinese community feared that the appointment of non-Mandarin-speaking headmasters was a subtle attempt by the regime to further undermine the status of the Chinese population. With the support of the Chinese schoolteachers' association, the Democratic Action Party (an ostensibly multiracial but predominantly Chinese party) launched public protests against the government's actions, which in turn prompted UMNO to undertake counterdemonstrations. Some UMNO leaders, in particular Sanusi Junid, the party's secretary-general, called for a major rally in the capital, Kuala Lumpur.[35] Communal passions again began to flare, and the possibility of another ethnic conflagration loomed. The UMNO-led rally failed to materialize, however; Mahathir, by then the

---

tails, see Kua Kia Soong, ed., *A Protean Saga: The Chinese Schools of Malaysia* (Kuala Lumpur: Resource and Research Centre, Selangor Chinese Assembly Hall, 1990), pp. 130–131.

35.   Harold Crouch, *Government and Society in Malaysia* (Ithaca, N.Y.: Cornell University Press, 1996), pp. 108–109.

prime minister, squelched it immediately upon returning from a foreign trip. Agitation was muted when Mahathir launched Operasi Lalang to quell the protests and incarcerated a number of political leaders and opponents under the terms of Malaysia's sweeping Internal Security Act.[36]

THE FUTURE OF LANGUAGE POLICY IN MALAYSIA

Just before Malaysia's 1990 national election, the government announced that it would introduce new educational legislation. This bill was supposed to address some of the grievances of the Chinese and Indian minority communities. Accordingly, key activists from both communities submitted various memoranda to the government. In the end, however, the bill was withdrawn.

In 1993 the UMNO-dominated government seemed to make a concession to the Chinese and Indian communities: Mahathir announced that the government would allow the use of English in Malaysian universities for the purposes of teaching in the areas of science, technology, and medicine.[37] In all likelihood, however, this policy change was driven more by the imperative of competitiveness in an increasingly global economy than by the need to address the misgivings of the country's minority communities. Not surprisingly, Mahathir's government did little to pacify opponents of single-language education. They correctly perceived the switch to English as a purely instrumental move.[38]

In 1996 Malaysia passed yet another education bill. Based on the 1990 education bill, but without any of the modifications called for by ethnic minorities, this legislation did little to address extant misgivings. The bill was introduced in parliament after the UMNO-dominated coalition won a landslide victory in 1995. The provisions of this law are sweeping. Some minority-language activists in Malaysia contend that its key provisions are quite retrograde. They argue, for example, that the new law requires every school in the National Education System to use Bahasa Malaysia.[39]

---

36. R.S. Milne and Diane K. Mauzy, *Malaysian Politics under Mahathir* (London: Routledge, 1999), p. 108.

37. P. Ramasamy, "The Politics of Language in Malaysia," Jabatan Sains Politik (Department of Political Science), Universiti Kebangsaan Malaysia, Bangi, Selangor, undated.

38. Interview with a Malaysian university professor of Tamil origin, Kuala Lumpur, Malaysia, May 16, 2000.

39. The schools in the National Education System include government, government-aided, and all private educational institutions. Only expatriate schools remain outside its purview. For a detailed discussion of this and other contentious aspects of the 1996 education act, see Kua, *Mother Tongue Education of Malaysian Ethnic Minorities*, pp. 47–51.

Previously, under the repealed Education Act of 1961, only primary schools were so required. The law also stipulates that, in government-aided or government-run schools, facilities for teaching students in their mother tongue can be made available if the parents of at least fifteen students so request. The languages of indigenous groups, such as Orang Asli or Kadazan, can be taught only if it is "reasonable and practicable" to do so. If past policies toward the Orang Asli are any indicator of future trends, it is unlikely that the government will make a concerted effort to address the educational needs of the aboriginal population.[40]

Interestingly, the 1996 legislation shows much greater sensitivity toward Islamic education. Specifically, if any school has five or more students who profess to be Muslim, these students must be given religious instruction during the school day at least two hours per week. This component of the law was no doubt aimed at appeasing the rising strength of Islamic activists in Malaysia in the 1990s.[41]

At the dawn of the twenty-first century, Malaysia is at a critical juncture. The country's political leadership, most notably Prime Minister Mahathir, has articulated a vision of transforming Malaysia into a developed state by 2020.[42] In some measure, he has already succeeded: Malaysia's per capita income remains at about U.S.$8,000 despite the financial crisis of the late 1990s.[43] To continue on this path, Malaysia will increasingly have to depend on trained personnel with adequate English-language skills. Thus far, it has managed to pursue rapid industrial development by relying on substantial numbers of trained expatriates.[44]

The commitment to the use of Bahasa Malaysia in public life nevertheless remains a professed goal of the government. The promotion of Bahasa Malaysia at the primary, secondary, and college levels commands widespread political support among the Malay population. Despite the notable progress that Malays have made under the NEP, a sense of inse-

---

40. On this point, see Means, "The Orang Asli."

41. On the attempts of UMNO to blunt the rise of radical Islamic sentiment in Malaysia, see Anthony Milner, "Constructing the Malay Majority," in Dru C. Gladney, ed., *Making Majorities: Constituting the Nation in Japan, Korea, China, Malaysia, Fiji, Turkey, and the United States* (Stanford, Calif.: Stanford University Press, 1998), pp. 151–169. See also Michael Vatikiotis, "Islam Makes Inroads," *Far Eastern Economic Review*, December 9, 1999, p. 18.

42. On this point, see Ahmad Sarji Abdul Hamid, ed., *Malaysia's Vision, 2020: Understanding the Concept, Implications, and Challenges* (Petaling Jaya, Selangor, Malaysia: Pelanduk, 1993).

43. S. Jayasankaran, "Miracle Cure," *Far Eastern Economic Review*, May 11, 2000, p. 30.

44. James Kynge, "A Shake-Up on Campuses," *Financial Times*, June 19, 1996, p. iv.

curity still pervades a significant segment of this community. Any attempt to dilute the standing of the Malay language is consequently seen as an assault on their standing within Malaysia.[45] Malay nationalists insist that if Japan made striking industrial progress both before and after World War II without the widespread adoption of English, Malaysia can as well.[46]

The Politics of Language in Singapore

Singapore's language policies provide a fascinating contrast to those of Malaysia. Even though speakers of Chinese dialects constitute nearly 77 percent of the population of Singapore, the country has long accepted Malay (as Bahasa Malaysia is referred to in Singapore) as its national language and English as the de facto official language of the state. Singapore's unusual linguistic choices arise from the political leadership's recognition of the country's unique ethnic composition, its choice of an ideology based on multiracialism and multiculturalism, its geographic location in a predominantly Malay cultural region, its historical ties to Malaysia, and its strategy of economic development.[47]

THE COLONIAL HERITAGE IN SINGAPORE

The origins of modern-day Singapore can be traced to January 30, 1819, when Sir Thomas Stamford Raffles, a British adventurer and servant of the East India Company, obtained the right to open a trading post from the local ruler, the Temenggong of Johore.[48] Over the course of the century, Singapore became an integral part of the British colonial empire in Asia and an important entrepôt. Independent Singapore's language policies both reflect its colonial heritage and mark important departures from

---

45. Systematic evidence to this end is hard to adduce. A series of interviews conducted with prominent university professors in several social science disciplines suggests, however, that this sense of insecurity persists. Interviews, University of Malaya, Kuala Lumpur, Malaysia, May 2000.

46. Interview with a member of the editorial staff of the *New Straits Times*, Kuala Lumpur, Malaysia, May 17, 2000.

47. The official language of Indonesia, Bahasa Indonesia, is fundamentally the same as Bahasa Malaysia. See, for example, chapter 9 in this volume. For a discussion of multilingualism in Singapore, see Eddie C.Y. Kuo and Bjorn H. Jernudd, "Balancing Micro- and Macro-Linguistic Perspectives in Language Management: The Case of Singapore," in Thiru Kandiah and John Kwan-Terry, eds., *English and Language-Planning: A Southeast Asian Contribution* (Singapore: Times Academic Press, 1991), pp. 70–89.

48. C.M Turnbull, *A History of Singapore, 1819–1988* (Singapore: Oxford University Press, 1999), p. 1.

the policies and practices of the colonial state. Until the outbreak of World War II and the subsequent Japanese occupation of Malaya and Singapore, English-language education was the preserve of the elite. Such education was imparted to a select few and mostly in Christian mission schools. Chinese-language education was pursued in community-based and private schools, Tamil education in estate-run schools, and Malay education in government-supported schools. A consequence of colonial education policy was the creation of two distinct classes of students: those who had the benefits of an English-language education and those who were educated in vernacular languages.[49]

As the possibility of British withdrawal approached in the wake of World War II, British colonial authorities belatedly concluded that universal English-language education would reduce communal divisions in a pluralist society. The resources for providing such education, however, were acutely lacking. As a compromise, the British fashioned a ten-year program in 1947 that sought to promote schooling in the three major vernaculars—Chinese, Malay, and Tamil—while expanding English-language schools.[50] The principal objectives of this new educational policy were to foster a sense of loyalty to the state and to prepare Singaporeans for eventual self-government. Faced with resource constraints, the program also called for the introduction of English in the third grade in Chinese, Indian, and Malay primary schools.

The first direct challenge to these educational and language policies came in 1954. Protests ensued when Singaporean authorities called up young men for military service. When student protesters were arrested, more than 1,000 of their fellow students took over the Chinese High School of Singapore. The authorities were loath to crack down for fear of provoking a more powerful backlash by the Chinese community. Protests continued through the end of the year, and in 1955 the students linked their efforts to the cause of striking bus drivers. It is widely believed that local communist unions sought to make common cause with the students and the striking bus drivers. Fearing the possibility of a wider communal conflagration, the government chose not to confront the students. Instead it appointed an all-party committee that included Lee Kuan Yew, a subsequent prime minister of Singapore, to examine the grievances of the students and Chinese-language educators.

The all-party committee issued a report recommending that no disciplinary action be taken against the students and their schools. It also

49.   Michael Hill and Lian Kwen Fee, *The Politics of Nation-Building and Citizenship in Singapore* (London: Routledge, 1995), p. 69.

50.   This discussion draws on ibid., pp. 67–90.

made sweeping recommendations for the transformation of the educational system in Singapore. Most significantly, the report stated that educational policies would have to recognize that Singapore was a multiracial society. To this end, it called for equal treatment for four streams of education—Chinese, English, Malay, and Tamil. It also recommended that bilingual education be encouraged in primary schools and trilingual education in secondary schools. The government accepted most of these proposals. Even after a brief and ill-fated merger with Malaysia, the policies based on these proposals did not change significantly.

THE ENSHRINEMENT OF MALAY IN LETTER BUT NOT IN SPIRIT

After a merger of less than two years, Singapore was ousted from the Federation of Malaysia on August 9, 1965.[51] Almost immediately, Singapore adopted its unique language policy, one that has held the country in good stead in both social and economic terms.

Shortly after the separation from Malaysia, the People's Action Party (PAP) prime minister, Lee Kuan Yew, declared that four languages—Chinese, English, Malay, and Tamil—would be granted official status. Malay was also accorded the status of a national language.[52] The decision to grant Malay this status while denying the same privilege to Chinese was indicative of Lee's political pragmatism, shrewdness, and tough-mindedness.[53] He was concerned that overt favoritism toward the Chinese community would be construed as pandering to the forces of Chinese chauvinism in a predominantly Malay region. This could incur the displeasure of Singapore's powerful neighbors.[54] Accordingly, early in Singapore's independent history, Lee successfully fended off demands by the Chinese chamber of commerce to grant Chinese the status of a national language—even though at the time close to 80 percent of the population of Singapore was ethnically Chinese.

---

51. For a succinct discussion of the politics surrounding the ouster, see Case, *Elites and Regimes in Malaysia*, pp. 103–105.

52. Chan Heng Chee, "Political Developments, 1965–1979," in Ernest C.T. Chew and Edwin Lee, eds., *A History of Singapore* (Singapore: Oxford University Press, 1991), p. 158.

53. This position was consistent with Lee's stance on educational policies prior to the independence of Malaysia and Singapore. His views harked back to his participation in the "All-Party Report on Chinese Education of 1956," which had called for the equal treatment of all four languages, the introduction of bilingual education in primary schools and trilingual education in secondary schools, and the designation of Malay as the national language. On this point, see R.S. Milne and Diane K. Mauzy, *Singapore: The Legacy of Lee Kuan Yew* (Boulder, Colo.: Westview, 1990), p. 18.

54. Chan, "Political Developments, 1965–1979," p. 171.

Lee and the PAP also understood the vital importance of binding the loyalties of the country's three main linguistic and cultural communities to the nascent Singaporean state. To this end, work started on the writing of primary-school textbooks that presented heroic and romanticized accounts of Singapore's historical evolution as a state and as a community.[55] Permanent exhibits at Singapore's National History Museum, frequented by schoolchildren, glorified the country's multiethnic makeup.[56]

During the 1960s the PAP formulated a clear-cut language policy that has endured, with some vital modifications, until the present day. Under the terms of this policy, every child in Singapore is expected to learn English as well as his or her mother tongue. This policy at first encountered some resistance from both the Chinese and the Malay communities. The Malay community proposed that every student be required to learn Malay in addition to English, as the former was the national language. Lee rejected this proposal, arguing that the adoption of such a policy would consign Chinese, the language of the majority community, to a distant third place.

Nevertheless, Chinese-language chauvinists did not think that the government's rebuff was strong enough. They vigorously expressed their discontent and reiterated their demands in the pages of a Chinese-language newspaper, the *Nanyang Siang Pau*. Taking a dim view of these demands, the PAP government moved to suppress them. In 1971 it shut down the *Nanyang Siang Pau* on the grounds that its vilification of the government's language policy amounted to the promotion of racial and ethnic discord.[57] Such harsh suppression made clear the PAP government's limited tolerance of criticism of its language policy.

Attempts to inculcate a set of cohesive values among the Singaporean population continued through the 1970s. As early as 1965, Lee had expressed his view that education policy should not produce a deculturalized population. To this end, he had insisted on the teaching of a second language—in addition to English—in secondary schools. This practice, he believed, would encourage interethnic communication. In an attempt to promote what the Singaporean state believed were civic virtues, the ministry of education introduced primary history textbooks in four languages (Chinese, English, Malay, and Tamil). These books not only

55. S. Gopinathan, "Education," in Chew and Lee, *A History of Singapore*, p. 277.

56. Author's visit to Singapore National History Museum, June 7, 2000. Benedict R.O.G. Anderson discusses the role and significance of museums in forging and promoting particular visions of national identity. Anderson, *Imagined Communities: Reflections on the Origin and Spread of Nationalism* (London: Verso, 1991).

57. Chan, "Political Developments, 1965–1979," pp. 172–173.

extolled the contributions of multiple ethnic groups to Singapore's development but also emphasized the importance of hard work, perseverance, and the rewards that flowed from such efforts. In 1974 the government introduced a new course, "Education for the Living," taught in the mother tongue of all students. The course was an amalgam of civics, history, and geography, and was designed to instill ideas about the rights and obligations of citizenship in Singapore.

The PAP government's attempt to forge civic loyalties to the Singaporean state faced a final challenge in the mid-1970s. A last bastion of opposition to the government's language policy included students and faculty at Nanyang University, an epicenter of anti-PAP, pro-Chinese, and procommunist sentiment. Starting in 1975 the government pressed the university to switch from Chinese to English as the medium of instruction. It encountered some minor resistance mostly in the form of malingering. By 1978, however, even this limited resistance was overcome. In 1980 Nanyang University merged with the University of Singapore to create the National University of Singapore.[58]

THE GOH REPORT AND ITS AFTERMATH

In 1978 the deputy prime minister of Singapore, Goh Keng Swee, received a broad mandate to examine problems in the ministry of education. In 1979 his committee produced a report that was extremely critical of the status of bilingual education in Singapore. It underscored the high attrition rates under bilingual education and argued that a uniform education system imposed on children with differential language-learning abilities was producing disastrous results.

Despite this critique of bilingualism, the report cautioned against wholesale rejection of the policy. It stressed that bilingual education was vital for the promotion of interethnic communication and the principles of multiculturalism. In addition, it proposed several modifications, including the "streaming" of students based on their performance in school by the fourth grade.

The Singaporean government subsequently adopted a new set of language policies. Malay and Tamil were offered to children whose parents wanted them to learn their mother tongues. Otherwise the emphasis was on the learning of English and Chinese (Mandarin). Beginning in 1982, English-stream students had to meet a second-language requirement to enter university. In so doing, they would be demonstrating the government's commitment to making the new bilingual policy work.

---

58. Ibid., p. 174.

THE "SPEAK MORE MANDARIN, USE LESS DIALECTS" CAMPAIGN

The government's pragmatic, technocratic approach to language policy was also evident in a campaign launched in 1979 to standardize the form of Chinese spoken by Singaporeans.[59] Lee Kuan Yew started this campaign because he believed that there were too many schisms in the Chinese community in Singapore.[60] Lee felt that the Chinese community was deeply divided along the lines of the various dialects spoken in Singapore. These linguistic divisions, he contended, could create new social cleavages and tensions. Lee was also concerned that, given Singaporeans' growing exposure to Western cultural values through various mass media, the lack of a shared linguistic ethos could undermine the country's cultural identity.[61]

A key development in the international arena reinforced the choice of Mandarin as the dialect to promote. Beginning with the U.S. opening to China in the early 1970s, Singapore watched the rise of Chinese economic and political clout in regional and global affairs. Lee reasoned that a Singaporean population that spoke Mandarin (the preeminent dialect spoken by Chinese officials) would be well positioned to take advantage of economic opportunities generated by China.

To this end, Lee created the Speak Mandarin Campaign Secretariat under the aegis of the ministry of information and the arts. The secretariat had close links with the ministry of education and organized a variety of activities designed to promote the use of Mandarin. Initial surveys conducted in the late 1980s revealed that the campaign was effective: Close to 87 percent of the Chinese population identified itself as Mandarin speaking, whereas only 26 percent had done so in 1980.[62]

THE FUTURE OF LANGUAGE POLICY IN SINGAPORE

There is little question that English has become intricately woven into the fabric of Singapore's social, cultural, and political life.[63] Yet there are periodic demands to further enhance the status of Mandarin—for instance,

---

59. For a nuanced discussion of this form of pragmatism, see Cho-Oon Khong, "Singapore: Political Legitimacy through Managing Conformity," in Muthiah Alagappa, ed., *Political Legitimacy in Southeast Asia: The Quest for Moral Authority* (Stanford, Calif.: Stanford University Press, 1995), pp. 124–125.

60. Gopinathan, "Education," p. 283.

61. Anne Pakir, "Education and Invisible Language Planning: The Case of English in Singapore," in Kandiah and Kwan-Terry, *English and Language-Planning*, p. 167.

62. Kuo and Jernudd, "Balancing Micro- and Macro-Linguistic Perspectives in Language Management," p. 81.

63. Interviews, Department of English, National University of Singapore, May 2000.

by replacing English with Mandarin as the primary medium of instruction.[64] Given Singapore's extraordinary integration into the global economy, however, it is unlikely that the country's political leadership will make more than symbolic concessions to these demands. Moreover, it can ill afford to alienate its Malay population, which remains conscious of its limited position in Singapore.[65]

Conclusion

What steps should Malaysia and Singapore take to alter the orientation of their language policies? In Malaysia the government could continue to rely on foreign expertise to fill the gap created by the lack of a skilled indigenous labor force. Such a strategy, however, will not serve Malaysian interests in the future. Given that Malaysia is already well on the pathway to industrialization, it behooves its leadership to consider the advantages of creating an indigenous workforce that is trained to meet the demands of a more sophisticated postindustrial economy. Such training cannot be adequately imparted when substantial portions of the population are not proficient in the English language. To achieve proficiency, schooling in English needs to start at least at the secondary level. Such a policy would serve every group in Malaysia, especially the marginalized Orang Asli and the economically backward Indian community.[66] A policy change along these lines, however, may provoke the wrath of Malay nationalists.

Prime Minister Mahathir is uniquely positioned to implement this policy shift. His credentials as an advocate of the Malays are beyond question. He is also the principal architect of Malaysia's industrial transformation. Consequently, he can articulate the case for the advancement of English-language teaching in primary and secondary education on economic development grounds and override the objections of Malay nationalists.

Language policy in Singapore seems to be on the right course. Singapore's literacy rate in 1998 was 93.1 percent, and its per capita income was nearly U.S.$35,000.[67] There is little in its present policies that calls for substantial change. The only area where the government could take ac-

---

64. Khong, "Singapore," p. 130.

65. Ganguly, "Ethnic Politics and Political Quiescence," pp. 269–270.

66. Simon Elegant, "Big Daddy," *Far Eastern Economic Review*, April 20, 2000, pp. 29–30.

67. For these figures, go to http://www.sg/flavour/profile/pro-people2.html.

tion would be to reduce its inordinate emphasis on learning Mandarin. Although attempts to promote the speaking of Mandarin have met with success, the impact of the campaign remains questionable.[68] As long as efforts to learn English proceed apace, however, interethnic communication should encounter few obstacles. Also, Singapore does not face the divisive interethnic tensions that it encountered in the 1970s. The PAP regime has successfully forged a sense of a Singaporean identity in a predominantly Chinese city-state.[69] It should therefore be able to allow for some linguistic diversity without fear of inter- and intracommunal polarization.

---

68.   One is forced to wonder about the validity of official statistical surveys that suggest the dramatic increase in the growth of households speaking Mandarin. Citizens facing intense governmental pressure to adopt Mandarin might not admit that they were willfully violating this policy.

69.   K.S. Sandhu and P. Wheatley, eds., *Management of Success: The Moulding of Modern Singapore* (Singapore: Institute of Southeast Asian Studies, 1989).

Chapter 9

Language Policy and the Promotion of National Identity in Indonesia

Jacques Bertrand

Indonesia is one of the most ethnically diverse countries in the world. Its population of more than 200 million people is spread over hundreds of islands. More than 400 languages and associated dialects are spoken among dozens of ethnic groups. Five major world religions are represented among these groups, although Muslims are a clear majority. Multiple and overlapping identities characterize most Indonesians in such a way that ethnic boundaries and cleavages are highly fluid. Many aspects of ethnicity, including religious, cultural, linguistic, racial, and regional identities, have been politicized at various times.

Unlike many other ethnically diverse countries, however, Indonesia has experienced little violent conflict around language issues. Although there is a strong coincidence between ethnic and linguistic groups in Indonesia, language issues have not been politicized. Ethnic conflicts have erupted in various parts of the archipelago: Examples include Aceh, Irian Jaya, East Timor, and more recently, Ambon (Moluccas) and Kalimantan—but language has not been a major source of intergroup resentment. Other cleavages—such as inequalities in the distribution of economic resources, overcentralization of political power, and more general cultural differences—have had greater prominence.

The policy of adopting and promoting Bahasa Indonesia has generally been successful in preventing intensely violent ethnic conflict in Indonesia.[1] This argument is developed around five points. First, crucial

---

1. "Bahasa" is the Malay term for "language." It is often incorrectly used alone to identify the Indonesian language. I use the Indonesian form "Bahasa Jawa/Indonesia" interchangeably with the English equivalent Indonesian/Javanese (language).

debates over Indonesia's language policy occurred during the rise of nationalism in the 1920s, when *pasar* (bazaar) Malay (later named "Bahasa Indonesia") became the language of the nationalist movement. Bahasa Indonesia was a more democratic language than either of its contenders, Javanese or Dutch. It was a lingua franca spoken by a large number of people across ethnic groups, as opposed to the restricted number of speakers of Dutch or Javanese—and it was easier to learn than Javanese.

Second, following Indonesia's independence in 1945 and the adoption of Bahasa Indonesia as the country's official language, linguistic conflict became less apparent. There was continuity in language policy under the successive regimes of Presidents Sukarno and Suharto. This included ongoing promotion of Bahasa Indonesia through education and as the language of government and business; official protection of local languages, but with only limited resources devoted to them; and a gradualist approach to implementation, allowing for some flexibility in the language of instruction in the early postindependence period. In general, education policies enhanced Bahasa Indonesia at the expense of local vernaculars.

Third, these policies were well received by most of the country's ethnic groups. Various groups continued to use local vernaculars while increasingly using Bahasa Indonesia for official purposes and for intergroup communication. Many adopted it as a primary language. For a large number of Indonesians, Bahasa Indonesia came to be seen as the language of modernity, advancement, and national unity.

Fourth, significant policy implementation problems generated resentments among some groups. Most notably, government policies systematically prevented the use and spread of the Chinese language. This remains the most repressive and discriminatory aspect of the government's language policy. In cases where separatist movements emerged, such as in Aceh, Irian Jaya, and East Timor, the government implemented its policies more forcefully. These movements also resisted Bahasa Indonesia more systematically, at least at first. Over time, group reactions to the government's language policies and the spread of Bahasa Indonesia have been more ambiguous. These reactions cannot be interpreted only as the acceptance of Bahasa Indonesia under threat of repression because, despite their conflicts with the Indonesian state, these groups may have seen some benefit in adopting and using Bahasa Indonesia.

Fifth, the government's language policy does have some weaknesses. Because of a lack of resources, small ethnic groups have been losing their languages as pressures to use Bahasa Indonesia or regional lingua francas have increased. Also, even though local languages are widely used by ethnic groups for many purposes, most of these languages are not taught in schools. The exceptions are the languages of large ethnic groups. In some cases, these languages are taught as optional courses in addition to the standard curricula. Also, there are not enough textbooks for teaching local languages. Finally, in recent years Javanese words have begun to penetrate Bahasa Indonesia. This trend has occurred in part because of the government's use of Old Javanese words for official names, which in turn has created resentment among non-Javanese.

During most of Indonesia's postindependence history, language policy has developed under authoritarian rule. It is therefore possible that linguistic policies met with little open resistance because of the government's tight hold on power. At the same time, there are some significant strengths in the government's language policy.

Language and Ethnicity

Indonesia comprises several hundred ethnolinguistic groups. According to a 1972 report by the National Language Institute, 418 different languages could be found across the archipelago.[2] More recently, the number was put at 712. Of these, 256 were spoken by groups scattered across the vast province of Irian Jaya (Papua); 14 were spoken as mother tongues by Indonesia's main ethnic groups (who comprise nearly 94 percent of the population), and the other 698 were spoken by groups representing 6 percent of the population. (See Table 9.1.)

Boundaries between ethnic groups in Indonesia are fluid, as is the extent to which various groups use language as an ethnic marker. Some groups, such as the Javanese, the Sundanese, and the Acehnese, clearly identify themselves as such and differentiate themselves from others in part through language. Other groups appear to have adopted ethnic identities that supersede linguistic groups. For example, a "Papuan" identity has emerged that distinguishes the various tribes of Irian Jaya from other ethnic groups in Indonesia, yet these groups speak more than 200 different languages. This identity has become more important in political terms than have the differences among tribal groups within the province. Similar multilinguistic groups have developed in other parts of eastern Indonesia. In some cases, a local lingua franca, such as Tetum in East Timor, has become an identifier of these "new" ethnic groups.

---

2. Reported in P.W.J. Nababan, "Language in Education: The Case of Indonesia," *International Review of Education/Internationale Zeitschrift für Erziehungswissenschaft/Revue Internationale de pédagogie,* Vol. 37, No. 1 (1991), p. 115. The report excluded many of the languages of Irian Jaya (West Papua) that had not yet been mapped.

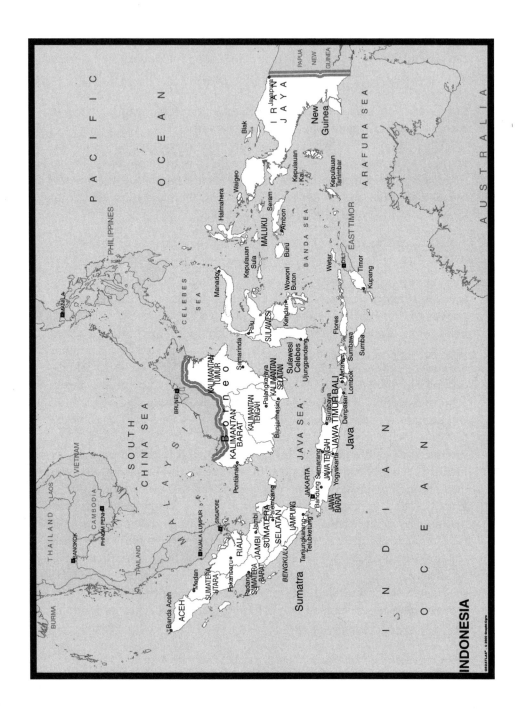

INDONESIA

Table 9.1. Language Groups in Indonesia.

Language[a]	Number of Speakers[b]	Main Concentration	Percentage[c]
Javanese	75,200,000	Central, eastern, and southwestern Java	38.44
Indonesian (Bahasa Indonesia)[d]	30,000,000	Various	15.34
Sundanese	27,000,000	Western third of Java	13.80
Madura (Madurese)[e]	10,000,000	Madura, Sapudi Islands, northern coast of eastern Java	5.11
Malay (Bahasa Melayu)[f]	10,000,000	Riau, Bangka	5.11
Minangkabau (Padang)[g]	6,500,000	West Sumatra and Central Sumatra	3.32
Batak[h]	5,830,000	North Sumatra	2.98
Balinese	3,800,000	Bali, Lombok, East Java	1.94
Bugis (Buginese)[i]	3,500,000	South Sulawesi	1.79
Aceh (Acehnese)	3,000,000	North Sumatra	1.53
Betawi	2,700,000	Jakarta, Java	1.38
Banjar (Banjarese)	2,100,000	Banjarmasin, Kalimantan	1.07
Sasak (Lombok)	2,100,000	Lombok	1.07
Chinese[j]	2,000,000	Throughout Indonesia	1.02
Total	**183,730,000**		**93.92**

SOURCE: Barbara F. Grimes, ed., *Ethnologue: Languages of the World,* 12th ed. (Dallas, Tex.: Summer Institute of Linguistics, 1992).
[a]According to Grimes, 712 languages were spoken in Indonesia in 1996.
[b]Figures refer to the estimated number of mother-tongue speakers. Where Grimes gives a numeric range, the highest figure is used.
[c]Percentages are based on a 1995 national population of 195,623,000.
[d]Grimes reports that there are more than 140,000,000 second-language users of Bahasa Indonesia with varying levels of speaking and reading proficiency.
[e]This statistic is for all countries, with most speakers living in Indonesia.
[f]This includes 2 million Bahasa Melayu speakers in Riau.
[g]This includes 500,000 Minangkabau speakers in Jakarta.
[h]Grimes reports that seven dialects of Batak are spoken. The largest linguistic group is Toba Batak with 2 million speakers.
[i]This statistic is for all countries, with most speakers residing in Indonesia.
[j]Major dialects include Mandarin, Min Nan, Min Dong, and Yeu (Cantonese).

In Indonesia, religion and region have been more influential ethnic markers than has language. Although groups identify themselves as speakers of different local languages (*bahasa daerah*) and proudly distinguish Bahasa Bali (Balinese), Bahasa Jawa (Javanese), and other local languages or dialects from the national language—Bahasa Indonesia—these distinctions have not been politicized. Groups maintain their local languages while learning and using Indonesian. Conflicts have mainly involved other ethnic markers. During the 1950s, for example, rebellions in South Sulawesi and West Sumatra targeted the centralizing tendencies of Jakarta and Javanese domination. Rebels were just as likely, however, to uphold the ideals of the Indonesian constitution and Bahasa Indonesia.[3]

Religion has been a much more sensitive issue than language in Indonesian politics. Since independence, when several groups rejected the idea of a secular Indonesian state, the role of Islam in the country has been a source of tension. Religious agendas in the 1950s gave rise to the Masyumi Party, which sought the establishment of an Islamic state in Indonesia. Violent groups fought a guerrilla war for more than a decade to advance this cause.[4] In more recent years, violence between Christians and Muslims in the Moluccas, church and mosque burnings since 1996, and other sporadic bouts of violence between religious groups have led to the deaths of several hundred people. These conflicts have often involved groups with the same local languages but different religions.

Regional distinctions have also been forms of ethnic identification and sources of resentment in Indonesia. But since the rebellions of the 1950s, which saw a demand for a reduced Javanese role in the country, regional actions have declined dramatically. After Suharto became president in 1965, the central government greatly increased its powers. Bolstered by the military, the Suharto regime established a hierarchical, authoritarian system of policymaking that left the country's regions little freedom to advance their particular interests. Decisions were made in Jakarta and then implemented through a bureaucracy that extended from the central government down to individual villages. Laws passed in 1974 and 1979 homogenized the forms of regional and local government across the archipelago, replacing local institutions that had once varied from place to place. Over time, several regions called for greater decentralization of political and economic power. Only with the fall of Suharto in May 1998 and the transition to democracy did the central government begin to address these demands.

---

3. For an overview of these issues, see R. William Liddle, "Coercion, Co-Optation, and the Management of Ethnic Relations in Indonesia," in Michael E. Brown and Šumit Ganguly, eds., *Government Policies and Ethnic Relations in Asia and the Pacific* (Cambridge, Mass.: MIT Press, 1997), pp. 273–319. On the regional rebellions, see Ichlasul Amal, *Regional and Central Government in Indonesian Politics: West Sumatra and South Sulawesi, 1949–1979* (Yogyakarta: Gadjah Mada University Press, 1992); and Barbara Harvey, *Permesta: Half a Rebellion* (Ithaca, N.Y.: Cornell Modern Indonesia Project, Southeast Asia Program, Cornell University, 1977).

4. On the 1950s, see Herbert Feith, *The Decline of Constitutional Democracy in Indonesia* (Ithaca, N.Y.: Cornell University Press, 1962). On the Darul Islam rebellion, see Cornelis van Dijk, *Rebellion under the Banner of Islam: The Darul Islam in Indonesia* (The Hague: Martinus Nijhoff, 1981).

Various regions have also resented the government's management of the economy. The regime legitimized its authoritarian rule by emphasizing the need for order to achieve progress. Having made large investments in the exploitation of Indonesia's natural resources, especially oil, gas, and minerals, the central government generated decades of high growth rates. When profits from oil and gas declined, it responded by diversifying Indonesia's exports, increasing labor-intensive manufacturing, and deregulating the financial sector. These actions bolstered the economy until the Asian financial crisis unfolded in 1997–98.

During the boom years, however, profits were concentrated in the hands of a small elite around President Suharto. Although some regional elites were co-opted by the regime and profited from presidential "largesse," many of Indonesia's regions reaped few benefits from the exploitation of their natural resources. Rich provinces such as Aceh and Irian Jaya witnessed the emergence of resistance groups whose main grievance was this highly uneven distribution of the proceeds from economic development.

The Origins of Indonesia's Language Policy

Language policy in Indonesia has its roots in the rise of Indonesian nationalism. Bahasa Indonesia was one of the pillars of nationalist expression and an important source of unity for the diverse ethnic groups that lived in the Dutch East Indies. The adoption of Bahasa Indonesia was contested when it was first proposed as the language of the young nationalist movement. It eventually won out against Dutch and Javanese, however, mainly because of its potential to garner the greatest support. The recognition of Bahasa Indonesia as the official language of independent Indonesia in 1945 led to a language policy that focused on both reinforcing its use through education and promoting it in official communications and intergroup interaction. Local languages were protected by the constitution and were expected to be promoted as well.

Malay became an important language under Dutch colonial rule. Pasar Malay developed as a lingua franca in the archipelago, and its use increased with the spread of commercial ties among the islands. The Dutch East India Company gained control over trade in the archipelago during the late seventeenth and eighteenth centuries, but the focus of its colonial ventures was mainly the Spice Islands (the Moluccas) and Java. Other areas under Dutch control were generally ruled indirectly, allowing native local rulers to preserve their power and status. Pasar Malay remained an important lingua franca, while Dutch continued to be the language of Europeans and a small number of native officials who acted as intermediaries between the Dutch and the colony's vast native population.

Education policy under the Dutch colonial government reinforced the position of Malay relative to Dutch among the native population. Before the nineteenth century, there were virtually no schools in the archipelago other than local, traditional Islamic schools (*pesantren*). There were, however, a few missionary schools that used the local vernacular as the language of instruction. A secular education system was established only when the Kingdom of the Netherlands assumed direct control of the Dutch East Indies in 1816 and the Dutch East India Company was abolished. In the late 1840s, the government opened a few elementary schools and teacher-training schools mainly for Dutch settlers. Only in 1854 did the colonial government begin to acknowledge its duty to offer educational opportunities to the native population. At that time, only a few schools provided three years of elementary education. In 1892 just 52,700 children attended government schools; another 15,750 attended schools that had been established by Christian missionaries.[5]

When the school system expanded toward the end of the nineteenth century, the Dutch ensured that it would reinforce the desired division among racial groups. Europeans were considered superior to every other group. The mixed Indo-Europeans (Indos) and ethnic Chinese, who were treated as an intermediary group of commercial collaborators, fell in the middle of the hierarchy. The vast native population was lumped together at the bottom.

The Dutch colonial school system evolved into a complex network reflecting this hierarchy. In 1864 the Europeesche Lagere School (Dutch elementary school, literally European elementary school), or ELS, was opened for Dutch settlers; its main language of instruction was Dutch. In 1893 schools for natives were divided among First Class schools, for children of the aristocratic class of native traditional leaders, and Second Class schools, for children of the population at large. Only in 1907 did the Dutch open up the Volksschool in villages; these "schools of the people" provided three years of Western-style elementary education to local children. The Vervolgschool (continuation school) offered two additional years of education beyond the Volksschool. By the 1920s the Second Class schools had been folded into the Volksschool and Vervolgschool, in which the language of instruction was the local language or Malay. Children of high-level Indonesian officials went to the Hollandsch-

---

5. Paul van der Veur, *Education and Social Change in Colonial Indonesia*, Papers in International Studies, Southeast Asia Series No. 12 (Athens: Southeast Asia Program, Ohio University Center for International Studies, 1969), p. 1.

Inlandsche School (HIS or Dutch-Indonesian school), which had a curriculum similar to the ELS. The languages of instruction at the HIS were the local language and Malay in the first few years, and then Dutch.[6]

The Dutch severely restricted access to secondary education in the colony. Until 1921 children from the Volksschool and Vervolgschool could not go on to secondary school because these schools used Dutch as the language of instruction. The Schalkelschool (Link school) system was established so that these children could learn enough Dutch (through participation in a five-year program) to attend secondary school. Under this system, most students were not allowed to pursue higher education. Although enrollments in vernacular and Malay schools grew from 100,000 in 1900 to 2.2 million in 1940, the number of graduates per year was often much lower than new enrollments. For example, enrollment in the Vervolgschool in 1940 was 287,126, but only 102,000 pupils graduated that year. Such low ratios were typical across the native school system.[7] From a population of 70 million in 1940, only 34,550 children attended secondary school; this figure includes enrollments in both public and private schools. Of those, 37 percent were Europeans or Indos, 17 percent were Chinese, and 46 percent were natives.[8]

As a result of pressure from the Chinese community, the Dutch established the Hollandsch-Chineesche School (HCS or Dutch-Chinese school) in 1908. The HCS was similar to the HIS, providing a Western-style education similar to that of the ELS. The language of instruction was Dutch, but the teaching of Chinese was permitted.[9] In addition, the Chinese were allowed to establish a network of private schools where the language of instruction was Chinese and the focus of the curriculum was on China rather than the Indies. The latter reflected differences in the Chinese community between the *peranakan* (mixed ethnic origin) Chinese, whose ancestors had come long before and who used local languages or Dutch as their principal language, and the *totok*, who were more recent immigrants and who spoke Chinese and continued to honor Chinese traditions.[10]

---

6. Ibid., pp. 1–26; and Murray Thomas, "Who Shall Be Educated? The Indonesian Case," in Joseph Fischer, ed., *The Social Sciences and the Comparative Study of Educational Systems* (Scranton, Penn.: International Textbook Co., 1970), pp. 282–293.

7. Van der Veur, *Education and Social Change in Colonial Indonesia*, pp. 5–6; and Thomas, "Who Shall Be Educated?" pp. 282–293.

8. Thomas, "Who Shall Be Educated?" p. 295.

9. Van der Veur, *Education and Social Change in Colonial Indonesia*, p. 3; and Thomas, "Who Shall Be Educated?" p. 291.

10. Thomas, "Who Shall Be Educated?" p. 295.

As the Indonesian nationalist movement began to emerge in the 1920s, Malay came to be seen as increasingly important. Many national-ists favored Malay because it was spoken by more people than Dutch and because it was perceived as a language of the natives, while Dutch was reserved for Europeans and native collaborators.[11] Nevertheless, it was not clear in the 1920s that Malay would become the principal language of the independence movement.

Early nationalist groups had made extensive use of Malay. The Budi Utomo, for example, was created in 1908 to foster the advancement of Ja-vanese society. Yet most of its members were civil servants, and many of its leaders used Dutch as their main language because of their poor com-mand of native languages. When the question of the Budi Utomo's prin-cipal medium of communication was raised, Malay was adopted because too few in the broader membership had mastered Dutch, and Javanese was considered too difficult for Sundanese and Madurese members to learn.[12] The Taman Siswa Movement established private schools for na-tives across the Indies to foster Western education; Malay was the pri-mary language of instruction in these schools. The Sarekat Islam, a Muslim organization formed in 1912, developed into one of the strongest nationalist challenges to the Dutch; Malay played an important role as the language of communication within the movement. When the Dutch established the People's Council (Volksraad) in 1918 in response to liberal policies emanating from the Netherlands, a prominent member of the council, Mohammad Thamrin, was able to press for the adoption of Ma-lay as a second official language, even though most native representa-tives in the council used Dutch. Student organizations, such as Jong Minahasa (1918), Jong Ambon (1920), and even Jong Java (1918), prompted use of their vernacular languages as well as the use of Malay. Indonesian students in the Netherlands, who played an important role in the nationalist movement, used Dutch or their mother tongues, yet their organization was renamed Perhimpoenan Indonesia (a Malay name) in 1924.[13]

11.   George McTurnan Kahin, *Nationalism and Revolution in Indonesia* (Ithaca, N.Y.: Cornell University Press, 1963), p. 39.

12.   Akira Nagazumi, *The Dawn of Indonesian Nationalism: The Early Years of the Budi Utomo, 1908–1918* (Tokyo: Institute of Developing Economies, 1972), p. 72

13.   Anton Moeliono, "The First Efforts to Promote and Develop Indonesian," in Joshua Fishman, ed., *The Earliest Stage of Language Planning: The "First Congress" Phe-nomenon* (Berlin: Mouton de Gruyter, 1993), pp. 129–137; and Kahin, *Nationalism and Revolution in Indonesia*, pp. 37–63.

Malay increasingly became the language of unity against the Dutch. Although many members of the nationalist elite continued to use Dutch among themselves, as it was often their primary language, they recognized the greater potential of Malay to unify the native population. Dutch had always been the language of the colonial masters and inaccessible to natives. Nationalist newspapers began to publish in Malay, as did some local writers. The Nationalist Party of Indonesia adopted Malay when it was formed in 1927. In 1926 the First Indonesian Youth Congress discussed Malay and Javanese as possible options for inter-island communication. Javanese was still a potential contender at that point. At the Second Youth Congress in 1928, Malay (renamed "Indonesian") was adopted as the language of the Indonesian nation. As political parties were subsequently formed, they adopted Malay as their principal language of communication in addition to Dutch, as no major party was organized along ethnic lines.

Pasar Malay moved to the fore for several reasons. As a lingua franca, it already played a much greater role in the archipelago than Dutch or any local vernacular. Moreover, Dutch had several disadvantages: It was the language of the colonizer; it was restricted to a small elite; and it had the connotation of being a high-status language, yet it was unfamiliar to most of the population. Malay was favored over Javanese because it was (and is) a relatively easy language to learn. Malay also conveyed a message of democratic inclusiveness, unlike the more hierarchical Javanese, in which levels of language are used to reinforce status differences between the aristocracy and the lower classes.[14] Furthermore, Malay was not associated with any particular ethnic group, whereas Javanese was the language of the archipelago's largest group (45 percent of the total population). Many nationalists believed that the adoption of Javanese as the national language would have eroded non-Javanese support for the nationalist movement. Malay was thus the logical choice.

During the Japanese occupation in the 1940s, the position of Bahasa Indonesia in the archipelago was further strengthened. The Japanese curtailed the use of Dutch, and they eliminated the hierarchical school system that favored Dutch-language schools.[15]

When Indonesia proclaimed independence on August 17, 1945, it adopted Bahasa Indonesia as its sole official language. After 1928 the use

---

14.   Khaidir Anwar, *Indonesian: The Development and Use of a National Language* (Yogyakarta: Gadjah Mada University Press, 1985), pp. 17–18.

15.   Ibid., p. 46.

of Bahasa Indonesia became increasingly widespread, as it had come to represent the language of national unity. For nationalist leaders, the promotion and spread of Bahasa Indonesia in independent Indonesia was a key component of their campaign to nurture an Indonesian national culture. The Indonesian language was the principal bond between the various peoples of Indonesia. It would provide the base from which a nationalist ideology and a common set of values could be promoted.

There was some resistance to this position, even from organizations that proposed visions of an independent Indonesia that were very different from the nationalist program. Muslim organizations such as the Masyumi Party and the armed rebel movement Darul Islam shared the nationalist vision of a common opposition to colonial rule and a united, independent Indonesia. The Darul Islam proposed the establishment of an Islamic state with Bahasa Indonesia as its national language.[16] The communists espoused a different ideological program, but they also favored Bahasa Indonesia as the principal language of communication, and they accepted the basic assumption of "Indonesia" as a united, independent country.

The only threat to Bahasa Indonesia came from the Dutch, who sought to reestablish control over the archipelago after the end of World War II in 1945. For four years, the new republic fought the Dutch, who supported the establishment of small states along ethnic lines as a way to divide and reconquer the former colony. Toward this end, they created a state called "Pasundan" in West Java, based on Sundanese ethnicity.[17] In Bali several noble houses rejected the rising Republican nationalism and favored the Dutch. The Dutch had supported the growth of Balinese nationalism with the adoption of a policy of "Balinization" (*Baliseering*) beginning in the 1920s. This policy had strengthened and reshaped Balinese cultural traditions, including the Balinese language. Throughout the 1930s and 1940s, part of the Balinese nobility continued to support Balinese culture and the Dutch against the rise of Republican ideals and Bahasa Indonesia.[18]

After the defeat of the Dutch in 1949, the government used Bahasa Indonesia to help unify the country. Because it originated from Pasar Malay, Bahasa Indonesia was a relatively undeveloped language. Literature in Bahasa Indonesia was nascent, vocabulary was limited, and there was

---

16. Ibid., pp. 60–61.

17. Van Dijk, *Rebellion under the Banner of Islam*, pp. 98–99.

18. Geoffrey Robinson, *The Dark Side of Paradise: Political Violence in Bali* (Ithaca, N.Y.: Cornell University Press, 1995).

no uniform grammar. Thus nationalist leaders and subsequently the government of Indonesia could create new words or manipulate the vocabulary to serve the purposes of national unity. For example, in formulating the five principles of the nationalist ideology of Pancasila (which would become the foundation of the Indonesian state), they took words such as *permusyawaratan* (deliberation) from the Qur'an to attract Muslims and *gotong royong* (mutual cooperation), which resonated among the Javanese.[19] By deliberately importing words from a variety of languages to compensate for gaps in the vocabulary of Bahasa Indonesia, the government was able to claim that Bahasa Indonesia was representative of ethnic groups throughout the archipelago. The idea was to make Bahasa Indonesia the language of the Indonesian nation, without favoring any particular ethnic group.

This language policy also recognized the importance of local languages. Although nationalists promoted Bahasa Indonesia to unify the nation, they also favored the concept of "unity in diversity," which became the national motto. Local languages were adopted as part of the cultural heritage of the new nation and promoted in that role. The 1945 constitution recognized the role of local vernaculars and guaranteed their existence and development, where they were "spoken and well nourished by their respective speakers."[20]

Language Policy, 1949–98

Language policy had a relatively low profile in Indonesia after independence. This trend continued from the Old Order regime of President Sukarno (1945–65) to the New Order regime of President Suharto (1965–98). In both periods, language policy emphasized the development and spread of Bahasa Indonesia as the language of education, government, and business, while ensuring that local languages were protected. These policies displayed remarkable continuity as Bahasa Indonesia progressed steadily under both regimes. It became the first language of a growing number of Indonesians, mainly in urban areas.

Although committed in principle to protecting local languages, the government's policy varied among ethnic groups. The Chinese language,

---

19. The five principles of Pancasila in their most recent formulation are (1) belief in a supreme God, (2) justice and civility among peoples, (3) the unity of Indonesia, (4) democracy through deliberation and consensus among representatives, and (5) social justice for all. Anwar, *Indonesian*, pp. 48–49.

20. Soenjono Dardjowidjojo, "Strategies for a Successful National Language Policy: The Indonesian Case," *International Journal of the Sociology of Language*, Vol. 130 (1998), p. 46.

for example, was banned altogether under the Suharto regime. Languages of large ethnic groups, such as the Javanese and the Sundanese, were given minimal support, while many languages of smaller groups were neglected despite the threat of extinction. Overall, the government's language policies generated little ethnic friction.

The basic tenets of Indonesia's language policy were established under the Old Order regime of President Sukarno and implemented gradually. During the period of liberal democracy in the early 1950s, most Dutch-language schools were closed, though 125 remained open for some time. The language of instruction at the University of Indonesia continued to be Dutch but was eventually changed to Bahasa Indonesia. Political parties, especially Christian and Muslim parties, opened their own schools, with Bahasa Indonesia as the language of instruction. Political parties, though divided on fundamental questions about the nature of the Indonesian state, did not question the promotion of Bahasa Indonesia as the country's sole national language.[21]

Local languages were not neglected in the development of official policy. The ministry of education and culture issued a directive on the functions and tasks of its language section. These included the continued development of the Indonesian language as well as local languages and their literatures.[22] In taking this step, the government was seeking the support of various ethnic groups—especially larger groups with distinct languages and literary traditions, such as the Javanese, Sundanese, and Madurese.

When the liberal democratic regime was abandoned in 1957, the Old Order government accelerated the implementation of its policies. Following the formation of the Constituent Assembly in 1955 to adopt a new constitution, it became clear that the communists, nationalists, and Islamists were deeply divided over the basic principles of the Indonesian state. Impatient with the pace of discussions, Sukarno suspended the assembly and the parliament, restored the constitution of 1945, and imposed an authoritarian regime known as Guided Democracy. Under this regime, Sukarno moved against the last vestiges of Dutch colonialism. He nationalized Dutch businesses, asked the Dutch and Indos who had chosen Dutch citizenship to leave the country, and closed most of the remaining Dutch-language schools.

Also during this period, a repressive policy toward Indonesia's ethnic Chinese began to take shape. The Chinese, especially the *totok*, had

---

21. Thomas, "Who Shall Be Educated?" pp. 325–327.

22. Anwar, *Indonesian*, p. 80.

difficulty integrating into Indonesian society, and their loyalty to the state was often questioned. The Dutch had created a special category for the Chinese as "Foreign Orientals," alongside two others: "Natives" and "Europeans." Even Chinese who had adopted local languages and customs (*peranakan*) were lumped into this category, effectively prohibiting them from integrating into the native population. The Chinese were also subjected to discriminatory legislation, such as the Agricultural Law of 1870, which prevented them from acquiring land in rural areas. During the rise of the nationalist movement and subsequently after independence, the Chinese were divided on how to achieve the best future for their community. "Assimilationists" argued in favor of dropping the Chinese language and Chinese traditions, adopting Indonesian names, and speaking Bahasa Indonesia. Others preferred political mobilization to preserve their language and culture.

A significant proportion of the Chinese community in Indonesia had retained their Chinese identity and looked to China as their homeland, even after years and sometimes decades of settlement in the Dutch East Indies. China's extension of citizenship to all overseas Chinese and questions of dual citizenship were controversial in Indonesia. After considering a range of compromises, the Indonesian government adopted a law that forced Chinese inhabitants of Indonesia to choose between Indonesian and Chinese citizenship. Sukarno wanted to force ethnic Chinese to declare and affirm their loyalty to Indonesia.[23]

Other measures were also taken against ethnic Chinese. The government prevented Chinese with Indonesian citizenship from attending Chinese schools and greatly curtailed the use of Chinese as a medium of communication. By early 1959, only 510 of Indonesia's 1,800 Chinese schools remained open, and over time these were converted to Indonesian "national" schools, where the language of instruction became Bahasa Indonesia.[24]

Although most Chinese favored integration into Indonesian society, no single approach emerged. The Chinese involved in Baperki, the political movement for the protection of the Chinese community, continued to argue for the rights of the Chinese community. Meanwhile, the assimilationists argued for complete integration and the dismantlement of Chinese organizations. Baperki became associated with the Left, especially

---

23.   J.A.C. Mackie and Charles A. Coppel, "A Preliminary Survey," in Mackie, *The Chinese in Indonesia* (Melbourne, Victoria: Nelson, in association with the Australian Institute of International Affairs, 1976), pp. 1–18; and Charles A. Coppel, "Patterns of Chinese Political Activity in Indonesia," in ibid., pp. 19–62.

24.   Thomas, "Who Shall Be Educated?" p. 328.

the Communist Party of Indonesia, while others sided increasingly with groups in the armed forces.[25]

The year 1965 was a turning point for Indonesia's ethnic Chinese, when a failed Communist Party coup brought the military to power. After successfully undercutting Sukarno's position, General Suharto was named president in 1966. In addition, the armed forces eliminated the Communist Party. Thousands of people were killed, and many others imprisoned. The Chinese, many of whom were suspected of being communist sympathizers and of being more loyal to the People's Republic of China than to Indonesia, lost the right to organize their own political groups. They were also stripped of their language and cultural rights.

The Suharto government pursued the same basic language policies as its predecessor. The priority remained the advancement of Bahasa Indonesia as the principal means of communication. At the same time, the government showed leniency toward some transgressions, and it adopted a gradualist approach to the promotion of Bahasa Indonesia. Local languages were officially respected and supported by the state, although in practice little was done to protect them. The Chinese were the biggest losers in this regard, as the government forcibly prevented the use and spread of the Chinese language.

The government's policy aimed at further advancing the unity of the country through the promotion of Indonesian nationalism. The common language of Bahasa Indonesia, combined with efforts to build an Indonesian national culture around the state ideology of Pancasila, was favored over local languages. Although some of the measures to advance these goals were repressive, many others were benign. It has consequently become difficult to assess in postauthoritarian Indonesia the degree to which the government's language policy has been genuinely embraced.

The cornerstone of this policy continued to be education. The sole language of instruction from primary school to university was Indonesian.[26] Exceptions were made for the first three grades of elementary school, where local languages could be used in areas where students lacked a good command of Indonesian. (In these cases, local languages were considered transitional media of instruction.) This option could be employed, of course, only in regions where classes were linguistically homogeneous.[27] As for foreign languages, only English was taught in

---

25.   Coppel, "Patterns of Chinese Political Activity in Indonesia," pp. 63–73.

26.   Dardjowidjojo, "Strategies for a Successful National Language Policy," p. 36.

27.   Nababan, "Language in Education," p. 121.

junior high school; other languages were taught in senior high school and at university.[28]

The curriculum, which was designed by the ministry of education, focused on national unity. In primary school, a textbook entitled *History of the National Struggle* emphasized the importance of national unity and a common history. Another textbook, *Morals of Pancasila,* included a chapter entitled "Implementation of the Principle of the Unity of Indonesia" and was used in secondary schools.[29]

The use of Indonesian as the medium of instruction was linked to objectives espoused in these texts. As Barbara Leigh has argued: "The aim of 'morals of Pancasila' is to engender self-control and restraint for the perceived national good. The language used is Indonesian, for the national good is defined as emanating from Jakarta and it embodies all that is needed to maintain national unity."[30] The Indonesian language was the strongest symbol of national unity, and its use in the classroom to convey political messages as well as further strengthen national unity was particularly effective.

In 1987 the government began to reform Indonesia's curriculum. Among other things, it permitted instruction in local languages and, in so doing, hoped to preserve the values and cultures of local ethnic groups.[31] As one scholar put it: "The knowledge and understanding of the culture through the use of the language [were] expected to create or strengthen the learners' sense of belonging and pride in their basic or ethnic identity."[32] The leadership in Jakarta had come to recognize that local cultures and their languages were assets that could complement the spread of Bahasa Indonesia.

Although the government officially promoted the preservation of local languages, it did little to implement this policy. Furthermore, it approved only five local languages—Balinese, Batak, Buginese, Javanese, and Sundanese—for optional instruction.[33] Many other languages had no place in local curricula.

---

28. Ibid., p. 126.

29. Barbara Leigh, "Making the Indonesian State: The Role of School Texts," *Review of Indonesian and Malaysian Affairs,* Vol. 25, No. 1 (Winter 1991), p. 18.

30. Ibid., p. 35.

31. Nababan, "Language in Education," p. 125.

32. Ibid., p. 123.

33. Gary Theisen, James Hughes, and Paul Spector, *An Analysis of the Status of Curriculum Reform and Textbook Production in Indonesia* (Jakarta: Center for Informatics, Office of Educational and Cultural Research and Development, Ministry of Education and Culture, 1990), pp. 9–11.

During the Suharto era, the government's policy on the Chinese language became even more repressive. No new Chinese settlers were admitted into Indonesia. The children of Chinese who did not have Indonesian citizenship were sent to Indonesian national schools, and the remaining Chinese-language schools were closed. Jakarta issued a mandate that Indonesians of non-Chinese descent should constitute a majority in every classroom. One Chinese-language newspaper could be published, but only under tight government control. Many of its articles, in any event, were in Bahasa Indonesia. The government slightly relaxed its policy after 1968 by passing a measure that allowed a few schools to teach some Chinese language. The measure was abolished, however, in 1975.[34] The Chinese were asked to adopt Indonesian names and to eliminate the use of the Chinese language altogether. Official intimidation and public resentment of the Chinese further strengthened discrimination against the use of their language.

Another aspect of the New Order government's approach to language policy was the continued effort to increase the use of Bahasa Indonesia as the language of government and business. Indonesian was the official language for all civil service positions, and it continued to be widely promoted in formal gatherings (e.g., business meetings, scientific seminars, and various conferences).[35] The policy was flexible because enforcement was limited, relying to a large degree on social pressure.

To further promote Bahasa Indonesia, the New Order government followed its predecessors by employing a variety of methods to standardize the national language. In 1947 the Sukarno government had instituted a spelling reform to standardize the language across the archipelago. This reform was extended in 1972 and again in 1987.[36] The responsibility for ensuring greater standardization was given to the National Center for Language Cultivation and Development, which in 1993 began answering directly to the president. In addition, the center published a standard dictionary and grammar of Indonesian.[37] These efforts were reinforced by a campaign to reduce regional differences in the use of Indonesian in the public-school system, the government and military, and the mass media.

---

34. Charles A. Coppel, *Indonesian Chinese in Crisis* (Kuala Lumpur: Oxford University Press, 1983), pp. 13, 161.

35. Dardjowidjojo, "Strategies for a Successful National Language Policy," p. 36.

36. Nababan, "Language in Education," p. 120; and Dardjowidjojo, "Strategies for a Successful National Language Policy," p. 41.

37. Dardjowidjojo, "Strategies for a Successful National Language Policy," pp. 40, 42–43.

The increasing mobility of the population contributed to the standardization of Bahasa Indonesia as well.[38]

Successes and Failures

The government's language policy has been applied unevenly from region to region, achieving some of its objectives but also eliciting mixed responses. Language policy in Indonesia has produced virtually no violent conflict among the vast number of ethnic groups spread across the archipelago. The ethnic violence that has erupted has had little to do with linguistic issues.

The government has succeeded in creating a strong sense of loyalty to Bahasa Indonesia as a symbol of national unity, in part because the national language has remained fairly neutral in ethnic terms. The government's gradualist approach to language issues has also helped to prevent the outbreak of ethnic conflict. The government has encountered resistance only when it has pushed its policies forcefully, for example, in East Timor and Irian Jaya. In addition, while the use of Indonesian has increased, local languages have remained strong.

Bahasa Indonesia has helped to reinforce common bonds among the many peoples of Indonesia. One can question the depth and breadth of these bonds, but the role of Bahasa Indonesia and its subsequent use by nationalist groups of all ideological orientations has clearly helped to unify the country. Although its use was contested by a few groups in the years immediately before and after independence, these groups were mainly dependent on the Dutch and had little support among the population. The Sukarno and Suharto regimes capitalized on these advantages and took steps in education and linguistic standardization that have contributed to the development of harmonious relations among most ethnic groups.

The absence of violence stemming from the government's language policy may well be explained by Bahasa Indonesia's relationship to other languages. Instead of replacing local languages, Bahasa Indonesia has evolved with them and produced diglossia.[39] Indonesian is the language of officialdom and supra-ethnic communication, while local languages

---

38. Nababan, "Language in Education," p. 118.

39. Diglossia is "a sociolinguistic phenomenon in which complementary social functions are distributed between a prestigious or formal variety and a common or colloquial variety of a language, as in Greek, Tamil, or Scottish English." See http://www.dictionary.com/search?q-diglossia (accessed May 31, 2002).

are used in other situations. Indonesian is perceived as appropriate in a variety of public domains, including mass communication, mass education, government institutions, and even some religious institutions where different ethnic groups meet under a common religious umbrella.[40]

For many Indonesians, Bahasa Indonesia has represented advancement and modernization. Webb Keane relates the experience of a small ethnic group, the Anakalangese. Even without formal education, Keane maintains, some members of this group use Indonesian not in competition with or as a replacement of the local language, but to enhance their status. Indonesian is seen as an asset—not as a threat to local identity or language.[41] Almost every ethnic group in Indonesia similarly recognizes its value for modernization and interethnic communication.

These developments may be a result of the government's broader political strategy. In the 1980s the Suharto regime was at the height of its power. The parties that remained active, the Democratic Party of Indonesia and the Unity Development Party, were weak. A well-tuned bureaucratic, military, and political apparatus provided political direction across the archipelago. The Suharto regime relied on these institutional instruments to maintain national unity, but it also used ideology to reinforce its power base. Pancasila was elevated to the level of a state ideology that infused every aspect of Indonesia's political and social life. Civil servants were required to take courses on Pancasila and its applications, and the school curricula obliged students to learn it as well. Opposition to the regime was depicted as anti-Pancasila and deserving of opprobrium.

"Development" (*Pembangunan*) was another key concept in the New Order's philosophy. Indeed economic development was the regime's primary justification. Learning Bahasa Indonesia was said to be an essential part of becoming a modern Indonesian. It was also the medium through which the New Order state communicated its economic vision. In this capacity, Indonesian would be acquired by those seeking a place in the modern world. Local languages would be preserved for their cultural value, but they represented traditional society. According to James Errington, "As New Order development has been superposed ('from above') on communities which were recently peripheral to state control, Indonesian territory has become the scene of many such 'projects of modernity.' These can be thought of as emerging situations of 'contact'— between local community and national polity, between citizen and au-

---

40.   Hein Steinhauer, "The Indonesian Language Situation and Linguistics Problems," *Bijdragen tot de taal-, land-, en volkenkunde,* Vol. 150, No. 4 (1994), p. 773.

41.   Webb Keane, "Knowing One's Place: National Language and the Idea of the Local in Eastern Indonesia," *Cultural Anthropology,* Vol. 12, No. 1 (February 1997), p. 44.

thoritarian state—which are mediated and shaped by the Indonesian language."[42] Errington went on to observe that "state language policy has long been framed in terms consonant with those which serve in other spheres of modernization." The "politics of national language" was integral to the regime's objectives of order and social control to foster development.[43]

To what extent do Indonesians view Bahasa Indonesia as a positive acquisition, as opposed to an imposition from the state? The spread of Bahasa Indonesia relative to local languages illustrates the degree to which it is replacing or complementing local vernaculars. P.W.J. Nababan and several colleagues estimate that 40.7 percent of the total population of Indonesia could speak Bahasa Indonesia in 1971, and that 61 percent of the population could speak it in 1980. According to Hein Steinhauer, 34.8 percent of men older than fifty could speak Indonesian in 1990, whereas 92.8 percent of men and 85.1 percent of women between the ages of ten and forty-nine could speak it. In urban areas, these figures reached nearly 100 percent for men and women between ten and forty-nine years of age.[44] The government's language policies clearly contributed to a large increase in the number of Indonesian speakers, thereby reinforcing its role as the national language.

As a mother tongue, Bahasa Indonesia has progressed much more slowly. Speakers of Indonesian as a mother tongue reside mainly in urban areas. Nababan's survey in 1980–83 showed that 35 percent of people in Jakarta spoke Bahasa Indonesia as their first language, compared with 29 percent in Medan, 23 percent in Ujung Pandang, and 20 percent in Jayapura. In many urban areas, especially in Jakarta, Bahasa Indonesia was widely used because it served as a lingua franca for their ethnically diverse populations. Overall, however, local languages were dominant across all linguistic groups, though more children than adults were found to speak Indonesian at home.

This was not the case, however, in Bali, where there appears to have been greater resistance to learning Indonesian.[45] A possible explanation is

---

42.   James J. Errington, *Shifting Languages: Interaction and Identity in Javanese Indonesia* (Cambridge: Cambridge University Press, 1998), p. 3.

43.   Ibid., pp. 58–60.

44.   P.W.J. Nababan, Erwina Burhanudin, Tony Rachmadie et al., *Survei Kedwibahasaan Di Indonesia* [Survey on bilingualism in Indonesia] (Jakarta: Pusat Pembinaan dan Pengembangan Bahasa, Departemen Pendidikan dan Kebuyaan, 1992), p. 2; and Steinhauer, "The Indonesian Language Situation and Linguistics Problems," p. 760.

45.   Nababan, *Survei Kedwibahasaan Di Indonesia*, pp. 33, 38.

that the Balinese mixed less than other ethnic groups because of their Hindu-Buddhist religion. Most other groups in Indonesia are Muslim or include members of mixed religions. Among other groups, there might also be more mixed marriages in which Bahasa Indonesia would be the main language of communication at home. In addition, the Balinese have strongly advocated the preservation and promotion of their language.

In some areas, the use of local languages at home has declined without a corresponding increase in Bahasa Indonesia. The 46 percent of speakers in Irian Jaya who spoke their mother tongue, for example, is a low figure. This can be explained by the large number of languages in the area and the high probability of mixed marriages between speakers of different languages. In these cases and as a general means of communication, a local lingua franca has emerged. Some speakers adopt Bahasa Indonesia between speakers of different groups, but others adopt languages of dominant local groups (or the local form of Malay). This is leading to the disappearance of languages spoken by small groups, such as the Moi, the Inanwatan, and the Waropen. A similar trend has occurred in Kalimantan, where many small groups (such as the Paku and Bayan Dayak) were moved to areas where Banjarese has emerged as a local lingua franca.[46]

The use of local languages varies enormously from one region to another. Although the Indonesian constitution calls for the protection of local languages, this is done only when ethnolinguistic groups make the effort to do so. As a result, only the languages of large groups have received some protection or support. As noted earlier, only Balinese, Batak, Buginese, Javanese, and Sundanese received government approval to be taught as optional curricula in schools. Only Balinese, Javanese, and Sundanese have textbooks for instruction in their languages. Textbooks in other subjects are in Bahasa Indonesia.[47] The capacity to teach languages outside of the home has therefore been limited. As a result, the languages of smaller groups have been undercut by migration.

The use of Indonesian also varies. Among all ethnic groups, local languages are primarily used at home and in informal relations. More surprising, Nababan found that local languages were dominant even in public places, including the workplace.[48] Among some groups, this is

---

46. Steinhauer, "The Indonesian Language Situation and Linguistics Problems," pp. 769–772.

47. Theisen, Hughes, and Spector, *An Analysis of the Status of Curriculum Reform and Textbook Production in Indonesia*, p. 13.

48. Nababan, *Survei Kedwibahasaan Di Indonesia*, p. 41.

very significant. For example, a government survey in 1976 found that among the Acehnese, there was little use of Bahasa Indonesia. Acehnese was used by more than 80 percent of speakers in the family, among students, with teachers, in religious activities, in the workplace, in public speeches, and in the market. Everyone who was surveyed stated that they would use the local language with other Acehnese, and 84 percent said that they would reply in Acehnese if another Acehnese started the conversation in Indonesian. Among civil servants, 86 percent used Acehnese with their superiors and 94 percent with their peers.[49] Aceh is an important example of resistance to the use of Bahasa Indonesia in an area that has a strong separatist movement.

These trends appeared to change somewhat over time. For example, in a study conducted in 1990, Leigh discovered a pattern of language use in Aceh similar to that found in other parts of Indonesia: Bahasa Indonesia was used in all schools, and the mass media played a strong role in spreading Bahasa Indonesia to villagers. Although Acehnese continued to be used in the home, the fields, and the marketplace, Bahasa Indonesia was increasingly being used in public settings. It had even been introduced in sermons in local mosques. After-school meetings for religious instruction were delivered mainly in Indonesian. Overall, there was an acceptance of Indonesian as the "language of getting ahead." Even members of the Free Aceh Movement communicated regularly in Bahasa Indonesia despite their struggle against the Indonesian state.[50] It is not altogether clear to what extent earlier resistance to Indonesian was due to lagging education as opposed to deliberate political resistance. It is likely, however, that the increase in the use of Bahasa Indonesia was largely a result of intimidation and coercion.

In some cases, the government clearly used coercion to spread Bahasa Indonesia. In East Timor, for example, the government's language policies were not well received. After Indonesian troops invaded the island in 1975, an education program in Bahasa Indonesia was implemented, as were courses to create a new loyalty to the Indonesian state. The military brought more than 400 teachers from Java and Bali to East Timor, citing a near-absence of instructors on the island. Tetum, the lingua franca that united various linguistic groups in East Timor, was

---

49.   Budiman Sulaiman, Abdullah Faridan, Syarifah Hanum, and Razali Cut Lani, *Kedudukan Dan Fungsi Bahasa Aceh Di Indonesia* [The status and function of the Acehnese language in Aceh] (Jakarta: Pusat Pembinaan dan Pengembangan Bahasa, Departemen Pendidikan dan Kebuyaan, 1981), pp. 20–21, 60–72.

50.   Leigh, "Making the Indonesian State," pp. 35–36.

banned outside the Catholic school system. In 1985, out of 274,971 copies of textbooks used in elementary schools in East Timor, 200,670 copies stressed either the Indonesian language or the principles of Pancasila; textbooks on other subjects were extremely scarce.[51] Thus according to Alberto Arenas, "Through the imposition of the Indonesian language, the national Pancasila ideology, the respect for typical Indonesian symbols of patriotism such as the flag and the national anthem, and the dissemination of a new version of history, Indonesia sought to ensure that young Timorese could eventually come to view themselves as full-fledged Indonesian citizens."[52] But even after a full generation of Timorese was educated in Indonesian, they still resisted Jakarta by speaking Tetum. Tetum, Catholicism, a common history, and a sense of victimization defined Timorese nationalism in opposition to Indonesia.[53] The Timorese resistance was so strong that the Pope was asked not to celebrate his public mass in Bahasa Indonesia during a visit to the island in 1989. He celebrated it instead in Tetum.[54]

In East Timor the Indonesian government's language policies were seen as aggressively assimilationist. As a former Portuguese colony, it neither shared the Dutch colonial legacy nor participated in the movement that led other parts of the archipelago to embrace Indonesian nationalism. To the Timorese, Bahasa Indonesia, Indonesian culture, and Indonesian nationalism represented the forces of conquest. Jakarta's language policies, forcefully implemented and accompanied by harsh forms of political control, led to resentment and resistance.

A similar pattern developed in Irian Jaya. Some have argued that Papuans use Indonesian because they are afraid to express themselves in their local language—even in song: "While in other provinces people freely express their inner feelings through regional songs, the Papuans are not allowed to do so. There are no written prohibitions, but the condition created and experienced by Papuans is one of fear to express themselves through regional songs. . . . Many Papuans have been intimidated, beaten, tortured and killed only for having sung Papuan songs."[55]

---

51. John G. Taylor, *Indonesia's Forgotten War: The Hidden History of East Timor* (London: Zed, 1991), pp. 128–129.

52. Alberto Arenas, "Education and Nationalism in East Timor," *Social Justice*, Vol. 25, No. 2 (Summer 1998), pp. 131–132.

53. Ibid., pp. 137–139, 141–146.

54. Taylor, *Indonesia's Forgotten War*, pp. 155–156; and Arenas, "Education and Nationalism in East Timor."

55. Neles Kebadabi Tebay, "Explaining the Papuans' Wish to Secede from Indonesia," *Jakarta Post*, December 1, 1999.

Irian Jaya has experienced more military repression and control than most of Indonesia's other provinces because of the presence of a separatist movement, the Free Papua Movement. Like East Timor, Irian Jaya did not participate in the Indonesian nationalist movement, having been integrated into the country only in 1969. Furthermore, Indonesians have always thought of Papuans as racially and culturally distinct, and Papuans themselves argue that they are different from other ethnic groups in the archipelago. Attempts to spread the use of Bahasa Indonesia in Irian Jaya have therefore met with resistance.

One might have expected more resistance from Chinese Indonesians to the government's language policies. Although targeted in mob rioting and subjected to discrimination, the Chinese have tended to accede to the government's linguistic demands. Under the New Order regime of President Suharto, the Chinese had no ability to organize politically, and severe restrictions were placed on the use of the Chinese language. Even before these repressive policies, Malay and (later Bahasa Indonesia) was the first language of many Chinese. Some Chinese viewed assimilation in a positive light, believing that it would reduce discrimination directed against them. In any event, the government's repressive policies took away the ability of the Chinese to choose.

One potential problem may be Javanese influence on Bahasa Indonesia. Although Indonesian was intended to be ethnically neutral, the New Order's language policy has occasionally reflected the dominance of the Javanese. In urban elite circles, upwardly mobile Indonesians have adopted some Javanese practices, including the use of honorific titles and polite forms of official interaction. The use of "Pak," "Bu," and "Mas" in front of names to identify status is a Javanese practice that has become part of the expected etiquette beyond Java. The use of "mari-mari" or "permisi" when taking one's leave is an example of non-Javanese mimicking Javanese behavior. Words such as *memohon* (to put forward a request humbly) and *restu* (endorsement) are Javanese words used with increasing frequency by non-Javanese. Technocratic words taken from old Javanese include *buana* (cosmos), *wawasan* (vision), *citra* (image), *wisma* (house), *dharam* (obligation), and *pamrih* (self- interest).

Many Javanese words have entered Jakartanese Indonesian. Words such as *nongkrong* (squat) and *mbopong* (carry on the chest) have enriched the vocabulary, because there are no Indonesian equivalents for these terms. In other cases, however, they replace existing Indonesian words. As the use of Jakartanese has spread among Indonesia's youth and as a common language on television, so too have Javanese words.

Some old Javanese has been used for national symbols and institutions. The Indonesian motto *Bhinneka Tunggal Ika* (Unity in Diversity) is a

Javanese expression.[56] Other examples include the army's dual-function ideology (*dwi fungsi*), the women's organization Dharma Wanita, the word for retired officer (*purnawirawan*), and an award given to provinces that are most successful in implementing development (*Parasamya Pernakarya Nugraha*).[57]

The influence of Javanese on Bahasa Indonesia has been an irritant for non-Javanese groups. Although the latter mainly complain about the growing imposition of norms, values, and expected behavior among the elite in what is becoming the new standard, there are also some signs of discontent at the relative influence of Javanese within the Indonesian language. Although the influence of Javanese in Bahasa Indonesia has yet to be a source of open conflict, there are risks that some groups may begin to express more forcefully their resentment in post–New Order Indonesia.

Conclusion

The language policies of the central government of Indonesia have generally helped to dampen violent ethnic conflict in the country. Since independence successive governments have embraced similar linguistic principles and made the national language, Bahasa Indonesia, a source of unification rather than division.

Bahasa Indonesia has spread to most areas of the country because it is generally seen as being ethnically neutral. Indonesia began its postcolonial history with an enormous historical advantage over other countries because it already had a lingua franca: Malay. The Javanese, however, could be praised for resisting the temptation to push for the adoption of Javanese, which is spoken by nearly half of Indonesia's population, as the country's official language. They realized early on that Javanese was too difficult to learn and too hierarchical to draw strong support from non-Javanese. They also understood that Dutch should not be adopted because its use had been restricted and because it was intimately associated with colonial power.

---

56. Michael van Langenberg, "The New Order State: Language, Ideology, Hegemony," in Arief Budiman, ed., *State and Civil Society in Indonesia*, Monash Papers on Southeast Asia No. 22 (Clayton, Australia: Centre of Southeast Asian Studies, Monash University, 1990), p. 124; and Errington, *Shifting Languages*, p. 1.

57. See Joseph J. Errington, "Continuity and Change in Indonesian Language Development," *Journal of Asian Studies*, Vol. 45, No. 2 (May 1986), pp. 339, 343; and Ariel Heryanto, *Language of Development and Development of Language: The Case of Indonesia* (Canberra, New South Wales: Department of Linguistics, Research School of Pacific and Asian Studies, Australian National University, 1995), pp. 43–44.

Education has been a cornerstone of the government's language policy, with Indonesian used as the sole language of instruction. At the same time, exceptions have been tolerated. Civil servants have been allowed to continue their use of local languages, as have students in early education, without fear of punishment. The use of Indonesian has been encouraged but not forced. Its status as the language of national unity and modernity has been the driving force behind its widespread adoption.

Official support of other languages has softened opposition to Bahasa Indonesia. Constitutional recognition of the place of local languages, some allowance in the school curriculum for these languages, and the expectation of their continued use in private circles have strengthened the stability of linguistic relations in Indonesia.

Continuity in these basic tenets is probably the best recommendation one can make to ensure that linguistic issues remain relatively uncontentious in Indonesia. It is therefore not surprising that after Suharto's fall, the governments of Abdurrahman Wahid and Megawati Sukarnoputri chose to maintain the language policies of their predecessors.

There are some important areas of concern, however. Government policies toward the country's ethnic Chinese have been repressive and discriminatory, despite the fact that many Chinese have embraced Bahasa Indonesia as their first language and have supported restrictions on the use of the Chinese language. In what could be seen as a useful step, the Wahid government eliminated many of the existing restrictions on the Chinese language and Chinese-language newspapers. Though where language policies have been implemented in broader, more coercive contexts—as in Irian Jaya and Aceh—they have continued to meet with resistance.

In recent years, the lack of resources to preserve and strengthen local languages has become increasingly problematic. The government should provide more support for small ethnic groups to preserve their languages. Also, more space could be provided in the school curricula for teaching local languages. A related problem is the lack of textbooks in less-popular local languages. Many languages spoken by small groups have only recently become written languages, mainly through the work of foreign missionaries translating the Bible into these languages. Others have better-developed written languages but poor literary traditions and no textbooks suitable for school use. Only larger groups, such as the Javanese and the Sundanese, have been able to publish textbooks to teach local languages and associated courses. A continued lack of textbooks could increase the divide between local languages that are strengthened and those in danger of disappearing.

The government could take a more balanced approach in deciding which words to include in the vocabulary of Bahasa Indonesia. In the first years of the development of Indonesian, words were imported from languages across the archipelago in an attempt to establish the language's ethnic neutrality. More recently Javanese words have been introduced into Indonesian, giving rise to new tensions. The government could consider reducing the use of Old Javanese to identify national symbols, institutions, awards, and other official names. This would help to dampen resentment of "Javanization."

The Indonesian case suggests several general lessons for language policy and ethnic conflict. First, the adoption of a lingua franca that is relatively neutral in ethnic terms may meet with less resistance than one identified with a particular group. It can promote unity in countries with diverse ethnic populations and avoid conflicts over the dominance of one or several ethnic groups. It can also facilitate the adoption of a single official language, which in turn can enhance common education and governmental processes.

Second, a gradualist approach to policy implementation can facilitate broader and deeper acceptance of an official language. Bahasa Indonesia spread among Indonesia's population through its adoption as the language of government, business, and education. It was embraced most enthusiastically when it was not forced on the groups in question. Flexibility with respect to the use of local languages in education alongside the use of the official language can enhance support for the latter. The gradual implementation of national language policies can reassure minority groups that the official language does not pose a threat. Furthermore, the promotion of an official language for purposes that are distinct from those of local languages may be more acceptable to ethnic groups.

Third, while the adoption of a single official language has advantages, the neglect of local languages can stir resentment. The Indonesian case shows how government policy has been associated with the disappearance of some languages due to the allocation of insufficient resources for their promotion. Official language policies will be stronger and more effective if they are combined with policies to enhance local languages.

Finally, assimilationist policies are counterproductive. Jakarta's policies toward the Chinese and groups with secessionist movements have met with resistance. Less oppressive policies are more likely to lead to the use and spread of official languages while preserving the specific languages of ethnic groups. The preservation of minority languages does not necessarily pose difficulties for the promulgation of official languages.

Chapter 10

Harmonizing Linguistic Diversity in Papua New Guinea

R.J. May

Papua New Guinea is the most linguistically diverse country on earth. Its roughly 4 million people speak more than 850 separate languages, around 15 percent of the world's stock. In the words of linguist Stephen Wurm, this makes Papua New Guinea something of a "sociolinguistics laboratory."[1] It is also a country characterized by a fairly high level of social tension. For some time the country has been plagued by urban and rural lawlessness, including intergroup fighting in the highlands, and since 1988 a rebellion on the island of Bougainville. Yet despite Papua New Guinea's linguistic fragmentation, language has not been a fault line in the country's social unrest, and it has never been a significant point of political contention. Indeed Papua New Guinea is unusual in that its constitution barely mentions language, and it has never elaborated a coherent language policy.

Paradoxically, the explanation for the absence of conflict along linguistic lines may be found in the fact of Papua New Guinea's extreme linguistic diversity. In precolonial times there was only limited contact among the typically small Melanesian societies, which tended to differentiate themselves from their neighbors through language. With European contact, pidgin languages developed, separately in New Guinea (initially a German colony and later a mandated territory under Australian administration) and Papua (a British and then an Australian colony), as a means of communication both between Europeans and Papua New Guineans and, more important, among Papua New Guineans themselves. When

---

1. Stephen A. Wurm, *New Guinea and Neighboring Areas: A Sociolinguistics Laboratory* (The Hague: Mouton, 1979).

both territories came under a single (Australian) administration during and after World War II, the two lingua francas—Tokpisin and Police/Hiri Motu—were officially maintained, although English was the dominant language of government, education, and commerce. Tokpisin, however, was widely adopted as the language of daily exchange, even in Papua. On the eve of independence in 1975, some advocated the adoption of Tokpisin as Papua New Guinea's national language.

In effectively deciding against the creation of a national-language policy at independence, Papua New Guineans implicitly acknowledged the potential for conflict if one lingua franca were chosen over another. At the same time, they recognized the value of maintaining English as an international language, and they specifically endorsed the value that Papua New Guinean communities placed on maintaining the diversity of their vernacular (*tokples*) languages, which are now widely used in early education and adult literacy programs.

This "nonpolicy" provided an opening for the continued natural spread of Tokpisin, and virtually ensured that language never became an issue of political dispute. Tokpisin is now spoken by around three-quarters of the population of Papua New Guinea, some 85 percent of whom are predominantly subsistence agriculturalists, and among whom the national print literacy rate in 1990 was 45 percent.

The Social and Historical Context

Until the latter part of the nineteenth century, Papua New Guinea's fragmented small societies were characterized by endemic intergroup fighting. Individual societies were linked by relations of exchange (including intermarriage) and temporary military alliances. Trading relations generally extended along attenuated "chains" (the Tokpisin word *rop* [rope] is commonly used in relation to trade links), with one village or group of villages exchanging goods with the next village or group on the chain, often unaware of the ultimate origin (or destination) of the goods traded.[2] At each link along the chain at least some villagers were bilin-

---

2. The linguist Donald C. Laycock described the situation in one province: "In the Sepik area the main social unit was the village, and even trading with other villages of the same linguistic community was fraught with suspicion. Trading was carried across linguistic groups—often in the form of 'silent trading,' where, for example, hills natives would lay down their yams and sweet potato against the fish from the river, until an agreement was reached—but the more normal social interaction was warfare, where a knowledge of the other language was not necessary." Laycock, "Papuans and Pidgin: Aspects of Bilingualism in New Guinea," *Te Reo*, Vol. 9 (1966), p. 44. Thomas G. Harding describes similar "silent trading" on the Rai Coast. Harding, *Voyagers of the*

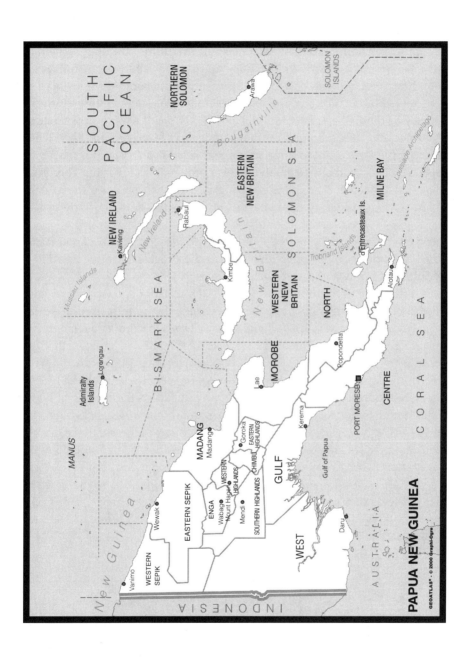

PAPUA NEW GUINEA

GEOATLAS* - © 2000 Graph-Ogre

gual, speaking their own language and that (or at least a simplified version) of their trading partners. In some cases, young boys were sent to live in the villages of these trading partners to learn other languages. Venturing beyond established chains was extremely hazardous.

In a few, more extensive and usually maritime, trading networks, "the language of one of the trading groups, sometimes in a somewhat simplified version, was used as a lingua franca throughout the whole circuit in question."[3] One of the more celebrated of such trading relationships was that between the Motu-speaking people of what is now Central Province and the National Capital District (Port Moresby) and the Elema and Koriki people of the Papuan Gulf. Every couple of years, the Motu people set off in their distinctive oceangoing canoes, carrying clay pots that they traded for sago and canoe logs with the people of the gulf in what was known as the Hiri trade. Another was the Kula trade of the Milne Bay islands. Along the north coast, trade networks linked the peoples of what is now Papua New Guinea with those of (West) Papua (Irian Jaya) and the Indonesian archipelago, in the process introducing Malay words into trade languages.

Although intergroup fighting was endemic, language was not always the marker that distinguished friend from foe. Frequently, fighting took place (and still does) among clans or lineages of the same language group, and sometimes alliances were formed across language divides. Language groups, in other words, were not necessarily political units.

In the latter part of the nineteenth century, limited European settlement began in eastern New Guinea,[4] particularly on the islands of New Britain and New Ireland, where copra plantations were established. In 1884 Germany annexed the northeastern segment of New Guinea, along with its offshore islands. Under pressure from the Australian colony of Queensland, Britain annexed the southeastern segment. In 1906 British New Guinea (Papua) was transferred to Australia and became an Australian protectorate. In 1914 an Australian Expeditionary Force "captured" German New Guinea, which subsequently became a League of Nations

---

Vitiaz Strait: A Study of New Guinea Trade Systems (Seattle: University of Washington Press, 1967), pp. 63–64. See also Stephen W. Reed, *The Making of Modern New Guinea* (Philadelphia: American Philosophical Society, 1943), p. 45; and Gillian Sankoff, "Multilingualism in Papua New Guinea," in Stephen A. Wurm, ed., *Language, Culture, Society, and the Modern World*, Pacific Linguistics Series C–No. 40, Vol. 3 (Canberra, Australian Capital Territory [ACT]: Department of Linguistics, Research School of Pacific Studies, Australian National University, 1977), p. 285.

3. Sankoff, "Multilingualism in Papua New Guinea," p. 270.

4. Western New Guinea was colonized at this time by the Dutch and eventually became part of the Republic of Indonesia; it is therefore beyond the scope of this chapter.

trust territory under Australia's mandate. Although both parts of eastern New Guinea were formally put under Australian jurisdiction, the two territories initially maintained separate administrations and distinct administrative cultures. During World War II, both territories came under a single Australian military administration. After the war the joint administration continued, though some elements of the separate administrative cultures lingered on. From the end of World War II until the latter part of the 1960s, a "Pax Australiana" was gradually extended—if sometimes tenuously—throughout Papua New Guinea, particularly into the populous highlands of the interior, where prewar European contact had been fleeting. In 1975 Papua New Guinea became an independent state.

Linguistic Diversity and Lingua Francas

Until the 1980s Papua New Guinea was generally described as having "over 700" vernacular languages. Although, even then, some of the less popular languages were heading for extinction, more recent research has set the number at around 850.[5] Of these, the largest language group is Enga, a non-Austronesian (or "Papuan") language spoken in the highlands, which has around 250,000 speakers, who speak several dialects. The next largest are Melpa, with about 150,000 speakers, and Kuman, with approximately 75,000; both are non-Austronesian languages of the highlands. There are probably another 8 languages with more than 50,000 speakers each; 7 are non-Austronesian highlands languages, and 1 (Kuanua) is an Austronesian language of the New Guinea islands. (See Table 10.1.) Not surprisingly, estimates of the numbers of speakers of these languages come from different sources and relate to different time periods; thus reliable comparative figures are unavailable. Such linguistic diversity reflected and reinforced the fragmentation of traditional societies. It also posed an obvious problem for the Europeans who came to trade, convert, and colonize.

NEW GUINEA

In New Guinea a pidgin language had developed before the establishment of the German colonial regime in 1884.[6] Melanesian pidgin (or

---

5.   Linguist Barbara F. Grimes has given a figure of 854, which the government of Papua New Guinea seems to have adopted. Grimes, ed., *Ethnologue: Languages of the World*, 11th ed. (Dallas, Tex.: Summer Institute of Linguistics, 1988). Grimes's data, however, are very much a "best estimate."

6.   For a useful survey of administration and language policy under both the German and Australian colonial regimes, see R.K. Johnson, "Administration and Lan-

Table 10.1. Vernacular (*Tokples*) Languages in Papua New Guinea.

Number of Speakers	Number of Vernacular Languages
Fewer than 100	50
101–500	226
501–1,000	135
1,001–10,000	331
10,001 or more	73
Unknown	25
Total	**840**

SOURCE: Otto M. Nekitel, *Voices of Yesterday, Today, and Tomorrow: Language, Culture, and Identity* (New Delhi: UBS Publishers' Distribution, in association with Nekitel Pty. Ltd., 1998), shap. 7. Nekitel draws substantially on Barbara F. Grimes, ed., *Ethnologue: Languages of the World*, 12th. ed. (Dallas, Tex.: Summer Institute of Linguistics, 1992), which itself draws on earlier data.

neo-Melanesian or, later, Tokpisin) originated in the Pacific islands labor trade of the late nineteenth century and was probably brought back to New Guinea by indentured laborers who had worked on plantations in Queensland and Samoa.[7] The language had a simplified grammatical structure and a vocabulary based on English but also drawing on German, Malay, and local vernacular sources (especially that of the dominant Kuanua-speaking Tolai group of East New Britain). By the 1880s Tokpisin was well established in the islands and north coast of New Guinea, and was being spread by the movement of indentured laborers and promoted through the trading activities of the German New Guinea Company. When Catholic missionaries of the Society of the Divine Word (SVD) arrived in northern New Guinea in 1896, the mission's founder, Fr. Eberhard Limbrock, reported: "There is a kind of English around that is already fairly well established along our coast. . . . It is going to be hard to

guage Policy in Papua New Guinea," in Wurm, *Language, Culture, Society, and the Modern World*, pp. 429–468.

7. For a detailed account of the development of Tokpisin, see Reed, *The Making of Modern New Guinea*, App. 1; Stephen A. Wurm, "Pidgin English," in Peter Ryan, ed., *The Encyclopaedia of Papua New Guinea* (Melbourne, Victoria, Australia: Melbourne University Press, 1972), pp. 902–905; Peter Muhlhausler, "The History of New Guinea Pidgin," in Wurm, *Language, Culture, Society, and the Modern World*, pp. 497–510; and Stephen A. Wurm and Peter Muhlhausler, eds., *Handbook of Tok Pisin (New Guinea Pidgin)*, Pacific Linguistics Series C–No. 70, Vol. 3 (Canberra, ACT: Department of Linguistics, Research School of Pacific Studies, Australian National University, 1985).

supplant. . . . This kanaka [native] English is more widely spoken than German."[8]

The government's official policy was to promote the usage of the German language, and colonial governors in New Guinea were ordered to encourage adherence to this policy. In practice, the policy was not effectively pursued (the first German administration school opened in 1908, began its German language program in 1911, and closed in 1914). Indeed mission-run schools taught mostly in Tokpisin, which was also the language of commerce and that commonly used by administration officers. By 1909, despite the colonial governor's dislike of a language that many considered brutish, the German administration had established a Tokpisin language school in Alexishafen (Madang) and was encouraging village leaders to learn Tokpisin.

Meanwhile the missions used both Tokpisin and local languages in their evangelical work. In East New Britain, both the Marist Catholics and the Methodists employed Kuanua. On the New Guinea mainland, missionaries in the latter part of the nineteenth century, and later pastors, frequently used the languages of coastal groups with whom they had first contact (and who often served as their guides), as they ventured further inland. On the north coast, between the Catholic mission's headquarters at Alexishafen and the Dutch New Guinea border (a distance of some 350 miles), there were reported to be 45 local languages. In 1904 pioneer missionary Fr. Andreas Puff wrote that of the mission's seventeen stations, only three shared a common language with the station next to them.[9] The SVD mission initially adopted Boiken, the language of the people living on the coast and islands around what is now Wewak, East Sepik, as the language of evangelization. In 1931, however, the mission decided to adopt Tokpisin as the language of communication and evangelization. Mission leader Fr. Francis Kirschbaum observed that although neither the German government nor the mission had done anything to promote Tokpisin, the people themselves had adopted it: "Pidgin is today the medium of communication between Whites and Blacks, and between Blacks and Blacks everywhere. No power on earth will ever stamp it out. Pidgin is modern and liked!"[10]

The Evangelical Lutheran Church, which arrived in New Guinea in

---

8. Quoted in Francis Mihalic, *Readings in PNG Mission History: A Chronicle of SVD and SSpS Mission Involvement on Mainland New Guinea between 1946 and 1996* (Madang: Divine Word University Press, 1999), p. 287.

9. Ibid.

10. Quoted in ibid., p. 290.

1886, initially rejected Tokpisin—the mission's founder describing it as "worthless gibberish unworthy of communicating the word of God."[11] The church used local languages instead, particularly Jabem (Yabim), the language of the villages around its headquarters at Finschhafen; Kate (Kote), the language of a small group in the mountains of the Huon Peninsula in Morobe Province; and the Graged (Bel) and Amele languages in the Alexishafen area.[12] Later, Kate was used as a lingua franca when the Lutheran Church expanded into the New Guinea highlands. The church maintained this policy until 1956, when it officially recognized Tokpisin—though it continued to use "church languages" until well into the 1970s.[13]

In 1921 Australia officially took over the administration of former German New Guinea (New Guinea). In the same year, it adopted the already well-established Tokpisin as its principal (unofficial) language.

SVD historian Fr. James Noss recalls that in 1931 Father Kirschbaum established a committee to standardize and systematize Tokpisin; the committee produced a Tokpisin primer, several textbooks, and a monthly magazine. There were at this stage three main streams of Tokpisin: administration Pidgin (used by government officers and others and containing more English words);[14] Alexishafen Catholic Mission Pidgin (used by the SVD mission and drawing on transliterated Latin vocabulary); and Rabaul Catholic Mission Pidgin, or "Tok Boi" (used by the Marist order in Rabaul, East New Britain, and drawing on the local Kuanua language).[15] In 1957 SVD Fr. Francis Mihalic, in collaboration with the Papua New Guinea Department of Education, produced the first official dictionary and grammar of Tokpisin; it was based on the Alexishafen (Madang/Sepik) stream.[16] Twelve years later Mihalic collaborated with

---

11. Quoted in ibid., p. 293.

12. Jabem and Graged are Austronesian languages; Kate and Amele are non-Austronesian.

13. See Herwig Wagner and Hermann Reiner, eds., *The Lutheran Church in Papua New Guinea: The First Hundred Years, 1886–1986* (Adelaide, South Australia: Lutheran Publishing House, 1986). For an overview of "church languages," see A.J. Taylor, "Missionary Lingue Franche: General Overview," in Wurm, *Language, Culture, Society, and the Modern World*, pp. 833–838.

14. After independence, this was often referred to as "Urbanized Pidgin," and the content of English words steadily increased.

15. Mihalic, *Readings in PNG Mission History*, pp. 290–291.

16. Considering Mihalic's important role in the propagation of Tokpisin, it is interesting that in his preface to the dictionary he declared that he was "looking forward to the day when Neo-Melanesian and the book would be buried and forgotten, when

the Lutheran Church in producing a Tokpisin *Nupela Testamen* (New Testament), 32,000 copies of which were sold within six months.

PAPUA

In British New Guinea, or Papua, where missionary and commercial contacts began in the 1870s, "broken" English was the first "unofficial language," spread by miners and traders. The early missions and some traders, however, also used local languages (particularly Suau, Wedau, and Dobu [the language of the Kula trade] in the east and Kiwai and Toaripi in the west). As the Germans had done in German New Guinea, the British and Australian administrations in Papua adopted English as the official language and sought to have mission schools teach in English.

From an early stage, however, the administration (based in Port Moresby) adopted a pidginized form of Motu, the language of the people of the Port Moresby area. Thomas Dutton records that a "simplified Motu," used in transactions between the Motu and visiting strangers, existed before the British administration came to Papua. Beginning in the 1880s, this "indigenous pidginized language" was adopted by the administration and others, including the London Missionary Society (LMS), the dominant mission in Papua.[17] Following the establishment of the Armed Native Constabulary in Papua in 1890, "Pidgin Motu" effectively became the official language and "the principal instrument of the spread of law and order" in Papua.[18] Thereafter it became known as "Police Motu," until 1970 when it was renamed "Hiri Motu."[19] Police or Hiri Motu differed from "pure" Motu in having a simpler grammar and a vocabulary less rich and containing words drawn from other Papuan and Torres Strait

---

standard English and the *Oxford Dictionary* will completely replace both" (1971 ed., p. ix).

17. Thomas E. Dutton, *Police Motu: Lena Sivarai* (Port Moresby: University of Papua New Guinea Press, 1985), p. x.

18. Ibid., p. 1.

19. Dutton notes, however, that contrary to popular belief, Police/Hiri Motu was probably not the language of the Hiri trade. Rather it was "most probably a continuation of the simplified form of Motu used by the Motu in trading with or talking to linguistically related and unrelated peoples in their immediate area, before the arrival of Europeans." Ibid., p. 1. Elsewhere he suggests that the Hiri trade employed two pidginized Gulf languages, which he calls Hiri Trading Language (Elema variety) and Hiri Trading Language (Koriki variety), and that the use of these languages rather than Motu "reflects the weak or inferior position of the Motu vis-à-vis their hosts." Thomas E. Dutton, "Towards a History of the Hiri: Some Beginning Linguistic Observations," in Dutton, ed., *The Hiri in History: Further Aspects of Long Distance Motu Trade in Central Papua,* Pacific Research Monograph No. 8 (Canberra, ACT: Australian National University, 1982), p. 70.

languages (e.g., Suau, Koriki, and Binandere), Polynesian languages (brought in by the Polynesian missionaries of the LMS), and "broken" English. The 1906/07 annual report of British New Guinea referred to Police/Hiri Motu as "a kind of dog Motu—hardly intelligible to those who speak Motu as their native language."[20] In the same year, however, a royal commission noted that "Motuan . . . has practically been constituted the official language, and . . . Government Officials are supposed to be proficient in its use."[21]

The Australian lieutenant governor of Papua from 1909 to 1940, Sir Hubert Murray, was particularly antipathetic to Pidgin English—describing it in 1924 as "vile gibberish"[22]—and fostered Police/Hiri Motu as an alternative. Nor did he see value in preserving the "native languages." However, even though Police/Hiri Motu became the unofficial official language of the administration and most missions in Papua, English remained the official language and the official medium of instruction in schools.

THE COMBINED ADMINISTRATION OF PAPUA AND NEW GUINEA

As noted above, when the two territories came under Australian administration, they retained their separate administrative cultures—and this included language. Thus, at the outbreak of World War II, the language policies of Papua and New Guinea were broadly similar: English was the official language in both territories; however, Tokpisin remained the lingua franca and language of field administration in New Guinea, while Police/Hiri Motu continued as the administrative lingua franca of Papua.[23] Indeed, to a substantial extent, Tokpisin was part of a New Guinean identity and Police/Hiri Motu part of a Papuan identity. Educa-

---

20.   *Annual Report of British New Guinea, 1906–07*, p. 21. See Stephen A. Wurm, "Motu and Police Motu: A Study in Typographical Contrasts," Papers in New Guinea Linguistics No. 2 (Canberra, ACT: Australian National University, 1964), p. 33. According to Wurm, "The level of mutual intelligibility between Motu and Police Motu [is] predominantly low to very low." Ibid.

21.   Quoted in Dutton, *Police Motu*, p. 80.

22.   J.H.P. Murray, *Notes on Colonel Ainsworth's Report on the Mandated Territory of New Guinea* (Port Moresby: Government Printer, 1924), p. 10.

23.   Southern Highlands Province is a special case. Although administratively part of Papua (and in the 1970s a source of some support for Papuan separatism), it is culturally part of the New Guinea highlands. Moreover, large parts of the province had little contact with any administration until well into the 1950s. Consequently, it was exposed to both Police/Hiri Motu and Tokpisin (but of all of Papua New Guinea's provinces, it has the highest proportion of people who speak neither).

tion in both territories was left largely to the missions, which determined their own policies on language (see below). However, while Tokpisin was widely spoken in New Guinea (especially among those—primarily from the Sepik [in the north] and the relatively recently contacted central highlands—who had migrated temporarily to other parts of the country as indentured laborers),[24] Police/Hiri Motu had much more restricted usage in Papua, having limited currency in wide areas of inland and eastern and western Papua.

World War II boosted the use of both Police/Hiri Motu and Tokpisin, when large numbers of Papuans and New Guineans, serving mostly on carriers, adopted them as lingua francas. Also during this period, radio broadcasting commenced in both Tokpisin and Police/Hiri Motu. In the postwar period, however, Tokpisin became increasingly widespread (even in Papua) as in-country migration—especially from the highlands to the national capital, Port Moresby—grew during the late 1960s and 1970s. Census figures for 1966 suggested that 37 percent of the population spoke Tokpisin, 8 percent Police/Hiri Motu, and 13 percent English. Nationally, however, 55 percent spoke none of these three languages (and this national figure ranged from 5 percent in New Ireland to 91 percent in Southern Highlands and 86 percent in Western Highlands).

The Question of a National Language

After World War II, the movement toward self-government and independence gradually accelerated in Papua and New Guinea. Local governments were established progressively across the Australian-controlled territory as part of the process of creating democratic institutions. In some areas—especially around Port Moresby—English was the principal working language. Tokpisin, however, was the most common working language in New Guinea, and Police/Hiri Motu was often used in Papua. Records were normally kept in English.

When a representative (part-appointed, part-elected) legislative council was set up in 1961, English, Tokpisin, and Police/Hiri Motu were the common languages of debate, and simultaneous translation was provided. This remained the situation when Papua New Guinea's first predominantly elected parliament was established in 1964. Of the 54 elected (38 indigenous and 16 "European") and 10 administration-appointed ("official") members, 15 indigenous and the 16 elected European and 10

---

24. In 1942 Reed estimated that one-fifth of the "native population" spoke Pidgin. Reed, *The Making of Modern New Guinea*, p. 284.

official members spoke English; 37 indigenous, 14 elected European, and 6 official members spoke Tokpisin; and only 9 indigenous, 4 elected European, and no official members spoke Police/Hiri Motu. One member, from the Southern Highlands, spoke only vernaculars (and so was provided with a simultaneous translator). In other words, 89 percent of parliamentary members spoke Tokpisin, 63 percent spoke English, and 20 percent spoke Police/Hiri Motu.

In reporting these data, the senior interpreter of the House of Assembly observed: "Certain members, both European and Indigenous, use English when they want a particular point to be given publicity. . . . Most Members use Pidgin to catch votes and sway opinion in the House. . . . There is more and more overt frustration with debates in English. . . . The Papuan Members very early in the life of the House realized this National flavour of Pidgin and virtually dropped using Motu. They, as do the European members, always use Pidgin when they want support."[25] By the time the second House of Assembly convened in 1967, every member spoke at least English, Tokpisin, or Police/Hiri Motu, but Tokpisin increasingly dominated parliamentary debate.

When a Pacific Islands Regiment (PIR, the forerunner of the post-independence Papua New Guinea Defence Force) was formed in 1951, Tokpisin was adopted as its lingua franca and was used by both New Guineans and Papuans. Harry Bell has noted that Tokpisin "appears to have been speedily assimilated by the Papuans."[26] As the defense force expanded in the mid-1960s and a major education effort was mounted to train new recruits (many of whom were illiterate), the official policy became the promotion of English. Tokpisin, however, was the language commonly spoken among soldiers. Bell has also observed that Papuan soldiers from different language groups used Tokpisin among themselves even when no New Guinean was present, and that the percentage of fluent Police/Hiri Motu speakers was "drastically dwindling."[27]

Moreover, with the growth of nationalist sentiment in the late 1960s and early 1970s, Tokpisin rose in status from an "inferior" language of the colonial regime to an expression of Papua New Guinean nationalism. This was reflected in the 1970s in a corpus of Tokpisin (and, to a minor ex-

---

25. Quoted in Brian Hull, "The Use of Pidgin in the House of Assembly," *Journal of the Papua and New Guinea Society*, Vol. 2, No. 1 (1968), pp. 22–25.

26. Harry L. Bell, "New Guinea Pidgin Teaching: Pidgin and the Army—An Example of Pidgin in a Technically-Oriented Environment," in Wurm, *Language, Culture, Society, and the Modern World*, p. 672.

27. Ibid., p. 675.

tent, Police/Hiri Motu, hereafter Hiri Motu) writing.[28] Bell observed that for the PIR, "the educated soldier tends to resent being addressed in Pidgin by a strange European, presumably on grounds that as a black man, he is automatically assumed to be uneducated. The same man, however, when addressed by a trusted European in English is as often likely to reply in Pidgin."[29] His observation was equally applicable outside the PIR.

By the late 1960s, there was evidence of growing support for Tokpisin as a national language. Two recently emerged political parties, the Christian Democrats and Pangu Pati, included this in their political platforms. In 1966 Wurm wrote a paper addressing the question of a national language, and though he stopped short of advocacy, his preference seemed to lie with Tokpisin.[30] With the establishment of the University of Papua New Guinea at this time, there was further discussion of a prospective language policy and even more evidence of support for Tokpisin. In 1971, however, at a conference on the future of Hiri Motu arranged by the administration's Department of Information and Extension Services, prominent politician (and subsequently Papua New Guinea's first governor-general) John Guise warned that the use of Hiri Motu "could become a political issue." "Police Motu had been rubbished for too long," Guise said, and "if this continued there could be trouble."[31]

In 1973 a surge of Papuan ethnic identity—prompted in part by fears that the better-educated Papuans would be swamped by migrants from the highlands—resulted in the formation of a Papuan subnationalist movement, Papua Besena, headed by the parliamentary member for Central (Province), Josephine Abaijah. On the eve of independence in 1975, Abaijah made a unilateral declaration of Papuan independence.[32] News-

28.   See, for example, R.J. May, "'Nationalism and Papua New Guinea Writing," *Australian Quarterly*, Vol. 43, No. 2 (1971), pp. 55–63.

29.   Bell, "New Guinea Pidgin Teaching," p. 676.

30.   Stephen A. Wurm, "Papua–New Guinea Nationhood: The Problem of a National Language," *Journal of the Papua and New Guinea Society*, Vol. 1, No. 1 (1966–67), pp. 7–19.

31.   Reported in "Motu: A Future Political Issue?" *Post-Courier*, May 26, 1971, p. 4.

32.   For accounts of this movement, see Boio B. Daro, "The Papua Besena Movement: Papua Dainai, Tano Dainai, Mauri Dainai," IASER Discussion Paper 7 (Port Moresby: Institute of Applied Social and Economic Research, 1976); Robert McKillop, "Papua Besena and Papuan Separatism," in R.J. May, ed., *Micronationalist Movements in Papua New Guinea*, Political and Social Change Monograph 1 (Canberra, ACT: Department of Political and Social Change, Research School of Pacific Studies, Australian National University, 1982), pp. 329–358; and Josephine M. Abaijah, *A Thousand Coloured Dreams:*

paper reports on Papua Besena briefly mentioned concern about the decline Hiri Motu.[33] But even though Papua Besena generally held its meetings in Hiri Motu, language was not a major issue in the politics of Papuan separatism (Abaijah herself advocating the use of English).[34] By the early 1980s, the Papua Besena movement waned.

In the lead-up to independence, the country's Constitutional Planning Committee (CPC) undertook extensive public consultation prior to the drafting of its final report. The subject of language did not feature in this discussion, except in the limited context of citizenship by naturalization. The CPC's comparatively brief comment on language appeared in a section on national goals and directive principles. In point 61, under the heading "National Languages," the report stated: "We strongly recommend that the State clearly recognize Pidgin, Hiri Motu and English, as national languages. Literacy in these languages should be actively promoted to encourage better communication between many different groups of our people, and enable them to participate more fully in the affairs of the country." In point 62, under the same heading, it stated: "Literacy in local languages should not, however, be discouraged as they should be safeguarded from falling into disuse. Thus we envisage that as many as possible of our people will be multi-lingual."[35] In the section entitled "Papua New Guinean Ways," it added: "We recognize our ethnic diversity and its varying forms of cultural expression as positive strengths."[36]

Reflecting this recognition, the constitution calls for "all persons and governmental bodies to endeavour to achieve universal literacy in *Pisin, Hiri Motu,* or English, and in *'tok ples'* or *'ita eda tano gado'* [the Tokpisin and Motu terms for vernaculars]." The constitution's section on citizenship by naturalization stipulates: "To be eligible for naturalization, a person must . . . speak and understand Pisin or Hiri Motu, or a vernacular of the country, sufficiently for normal conversational purposes." Apart from brief provisions requiring that a person who is arrested or detained be in-

---

The Story of a Young Girl Growing Up in Papua (Mount Waverley, Victoria, Australia: Dellasta Pacific, 1991).

33. See "Motu: A Future Political Issue?" *Post-Courier,* June 5, 7, 13, 1973, p. 4.

34. Abaijah's autobiography contains only one reference to language. In describing an incident in which a policeman took exception to her addressing him in English, she says, "The police liked to make Papuans talk in Pidgin English, a colonial language used in ex-German New Guinea." Abaijah, *A Thousand Coloured Dreams,* p. 47.

35. Constitutional Planning Committee, *Final Report* (Port Moresby, 1974), p. 2/8, mimeo.

36. Ibid., p. 2/14.

formed of the reasons "in a language that he understands," these are the only references to language in an otherwise detailed constitution.

Significantly, there is no provision for a national language in either the constitution or the National Identity Act (passed before independence and substantially unchanged since). Nor is the question of language mentioned in the extensive provisions relating to the National Parliament or in its standing orders. In practice, English, Tokpisin and, rarely, Hiri Motu are the languages of parliamentary debate, though there is no formal restriction on language use. Much of the proceedings of parliament in fact take place in a mix of English and Tokpisin. Simultaneous translation is provided, but the record of debate is published in English only.[37] In a 1988 sample of five ninety-minute sessions of question time, covering fifty-two parliamentary "utterances," 15 percent were in English, 34 percent in Tokpisin, and 51 percent in a mixture of English and Tokpisin; no use of Hiri Motu was recorded. The speaker began in Tokpisin 79 percent of the time.[38]

Although language was not a significant issue in the lead-up to independence, it surfaced in a long-running public debate soon after. A newly appointed professor of linguistics, Thomas Dutton, prompted the debate in a public lecture at the University of Papua New Guinea in May 1976. He started with the observation that Papua New Guinea had no policy on national language and argued that "in practice English functions as a national language," complemented by Tokpisin and Hiri Motu. He went on to advocate the adoption of Tokpisin as the national language "for all internal communication and administrative purposes and for formal education at *all* levels—primary, secondary and tertiary."[39] Dutton accused the more zealous supporters of English of "cultural and linguistic imperialism,"[40] and described attempts to make English a national language as

---

37. Vere Bau provides a brief profile of the parliamentary interpretation service. Bau, "A Mini 'United Nations' Interpreting Service," *Bikmaus*, Vol. 2, No. 2 (1981), pp. 83–93.

38. Otto M. Nekitel, *Voices of Yesterday, Today, and Tomorrow: Language, Culture, and Identity* (New Delhi: UBS Publishers' Distribution, in association with Nekitelson Pty. Ltd., 1998), chap. 9.

39. Dutton's lecture and a selection of media responses are reproduced in B. Mac-Donald, *Language and National Development: The Public Debate, 1976*, Occasional Paper No. 11 (Port Moresby: Department of Language, University of Papua New Guinea, 1976) (emphasis in original). Some of Dutton's argument had been anticipated in Ranier Lang, "A Plea for Language Planning in Papua New Guinea," IASER Discussion Paper 1 (Port Moresby: Institute of Applied Social and Economic Research, 1976).

40. Dutton, in MacDonald, *Language and National Development*, p. 9.

"an expensive mistake."[41] Although acknowledging the importance of language in fostering "group ties and unifying forces," Dutton said: "It is not true that English is necessarily the best candidate. . . . It creates divisions while it supposedly unifies; it isolates people and separates them from their traditional societies; it creates elites who get further and further away from their relatives the higher they go and causes them to congregate in ugly unfriendly towns. And finally it does nothing for the self-respect of the nation for while it attempts to remain English-speaking it remains but a second-rate Western country without real identity."[42]

Looking at the alternatives to English as a national language, Dutton recognized the practical difficulties of using any of the local vernaculars (the largest of them, Enga, then having an estimated 150,000 speakers) or the village-based "church languages." Comparing the two lingua francas, he argued that on the basis of 1971 census figures, Tokpisin was much more widely spoken than Hiri Motu (750,000 speakers as opposed to 150,000—about the same as Enga). He also noted that Tokpisin was gaining ground (Dutton claimed that in 1976 there were some 10,000 Papua New Guineans who spoke Tokpisin as their mother tongue), and that it was the dominant language in parliamentary debate and on radio. To overcome the problem that "there is a lot of idiosyncratic variation which may interfere with communication between different speakers," Dutton proposed the creation of a national-language planning committee to draw up an "improved variety" of Tokpisin, incorporating new vocabulary for new concepts. He suggested, however, that at the primary-school level the national language be introduced "after students have learned to read and write in their own language or mother tongue," and that English and other foreign languages be introduced at a later stage of the education process, probably late secondary or early tertiary, "for those wishing to specialize in certain careers."[43] English, Dutton maintained, should remain "the language of external communication."[44]

Dutton anticipated resistance to his proposal (specifically, that "the community will feel cheated out of a 'real' education" and that teachers would resist").[45] He did not, however, foresee the extent to which his lecture would (to borrow the phrase of a contributor to an earlier debate)

---

41. Ibid., p. 3.
42. Ibid., pp. 9–10.
43. Ibid., p. 24.
44. Ibid., p. 25.
45. Ibid., p. 29.

put a cat among the pidgins.[46] For the next several weeks, the debate over Dutton's proposal was featured prominently in the national media. Many of the contributors supported the use of Tokpisin as the national language or argued instead in support of English. A smaller proportion disputed the claims for Tokpisin and argued for Hiri Motu, at least in Papua, or local vernaculars. The minister for primary industry, Boyamo Sali, objected that Tokpisin "was not spoken by the great grandfathers of the Papua New Guinea people" and pushed for "one of the country's 700 dialects [sic]," specifically recommending Motu, Kuanua, Kate, or Jabem (reflecting, perhaps, his Morobean Lutheran allegiance). Sali, however, seems to have been a lone voice. More representative was Papua Besena leader Abaijah. Dismissing Tokpisin as a "mutilated foreign language" and "the language of colonialism," and Dutton as a "visiting foreigner," Abaijah argued that "Motu should be the national language, in Papua at least."[47]

Another Papuan pointed out, however, that "the Motu referred to was, in fact, not Motu, at all, but a colonial relic of the past [Hiri Motu] that ensured that our erstwhile masters were able to pass on their orders to us." This commentator supported English as the national language.[48] In a later letter, in which she described "pidgin English" as "a comic opera language," Abaijah also supported English, attacking Tokpisin as a "spoiler" that "prevents the less privileged people from becoming fluent in our international language, which is English." "I look forward to the day," she said, "when it will be official policy to stamp out pidgin English in Papua."[49] Percy Chatterton, an English-born longtime resident (of Papua), former missionary, and member of parliament, was more circumspect. Chatterton believed that "Pidgin, as it is now, is an inadequate medium for conducting the business of a modern nation"; and he described the attitude of Papuans toward Tokpisin as "one of tolerance rather than of acceptance." His own preference was for English, but he warned: "The formal adoption of any one language would be premature at the present time and might provoke a strong reaction from those who disagreed with the choice. It seems to me far better to continue the three language policy and allow each language to find its own level and area of

46. John T. Gunther, "More English, More Teachers! Putting a Cat among the Pidgins," *New Guinea*, Vol. 4, No. 2 (1969), pp. 43–53.

47. "Say 'No' to Pidgin," *Post-Courier*, May 17, 1976, p. 3.

48. "English Should Be PNG's National Language," *Post-Courier*, July 14, 1976, p. 14.

49. Josephine M. Abaijah, "English Is Our National Language," *Post-Courier*, June 25, 1976, p. 2.

usage. . . . We don't want any language riots here."[50] An editorial in the daily *Post-Courier* commented, "In Papua New Guinea the idea of a national language is a utopian dream."[51]

In June 1976 the ongoing debate prompted a question in the National Parliament about the government's plans for creating a national-language policy. Prime Minister Michael Somare's response was statesmanlike: After acknowledging that there were difficulties in the selection of a national language, he said: "I feel that Motu and Pidgin should be spoken by the people as a means of communication in this country, but English should be the language for education, commerce, and trade."[52] The prime minister's answer was reportedly delivered in Tokpisin.[53]

The situation has changed little since independence: Papua New Guinea still has no explicit national-language policy. English remains the principal language of government, education, and commerce, and it is becoming widely spoken. Tokpisin and Hiri Motu are the popular lingua francas. As observed and predicted by some of the contributors to the national-language debate in 1976, however, there appears to have been a steady decline in the use of Hiri Motu, even among coastal Papuans, and a corresponding—and uncontested—rise in the use of Tokpisin, which has become by far the most commonly spoken language. Papua New Guinean linguist Otto Nekitel estimated that in the late 1990s, three-quarters of the country's people spoke Tokpisin.[54] Although still widely spoken locally, "church languages" and the less popular vernaculars appear to be declining in use. (See Table 10.2.) Despite occasional calls since 1976 for an explicit language policy—mostly from academic linguists[55]— language has remained something of a nonissue in Papua New Guinea.

---

50. NBC, June 23, 1976. See also Percy Chatterton, "Bipo tru Kila Kila Primary dekenai Dutton taught tok English [Some time ago, Dutton taught English at Kila Kila primary (school)], *Post-Courier,* July 15, 1976, p. 2.

51. Editorial, *Post-Courier,* May 17, 1976, p. 2.

52. *National Parliamentary Debates,* First Parliament, Vol. 1, No. 10 (June 18, 1976), p. 1130.

53. Terry Stayte, "Long Niugini ol I tok tok long pisin [In Papua New Guinea they speak Tokpisin]," *Canberra Times,* July 21, 1976, p. 17.

54. Nekitel, *Voices of Yesterday, Today, and Tomorrow,* p. 82.

55. In 1982 Nekitel called for an explicit statement on "national and/or official language policy"—even if it were only an endorsement of "the current unofficial trilingual policy." He blamed "the English medium educational policy" for Papua New Guinea's "increasing social problems" and advocated "a dual language policy based on our two national lingua francas." See Otto M. Nekitel, "Language Planning in Papua New Guinea: A Nationalist Viewpoint," *Yagl-Ambu,* Vol. 11, No. 1 (1984), pp. 1–24.

Table 10.2. Speakers of Major "Church Languages" in Papua New Guinea.

Church Language	First-Language Speakers	Second-Language Speakers
Dobu	8,000	10,000
Jabem	2,084	60,000
Kate	6,125	80,000
Kuanua	60,000	20,000
Suau	6,795	14,000

SOURCE: Otto M. Nekitel, *Voices of Yesterday, Today, and Tomorrow: Language, Culture, and Identity* (New Delhi: UBS Publishers' Distribution, in association with Nekitelson Pty. Ltd., 1998), p. 16.

Papua New Guinea currently has two daily newspapers—both in English—and two weekly newspapers—one in English and one in Tokpisin[56]—though the latter (*Wantok*), originally published by the SVD mission press in Wewak, has only a small circulation (around 10,000). National radio and television use both English and Tokpisin with some Hiri Motu. Government-run provincial radio stations (where they still operate—many have closed because of lack of funds) broadcast in English, Tokpisin, Hiri Motu, and local vernaculars, depending on their capacity and their audience.

As in public administration generally, English is the working language of the national judiciary, and court records are kept in English. At the provincial and district levels, however, court proceedings are usually held in Tokpisin or Hiri Motu. The courts provide interpreters when necessary. There is also a less formal village court system, in which proceedings are usually in Tokpisin, Hiri Motu or, most commonly, local vernaculars.

Language at the Subnational Level

In most of Papua New Guinea's nineteen provinces, the mix of languages is such that no single vernacular prevails. In a few provinces, however, the dominance of one language is noticeable. This is particularly true in the Enga and East New Britain Provinces. In Enga the dominance of one language does not appear to have posed a problem.[57] The predominance

56.   There is also at least one provincial paper, the *Milne Bay Star,* that employs a regional ("church") language (Dobu) as well as English and Police/Hiri Motu.

57.   Before 1975 Enga was part of the Western Highlands District, and its separation was in part a recognition of demands by Enga speakers. In 1976, however, the Enga Area Authority (the precursor of provincial government) voted to adopt Tokpisin as its official language. Lang, "A Plea for Language Planning in Papua New Guinea," p. 13.

of the Kuanua-speaking Tolai in East New Britain politics and administration, however, has led to complaints of "Tolai imperialism" by minority Bainings and Sulka people in that province.

A few other minor instances of language politics have arisen at the
provincial level. When around 1980 it was proposed in the East Sepik
Province to establish a council of "chiefs" (among societies that had been
regarded as generally being without hereditary leadership), the word
chosen, *kokal* (a Boiken term), was regarded by most others in the province as a "foreign" term. The proposal was not pursued. In Bougainville a
declaration in 1990 by Francis Ona's Bougainville Revolutionary Army
(BRA) of the "Republic of Meekamui" was a source of some contention
within the BRA.[58] Meekamui was drawn from the Nasioi language, the
language of those around a disputed gold and copper mine, but it was
only 1 of Bougainville's 21 languages. Even in these extremely minor inci-
dents, language has not been a highly contentious issue.

At the district and village levels, Tokpisin, Hiri Motu, "church languages," and especially local vernaculars are widely used in community
schools and village courts as well as in daily communication, though, as
noted, all but Tokpisin are declining in use. Nekitel observed that by 1980
there had been an "alarming shift" from vernaculars to Tokpisin in his
Sepik (Abu'-speaking) village: "Tokpisin is used in most situations for
perhaps 60 to 70 percent of the time."[59] Local government council and
school board meetings, church services, and religious instruction were all
conducted in Tokpisin. Nekitel suggested several reasons for this change:
colonial attitudes toward Abu'; interethnic marriage; loss of language
skills as a result of being away from the village; ease of articulation in
Tokpisin; consideration for others; and parents' failure to foster Abu'.[60]
There has been support for vernacular languages, however, especially in
early education.

Language, Education, and Tokples Skuls

At first, both the German and the British/Australian administrations
used their own languages as the official languages of education in their

---

58. Anthony Regan, personal communication, Canberra, ACT, Australia, 1999.

59. Nekitel, *Voices of Yesterday, Today, and Tomorrow*, p. 52.

60. Ibid., chap. 5. See also Otto M. Nekitel, "Culture Change, Language Change: The
Case of Abu' Arapesh, Sandaun Province, Papua New Guinea," in Thomas E. Dutton,
ed., *Culture Change, Language Change: Case Studies from Melanesia*, Pacific Linguistics Series C–No. 120 (Canberra, ACT: Department of Linguistics, Research School of Pacific
Studies, Australian National University, 1992), pp. 49–58.

territories. For the most part, however, education was in the hands of the missions, which used whatever language—principally Tokpisin and local vernaculars or "church languages"—that would help them to achieve their primary objective: evangelization.[61] Before World War II, the administrations of the two territories occasionally attempted to encourage the teaching of English in mission-run schools through education subsidies to missions fulfilling certain prescribed syllabus requirements. The amounts involved were too small, however, to provide sufficient incentives to persuade the missions to change their practices. In fact, the missions opposed moves to extend conditional education subsidies to their schools. Following the establishment of the New Guinean administration's first school in 1922, a report to the Australian government by Col. John Ainsworth recommended that classes be conducted in the vernacular, and that administration officers learn the vernacular of the areas in which they served. This never became official policy.

After World War II, a director of education for the joint territories was appointed; the first director, W.C. Groves held the post until 1958. Groves promoted increased government involvement in education, and he emphasized the need for education to be attuned to local cultures.[62] A five-year plan for "native education," circulated in 1948, suggested that the first few years of education should be provided primarily by mission-run schools using local vernaculars, but that English should be introduced progressively, equipping students to go on to district-level schools where English would be the medium of instruction. Expert opinion in education generally agreed with this position.[63]

The Australian government and its administration in Papua New Guinea supported this policy until a change of government in Canberra in 1949 brought a change in policy. Although in 1952 an education ordi-

---

61.   On the eve of World War II, some 80,000 pupils attended mission schools in Papua New Guinea. At the same time, there were fewer than 600 indigenous pupils in government schools in New Guinea and no government schools for indigenous children in Papua. "Education, Missions," in Ryan, *The Encyclopaedia of Papua New Guinea,* p. 330.

62.   Groves arrived in New Guinea in 1922, as the first European teacher in the colonial administration's education system. Johnson, "Administration and Language Policy in Papua New Guinea," p. 436. He set out his views on language in education in a publication entitled *Native Education and Culture-Contact in New Guinea* (Melbourne, Victoria, Australia: Melbourne University Press, 1936).

63.   Notable examples include independent reports by anthropologist Camilla H. Wedgewood ("Suggested Organization of Native Education in New Guinea" [typescript 1945]) and linguist Arthur Capell ("Papua New Guinea Report on Linguistics" [typescript 1951]). Neither Wedgewood nor Capell saw much of a role for Tokpisin or Police/Hiri Motu.

nance was passed that empowered the director of education to determine language usage in schools, views in Australia on the use of languages other than English in the education system were mixed. The following year the United Nations Trusteeship Council urged the Australian administration to eliminate the use of Pidgin English, which it saw as un-democratic and colonialist.[64] In 1955 an education policy directive was issued that listed as its first goal the teaching of all children in administra-tion-controlled areas to read and write in English. The previous year an education ordinance had provided the basis for the administration's as-suming responsibility for education in nongovernment schools; Tokpisin was permitted in areas recently coming under administration influence, but not to the detriment of eventually teaching in English, which was seen as a "unifying language."[65] By 1959—in the face of strong opposition from some churches—the administration had threatened to close down all schools teaching in a "foreign vernacular" (essentially "church lan-guages") and effectively forced mission schools to accept English as the medium of instruction. Mihalic recalls that in the Sepik, "pupils caught speaking Pidgin received demerits."[66] Nekitel remembers "being belted" for violating the "English only" regulation.[67] Vernacular broadcasts by the Education Services Division were also discontinued. By 1970 the mis-sion schools—even the Lutheran schools—had joined the Territory education system and were shifting to English.

There has been much discussion about the "failure" of vernacular education in Papua New Guinea in the 1950s and 1960s.[68] A lack of com-mitment by the Australian administration and the paucity of teaching materials in local languages were significant factors. Another important factor, however, appears to have been opposition from parents and teach-ers, who frequently saw education other than in English as inferior. A

64. See Johnson, "Administration and Language Policy in Papua New Guinea," p. 444. The Australian minister for territories at the time, Sir Paul Hasluck, has re-called: "A decision had been made that education should be in the English language. This decision had little to do with education theory. Indeed I conceded to mission schools, against the advice of my own experts, that they could use their vernacular as a transition to eventual teaching in English." Hasluck, *A Time for Building: Australian Administration in Papua and New Guinea, 1951–1963* (Melbourne, Victoria, Australia: Melbourne University Press, 1976), p. 89.

65. Ibid., p. 445.

66. Mihalic, *Readings in PNG Mission History,* p. 76.

67. Nekitel, *Voices of Yesterday, Today, and Tomorrow,* p. 179.

68. See, for example, Kenneth R. McKinnon, "Education in Papua New Guinea—The Years Ahead," *Papua New Guinea Journal of Education,* Vol. 7, No. 1 (1971), pp. 7–21. McKinnon was the last non–Papua New Guinean director of education.

1988 survey of teachers' attitudes reported that although the majority of teachers rated themselves more fluent in their mother tongue than in Tokpisin, English, or Hiri Motu, and agreed that the use of Tokpisin would facilitate communication and improve student understanding, 91 percent preferred to retain English as the medium of education.

In the 1960s, however, responding to increasing nationalist sentiments and a growing weight of evidence from research, education policy began to swing back toward the use of vernaculars and Tokpisin in early schooling and adult literacy programs. In 1973 a proposed five-year development plan recommended that the language of primary education should be "selected by the community which the school serves," provided that instructors and teaching materials were available. English, however, should remain the language of instruction at the secondary and tertiary levels.[69] The education department's ensuing Education Plan of 1975, however, was rejected by the government, which directed that English be the sole language of instruction at all levels. A subsequent ministerial statement, though, did allow for the teaching of local languages, in addition to the normal syllabus, subject to approval by the provincial education boards (provincial government was being introduced in 1976) and the availability of adequate teaching and financial resources.

Following the establishment of provincial governments and the transfer of a large part of education policymaking to these governments, the use of vernaculars in early education gained widespread support. Several provinces, notably North Solomons (Bougainville) and East New Britain, introduced *viles tokples skul* (local vernacular school) programs.[70] Although their record was mixed, the idea of early education in vernaculars was widely endorsed. In 1989 the National Literacy Board passed a resolution calling for the teaching of initial literacy and numeracy in *tokples*. This was endorsed as government policy the following year. In 1991 the department of education issued its *Education Sector Review Ministerial Brief*, which stated: "The policy that learners should acquire initial

---

69. Department of Education, *Proposed Five-Year Development Plan* (Port Moresby: Department of Education, 1973).

70. See, for example, papers in John Brammall and R.J. May, eds., *Education in Melanesia* (Canberra, ACT: University of Papua New Guinea and Research School of Pacific Studies, Australian National University, 1975), sec. 7; L.D. Delpit and Graeme Kemelfield, *An Evaluation of the Viles Tok Ples Skul Scheme in the North Solomons Province*, Educational Research Unit Report No. 51 (Port Moresby: University of Papua New Guinea, 1985); Sheldon G. Weeks and John Waninara, *Review of the Education System in East New Britain*, Research Report No. 60 (Port Moresby: Educational Research Division, National Research Institute, 1988); and papers by Naihuwo Ahai and Micael Olsson in *Yagl-Ambu*, Vol. 11, No. 1 (1984).

literacy in a language they speak and then transfer this literacy to English or any other of the national languages has been adopted."[71] By 1993 there were provincial literacy programs in about 200 languages in 1,800 *tokples skuls,* reaching 27,300 pupils.[72] Subsequent policy documents have broadly repeated the substance of the 1991 statement. The department of education's Corporate Plan of 1998–2002, based on the National Education Plan of 1995–2004, for example, states that among its policies on elementary education: "The language for instruction in elementary schools will be that which the children speak and will be determined by the community."[73]

In September 1999 the minister for education, research, science, and technology, John Waiko, announced a new language policy that he said would "start making a significant contribution to literacy . . . both in English and, importantly, in our many Papua New Guinean languages";[74] 837 languages have since been declared official languages in the education system.[75] These will be the basic languages of instruction in community schools from the elementary preparatory level to grade two, after which there will be a transition (grades three to five) to English.

In a country with an estimated 850 languages, some of which are spoken by small groups in remote areas, the more widespread use of vernaculars poses problems. In particular, it seems inevitable that in some community schools, small vernacular groups will not be given much attention and more frequently used vernaculars will triumph over less popular ones—as was the experience in the early days of mission expansion with the adoption of "church languages." To date, there is little evidence that such problems have arisen, but in the East Sepik Province, Kwoma children in some community schools around Ambunti are receiving ver-

---

71. The use of the phrase "any other of the national languages" is interesting. There is a widespread popular perception in Papua New Guinea that English, Tokpisin, and Hiri Motu are "national languages," though there is no statutory basis for this. For an elaboration of the policy, see Department of Education, *Education Sector Review,* Vol. 2 (1991), pp. 169–170.

72. W. Jonduo, "Evaluation Samples of Literacy Programmes: Preliminary Findings," in O.I.M.S. Nekitel, S.E. Winduo, and S. Kamene, eds., *Critical and Developmental Literacy* (Port Moresby: University of Papua New Guinea Press, 1995), pp. 41–57.

73. Department of Education, *Corporate Plan, 1998–2002* (Port Moresby: Department of Education, 1998), p. 9.

74. "Education Reform and Language Policy in Schools," statement to the press by the minister for education, research, science, and technology, the Hon. Professor John Waiko, September 3, 1999.

75. Jacqueline Kapigeno, "PNG World Leader in Language, Culture," *Post-Courier,* April 13, 2000, p. 4.

nacular teaching in the language of the neighboring Iatmul (a group with whom they had been traditional enemies); this is emerging as a source of grievance among the Kwoma.[76] It is possible that the well-intentioned policy of vernacular use in schools could give rise to low-level local tensions.

Conclusion

Given the great linguistic diversity in Papua New Guinea, language might have been expected to provide a source of ethnic cleavage and conflict. It has not.

Precolonial Papua New Guinean societies were marked by endemic warfare, and contemporary Papua New Guinean society has been plagued by intergroup fighting. Much of this fighting, however, takes place within the same language group (especially among the larger language groups of the highlands) over issues such as land, compensation claims (resulting, for example, from road accidents), and election outcomes. Some conflicts follow linguistic divisions, but there has been no instance since independence in which language per se has been a source of major disagreement. Similarly, the Bougainville conflict, which from at least as early as 1990 was associated with demands for Bougainville independence, has never been concerned with language—partly because the Bougainville Revolutionary Army itself drew supporters from almost all of Bougainville's twenty-one vernacular language groups (representing itself in Tokpisin and English). "Bougainville" identity, in other words, transcends linguistic boundaries.

It might be argued, more generally, that Papua New Guinea's extreme linguistic fragmentation—and, to the extent that linguistic boundaries define ethnicity, its extreme ethnic fragmentation—has dissipated the potential for ethnic conflict. Because Papua New Guinea has so many small ethnolinguistic groups, language does not provide an effective basis for political mobilization except, on occasion, in local contexts.[77] Moreover, Papua New Guinea's small-scale societies have tended to dif-

---

76. Angela Mande-Filer, personal communication, Canberra, ACT, Australia, 2000.

77. Even at the subnational level, ethnic tensions have tended to follow administrative/geographic rather than linguistic lines. Tensions, for example, between highlanders and "coastals," New Guinea Islanders and mainlanders, or Bougainvilleans and mainlanders, cut across linguistic divides. And at the subprovincial level, regional divisions (within and across linguistic boundaries) have been more salient than linguistic ones. See R.J. May and A.J. Regan with A. Ley, eds., *Political Decentralisation in a New State: The Experience of Provincial Government in Papua New Guinea* (Bathurst, New South Wales: Crawford House, 1997).

ferentiate themselves from their neighbors through language use, rather than seek to extend their linguistic domain.[78] No vernacular language group, however, is large enough—even if it were imperially inclined—to push for the adoption of its language as a national language. Thus, as contact between different communities increased following European colonization, lingua francas developed naturally as a means of inter-group communication.

Among the lingua francas, "church languages" have declined in use since the Lutheran Church's adoption of Tokpisin. Even Hiri Motu, which was never comprehensively accepted as the lingua franca of Papua, appears to have given way to Tokpisin and English. Tokpisin has become by far the most widely spoken language, with growing numbers speaking Tokpisin as a mother tongue. As Father Kirschbaum observed in 1931, the people themselves have chosen Tokpisin as the language of communication.

By declining to formally choose a national language (or national languages), Papua New Guineans avoided the conflict that would almost certainly have occurred in 1975 if, say, Tokpisin had been chosen over Hiri Motu, or if English had been given an official status above Tokpisin or Hiri Motu. In the absence of an explicit national policy, Tokpisin has naturally assumed its dominant position in popular communication (and, to a large extent, parliamentary debate). Meanwhile English has been retained as the principal language of education, commerce, and administration, and local vernaculars have been officially recognized with a view both to promoting literacy at the communal level and to acknowledging the cultural value of local languages in accordance with the constitution's directive principles. In this way, Papua New Guinea has evolved as a special sort of multilingual society, and may have ensured that in a society marked by extreme linguistic diversity and two potentially competing lingua francas, language has not been a source of conflict.

Whether the Papua New Guinean experience contains lessons for other multilingual states is less easy to say. Clearly, Papua New Guinea is very unusual in several respects: First, it boasts extreme linguistic diversity; second, no vernacular language has much currency outside its local area; third, literacy rates are fairly low, and there is no great tradition of a vernacular literature; and fourth, English and Tokpisin, to an increasing extent, are widely accepted as politically neutral languages. These factors

---

78.   Donald C. Laycock, "Melanesian Linguistic Diversity: A Melanesian Choice?" in R.J. May and Hank Nelson, eds., *Melanesia beyond Diversity* (Canberra, ACT: Research School of Pacific Studies, Australian National University, 1982), pp. 33–38.

have facilitated the spread of Tokpisin as a lingua franca of the people and of English among a more restricted group.

One general lesson does emerge from the Papua New Guinean experience: In states where language has been a source of conflict, tension has frequently arisen because one numerically or culturally dominant group has imposed its language on minority groups through official national-language policies. The experience of Papua New Guinea suggests that in multilingual societies, it may be wiser not to elaborate a national-language policy but, in effect, to let market forces determine language use. A misguided language policy may create more problems than no policy at all.

Chapter 11

Language Policy and Ethnic Relations in the Philippines

Caroline S. Hau and Victoria L. Tinio

The vicissitudes of language-policy planning and implementation in the Philippines underscore the challenges posed by the coexistence of nationalist aspirations, subnational group loyalties, and pragmatic concerns in a multilingual country. Since 1935 the Philippine state has worked to develop a *wikang pambansa,* or national language. Initially called "Pilipino" and based on one of the country's major languages (Tagalog), the national language was renamed "Filipino" in 1973 and made inclusive of all existing Philippine languages and dialects. This policy shift occurred largely as a consequence of the objections raised by non-Tagalog speakers to the "ethnic bias" of a Tagalog-based national language. State efforts to promote the national language have been complicated by the existence of a hierarchy of languages that privileges English above Filipino and other indigenous languages and enshrines the former as the language of power in the country.

The national-language project has its origins in the country's colonial history. This effort recognizes the symbolic and unifying power of a common language to facilitate social exchanges across class, ethnic, religious, and other divides within a markedly heterogeneous population. The Philippine case illustrates the extent to which language has been used in conflicts involving groups such as the Muslims, indigenous peoples, and the Chinese. Officially, the state has generally accommodated the demands of the country's various ethnic groups. Poor implementation and scarce resources, however, have undermined whatever goodwill that government policies have generated. These policies have ended up as palliatives that, in more than one case, served only to aggravate the original problem. Ironically, the state's partial failures to implement its language policies have helped to ease rather than exacerbate interethnic tensions: These limited efforts have helped to prevent languages from becoming a source of ethnic mobilization in the Philippines.

The mitigating effects of these policy failures, however, have been canceled out by the wasted opportunities afforded by a common language. While the use of English, for example, has dampened ethnic differences, it has reinforced class divisions across ethnic groups. English's preeminence, rooted in a policy of bilingual education, has hindered the ability of the state to fully develop a national lingua franca, Filipino. By promoting this lingua franca as a national language, the state could tap its potential for promoting social justice and facilitating dialogue across social groups.

Discussions of the links between language policies and ethnic relations must consider the larger complex of political, economic, and cultural institutions that influence this relationship. This chapter focuses on the cornerstone of the national-language project, the educational system, and how the choice of a language as a medium of instruction influenced and in turn was influenced by social and ethnic relations.

The chapter is divided into three main sections. The first section presents an overview of the ethnic and linguistic profile of the Filipino population and the historical, economic, and political contexts in which ethnic identification and social relations among ethnolinguistic groups took shape and continue to be articulated. The second section discusses language policies in the Philippines, particularly the national-language project, and their implications for interethnic relations. In the conclusion, we provide a critique of the potential of Filipino to be an inclusive national language and outline a number of recommendations for developing such a language.

Ethnic and Linguistic Overview

One of the most noteworthy features of Philippine society is its cultural and linguistic diversity. This diversity, however, has long been acknowledged by scholars to have sprung from a common linguistic stock—that is, from an Austronesian and Malayo-Polynesian "base culture" extending from the Easter Islands and Hawaii off the coast of America across the Pacific, Southeast Asia, and the Indian Ocean up to Madagascar off the eastern coast of Africa.[1] This presumed commonality is borne out by the

---

1.   Zeus A. Salazar, "The Matter with Influence: Our Asian Linguistic Ties," *The Malayan Connection: Ang Pilipinas sa Dunia Melayu* (Quezon City, Luzon: Palimbagan ng Lahi, 1998), p. 72.

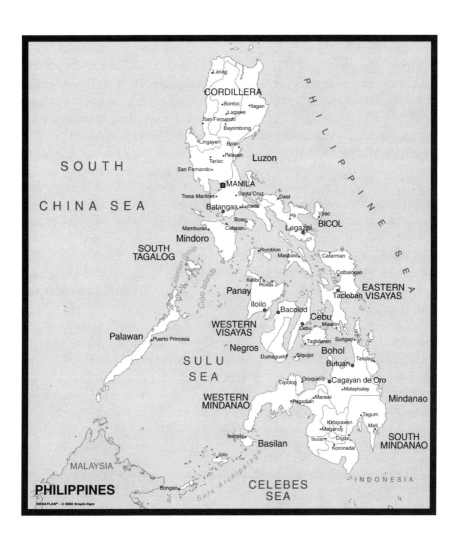

CORDILLERA

Laoag

Bontoc
Ilagan
Lagawe
San Fernando
Bayombong

Lingayen
Balen
Palayan
Tarlac
Luzon
San Fernando

MANILA
Trece Martires
Santa Cruz
Daet
Batangas
Lucena
Boac
Pili
Virac
Mamburao
Calapan
Legazpi
BICOL
Mindoro

SOUTH
TAGALOG

Romblon
Masbate
Catarman

Catbalogan

Kalibo
Roxas
Panay
Tacloban
EASTERN
VISAYAS
Iloilo
Bacolod
Cebu

WESTERN
VISAYAS
Cebu
Maasin

Palawan
Puerto Princesa
Negros
Tagbilaran
Surigao
Bohol
Dumaguete
Siquijor
Tandag
Butuan

Dipolog
Oroquieta
Cagayan de Oro
Malaybalay

WESTERN
MINDANAO
Marawi
Pagadian
Mindanao
Tagum

Kidapawan
Maganoy
Mati
Isabela
Isulan
Digos
SOUTH
Basilan
Koronadal
MINDANAO

Jolo

MALAYSIA

PHILIPPINES
GEOATLAS® - © 2000 Graphi-Ogre
Bongao
Sulu Archipelago
CELEBES
SEA
INDONESIA

SOUTH

CHINA SEA

PHILIPPINE

SEA

SULU

SEA

Calamian Group

Cuyo Islands

fact that nearly 40 percent of the vocabulary of Philippine languages is shared by languages in Indo-Malaysia, the Pacific island world, and Madagascar.[2]

Scholars disagree, however, on the exact number of Philippine languages, largely because of differences in the application of the terms "language" and "dialect."[3] Two hundred languages were said to have been spoken at the time of first European contact in the sixteenth century.[4] One estimate, based on research conducted in 1991, placed the number of Philippine languages at 171, of which 168 are "living" and 3 "extinct."[5] The 1995 census identified 12 "major" languages—that is, those spoken by more than half a million people as a mother tongue: In descending order, they are Tagalog, Cebuano, Ilocano, Hiligaynon/Ilonggo, Bikol, Waray, Kapampangan, Boholano, Pangasinan, Maranao, Maguindanao, and Tausug. (See Table 11.1.)

Of these major languages, 5 have emerged as regional lingua francas: Tagalog in central and southern Luzon, Bicol, and Palawan; Cebuano and Hiligaynon/Ilonggo in the Visayas and most of Mindanao; Ilocano in northern Luzon; and Tausug in the Sulu Archipelago.[6] Internal migration, the media, and the government's bilingual education policy have spurred the dissemination of Filipino nationwide, particularly in urban areas. The 1987 constitution designates Filipino as the national language and, along with English, as the language of official communication and instruction.

Given the multilingual setting of the country, many Filipinos have learned to communicate, with varying degrees of fluency, in three to four languages. A typical Filipino may use a vernacular language with his or her family; a regional lingua franca and/or Filipino with peers or coworkers; and English in business, industry, academia, and international arenas.[7] These languages exist in a hierarchical relationship, with English

---

2. Ibid., pp. 72–73.

3. Ernestina C. Nadela, "An Annotated Bibliography on Philippine Linguistics in the Library of Congress," M.S. thesis, Catholic University of America, 1967.

4. Laura Lee Junker, *Raiding, Trading, and Feasting: The Political Economy of Philippine Chiefdoms* (Honolulu: University of Hawaii Press, 1999), p. 61.

5. Barbara F. Grimes, ed., "The Philippines," *Ethnologue: Languages of the World,* 12th ed. (Dallas, Tex.: Summer Institute of Linguistics, 1992), pp. 747–765.

6. Consuelo J. Paz, *Ang Wikang Filipino: Atin Ito* [The Filipino language: it's ours] (Quezon City, Luzon: Sentro ng Wikang Pambansa, Sistemang Unibersidad ng Pilipinas, 1995), p. 4.

7. Andrew B. Gonzalez, *Language and Nationalism: The Philippine Experience Thus Far* (Quezon City, Luzon: Ateneo de Manila University Press, 1980), p. 149.

Table 11.1. Major Languages Spoken as Mother Tongues in the Philippines, 1995 (population 68,431,213).

Language	Percentage
Tagalog	29.29
Cebuano	21.17
Ilocano	9.31
Hiligaynon/Ilonggo	9.11
Bikol	5.69
Waray	3.81
Kapampangan	2.98
Boholano	2.10
Pangasinan	1.81
Maranao	1.27
Maguindanao	1.24
Tausug	1.15
English	0.04
Chinese*	0.09
Other	10.94
Total	**100.00**

SOURCE: National Statistics Office, Republic of the Philippines, *1995 Census of Population*, Report No. 2: *Socio-Economic and Demographic Characteristics* (Manila: National Statistics Office, 1997), pp. 79–80.
*The term "Chinese" encompasses the Hokkien dialect spoken by the majority of the Philippine Chinese, putonghua (Mandarin Chinese), and other dialects.

being the most prestigious and the vernacular (when not the regional lingua franca) the least.

Research suggests that language use in the Philippines should not be viewed in strict categorical terms because borrowing and code-switching are common.[8] (Code-switching occurs when a multilingual person alternates between two or more languages while speaking to another multilingual person.) Although code-switching in both oral and written communication is employed to establish rapport as the social situation demands, in the classroom code-switching serves a primarily utilitarian function.[9] With the 1974 institution of the bilingual education policy— which designated English as the medium of instruction in science, mathematics, and English language classes, and Filipino as the language of instruction in social studies, work education, character education, health

8.   Andrew B. Gonzalez and Lourdes Bautista, *Language Surveys in the Philippines (1966–1984)*, Vol. 1 (Manila: De La Salle University Press, 1986), p. 23.

9.   Ibid., pp. 24–25.

education, and physical education—many first graders who do not have sufficient skills in English (or, in non-Tagalog areas, in Filipino) are taught in two or more languages, with the vernacular acting as the bridge language. At present, few Philippine classrooms are monolingual.

In government and the courts, English remains the dominant language. Although the law encourages the use of Filipino, the regional languages, and the vernacular in these settings, efforts at indigenizing official written communication have not been comprehensive, with local governments having greater success than the national government. Court trials and deliberations in Congress are usually conducted in English, with other languages used intermittently. Political campaigns, however, are conducted in a combination of Filipino and the relevant regional language. The government's public information campaigns are generally trilingual (in English, Filipino, and regional languages).[10]

In recent years, mass media, particularly broadcasting, have shifted to Filipino. The two biggest networks in the Philippines have almost entirely Filipino programming. National broadsheets are still predominantly in English, while national tabloids are mostly in Filipino. Community newspapers generally use the regional language in combination with English, except in Mindanao, where most are in English.[11] The most popular comics and weekly magazines are in Filipino, although vernacular magazines are also widely read.[12] Radio programming is usually bilingual, with Filipino being more dominant except in some Cebuano- and Hiligaynon/Ilonggo–speaking areas and in metropolitan Manila,[13] where English is preferred.[14]

In the Philippines, the language first learned by an individual is typically one of the bases of his or her ethnic identity, in some cases even more so than the parents' ethnicity. But although the mother tongue is a significant determinant of ethnic identification, this determination depends in part on who is doing the evaluation—a Tagalog speaker of non-Tagalog parentage is, for example, considered a Tagalog by Tagalogs, but less so by non-Tagalogs. This example suggests that "although clearly interrelated, language and ethnicity do not enjoy a one-to-one relationship, that is, as the situation shifts, a person can shift his ethnic identity

10. Adriano Arcelo, "The Role of Language in Philippine Society," *Philippine Journal of Linguistics*, Vol. 21, No. 1 (June 1990), pp. 53–54.

11. Crispin C. Maslog, ed., *The Rise and Fall of Philippine Community Newspapers* (Manila: Philippine Press Institute, 1993), p. 3.

12. Gonzalez and Bautista, *Language Surveys in the Philippines (1966–1984)*, p. 15.

13. Arcelo, "The Role of Language in Philippine Society," p. 54.

14. Gonzalez and Bautista, *Language Surveys in the Philippines (1966–1984)*, p. 15.

especially if he is multilingual."[15] We therefore need to examine the nonlinguistic factors that determine the ways—if any—in which language is used by different groups to assert their ethnic differentiation vis-à-vis other groups.

The present hierarchy of languages in the Philippines is the product of a history shaped by interactions with the outside world. Centuries of trade with Asia and other regions brought to the Philippines a relatively small number of settlers from China, India, and the Middle East. Arab and Indo-Malaysian traders and settlers helped to spread Islam in the southern part of the Philippines, while Chinese immigration increased with Spanish colonization and the demand for Chinese artisans and merchants that came with the establishment of the galleon trade between Spanish Mexico and China. In the wake of European and American colonialism in the Philippines, social divisions came to be organized not just around economic background or class status but also around distinctions between Christian and non-Christian populations, and between indigenous and nonindigenous peoples.

The Philippines has four main social blocs: Christian Filipinos (about 92 percent of the population) belonging to numerous ethnolinguistic groups but collectively making up what Ronald May has called a "cohesive 'super ethnie'"; tribal Filipinos, or indigenous cultural communities (also called Lumads, highlanders, uplanders, and indigenous peoples) of the same ethnic stock, and Negritos, numbering more than forty ethnolinguistic groups (3 percent); Muslim Filipinos, comprising thirteen ethnolinguistic groups of the same ethnic stock but differentiated by religion and degree of Islamization (4–5 percent); and Chinese Filipinos, relatively homogeneous and predominantly Hokkien speaking, with a Cantonese-speaking minority (0.5 percent).[16] (See Table 11.2 for a breakdown of religious groups in the Philippines.)

The Spanish and American colonizers and the postcolonial Philippine state played an important role in framing the ethnic question, in classifying groups, and in fostering group consciousness. The first 200 years of Spanish rule were characterized by the relatively slow growth of "ethnic" consciousness,[17] which was influenced by Spanish-introduced

---

15. Ibid., p. 38.

16. R.J. May, "Ethnicity and Public Policy in the Philippines," in Michael E. Brown and Šumit Ganguly, eds., *Government Policies and Ethnic Relations in Asia and the Pacific* (Cambridge, Mass.: MIT Press, 1997), pp. 321–322.

17. William Henry Scott, "The Creation of a Cultural Minority," *Cracks in the Parchment Curtain and Other Essays in Philippine History* (Quezon City, Luzon: New Day, 1985), p. 29.

Table 11.2. Religious Groups in the Philippines, 1990.

Religion	Number	Percentage
Roman Catholic	50,219,801	82.92
Protestant	3,287,355	5.43
Muslim	2,769,643	4.57
Aglipay	1,590,208	2.62
Iglesia ni Kristo	1,414,393	2.34
Born-again Christian	323,789	0.53
Buddhist	22,681	0.04
Other	736,239	1.22
Not stated	197,007	0.33
Total	**60,561,116**	**100.00**

SOURCE: *Philippine Yearbook, 1994* (Manila: National Statistics Office, n.d.).

---

distinctions between Christian and non-Christian populations. These distinctions, along with those between indigenous and nonindigenous peoples, were later amplified by the Americans, and constitute an important legacy of colonialism that continues to influence relations between the Philippine state and the people in the country.

INDIGENOUS PEOPLES

Early Spanish accounts of the so-called highlanders in the northern Philippines were more interested in differentiating between Spaniards and colonized "natives" than in distinguishing between one "native" and another. These "natives" were distinguished from one another mainly by whether they submitted to Spanish rule or not; in censuses, vassals were called *indios* while the rest were called *tribus independientes.* The Spanish census also categorized people on the basis of their submission to Catholic missionization or baptism, with *bautizados* and *convertidos* being counted separately from *infieles.* The twin logic of conversion and separation of rulers from ruled lay behind the Spanish decision to create the intermediate category of *mestizo* and to apply it to the offspring not just of European and native unions but of Chinese and native ones as well.

The emergence of a cultural concept of the highlanders during the seventeenth century can be traced to Spanish missionary work among "pagans" and to Spanish gold-mining efforts in the Cordillera region.[18]

---

18. William Henry Scott, *The Discovery of the Igorots: Spanish Contacts with the Pagans of Northern Luzon,* rev. ed. (Quezon City, Luzon: New Day, 1974), pp. 3, 329.

This concept was fluid and highly arbitrary. The term "Igorot," for example, actually encompassed six ethnolinguistic groups (Bontoc, Ibalog, Ifugao, Isneg, Kalinga, and Kankanay).[19] In the eighteenth century, the word "Igorot" acquired a more specific meaning and came to refer to the people of Benguet, Ifugao, Mountain Province, and the Kayapa municipality of Nueva Vizcaya.[20] It was not until the first half of the nineteenth century that the Spaniards attempted to extend political control over northern Luzon. Their limited success reinforced the perceived difference between the highland and lowland inhabitants, but failed to arouse awareness that various Cordillera peoples were different from one another.[21]

Ethnological science, education, and colonial policy coalesced during the American period. American ethnographic discourse on the "non-Christian tribes" was institutionalized through the establishment of the Bureau of Non-Christian Tribes in 1901. The bureau played a crucial role in advancing the annexation debates by providing the rationale that justified American presence and intervention in the Philippines.[22] The bureau called for "systematic investigations with reference to the non-Christian tribes of the Philippine Islands, in order to ascertain the name of each tribe, the limits of the territory which it occupies, the approximate number of individuals which compose it, their social organizations and their languages, beliefs, manners and customs, with special view to determining the most practicable means of bringing about their advancement in civilization and material prosperity."[23] Where the Spaniards had met with limited success, the Americans embarked on an ambitious project to map the hitherto "outside" and "unknown" areas in the Philippines and place these areas within the administrative reach of the colonial state. The American colonial government was instrumental in fleshing out the cartographic creation "Filipinas" (anglicized into the "Philippine islands" and later the "Philippines"), first wrought by the Spaniards.

A leading American colonial official of the time, Dean Worcester, wrote of the "great confusion" that attended American efforts to classify

---

19. Ibid., pp. 2–3.

20. Ibid., p. 171.

21. Ibid., p. 305.

22. Paul A. Kramer, "The Pragmatic Empire: United States Anthropology and Colonial Politics in the Occupied Philippines, 1898–1916," Ph.D. dissertation, Princeton University, 1998, pp. 167–174.

23. Ibid., p. 175.

the islands' non-Christian peoples.[24] Ethnologist and educator David Barrows, who headed the 1903 census mission, advocated the use of the term "culture areas," but it was Worcester's preferred term, "tribes," that was adopted by the colonial administration. Worcester counted seven "tribes" (Bontocs, Igorots, Ilongots, Kalingas, Lepanto-Benguets, Negritos, and Tinguians) in northern Luzon, a number that corresponded rather conveniently with the "subprovince" and administrative structure of Mountain Province as designated by the colonial state.[25] Through this administrative readjustment, the 116 groups of earlier Spanish ethnographic accounts were subsequently reduced to 27.

American attitudes toward indigenous peoples differed from those of their colonial predecessors. Whereas Spaniards looked upon the pagans and Muslims as *feroces,* the United States' "civilizing mission" was informed by a "noble-savage" discourse that aimed to rescue the non-Christian tribes from the "corrupt" culture of lowland, Hispanized Filipinos, whom Americans regarded as purveyors of the *"cacique* system" (the domination of local and provincial politics by a class of landed mestizos [of Spanish and Chinese ancestry]) and whose economic elite had been co-opted by the Spanish colonial state. This so-called Malay society was frequently characterized as "feudal" and "aristocratic."[26]

Schools and public education were seen as the principal solutions to—and the indigenous peoples' means of circumventing—the *cacique* system and the "congenital incapacity and inhumanity of lowland Filipinos."[27] Public education, conducted in English and in institutions such as the Trinidad Agricultural School, coupled with the mining boom of the 1930s and the development of Baguio City as a summer capital, helped to bring people together and foster a regional, ethnic Igorot consciousness among the inhabitants of the Cordilleras. The presence of lowlanders, especially Ilocano settlements surrounding the highlands, also drew attention to social differences between highlanders and lowlanders.[28]

---

24. Quoted in ibid., p. 278.

25. Rodney J. Sullivan, *Exemplar of Americanism: The Philippine Career of Dean C. Worcester,* Michigan Papers on South and Southeast Asia No. 36 (Ann Arbor: Center for South and Southeast Asian Studies, University of Michigan, 1991), p. 153.

26. Kramer, "The Pragmatic Empire," pp. 183–184.

27. Sullivan, *Exemplar of Americanism,* p. 150. See also Gerard A. Finin, "Regional Consciousness and Administrative Grids: Understanding the Role of Planning in the Philippines' Gran Cordillera Central," Ph.D. dissertation, Cornell University, 1991, pp. 103–148.

28. Patricia O. Afable, "Language, Culture, and Society in a Kallahan Community, Northern Luzon, Philippines," Ph.D. dissertation, Yale University, 1989.

Worcester organized the Cordilleras into the Mountain Province. Like the "Moro" (Muslim) territories in the south yet unlike the Christian territories elsewhere in the country, it was not put under the jurisdiction of the Filipino-run Philippine Assembly. Instead it was administered directly by the U.S. secretary of the interior. Its governance was modeled on U.S. treatment of North American Indians, with instructions to colonial officials to "maintain . . . tribal organizations and government."[29] This administrative arrangement emphasized similarities rather than differences among tribal Filipinos.

Worcester's territorial-administrative divisions, however, based on an imprecise cartographic and ethnographic notion of "tribal areas" in which language played a key classificatory role, proved to be durable.[30] Inhabitants of these tribal areas moved toward integration into the national political system on the basis of firm subnational group identities, with their "territories" remaining substantially the same as those officially recognized by Worcester. Ethnic consciousness, which had its origins in the American penchant for emphasizing tribal divisions, remains a factor in contemporary Philippine politics.

In the postindependence era, conflicts with "outsiders" became more pronounced and led to political mobilization and activism on the part of the indigenous peoples. Under the administration of Ferdinand Marcos, the office of the Presidential Assistant on National Minorities, formed in 1975, promoted Igorotlandia as a tourist attraction—the home of "authentic natives."[31] In 1978 the ministry of tourism embarked on a cultural enhancement program that was meant to highlight the distinctiveness and cultural attractions of ethnic minorities.

Although the government took pains to showcase the cultures of indigenous peoples, it was unable to redress the grievances of these communities. Cordillera activists resisted the Chico River Basin Development Project in the mid-1970s and criticized Cellophil Corporation's pulp mill operations in Abra in 1977 for encroaching on communal lands and damaging irrigation systems. Indigenous peoples also clashed with loggers who conducted operations on ancestral lands.[32]

In the late 1960s, the country experienced the growth of militant student nationalism, which came to be linked to the anti-Marcos struggle in the 1970s and resulted in political mobilization under the auspices of the

29. Sullivan, *Exemplar of Americanism*, p. 141.

30. Finin, "Regional Consciousness and Administrative Grids," p. 63.

31. Ibid., p. 475.

32. Ibid., pp. 423–431, 440, 471.

Communist Party of the Philippines–New People's Army in the Cordilleras. In 1979 the communist arm, the National Democratic Front, gave special prominence to the plight of "minority people."[33] Anti-Marcos groups flourished and formed coalitions with cause-oriented groups. The formation of the Cordillera People's Alliance and Regional Autonomy closed the gap between anti-Marcos, educated urban highlanders, and rural highlanders who resisted the government because they had local grievances.

In the 1980s the Cordillera People's Liberation Army proposed the creation of a Cordillera Autonomous Region that would be governed according to local highland traditions.[34] In 1984 this proposal was brought up as one of the Marcos administration's peace initiatives and was later included in the peace agenda of Corazon Aquino's government. Internecine conflict within the Left resulted in a split, two years later, between the Cordillera People's Liberation Army and the Communist Party–New People's Army. Nevertheless, in 1997 President Fidel Ramos signed an executive order creating the Cordillera Administrative Region, based on the administrative organization bequeathed by the Americans.[35]

Both the American colonial state and the Philippine state opposed the assimilation of tribal Filipinos into the dominant Filipino culture. Indeed the participation of these groups in the political system and in civil society was premised on their communal differences. A look at the Rules and Regulations Implementing Republic Act No. 8371 (Indigenous Peoples' Rights Act of 1997), for example, reveals that the government, in theory, "recognize[s] and respect[s] the rights of the ICCs/IPs [indigenous cultural communities/indigenous peoples] to preserve and develop their cultures, traditions, and institutions." Respect for "cultural integrity" extended to allowing ICCs/IPs "to exercise their rights to establish and control their educational systems and institutions," and pledging to establish, maintain, and support a system of education "relevant to the needs of the ICCs/IPs, particularly their children and young people," and to develop school curricula "using their language, learning systems, histories, and culture."

Land problems (encroachment on ancestral or communal lands) and livelihood issues (problems concerning employment and income) continue to preoccupy these groups. Concerns about education

---

33. Ibid., p. 478.

34. Ibid., p. 524.

35. Ibid., p. 924.

revolve mainly around inadequate infrastructure, the lack of textbooks and qualified teachers, and the need for more scholarship as well as more adult and community education. Long-range planning is also deficient.

These issues suggest two conclusions. First, cultural issues, such as language, do not play a major role in debates between the state and indigenous peoples because other issues—including land rights, development, and poverty alleviation—are more pressing. Second, where cultural issues are at stake, the biggest problem has been the state's inability—owing to scarce resources and inefficient implementation—to make good on its promises to groups whose cultures it seeks to preserve and whose grievances it seeks to redress.

THE MOROS

The term "Moros" (Muslims), first used by the Portuguese, was applied to most inhabitants in the southern region of the Philippines with little regard for linguistic differences among the region's Muslims. In fact, there are at least thirteen ethnolinguistic groups spread over a wide area in Mindanao, and considerable differences exist in the degree to which these groups are "Islamicized."[36]

Throughout the Spanish era, from 1565 to 1898, Spaniards organized expeditions to Muslim lands and clashed with Muslims in sea battles. Forts were built, lost, and retaken in the colonial outpost in Zamboanga, but the Spaniards never succeeded in subjugating the region. Even in the late 1800s, Muslim slave-raiding ventures made frequent incursions into Spanish-held territories in the Visayas.

Religion is said to have played an important role in cementing Sulu, Maguindanao, and Maranao awareness of their differences from Spaniards and Spanish-ruled "natives,"[37] but it hardly constitutes a primordial tie that binds one group ineluctably to another across time and space. Thomas McKenna argues that "Spanish aggression against Muslim polities did not stimulate the development of an overarching ethno-religious identity self-consciously shared by various Muslim ethnolinguistic groups."[38] Nonreligious motives—for example, control of the profitable Sino-Sulu trade, the appropriation of resources, and the collection of

36. Cesar Adib Majul, *Muslims in the Philippines* (Quezon City, Luzon: University of the Philippines Press, 1999), pp. 89–90.

37. Ibid., p. 99.

38. Thomas M. McKenna, *Muslim Rulers and Rebels: Everyday Politics and Armed Separatism in the Southern Philippines* (Berkeley: University of California Press, 1989), p. 81.

tributes—were equally important in accounting for the fervid resistance put up by the Muslims against the Spaniards.

Moro identity was nurtured during the American colonial period—with the active encouragement of the colonial government.[39] Collaboration with American colonial authorities allowed *datus* (chieftains) to retain their power and wealth and to enhance their trading status. Najeeb Saleeby argues that Muslim unity was promoted not through the preservation or restoration of individual trading polities but through the formation of a transcendent Philippine Muslim identity.[40]

Education was an important element in the development of Moro identity. Through contact with one another and with other Filipinos, Muslims educated in Philippine public schools and colleges during the American and postindependence periods grew to be self-conscious of an ethnoreligious identity that transcended ethnolinguistic and geographical boundaries. This identity was further strengthened when government policies that favored Christian settlers (in logging and development, for example) generated an influx of postwar migrants and created profound economic and social gaps between Muslim and Christian communities throughout Mindanao. This, along with latent distrust and stereotyping of Muslims by non-Muslim Filipinos, sowed the seeds of the secessionist movement that culminated in the violent clash between the Moro National Liberation Front (MNLF) and the Marcos regime from 1972 to 1977.

The Tripoli Agreement of 1976 enunciated general principles for Muslim autonomy in thirteen provinces in Mindanao, but did nothing to hinder the emergence of a unified and reinvigorated Muslim elite that was critical of *datu*-led development. Self-defense, control of economic resources, and better access to economic opportunities were as important as religious motives in explaining the actions of ordinary Muslims.

In the cultural arena, the emergence of a popular Muslim nationalism led by a newly ascendant elite under the Islamic guidance of politically active *ulama* (specialists in Islamic law and theology) independent of *datu* supervision led to an Islamic renewal. Education played a leading role in this renewal through the reestablishment of ties with Islamic religious centers in the other countries. The strengthening of linkages with al-Azhar University in Egypt and with universities in Sudan, Kuwait, Saudi Arabia, and Pakistan bore fruit in the 1980s with the unparalleled growth of Islamic education in the region.

---

39. Ibid., p. 85.

40. Ibid., p. 106.

The growing religious dimension of the conflict reached a milestone when a splinter group, the Moro Islamic Liberation Front (MILF), broke away from the MNLF over the Tripoli agreement and became an independent organization in 1978. The rise of the MILF marked the entrance of Islamic phraseology into everyday political discourse in Muslim Cotabato, but it is also striking that most Muslims resisted their leaders' attempts to "purify" their rituals.[41] The creation of the Autonomous Region of Muslim Mindanao under the Aquino administration in 1989 was hobbled when in a plebiscite only four of thirteen provinces voted for autonomy. A 1996 peace accord between the Ramos government and the MNLF has not stopped hostilities, with the MILF still active on the military front. Shadowed by charges of corruption and mismanagement, the Autonomous Region government has had limited success in ensuring that the goodwill and resources of the Philippine state filter down to the people of the region.

In matters of language, the Muslim case represents an extreme version of the experience of the indigenous peoples of the Philippines. Compulsory education under the American public school system, where English was the medium of instruction, was not properly enforced. Ironically, the lack of school facilities and poor socioeconomic conditions helped to lessen Muslim resistance to American-sponsored education, which was perceived at the time as "a device to alienate them [the Muslims] eventually from their Islamic faith and convert them to Christianity."[42] The problem of inadequate facilities persisted through the postwar years, pointing up the government's failure to educate the majority of Muslims. The situation was a time bomb that never exploded because vernacular languages remained the medium of instruction in most Muslim schools. In the 1950s and 1960s, most Muslims received their educations mainly through the *madrasas* (sectarian schools) run by local religious leaders.

The Muslims were (mis)handled by the state not as ethnic groups, but as "religious deviants."[43] The conflict between Muslim and Christian Filipinos was reflected in debates over language. It is not unusual, for example, for Muslim leaders to communicate with each other in English and to use Filipino when being interviewed by Christian Filipinos, say, over the radio. Studies show that Muslims joined the Moro rebellion for reasons other than simple devotion to Islam or their Moro identity.

41. Ibid., p. 228.

42. Antonio Isidro and Mamitua Saber, *Muslim Philippines* (Marawi City: University Research Center, Mindanao State University, 1968), p. 95.

43. May, "Ethnicity and Public Policy in the Philippines," p. 349.

Self-defense, not Islamic reform, was a key motivation for many ordinary people who joined the MILF or MNLF.[44]

Cultural similarities between Muslims and Christians raise doubts about the explanatory power of identity politics in the Philippines. Communal identity has often been used not to separate Muslims or assimilate them into the mainstream but to integrate them into the larger Philippine body politic through the co-optation of "brokering" Muslim elites. As in the case of the indigenous peoples, the government had an interest in preserving cultural differences rather than erasing them as part of the process of nation building and state construction through "electoral democracy."[45] Integration was in many ways a form of "ethnic juggling" that served to frustrate separatist appeals while providing mechanisms for the government to work with "loyal" Muslim allies.

THE CHINESE

Until the mid-nineteenth century, the Spaniards used the term *sangley*—from the Mandarin *shang-lü*, meaning merchant-traveler,[46] or from the Hokkien *sengdi*, meaning business—to refer to the Chinese who lived in the Philippines. This term points to the historical conflation of ethnicity and merchant capitalism that began with the Spanish regime and continues to this day. The Chinese were middlemen in an economy based on profits accrued from the galleon trade between China and Spanish Mexico. Furthermore, the Chinese supplied the Spaniards with provisions and artisanal labor for the colonial city of Manila.

With the abolition of the galleon trade in the early 1800s, the colonial state shifted to an agricultural-export economy, with the Chinese acting as middlemen who collected Philippine produce and export products and sold them to European firms for shipment to the world market. The Chinese also engaged in the wholesale trade of imported goods and their retail distribution in the cities and provinces. During the first half of the Spanish period, Spanish dependence on the Chinese and Spain's initial attempts to establish itself in the Philippines, laced with Spanish paranoia about the presence and power of the Chinese empire in Southeast Asia, periodically exploded into anti-Chinese pogroms—notably in 1586, 1603, 1639, 1662, and 1686. But by the nineteenth century, the transformation of the Philippines into a cash crop, export-based economy and its

---

44. McKenna, *Muslim Rulers and Rebels*, p. 11.

45. Patricio N. Abinales, "State Authority and Local Power in Southern Philippines, 1900–1972," Ph.D. dissertation, Cornell University, 1997, p. 7.

46. Edgar Wickberg, *The Chinese in Philippine Life, 1850–1898* (New Haven, Conn.: Yale University Press, 1965), p. 9.

integration into the global market created a demand for an expanded Chinese mercantile network, which, along with advances in steamship travel, led to a sharp increase in Chinese immigration.

The American colonial government encouraged the expansion of Chinese economic activities but barred the Chinese from political partici-pation.[47] The tension between high levels of economic integration and low levels of political participation strengthened the ethnic consciousness of the Chinese while cementing the image of the Chinese community as "alien" to the Philippines in both its political and cultural orientations. The influx of women immigrants and the growth of Chinese nationalism in the waning years of the Qing dynasty during the first decade of the twentieth century created stable family structures within the Chinese community and encouraged a movement toward re-Sinification. This led to the establishment of Chinese schools, newspapers, and chambers of commerce, the last serving as spokesperson organizations for the local Chinese community.

The problematic legal status of the Chinese meant that they were confined to mercantile operations, because professions such as law, medi-cine, and architecture could be practiced only by Filipino citizens. As eco-nomic anthropologist John Omohundro noted, "By different methods, and for different motives, the Spanish, the Filipinos, and the Americans each contributed to the specialization of the Chinese in a merchant niche."[48]

The economic specialization of the Chinese, most notably in retail trade and wholesale distribution, was a source of Filipino resentment. Part of the nationalist critique of Filipinos' economic "alienation" from retail trade—one of the most visible economic niches in the Philippines—expressed itself in a tide of nationalist legislation in the 1950s aimed at breaking the Chinese "stranglehold" over retail trade. One manifestation of this nationalist sentiment was the Filipinization of Chinese schools, which had flourished under American rule. Filipinization meant cutting hours of Chinese-language study, putting schools in majority Filipino ownership, and supervising textbook production.

The normalization of Philippine diplomatic relations with China in 1975 smoothed the way for the passage of the Naturalization Law, which relaxed constraints against citizenship and enabled Chinese Filipinos to

---

47. James Blaker, "The Chinese in the Philippines: A Study of Power and Change," Ph.D. dissertation, Ohio State University, 1970, p. 82.

48. John T. Omohundro, *Chinese Merchant Families in Iloilo: Commerce and Kin in a Central Philippine City* (Quezon City, Luzon: Ateneo de Manila University Press, 1981), pp. 43–44.

participate in the political process. The late 1980s and early 1990s, however, bore out the stereotype that identified Chinese ethnicity with money, as the government offered permanent residency status to aliens in exchange for a fee.[49] Since the late 1980s, however, the Chinese have become as visible a presence in the political arena as in business.

The Philippine government's policies toward the Chinese community have focused mostly on economic and political issues. Unlike in Indonesia, there was no outright ban on Chinese schools or prohibitions concerning the teaching of Chinese. State supervision was extended to Chinese schools starting in 1956, but this was done mainly through the Filipinization of Chinese textbooks, which basically consisted of adapting Chinese-language courses by using Philippine topics and references. The Filipinization of Chinese schools in 1971–72 simply put the schools in the hands of the majority. The shortening of hours of language instruction in Chinese created practical problems having to do with the educators' failure to teach Chinese students the rudiments of reading and writing in Chinese. Few schools teach Chinese as a second language. This has produced functionally illiterate schoolchildren who are unable to read, speak, or write Chinese well.

Chinese integration—especially of the younger generation—is much more widespread than is evident from the way this minority is depicted by the mass media. The relaxation of laws stigmatizing the Chinese as illegal aliens and the subsequent entry of the Chinese into Philippine politics during the martial-law years have highlighted the incorporation of the Chinese into the mainstream. This seems to be confirmed by the fact that younger generations of Chinese Filipinos write almost exclusively in English or Filipino.

LANGUAGE AND CONFLICT

In general, there seems to be little direct correlation between language issues and ethnic conflict in the Philippines. Benedict Anderson observes that although the Philippines contains far more ethnolinguistic groups than Burma, for example, "ethnicity" as such has played only a minor role in Philippine politics.[50] Ronald May argues that the Philippine elec-

---

49.   Caroline S. Hau, "Who Will Save Us from the 'Law'? The Criminal State and the Illegal Alien in Post-1986 Philippines," in Vicente L. Rafael, ed., *Figures of Criminality in Indonesia, the Philippines, and Colonial Vietnam* (Ithaca, N.Y.: Southeast Asian Studies Program, Cornell University, 1999), pp. 128–151.

50.   Benedict Anderson, "Introduction," *Southeast Asian Tribal Groups and Ethnic Minorities: Prospects for the Eighties and Beyond*, Cultural Survival Report No. 22 (Cambridge, Mass.: Cultural Survival, 1987), p. 9.

toral system and parochial politics have impeded the effective implementation of the same state-sponsored assimilationist policies that were successfully adopted by other states in Southeast Asia.[51] The idea of participation in the national body politic did not entail the assimilation of ethnic groups to the dominant culture and the attendant loss of their identities. Rather it assumed and encouraged the integration of these groups as distinct communal entities. Thus the Philippine government has, at least on paper, formulated policies that seek to accommodate the demands of various ethnolinguistic groups. These policies are vitiated, however, by scarce resources and by the state's own failure to implement these initiatives effectively because of mismanagement, corruption, and lack of political will.

This policy failure has important implications for the government's national-language project: Although language has not been a major source of ethnic conflict in the Philippines, implementation failures have prevented the government from taking advantage of linguistic resources that may aid it in its efforts to address the larger socioeconomic and political problems facing the country.

The National-Language Project

If there is a lesson to be learned from the decades of national-language policy in the Philippines, suggests noted linguist and Philippine Secretary of Education Andrew Gonzalez, it is that "benign neglect is better than deliberate language planning."[52] The tension between nationalist aspirations and enduring ethnic loyalties is the backdrop to this story.

The effort to develop a national language based on only one Philippine language, Tagalog—as was done in 1940—was bound to generate interethnic friction. What is remarkable about the Philippine case is the degree to which anti-Tagalog forces have allied with the pro-English lobby, particularly within the elite. The biggest outcry against a Tagalog-based national language has come from the Visayan elite. While they have recognized the need to fashion a linguistic symbol of unity, they have either favored English over Tagalog or advocated their regional language. Gonzalez and Lourdes Bautista explain the dilemma: "The problem is more that, on the societal level, there are conflicting demands between ethnic loyalties which make for attachment to the ethnic language, nationalist sentiments which foster the longing for a linguistic

---

51. May, "Ethnicity and Public Policy in the Philippines," p. 350.

52. Gonzalez and Bautista, *Language Surveys in the Philippines (1966–1984)*, p. 47.

symbol of national unity, and pragmatic considerations which necessitate the maintenance of an international language for business and trade, science and technology."[53]

In the Philippines, language issues are part of a social structure that evolved in colonial times and persist in the postcolonial era. Framing language-policy debates in simple "ethnic" terms therefore misses an important historical point: Languages in the Philippines exist in a hierarchy (or hierarchies) influenced to an enormous degree by the relative status of the colonial language—English.

It was only in the 1930s, as the Philippines was looking ahead to political independence, that a consensus was reached on the feasibility and desirability of developing a national language. For the first time, a national language was seen as a key to nationhood, and the country's ethnic and linguistic diversity was viewed as a distinct liability.[54]

Before then, the two colonial languages—Spanish and English—occupied dominant positions in the country's linguistic hierarchy. The debates on English have been more intense and protracted because of the relative success with which it was disseminated in the Philippines. The 1903 census reported that after more than three centuries of Spanish rule, less than 10 percent of the population spoke Spanish as a first or second language. The 1870 census found that only 2.46 percent of the population could "talk Castilian."[55]

The lack of Spanish usage resulted from a decision by the Spanish Crown that initially encouraged friars to work in native languages, which they hoped would speed up religious conversion.[56] In the sixteenth century, the Crown reversed course and instructed the friars to teach Castilian.[57] In 1550 Carlos I decreed that colonies be instructed in Christian doctrine in the Castilian language and not in native languages.[58] Felipe II later issued another decree making instruction in Castilian a re-

---

53.   Ibid., p. 46.

54.   Gonzalez, *Language and Nationalism*, pp. 45–46.

55.   Emma H. Blair and James A. Robertson, eds., *The Philippine Islands*, Vol. 45 (Ohio: Arthur H. Clarke, 1907), pp. 299–303. The country's foremost "national hero," José Rizal, wrote all of his major works in Spanish. It is a sign of how inaccessible Spanish has become to present-day Filipinos that Rizal's masterpieces—as well as many other works written in Spanish by Filipinos—are read only in translation.

56.   John L. Phelan, *The Hispanization of the Philippines* (Madison: University of Wisconsin Press, 1959), p. 131.

57.   Emma H. Blair and James A. Robertson, eds., *The Philippine Islands*, Vol. 9 (Ohio: Arthur H. Clarke, 1907), pp. 255–256.

58.   Blair and Robertson, *The Philippine Islands*, Vol. 45, p. 185.

quirement for all natives. This would be reiterated in subsequent decrees throughout the Spanish period.

Efforts to teach Spanish were hampered by a lack of funds, the paucity of teachers, the absence of an organized system of primary education, and scarcities of teaching materials.[59] It was not until 1863 that an educational decree was passed establishing a system of primary education and including regulations for a normal school for teachers. Its objectives included the teaching of Spanish. Spanish was to be used as the sole medium of instruction, and literacy in Spanish was to be the major objective of the school curriculum.[60] Native languages, however, continued to be used in primary schools,[61] and the 1863 decree—like its many predecessors—was hampered by poor implementation.

This is not to say that the Spanish language had no impact on Philippine society. A Hispanized elite evolved that could afford to send its sons to Europe to pursue a higher education. Filipino nationalism in the late nineteenth century was not articulated in terms of the debate between "foreign" and "native" languages. The language of elite-based Philippine nationalism was Spanish; the vernacular was used by other populist movements.

During the Revolutionary Period that followed the Filipino war of independence against Spain, nationalist leaders did not concern themselves with the issue of a national language. The 1897 Provisional Constitution of Biak-na-Bato made Tagalog the "official language" of the republic and the medium of elementary-school instruction. English and French were to be taught as high school courses. The constitution further provided that English would replace Tagalog as the official language once the former was disseminated throughout the archipelago. Similarly, the 1899 Malolos Constitution, which superseded the Biak-na-Bato Constitution, did not make any provisions for a national language. Spanish was designated the temporary official language, although Philippine languages were allowed in some official settings.

The trajectory of English as an official language and medium of instruction differed significantly from that of Spanish: English was disseminated more widely and entrenched more effectively in state policies and the public imagination. By the end of the American period, according to the 1939 census, 26.6 percent of the population claimed ability to speak

---

59.   Encarnacion Alzona, *A History of Education in the Philippines, 1565–1930* (Manila: University of the Philippines, 1932), pp. 22–23.

60.   Emma H. Blair and James A. Robertson, *A History of the Philippines*, Vol. 46 (Ohio: Arthur H. Clarke, 1907), pp. 78, 85.

61.   Alzona, *A History of Education in the Philippines*, p. 95.

English. In 1939 Tagalog was spoken by 25.4 percent of the population, Waray by 19.1 percent, Cebuano by 16.9 percent, and Hiligaynon/ Ilonggo by 14.1 percent.[62] These statistics suggest the relative preeminence of English over the Philippine languages while underscoring the fact that no single language, not even English, was spoken by a majority of the Filipino people.

The English language's lofty status owed much to the Office of the Superintendent of Public Instruction, created in 1900, which mandated the teaching of English in Philippine classrooms. Despite faulty teaching methods and a lack of funds, it was clear that the American colonial government viewed education as a priority.[63] U.S. President William McKinley's instructions to the Schurman fact-finding commission envisioned Filipino participation in legislation and administration, the education of the masses, and the training of Filipinos for leadership, and it was generally acknowledged that education was a key factor in realizing these goals.[64]

Although McKinley recognized the practical need to use Philippine languages, Act No. 74 (An Act Establishing a Department of Instruction in the Philippines) made English the basis of all public school instruction.[65] Language was believed to be inseparable from the inculcation of "progressive" ideas about business and civil government.[66] Six hundred American teachers were brought to the Philippines on board the USS *Thomas* in 1901 and thereafter came to be known as Thomasites. A normal school was established that same year, provincial secondary schools in 1902, and the University of the Philippines in 1908. A generation of young Filipino *pensionados*, or scholars, was sent to the United States to obtain higher education.

Instruction in the vernacular was discussed during the incumbency of the third director of education (1903–09), David Barrows, and experimental classes were conducted among the Manobo ethnic group in Agusan and Butuan, in the Mindanao region. Tagalog was offered as a

---

62.   Gonzalez, *Language and Nationalism*, pp. 62–63.

63.   Glenn A. May, *Social Engineering in the Philippines: The Aims, Execution, and Impact of American Colonial Policy, 1900–1913* (Quezon City, Luzon: New Day, 1984), p. 125.

64.   Charles A. Elliott, *The Philippines to the End of the Commission Government: A Study in Tropical Democracy* (Indianapolis: Bobbs-Merrill, 1917), pp. 407–409.

65.   Homer Stuntz, *The Philippines and the Far East* (New York: Jennings and Pye, 1904), p. 190.

66.   *Report of the Philippine Commission to the President*, Vol. 2 (Washington, D.C.: Government Printing Office, 1900), p. 300.

course to American and Philippine teachers at the Philippine Normal School in 1906 and 1907.

It has been claimed that English instruction suffered because of this ambivalence about teaching a foreign language.[67] There was a movement in some quarters to teach in the vernacular while retaining English as the medium of instruction in higher grades. But educators worried about creating a divisive class system discouraged the use of the vernacular.[68]

During the American colonial era, English was made the official language of the civil government, while Spanish was retained as the official language of the courts. During the first decade of American rule, Spanish continued to be used by educated Filipinos who filled positions in the government bureaucracy.

The results of these educational initiatives were substantial. After twenty years of American rule, more people spoke English than Spanish.[69] As early as 1925, however, the Monroe survey noted that Filipino students had problems learning English and recommended the use of the vernacular for teaching manners and morals.[70] Vice Governor-General George Butte, concurrently secretary of public instruction, also advocated use of the vernacular in 1931. A Filipino educator, Cecilio Lopez, promoted the use of vernacular languages, with Tagalog and English being taught in higher grades and English used as the medium of instruction in high schools.[71] These recommendations were ignored, and English remained the sole medium of instruction and the official language during the American period.

In 1934 a national assembly was called to frame the Philippine constitution in preparation for formal political independence from the United States. Spirited debates among members of the assembly led to a compromise proposal that adopted a "multi-based" approach to the national-language issue. The compromise called for the national language to be "based on all existing native dialects." When the proposal came before the Style committee responsible for refining the language of the constitution, however, the basis of the national language was changed from "all

67.   Benigno Aldana, *The Philippine Public School Curriculum* (Manila: Philippine Teachers' Digest, 1935), p. 109.

68.   Bureau of Education, *Twenty-first Annual Report of the Director of Education* (Manila: Bureau of Printing, 1921), p. 69.

69.   Ibid., p. 19.

70.   Gonzalez, *Language and Nationalism*, p. 35.

71.   Cecilio Lopez, *The Language Situation in the Philippine Islands* (Manila: n.p., 1931).

existing native dialects" to "one of the existing native languages."[72] Thus the 1935 constitution mandated the development of a national language based on only one Philippine language, and it designated English and Spanish as official languages. The constitution made provisions for setting up the Institute of National Language to study the chief languages spoken by half a million Filipinos, their vocabulary, phonetics, and orthography. In 1937 the institute recommended Tagalog as the basis for the national language.

Commonwealth Act 570 of 1940 called for the development of a national language based on Tagalog. Tagalog was chosen because it was used in the capital, Manila, and because it had spread to other areas through nationalist efforts. Although Visayan was used by more people than Tagalog, the term "Visayan" was problematic because it referred to a region, not a unitary language; in fact, there were considerable differences among Visayan languages such as Cebuano, Hiligaynon/Ilonggo, and Waray. This picture was complicated, because although the Visayan languages were not mutually intelligible, ethnic unity among Visayans was nevertheless conceivable: This led some to oppose the use of Tagalog as a basis for the national language.[73]

This opposition to Tagalog, however, should not be interpreted as a manifestation of ethnic conflict. The debate over Tagalog—one that continues to this day—reflects intra-elite rivalry and internecine battles over resource allocations that happened to be parceled out by region.

In 1940 Tagalog (renamed Pilipino in 1959) was designated an official language alongside Spanish and English. On the eve of World War II, the new national language was introduced in schools. The use of local dialects was permitted in the first and second grades as an auxiliary medium of instruction. English, though, remained the de facto principal medium of instruction throughout the Philippines.

After the war, language issues were low priorities. Local or regional vernaculars were used in the first and second grades in accordance with the recommendation of the United Nations Educational, Scientific, and Cultural Organization's Consultative Educational Mission in 1957–58. The national language was introduced as a required subject for the first time. It is telling, for instance, that not until 1963 was the national anthem sung in Pilipino.

---

72. Pamela C. Constantino, *Pagplaplanong Pangwika tungo sa Modernisasyon: Karanasan ng Malaysia, Indonesia at Pilipinas* [Language planning toward modernization: the Malaysian, Indonesian, and Philippine experiences] (Quezon City, Luzon: Sentro ng Wikang Filipino, Unibersidad ng Pilipinas, 1991), p. 56–59.

73. Gonzalez, *Language and Nationalism*, p. 46.

The difficulties of teaching two unfamiliar languages—English and the Tagalog-based national language—quickly became obvious in non-Tagalog regions. The lack of proper teacher training and the unavailability of books exacerbated these problems. The dropout rate from compulsory public education further undermined the government's efforts to expand the use of the national language.[74] In addition, debates on what kind of Tagalog was to be used, coupled with objections from some Cebuano lawmakers and professionals about the use of Tagalog as the national language, made the language issue contentious.

The teaching of English as a second language was first attempted in 1957, but students made little progress in either English or Pilipino. Matters eventually took their own course. In the post–World War II period, a Manila-based Tagalog lingua franca spread via the mass media and massive migration to the capital. By 1970, 56.2 percent of the population spoke Tagalog, up from 39.4 percent in 1948.[75]

The self-conscious use of Pilipino in support of radical nationalism by students and the Left began to take hold in the late 1960s. In 1970 the Board of National Education broached a tentative proposal to use Pilipino as the medium of instruction in primary grades, but a study committee postponed its recommendations.

The 1973 constitution, promulgated under martial law, marked another shift in state policy. It represented a return to the hijacked compromise agreement of 1934 in that it advocated a multidimensional approach to the national-language issue. The new constitution declared English and Pilipino to be official languages, but it also mandated a new search for a national language, known as "Filipino," which would be based not on Tagalog but on other Philippine languages and dialects "without precluding the assimilation of words from foreign languages." In effect, the constitution was legislating a linguistic fiction rather than the development of one Philippine language into a national lingua franca. The propagation of Pilipino (which many non-Tagalogs viewed as nothing more than another name for Tagalog), coupled with the purist approach to its teaching in schools, heightened ethnic tensions.[76] This policy shift was the constitutional convention's problematic attempt to pacify non-Tagalog groups. Vernacular languages continued to be used as the media

---

74. Constantino, *Pagplaplanong Pangwika tungo sa Modernisasyon*, p. 193.

75. Gonzalez, *Language and Nationalism*, p. 103.

76. Ernesto Constantino, "Ang 'Universal Approach' at ang Wikang Pambansa ng Pilipinas" [The "universal approach" and the national language in the Philippines], in Constantino, Rogelio Cruz, and Pamela D. Cruz, eds., *Filipino o Pilipino?* [Filipino or Pilipino?] (Manila: Rex Book Store, 1974), p. 28.

of instruction in grades one and two, until a bilingual education policy was officially put into effect in 1974.[77]

When Corazon Aquino assumed the presidency following the toppling of the Marcos dictatorship in 1986, a new constitutional convention was convened. Whereas debates over the national language during the 1972 constitutional convention were extremely heated, the tone of the 1986 proceedings was relatively conciliatory.[78] There was general acknowledgment that Filipino had become a national lingua franca. Representatives to the convention were consequently more concerned about language use in official communications and instruction. The presence of a strong English-language lobby during the convention's deliberations secured the use of English in government and in the classroom. The 1987 constitution acknowledged the necessity of retaining English as an official language, but accorded primacy to Filipino as both the national and official language. Furthermore, it empowered Congress to strip English of its official language status should circumstances warrant.

The continuing special status of English has implications for the full development of Filipino as well as other Philippine languages. English stands in a hierarchical relationship to other Philippine languages, fostering linkages within a social class that cuts across ethnic groups while widening the gap between social classes. Despite the fact that the Philippines has a vibrant literary and pop culture in English, the continued use of English has preserved the gap between the urbanized, educated elite and the majority of people who are not functionally literate in English.

English is the most prestigious language in the Philippines, and proficiency in English is associated with the Filipino elite. Bonifacio Sibayan has argued that English is seen as the language of the rich.[79] Fluency in English is also considered an index of educational attainment and is acknowledged to be the key to power and social mobility.[80] The moti-

---

77. Emma J. Fonacier Bernabe, *Language Policy Formulation, Programming, Implementation, and Evaluation in Philippine Education (1565–1974)* (Manila: Linguistic Society of the Philippines, 1987), p. 159.

78. For a discussion of the 1986 constitutional convention debates over the language provisions in the 1987 constitution, see Maria Ela L. Atienza, "The National Language Policy in the 1987 Constitution: The Politics of Language in Constitution Drafting," M.A. thesis, College of Social Sciences and Philosophy, University of the Philippines–Diliman, 1993.

79. Bonifacio P. Sibayan, "Views on Language and Identity: Limited Metro-Manila Example," in Arthur Yap, ed., *Language Education in Multilingual Societies* (Singapore: SEAMEO [Southeast Asian Ministers of Education Organization] Regional Language Centre and University of Singapore Press, 1978), pp. 3–52.

80. Bonifacio P. Sibayan and Lorna Z. Segovia, "Languages and Socioeconomic De-

vations for learning English, therefore, are both instrumental and integrative: to be able to afford better economic opportunities on the one hand, and to identify with the educated Filipino elite on the other.[81]

The commitment to English—from the government and an influential segment of the population—is justified on economic grounds. The remittances of more than 6 million overseas Filipino workers have poured billions of dollars of revenues into government coffers. This has produced and sustained a preference among Filipino students for English language classes in the country's universities. This, it is believed, will better equip them for work abroad.

Given English's economic value, nationalist critiques of this linguistic situation have been only marginally influential. Indeed the resiliency of the bilingual education policy, despite compelling arguments marshaled against the use of English as a medium of instruction,[82] is indicative of the compromises that educators and language planners have been forced to adopt. Ironically, since the bilingual policy was first implemented in 1974, the Philippine educational system has been in steady decline. What the bilingual experiment has wrought is a generation of young Filipinos who are proficient in neither English nor Filipino. Despite a national literacy rate of 83.8 percent, the failure of bilingual education is evident in the frequent code-switching to which teachers resort in the classroom.[83] In general, little comprehension exists beyond surface meaning because none of the languages is acquired well enough to apply in either a conventional or scholarly context.[84]

Despite the informal dissemination of Filipino as a national lingua franca, the spread of this language has not been maximized by the state through sustained efforts at standardization and intellectualization (i.e., the process of developing the language by creating registers specific to the various domains of knowledge and their fields of specialization). The University of the Philippines system has started to write social sciences

velopment: Resulting Patterns of Bilingualism/Multilingualism," paper presented at the Fourteenth Regional Seminar of the SEAMEO Regional Language Centre, Singapore, 1979.

81.   Gonzalez and Bautista, *Language Surveys in the Philippines*, pp. 47–48.

82.   Gregorio del Pilar II, "Isang Rebista ng mga Empirikal na Pag-aaral sa Pinagkumparang Bisa ng Ingles at Wikang Pilipino" [A review of empirical studies on the comparative efficacy of English and Filipino], University of the Philippines, 1991.

83.   Martha A. Adler, "Language, Literacy, and Culture as Grade One Teachers Carry Out National Educational Reform Policies: A Philippine Ethnography," Ph.D. dissertation, University of Michigan, 1997.

84.   Ibid., pp. 252, 255.

and science textbooks in Filipino, but most schools still use English text-books to teach science and mathematics courses, and only a small number of Filipino scholars write articles or conduct scholarly discourse in Philippine languages.

Vernacular languages have been similarly neglected, and have not been developed in ways that make them effective pedagogical tools in primary school. This may mean that although vernacular languages are not moving toward extinction, they will remain "private" rather than public media.

Conclusion

Just as the preeminence of English has constituted a major impediment to national-language development in the Philippines, the conflict over the nature and status of Filipino has been problematic. Some claim that Filipino remains a legal fiction, a language that is yet to be created and thus one that cannot be used as the country's primary medium of instruction. Others insist that Filipino is no different from Tagalog-based Pilipino—that the change of the language's name was a ploy to gain wider acceptance for it—and they question its exclusiveness and therefore its constitutionality.

Yet another faction, based in the linguistics department of the University of the Philippines and pivotal during the constitutional debates of 1972 and 1986,[85] argues that Filipino does exist in the form of the lingua franca spoken throughout the country, especially in cities, and as such should be elevated to the status of national language and primary medium of instruction. Filipino, it is said, is "democratic" in character because, as a lingua franca, it is "used freely and without reservation or anxiety, and it assimilates words and strategies just as freely from the native languages of its speakers. In this manner, the majority is able to play a determining role (in its development)."[86]

This Filipino is defined as an inclusive rather than exclusive language that draws, at least in principle, from all major Philippine languages and dialects (all closely related in terms of sound, lexicon, syntax, and meaning), and borrows from foreign languages (primarily English and Spanish). This so-called universal approach to language building exists as a

---

85. Jovita H. Orara, *Ang Papel ng UP sa Kilusan para sa Wikang Pambansa (1908–1973)* [The role of the University of the Philippines in the national language movement (1908–1973)] (Quezon City, Luzon: Unibersidad ng Pilipinas Sentro ng Wikang Filipino, 1993).

86. Paz, *Ang Wikang Filipino*, p. 3.

potential alongside the reality of language activism; this approach is part of the cultural framework propagated by student movements and the Philippine Left, which actively espouses the use of the lingua franca as a language of communication across linguistic divides, and as a language of political thinking and action.

As a lingua franca, Filipino is the language of everyday speech, evolving out of social necessity and belonging not to any one ethno-linguistic group but to all who use it. Two parallel processes are presently guiding the evolution of Filipino: simplification (both spelling and grammar) and competition (e.g., in the case of three competing words, all may eventually become accepted synonyms, or one can drop out, or the meaning of one can change). This evolutionary process has the potential to overcome existing hierarchies among Philippine languages. As the lingua franca is cast and recast in everyday speech, different kinds of Filipino—dialects, as it were—are emerging in different parts of the country. Linguist Consuelo Paz argues that at this point in Filipino's evolution, standardization would be anathema to its democratic nature, if standardization would privilege one ethnolinguistic group over another.[87]

The issue that could derail the widespread acceptance of Filipino as a national language and as the primary medium of instruction is the perception, held by many, that Filipino is based primarily on Tagalog. Its proponents concede that Filipino draws most heavily from Tagalog, yet they argue that Filipino is based on a "universal nucleus" found in most Philippine languages. Hence elements found in Tagalog can also be found in other Philippine languages. This technical debate is secondary. What is key is that as long as many continue to believe that Filipino is Tagalog, then ethnic rivalries of decades past come into play.

Another criticism of Filipino is that it is too inclusive—that it is little more than legitimized Taglish (a mix of Tagalog and English), so liberal is its use of words and idioms from English. This critique underscores the sensitivity of language issues in the Philippines, especially where colonial legacies are concerned.

The issue is not just the question of replacing English with Filipino. Just as English creates linguistic hierarchies that separate those who speak the language from those who do not, Filipino has the potential to be as exclusionary as English. Even so, the linguistic space created by Filipino is wider than that of English; it need not be constrained by class or even ethnolinguistic differences, given that Filipino does not belong, strictly speaking, to the Tagalogs.

---

87. Ibid., pp. 38–43.

There is a compelling need in the Philippines to create linguistic public spaces where different classes and groups can meet on a common linguistic ground. English was supposed to play this role, but it only succeeded in reinforcing class differences. Filipino appears to stand a better chance.

Ethnic identity per se will probably not determine the direction of debates on language use in the Philippines. Other factors—economic and political—will exercise more influence. For the government, the most pressing problems are social injustice and the unequal distribution of resources.

Although Andrew Gonzalez has argued that "benign neglect is better than deliberate language planning," this kind of fatalism ignores the difficult challenge of crafting implementable policies amid continuing debates over the specific form, substance, and direction of language policy. Even though policymakers have reached a consensus on the desirability of a national language, they have had to contend with an equally strong demand to maintain the country's perceived "comparative advantage" as an English-speaking nation.

Those who argue in favor of the retention of English as the official language of education invoke a nationalism that conceives of development in terms of integration with the global economy, facilitated in part by a labor force proficient in the world's dominant language. Those who argue for Filipino invoke the legacy of colonialism and the role played by English in reproducing historic patterns of social and economic inequality that account for so many of the problems afflicting the country today.

The country's bilingual policy in education and government represented a compromise between these two positions, both of which are rooted in perceptions of national interests. The state sought to promote Filipino while retaining English, but given its limited resources and its limited capacity to fully implement its own policies, the effort to promote both languages has resulted not in genuine bilingualism, but in semilingualism in which neither of the two languages is spoken with any real facility by the majority of the population.

The failure of the bilingual education policy has been attributed not so much to flaws in the policy itself but to poor implementation.[88] An evaluation of the policy suggests that insufficient resource allocations for increasing the salaries of teachers, teacher training, development of

---

88. Wilfredo L. Alberca, "The Continuing Controversy: Agreement or Disagreement over the Bilingual Education Policy?" *Philippine Journal of Linguistics,* Vol. 21, No. 1 (June 1990), p. 73.

teaching materials, and upgrading facilities have contributed to the deterioration of the quality of education in general.[89] Moreover, in cases where the government earmarked funds for the education sector, some funds have either been mismanaged or siphoned off by corrupt officials.

The most feasible course of action is a two-pronged approach. First, the government should prioritize programs aimed at maximizing the use of Filipino as the national lingua franca while minimizing the divisive effects of ethnic-language loyalties. Second, it should upgrade the teaching of English, but strictly as a second language.

Even as the debate over the exact nature and use of the national language continues, the government should promote the development of the national lingua franca by encouraging its codification, and when appropriate, its standardization. This would entail the establishment of a vastly improved and fully functioning national-language institute that would coordinate regional efforts to compile, publish, and distribute dictionaries, grammar books, teaching aids, and other learning materials in Filipino. These efforts should be responsive to the ways by which the language is evolving in daily usage.

Perhaps most crucial to Filipino's acceptance as a national language will be efforts to change public perception of the language—both its ethnic derivations and its use in different situations—through a massive information campaign, a large-scale translation program, the development of literature in Filipino, and its use as a primary medium of instruction.

The bilingual policy in education should be terminated. Instead Filipino should be used as the primary language of instruction. At the same time, vernacular languages should be allowed to flourish and their potential as auxiliary media of instruction should be fully developed. English should be taught as a second language, with proper institutional support. Knowledge of other foreign languages should be encouraged as well. These steps would form the main pillars of a more effective language policy for the Philippines.

---

89. Ibid.

Part III
East Asia

Chapter 12

The Evolution of Language Policies in China

June Teufel Dreyer

Language policies in the People's Republic of China (PRC) have been shaped by a variety of sometimes conflicting interests, including a commitment to communist ideology, the goal of creating a strong nation and state, the desire for rapid economic development, and the need for social stability. In general, China's language policies have been repressive when ideological considerations were paramount, and less so at other times.

China's communist ideology held that ethnic and linguistic differences would wither away, as would the state itself, as socialism evolved into communism. In theory, the imposition of a common language on the people was unnecessary. At the same time, the needs of nation building and the desire for rapid economic development seemed to call for the imposition of a common language on the country's many ethnic groups. A commitment made in the early years of communist rule to provide all of China's fifty-five ethnic minorities with written languages proved to be impractical. Two subsequent efforts to impose linguistic conformity in the late 1950s and mid-1960s sparked resistance in many areas and contributed to ethnic unrest in some regions.

In the 1970s and, more noticeably, in the 1980s, China's leaders attempted to repair the damage to relations with minorities by easing restrictions on minority languages and reassuming the party's earlier self-proclaimed role of protector and developer of ethnic literature and culture. The central government's desire to encourage tourism also led it to support many of the unique contributions of minorities, in particular those associated with language and literature. These policies, however, fostered the growth of outward pressures, including separatist demands among minority groups that alarmed the central government.

China's official language policy is bilingualism: People are encouraged to use putonghua, which is loosely based on Beijing Mandarin;[1] and minorities are allowed to use their own languages. Han Chinese who live in minority areas are supposed to learn local minority languages. There is a considerable gap, however, between policy and practice. Where an ethnic group has a well-developed language and literature and is perceived as threatening to the central government, minority interest in that language and culture is considered suspect. Where a group with a well-developed language and literature is not perceived as threatening, its broadcasts and publications are subject to less scrutiny and even given a modest degree of government encouragement. In the case of the Zhuang, China's most populous minority and one of its best assimilated, the government has created a script for the group and has been more enthusiastic about its propagation than have most Zhuang. The government has also supported the spoken and written languages of several small southwestern minorities. At the other end of the spectrum, the central government considers Tibetan, the languages of the Turkic Muslim minorities and, to a lesser extent, Mongolian to be potentially subversive.

Many government documents are regularly translated into seven minority languages: Kazak, Korean, Mongolian, Tibetan, Uygur, Yi, and Zhuangand. Whatever the linguistic medium, Beijing wants to control the content of the message. Although bilingualism is officially advocated, Han who live in minority areas rarely learn local spoken languages, and they almost never learn local written languages. This is due in part to what official sources regularly criticize as "great nation chauvinism." Another explanation for Han resistance to learning minority languages is that, because any given minority is small compared with the Han majority, it is more useful for minorities to learn putonghua than it is for Han to learn minority languages. China's language planners have also argued that, if China is to modernize quickly, it needs to make rapid advances in science and technology; therefore the second language taught in schools should be English or Japanese. Members of some minorities agree, but they contend that it is putonghua that should be dropped in minority schools, not minority languages.

The use of putonghua in Han areas has eroded as well. The loosening of central government control that accompanied Deng Xiaoping's reforms in the 1970s encouraged regional tendencies even within Han ar-

---

1. Because the term "Mandarin" conjured images of the official class of traditional China that Mao Zedong despised, "putonghua" (common speech) was used instead. The term "kuo-yü" (guoyü in pinyin transliteration) or "national language," is the preferred term in the Republic of China on Taiwan.

eas. Beijing subsequently became worried by the resurgence of local dialects and decreed that student success in learning putonghua would be an important criterion in evaluations of their teachers' qualifications.

Language policies and practices in China are the result of trial and error over the past half-century and are still evolving. This chapter analyzes the development of these practices since 1949 to the dawn of the twenty-first century.

Background

The Chinese Communist Party (CCP) came to power in 1949 vowing to create a strong nation—in Mao's phrase, a "China that has stood up [in the family of nations]." This entailed, among other things, imposing a common national language, putonghua, on the entire country. It also meant teaching a simplified version of traditional Chinese characters to the entire population. At the same time, the party pledged to allow every ethnic group in the country to develop according to its own historical characteristics. Minority languages were said to be important parts of this ethnic-cultural complex. Several factors helped to shape language policy in the PRC.

First, the Soviet Union, whose experience provided the CCP with a model for formulating ethnic policies, had made similar promises to its own non-Russian minority groups. Second, it would have been difficult to enforce any other policy. The CCP had assumed control over most of China's minority areas either through force or last-minute surrenders by local elites when the futility of resistance had become obvious. Most of these areas were located on or near the country's land borders, far from such roads and railways as then existed, characterized by difficult terrain, and sparsely populated. The new PRC was still internally fragile, it had both domestic and international enemies, and it could ill afford to devote scarce resources to the suppression of local languages.

A third factor shaping China's language policy was ideology. Karl Marx had predicted that ethnic differences, including those involving linguistics, would wither away under the dictatorship of the proletariat. Because minority groups constituted a small percentage of China's population, and because none was as economically or educationally advanced as the majority Han (with the exception of ethnic Korean residents of China), minorities could be expected to freely accept the benefits of learning putonghua and adopting the country's new social system.

A fourth factor was the CCP's desire to present its policies toward minorities as a benign alternative to those of its predecessor, the Kuomintang (KMT). The KMT, whose name literally translates as "Nationalist

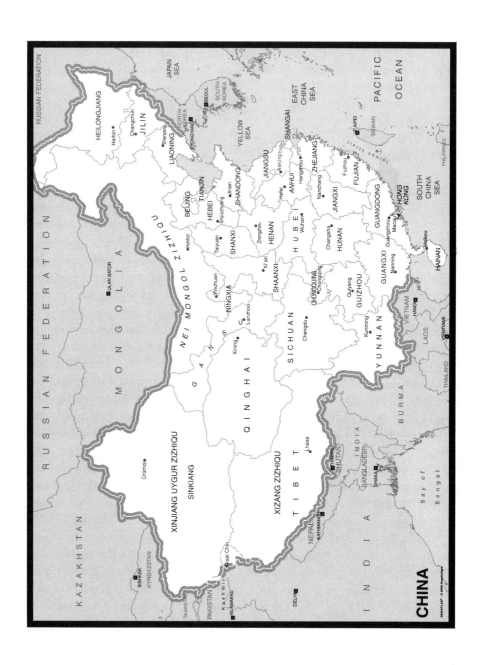

Party," was formed at the turn of the twentieth century, when ethnic nationalism in the West was growing. Its cosmopolitan founder, Sun Yat-sen, had been greatly influenced by the power of nationalist sentiments. The KMT's language policy was unabashedly assimilative: It held that minorities should speak standard Chinese and, generally, accept Chinese ways as the nation strove for modernization.[2] Because the KMT had barely begun to assert its administrative authority over China when the war with Japan began, its language policies were implemented weakly or not at all.

Fifth, party leaders were aware that they knew relatively little about the country's minority groups and their languages. They therefore realized that it could be counterproductive to impose harsh language policies on minorities until they had a better understanding of the linguistic tasks involved.

Subsequent anthropological research found hundreds of groups in China that identified themselves as distinct minorities. Considering this number excessive, Beijing arbitrarily combined several groups into larger groups even where, as in the case of the Zhuang, this meant combining groups that spoke mutually unintelligible languages and that had had little contact with one other. Not surprisingly, these forced mergers caused problems when it came time to devise both a spoken and a standard written language.

After considerable political debate, the CCP decided that China had fifty-four ethnic minorities; a fifty-fifth, the Jinuo of Yunnan Province, was added in 1979. (See Table 12.1.) Dialect groups were not classified as minority groups, even when their languages were mutually unintelligible with putonghua, which the government had decreed would be the official language of the PRC. This excluded, among others, the Hakka and the Hoklo, both of which are considered ethnic groups in the Republic of China on Taiwan. The 1954 census revealed that the PRC's minorities totaled 40 million people, or 6 percent of the total population of the

---

2. There are important caveats here. Ironically, neither Sun Yat-sen nor his successor, Chiang Kai-shek, was a fluent speaker of Mandarin. Sun was born to a Cantonese-speaking family; the difference between Mandarin and Cantonese has been compared with that between Spanish and Dutch. He was educated at an English-language school in Hawaii and spoke Japanese well enough to pass as a native in Japan. Chiang attended a Japanese military academy and also spoke Japanese well. His nearly impenetrable Zhejiang dialect was a source of merriment to some educated Mandarin speakers and an acute embarrassment to others. Sun endured constant criticism from rivals who complained that he was ignorant of Chinese culture, which indeed he had rebelled against at an early age. Both Sun and Chiang were more concerned with modernizing the country than with forcing traditional Chinese ways on either minorities or Han Chinese.

Table 12.1. Ethnic Minorities in China, 1990.

Group	Number	Main Concentration
Zhuang	15,489,630	Guangxi, Yunnan
Manchu	9,821,180	Liaoning, Jilin, Heilongjiang
Hui	8,602,978	Ningxia, Gansu
Miao	7,398,035	Guizhou, Hunan, Yunnan
Uygur	7,214,431	Xinjiang
Yi	6,572,173	Sichuan, Yunnan
Tujia	5,704,223	Hunan, Hubei
Mongol	4,806,849	Inner Mongolia, Liaoning
Tibetan	4,593,330	Tibet, Sichuan, Qinghai
Bouyei	2,545,059	Guizhou
Dong	2,514,014	Guizhou
Yao	2,134,013	Guangxi, Guangdong
Korean	1,920,597	Jilin, Liaoning, Helongjiang
Bai	1,594,827	Yunnan
Hani/Akha	1,253,952	Yunnan
Kazak	1,111,718	Xinjiang, Qinghai
Li	1,110,900	Hainan
Dai/Thai	1,025,128	Yunnan
She	630,378	Fujian
Lisu	574,856	Yunnan
Gelao	437,997	Guizhou
Lahu	411,476	Yunnan
Dongxiang	373,872	Gansu
Va/Wa	351,974	Yunnan
Shui,Sui	345,993	Guizhou
Naxi	278,009	Yunnan
Qiang	198,252	Sichuan
Tu	191,624	Qinghai, Gansu
Xibo/Xibe	172,847	Xinjiang
Mulam/Molao	159,328	Guangxi
Kirghiz	141,549	Xinjiang
Daur	121,357	Inner Mongolia, Heilongjiang
Jingpo	119,209	Yunnan
Salar	87,697	Qinghai, Gansu
Blang/Bulang	82,280	Yunnan
Maonan	71,968	Guangxi
Tajik	33,538	Xinjiang
Primi/Pumi	29,657	Yunnan
Achang	27,708	Yunnan
Nu	27,123	Yunnan
Ewenki	26,315	Inner Mongolia
Gin/Jing	18,915	Guangdong
Jino	18,021	Yunnan
De'ang/Benglong	15,462	Yunnan
Uzbek	14,502	Xinjiang

Table 12.1. *(continued)*

Group	Number	Main Concentration
Russian	13,504	Xinjiang
Yugu	12,297	Gansu
Bonan/Baoan	12,212	Gansu
Monba	7,475	Tibet
Orogen	6,965	Inner Mongolia
Derung/Dulong	5,816	Yunnan
Tatar	4,873	Xinjiang
Hezhen	4,245	Heilongjiang
Lhoba	2,312	Tibet

SOURCE: Census data were published in 1991 by the State Statistical Bureau.

country. By 1999 the minority population had risen to 110 million, or 8.74 percent of the whole.

Phase One: Language Policy in the Early Years of the PRC

The 1949 Common Program of the newly founded PRC granted, at least on paper, "each of the minorities alike . . . the freedom to develop its own language." The 1954 constitution went considerably further, stipulating that minority areas could use one or more of the languages commonly used in those areas to transact official business. Courts were to use local languages in judging and sentencing, and minorities were given the right to use their own spoken and written languages in litigation.

The All-China Minorities Education Conference, held in 1951, advocated that minorities with written languages be taught in those languages at the primary- and secondary-school levels. Those who did not have a written language, or whose written languages were "imperfect," were to be helped to develop and reform their written languages; these minorities could be taught with Chinese-language or minority-language textbooks where the latter existed. The conference also voted unanimously to establish putonghua classes in "various" grades of minorities schools "in accordance with the needs of the minorities concerned."[3]

Because the CCP realized that it needed to learn much more about minority peoples before it could consolidate its rule over them, there was much interest in Beijing in minority languages in the early 1950s. Schol-

---

3. United States Consulate General, Hong Kong, *Current Background (CB)*, No. 152 (1951), pp. 11–15.

arly research on minority languages was part of the 1951 Work Plan of the Chinese Academy of Sciences.[4] When the Central Nationalities Institute was founded in 1950 in Beijing, it included a department for such research, and several prominent linguistics experts and anthropologists were assigned to it. Investigation teams were formed and sent to conduct fieldwork in minority areas. Their expertise was to be used in collecting materials for the formulation of written minority languages, the compilation of corresponding dictionaries, and the preparation of courses of study to train cadres in minority languages. Minority-group members who wished to study putonghua were to be given opportunities to do so, but there was to be no compulsion "at the present moment."[5]

By 1952 the CCP claimed to have published more than 700,000 books and magazines in the Mongolian, Tibetan, and Uygur languages, and to be producing radio broadcasts and dubbed films in several minority languages. Work was proceeding on a written language for the Yi, a group whose 3 million members lived in rural areas in several southwestern Chinese provinces. The founding of Nationalities Press in Beijing in 1953 facilitated the preparation of works in minority languages: In 1954, 8.73 million such books were published, an increase of 13 percent over the previous year.[6]

Newspapers and magazines also became a focus of the party's efforts. In 1955 one source reported that twenty newspapers and twenty-eight magazines were being published in seven minority languages (Kazak, Korean, Mongolian, Tibetan, Uygur, Xibo, and Yi).[7] Another source reported the founding of a small newspaper in 1955 in the then-Dehong Dai (Thai) Autonomous Prefecture.[8] Every issue included one page each of putonghua, Dai, Jingpo, and Lisu. For the first year, the Dai page had to be handwritten because there was no print matrix available for the language. The first head of the prefecture later had one made out of steel.[9]

Also in 1955, a conference on minority languages in Beijing drew up a three-year plan for its work. This included the popularization of a new

---

4.   United States Consulate General, Hong Kong, *Survey of the China Mainland Press* (*SCMP*), No. 194 (1951), p. 20.

5.   *CB*, No. 264 (1951), pp. 9–13.

6.   *CB*, No. 360 (1953), p. 15.

7.   *Guangming Ribao* (*GMRB*), May 20, 1955, p. 3.

8.   It became the Dai-Jingpo Autonomous Prefecture in 1956.

9.   Xinhua, April 13, 1989, in Foreign Broadcast Information Service (FBIS), April 14, 1989, p. 45.

script for the Zhuang, the PRC's largest minority, which then numbered 7 million. In addition, a script was to be created for the Hani, a small group of approximately half a million people. The conferees opted for a simplified version of Mongolian, which would be written horizontally rather than vertically.[10] Elsewhere, party and government officials adopted horizontal rather than vertical writing for putonghua as well.

These events suggest that the new communist government was fairly tolerant of ethnic minorities and their languages. Statements in the Chinese media, however, implied that the bilingual facilities called for by the party's program often existed on paper only.[11] In 1956, a year after the conference on minority languages was held, the PRC's highest-ranking member of an ethnic minority, Ulanfu, complained openly to the National Party Congress that "no vigorous and practical support is given to devising and promoting [those] languages."[12] Ulanfu, an ethnic Mongol who had been educated in Beijing and had joined the party in the 1920s, only a few years after it was founded, was far more comfortable in putonghua than his native tongue. He was also an alternate member of the CCP's political bureau, first party secretary of the Inner Mongolia Autonomous Region, chair of the IMAR's government, and head of its defense operations. Ulanfu was not a disgruntled ethnic chauvinist, and his position in the power structure meant that his words had to be taken seriously.

A month after Ulanfu's speech, the government announced a five-year plan for minority languages. It reiterated familiar themes: Ethnic minorities without a written language must be helped to create one as soon as possible; more magazines, newspapers, and documents should be published in minority languages; the central broadcasting station should increase its programming in minority languages; more radio receiving stations should be set up in minority areas; and more films should be dubbed into minority languages. Acknowledging that the quality of translations was low, party and government sources agreed to expand training programs for translators.[13] Separately, a decision was made to write the scripts of the country's Muslim minorities in Cyrillic rather than in Arabic.[14] This represented a gesture of solidarity with the

---

10.   *SCMP,* No. 1130 (1955), p. 16.

11.   See, for example, *CB,* No. 264 (1951), pp. 9–13; *SCMP,* No. 1456 (1956), p. 13; and *Renmin Ribao (RMRB),* February 10, 1957, p. 3.

12.   *CB,* No. 418 (1956), p. 18.

13.   *Minzu Tuanjie (MZTJ),* No. 7 (July 1959), pp. 23–25.

14.   *SCMP,* No. 1361 (1956), p. 12.

Soviet Union and an attempt to insulate China's Islamic minorities from pan-Muslim feelings emanating from the Middle East.

Many of these projects were halted or reversed in 1957. A country-wide "Hundred Flowers" campaign to encourage citizens of the PRC to voice their grievances against the party and the government had produced criticism that the ruling elite felt it could not tolerate. An investigation of the party's minorities program showed that much of this criticism was disproportionately—though far from exclusively—leveled by minorities.

An examination of books and papers that had been translated into minority languages revealed many developments that aroused the party's ire. One problem involved translations that gave minority readers misleading impressions that could cause problems later. Most of the examples given, however, were probably caused by translation glitches—not counterrevolutionary zeal. For example, it was discovered that the same term had been used both for the "liberation" of the city of Shanghai by the CCP in 1949 and for Ghana's "liberation" from British colonialism. "Central People's Government" had been translated as "the imperial house," and "capital" as "the palace in Beijing."

A second problem was resistance to borrowing vocabulary from putonghua on the grounds that it was structurally inappropriate to the minority language concerned. When the minority language did not have a term for a new concept, translators were criticized for going to unacceptable lengths to coin a new word or phrase from existing elements of that language. Worse yet, in the ideologically fervent atmosphere of the times, translators had occasionally adopted a word or phrase from a foreign language.[15] "Errors" such as these were said to be covert slanders against putonghua and its literature.[16]

It was also said that books in minority languages belittled "the advanced experiences of the Han elder brother" through such acts as placing the verses of minority poets in the front while relegating the poems of Han communist leaders Mao Zedong and Zhu De to the back. In general, books for minorities were deemed to exhibit objectionable levels of local nationalism, religious sentiment, capitalist thought, and "aloofness from politics, reality, and production."[17]

The leadership in Beijing replaced its mass campaign to elicit people's opinions with another mass campaign to correct danger-

15. *RMRB,* February 15, 1958, p. 2.

16. *Minzu Yanjiu (MZYJ),* No. 6 (June 1959), p. 5.

17. *MZYC,* No. 6 (June 1959), p. 5.

ous thoughts: The era when a "hundred flowers" were encouraged to bloom was succeeded by an anti-rightist movement in which only one ideology—communism—and one language—putonghua—would henceforth be tolerated.

Phase Two: The Great Leap Forward and Its Aftermath

The Great Leap Forward, launched in 1958, sought to move the PRC's economy to a higher stage of socialism while raising productivity. Although language issues were not the driving force behind the Great Leap Forward, the campaign nonetheless had a profound effect on China's language policies. Tremendous emphasis was placed on rapid growth and ideological purity, and government toleration of ethnic diversity consequently diminished drastically.

As part of the campaign, Beijing required ethnic minorities to learn putonghua, though the official press described minorities as clamoring to do so. Some resistance to this initiative was acknowledged, but it was explained away as the result of misunderstandings. When minorities complained that they did not want to learn putonghua because it was too difficult, they were told to overcome their resistance. If minorities argued that only those who worked in Han areas should have to study the Han language, they were told that "such people regard the Han language as only a means to explain things to Han people. They neglect the important aspect of Han being a means through which to study the [wisdom of the] Han elder brother." Minority cadres were described as realizing, "'If you can't speak Han, you're deaf. If you can't read Han, you're blind.'"[18]

According to the official media, a new "high tide of enthusiasm" for learning putonghua emerged within minority communities. For this reason, and because translation facilities not only were expensive to maintain but also took people away from more productive activities, it was deemed useless to continue research work on minority languages. Articles, radio broadcasts, and mass meetings criticized "fuzzy thinking" on language planning, including the idea that every minority group ought to have its own spoken and written language. In cases where one nationality had been using the language of another, it was said to be acceptable to continue doing so. In cases where two nationalities had similar languages, choosing one or the other—or creating an "alliance" between the two—was the suggested solution. Every minority language had to be

18. *MZYJ*, No. 7 (July 1958), p. 30.

standardized in accordance with the pinyin alphabet, based on Latin script, that had been developed for putonghua.[19]

This edict was also applied to Uygur and Kazak, thus negating the 1956 decision to use Cyrillic in transcribing both languages.[20] Although eyewitnesses described the 1956 decision as widely ignored, the new policy had enormous political and symbolic significance. Growing out of and reflecting not-yet-public disagreements between the PRC and the Soviet Union, this decision further separated Chinese Uygurs and Kazaks from their counterparts in the Soviet Union by making cross-border communications more difficult.

Research projects on minority languages were either curtailed or terminated. Linguistics experts were said to have thought "without evidence" and told that they had to "catch up to an international standard, write huge books, and collect ever more material." In seeking to compile a 50,000-character Han-Yi dictionary "to rival that of [the huge compendium of the Chinese language commissioned by the Qing (Manchu) dynasty emperor] Kangxi," these experts were said to have wasted eight years, during which time the Yi nationality had been without a written language (contradicting earlier government claims).[21] Similar delays were said to have characterized the work of the group commissioned to study the Dai language.

Researchers also were accused of exaggerating the uniqueness of minority languages while neglecting the ways in which they were similar to each other and to putonghua. Insistence on producing detailed, comprehensive dictionaries was cited as evidence that compilers wanted to "throw off politics, reality, and the masses." Dictionaries of a few thousand characters, which would meet basic economic needs, were considered to be suitably socialist and practical: The new policy favored basic dictionaries that contained simple terms related to economic production (e.g., plows and machinery) as well as to politics (e.g., exploitation and the dictatorship of the proletariat). Minority-group members who protested were accused of being "local nationalists" who espoused "national splittism" at the expense of national unity. Linguistics experts who objected to project cutbacks were labeled "bourgeois scientific objectivists" who were using capitalist techniques.[22]

---

19.   *MZTJ*, No. 2 (February 1958), pp. 6–7.

20.   *SCMP*, No. 1799 (1958), p. 28.

21.   *MZTJ*, No. 5 (May 1958), pp. 4–5.

22.   Ibid.

The policies of the Great Leap Forward produced intense resistance both in Han areas and in ethnic-minority areas. Mass hunger and starvation, economic chaos, and political dissension ensued. In a few cases, resistance took the form of outright rebellion. Many of the government's policies, including those on minority languages, were subsequently modified or reversed. In view of Ulanfu's previous defense of the role of language planning, it is interesting to note that one of the first manifestations of the new, more benign, view of minority-language study came from his province, the Inner Mongolia Autonomous Region.

In January 1962, a conference on language and education was held "under the direct supervision of the regional party committee" in Huhhot, the capital of the IMAR. Conference participants actually praised the party's efforts in encouraging and developing the study of Mongolian, as well as its achievements in researching Mongolian dialects and in unearthing, collating, and translating Mongolian literature. Statistics were released on the number of Mongolian-language broadcasting stations and on the numbers and circulation of Mongolian-language newspapers and magazines. Mongolian was described as the language of instruction in primary and secondary schools, though students were "also paying attention to learning putonghua."[23]

A few months later, Fu Mouji, a linguistics specialist writing in the journal *Minzu Tuanjie*,[24] expressed views different from those heard at the 1962 conference, especially those involving the borrowing of vocabulary from putonghua. Fu acknowledged that minority languages would likely absorb increasing numbers of words from putonghua, but he cautioned that borrowing should be done carefully, taking into consideration the structure and past development of the languages in question. With minority languages such as Dai, Lisu, Miao, and Zhuang, many words and terms could be absorbed easily. This was not true, however, of Kazak, Mongolian, Tibetan, and Uygur. Fu cautioned, "We must take a long look at the influence of putonghua on specific minority languages . . . we must be meticulous and keep close relations with the masses, not simply decide for them."[25]

---

23. *GMRB*, February 15, 1962, p. 1.

24. The journal had only recently reappeared after publication was suspended during the latter part of the Great Leap Forward. This disruption may have been more a function of paper shortages than of a conscious desire to stop communications with ethnic minorities. *Minzu Tuanjie*'s more scholarly sibling publication, *Minzu Yanjiu*, also suspended operations, for an even longer period of time.

25. *MZTJ*, No. 3 (March 1962), pp. 25–27, 36–37.

In 1963 *Minzu Tuanjie* published an article about a Mongol poet, quoting a speech he had made in 1956—that is, before the anti-rightist campaign and the Great Leap Forward—to the effect that "one's own nationality language is best able to express that nationality's life, feelings, and character. Using it in one's works not only can directly enthuse one's own people to work and struggle, it can also add unique fresh flowers to the literary garden of the ancestral land which no other nationality's can be substituted for."[26] It was argued, in other words, that the development and use of minority languages would be promoted not only for literary reasons but also for economic and patriotic reasons. *Minzu Tuanjie* also ran an article entitled "Strengthen Nationalities Press Work," which again advocated careful training of translators.[27]

Central government toleration of minority languages continued until the mid-1960s. The nationally circulated putonghua magazine, *Zhongguo Qingnian*, proudly announced in 1963 that "since liberation, more than ten nationalities had been helped to create national scripts," and an additional three had received advice on how to improve existing written languages. Eleven minorities were said to be publishing newspapers and magazines.[28] Han who lived or worked in areas where there were ethnic minorities were officially encouraged to learn minority languages. In March 1966 a Chinese newspaper carried an article entitled "Learn to Speak Minority Nationalities for the Revolution." In it, a Han employee of a branch of the People's Bank located in the Xinjiang Uygur Autonomous Region, explained how learning Kazak had facilitated his dealings with Kazak speakers and simultaneously advanced the cause of socialism.[29]

Phase Three: Resurgence of Linguistic Assimilation, 1966–70

The Great Proletarian Cultural Revolution began to unfold in 1966 and, with it, another and much more energetic attack on minority languages was launched. The four minority-language editions in which the glossy *China Pictorial* had been published (Mongol, Tibetan, Uygur, and Zhuang) disappeared from bookstores at the beginning of 1967, and much broadcasting in minority languages ended. Ulanfu was purged. Among his long list of alleged crimes was giving orders "to organize a movement in

---

26. *MZTJ*, No. 5 (May 1963), pp. 37–40.

27. *MZTJ*, No. 1 (January 1963), pp. 9–12.

28. *Zhongguo Qingnian*, November 1963, p. 4.

29. *Dagong Bao*, March 3, 1966, p. 4.

the whole IMAR to study Mongol in order to compete with and resist the mass movement for the creative study and application of Chairman Mao's works." This was held to be part of Ulanfu's larger plot to encourage the separation of the IMAR from China and its incorporation into the Mongol People's Republic, with himself as emperor.[30] Ulanfu's removal from his posts presumably also meant the end of efforts to study the Mongol language. The size of the IMAR region was reduced by two-fifths.

Beijing's new policies were met with resistance and incomprehension from minorities who did not understand putonghua. *Renmin Ribao*, the official organ of the Communist Party, published an article in late 1968 detailing the efforts of People's Liberation Army (PLA) cadres in bringing Cultural Revolution propaganda to Mongol herders:

All of a sudden, a number of commune members failed to turn up for several successive evenings. A poor herdsman went to look for them, but they would not come. When comrades of the Third Machine Gun Company went to ask them, they still would not come, claiming that they were "sick." With each day, more and more people used this pretext to absent themselves from the study class. . . . a whisper was going around the village: the PLA soldiers speak putonghua. We can't understand them. If we want to study, we will find people who read the Mongol language to instruct us. The company's party branch quickly became aware that class enemies were attempting to exploit ethnic and linguistic difficulties to sow dissension between the soldiers and the people and destroy the Mao Zedong study class.[31]

The article ends with the PLA ferreting out the individuals who started and continued to participate in the whisper campaign, forcing the herders to denounce them, and reassembling the study group—presumably still in putonghua, and still not understood by the majority of attendees, who were now more worried about being denounced as class enemies than not understanding what was being said.

The policy of restricting minorities' languages remained in force for the next several years. Programming and publications in minority languages disappeared. A *Renmin Ribao* article in 1970, describing the visit of an elderly Mongol woman to Beijing for medical treatment, made a point of mentioning that she had repeatedly chanted to herself in putonghua good wishes to the party and to Chairman Mao for their concern.[32] A language forum held in Xinjiang in 1971 concentrated on the absorption of

30. Radio Huhhot, January 12, 1968.

31. *RMRB*, October 21, 1968, p. 1.

32. *RMRB*, February 8, 1970, p. 4.

new words, presumably borrowed from putonghua, into Uygur and Kazak.[33] Also in 1971, *Renmin Ribao* urged people to "quickly overcome all the obstacles which prevent the national minorities from reading the works of Mao Zedong in putonghua."[34]

Phase Four: Linguistic Liberalization, 1971–77

The official attitude toward minority languages was changing even as the *Renmin Ribao* article was being written. Radio Beijing began a series of broadcasts in May 1971 in Uygur and Kazak. In October the Guangxi provincial broadcasting system resumed Zhuang-language programming, which had been terminated in 1967. Also in October, two of the Mongol areas that had been removed from the IMAR in 1969 and attached to other provinces started broadcasting in Mongolian. The media began making frequent references to the activities of minority presses, citing impressive statistics on numbers of columns being published and large increases in the circulation of ethnic-languages newspapers.

In January 1972 the Central Institute of Nationalities reopened, with a class of 700 representing forty-six of the country's then-recognized fifty-four ethnic minorities. By October the institute was hosting 1,100 students representing forty-eight nationalities. Teachers reportedly spoke in their native languages in class.[35] The numbers of primary and secondary schools designed specifically for minority students and using minority languages also increased. Modern Tibetan–language printing equipment went into operation in the Tibet Autonomous Region in 1972, work began on revising the 1964 edition of the putonghua-Tibetan dictionary, and a decision to manufacture more Tibetan typewriters was announced.[36]

The new revolutionary operas introduced during the Cultural Revolution under the auspices of Mao Zedong's wife, Jiang Qing, were modified. They had originally been sung in putonghua to the accompaniment of piano music; by the mid-1970s, it had become acceptable to adapt dialogues to minority folk-song forms sung in minority languages and to use traditional musical instruments. The adaptations in Bai, Korean, Uygur, and Kazak were said to be particularly popular. The Uygur version utilized the "twelve mucam" form, while the Kazak variant

---

33. Radio Urumqi, December 30, 1971.

34. *RMRB* May 22, 1971, p. 1.

35. Xinhua, December 13, 1972.

36. Radio Beijing, August 3, 1974; and Radio Lhasa, June 9, 1975.

employed a poem-recitation style said to be unique to that nationality's folklore.[37] The plots remained the same—exploited and downtrodden masses joining forces with heroic Communist Party members to vanquish evil landlords, capitalists, Japanese imperialists, and other unsavory characters—but the modes of presentation were radically different.

Local writers who used local vernaculars were lavishly praised. *At the Foot of Kyzyl Mountain*, a novel singled out for special attention, was described as "richly portraying Uygur life and characteristics . . . using a wealth of Uygur proverbs" in the execution of its standard socialist plot.[38] In addition, a major effort was begun to induce Uygurs and Kazaks into using the pinyin version of their scripts,[39] previous efforts having fallen into abeyance because of the weakening of central government controls in the chaos of the Cultural Revolution.

These changes closely coincided with the fall from power of Lin Biao, the man who had emerged from the Cultural Revolution as second in power only to Mao, and who had been explicitly named in the constitution as Mao's successor. Lin disappeared from public view in May 1971, and was later reported to have died in a plane crash in September of that year. A subsequent campaign to vilify Lin charged him with a lengthy list of errors on virtually every aspect of policy. These included "twaddling nonsense" about minorities and accusations that caused splits among China's nationalities. Lin's attitude toward nationalities' languages, however, was not listed on this bill of charges. Apart from his demise coinciding with the revival in minority languages, there is no evidence linking Lin to the linguistic intolerance of the Cultural Revolution.

In January 1975, the Fourth National People's Congress met and approved a new constitution that reaffirmed the right of every nationality to use its own spoken and written languages.[40] This guarantee was less explicit, however, than those contained in the 1954 constitution that it replaced, which declared: "Citizens of all nationalities have the right to use their own spoken and written languages in court proceedings. The people's courts are required to provide interpreters for any party unacquainted with the spoken or written languages commonly used in the locality. In an area entirely or largely inhabited by a minority or where a number of nationalities live together, hearings in the people's courts are

---

37. Radio Beijing, May 26, 1976.

38. Radio Beijing, March 17, 1976, and April 21, 1976.

39. Radio Beijing, August 23, 1976, devoted half an hour to a discussion of the steps leading to the adaptation of Uygur and Kazak to pinyin and the continuing efforts to popularize the pinyin script.

40. Cited in *Beijing Review*, January 24, 1975, p. 14.

to be conducted in the language commonly used in the locality, and judgments, notices, and all other documents of the people's courts are to be promulgated in that language."[41]

It may be unwise to attach too much significance to the new constitution because the more benign 1954 constitution was in force during both the Great Leap Forward and the Cultural Revolution, when the use of minority languages was severely restricted. At the very least, however, the wording of the 1975 constitution represented a consensus opinion among the framers at the time it was promulgated—and the promises of the 1975 constitution were significantly weaker than those of its 1954 counterpart. In the mid-1970s, a major ideological cleavage emerged between the ultra-radical Gang of Four, which included Mao Zedong's wife, Jiang Qing, and a less ideologically rigid group headed by Premier Zhou Enlai. The looser wording of the 1975 constitution may have represented a compromise between the two factions on the minority-language question.

Zhou died in early 1976, followed by Mao in September of the same year. Barely a month later, the Gang of Four was purged. The Gang's fall from power was accompanied by a massive denunciation campaign that included criticisms of its negative attitudes toward minority languages. It was said, for example, that when a minority group member from Xinjiang used an interpreter to deliver his work report to a group including Jiang Qing, the latter was deeply offended. She commented, "Next time you talk to us, will you speak without an interpreter? You make me feel like a foreigner."[42]

The Gang of Four was thought to have called for the elimination of minority languages for two reasons: (1) these languages were said to be "useless" and (2) their use amounted to "retrogression."[43] Other allegations included the charge that, although the adaptation of the revolutionary opera *Red Lantern* was done with the personal approval of Zhou, the Gang of Four had opposed it, with Jiang Qing only "pretending" to voice her support.[44]

The consequences of the Gang of Four's policy on minority languages after 1971 are not clear. A 1978 report accused both Lin Biao and the Gang of Four of burning minority literary and artwork.[45] Although

---

41. *Constitution of the People's Republic of China* (Beijing: People's Publishing House, 1954), Article 77.

42. Radio Beijing, January 30, 1977.

43. Radio Beijing, May 16, 1977.

44. Radio Urumqi, December 16, 1977.

45. Xinhua, November 25, 1978, in FBIS, November 30, 1978, p. E21.

this may be true, it is also true that Han Chinese works of art and literature were destroyed wantonly during the Cultural Revolution; anything old was considered decadent.[46] It is certain that modified revolutionary operas were performed in minority languages, and that the official press frequently praised Han cadres who had learned to speak the languages of the areas in which they worked.[47] Although these cadres may have received praise because they were the exception rather than the rule, that they were praised at all is indicative of the official attitude toward minority languages. The Gang of Four may have been responsible for the less-explicit language guarantees contained in the 1975 constitution, and they may have also figured in conferences on the arts held in Xinjiang in August 1975 and July 1976. The reports of each conference dwelt on the weeding out of old, erroneous manifestations of feudalism, capitalism, and revisionism in literature and said virtually nothing about the adaptation of art forms.[48]

In any case, policy toward minority languages seemed to improve modestly after the Gang of Four's fall. Meetings were held in 1977 to discuss the publication of Mongolian-language books, drawing together representatives of the eight provinces in which China's Mongols live. Compilation of a new Mongolian-Han dictionary began, and Mongolian-language books were said to be less expensive than their putonghua counterparts because the were given government subsidies.[49] New regulations on admission to institutions of higher learning and vocational schools that were issued by the IMAR in 1977 allowed minorities to take entrance exams in their own languages. Those applying to the Han (putonghua) or Mongolian language departments, however, still had to take their exams in putonghua or Mongolian, respectively.[50] Ulanfu was rehabilitated and cleared of the charges that had been leveled against him.

In Sichuan, an experimental program was started to teach the Yi to read Yi-language materials, thereby solving "a big problem in the cultural emancipation of the Yi people." A new version of standardized Yi was used to dub films, translate books and government documents, and pro-

---

46. Eyewitnesses describe priceless manuscripts and works of art being burned or destroyed with hammers. See, for example, Nien Cheng, *Life and Death in Shanghai* (New York: Grove, 1986), pp. 73–79.

47. See, for example, Radio Huhhot, October 6, 1974.

48. Radio Urumqi, August 27, 1975, and July 22, 1976.

49. Radio Huhhot, May 17, 1977.

50. Radio Huhhot, November 8, 1977.

duce "creative literary works."[51] Volume five of the *Selected Works of Mao Zedong* was published in Kazak, Korean, Mongolian, Tibetan, and Uygur at approximately the same time as its putonghua version appeared.[52] A new constitution introduced in January 1978 and ratified two months later contained the 1975 constitution's protection that allowed minorities to develop and use their spoken and written languages.[53]

Phase Five: Linguistic Liberalization under Deng Xiaoping

The government's policies became even more tolerant after Deng Xiaoping was rehabilitated and returned to power. In 1977 Deng was cleared of all charges that had been brought against him. By mid-1978 he had eclipsed Hua Guofeng (who had succeeded Mao) to become China's paramount leader—a position that he would hold until his death in February 1997.

Whereas the leaders of the Great Leap Forward had repressed minority languages in the name of ideology and economic production, and those responsible for the Cultural Revolution had done the same in the name of ideology, Deng believed that encouraging minority languages and their cultures would stimulate production. His reasoning, which also applied to Han areas, was that repressive policies had led to economic stagnation. It followed that allowing more freedoms—which, in the case of minorities, would include greater freedom to use and develop their languages and literatures—would generate increased production. Deng further believed that economic backwardness rather than class friction was the main source of interethnic tensions in China.

There were limits to Deng's comparatively liberal policies. His "special economic zones," which received tax breaks and other privileges were all located on the east coast of China; none were in or even near minority areas. Except for China's Korean minority, whose income and educational levels exceeded those of the Han, minorities trailed behind the Han in both categories. As the economy of the east coast subsequently boomed, minority areas fell further behind. Beijing began to encourage tourism in minority areas to help redress this imbalance. The stark beauty of the Central Asian steppe, the lush tropical flora and fauna of Dai areas of Yunnan, and the magnificent Himalayan setting of Tibet's Potala Palace contrasted sharply with the more uniform appearance of Chinese

---

51.   Radio Beijing, May 16, 1977.

52.   Radio Beijing, July 1, 1977.

53.   See "Constitution of the People's Republic of China," *Beijing Review*, March 17, 1978, Article 4, pp. 6–7.

cities. Tourists had to be entertained, of course, and this gave further impetus to the development of minority cultures, including language.

Researchers interested in minority languages describe the 1980s as a "golden age" for their work. A project was begun—revived according to some sources—to collect and study the Dongba script of the Naxi people of Yunnan Province. This effort included the collection of pictographs used by the ancient priests, or Dongba, of the Naxi. Storyboards with translations in English, Japanese, and putonghua appeared in "minority villages," where tourists could also view what purported to be traditional costumes, dances, and handicrafts. Cultural works—including the *King Gesar* epic of Tibet, the Hani nationality's *Ashma,* and the Dai *Zhaoshutun*—were published both in their original versions and in putonghua. The central government stated that these materials were being collated and published because they belonged "to the whole of China and to the world."[54] These materials were not intended to instill pride in the achievement of specific ethnic groups, but in all of China.

In 1981 a prize competition was established for minority writers, though most of their stories seem to have been written in putonghua. Fittingly, the first awards were presented by Ulanfu. To provide these writers with better access to nationwide readership, a new journal, *Minzu Wenyi,* was founded; at first a bimonthly, it later became a monthly. In the same year, a project to "save" Manchu was also begun. Researchers located the only people left in China—nine of them, all elderly—who remembered the language of the last (Qing) dynasty. Eighty linguistics experts attended a two-month course in Shuangcheng County, Heilongjiang Province, to acquaint themselves with Manchu lexicographical works; a second course was held the following year for more advanced work in Manchu grammar.[55]

By 1981, 10 million minority children, representing 70 percent of the school-age population, were reported to be attending classes. Boarding schools were being established for those who lived in areas too isolated for local schools. More than thirty of the fifty-five minorities had their own spoken languages, and twenty of those had their own writing systems. It was still impossible to produce textbooks in all the minority languages, although a number of publishing houses in various parts of the PRC were translating and printing textbooks in many of them.[56] At the same time, the central government was concerned about the drift away

54. Xinhua, November 25, 1981, in FBIS, December 31,1981, p. K11.

55. Xinhua, November 2, 1981, in FBIS, November 2, 1981, p. S1.

56. Xinhua, November 11, 1981, in FBIS, November 12, 1981, pp. K17–K18.

from putonghua in China as a whole. The press lamented that, in the "ten chaotic years [of the Cultural Revolution], many schools that had formerly used the common spoken language in teaching have once again made use of local dialects" in their place. It was said that those who tried to use putonghua, even in large cities such as Shanghai and Guangzhou (Canton) "often encountered difficulties."[57]

Under party and government sponsorship, societies for Manchu, Mongol, Tibetan, and Zhuang studies were established. Yunnan, with its high number of small and diverse minority groups, was said to have set aside a substantial (but unspecified) portion of its budget for minority-language education. Dai, Jingpo, Lisi, Tibetan, and Va (Wa) primary-school textbooks were published. Primary schools teaching in those languages were permitted to extend instruction for an additional year or two.[58] What parents, who often preferred to have their children in the workforce than in school, thought of this was not recorded.

Phase Six: Dealing With Problems of the Reforms

Although the central government produced a deluge of statistics in the 1980s on how many books, magazines, and newspapers were published in how many languages, and how many films or television specials were dubbed in these languages, all was not going as the government wished. Ulanfu, demonized under the Cultural Revolution for his Mongol chauvinism, began to complain publicly about Han chauvinism. He charged that the cadres and masses of minority nationalities "demand that the cultural heritage of national minorities be rescued and sorted out, and that the spoken and written languages of the minorities be used and developed."[59]

Some indication of these problems may be gleaned from an unusually frank article in the journal of the Central Institute of Nationalities in 1985. According to the article, although language development and education for minorities were important themes during the 1980s, they were subordinate to the higher priority of economic development. In contrast to official claims that Han/minority problems would be solved through economic development, the author of the article argued that ethnic minorities could not begin to approach the level of development in Han areas until the educational gap between Han and others had been bridged.

---

57. Xinhua, December 11, 1981, in FBIS, December 14, 1981, p. K7.

58. Xinhua, August 24, 1981, in FBIS, August 25, 1981, p. Q1.

59. *RMRB*, July 14, 1981, pp. 2–3.

This was not happening, he stated, and it was unlikely to happen unless a number of problems were addressed.

After an obligatory preface praising the PRC's tremendous achievements since 1949, the author blamed "historical factors and certain mistakes in our work" for the low level of education in minority areas. For every 10,000 people in China in 1984, 13 were in college; for minorities, the figure was only 7 or 8. Whereas the illiteracy rate in the PRC as a whole was 23 percent, it was twice as high in minority areas. Thus, among the many problems that would have to be corrected, the author claimed, was the insufficient attention paid to education in minority areas. Provincial and local authorities had diverted central government funds for minority education to finance housing projects for education bureaucrats. Some teachers assigned to minority schools were themselves semiliterate; not surprisingly, they were poor teachers. Teaching conditions in minority-area schools were abysmal: The school in Guangxi, to which the author had been assigned, had only a single small restroom for nearly 2,000 students, and many schools were structurally unsafe. In a minority area of Qinghai—known for its harsh climate—there were no school buildings at all. Classes were held outdoors, with students sitting on the ground and using their folded legs as desks. In Guangxi, some classes were held in cattle pens. Some school roofs leaked so badly that students and teachers needed umbrellas when it rained. The recurrence of interest in religion meant that parents preferred to send their children to temple schools, where students learned to recite scriptures or chant sutras rather than learn either putonghua or the contemporary form of their native languages. Students did not learn about science and technology, which might enable their region to advance economically.[60]

Other sources paint a different picture. For example, although the government had claimed for years that there was universal literacy in both Korean and putonghua among the country's Korean minority,[61] a 1990 source stated that the tiny Hezhen minority (population 2,000) had just become the PRC's first minority to free itself of illiteracy. The Hezhen language had no written form, but 98 percent of school-age Hezhen children attended classes and had learned to read and write in putonghua.[62]

Bilingualism—defined by Beijing as minorities learning both their own language and putonghua, not Han and minorities learning each

---

60.   Kuang Haolin, "For the Minority Nationalities to Develop Economically, Their Education Must Come First," *Zhongyang Minzu Xueyuan Xuebao* [Bulletin of the Central Institute of Nationalities], May 15, 1985, pp. 43–47.

61.   See, for example, Xinhua, November 11, 1981.

62.   Xinhua, December 12, 1990.

other's language—had become standard policy by 1980. Schools in minority areas would teach children in their native languages starting in kindergarten, where it existed, or first grade. Putonghua was to be introduced gradually until it became the main or even the exclusive language for teaching and learning in secondary schools. Phasing in putonghua while phasing out ethnic-minority languages indicates, as one Han researcher put it, that native languages functioned as a "crutch" enabling minority children to transition into putonghua. By the time putonghua had been phased in, however, the students were deficient in both it and their native language.

There were many other problems associated with teaching in minority languages.[63] China's education policies and curricula were set in Beijing. This meant that every textbook in every language had to teach the same things. This top-down system caused several difficulties. For example, books in minority languages were simply translations of their putonghua counterparts. Typically, they would be as much as 50 percent longer than putonghua textbooks and also printed in fewer numbers. This drove up the costs of publishing books in minority languages. Yet, according to law, the prices of minority-language textbooks could not be set higher than their putonghua counterparts. As a result, publishing houses lost money on textbooks in minority languages. The difference was supposed to be made up through government subsidies, but these subsidies were often insufficient, and they often failed to materialize altogether. Publishing houses consequently had little economic incentive to produce minority-language textbooks.

A second problem with the top-down system was the poor quality of the translations. Teachers, many poorly trained themselves, inadvertently transmitted misinformation, which later hurt students on standardized nationwide examinations. A third problem was that the authors of textbooks assumed that readers had knowledge of Han myths and stories. In practice, however, many minority children were unfamiliar with these stories.[64] Their ability to understand their textbooks was consequently constrained. Minority students were bewildered rather than edified, and they left schools in droves.

---

63.   Jing Lin, "Policies and Practices of Bilingual Education for the Minorities in China," *Journal of Multilingual and Multicultural Development*, Vol. 18, No. 3 (Fall 1997), pp. 193–205, contains an excellent summary of these problems.

64.   This point is made in ibid., p. 198, as well as by Zhou Yaowen, "Bilingualism and Bilingual Education in China," *International Journal of the Sociology of Language*, Vol. 92 (1992), p. 43.

Some officials felt that minority students performed poorly in school because they were stupid. Teachers pointed out, however, that some of their young Dai and Tibetan dropouts entered monasteries where they subsequently learned to read sutras. Surely this took considerable intelligence. A young Zhuang woman who was illiterate in Han and Zhuang had nonetheless managed to learn fluent, grammatically correct English; she explained that she had picked it up from Western backpackers.[65]

Although by 1985 the central government had acknowledged that curricula must respect minority cultures, very little changed at the local level. The appalling condition of minority-area schools and poor training of teachers were constant themes,[66] as was the high minority dropout rate. There were also reports that the government's promises to allow certain minorities to take college entrance examinations in their native languages were not being honored.[67]

Not only did the government's minority education policy fail in terms of test scores and school graduation rates; it also failed to achieve the government's most cherished aims. First, economic development in ethnic minority areas continued to lag far behind that of Han areas, particularly those on the eastern coast. Indeed the economic gap widened over time. Second, social instability in minority areas continued to intensify. Mao's economic policies had been redistributive—transferring substantial sums of money from affluent places such as Shanghai to poorer areas such as Tibet and Guizhou to help alleviate poverty. Deng, on the other hand, gave special incentives to some areas—all initially on the east coast—to induce rapid development. These policies were resented by those who felt disadvantaged by them. Central government officials worried that social instability would intensify if these income gaps continued to widen. In Han areas, the less restrictive social policies introduced by Deng produced a population more willing to voice its grievances publicly. Many of these were economic grievances, although the 1980s also saw protests by Turkic Muslims against nuclear testing in their part of the country and protests against literature and art that different groups found offensive. Tibetans were angered by a literary

---

65. Jasper Becker, "Guangxi Backpacker Haunt Offers Fresh Perspective," *South China Morning Post*, October 7, 1999.

66. It should be noted that education in rural areas in general has suffered in the post-Mao era: Scarce resources have been poured into elite urban schools, and most minorities do not live in urban areas.

67. Jing Lin, "Policies and Practices of Bilingual Education for the Minorities in China," p. 196.

work that they believed made fun of their traditional greeting of sticking one's tongue out at visitors.[68] Muslims became violent over the publication of a book alleging that pilgrimages to Mecca involved orgiastic practices.[69]

Lhasa, the capital of Tibet, was already under martial law when demonstrations began in Tiananmen Square in the spring of 1989. The foreign media's subsequent concentration on Tiananmen led it to ignore Muslim rioting in the capital of Xinjiang at the same time. The concern of the CCP and government elites that they were losing control of the country was exacerbated by the collapse of the Soviet empire in Eastern Europe. The Soviet-dominated Mongolian People's Republic was replaced by the independent republic of Mongolia, after which students could elect to study Tibetan (not Russian, as in the past). This was accompanied by a revival of interest in the Tibetan form of Buddhism that most Mongols had practiced before their country had become a Soviet client state. The Dalai Lama, who fled Tibet after the failure of a rebellion against Beijing in 1959, received the Nobel Peace Prize in 1989 and was invited to visit Mongolia. The disintegration of the Soviet Union in 1991 led to the creation of Muslim successor states on the borders of the PRC, several of which had ethnic kin in China. Islamic fundamentalism appeared to be growing as well, and it was rumored that groups such as Hezbollah and Hamas were aiding Muslim dissidents in China.[70]

The government's public encouragement of minority languages continued into the 1990s, albeit with a higher degree of wariness. At the Third Minority Writers' Award Ceremony in 1990, Nationalities Affairs Minister Ismail Aymat, himself a Uygur, praised the work of the eighty-four winners representing forty-one nationalities, while issuing some guidelines for future output. Henceforth, he said, minority literatures should enhance the historical advance and social progress of the minorities in question, as well as promote unity and cooperation among all of China's nationalities. Demonstrations and petitions were not, he admonished, the way to protest against literary works that minorities found offensive. These tactics were deemed illegal because they could trigger social unrest. He accused some writers of holding chauvinistic views and

68. Cheng Hong, "Writers Urged to Respect Minority Nationalities," *China Daily,* April 7, 1989, p. 3.

69. Radio Xinjiang, May 26, 1989, in FBIS, June 2, 1989, pp. 61–62; and Carl Goldstein, "Letter from Xinjiang," *Far Eastern Economic Review,* August 9, 1989, p. 37.

70. See, for example, "Smouldering Grievances," *Far Eastern Economic Review,* September 23, 1993, p. 9; and Lincoln Kaye and John McBeth, "Peace Dividend: Asia's Big Two Adjust to Israel-PLA Accord," in ibid., p. 18.

urged them to think more seriously about the possible effects of their writings. Aymat's deputy minister added that, although the general situation in minority areas was good, "some unstable factors still exist." She worried that "increasingly sharp ethnic conflicts in neighboring nations have had some impact on China's border areas."[71]

In early 1991 two Mongol intellectuals were arrested in the IMAR, and the organization they had founded—the Ih Ru League Society of Mongol Culture Studies—was declared illegal.[72] The society, founded in 1990 by twenty-eight individuals, most of them bureaucrats and teachers, had been registered with the authorities according to the law. Also in accordance with the the law, the society had forwarded summaries of its meetings as well as appeals letters that it had sent to prospective members. They complained that Mongol culture was being neglected, that educational conditions were poor, and that the environment was deteriorating.[73] Since all of these problems had been admitted elsewhere by official sources, one is left to conclude that the government's objections lay more with individuals who were trying to assert independent rights to protect and shape their culture. Interestingly, the arrested leaders of the society had all received their introduction to Mongolian culture at schools and institutes founded and run by the government.

Events in two other areas of China reinforced the impression that ethnic instability was on the rise as the 1990s unfolded. In 1990 a major rebellion broke out in the Baren area of the Xinjiang Uygur Autonomous Region, precipitated by the closing of mosques that had been built without official permission. The mullahs of these mosques were accused of subversive teachings designed to sow disunity and promote separatism. In 1991 three Uygur-language books were banned because they allegedly spread separatist ideas and imperiled the unity of the country.[74] Similar charges were made against the abbots of Tibetan monasteries. At the same time, it was declared that when the needs of socialism conflicted with the dictates of culture and religion, the needs of socialism would prevail. The CCP and the government reserved unto themselves the right to decide when such a conflict existed.

---

71. Quoted in Xie Liangjun, "Ismail Aymat Discusses Ethnic Literary Creation," *China Daily*, November 19, 1990, p. 1.

72. Administrative units in the IMAR have traditional Mongolian names such as "league" and "banner."

73. "Two Inner Mongolian Intellectuals Arrested for Organizing Society to Study Mongolian Culture and Protect Grassland," *Ming Pao* [Bright Report], June 11, 1991, in FBIS, June 14, 1991, p. 45.

74. Xinjiang Television, February 7, 1991, in FBIS, February 8, 1992, pp. 52–53.

Language Policy at the Turn of the Century

Given that these allegedly subversive activities had been going on for several years before the authorities discovered them, it appears that Beijing was not carefully monitoring what was being said in minority languages. Han are still told to learn the minority languages of the areas they live in, but in general Han continue to avoid doing so. A researcher who attended several training schools for teachers in minority areas in Yunnan reports that she did not see any Han learning minority languages in those schools. In addition, few of the Han teachers she observed could speak the local language.[75]

There are exceptions. A Kazak woman describes visiting her grandparents in the Altai region of Xinjiang and being told that their Han neighbor had learned some Kazak. Some Han artists and intellectuals have become interested in Tibetan culture, prompting them to learn the Tibetan language. One researcher estimates that about 2 percent of the Han in Xinjiang are able to speak Uygur.[76] Another reports that resentment in Uygur areas mounted when government-supplied textbooks for teaching Uygur to read putonghua arrived on schedule, while those that would teach Han to read putonghua were delayed.[77] Most Uygurs in Urumqi, the capital of Xinjiang, can speak putonghua, though those in rural areas either cannot or choose not to do so.

The Korean case is an anomaly. Given the booming economy in South Korea and the possibility of lucrative joint ventures with South Korean partners, some Han parents have been encouraging their children to study Korean.

The Kazak woman mentioned above opines that, apart from those who want to rise in the Han-dominated power hierarchy, most people feel that there is little to be gained from studying each other's language. The Han lifestyle is unattractive to Kazaks. Han live with their animals in their homes and, in general, behave in ways that repel Kazaks. The Han argument that they are superior because they have had 5,000 years of civilization sounds ridiculous to Kazaks. "If this is civilization," she says, "we don't want it." Moreover, she notes, the gap between Han and Kazak

---

75.   Assistant Professor Linda Tsung, Hong Kong University of Science and Technology, personal communication, April 7, 2000.

76.   Assistant Professor Barry Sautman, Hong Kong University of Science and Technology, personal communication, March 29, 2000.

77.   Visiting Assistant Professor Gardner Bovingdon, Yale University, personal communication, March 11, 2000.

has increased over the years.[78] Efforts at integration were pushed hard during the Cultural Revolution but have virtually ceased since the fall of the Soviet Union. Because Han and Kazaks live in different neighborhoods, shop at different stores, and visit different cinemas, there is little incentive to learn each other's language.

In other cases, promising young Tibetans and other minorities are sent to boarding schools in the interior of China. They study their own languages for perhaps three hours a week and putonghua the rest of the time. The aim, particularly important in the case of the frequently restive Tibetans, is to produce a contingent of ethnic Tibetans who are fluent in putonghua and who appreciate the values of Han/socialist society. These students are expected to return to Tibet to become its next generation of leaders. If the government is worried that these individuals will lose their ability to relate to their ethnic kin, it has not voiced this concern publicly. Government efforts to create a Tibetan elite with little knowledge of its own language and culture could create a gap between these Tibetan officials and ordinary Tibetans. There is a countertrend, however: Many Tibetan officials and ordinary Tibetans fear that their children will lose their native culture either in the boarding schools or in the government-controlled educational system in Tibet. They have arranged to send their offspring to schools in India, run by the exiled Dalai Lama, for what they perceive to be a more authentically Tibetan education.[79]

The central government is becoming more vigilant about what is being said and written in Kazak, Mongolian, Tibetan, Uygur, and other minority languages. Although a number of cultural organizations have been closed and repressive measures have been taken against some minorities in these areas, official support for minority languages and literature has continued. Each year, the government produces volumes of statistics on the numbers of titles published and films produced by and for minorities in their languages.

The acute sensitivity to language that characterized the first three decades of communist rule in China has abated. The government's emphasis has shifted to controlling the message rather than the medium in which it is expressed. Unfortunately, it has proved difficult to educate mi-

---

78   Conversation with author, June 14, 1990.

79.   Standard curricula as they appear in Tibetan-exile publications such as *Tibetan Review* seem to indicate a British boarding school–style education, including instruction in the English language, mathematics, and science, plus Tibetan language, Buddhist studies, and Tibetan culture and crafts. This might be called Tibetan education with modern characteristics.

norities—in whatever language. The minority illiteracy rate in 1999 was said to be 30.8 percent, or 9.3 percent higher than that of the Han.[80] This was down from the 46 percent illiteracy rate for minorities mentioned in the 1985 source quoted above, though one should be wary of accepting official statistics at face value.[81] Government officials, given certain targets and knowing that their superiors will base job evaluations on meeting these targets, have incentives to report success whether or not they have achieved it.

The central government's formal commitment to bilingualism notwithstanding, provincial leaders have been increasingly open in voicing their discontent. In an April 1998 speech, Xinjiang's party head, a Han, said that "we say the constitution provides that all nationalities have the freedom to use and develop their spoken and written languages, but this in no way means advocating the use of their own spoken and written languages." He went on to say that "since it is impossible to promptly translate many things into minority languages, it is a very urgent task for cadres of minorities to learn and have a good command of the Chinese language."[82] At the National People's Congress meeting in March 2000, the leading party figure in Sichuan complained about promoting minority education when it was so much less useful than learning a foreign language: "The whole world is learning English. Why bother so much [with minority languages]?" This party leader also castigated the Tibetans for their high level of poverty and widespread illiteracy, blaming these problems on Tibetan donations to monasteries. He suggested that they spend their money on their children's education instead.[83]

In interviews, several members of ethnic minorities stated that they want to learn English and/or Japanese but not at the expense of their own languages. Putonghua, they argued, could and should be dropped from the equation. Individuals whose written languages are phonetically based remarked that they found English easier to learn than putonghua, because the latter is based on ideographs. People who had studied in bilingual schools complained that they were not truly bilingual: Although

80. Yü Fei, "Development Gap in Minority Regions," Xinhua, May 19, 1999, in FBIS May 22, 1999.

81. Kuang, "For the Minority Nationalities to Develop Economically, Their Education Must Come First."

82. Quoted in Wang Lequan, "Strive to Build a Contingent of High-Quality Cadres," Radio Urumqi, April 26, 1998, in FBIS, May 27, 1998.

83. Zhou Yongkang, quoted in Josephine Ma, "Tibetans 'Wasting Money' on Donations to Monasteries," South China Morning Post, March 14, 2000.

they could speak their own languages, because they had done so at home since infancy, they had not been taught to read and write them.

A government initiative to develop China's western regions, where most minorities live and whose economic levels have fallen far behind those of the east coast, was ratified at the March 2000 meeting of the National People's Congress. This plan has caused anxiety among minorities, who fear that Han will be sent in to "help" minorities and that this will swamp minority languages and cultures. Central authorities have denied that this is their intent, stressing that the new culture will "combine local traditions with the most outstanding features of other cultures" so as to bring about economic prosperity.[84] Minorities remain skeptical.

Government efforts to establish putonghua as the national language face resistance in Han areas as well. In March 2000 the ministry of education issued a directive requiring that, by 2005 in cities and 2010 in rural areas, every teacher and student be able to speak putonghua fluently and write simplified characters. Local Han dialects must be dropped, and teachers who do not comply will receive poor evaluations that could mean reduced pay or diminished job security.[85] A similar directive was issued when China emerged from the Cultural Revolution. Then, as now, the central government has experienced some difficulty in having its orders obeyed at the local level. Several observers in different parts of the country have noticed that, although local people—both minorities and Han—could speak putonghua, they preferred to converse in the local dialect.[86]

Conclusion

Considering China's huge size and disparate regional cultures and languages, the central government has been effective in imposing putonghua and the Han writing system as a lingua franca. Ever-present tendencies to use local languages and dialects, however, have been reinforced by the economic policies introduced by Deng Xiaoping. The cen-

---

84. See, for example, "NPC Deputies Discuss Ethnic Cultural Protection," Xinhua, March 14, 2000; "Nationalities Affairs Commission to Run Exhibition," Xinhua, March 28, 2000; and "New Cultural Revolution Plan for West," Xinhua, March 29, 2000.

85. Daniel Kwan, "Pressure On for Putonghua," *South China Morning Post*, March 9, 2000.

86. I noticed this phenomenon in the Xishuangbanna Dai Autonomous Region during a 1994 visit; Linda Tsung reports the same in several other areas of Yunnan based on experiences from 1995 to 1998.

tral authorities should carefully monitor these tendencies, still minor, to ensure that they do not become a major trend that could undo the gains of previous decades. They should also avoid heavy-handed enforcement of policies that support the use of putonghua: They should emphasize the benefits of becoming fluent in putonghua rather than the penalties for not doing so.

Although the central government is keen to maintain the purity of putonghua, it must also keep its promises to protect and develop minority languages and literatures. Fulfilling these promises will not be easy. Indeed the government has to manage a difficult balancing act: It has to meet its commitments to minorities without appearing to play favorites. The appearance of favoritism—giving some minorities preferential treatment—has already caused problems with respect to family planning and university admissions. The central government's leaders should try to avoid creating the appearance of linguistic favoritism. This requires a degree of fine-tuning and a level of political skill that has so far proved elusive to policymakers in Beijing.

Chapter 13

The Evolution of Language Policies and National Identity in Taiwan

June Teufel Dreyer

Like many countries, Taiwan was buffeted by colonial experiences that influenced its ethnolinguistic composition and political development. Taiwan's colonial experiences were especially complex, however, and their effects particularly profound. Although Portuguese, Dutch, and Spanish occupiers were mainly interested in trade, making little conscious effort to change the languages and cultures of the natives, the period of Japanese colonization (1895–1945) was characterized by a harsh but successful effort to educate all Sinic groups in the Japanese language. The targeted groups were primarily the Hakka (or "guest people"), whose ancestors had emigrated from the mainland's Guangdong Province many centuries earlier, and the Hoklo, from southern Fujian Province.

Following Japan's defeat in World War II, Taiwan was administered by the Kuomintang (KMT, or Chinese Nationalist) government of Chiang Kai-shek. After losing the battle for control of the mainland to the Chinese Communist Party (CCP) in 1949, Chiang and nearly 2 million mainlanders arrived in Taiwan. Fearing an imminent invasion from the communist mainland, the KMT began a massive nation-building effort in Taiwan. Linguistically, this involved forcing every resident of Taiwan to speak and write in standard Mandarin (generally referred to as "kuo-yü" on Taiwan and "putonghua" on the mainland).

Since the 1940s two sets of forces—internal pressures for democratization and external pressures from the mainland for unification—have combined to bring about an evolutionary process of "Taiwanization" in Taiwan. As Taiwan's political system became more democratic and as Taiwan natives moved into positions of power, politicians—even those who originally came from the mainland—found it increasingly expedient to campaign in Hokkien, the native language of most residents of Taiwan. At the same time, pressures from the mainland for unification under Beijing's rule stiffened resistance and led Taiwan's leaders to embrace a distinctive Taiwan identity.

Taiwan's identity is still evolving. The country's current language policies encourage the study and use of native languages while retaining kuo-yü, or perhaps Hokkien, as a lingua franca. There is also a noticeable trend toward incorporating phrases and expressions from one language into others. English words often find their way into conversation as well. Some observers predict that, within a generation, a common spoken language will evolve that is an amalgam of all the above and quite different from the kuo-yü advocated under Chiang Kai-shek's government or the standard putonghua of the mainland.[1] The evolution of a linguistic and cultural identity distinct from that of the mainland has been expedited by the KMT's defeat by the Democratic Progressive Party (DPP) in the March 2000 presidential election. Few members of the DPP are mainlanders, and the new government has encouraged the formation of a distinctive Taiwanese identity.

This chapter begins with an overview of Taiwan's ethnolinguistic composition and its early colonial experiences. It then reviews the Japanese colonial period. The main phases of Taiwan's post-1945 story are then examined: the period of "hard authoritarianism," 1945–69; the era of "soft authoritarianism," 1969–86; the unfolding of democratization, 1986–96; and the advent of full democracy in 1996. The chapter concludes with a brief assessment of the prospects for ethnolinguistic harmony in Taiwan.

The Ethnic Setting and Early Colonial Experiences

The nearly 22 million people of the Republic of China (ROC) on Taiwan belong to four main ethnolinguistic groups.

- Less than 2 percent are aborigines, the earliest known inhabitants of the island. Aborigines belong to nine major surviving groups. Their languages and cultures are broadly Malay-Polynesian.

---

1. These observers include Richard Kagan of Hamline University, St. Paul, Minnesota, in a personal communication to the author, April 28, 2000. Kagan notes that when Taiwan's president, Chen Shu-bian, gives a speech in kuo-yü, he uses Hokkien expressions, which makes it difficult for newspapers to report because they have no equivalent Chinese characters. Another source, a political analyst of mainlander origin, says that he regularly watches Hakka-language television broadcasts to pick up new expressions that he finds clever and useful.

- Approximately 14 percent are mainlanders, people who emigrated from the mainland to Taiwan in or around 1949. They represent a wide variety of dialects and cultural groups.
- Approximately 15 percent are Hakka, whose ancestors emigrated from the mainland, some from the mainland's Fujian Province but mostly from Mei County of Guangdong Province, several hundred years ago.
- Approximately 70 percent are Hoklo, whose ancestors emigrated from Fujian Province hundreds of years ago.

With the exception of the aborigines, for whom careful statistics are kept, population figures for other groups are approximations. Particularly since the 1980s, there has been substantial intermarriage among groups, which further complicates the picture. Aboriginal population statistics, however, are misleading: The government does not classify children of aborigines and nonaborigines as aborigines, although they may consider themselves to be either aborigines or of mixed ethnicity.

Some, including the government of the People's Republic of China (PRC), argue that mainlanders, Hakka, and Hoklo are not separate ethnic groups but rather subgroups of the Han. Although all three groups use Chinese characters to write their languages,[2] their spoken languages are mutually unintelligible. The difference between kuo-yü and Hokkien (or minnan), the language spoken by the Hoklo, has been compared with the difference between English and German.[3] Those who believe that these groups constitute separate ethnicities disagree that Hakka and Hokkien are offshoots of kuo-yü. They regard all three as offshoots of a common tree of Sinitic languages. Other linguists point out that Hakka was the kuo-yü, or national language, of its day: The Hakka, fleeing to south China to escape the barbarian invasions ravaging the north, retained the then-standard language in its pure form. What is currently referred to as kuo-yü reflects later linguistic developments. The languages of the indigenous groups are also mutually unintelligible.

Taiwan's prehistoric record goes back thousands of years, but the origins of the island's indigenous inhabitants are uncertain because of the lack of written records. Anthropological evidence indicates that Taiwan's indigenous peoples had ties to islands now under the jurisdiction of In-

---

2. Because Chinese characters are ideographs, they can in theory be used to write any language. The characters are better suited than most, however, to rendering the monosyllabic, uninflected Sinitic languages. Even here, though, they are imperfect.

3. Shih Cheng-feng, "Ethnic Differentiation in Taiwan," *Journal of Law and Political Science*, No. 4 (1995), pp. 89–111, available at http://www.wufi.org.tw. Citation is from website, p. 7.

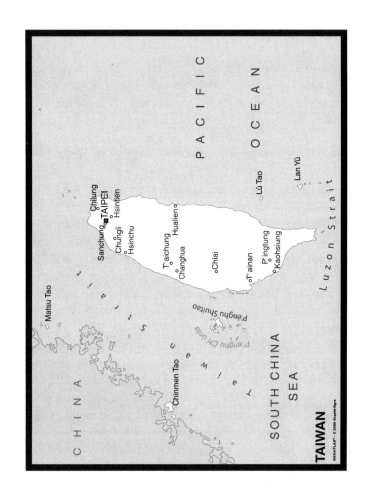

donesia. Indigenous groups both there and in Taiwan practiced tattooing, gerontocracy, spirit worship, and indoor burial. They regularly gave identical names to father and son. Such vocabulary and grammar as can be ascertained indicate that the indigenous people of Taiwan spoke Malay-Polynesian languages. Most of these Australoid settlements have been found in southern Taiwan or along its eastern coast. In northern and central Taiwan, anthropologists have discovered black pottery, tripods, and stone halberds that are characteristic of areas of the mainland. Some have suggested that there are connections with the Ainu of Japan. It is not even certain that the prehistoric remains found on Taiwan were left by the ancestors of the modern aborigines who inhabited the island. Yet another theory, based on analyses of genetic markers, holds that both the Taiwanese and the Polynesians originated in Southeast Asia but dispersed independently of each other.[4] Some geological evidence indicates that the Ryukyu Arc, which includes Taiwan, was once linked to the American continent, spawning additional theories.[5]

It is known that about 800 years ago, different groups of people began to arrive from the Chinese mainland. They came not to establish colonies but to escape barbarian invasions, oppressive governments, and high taxes. The Hoklo came from Ch'uan-chou (Quanzhou) or Chang-chou (Zhangzhou) in southern Fujian. Some Hakka also came from southern Fujian; others came from Mei County in Guangdong Province. At first, each group was torn by clan feuds, though these eventually subsided.[6] Ancestral tablets were carefully tended, thus preserving elaborate genealogical connections with forebears. Physical ties with the mainland, however, were severed. Bloodlines rather than geographical areas served as objects of reverence. Over the centuries, adaptations of the groups' respective cultures took place to accommodate differences in climate and building materials between their places of origin and Taiwan.

The Hoklo and Hakka classified Taiwan's indigenous population as *p'ing-pu* (plains people) or *kao-shan* (high mountain [people]). By the early twentieth century, many of the plains people—including the Ketagalan, Luilang, Favorlang, Kavalan, Taokas, Pazeh, Papora, Babuza, Hoana, Siraya, and Sao—had disappeared either through extermination or intermarriage. Because of their relative isolation, the mountain peoples were better able to retain their cultural identities. There are currently nine

4.   Randolph A. Schmid, "New Theory on Polynesian Migration," *Washington Post,* July 17, 2000, http://www.washingtonpost.com/wp-srv/aponline170129_000.htm.

5.   Larry Teo, "Was Taiwan Once Linked to Americas?" *Straits Times* (Singapore), July 24, 2000, http://www.straitstimes.asia1.com.sg.

6.   Shih, "Ethnic Differentiation in Taiwan," p. 5.

major indigenous groups in Taiwan, totaling slightly more than 389,900 people. The largest group, the Ami, comprise more than a third of the indigenous population, followed by the Atayal and Paiwan. The Yami, numbering only 4,500, are the smallest. (See Table 13.1.)

Each group has its own tribal language, generally including several dialects. These languages are often referred to as "Formosan" to avoid confusion with "Taiwanese," which refers to Hokkien. All Formosan languages belong to the Proto-Austronesian linguistic family, an agglutinative language type that also includes Malay and Hawaiian. The Formosan languages are subdivided into three branches: Atayalic, Tsouic, and Paiwanic. Collectively, they exhibit more diversity than the Philippine languages to which they are related, leading to speculation that the huge Austronesian speech community may have originated in Taiwan.[7]

In the sixteenth century, Western powers began to arrive in Taiwan, adding their linguistic and cultural influences to the mix. The Portuguese were first. Legend has it that the first Portuguese sailor to glimpse Taiwan called to his mates "Ilha Formosa," or beautiful island. The Spaniards later established an outpost on Taiwan's northeastern cape, calling it "Santiago." The name survives today in transliteration as "Sandiao."

It was Dutch influence, however, that was of primary importance in the seventeenth century. After establishing a fort in southwest Taiwan in 1624, the Dutch brought in not only soldiers and sailors but also merchants, technicians, missionaries, and officials. The new residents proceeded to develop idle land, plant sugar cane, produce camphor, convert local inhabitants to Christianity, and collect taxes. Periodic fighting between Dutch and Spanish occupiers ended in Dutch victory in 1642. The Dutch government then strengthened its hold on Taiwan, dividing the native peoples' territory into seven districts, each headed by a local elder chosen by his own people according to their preferred practices. Many of the colonizers were single men, and official policy encouraged intermarriage. In general, the Dutch were respectful of the languages and cultures that they found on the island.

At the same time, turmoil on the mainland brought new immigrants to Taiwan. This new external influence was soon to overwhelm the Dutch. Fleeing the Manchu invaders who had established the Qing dynasty, the refugees were at first welcomed by the Dutch. In 1652, however, when the settlers' demand to buy the land they tilled rather than pay rent on it was rebuffed, a rebellion ensued. The Dutch put down the rebellion, but shortly thereafter were themselves defeated by the

---

7. See, for example, Jared M. Diamond, "Taiwan's Gift to the World," *Nature*, February 17, 2000, pp. 709–710.

Table 13.1. Indigenous Minorities in Taiwan, 1998.

Tribe	Number	Taiwan Province	Taipei	Kaohsiung
Ami	150,236	142,092	4,469	3,675
Atal	92,273	90,364	1,337	572
Bunun	42,495	41,525	514	456
Paiwan	69,529	67,783	596	1,150
Puyuma	10,462	10,042	223	197
Rukai	12,614	12,124	118	372
Saisiyat	7,361	7,266	88	7
Tsou	7,116	6,982	101	33
Yami	4,009	3,887	60	62
Total	**369,095**	**382,065**	**7,506**	**6,524**

SOURCE: Council on Aboriginal Affairs, Executive Yuan, Republic of China on Taiwan.

half-Japanese son of a Chinese pirate, Cheng Ch'eng-kung (Zheng Chenggong). Cheng's family had belatedly pledged allegiance to the dynasty that preceded the Qing, and he hoped to use Taiwan as a base to reconquer the mainland. It was this unlikely individual who brought Chinese civilization to Taiwan. Cheng, also known as Koxinga, built the first Confucian temple in Taiwan to symbolize the introduction of Chinese culture. He also established Chinese-style schools, introduced Chinese laws and customs, and transplanted mainland traditions. Although Cheng's stated aim, and that of this son and successor, was reconquering the mainland on behalf of the Ming,[8] the raids they made on the mainland more closely resembled pirate attacks than attempts at restoring the dynasty.

In 1683 the Qing defeated Cheng's grandson, and Taiwan was administered, though rather loosely, as part of Fujian Province. Some Qing officials advocated the immediate abandonment of the island, given its wildness and remoteness. The native peoples proved rebellious, with officials complaining of a small revolt every three years and a large one every five years. The island nonetheless remained an important source of rice, sugar, deerskin, and camphor for the mainland.

---

8. Doubtless savoring the linguistic symbolism, the ROC government named its first Perry-class frigate the *Cheng-kung*, after Cheng. The official communist attitude toward Koxinga has vacillated between praise because he conquered the foreign imperialist Dutch and opprobrium because he sought to use Taiwan as a base to conquer the mainland, just as the KMT did.

By the nineteenth century, Taiwan's wealth had attracted the attention of various foreign powers, most notably Japan. Hoping to thwart the outsiders' ambitions, the Qing in 1885 made Taiwan a province of China. Its first governor attempted to establish defenses against foreign aggression, reform the tax system to make the island financially independent, and educate its indigenous peoples in Chinese. Children of affluent families received instruction in classical Chinese, although they retained their native languages for oral communication.

The Japanese Colonial Period, 1895–1945

Beijing's efforts to bind Taiwan to the mainland by making it a province did not succeed: Japan decisively defeated its larger neighbor in the Sino-Japanese War of 1894–95. Under the terms of the Treaty of Shimonoseki, signed in 1895, China formally ceded Taiwan to Japan. The island had been a province of China for barely a decade. The Japanese army landed on Taiwan and was immediately confronted by an independence movement. It took the Imperial Japanese Army four months to capture the city of Tainan from the rebels. Guerrilla resistance against the invaders continued intermittently for the next twenty years.

With characteristic thoroughness, the Japanese set about transforming the inhabitants of Taiwan into loyal subjects of the emperor. Government buildings were constructed for the new rulers. Streets were paved and given Japanese names. The Japanese language and writing system were taught from elementary school onward. The urban middle class wore Japanese clothing. A few of the literati resisted, even going to the mainland so that they could continue to write freely in the classical Chinese style. Others who were averse to Japanization stayed and attempted to preserve their languages and literatures as best they could. They founded the Li Poetry Society, whose politics-infused journal, *Taiwan Wen-i Chiu-chih,* became a force for Taiwanese nationalism. One of its members wrote a comprehensive history of Taiwan that was to become the standard reference work on the topic.

Another trend, the Taiwanese New Literature Movement, emerged in the 1920s. Many of its products were published in Japanese. A Taiwanese language movement that dates from the 1930s advocated the use of a new written language based on Hokkien. Classical Chinese is the written language used by the educated class prior to the twentieth century. It differs from all forms of the spoken language. Many words in Hokkien do not have corresponding Chinese characters, making the development of a new writing system exceedingly difficult. The Japanese colonial government did not encourage such experiments: Not only were they tinged with nationalism but they hindered the establishment of the primacy of the Japanese language. However, insofar as proponents of the new written language avoided the appearance of challenging Japanese rule or the paramount position of the Japanese language, they were tolerated. Promising students gained admission to prestigious Japanese universities, where they were influenced by the celebrated writers of the time. In the view of present-day Taiwan scholars, a hybrid culture evolved.[9]

Students from Taiwan were encouraged to study subjects with practical use to the colony, such as medicine, rather than literature, politics, or philosophy. Nonetheless, many Taiwanese youth at Japanese universities were intrigued by the debates of the day on such topics as nationality, race, and the nature of good government. They also discussed how to apply their ideas to the situation at hand. P'eng Ming-min, who later became an outspoken advocate of Taiwan independence and a presidential candidate, recalls being attracted to the theories of Ernest Renan while a student at Japan's most prestigious university. Renan argued that modern nationhood is based not on a shared language, culture, or ethnic origin but on a shared sense of destiny.[10]

Aboriginal peoples were also educated in Japanese. European missionaries had been active in some aboriginal areas, devising romanized scripts for aboriginal languages and translating the Bible and other important books into these languages. But the Japanese brought the first schools to other aboriginal areas. As opposed to the rather dismissive attitude evinced by Chinese toward the aborigines, Japanese anthropologists found them fascinating—so fascinating that the colonial government restricted access to Lan Yü (Orchid Island), the home of the Yami, to officials and anthropologists. The latter discovered that the Yami language and animist beliefs bore a striking resemblance to those of a tribe in the Philippines.[11] Much later, representatives of the Yami visited the Philippine tribe, the Ivatne of Bataan, and discovered a 70–80 percent overlap in languages as well as startling physical resemblances.[12]

---

9.   Government Information Office, *1999: The Republic of China Yearbook* (Taipei: Government Information Office, 1999), p. 421.

10.   See Lai Tse-han, Ramon H. Myers, and Wei Wou, *A Tragic Beginning: The Taiwan Uprising of February 28, 1947* (Stanford, Calif.: Stanford University Press, 1991), p. 20.

11.   Henry Kamm, "Culture of Taiwan's Aborigines Eroding as Modern Ways Seep In," *New York Times*, June 3, 1981, p. A13. See also J. Raymond Dyer, "Who Are the Formosans?" *Reporter*, March 10, 1955, pp. 14–17.

12.   Deborah Kuo, "Local Tribe Tries to Find Ancient Relatives in Philippines," report in two parts, Central News Agency (Taipei), July 4 and July 6, 1999. The Yami were given their name by a Japanese anthropologist, and call themselves Dahwu. According

A Japanese naturalist who roamed the island searching for new species of wildlife also produced the classic work on aboriginal culture, *Wanderings among Aborigines,* which is still read today. Publication was financed not by a Chinese-language source but by a Japanese newspaper, *Mainichi Shimbun* of Osaka.[13] It was also a Japanese scholar who discovered the oldest cultural strata on the island, at Fengpitou near present-day Kaohsiung. The deepest layer dates back 35,000 years, or 20,000 years earlier than other discoveries.[14]

In 1937 the intensification of the Japan-China confrontation that had begun in 1931 led Tokyo to impose a more thoroughly assimilationist policy on Taiwan. Huge amounts of social resources were devoted to an intensified program of Japanization. One program, for example, taught young Taiwanese women how to behave like proper Japanese ladies. Another banned Chinese-language publications, even the literary supplements that had theretofore appeared in Japanese-language newspapers.

Upholding civil liberties in its colonial territories was low on the list of priorities of the Japanese government before the war intensified, and dropped even further afterward. Overt resistance to Japan's assimilative policies was futile; thus the population's reactions ranged from sullen compliance to eager enthusiasm. Some of the latter sentiment was no doubt feigned; those who favored sullen compliance tended to look on the enthusiasts as motivated by careerism or other forms of self-aggrandizement. Only Japanese was spoken in public. There was an outpouring of propagandistic plays, songs, and stories praising the imperial government's efforts to bring peace and prosperity to greater East Asia. This was a wrenching experience. According to a contemporary analysis, it led writers "to directly confront oppressive relationships within the colonial structure. For these writers, who had been partially nourished by Japanese culture in their formative years and to which they held various degrees of allegiance, this experience must have been simultaneously disillusioning and educating. Above all, it became clear to them that artistic approaches were not ideologically innocent."[15]

---

to tribal legend, the groups maintained close trade and cultural contacts across the treacherous Bashi Channel, but they had a falling out several hundred years ago.

13. Joyce Yen, "What Taiwan Is Reading," *Taipei Times,* April 16, 2000. For articles from the *Taipei Times,* go to http://www.taipeitimes.com.

14. Chen Kuang-fu, "Preserving Our Heritage Is Key to Identity," *Taipei Times,* April 15, 2000.

15. Government Information Office, *1999: The Republic of China Yearbook,* p. 428.

Hard Authoritarianism, 1945–69

After Japan surrendered to the Allies in 1945, Taiwan was handed over to Chiang Kai-shek's Kuomintang government. Initial hopes in Taiwan for self-government were dashed. Disillusionment deepened with the arrival of Chiang's troops and administrators. The father of the aforementioned P'eng Ming-min was mortified by the spectacle of ill-kempt, poorly disciplined KMT troops disembarking from troop ships and being saluted by immaculately attired and impeccably behaved Japanese troops. "If there had been a hole nearby, I would have crawled in," he stated.[16] Among the more widespread derogatory names given to the newcomers by Taiwan residents was "taros." The scraggly black roots of the taro reminded them of the disheveled hair of the mainlanders. Natives became known as "yams," because the vegetable is not only a staple food on Taiwan but also happens to resemble the shape of the island itself.

Chiang's troops and administrators proved to be insensitive, inept, and corrupt, soon destroying the island's infrastructure and economy. Natives contrasted Chinese administration unfavorably with Japanese rule, which had been draconian but efficient and generally free of corruption. Mainlanders thought of native Taiwan residents as collaborators; Taiwan residents thought of mainlanders as carpetbaggers. Accumulated tensions burst into demonstrations when KMT troops roughed up an elderly woman who had been selling cigarettes without a license. Chiang used the incident as an excuse to stifle all dissent on Taiwan. Thousands of people were executed in a systematic attempt to wipe out the island's intelligentsia. For several decades, it was dangerous even to mention the matter, known as the 2-2-8 (February 28, 1947) incident.[17]

The KMT's defeat on the mainland in 1949 brought a huge exodus of immigrants to Taiwan, including Chiang Kai-shek himself. Nearly 2 million people, representing many different dialect and language groups from the mainland, flooded in. Faced with a communist government preparing to launch an invasion from the mainland and a sullen population on Taiwan, Chiang embarked on an ambitious program of nation building on the island. Language was a crucial component of this effort.

Kuo-yü, or national language, was to replace Japanese as the language of instruction from kindergarten on. It is essentially the same language as that chosen as standard by the communist government on the

---

16.   Quoted in Lai, Meyers, and Wei, *A Tragic Beginning,* p. 21.

17.   For an eyewitness account, see George H. Kerr, *Formosa Betrayed* (Boston: Houghton Mifflin, 1965).

mainland. Children who attempted to speak Hokkien, Hakka, or aboriginal tongues were slapped, fined, or subjected to other disciplinary actions. Films were produced in kuo-yü, with subtitles in Chinese characters for those who could not understand the spoken form of the language. Although there was no direct prohibition against the use of other languages or dialects in film production, the KMT government restricted language usage in other ways. The Central Film Production Company, affiliated with the KMT, provided funding for films in kuo-yü. And it was understood that kuo-yü films would receive preferential treatment in the government-sponsored annual film awards.

As for radio, so-called dialect programming—meaning the total of all local dialects and languages—was limited to 45 percent on AM radio and 33 percent on FM radio. When television was introduced, non–kuo-yü programming was limited to 30 percent on the island's three stations, all of them government affiliated.[18] Budgets for these programs were lower than for kuo-yü programs. Actors and actresses who spoke Hokkien or Hakka in kuo-yü productions had the parts of maids, construction workers, or rascals, to give the impression that speaking these languages marked one as lower class.[19]

Streets were given traditional Chinese names. For example, major thoroughfares in the capital, Taipei, were named after the Confucian virtues. The street running in front of the presidential palace and other major government buildings was renamed "chieh-shou," or long life, in honor of Chiang Kai-shek.

The island's history and culture were ignored. Students learned the history of the mainland and its culture, memorizing long lists of dynasties and emperors to whom they had little or no emotional ties. They studied Beijing opera rather than Taiwan opera or traditional Taiwan puppet theater. Chiang repeatedly declared his intention to reconquer the mainland. To borrow Renan's terminology, the system that he created was designed to emphasize the shared destiny of the different peoples on Taiwan.[20] Emergency decrees, said to be necessary for the duration of the period of communist insurgency, gave legal sanction to the repression of freedom of speech. The number of newspapers, magazines, and radio and television statements was controlled by the government, which set limits even on how many pages newspapers could have. It was illegal to

---

18. Eugenia Yun, "The Hakka: The Invisible Group," *Free China Review,* Vol. 43, No. 10 (October 1993), p. 16.

19. Shih Cheng-feng, personal communication, August 15, 2000.

20. Lai, Myers, and Wei, *A Tragic Beginning,* p. 20.

advocate independence, and risky to even mention the word. The Taiwanese chafed under these restrictions, but they had to do so quietly to avoid arrest and imprisonment. The KMT had a network of spies, even among Taiwanese who were studying abroad, to report on manifestations of disloyalty. Identity cards allowed the authorities to easily distinguish those whose origin was mainland from those whose origin was Taiwanese.

The Formosan peoples were also required to learn kuo-yü, and they too had to show loyalty to the KMT government. Otherwise, there was little pressure on Formosans to assimilate, perhaps because their distinct cultures and intricate artwork proved to be valuable in attracting tourists to the island. The Formosan Aboriginal Culture Center, featuring daily performances of native dance and music, was established at the resort area of Sun Moon Lake in central Taiwan. Westerners who lived in Taiwan during the 1950s and 1960s reported that the aborigines were treated as curiosities and predicted that they would soon disappear. A government-issued reference book published in 1983 had only one paragraph on the Formosans, in the context of explaining that most of China's Austronesian and Malay-Polynesian speakers were to be found on Taiwan.[21] Hakka and Hokkien were mentioned in a single sentence listing Kan-Hakka and Amoy-Swatow (i.e., Hokkien) among the nine dialects spoken in China.[22] At the same time, a good deal of attention was paid to minority groups on the mainland. The cabinet-level Mongolian and Tibetan Affairs Commission enjoyed a healthy budget and well- appointed offices decorated with scrolls in both Mongolian and Tibetan.

Soft Authoritarianism, 1969–86

For decades, the KMT was the only meaningful legal party in Taiwan, and it actively recruited natives of the island as party members. Its membership consequently became Taiwanized, reaching an estimated 85 percent by the 1970s. At the same time, the KMT underwent an evolution described by one scholar as a shift "from hard authoritarianism to soft authoritarianism."[23] Confirming its historical reputation for resistance to outside rule, the native-born population began to test the limits of the

21.   Government Information Office, *Republic of China: A Reference Book* (Taipei: United Pacific International, 1983), p. 4.

22.   Ibid., p. 5.

23.   The phrase was coined by Edwin Winckler.

government's tolerance. Opposition to the KMT, mostly from Hoklo,[24] coalesced into the "tangwai" (literally, outside the party) movement, since dissenters did not want to join the KMT, but were forbidden to form a party of their own.

Increasing Hoklo activism was also evident on the literary scene by the latter half of the 1960s. During the 1950s, literature had been dominated by mainland writers, who were often mobilized for state-sponsored cultural programs. In general, the works they produced were more notable for their anticommunist content than for their literary excellence. The persecution of the intelligensia that followed the February 28 incident intimidated or inhibited the creativity of those intellectuals who survived it. By the late 1960s, a nativist movement had begun to develop. Its main features were use of Hokkien, depictions of the difficulties of ordinary Taiwanese, and resistance to the "imperialist" presence in Taiwan.

The nativist movement essentially ended in 1979, in what proved to be a major sociopolitical turning point in Taiwan's history. A peaceful protest against the rule of the authoritarian mainland clique that controlled the KMT was held in the southern port city of Kaohsiung, whose population is overwhelmingly Hoklo. Finely attuned to symbolism, the organizers of the protest had chosen International Human Rights Day for their march. The gathering soon turned violent. Protestors blamed *agents provocateurs* sent by the KMT to stir up trouble, and the government blamed the demonstrators. Protest leaders, all of them Hoklo, were arrested and sentenced to long prison terms. Nativist writers subsequently began to play more explicitly political roles. The Kaohsiung incident, as it came to be known, provided the opposition with its next generation of leaders.

One contributing factor to the Kaohsiung protests was the growing isolation of the Republic of China on Taiwan from the international community. The United States had established full diplomatic relations with the PRC on January 1, 1979, and the KMT's claim to be the legitimate government of all of China was growing increasingly hollow. Although it was still illegal to speak of Taiwan's independence, the opposition became convinced that it was necessary to create a different persona for the island—an identity separate from that of the mainland. The imprisoned "Kaohsiung Eight" became heroes to those who considered themselves voiceless, and the opposition began to press the government in ways that tested the limits of its tolerance.

---

24.   Hakka sometimes describe themselves as "the quiet minority," as opposed to the more assertive Hoklo.

Writers continued to experiment with new literary forms that had political shadings. For example, Wang Der-wei, whose satirical *Rose, Rose, I Love You* was published in 1984, incorporated Hokkien, English, and Japanese words and expressions that natives actually used in their daily lives into his Chinese prose.[25] Although the desire to assert a distinct identity is primarily associated with the Hoklo, other minority groups in Taiwan participated as well. In 1985 several such groups converged to destroy a statue of Wu Feng, a fictional deity invented by the Han Chinese to domesticate the "barbaric" aborigines. Aboriginal intellectuals lamented that their children were opposed to learning their native languages and that, without government support, indigenous languages and literatures might soon disappear. Activists also lobbied successfully for a change in the formal term *shan-pao jen* (literally, mountain compatriots), asking that they be referred to as *yuan-chu jen* (original inhabitants) instead.[26] In short, the Formosan peoples were rejecting assimilation, and in contrast to the past, they were doing so collectively.

Another major turning point came in 1986. A combination of then-president Chiang Ching-kuo's preference for further liberalization and pressures from various ethnic groups within the population led him to declare that the emergency decrees would be rescinded the following year. Numerous political parties were founded, of which the most important by far was the Democratic Progressive Party. The DPP's members (nearly all of whom were Hoklo) were as likely to campaign in Hokkien as kuo-yü, particularly outside Taipei, where the majority of the mainlander population lived.

Democratization, 1986–96

After the emergency decrees were lifted in 1987, restrictions on the media were gradually removed. There was a subsequent explosion in programming, magazines, and newspapers for Taiwan's minority groups. For example, eleven writers immediately founded *Hakka Wind and Clouds* (renamed *Hakka Monthly* in 1990), a monthly magazine on Hakka news and culture. One of the founders, Chung Chun-lan, helped to launch the Give Us Back Our Mother Tongue movement. During the following year, 10,000 people demonstrated in Taipei on behalf of the cause. Many people were nevertheless reluctant to be publicly associated with the cam-

---

25.   A number of these works, including Wu's book, are being translated into English. See Rita Fang, "Taiwanese Novels Go English," *Taipei Journal*, August 11, 2000, p. 5.

26.   Government Information Office, *1999: The Republic of China Yearbook*, p. 419.

paign. For example, one prosperous physician gave financial aid to the movement to promote the Hakka language on the condition that his name not be mentioned. He was afraid that many of his patients would switch to other doctors if they discovered that he was a Hakka.[27]

Protests intensified in 1988, as groups previously constrained by the emergency decrees voiced their complaints. In addition to the Hakka, aboriginal peoples began to demonstrate not only about language and culture but also over land that they believed—with considerable justification—had been stolen from them.[28] The lucrative camphor trade had led émigrés to encroach on tribal forests for centuries, often destroying them in pursuit of quick profit. More recently, a large cement company was reported to have colluded with local officials to displace aborigines from their land without adequate compensation.[29]

A political milestone was reached in 1988. President Chiang Ching-kuo, the son of Chiang Kai-shek, died in office. In accordance with the constitution, he was succeeded by his vice president, Lee Teng-hui. Lee, native-born of Hakka ancestry, spoke fluent Hokkien. He had received his undergraduate education at one of Japan's most prestigious universities and earned a doctoral degree at Cornell University. There were slightly nervous jokes that Lee's kuo-yü was the least fluent of the numerous languages that he spoke. He moved decisively to advance the democratization process begun by Chiang. Given the ethnic mix of the country, democratization inevitably meant Taiwanization. Lee's autobiography, *The Road to Democracy*, is subtitled *Taiwan's Pursuit of Identity*. Although he was not explicit about the content of this identity or how it was to be pursued, Lee's actions reflected a concern with the creation of a national persona that would be distinct from that of the mainland. He states: "The 'new Taiwanese' who will create a new Taiwan include the original indigenous people, those whose ancestors came here four hundred years ago, and those who arrived only recently. Anyone who lives in and loves Taiwan is a 'new Taiwanese.'"[30]

---

27. Jim Hwang, "The Hakka: Silent No More," *Free China Review,* Vol. 43, No. 10 (October 1993), p. 19.

28. "Aborigines March for Land, Protection of Rights," Agence France-Presse (Hong Kong), August 25, 1988, in Foreign Broadcast Information Service (FBIS), August 26, 1988, p. 52; and "An Aboriginal March," Taipei International Service, August 29, 1988, in FBIS, September 2, 1988, p. 70.

29. Mark Munterhjelm, "Kowtowing to Big Business," *Taipei Times,* April 10, 2000.

30. Lee Teng-hui, *The Road to Democracy: Taiwan's Pursuit of Identity* (Tokyo: PHP Institute, 1999), p. 200.

Both this statement and Lee's actions indicated that he envisioned a pluralist society based on an amalgam of the country's languages and cultures. Lee's twelve-year presidency featured a number of measures taken in support of this end. For example, the designation of ancestral origins on identity cards was replaced with place of birth. As time went on, this would be Taiwan for the great majority of people, thus eroding the distinction between those who arrived long before the communist takeover of the mainland and those who came as a consequence of it. School curricula and official magazines and newspapers paid progressively less attention to the history of mainland China and more to that of Taiwan. The country's yearbooks did the same, and they began to include additional material on language, literature, and ethnicity in Taiwan.

In 1989 a pathbreaking film, *City of Sadness* (*Beiqing Chenshi*), won the Golden Lion award at the Venice Film Festival. Not only was the dialogue largely in Hokkien, but its young director had broken from the standard historical epics that evoked the mainland. *City of Sadness* dealt with the changing reality of life in Taiwan, the increasing divergence between rural and urban cultures, and it addressed the once taboo topic of the February 28 incident. Under Lee's presidency, it became possible to speak openly of 2-2-8. Classified archival materials were made available to scholars, and several historians were commissioned to write an investigative report on the executions. Lee's administration commissioned a memorial site to the victims of the massacre, and in a moving ceremony on the fiftieth anniversary of the incident in 1997, he personally dedicated the new memorial.

By 1990 ethnically driven demonstrations had largely ended. In December 1990 the Hakka Association for Public Affairs (HAPA) was founded. HAPA sponsors perhaps a dozen public seminars and lectures around the island each year, on topics that include Hakka television programming, ethnic songs and poetry, the language movement, and historical relics. Four-day cultural camps geared to three different age groups—children, teens, and adults—include Hakka speech contests; field trips to Hakka cultural sites; and classes on language, history, music, drama, and architecture. The organizers discovered, somewhat to their surprise, that non-Hakka were also interested in participating. HAPA funding also helped students at twelve of the island's universities to form Hakka clubs. School authorities, fearful that such organizations might promote segregation and/or ethnic discontent, sometimes had to be reassured. At least one student organizer had to agree to keep the club's office off-campus before obtaining permission to meet.

HAPA's efforts seem to have resulted in raising ethnic consciousness. Dictionaries and books on Hakka increased, as major publishing companies began to place Hakka projects on their agendas. Audio- and video-tapes on Hakka folk music and opera appeared, some of them the product of companies specializing in Hakka entertainment.

Still, some Hakka feared that the lifting of restrictions on ethnic languages and cultural offerings would result in their culture being over-shadowed by that of the Hoklo, given that the latter are by far the major-ity on the island. When the limitations on ethnic-language programming ended in July 1993, it was noted that most new programming was in Hokkien. A noted Hakka professor of linguistics warned that the Hakka could go the way of the p'ing-pu, who no longer exist as a separate group.[31]

In April 1993 the ministry of education announced that Hakka, Hokkien, and indigenous tribal languages could be offered as electives at the primary-school level. The central government was actually lagging behind local initiatives on this issue: Three counties had already put such programs into effect. An Ilan County order of June 1990 decreed that stu-dents should no longer be discouraged from, or punished for, speaking dialects at school. It was also the first local government to begin Hokkien courses in elementary and junior high school.

Also in 1990, Taipei County began extracurricular Atayal-language lessons in elementary and high schools where the majority of students were Atayal aborigines. Although the new approaches to Hakka and Hokkien instruction were far from ideal, there were no ready-made teaching materials at all for Atayal. Some Atayal teachers were not fluent in their own language and learned as they went along. In 1992 the county government ordered its bureau of education and its cultural center to compile teaching materials in Atayal, Ami, Hakka, and Hokkien.[32]

In 1991 P'ingtung introduced electives in Hokkien, Hakka, Paiwan, and Rukai in schools where families of those groups lived. Language classes were supplemented by native-language speech contests, singing competitions, and music and dance performances. P'ingtung groups later performed at other locations on the island.

Given the fact that most of Taiwan's ethnic groups were distributed in more than one county, it was inefficient to have county governments producing teaching materials. Hence the central government began to

---

31. Yun, "The Hakka," p. 16.

32. "Tiway Sayion—Taiwan's First Aboriginal School Principal," *Sinorama*, January 2000, http://www.db.sinorama.com.tw/em/docshow, chronicles the story of an Ami teacher trying to recapture his tribe's language and culture so that he can pass them on to his students. Another such story is Leu Chien-ai, "Tending the Roots," *Free China Review*, Vol. 42, No. 6 (June 1992), p. 37.

take a more active role. The central government had additional intellectual as well as financial resources to bring to bear on the problem, including the Council on Aboriginal Affairs of the Executive Yuan and the Institute of Ethnology of Academia Sinica (Taiwan's most prestigious research institute). The expertise of National Chengchi University's Graduate Institute of Ethnology was also utilized. Central government coordination also complemented the efforts of President Lee Teng-hui's plans to foster the development of a Taiwanese identity that was distinct from that of the mainland.

One vexing question was how to write some of the country's languages. Chinese characters are particularly ill suited to writing the aboriginal languages. There are no Chinese characters to represent some words in Hokkien and Hoklo. Romanization writing systems seem to be best suited for aboriginal languages and could be used for Hokkien and Hakka as well. More than 150 years ago, Western missionaries developed a romanization system for Hokkien that is still widely used. Several other systems exist as well, each with its group of learned advocates. The various methods, however, tended to start from scratch and contributed yet another idiosyncratic system to an already eclectic jumble. Responding to criticism that they were moving too slowly, government officials argued that what appeared to be reluctance to implement bilingual education was prompted more by uncertainty on how to proceed than by resistance to the goal of teaching languages.

In August 1994, the ministry of education established a task force composed of experts from Academia Sinica's Institute of History and Philology to research the languages and compile guidelines for teaching them. A system originally called *t'ung-yung p'in-yin* (common-use pinyin) was developed for writing Hokkien, Hakka, and the aboriginal languages. The system incorporated some features of the missionary-devised roman- ization scheme. Its principal creator, Academia Sinica's B.C. Yü, pointed out that the system could also be used to romanize kuo-yü and was compatible with the Han-yü pinyin used on the mainland.[33] In early 2000, feeling that the term *t'ung-yung p'in-yin* might cause confusion with the mainland's pinyin, government officials decided to call the new system "Taiwan p'in-yin." The new system was to be used in conjunction with Chinese characters for Hokkien and Hakka.[34] Adoption of the scheme was not made compulsory, and academic groups and private institutions were free to develop their own phonetic systems. In the

---

33. Government Information Office, *1999: The Republic of China Yearbook*, p. 41.

34. Shih Cheng-feng, personal communication, April 19, 2000.

summer of 2000, a comprehensive Hokkien–kuo-yü dictionary was published. It was expected to solve the problem of representing Hokkien in
written form.[35]

By the early 1990s, politicians who were born on the mainland or
who came from mainland families were taking lessons in Hokkien with
the intention of making campaign speeches and talking to their constituents in the language or dialect in which voters felt most comfortable. In
what must have been an intentionally ironic twist on producing films in
kuo-yü with subtitles, the DPP's 1991 campaign video was in Hokkien,
with subtitles for kuo-yü speakers. Hokkien began to lose its reputation
as the patois of the rude and the crude. It even gained a certain cachet.
The first popularly elected governor of Taiwan, James Soong Chu-yü, a
mainlander, was among those who campaigned in Hokkien.

In 1994 a major new figure emerged on Taiwan's political and ethnic
scene. A split in the KMT facilitated the election of the DPP candidate,
Chen Shui-bian, as mayor of Taipei City. Taipei is not only the capital of
the ROC and by far its largest city; it is also where most people of mainland origin live. Chen, a lawyer, had represented the Kaohsiung dissidents in 1980. The brilliant son of a poor Hoklo farming family, Chen is
unusual among members of the Taiwan elite in that he never studied
abroad. Among his numerous innovations was founding a bureau of
Hakka affairs in the city government. Another was renaming the street
that passes in front of the presidential palace. Chen, in a well-publicized
ceremony, changed it from chieh-shou to Ketagalan, the name of one of
the nearly extinct p'ing-pu (plains) aboriginal tribes that had lived and
hunted in the area. This linguistic insult to Chiang Kai-shek and symbolic
rejection of his attempt to assimilate Taiwan to Chinese culture led some
to criticize Chen for stirring up ethnic tensions. To others, he became a
hero.

The Advent of Democracy

Lee Teng-hui's election, by direct popular vote, to the presidency of the
Republic of China in 1996 marks the advent of full democracy in Taiwan.
By the time of the 1998 election for the mayor of Taipei, the KMT was able
to unite behind a popular mainlander candidate, Ma Ying-jeou. During a
campaign rally event, with obvious symbolism President Lee asked Ma,
in kuo-yü, whether he was a mainlander or a Taiwanese. Ma replied in
Hokkien that he was a "New Taiwanese," drinking Taiwan water and

---

35. William Hsu, "Scholar Unveils Taiwanese Dictionary," *Taipei Times*, August 13,
2000.

eating Taiwan rice. The press, both official and nonofficial, voiced general approval of the concept. Yam and taro had blended, and Ma won the election over Chen.

Despite his defeat, Chen decided to run for president in the March 2000 contest. This was to be the hardest-fought election in the history of the ROC. Power had first passed from Chiang Kai-shek to his son Chiang Ching-kuo at the time of the father's death. Ching-kuo himself died in office twelve years later and was succeeded by Lee, his vice president. Since Lee had announced his decision to retire, the campaign of 2000 was the most wide open in the country's history.

Corruption was the major issue in the election, not language or ethnic relations. All three major candidates nonetheless considered the votes of each ethnolinguistic group to be very important and fought hard for them. The KMT chose to feature aboriginal ceremonies on network television coverage beamed around the world to mark the new millennium. The DPP candidate Chen Shui-bian's campaign rallies often featured aboriginal singers.[36] His party's website also contained a lengthy policy statement detailing Chen's views on the injustices done to aboriginal peoples in the past and promising to integrate them into Taiwan's society while respecting and preserving their languages and cultures.[37] A foundation for advancing Bunun rights issued a Red Paper—its version of a White Paper—demanding that the Aboriginal Affairs Council be upgraded to ministerial level and that each of the major tribes receive one seat in the Legislative Yuan, with smaller tribes to be represented through seats that alternated among them.[38] Aborigines were also vocal in complaining that they had not received adequate attention after the devastating earthquake of September 1999, and in lobbying to have the study of their languages, Hokkien, and Hakka made compulsory rather than voluntary from elementary through senior high school.[39]

All three major candidates courted the Hakka vote with special care, given that statistics showed that one in four registered voters was either Hakka or directly related to one. The DPP, for example, calculated that Chen Shui-bian would need 300,000 Hakka votes to win the election. Hakka used this to their advantage. For example, an angry Hakka activist complained bitterly that the DPP was permeated by "great Hokkien-

---

36. "Chen Fans Pin Hopes on Graft Buster," *Taipei Times*, March 9, 2000.

37. See http://www.dpp.org (in Chinese).

38. "Bunun Tribe Calls for Reforms," *Taipei Times*, December 23, 1999.

39. "Activists Push for Native-Language School Teaching," *Taipei Times*, January 8, 2000.

language chauvinism."[40] After enduring decades of seeing their language suppressed in the name of the so-called national language, the Hoklo insisted on speaking Hokkien on all public occasions, including parliamentary and political party gatherings.

The KMT's standard-bearer, Lien Chan, a Hoklo who had been raised on the mainland, promised to appoint prominent Hakka politicians to his cabinet; and James Soong, a mainlander, held "Hakka-night" entertainment rallies in areas where Hakka were numerous. Chen Shui-bian campaigned in Hakka, becoming the first non-Hakka politician to do so. He lamented the fact that only half of Hakka, mostly over the age of forty,[41] can speak the language. He promised, if elected, to make it one of three official languages of the ROC[42]—the others being Hokkien and kuo-yü— and to establish a Hakka affairs bureau.[43] DPP representatives spoke of the need for reconciliation among mainlanders on the island and all those groups born on it. Echoing Lee Teng-hui's words, they vowed that every group that identified with the new country would be a respected part of it. Chen's biographer described his aim as the creation of a culturally and linguistically pluralistic society that avoided cultural chauvinism.[44] A Hong Kong magazine described Hakka voters as generally pleased with what they heard from the candidates.[45]

In the end, Chen Shui-bian eked out a narrow win over James Soong. He received an estimated 420,000 Hakka votes, not as many as Soong but 120,000 more than DPP calculations had indicated he needed. This was an important part of his modest margin of victory.[46]

In what was perceived as a gesture of conciliation, Chen made his acceptance speech in kuo-yü. His initial round of cabinet appointments included both mainlanders and Hoklo, prompting praise from those groups and immediate complaints from Hakka. Three Hakka

---

40. Chang Shih-hsien, "A Hakka View of Language Matters," *Taipei Times*, December 4, 1999.

41. Lin Chieh-yu, "Chen Aims for Hakka Vote with New Proposals," *Taipei Times*, December 28, 1999.

42. Mark O'Neill, "Taiwan Election," *South China Morning Post*, March 15, 2000.

43. See http://www.dpp.org (in Chinese).

44. Richard C. Kagan, *Chen Shui-bian: Building a Community and a Nation* (Taipei: Yeu Chen, 1999), pp. 217–218.

45. Steve Chen and Julian Baum, "Welcome Guests: Presidential Candidates Woo Hakka Minority," *Far Eastern Economic Review*, March 16, 2000, p. 32. See also Monique Chu, "Hakkas Are Still Sitting on the Fence ahead of Election," *Taipei Times*, March 2, 2000.

46. Shih Cheng-feng, personal communications, April 14, 2000, and May 1, 2000.

were appointed in the second round, and an Atayal was named chair of the Council on Aboriginal Affairs.[47] Another aborigine, the island's leading chanteuse, was chosen to sing the national anthem at Chen's inauguration.

Policy changes in favor of native groups and their languages continued during the election period and in the transition period between Chen's election and his inauguration. In January 2000 the ministry of education announced that voluntary mother-tongue classes would become compulsory throughout the nation's public school system. The choices were Hokkien, Hoklo, or an aboriginal language. Despite some parental concern, particularly from mainlanders, that this would add yet another requirement to the study calendars of their already academically burdened children, the media were generally approving. Supporters pointed out that not teaching native languages gave powerful negative messages about them and would eventually result in "linguicide."[48]

At the end of March 2002, the Legislative Yuan passed the Mass Transportation Language Equality Protection Law, requiring all vehicles engaged in public transportation, as well as stations servicing public transportation systems, to include Hokkien and Hakka in their public announcements. It also established fines from NT $30,000 to NT $300,000 (approximately U.S.$1,000 to U.S.$10,000) for those that did not comply. Critics complained about too much babble disturbing their commutes; supporters argued that the law would promote cultural pluralism and benefit minority groups.[49]

These changes went a long way toward meeting the concerns of those who feared linguicide. Ethnic bitterness in Taiwan has consequently been greatly reduced, but it is not entirely gone. In a speech during the presidential campaign, Chen Shui-bian vowed to establish a museum dedicated to the February 28 incident, saying that it was a tragedy of oppression by "foreign" aggressors, implying that he and others did not feel themselves to be the same as mainlanders. A participant in the commemorative service held on February 28, 2000, compared the occasion to the Jewish celebration of Passover. The 400-year occupation of Taiwan was likened to the Jewish people's 430-year-long bondage in Egypt, and

---

47.   "Yahani Isagagafat," *Taipei Times*, April 22, 2000.

48.   "Speaking in Tongues," *Taipei Times*, January 9, 2000; and Matthew Ward, "To Keep a Mother Tongue, Teach It!" *Taipei Times*, January 22, 2000.

49.   Joyce Lin discusses an earlier ruling in Taipei, where announcements are made in English as well. Lin, "Native Dialects Go Compulsory," *Taipei Journal*, February 3, 2000, p. 4. For the countrywide law, see "Language Equality Law Passed," *Taipei Times*, April 1, 2000.

the February 28 incident was said to be symbolic of Taiwan's suffering under four centuries of foreign rule.[50]

Moderation and multiculturalism are increasingly prevalent in Taiwan. The newspaper that compared "foreign" with mainland rule over Taiwan also contained an opinion piece arguing for mutual respect based on understanding and integrating racial and ethnic cultures. Its author suggested a symbiotic rather than competitive relationship among cultures, with children learning the languages and ways of other groups.[51] A sociologist speculated along similar lines, opining that the differences among groups in Taiwan could push progress forward so long as all groups—mainlanders, Hoklo, Hakka, and aborigines—identify themselves as an important part of the country.[52] When defeated presidential candidate James Soong, who had broken from the KMT to run as an independent, announced his plans to form a new party, he emphasized that it would not be oriented toward any ethnic group.[53]

It is possible that once the novelty of using minority languages freely and having children study those languages in school wears off, kuo-yü will retain its primacy. It is also possible to envision a Taiwanese identity with Hokkien as its major linguistic component, but also including elements of Hakka, kuo-yü, English, and Japanese. Kuo-yü could be retained as a lingua franca for communication with the mainland.

Conclusion

The democratization process in Taiwan that followed the lifting of the emergency decrees in 1987 included respect for and significant attention to languages other than the standard kuo-yü imported from the mainland. Development of these spoken and written languages was and is viewed as one of the keys to the creation of a unique Taiwanese identity separate from that of the mainland.

Although this "Taiwanization" process has been remarkably peaceful, it has created some ethnic and political tensions. Because the Hoklo constitute the majority in Taiwan by far, it is their culture that has

---

50. Wang Ming-jen, "Leaving the Darkness of 2-2-8 Behind," *Taipei Times*, February 29, 2000.

51. Hong Wan-long, "Learning Core Values Will Ease Ethnic Tensions," *Taipei Times*, February 29, 2000.

52. Huang Fu-san of Academia Sinica, quoted in Chiu Yü-tzu, "Hidden History Surfaces," *Taipei Times*, February 28, 2000.

53. Yü Sen-lun, "Soong Campaign Team Working on Founding New Party," *Taipei Times*, March 23, 2000.

received the most attention as the process unfolded. This has provoked anger and anxiety in other groups. Charges of Hokkien-language chauvinism have been made. At the same time, some parents oppose the attention being paid to bilingual education, arguing that the time devoted to learning Hakka or Atayal could be better spent on English, Japanese, or mathematics. Mainlanders worry that the diminution in the use of their language will result in a lessening of their status in Taiwan society. Others worry that the decline in the use of kuo-yü will exacerbate problems with the mainland.

Taiwan's democratic government has thus far been able to pacify those who have ethnolinguistic worries. Grievances have been aired through established legal channels. Ethnic problems have been most pronounced during election campaigns, because the country's ethnic groups tend to be well organized and vocal. One presidential candidate in the 2000 race accused his opponent of playing the ethnic card, though he was himself open to this charge.

The continued management of ethnolinguistic tensions in Taiwan will require sustained attention from the country's leadership. If Taiwan's leaders stay on the path that guided them in the final years of the twentieth century, there are good reasons for believing that the worst of the country's "culture wars" has passed. P'eng Ming-min's dream of a nation based not on a shared language, culture, or ethnic origin but on a shared destiny—opposition to rule by the mainland—may come to pass.

Part IV
Conclusions

Chapter 14

Language Policy and Ethnic Relations in Asia

Michael E. Brown

We have tried to accomplish two main objectives in this book. First, we have sought to advance scholarly understanding of the origins, evolution, and impact of language policies on ethnic relations. Although this volume examines problems and policies in fifteen countries in Asia, our hope and expectation is that these analyses will also shed light on ethnolinguistic problems elsewhere around the world. Most countries have to contend with ethnolinguistic diversity of one kind or another, and this volume has a broad, comparative base for assessing these issues. Second, we have strived to develop policy lessons and policy recommendations for countries in Asia as well as for policymakers who have to contend with ethnolinguistic problems in other parts of the world.

In this concluding chapter, I develop some general arguments about the perils of different kinds of ethnolinguistic settings, the challenges that confront policymakers in the ethnolinguistic arena, and the policy lessons that we should derive from the historical record.[1] One of the main arguments of this book is that government policies almost always influence the trajectories of ethnolinguistic relations in the countries in question. Some governments manage ethnolinguistic problems relatively well. Although ethnolinguistic issues are often highly contentious, ethnolinguistic diversity does not inevitably lead to violence, and some governments take actions that ameliorate ethnolinguistic tensions. Unfor-

---

1. This chapter draws on the analyses and assessments found elsewhere in this volume, but it is not a consensus report. These conclusions are my own. Other contributors to this volume may not agree with my judgments, forecasts, and policy recommendations; they should not be held accountable for the arguments developed herein.

tunately, this is not the universal pattern. Governments often tackle ethnolinguistic issues belatedly and tentatively, and some adopt misguided policies that exacerbate ethnolinguistic problems and contribute to the escalation of ethnic violence. As a general rule, governments that have embraced tolerant, inclusive, multilingual visions of their countries have fared better than those that have tried to impose hegemonic, exclusive, unilingual visions on their countries. In addition, governments that have emphasized inducement and persuasive policy instruments have fared better than those that have relied on coercion and the use of military force.

Many of the policy lessons that emerge from this study are straightforward. First, governments need to improve their efforts at collecting basic ethnolinguistic data on an ongoing basis. Governments lack fundamental ethnolinguistic and demographic facts. Second, political leaders need to develop viable "ethnic visions" of their countries. Many leaders do not have clear, long-term ethnolinguistic goals, while others pursue objectives that are sharply inconsistent with ethnolinguistic realities in their countries. Third, political leaders need to adopt long-term planning horizons with respect to ethnolinguistic issues. Many policymakers hope that ethnolinguistic problems can be solved quickly, easily, and permanently. In reality, however, most of these problems cannot be solved; they can only be managed. Policymakers must therefore prepare themselves for the long haul. Fourth, policy initiatives often fail because of resource constraints or misguided resource allocations. If political leaders are serious about addressing ethnolinguistic problems, they have to be more energetic about policy implementation. Although many governments are reasonably successful in managing ethnolinguistic problems in their countries, there is room for improvement everywhere—and many policymakers have yet to master the basics.

Linguistic Settings and Ethnic Conflict

The best starting point for studying ethnolinguistic problems is understanding the characteristics and perturbations of different kinds of ethnolinguistic settings. This is easier said than done. Indeed, one of the first challenges that scholars face is determining basic ethnolinguistic facts.[2]

THE TRUTH IS OUT THERE

There are two main reasons why it is difficult to determine basic facts about ethnolinguistic settings. First, ethnolinguistic settings are inher-

---

2. See the chapter by Jyotirindra Dasgupta in this volume.

ently complex. The dividing line between a "language" and a "dialect" is not always clear, and categorization is often a highly politicized issue. As one noted scholar observes, "A language is a dialect with an army and a navy."[3] In addition, some people speak two or more languages. In these cases, ethnolinguistic identities can be subtle and layered, with multiple overlapping identities. Moreover, some ethnolinguistic settings have been influenced by colonial rule. This was clearly the case in, for example, Burma, Malaysia, Singapore, Sri Lanka, and Taiwan. Many ethnolinguistic settings have been complicated by waves of in-country and cross-border migration; settlement patterns have consequently changed and become tangled over time. This has been an issue in Bangladesh, China, India, Indonesia, the Philippines, and Taiwan, for example. In some countries, the number of spoken languages is simply staggering: More than 400 languages and dialects are spoken in Indonesia, and more than 850 languages are spoken in Papua New Guinea, for example. Collecting accurate and comprehensive data on ethnolinguistic settings is therefore a formidable task under the best of circumstances. Unfortunately, many censuses are poorly designed and poorly executed.

Second, many governments want to keep secret the truth about the ethnolinguistic compositions of their countries. They may want to downplay the amount of ethnolinguistic diversity that exists in their countries because they seek to undercut minority groups. Minority groups that are portrayed as small have more difficulty claiming political standing for their causes. This makes it easier for central authorities to treat minorities as peripheral and inconsequential. This in turn makes it easier for central authorities to pander to larger ethnic groups and political constituencies. In addition, marginalizing ethnolinguistic minorities makes it easier for governments to impose homogeneous national identities on their countries. Many central authorities seek to do this because they have simplistic views about the nature and durability of national identity: They fear that, if a multiethnic conception of the nation is embraced, then disintegration of the nation is more likely. The sad irony is that the opposite is more likely to be true: Homogeneous national identities either marginalize or exclude ethnic minorities, which makes secession more attractive to these groups.

Although many central governments have genuine concerns about

---

3.   See Joshua A. Fishman, "Concluding Comments," in Fishman, ed., *Handbook of Language and Ethnic Identity* (Oxford: Oxford University Press, 1999), pp. 444–454 at p. 444. For more discussion of this definitional issue, see the "Introduction" in Barbara F. Grimes, ed., *Ethnologue: Languages of the World,* 14th ed. (Dallas, Tex.: Summer Institute of Linguistics International, 2000), especially pp. vii–ix.

the preservation of national unity, the imposition of uniform national identities also provides a mechanism and a smokescreen for authoritarian and corrupt leaders to impose their will on minority groups. It is not a coincidence, for example, that the last census that collected and released data on ethnolinguistic minorities in Burma was conducted in 1931— under British colonial rule.[4] In short, the political motivations of central authorities also impede efforts to develop comprehensive and accurate ethnolinguistic information.

Most governments have to contend with ethnolinguistic diversity of one kind or another. Few countries are ethnolinguistically homogeneous and, although some ethnolinguistic minorities assimilate and eventually cease to exist as groups with distinct identities and political agendas, this process usually unfolds slowly over many generations. In most countries, ethnolinguistic diversity is—and will continue to be—a fact of life.

LANGUAGE AND CONFLICT: TWO SCHOOLS OF THOUGHT

What is the relationship between ethnolinguistic diversity and conflict? There are two main schools of thought on this question: the pessimists and the optimists.

Pessimists believe that ethnolinguistic diversity and attendant language problems are pervasive sources of conflict in the modern world. Ronald Wardhaugh observes that in a world where billions of people speak thousands of languages, "competition between languages is to be expected." He argues that, because all of these people and languages are housed in fewer than 200 states, "the opportunities for competition to turn into conflict are considerable."[5] William Bostock complains that language grief "has been either overlooked or downplayed in its significance as a cause of ethnic conflict." He contends that language grief is often an important "raw material" of ethnic conflict.[6] Harold Schiffman observes that South and Southeast Asia have high levels of ethnolinguistic diversity and that cultures and languages in these regions have been deeply intertwined for centuries. As a result, postindependence governments in South and Southeast Asia have been acutely aware that ethnolinguistic diversity is "a source of conflict" that has to be managed.[7]

---

4. See the chapter by Mary P. Callahan in this volume.

5. Ronald Wardhaugh, *Languages in Competition: Dominance, Diversity, and Decline* (Oxford: Basil Blackwell, 1987), p. vii.

6. William W. Bostock, "Language Grief: A 'Raw Material' of Ethnic Conflict," *Nationalism and Ethnic Politics*, Vol. 3, No. 4 (Winter 1997), pp. 94–112 at p. 94.

7. Harold F. Schiffman, "South and Southeast Asia," in Fishman, *Handbook of Language and Ethnic Identity*, pp. 431–443 at pp. 432, 442.

Henry Bretton states the case boldly: "Language may indeed be the most explosive issue universally and over time." The reason, he says, is that fears of language deprivation "raise political passion to a fever pitch."[8] Looking ahead, Joshua Fishman predicts, "The evils of ethnolinguistic violence will probably never totally disappear."[9]

Optimists believe that language differences and language grievances do not lead automatically or even easily to violence. David Laitin is an energetic advocate of this position. He argues that language differences and language grievances "play no causal role" in the onset of ethnic violence. Although language grievances are "strongly associated with increased levels of political protest," he maintains that this kind of political conflict "does not translate inexorably into a higher probability of ethnic violence." Thus, "it is far more likely that language grievances will result in political protests than in military action." Laitin also argues that, under some conditions, language differences can actually "help to contain violence."[10] Similarly, William Beer contends, "Language differences do not in themselves lead to disruptions of national unity." Problems develop, he says, when ethnolinguistic minorities are blocked from achieving political, economic, and social equality.[11] Robert Phillipson, Mart Rannut, and Tove Skutnabb-Kangas agree that language differences themselves rarely lead to ethnic conflict. A lack of linguistic rights, however, is "one of the causal factors" in some conflicts.[12]

LANGUAGE AND CONFLICT: A SYNTHESIS

Both schools of thought make important contributions to scholarly understanding of the relationship between ethnolinguistic diversity and conflict, but both are only half-correct. The pessimists are correct in pointing out that ethnolinguistic diversity is widespread and that language issues are often contentious. Ethnolinguistic problems do not always lead

8. Henry R. Bretton, "Political Science, Language, and Politics," in William M. O'Barr and Jean F. O'Barr, eds., *Language and Politics* (The Hague: Mouton, 1976), pp. 431–447 at p. 447.

9. Fishman, "Concluding Comments," p. 453.

10. David D. Laitin, "Language Conflict and Violence: The Straw That Strengthens the Camel's Back," *Archives Européennes de Sociologie,* Vol. 41, No. 1 (2000), pp. 97–137 at pp. 98, 99, 134, 137.

11. William R. Beer, "Toward a Theory of Linguistic Mobilization," in Beer and James E. Jacob, eds., *Language Policy and National Unity* (Totowa, N.J.: Rowman and Allanheld, 1985), pp. 217–235 at p. 217.

12. Robert Phillipson, Mart Rannut, and Tove Skutnabb-Kangas, "Introduction," in Skutnabb-Kangas and Phillipson, eds., *Linguistic Human Rights: Overcoming Linguistic Discrimination* (Berlin: Mouton, 1995), pp. 1–19 at p. 7.

to intense, violent conflicts, however. If they did, the world would be a much deadlier place than it is. The optimists are correct in observing that language problems do not always lead to violence. It is a mistake, however, to extract language issues from the conflict equation altogether. Language issues are often important driving forces in ethnic disputes and even in violent conflicts. Three propositions emerge from the case studies in this volume.

First, ethnolinguistic diversity is widespread, but violent ethnolinguistic conflicts are not. This is not to say that language issues are unimportant or that they are usually resolved through the application of sweet reason. Many language issues are highly contentious. They often evolve into vigorous disputes in local and national politics. Most of these disputes, however, do not result in armed conflict. Many are resolved through normal political processes and compromise formulas. As a result, high levels of ethnolinguistic diversity have not led to widespread ethnolinguistic violence in India, Indonesia, Malaysia, Papua New Guinea, the Philippines, Singapore, and Thailand, for example.

Second, language issues are rarely the sole driving forces behind violent ethnic conflicts. Most violent ethnic conflicts are primarily contests over other issues: political power, economic resources, and social status. Political leaders and ethnic entrepreneurs often highlight language issues because of their great symbolic importance to ethnolinguistic groups; this makes it easier for leaders to rally support for their campaigns. It would be a mistake, however, for scholars to portray language issues as being more central than they really are. Language issues have been prominent in the conflict in Sri Lanka, for example, but even here other issues have come into play. This conflict has also been driven by disputes between the Sinhalese majority and the Tamil minority over Tamil political and administrative autonomy in Tamil-majority areas of the country, over Sinhalese migration to Tamil-majority areas, and over Tamil access to higher education.[13] Similarly, disputes between New Delhi and various ethnolinguistic groups in India have not been limited to language issues. Here, too, political, administrative, and economic autonomy was a key issue of contention.[14]

Third, conflicts between ethnic groups often have a language component. Language issues are deeply intertwined with political, economic, and other social issues. Groups that are discriminated against politically, economically, and socially are often discriminated against linguistically

---

13. See the chapter by Neil DeVotta in this volume. See also Laitin, "Language Conflict and Violence."

14. See the chapter by Jyotirindra Dasgupta in this volume.

as well. And groups that are discriminated against linguistically suffer political, economic, social, and educational consequences. Language can rarely be excised from the equation altogether.

In short, scholars should not overstate or understate the significance of language issues in ethnic conflicts. Some scholars overstate the importance of language issues because they are often prominent focal points in ethnic disputes. Others understate the importance of language issues in ethnic conflicts because these conflicts inevitably involve a range of other issues as well. Languages issues are often contentious issues in ethnic relations, but they are rarely the entire story.

LANGUAGE AND CONFLICT: TYPES OF ETHNOLINGUISTIC SETTINGS

The relationship between ethnolinguistic diversity and conflict is complex. One of the keys to understanding this issue is recognizing that different kinds of ethnolinguistic settings inherently pose different kinds of policy problems, especially when it comes to forging national identities and maintaining political stability.

More specifically, we can distinguish between countries that have unipolar, bipolar, or multipolar ethnolinguistic settings.[15] For the purposes of this discussion, a country can be categorized as ethnolinguistically unipolar if one group comprises roughly 90 percent or more of the total population; by this measure, Bangladesh, China, the Philippines, and perhaps Thailand and Vietnam can be described as being unipolar. Countries can be categorized as bipolar if two groups comprise approximately 90 percent or more of the total population: Malaysia, Singapore, Sri Lanka, and perhaps Laos can therefore be described as being ethnolinguistically bipolar. Countries can be categorized as multipolar if no two ethnic groups taken together comprise 90 percent or more of the total population: Burma, India, Indonesia, Pakistan, Papua New Guinea, and Taiwan can best be described as ethnolinguistically multipolar.

In countries with unipolar ethnolinguistic settings—where one group dominates the country demographically, politically, economically, and socially—the formation of national identities is comparatively easy, and nationwide ethnic wars are less likely to develop. Countries dominated by one group, however, are prone to mistreat minorities because the latter are small and weak. Sins of commission (oppression and forced assimila-

---

15. Categorization is difficult because ethnolinguistic data are unreliable in some cases and because some countries do not fit neatly into any one category. This discussion draws on Michael E. Brown, "The Impact of Government Policies on Ethnic Relations," in Brown and Šumit Ganguly, eds., *Government Policies and Ethnic Relations in Asia and the Pacific* (Cambridge, Mass.: MIT Press, 1997), pp. 511–575 at pp. 521–524.

tion) and omission (indifference and neglect) are both more likely. This has been a problem for minorities in Bangladesh, China, and the Philippines, for example.

Countries with bipolar settings have to contend with only one major ethnolinguistic cleavage; however, they lack the cross-cutting cleavages that are generated by the presence of large numbers of politically significant ethnolinguistic groups. As a result, confrontations between the two dominant groups can become intense, zero-sum competitions fueled by political leaders who pander to their respective ethnic constituencies. This dynamic has dominated political life in Sri Lanka since independence.

In countries with multipolar settings, cross-cutting cleavages make nationwide ethnic war unlikely. In fact, high levels of ethnolinguistic diversity can help to dampen intergroup disputes. In Papua New Guinea, for example, exceptionally high levels of ethnolinguistic diversity have aided in keeping intergroup conflicts localized. None of the hundreds of ethnolinguistic groups in Papua New Guinea is large enough to imagine that it could dominate the entire country, and none has tried to do so. Ethnolinguistic conflict in Papua New Guinea has therefore been limited.[16] In countries with multipolar settings, however, creating national identities is difficult, and fragmentation is often a worry. Forging and sustaining a national identity has been an inherently difficult policy challenge in Burma, India, Indonesia, Pakistan, Papua New Guinea, and Taiwan, for example. Preventing political disintegration has been a top policy concern for decades in Burma, India, Indonesia, and Pakistan. In addition, managing local and regional frictions is an ongoing, massive undertaking in highly diverse settings because large numbers of ethnolinguistic interactions regularly take place in many different policy arenas.

The geographic distribution of ethnolinguistic populations is another important factor in the stability equation. Ethnic groups that are concentrated geographically are more likely to seek regional autonomy arrangements, and groups that are concentrated near international borders are more likely to develop secessionist movements. Secessionist tendencies are even more likely to emerge if groups concentrated near international borders have ethnic compatriots living on the other side of the borders in question; these tendencies are likely to be especially pronounced if ethnic compatriots hold power in a neighboring state.

Most of the fifteen countries examined in this volume contain regionally concentrated ethnolinguistic groups. Only Singapore can be de-

16. See the chapter by R.J. May in this volume.

scribed as having highly intermingled ethnolinguistic populations, and Singapore is of course unique in many respects. Due to the arbitrary ways in which many borders were drawn in Asia, cross-border complications are common. Several countries have regionally concentrated ethnic groups that receive material and moral support from ethnic compatriots living in neighboring states. For example, Burma's rulers have had to contend with Karen rebels, some of whom use bases in Thailand as sanctuaries. The Chinese government worries about secessionist movements among Uygurs in Xinjiang, which abuts Kazakhstan. The Indian government has had to contend with a secessionist movement in Kashmir that has received support from Pakistan. Tamil rebels in Sri Lanka have received support from ethnic compatriots in the Indian state of Tamil Nadu.

For countries with regionally concentrated ethnolinguistic populations, regional autonomy arrangements and federalism are potential solutions to some ethnic problems. Central authorities are generally reluctant to go down this path, however, because they worry about encouraging secessionist movements. Governments in Burma, China, Indonesia, Malaysia, and Pakistan have favored highly centralized political systems for these and other more self-serving reasons. Governments in Bangladesh, the Philippines, and Sri Lanka have proposed regional autonomy packages only grudgingly.

Language Policy and Ethnic Conflict

One of the main arguments of this book is that the decisions and actions of political leaders and governments can significantly influence their countries' ethnolinguistic problems. Many others factors—including the contours of ethnolinguistic settings, historical interactions between ethnolinguistic groups, colonial legacies, and regional complications—must of course be taken into account. That said, government policies are almost always important, and they are often decisive factors in the evolution of ethnolinguistic issues.

Some factors that one might think of as independent "givens" that evolve entirely on their own, such as ethnolinguistic settings, are in fact influenced by government policies. Health care policies affect birth rates and death rates, for example, and government provision of health care can vary; in some countries, some ethnic groups receive better care than others. Similarly, population movements are not always propelled by purely economic forces. Governments often decide to try to change the ethnolinguistic composition of provinces and regions for political reasons. In particular, central authorities frequently worry about the loyalty of ethnolinguistic minorities, and they wory about secessionism in minority areas. Some central governments seek to strengthen their control over potentially rebellious areas by encouraging migration into these areas. These "ethnic flooding" programs are always highly contentious: Minorities correctly conclude that, as they come to be outnumbered in their traditional homelands, they are weakened politically and faced with extinction culturally. Many central governments have engaged in these kinds of campaigns. Governments in China have encouraged Han Chinese to settle in Tibet and Xinjiang. Governments in the Philippines have encouraged Christian Filipinos to settle in tribal and Moro areas. The Sri Lankan government has provided economic incentives for Sinhalese to move to Tamil areas. Governments in Bangladesh have encouraged Bengalis to settle in the tribal areas of the Chittagong Hill Tracts. Governments in Indonesia have urged people to move from Java and other crowded parts of the archipelago to Kalimantan and other less crowded parts of the country. In short, one should not think of ethnolinguistic settings as immutable; they are often influenced and even transformed by government initiatives and policies.

Governments influence ethnolinguistic relations through both general policies aimed at the country as a whole and specific policies targeted at particular groups and issues. The former include decisions about political representation and plans for economic development. Governments rarely make these decisions in an ethnic vacuum. Political leaders understand that decisions about these issues have ethnic ramifications, and they usually take these effects into account. This is not to say that political leaders always look at these issues in benign terms. To the contrary, they often seek to favor ethnic constituencies at the expense of ethnic rivals, and they frequently ignore small and politically unimportant ethnic minorities. Although specific language policies deserve special attention, one should not lose sight of the fact that other government policies also affect ethnolinguistic dynamics.

POLICY OUTCOMES

One of the most striking conclusions that comes from the case studies in this volume is that some governments are reasonably effective at managing ethnolinguistic problems. As discussed above, ethnolinguistic diversity does not automatically lead to violence, although it does have the potential to become highly problematic. Some governments devise and implement policies that address important ethnolinguistic problems and ease ethnolinguistic tensions. This is not to say that these governments are models of goodwill, effectiveness, and efficiency. Many governments tackle ethnolinguistic problems belatedly, and their subsequent efforts are often tentative. Others merely muddle through. Some aggravate ethnolinguistic problems and make difficult situations worse. Even so, some governments have had positive effects on ethnolinguistic problems.

Governments in four countries—India, Indonesia, Papua New Guinea, and the Philippines—have comparatively good records in this regard. India has an enormous population, tremendous ethnolinguistic diversity, and the potential for a great deal of ethnolinguistic friction. The country's democratic traditions and the government's relatively temperate language policies have helped to dampen ethnolinguistic tensions and keep a potentially fragile country from experiencing widespread ethnolinguistic violence. New Delhi's willingness to embrace multilanguage policies and its efforts to create linguistically defined states have been milestones in this effort.[17] Indonesia is another country with a large population and high levels of ethnolinguistic diversity. Although Indonesia's postindependence governments have often been noted for authoritarianism and corruption, they have nonetheless handled ethnolinguistic issues rather well. The government has successfully promoted Bahasa Indonesia as a national language, but it has done so without posing undue threats to minority languages. As a result, language issues have not become highly politicized, even though language and ethnic identity are closely linked in Indonesia. Language has not been a source of great political tension or violence in the country.[18] Similarly, the Philippines has experienced little violence over language issues, but it has had only mixed success in promoting a vibrant national language.[19] Papua New Guinea has charted a radically different but nonetheless successful policy course. Instead of trying to impose a robust language policy on the most ethnolinguistically diverse country in the world, Papua New Guinea's leaders have instead adopted a "nonpolicy" on language issues. The government has not instituted a national language program; rather, it has allowed English and lingua francas to develop at their own pace. This has kept language issues from becoming contentious.[20]

The track records in five other countries—Thailand, Malaysia, Singapore, Laos, and Vietnam—are mixed. Governments in Thailand have engaged in a sustained effort since the late 1800s to forge a strong national identity; development of Thai as a national language has been a central

---

17. See the chapter by Jyotirindra Dasgupta in this volume.

18. See the chapter by Jacques Bertrand in this volume.

19. See the chapter by Caroline S. Hau and Victoria L. Tinio in this volume.

20. See the chapter by R.J. May in this volume.

component of this effort. A national language has been successfully instituted without sparking a violent backlash, but the country's ethnic minorities have been deliberately marginalized along the way.[21]
Governments in Malaysia have successfully established Bahasa Malaysia
as the country's national language, but at a high cost to its Chinese and
Indian communities. The government in Singapore has successfully
created a distinct national identity, but its language policies have arti-
ficially imposed Malay and English on a predominately Chinese population.[22] Governments in Laos and Vietnam were preoccupied with war
until 1975 and have given language issues only intermittent attention
since then. Laos has tried to institute Lao as a national language, but
severe resource constraints have hampered this effort. Significant minority opposition to this effort has also emerged.[23] The government in
Hanoi adopted accommodating policies toward ethnolinguistic minorities during the war—when these groups and their homelands were
strategi- cally important—but it has been less sympathetic since the end
of the war. Institution of Vietnamese as a national language has been energetic, minority languages have not been adequately promoted, and
government-sponsored migration of Viet to minority areas has been
intense.[24]

China and Taiwan are in transition. Beijing's policies toward minorities have alternated between accommodation and annihilation since 1949.
Successive governments launched brutal assimilationist campaigns in the
late 1950s and again during the Cultural Revolution in the mid- to late
1960s. Since the late 1970s, the government's commitment to economic
development has led it to adopt more accommodating policies toward
minorities. Even so, China still bases its policies toward Tibet and
Xinjiang, in particular, on military occupation and "ethnic flooding" programs designed to consolidate and perpetuate Beijing's control over
these remote regions. Beijing's relations with China's ethnolinguistic minorities are better today than they were during the Cultural Revolution,
but many problems remain.

The ethnolinguistic situation in Taiwan has improved far more dramatically. After the Kuomintang fled the mainland and seized control of
Taiwan in 1949, it instituted a harsh, determined campaign to make Mandarin the island's common language. Starting in the 1980s, mounting

---

21. See the chapter by Charles F. Keyes in this volume.

22. See the chapter by Šumit Ganguly in this volume.

23. See the chapter by Charles F. Keyes in this volume.

24. See the chapter by Thaveeporn Vasavakul in this volume.

pressures for democratic rule combined with a growing desire to create a distinct identity for Taiwan led the government to adopt more tolerant language policies. As a result, multilingualism is increasingly prevalent in Taiwan, and ethnolinguistic tensions are declining. Taiwan appears to have turned the corner.[25]

Governments in four countries—Pakistan, Bangladesh, Sri Lanka, and Burma—have done a poor job of managing ethnolinguistic problems. In each case, government policy failures have significantly exacerbated ethnolinguistic tensions and contributed to ethnic violence. Successive governments in Pakistan adopted heavy-handed policies on language issues, promoting Urdu as the national language even though it was spoken by a minority of the country's population and seen as highly problematic by the rest. Many groups saw this policy as one element in a comprehensive strategy of political and economic discrimination. This, in turn, pushed the country's Bengali population to secede from Pakistan in 1971.[26] Although Bangladesh's leaders complained bitterly about language bias prior to 1971, they have adopted highly discriminatory language policies of their own since independence. Non-Bengalis have been marginalized linguistically, politically, and economically. These policies, combined with government programs to gain more control over minority areas, led to insurrectionist violence that lasted from the early 1970s through the late 1990s.[27]

In Sri Lanka, political opportunists among the Sinhalese majority exploited language issues to advance their political careers. Their campaign to make Sinhalese the country's national language became a focal point in Sri Lanka's increasingly polarized ethnic conflict. In addition to its symbolic ramifications, the language issue had material consequences because it limited Tamil access to higher education and government employment. The civil war that began in 1983 and subsequently claimed tens of thousands of lives was not driven entirely by language issues, but government mishandling of language policy was a significant part of the problem.[28] Finally, successive governments in Burma assumed that their campaign to promote Burmese as a national language and to create a common national identity would meet little resistance from minorities. This has proved to be a miscalculation. In Burma—as in Pakistan, Bangladesh, and Sri Lanka—the violent ethnic conflicts that ensued were not

---

25.   See the chapters by June Teufel Dreyer in this volume.

26.   See the chapter by Alyssa Ayres in this volume.

27.   See the chapter by Amena Mohsin in this volume.

28.   See the chapter by Neil DeVotta in this volume.

driven entirely by language issues. The desire of political leaders in Rangoon to establish and maintain strong, highly centralized control over the whole of the country was the overarching problem. That said, aggressive, hegemonic language policies have contributed significantly to Burma's ethnic tensions.[29]

In all of these cases, government policies on language issues and toward ethnolinguistic minorities have had significant effects on ethnic relations in the countries in question. In some cases, they have made difficult situations even worse by exacerbating ethnolinguistic tensions. In other cases, they have played important roles in instigating ethnic violence. To better understand these policy outcomes, we need to examine the strategic choices of these governments, along with specific decisions made about national language issues, minority language issues, and education issues.

STRATEGIC CHOICES

Strategic thinking is inherently difficult for most political leaders. It requires them to think ahead—not just years ahead, but decades ahead. It then entails defining overarching goals and developing long-term plans to bring about the realization of these goals. Most political leaders have shorter planning horizons: In democracies, elected officials focus on pending elections, and policymakers everywhere tend to be preoccupied with the crisis *du jour*. That said, most political leaders recognize the importance of having ethnolinguistic visions and long-term plans, and most make efforts to develop both.

Of the fifteen countries studied in this volume, Papua New Guinea is the notable exception to this general rule. When Papua New Guinea moved toward independence in the 1970s, its leaders made a conscious decision *not* to have a grand strategy or even a national policy on language issues. The country's constitution mentions language only in passing. English and the leading lingua francas (Tokpisin and Hiri Motu) are widely used, along with hundreds of local vernaculars. The rationale for adopting this approach was conflict avoidance: Papua New Guinea's leaders feared that, if they took a strong stand on national language and language-use questions, they would aggravate problems that did not require immediate action. It was better, they reasoned, to allow lingua francas to develop on their own. Although they did not implement a slew of government-sponsored programs on language issues, Papua New Guinea's leaders nonetheless made a strategic choice: They made a deci-

---

29. See the chapter by Mary P. Callahan in this volume.

sion to adopt a nonpolicy on language and to wait and see how ethnolinguistic developments would unfold.[30]

Political leaders who seek to develop more concrete ethnolinguistic strategies have to make two sets of choices.[31] First, they have to decide on long-term visions and goals. Most leaders have one of two basic ethnolinguistic visions of their countries: a unilingual vision, where one language is the country's dominant language; or a multilingual vision, where two or more languages are widely used. Ethnolinguistic settings do not determine decisions about these visions and goals. Many countries with considerable ethnolinguistic diversity have governments that have embraced unilingual visions for long periods of time. Unilingual visions are often favored for a combination of strategic and parochial political reasons. Some governments argue, often with justification, that their countries face external and internal threats to national security that behoove them to forge strong, uniform, national identities. Unilingual visions are also favored because they serve parochial political interests. Many political leaders need to maintain the support of specific ethnic constituencies to stay in power. Unilingual agendas often appeal to these leaders because they provide a mechanism for elevating ethnic constituents above other groups.[32]

Other governments, however, are either more tolerant of ethnolinguistic diversity or more resigned to diversity as a fact of life in their countries. Some go far to preserve linguistic and cultural diversity. Some governments are sensitive to ethnolinguistic problems and are interested in making good-faith efforts to promote political, economic, and social justice. One could say that such governments have multilingual visions of their countries.

Second, political leaders have to make choices about the policy instruments they will employ to turn their visions into realities. In broad terms, we can distinguish between policies based primarily on coercion and policies based primarily on inducement.[33] Coercive instruments in-

---

30. See the chapter by R.J. May in this volume.

31. For more discussion of these issues, see Brown, "The Impact of Government Policies on Ethnic Relations," pp. 534–543.

32. I would like to thank Ron May for suggesting this characterization of the problem.

33. Categorizing policy instruments is often difficult: Every government employs combinations of coercive and persuasive instruments; some governments employ different instruments with respect to different ethnic groups; and some governments favor different types of instruments at different times.

clude legal prohibitions, political repression, economic pressure, the imposition of martial law, and the use of military force. Policies based on inducement rely primarily on persuasion, co-optation, and the extension of political, economic, and educational opportunities. Coercion is often favored as a policy instrument in the ethnic arena. Authoritarian regimes, by definition, depend on the use of coercion and force, and they rarely hesitate to use it against what they see as ethnic troublemakers. Even in nonauthoritarian settings, governments often see coercion and military force as quick and permanent solutions to ethnic problems, especially when problems drag on or intensify.

Ethnolinguistic settings and ethnolinguistic problems vary considerably from country to country, so it is not surprising that there is no single, simple policy formula that policymakers everywhere should employ. That said, three general, strategic guidelines can be derived from the experiences of the countries studied in this volume.

First, governments that have embraced tolerant, inclusive, multilingual visions have generally fared better than those that have tried to impose hegemonic, exclusive, unilingual visions on their countries. Papua New Guinea and India have the best track records in this regard. As discussed above, Papua New Guinea's leaders made a conscious decision not to impose any particular ethnolinguistic vision on the country. They decided, in effect, to let nature take its course and to let a thousand ethnolinguistic flowers bloom. Political leaders in India, however, made a conscious decision to embrace a multilinguistic vision that allowed for multiple languages to be used in government and in schools, with specific language usage to vary from state to state. New Delhi's willingness to create linguistically defined states (belated and grudging, in some cases) helped to defuse ethnolinguistic tensions in many different parts of the country. India's implementation of this multilinguistic vision has helped to stabilize the country while providing opportunities for ethnolinguistic minorities to survive and even thrive as groups.[34] Singapore has officially embraced a form of civic nationalism that tolerates and even promotes the use of several languages, but its imposition of Malay and English on a predominantly Chinese population has not given great weight to the linguistic preferences of the public.[35]

Ethnolinguistic tensions in Taiwan eased considerably starting in the 1980s precisely because the central government began to abandon the aggressive, unilingual, assimilationist agenda it had instituted in 1949. The

---

34. See the chapter by Jyotirindra Dasgupta in this volume.

35. See the chapter by Šumit Ganguly in this volume.

adoption of more inclusive, tolerant policies toward the use of other languages has helped to defuse tensions that had been mounting among the
island's large, non-Mandarin groups. Ethnolinguistic tensions have also
eased in China due to a similar policy shift starting in the late 1970s. The
situation in Taiwan has improved more dramatically, however, because
its embrace of multilingualism has been more enthusiastic and because
political power in Taipei is now being shared more widely among the
country's main ethnolinguistic groups. Although Beijing has become
more relaxed about the use of minority languages in minority areas, it is
still committed to retaining political control over these regions, and the
government is Beijing is still dominated by Han Chinese. In short, language policy in Taiwan has undergone a transformation, and this dramatic policy change has brought about a substantial improvement in
ethnolinguistic relations. Policy changes in China have been more limited, and the policy benefits have been correspondingly modest.[36]

Other governments have adopted hybrid linguistic visions, and these
approaches have worked reasonably well. Governments in Indonesia
have worked energetically since independence to establish Bahasa Indonesia as the country's single national language, but they have not tried to
eliminate other languages or vernaculars. Instead, Bahasa Indonesia has
been added to the country's ethnolinguistic equation. In addition, Bahasa
Indonesia is seen as ethnically neutral; it does not privilege any one
ethnolinguistic group above the rest. This effort has consequently been a
policy success.[37] Governments in the Philippines have also tried to create
and institute a widely used national language, but with less success. The
national language project first tried to institute Pilipino as the country's
national language. Pilipino is based on Tagalog, however, and other
groups resented an initiative that gave important advantages to one
ethnolinguistic group. The national language was reconstituted in a more
inclusive form, Filipino, in the 1970s. The national language project has
subsequently been more successful. Although Manila has worked for decades to establish Pilipino/Filipino as a national language, it has not engaged in concerted efforts to eliminate minority languages. Its approach,
in short, has contained elements of both unilingualism and multilingualism.[38] Hanoi has labored for decades to promote Vietnamese as
the country's one and only national language, but it has also called for
the protection of minority languages. Unfortunately, these official decla-

---

36. See the chapters by June Teufel Dreyer in this volume.

37. See the chapter by Jacques Bertrand in this volume.

38. See the chapter by Caroline S. Hau and Victoria L. Tinio in this volume.

rations of support for minority languages have not been matched by sustained, energetic implementation efforts. In short, Hanoi's promises to support multilingualism have not been fully realized in practice.[39]

Many governments have embraced strict unilingual visions and worked to enshrine one language in a privileged national position. Minority languages have often been neglected or actively suppressed over the courses of these campaigns. The vast majority of these countries—Bangladesh, Burma, China, Laos, Malaysia, Pakistan, Sri Lanka, and Taiwan (until the mid-1980s)—have seen ethnolinguistic tensions rise as a result. Aggressive assimilationist policies often generate political backlashes among targeted minorities. As discussed above, the irony is that aggressive assimilationist campaigns are often counterproductive: Instead of generating ethnic harmony and national unity, they produce the opposite—minority mobilization and secessionist action.

A second strategic guideline that can be derived from the experiences of the countries studied in this volume is that inducement is more effective than coercion. Governments that have relied on persuasive policy instruments have generally fared better than those that have tried to impose their linguistic visions on unreceptive populations. India, Indonesia, Papua New Guinea, and the Philippines have all emphasized carrots over sticks, and they have experienced relatively few ethnolinguistic problems. Significantly, governments in Indonesia and Thailand have successfully established national languages under difficult circumstances; their reliance on inducement has been one of the keys to these policy successes. Taiwan's shift in the 1980s was not just a change in policy goals; it also involved a move away from the coercive policy approaches that Taipei had employed since 1949. This move contributed to the improvement in ethnolinguistic relations in Taiwan that began in the 1980s.

Governments that have relied heavily on coercion—Bangladesh, Burma, China, Laos, Malaysia, Pakistan, Singapore, Sri Lanka, and Vietnam—have experienced higher levels of ethnolinguistic tension because coercion creates more problems than it solves. Contrary to what policymakers hope and expect, coercive instruments rarely produce quick or permanent settlements to ethnolinguistic problems. Military clashes with ethnic minorities can degenerate into armed conflicts that last for decades. When governments employ coercive instruments, ethnic groups become more radicalized, and the prospects for political accommodation and conflict resolution consequently dim. Sadly but inevitably, governments usually take a long time to admit publicly that their coercive ef-

---

39. See the chapter by Thaveeporn Vasavakul in this volume.

forts have failed. Indeed, many governments are never able to take this step: It often takes a change in government before mistakes can be acknowledged, sunk costs can be set aside, and peace initiatives can be launched.

A third strategic guideline is that one particular strategic option—the combination of unilingual visions with coercive policy instruments—is particularly problematic. It is not a coincidence that, of the fifteen countries studied in this volume, the four with the most troubled ethnolinguistic histories—Bangladesh, Burma, Pakistan, and Sri Lanka—all adopted this policy package. The other four countries that went down this path—China, Laos, Malaysia, and Taiwan (until the mid-1980s)—experienced many problems as well. The reasons for this are easy to understand. The pursuit of unilingual goals leads governments to either assimilate or dominate ethnic minorities. Assimilation is a highly contentious undertaking even if it is pursued slowly and through inducement: It nonetheless threatens minorities with political diminishment and cultural extinction. Utilizing coercive policy instruments compounds the problem: It radicalizes minorities and stiffens resistance. Unless overwhelming force is used against small, weak, isolated minorities, long conflicts are likely to result.

One of the troubling conclusions that flows from this analysis is that if some governments do indeed tend to favor both unilingual visions (for national unity reasons or parochial political reasons) and coercive instruments (because of authoritarian impulses or misguided beliefs about the efficacy of force), then there is a tendency for some governments to gravitate toward their least salubrious strategic option. A categorization of the countries studied in this volume provides some support for this hypothesis. (See Table 14.1.) A related conclusion is that the most promising strategic option is the simultaneous adoption of inclusive, tolerant, multilingual goals and the pursuit of these goals through inducement and persuasive policy instruments. Embracing this option requires policymakers to have a long-term perspective on ethnolinguistic problems and a tolerance for slow, incremental policy progress. Unfortunately, as discussed above, governments often have powerful short-term incentives to do the opposite.

NATIONAL LANGUAGE ISSUES

Some of the most important decisions that governments make about language policies are national language decisions. In countries emerging from colonial rule, these decisions are usually made in the lead-up to or at independence, and they are often enshrined in constitutions. These early decisions frame language questions in these countries for years and

Table 14.1. Ethnolinguistic Strategies.

	Persuasive Instruments	Coercive Instruments
Unilingual Goals	Thailand	Bangladesh Burma China (until late 1970s) Laos Malaysia Pakistan Sri Lanka (until late 1970s) Taiwan (until mid-1980s)
Mixed Goals	Indonesia Philippines	China (since late 1970s) Vietnam
Multilingual Goals	India Papua New Guinea Taiwan (since mid-1980s)	Singapore Sri Lanka (since late 1970s)

NOTE: Categorizing government policies in this manner is inherently difficult. Some policies do not fit neatly into any one category, and some policies change over time. Classification inevitably simplifies complex situations. It is nonetheless useful to make some broad distinctions between different kinds of government policies.

    These categorizations are my own. The other contributors to this volume may not agree with them, and they should not be held accountable for them.

even decades to come. Their effects are widespread and long-lasting. Even if national language decisions are made later in a country's postindependence history or if they are revisited from time to time, they stand out as exceptionally important policy milestones.

Contrary to what one might think, the process of making national language decisions is complicated. There is much more to establishing a national language that picking one out and making a public declaration about its new status. As Charles Keyes observes, it is a multistep process.[40]

First, political leaders have to decide if a national language should be established. They have to weigh the advantages of having a national language (the promotion of national unity and the facilitation of political, economic, and social interactions) against the disadvantages (possible backlashes from ethnolinguistic minorities). Although national governments generally have the overarching goal of preserving the political unity and territorial integrity of their countries, many political leaders

---

40. The following is based on the analysis by Charles F. Keyes in this volume.

look at these issues primarily in parochial terms. For them, national language policies are mechanisms for facilitating centralized control over their countries and for rewarding ethnic constituencies. These cost-benefit calculations do not always put national interests first.

Second, if political leaders decide to establish a national language, they have to determine how many languages should have this status and which languages will be so designated. Although this is a relatively straightforward process in countries dominated by one ethnolinguistic group (e.g., Bangladesh, China, and Thailand), it is a much more complicated and contentious issue in countries where the ethnolinguistic picture is complex (e.g., India, Indonesia, Pakistan, Papua New Guinea, Singapore, and Taiwan). It is particularly contentious when ethnolinguistic minorities are large and highly sensitive to being treated as second-class citizens (e.g., Sri Lanka).

Third, political leaders have to make decisions about the specific roles and functions national languages will play. This is rarely a simple matter because designated national languages are often not spoken or understood by ethnolinguistic minorities. Decisions have to be made about how national languages will be used in government—not just in national parliaments but in local government agencies, courts, and police forces. Decisions also have to be made about language use in schools: Will national languages be the sole languages of instruction in schools? Will other languages and vernaculars be given an equal footing? Will other languages and vernaculars be used only in early primary education as bridges to instruction in national languages? Will any of these policies vary from region to region?

Finally, national language decisions have to be implemented. This is also a multistage process. As Charles Keyes explains, standardized forms of national languages often have to be devised. These standardized languages then have to be promulgated and inculcated among the general population. Those who use nonstandard forms of national languages have to be taught and brought around to use standardized models. Those who are unfamiliar with these languages have to be trained from scratch.[41]

The cases studied in this volume offer several guidelines for policymakers who have to contend with these issues. First, political leaders have to recognize that national language decisions are complicated, contentious issues. Some leaders take it as a given that their countries must have a national language, that only one language can be so designated, that one particular language should be enshrined as the national

---

41. See the chapter by Charles F. Keyes in this volume.

language of the country in question, and that ethnolinguistic minorities will go along quietly and happily with these decisions. National leaders in Bangladesh and Burma, for example, have tended to assume these problems away. All of these issues require careful deliberation. Policy ramifications and implementation challenges need to be assessed. And above all, the concerns of ethnolinguistic minorities have to be taken into account. The process of consulting with minorities will help to build a consensus and facilitate the implementation of national language decisions. It is naive to think that policy answers are self-evident, that policy problems will solve themselves, or that policy opponents will simply acquiesce.

Second, central authorities should endeavor to be as inclusive as possible when they formulate national language policies. They should strive to minimize ethnolinguistic marginalization, which can lead to alienation, polarization, mobilization, and in the most extreme cases, the rise of secessionism. This might entail selecting an ethnically neutral language as the country's national language. This has been one of the keys to Indonesia's success in promoting a national identity while minimizing ethnolinguistic tensions. Picking an ethnically neutral language might not make sense in countries with demographically dominant ethnolinguistic groups (as in China and Thailand), and it is certainly not a panacea, but it can help in countries where political leaders have to strike a balance between the need for national unity, on the one hand, and the preservation of ethnolinguistic harmony, on the other.

Another option is for central authorities to designate two or more languages to be national languages. This is more complicated for all of the obvious reasons, but it provides a way of co-opting and pacifying large ethnolinguistic minorities. It has certainly played a role in India's ethnolinguistic success. After embracing ethnolinguistic nationalism for decades, Sinhalese leaders in Sri Lanka have come to recognize that giving Tamil a national language status will help to facilitate ethnic accommodation and conflict resolution. Contrary to what many political leaders think, giving two or more languages the status and functions of national languages can help to promote the development of strong national identities: Ethnolinguistic minorities are more likely to identify with larger national entities if they perceive themselves to be respected, integral members of these communities. Conversely, they are more likely to feel alienated if they believe that they are being treated as second-class citizens in their own countries. It is a bit of a paradox, but designating a single language as a country's national language is not necessarily the best way to forge a strong national identity.

Third, implementation of a national language policy is more likely to be effective if it is based on inducement rather than coercion. This has been another of the keys to success in Indonesia and Thailand. If the national language comes to be seen as the language of political access, economic opportunity, and high social standing, it will be used and even eventually embraced by those who seek to get ahead. Coercive efforts to implement national language policies and forcibly assimilate minorities have provoked strong backlashes from minority groups in Burma, China, and Taiwan, for example.

Finally, implementation of a national language policy is more likely to be effective if it proceeds slowly, steadily, and incrementally over decades. Crash programs are to be avoided because they are more likely to spark backlashes from minority groups. In any event, crash programs have limited positive effects because language usage changes slowly. National language initiatives are massive undertakings that require sustained efforts over generations. This in turn requires sustained, high-level attention from policymakers as well as sustained, high levels of resources. National language projects require enormous commitments of time, economic resources, and political energy.

MINORITY LANGUAGE AND EDUCATION ISSUES
Even if national leaders ultimately decide to establish only one language as a country's national language, they still have to address an array of minority language issues. The broadest issue on the agenda is the way in which minority languages fit into the "ethnic vision" that national leaders have of their countries and the way in which central governments will treat these languages. There are two main options: "soft assimilation" and "hard assimilation."

At the benign end of the spectrum, national leaders strive to promote or at least protect minority languages. In these cases, national leaders value the cultural contributions that ethnolinguistic minorities make to the heritage and vibrancy of their countries. They recognize that, even if one language is elevated above all others, ethnolinguistic minorities should still be treated with respect and that concrete steps should be taken to promote, nurture, and protect minority languages. This might mean extending constitutional and statutory protections to minority languages and designating ways in which minority languages can be used in government and in schools. This in turn entails allocating government resources—technical and financial—to the promotion and protection of minority languages. This approach toward minority languages could be called "soft assimilation." New national languages and identities are created and placed on top of existing minority languages and identities, in the hope that these multiple linguistic identities will cohabit and endure.

Many countries have made formal commitments to protect minority languages, but they have failed to follow through on these commitments. China, for example, has had elaborate minority protections enshrined in its constitutions, but these provisions have been periodically trampled in practice. Hanoi has also made official commitments to preserve and protect minority languages, but these pledges have not always been reflected in government actions. Indonesia, the Philippines, and Taiwan (since the mid-1980s) have been more energetic in living up to their public declarations to support minority languages, but even in these cases, the national governments have devoted insufficient resources to minority language programs. Because minority groups are by definition relatively small, minority programs are often short-changed when resource allocation decisions are made. In short, good intentions are necessary but insufficient. Even if minority language protections are extended on paper, it is possible that minority groups will be mistreated.

At the other end of the spectrum, some central authorities seek to establish national languages as the exclusive or near-exclusive languages of their countries. In such cases, the use of other languages is strongly discouraged. Minority languages are not given constitutional or statutory protections. To the contrary, they are banned from use in government agencies and schools; they are prohibited for use by the mass media; they are delegitimized by designating them as "dialects"; they are ridiculed by national leaders and in the mass media; and those who use minority languages in public and in schools are derided.[42] The institution of a single national language and the corresponding elimination of minority languages—"hard assimilation"—is the goal. Bangladesh, Burma, China, Malaysia, and Taiwan have gone far in this direction at various times.

It is not surprising to see that inclusive, tolerant, "soft assimilation" policies generate less of a backlash from ethnolinguistic minorities than exclusive, aggressive, "hard assimilation" alternatives. Although large minority groups are likely to be disappointed if their languages are not given some form of national language status, they can often be placated if their political leaders reassure them that cherished languages and group identities will be given the support they need to survive. These kinds of policies have helped to keep ethnolinguistic tensions low in Indonesia for

---

42. Some governments preserve small, token minority enclaves for tourist and public relations purposes. These charades should not be equated with genuine efforts to preserve vibrant, viable minority communities.

decades, and they have helped to dampen ethnolinguistic tensions in Taiwan in recent decades. Conversely, ethnolinguistic minorities are much more likely to mobilize if they believe that their identities are under siege. Threats to group identity and survival generate powerful incentives for groups to mobilize and take action.[43] It is not a coincidence, therefore, that ethnolinguistic minorities have mobilized and agitated in Bangladesh, Burma, China, Malaysia, and Taiwan.

If central authorities seek to elevate the language of one group above others, they should recognize that successful implementation of this initiative will require high levels of determination and resources. Even if they combine this kind of national language policy with tolerance for minority languages, protecting and supporting minority languages will be an expensive, open-ended undertaking. If central authorities seek to marginalize and eventually eliminate minority languages, the costs will be even higher because ethnolinguistic opposition will be more intense.

One way for countries to try to manage minority language issues is to vary language policies on a regional basis, taking differences in local ethnolinguistic settings into account. National leaders who seek to support minority languages will inevitably have to do this, accommodating local language usage along the way.

The most extreme form of this policy is the creation of linguistically defined provinces, regions, or states. The idea is that, if large numbers of a particular ethnolinguistic group are concentrated in one part of a country, a separate administrative province or state can be created, and the language of the group in question can be given a special status within that province or state. This balances the need for national unity with the desires of many ethnolinguistic groups for political structures with which they can identify. The historical record offers some support for this approach. The creation of linguistically defined states in India has clearly helped to dampen ethnolinguistic tensions in Tamil Nadu, the Punjab, the Northeast, and elsewhere around the country.[44] In Burma, Pakistan, the Philippines, and Sri Lanka, for example, the refusal of central authorities to accept regional autonomy arrangements contributed mightily to ethnic dissatisfaction. Contrary to what leaders in many countries argue—usually for self-serving reasons—these kinds of regional autonomy arrangements do not necessarily lead to secession and political disintegration. To the contrary, they can help to reduce secessionist impulses.

43.　See Milton Esman, *Ethnic Politics* (Ithaca, N.Y.: Cornell University Press, 1994), chap. 2.

44.　See the chapter by Jyotirindra Dasgupta in this volume.

This is not to say that regional autonomy arrangements are a panacea.[45] First, they are difficult to implement because ethnolinguistic settings are complex. It is impossible to create regional borders that neatly place every member of one group on one side of the line and every member of other local groups on the other side of the line. Inevitably, some members of the targeted group have to be left out of "their" new province or state. And inevitably, these new entities are not ethnolinguistically homogeneous. Second, although the leaders of ethnolinguistic minorities usually claim to be the champions of ethnic justice and fairness when they are campaigning for the creation of their own political units, they often pursue discriminatory policies once they are in charge of their own regional governments. Many of these leaders are not champions of ethnolinguistic justice; they are merely the advocates of their own ethnolinguistic groups. The creation of ethnolinguistically defined provinces and states therefore solves some ethnic problems but gives rise to others. Finally, the creation of ethnolinguistically defined units can be potentially problematic because it can intensify ethnic identifications and polarize ethnic relations in the country in question. Political leaders who implement these regional arrangements have to monitor these problems carefully.

A critical implementation issue for language policy is education. Those who seek to implement national language policies must devise standardized forms of these languages and then inculcate them via schools, the mass media, and literary establishments. Those who also seek to preserve and promote minority languages face even more formidable challenges. Many minority languages are also in need of standardization, many have no written forms, and many lack terms for modern phenomena. All of these problems have to be overcome if minority languages are to be taught and widely used in schools. These are enormous challenges in countries with limited governmental resources and even modest numbers of ethnolinguistic minorities. The problems become quite staggering in countries with hundreds of distinct ethnolinguistic groups.

Because different countries have vastly different ethnolinguistic settings, and given that different governments have very different ethnolinguistic goals, there is no simple rule for using and teaching national and minority languages in schools. Some governments require the national language and only the national language be used as the language of instruction in all schools starting at the primary level. This of

---

45. See ibid.

course places ethnolinguistic minorities at a great disadvantage in school and, later, in the economic marketplace. Of the countries studied in this volume, Thailand is perhaps the most energetic practitioner of this approach. Taiwan also embraced this approach until its policy shifted in the 1980s and 1990s. Bangladesh pursued a similar policy until 1997, when it made some concessions to minorities as part of a peace package. Other governments allow minority languages and vernaculars to be used for several years; these languages are gradually phased out as instruction in the national language is phased in. Indonesia and, more unevenly, China have adopted this approach. Papua New Guinea allows instruction in 837 local languages and vernaculars until grade 2, when English is phased in as the language of instruction. Some governments allow minority languages to be used more extensively, and some place a heavy emphasis on bilingualism and multilingualism. India and the Philippines have favored this policy.

One lesson that can be derived from the disparate experiences of the countries studied in this volume is that the role of bilingualism in education tends to be misunderstood and underestimated. Bilingualism is misunderstood because many national leaders fear that instruction in minority languages and vernaculars will undercut their efforts to develop national languages. It appears that greater tolerance for local languages and vernaculars—at least in the first few years of instruction—might actually facilitate instruction in national languages later on. Bilingual instruction can provide a transitional instructional mechanism. In addition, minorities might be more likely to embrace national languages if their fears of linguistic annihilation are assuaged.[46] Total prohibitions on the use of local languages and vernaculars in schools therefore appear to be counterproductive in these settings.[47]

Policy Lessons

The overarching policy lesson of this study is that governments need to do more to acknowledge and face up to the policy challenges posed by ethnolinguistic diversity. Denial and wishful thinking are not effective policy options.

In addition, governments need to appreciate that different kinds of ethnolinguistic settings have different kinds of intrinsic advantages and

---

46.   See the chapter by Charles F. Keyes in this volume.

47.   The ethnic dynamics in countries with large immigrant populations—such as Australia, Canada, New Zealand, and the United States—might be different.

disadvantages. Forming or sustaining a national identity is intrinsically easier in a unipolar setting, but paying attention to the needs and preferences of minorities is more difficult because these groups are comparatively small and therefore politically less important. Bipolar settings are perhaps the most volatile of the lot because they are more likely to generate zero-sum competitions and countrywide civil wars. Multipolar settings are less likely to generate countrywide civil wars, but forming and sustaining a national identity is inherently more challenging in highly diverse settings. Understanding that structural problems vary from setting to setting will help governments to anticipate and prioritize policy problems.

Governments also need to make concerted, sustained efforts to tackle five sets of specific problems that undercut the effectiveness of government policies on ethnolinguistic issues: data problems, vision problems, timing problems, implementation problems, and learning problems.

DATA PROBLEMS

Some governments are either uninformed or in denial about basic ethnolinguistic facts in their countries. In Bangladesh and Pakistan, for example, many political leaders have idealized images of their countries as ethnically homogeneous entities.[48] Unfortunately, these unrealistic images form the basis for government policies that disregard the interests and preferences of minority groups. Ethnolinguistic minorities often respond to discrimination by mobilizing, with political tension as the result.

Central governments need to make concerted efforts to ascertain the facts about the number, size, composition, and regional distribution of the ethnolinguistic groups that reside in their countries. Collecting this data once is not sufficient. Ethnolinguistic settings change over time because groups grow and shrink at different rates, and because in-country and cross-border population movements can greatly influence ethnolinguistic distributions. Collecting ethnolinguistic data on a continuing, regular basis is difficult because censuses are conceptually challenging, economically expensive, and politically controversial.

These efforts are nonetheless essential. Even if central authorities merely seek to manage the ebb and flow of events, they need to be well informed about the magnitude and changing nature of the policy problems on their agendas. Understanding the basic facts about ethnolinguistic settings is even more important if governments seek to bring about changes in these settings.

---

48. See the chapters by Alyssa Ayres and Amena Mohsin in this volume.

VISION PROBLEMS

Political leaders need to have viable visions of how ethnolinguistic relations in their countries should be organized. Unfortunately, many political leaders do not have a good grasp of "the vision thing," as a former U.S. president once put it. The problem is a familiar one in the world of policymaking: Political leaders get caught up in the day-to-day business of governing, with periodic interruptions from policy crises breaking the routine. The urgent pushes the important to the side. As a result, leaders fail to define and pursue long-term policy goals. This problem is especially pronounced in the arena of ethnolinguistic relations: Because ethnolinguistic issues are complex, it is often difficult to determine what a country's long-term goals should be. These issues are also politically contentious; this gives leaders an added incentive to avoid them. Devising effective arrangements to manage ethnolinguistic problems is a long-term proposition, moreover. Bringing about fundamental changes in a country's patterns of ethnolinguistic interactions could take years, decades, even generations—if it can be done at all. Political leaders often find it difficult to focus on such long-term undertakings. They are more inclined to address issues that require—and respond to—immediate action. As a result, political leaders often fail to give sufficient attention to the development of long-term ethnolinguistic visions for their countries.

The only thing worse than having no vision is having a bad vision— that is, an unrealistic vision that cannot be realized peacefully because it is fundamentally at odds with the ethnolinguistic facts on the ground. Unfortunately, many political leaders embrace highly problematic ethnolinguistic visions. Central authorities often favor unilingual visions because they worry about maintaining the political unity and territorial integrity of their countries. Unilingual visions based on dominant ethnic identities also resonate well with large ethnic constituencies. Moreover, they provide rationales for strong central governments, which many political leaders favor for self-serving reasons. Unfortunately, these unilingual visions are seldom realistic. Governments in Bangladesh, Burma, China, Malaysia, Pakistan, and Taiwan have had considerable trouble trying to impose unilingual visions on ethnolinguistic minorities. Minority groups have resisted assimilationist campaigns even when the minorities in question have been small and weak, as in Bangladesh and China.

Flawed ethnolinguistic visions can be deeply counterproductive. As discussed above, unilingual visions and the "hard assimilationist" campaigns that follow often fail to produce the strong national identities and political stability that leaders ostensibly seek. To the contrary, unilingual visions marginalize and antagonize ethnolinguistic minorities, which frequently leads them to mobilize and, in some cases, seek to secede from the country in question.

TIMING PROBLEMS

Government efforts to address ethnolinguistic problems are often undercut by three timing problems.[49] Unfortunately, these problems tend to be inherent in the policymaking process.

First, political leaders often neglect policy problems; they hope that these problems will either resolve themselves or go away on their own. This is naive at best and dangerous at worst. Policy problems are rarely self-correcting. To the contrary, if left to themselves, policy problems usually get worse as time goes by. Wishful thinking is not a viable substitute for policy; it is the self-deluding refuge of the short-sighted. Unfortunately, governments often ignore policy problems until they become crises; then and only then do they find their way onto the agendas of busy policymakers. The result is that policy problems are neglected when they are relatively easy to solve, and they are addressed only after they become formidable. In effect, policymakers wait until problems become unsolvable before they try to solve them. This overstates the decision-making dynamic—but not by much. The policy lesson is to engage ethnic problems as soon as possible, even if these problems have not yet developed into deadly conflicts. Ethnic problems become much more formidable once the violence threshold is crossed.

Second, policymakers need to adopt longer planning horizons. In the arena of ethnolinguistic relations, policymakers must become accustomed to thinking five, ten, and twenty years into the future. This is inherently difficult for most policymakers; their planning horizons are tied to the daily press of events and pending political challenges, as discussed above. Many policymakers do not expect to be in office ten or twenty years in the future; it is consequently difficult for them to expend time, energy, and political capital in the short term when the policy benefits—if any—will be reaped by someone else in the long term. The costs of policy engagement are immediate and often quantifiable; the benefits of far-sighted actions are long term and often unquantifiable. These incentives and calculations are inherent in the policymaking process, and they will continue to discourage policymakers from strategic thinking. Wise policymakers will work to overcome these structural pressures. Those who simply react to events will be overtaken by them.

---

49. This discussion draws on Michael E. Brown, "Security Problems and Security Policy in a Grave New World," in Brown, ed., *Grave New World: Security Challenges in the 21st Century* (Washington, D.C.: Georgetown University Press, 2003).

Third, policymakers generally hope that ethnic problems can be solved quickly and permanently. Unfortunately, most ethnic problems are not amenable to quick fixes, and many cannot be solved at all; they can only be managed.[50] Ethnic problems will be facts of life for most countries throughout the twenty-first century. There is no light at the end of this tunnel. The policy lesson is that policymakers must prepare themselves psychologically and politically for the long haul. This means thinking about problems in long-term time frames, as discussed above, and it means making long-term and even open-ended policy commitments.

IMPLEMENTATION PROBLEMS

Even if informed, visionary policies are enunciated in a timely way, they must be effectively implemented if they are to have the desired results. Unfortunately, many policy initiatives collapse at the implementation stage. Two implementation problems are particularly notable with respect to ethnolinguistic issues.

First, political leaders often employ coercive policy instruments—the use of military force, in particular—because they believe that coercion will produce quick, permanent solutions to ethnic problems. This is usually a tragic miscalculation. Coercion generally fails to solve ethnic problems in the short term, and it compounds them in the long term. As leaders in Bangladesh, Burma, China, Indonesia, Pakistan, Sri Lanka, and other countries have discovered to their dismay, escalation is easy, de-escalation is hard, and the radicalization and militarization of ethnic minorities is exceedingly difficult to reverse. Coercion is more effective at conquering territory than winning hearts and minds. Coercion does not lead to ethnic accommodation; indeed, it makes accommodation more difficult. Political leaders often see the use of military force as necessary because they see minority mobilizations as threats to national survival. Unfortunately, military actions usually make ethnic problems worse, political reconciliation more difficult, and political fragmentation more likely. The use of military force is not the solution to most ethnic issues; to the contrary, it is the harbinger of more intense and more tenacious ethnic problems.

Second, many policy initiatives to address ethnolinguistic problems are undercut by crippling resource constraints or misguided resource allocations. In countries emerging from colonial rule and struggling to develop politically and economically, resource constraints naturally abound. Resources are far from unlimited, and difficult decisions have to be made about their allocation. Under these circumstances, central au-

---

50. See Esman, *Ethnic Politics*, p. 261.

thorities will inevitably be inclined to devote scarce resources to large and influential groups, rather than to small, weak minorities. The result is that programs devoted to helping small ethnolinguistic groups are often short-changed. This has been a chronic problem in Bangladesh, China, Indonesia, Thailand, and Vietnam, for example.

By themselves, grand, public pronouncements are worse than useless; unless they are followed by serious, sustained implementation efforts, they can be counterproductive. When policy initiatives are not implemented, when they are partially implemented, or when they are implemented in a delayed fashion, the problems they were meant to address fester, and the minorities they were meant to pacify become more resentful and radicalized over time. In addition, implementation failures undermine government credibility. As a result, governments are even less able to engage ethnolinguistic minorities constructively later on. In short, if political leaders talk the talk, they must also walk the walk: Policy implementation is critical.

LEARNING PROBLEMS

Some of the most common and persistent policy problems in the ethnolinguistic arena are learning problems. Some governments seem to learn little from policy failures or successes, while others learn very slowly.

It is not surprising that political leaders generally do not learn from the successes and failures of others. When other governments stumble, outsiders often attribute failure to the stupidity or venality of a particular set of political leaders or to the structural flaws of a particular political system. In addition, transferring policy lessons from one place and time to another can be conceptually difficult. Many political leaders believe, in any event, that the problems they face are uniquely complex and difficult, and that there is little point in learning lessons from the experiences of others.

What is surprising, however, is that political leaders are often slow to learn policy lessons from their *own* experiences in their *own* countries—even when misguided policies have led to catastrophic policy outcomes. Pakistan's leaders have remained attached to the promulgation of Urdu as the country's national language even though this was one of the factors that led to Bangladesh's secession in 1971. Their continued commitment to Urdu has been an important source of tension between the central government and the country's Sindhi minority.[51] Similarly, Bang-

---

51. See the chapter by Alyssa Ayres in this volume.

ladesh's leaders failed to learn a central lesson from their own experiences as citizens of Pakistan: Discriminatory language policies alienate ethnolinguistic minorities and can contribute to ethnic violence.[52]

The silver lining in this cloud is that political leaders and governments occasionally learn from their mistakes and modify their strategies and policies. China and Taiwan made notable policy shifts in the 1970s and 1980s, respectively. It is important to note, however, that high-level strategic calculations influenced these decisions: China's leaders determined that robust economic development was essential to the country's future; this pushed them to adopt more accommodating policies toward the country's ethnic minorities. Taiwan's leaders gave up the hope of reconquering the mainland and decided that the development of a distinct Taiwanese identity was one of the keys to maintaining the island's independence; this led them to adopt a different ethnic vision of the country and a fundamentally different set of policies on ethnolinguistic issues. Governments in Sri Lanka and Bangladesh eventually revisited their language policies due to outbreaks of ethnic violence. Sri Lanka's government made important constitutional provisions for the Tamil language in the late 1970s and again in the 1980s. Tragically, these concessions came after Sinhalese-Tamil relations had crossed the violence threshold. The government in Bangladesh made some concessions on language issues as part of the 1997 package that sought to bring an end to a quarter century of ethnic violence in the Chittagong Hill Tracts. Painful experiences can lead governments to recalibrate the costs and benefits of alternative strategic options.

The overarching policy lesson here is that the successful management of ethnolinguistic issues is an ongoing activity that will inevitably involve policy shifts and adjustments as ethnolinguistic circumstances evolve. If policy shifts, changes, and adjustments are inevitable, it follows that governments must engage in regular, sustained self-assessment and learning exercises.

This is easier said than done. Political leaders and bureaucratic administrators prefer to set policy directions and then stay on these courses. They do not like to revisit policy issues because this is both time consuming and an admission that their initial decisions were less than perfect. Political leaders and bureaucratic administrators generally like to think of themselves as infallible, and they certainly prefer to be seen as infallible. They consequently find it exceedingly difficult to admit policy mistakes. As discussed above, it often takes a change in government before mis-

---

52. See the chapter by Amena Mohsin in this volume.

takes can be acknowledged and new policies can be launched. Learning, therefore, will continue to be a policy problem in the ethnolinguistic arena.

Conclusions: The Politics of Language Policy

Most of the foregoing policy lessons and recommendations are common-sensical: Base decisions on accurate information, define policy objectives carefully, plan ahead, follow through on policy initiatives, and try to learn from one's mistakes. They need to be emphasized, however, because most policymakers fall short in one area or another at one time or another, and many commit basic policy blunders systematically and chronically.

There are two main reasons why there is substantial room for improvement in the language policy arena. First, there are analytical impediments to better policy. Ethnolinguistic settings are complicated, ethnic problems are complex, and government policies consequently have to be multifaceted. All of these issues are in motion, moreover, due to demographic and economic forces, group interactions, and the effects of governments' actions and regional developments on ethnolinguistic landscapes. Our hope is that this volume will shed some light on these analytical challenges, clarify strategic and policy choices, and provide some guidance for well-intentioned leaders with responsibilities for making decisions about these issues.

The second impediment to better language policy is political: Many policymakers have powerful political incentives to underestimate the amount of ethnolinguistic diversity that exists in their countries—or to deny that their countries contain any ethnolinguistic diversity. Central authorities often have powerful political incentives to embrace unilingual visions and adopt aggressive assimilationist strategic plans. They also have powerful political incentives to seek quick solutions to ethnolinguistic problems; this often leads them to view coercive policy instruments and the use of military force as attractive policy options. Policymakers everywhere tend to focus on day-to-day emergencies rather than on long-term strategic challenges; the urgent tends to dominate the important, and serious matters get pushed to the side. Planning horizons are often framed by political cycles such as electoral calendars. Issues that require longer-term planning do not get the attention they deserve.

Addressing ethnolinguistic problems more effectively, therefore, is not just an analytical challenge—it is a political challenge. The political incentives that frame and shape language policies are not going to disappear, but they are not immutable. The advent of democracy is not a panacea, to be sure, but it does generate more opportunities for group participation in political processes while holding policymakers more accountable for their decisions and actions. Although democracy has proved to be highly problematic in some multiethnic settings, it has helped to dampen ethnic tensions and promote ethnic accommodation in others.[53] To paraphrase Winston Churchill, democracy is the worst possible form of government for multiethnic countries—except for all the others.

---

53. For thoughtful discussions of the problems experienced by democracies in multiethnic settings, see Arend Lijphart, *Democracy in Plural Societies* (New Haven, Conn.: Yale University Press, 1977); Donald L. Horowitz, *Ethnic Groups in Conflict* (Berkeley: University of California Press, 1985); Larry Diamond and Marc F. Plattner, eds., *Nationalism, Ethnic Conflict, and Democracy* (Baltimore, Md.: Johns Hopkins University Press, 1994); Timothy D. Sisk, *Power Sharing and International Mediation in Ethnic Conflicts* (Washington, D.C.: U.S. Institute of Peace Press, 1996); and Jack L. Snyder, *From Voting to Violence: Democratization and Nationalist Conflict* (New York: W.W. Norton, 2000).

Suggestions for Further Reading

Ethnicity and Language: General Works

Anderson, Benedict. *Imagined Communities: Reflections on the Origins and Spread of Nationalism,* rev. ed. London: Verso, 1991.

Beer, William R., and James E. Jacobs, eds. *Language Policy and National Unity.* Totowa, N.J.: Rowman and Allanheld, 1985.

Bostok, William W. "Language Grief: A 'Raw Material' of Ethnic Conflict," *Nationalism and Ethnic Politics,* Vol. 3, No. 4 (Winter 1997), pp. 94–112.

Brass, Paul, ed. *Ethnic Groups and the State.* London: Croom Helm, 1985.

Brass, Paul. *Ethnicity and Nationalism: Theory and Comparison.* Newbury Park, Calif.: Sage, 1991.

Connor, Walker. *Ethnonationalism: The Quest for Understanding.* Princeton, N.J.: Princeton University Press, 1994.

Cooper, Robert L., ed. *Language Spread: Studies in Diffusion and Social Change.* Bloomington: Indiana University Press, 1982.

Corner, Trevor, *Education in Multicultural Societies.* New York: St. Martin's, 1984.

Crystal, David. *The Cambridge Encyclopedia of Language,* 2d ed. Cambridge: Cambridge University Press, 1997.

Danspeckgruber, Wolfgang, ed. *The Self-Determination of Peoples: Community, Nation, and State in an Interdependent World.* Boulder, Colo.: Lynne Rienner, 2002.

Deutsch, Karl. *Nationalism and Social Communication,* 2d ed. Cambridge, Mass.: MIT Press, 1966.

Edwards, John. *Language, Society, and Identity.* New York: Basil Blackwell, 1985.

Edwards, John, ed. *Linguistic Minorities, Policies, and Pluralism.* London: Academic Press, 1984.

Esman, Milton J. *Ethnic Politics.* Ithaca, N.Y.: Cornell University Press, 1994.

Fishman, Joshua A., ed. *Handbook of Language and Ethnic Identity.* Oxford: Oxford University Press, 1999.

Fishman, Joshua A. *Language and Nationalism: Two Integrative Essays.* Rowley, Mass.: Newbury House, 1972.

Fishman, Joshua A., Charles A. Ferguson, and Jyotirindra Das Gupta, eds. *Language Problems of Developing Nations*. New York: Wiley and Sons, 1968.

Fishman, Joshua A., Michael Gertner, Esther G. Lowy, and William Milan, eds. *The Rise and Fall of the Ethnic Revival: Perspectives on Language and Ethnicity*. Berlin: Mouton, 1986.

Glazer, Nathan, and Daniel Moynihan, eds. *Ethnicity: Theory and Experience*. Cambridge, Mass.: Harvard University Press, 1975.

Gurr, Ted Robert. *Minorities at Risk: A Global View of Ethnopolitical Conflicts*. Washington, D.C.: United States Institute of Peace, 1993.

Gurr, Ted Robert. *Peoples versus States: Minorities at Risk in the New Century*. Washington, D.C.: United States Institute of Peace, 2000.

Hannam, Hurst, *Autonomy, Sovereignty, and Self-Determination: The Accommodation of Conflicting Rights*. Philadelphia: University of Pennsylvania Press, 1990.

Haugen, Einar, J. Derrick McClure, and Derick Thomson, eds. *Minority Languages Today*. Edinburgh: Edinburgh University Press, 1981.

Horowitz, Donald L. *The Deadly Ethnic Riot*. Berkeley: University of California Press, 2001.

Horowitz, Donald L. *Ethnic Groups in Conflict*. Berkeley: University of California Press, 1985.

Hutchinson, John, and Anthony D. Smith, eds. *Ethnicity*. Oxford: Oxford University Press, 1996.

Issacs, Harold. *Idols of the Tribe: Group Identity and Political Change*. New York: Harper and Row, 1975.

Kennedy, Chris, ed. *Language Planning and Language Education*. London: Allen and Unwin, 1984.

Laitin, David D. "Language Conflict and Violence: The Straw That Strengths the Camel's Back," *Archives Européennes de Sociologie*, Vol. 41, No. 1 (2000), pp. 97–137.

Lieberson, Stanley. *Language Diversity and Language Contact*. Stanford, Calif.: Stanford University Press, 1981.

McNeill, William H. *Polyethnicity and National Unity in World History*. Toronto: University of Toronto Press, 1986.

Musgrave, Thomas D. *Self-Determination and National Minorities*. Oxford: Clarendon, 1997.

O'Barr, William M., and Jean F. O'Barr, eds. *Language and Politics*. The Hague: Mouton, 1976.

Rubin, Joan, and Björn H. Jernudd, eds. *Can Language Be Planned? Sociolinguistic Theory and Practice for Developing Nations*. Honolulu: University of Hawaii Press, 1971.

Schiffman, Harold F. *Linguistic Culture and Language Policy*. London: Routledge, 1996.

Seton-Watson, Hugh. *Language and National Consciousness*. Oxford: Oxford University Press, 1981.

Skutnabb-Kangas, Tove, and Robert Phillipson, eds. *Linguistic Human Rights: Overcoming Linguistic Discrimination*. Berlin: Mouton, 1995.

Smith, Anthony D. *The Ethnic Origins of Nations*. New York: Basil Blackwell, 1986.

Smith, Anthony D. *National Identity*. London: Penguin, 1991.

Stack, John F. *The Primordial Challenge: Ethnicity in the Contemporary World*. Westport, Conn.: Greenwood, 1986.

Taras, Ray. "Nations and Language-Building: Old Theories, Contemporary Cases," *Nationalism and Ethnic Politics*, Vol. 4, No. 3 (Autumn 1998), pp. 79–101.

Wardhaugh, Ronald. *Languages in Competition: Dominance, Diversity, and Decline.* Oxford: Basil Blackwell, 1987.

Weinstein, Brian, ed. *Language Policy and Political Development.* Norwood, N.J.: Ablex, 1990.

Young, Crawford. *The Politics of Cultural Pluralism.* Madison: University of Wisconsin Press, 1976.

Politics and Ethnic Relations in Asia: General Works

Alagappa, Muthiah, ed. *Political Legitimacy in Southeast Asia: The Quest for Moral Authority.* Stanford, Calif.: Stanford University Press, 1995.

Anderson, Benedict. *The Spectre of Comparisons: Nationalism, Southeast Asia, and the World.* London: Verso, 1998.

Barnes, R.H., Andrew Gray, and Benedict Kingsbury, eds. *Indigenous Peoples of Asia.* Ann Arbor, Mich.: Association of Asian Studies, 1995.

Brown, David. *The State and Ethnic Politics in Southeast Asia.* London: Routledge, 1994.

Brown, Michael E., and Šumit Ganguly, eds. *Government Policies and Ethnic Relations in Asia and the Pacific.* Cambridge, Mass.: MIT Press, 1997.

Christie, Clive J. *A Modern History of Southeast Asia: Decolonization, Nationalism, and Separatism.* London: I.B. Tauris, 1996.

Coulmas, Florian. "The Far East," in Joshua A. Fishman, ed. *Handbook of Language and Ethnic Identity.* Oxford: Oxford University Press, 1999, pp. 399–413.

Diamond, Larry, and Marc F. Plattner, eds. *Democracy in East Asia.* Baltimore, Md.: Johns Hopkins University Press, 1998.

Iftekharuzzman, ed. *Ethnicity and Constitutional Reform in South Asia.* New Delhi: Manohar, 1998.

Keyes, Charles F. *The Golden Peninsula: Culture and Adaptation in Mainland Southeast Asia.* Honolulu: University of Hawaii Press, 1995.

Liefer, Michael, ed. *Asian Nationalism:* London: Routledge, 2000.

McCloud, Donald G. *Southeast Asia: Tradition and Modernity in the Contemporary World.* Boulder, Colo.: Westview, 1995.

Mitra, Subrata K., and R. Allison Lewis, eds. *Subnational Movements in South Asia.* Boulder, Colo.: Westview, 1996.

Montgomery, John D., ed. *Human Rights: Positive Policies in Asia and the Pacific Rim.* Hollis, N.H.: Hollis, 1998.

Neher, Clark D., and Ross Marley. *Democracy and Development in Southeast Asia.* Boulder, Colo.: Westview, 1995.

Phadnis, Urmila. *Ethnicity and Nation-Building in South Asia.* Newbury Park, Calif.: Sage, 1990.

Pye, Lucian W. *Asian Power and Politics: The Cultural Dimensions of Authority.* Cambridge, Mass.: Belknap, 1985.

Schiffman, Harold. F. "South and Southeast Asia," in Joshua A. Fishman, ed. *Handbook of Language and Ethnic Identity.* Oxford: Oxford University Press, 1999, pp. 431–443.

Steinberg, David Joel, ed. *In Search of Southeast Asia: A Modern History,* rev. ed. Honolulu: University of Hawaii Press, 1987.

Tambiah, Stanley J. *Leveling Crowds: Ethnonationalist Conflicts and Collective Violence in South Asia.* Berkeley: University of California Press, 1996.

Tarling, Nicholas. *Nations and States in Southeast Asia.* Cambridge: Cambridge University Press, 1998.

Taylor, R.H., ed. *The Politics of Elections in Southeast Asia.* Cambridge: Cambridge University Press and Woodrow Wilson Center, 1996.

Tønnesson, Stein, and Hans Antlöv, eds. *Asian Forms of the Nation.* Richmond, U.K.: Corzon, 1996.

Bangladesh

Abecassis, David. *Identity Islam and Human Development in Rural Bangladesh.* Dhaka: University Press Ltd., 1990.

Ahmad, Nafis. *A New Economic Geography of Bangladesh.* Delhi: Vikas Publishing House Pvt. Ltd., 1976.

Ahmed, Moudud. *Democracy and the Challenge of Development: A Study of Politics and Military Interventions in Bangladesh.* Dhaka: University Press Ltd., 1995.

Ahmed, Rafiuddin, ed. *Religion: Nationalism and Politics in Bangladesh.* New Delhi: South Asian Publishers, 1990.

Barenstein, Jorge. *Overcoming Fuzzy Governance in Bangladesh: Policy Implementation in Least Developed Countries.* Dhaka: University Press Ltd., 1994.

Baxter, Craig. *Bangladesh: A New Nation in an Old Setting.* Boulder, Colo.: Westview, 1984.

Bhuiyan, Muhammad Wadud. *Emergence of Bangladesh and the Role of the Awami League.* Delhi: Vikas Publishing House Pvt. Ltd., 1982.

Burling, Robbins. *The Strong Women of Modhupur.* Dhaka: University Press Ltd., 1997.

Chowdhury, Mohammad Rafi, and A.R. Mushtaque, eds. *Counting the Hills: Assessing Development in Chittagong Hill Tracts.* Dhaka: University Press Ltd., 2001.

Faaland, Just, and J.R. Parkinson. *Bangladesh: The Test Case of Development.* Boulder, Colo.: Westview, 1976.

Gain, Philip, ed. *The Chittagong Hill Tracts: Life and Nature at Risk.* Dhaka: Society for Environment and Human Development, 2000.

Hakim, Muhammad A. *Bangladesh Politics: The Shahabuddin Interregnum.* Dhaka: University Press Ltd., 1993.

Hill Women's Federation (HWF), ed. *Kalpana Chakmar Diary* (The diary of Kalpana Chakma). Dhaka: HWF, 2001.

Kamal, Mesbah, and Sharmin Mridha, eds. *Parbattya Chattagram: Shonkot 'O Shombhabona* (The CHT: problems and prospects). Dhaka: Research and Development Collective, 1999.

Miah, Mohammad Maniruzzaman, Jasimuddin Ahmed, and Saeedur Rahman, eds. *Parbattya Chattagram Chukti 'O Jatiya Shartho* (The CHT accord and national interest). Dhaka: Boipara, 1999.

Mohsin, Amena, ed. *Ethnic Minorities of Bangladesh: Some Reflections—The Saontals and the Rakhaines.* Dhaka: Program for Research on Poverty Alleviation, Grameen Trust, 2002.

Nahar, Sultana. *A Comparative Study of Communalism in Bangladesh and India.* Dhaka: Dhaka Prakashan, 1994.

Osmany, Shireen Hasan. *Bangladeshi Nationalism: History of Dialectics and Dimensions*. Dhaka: University Press Ltd., 1992.

Pampu, Protim Roy. *Parbattya Ain: Totte 'O Proyoge* (The CHT laws: in theory and practice). Rangamati: Rangamati Prokashoni, 2001.

Quaderi, Fazlul Quader, ed. *Bangladesh Genocide and the World Press.* Dacca: Alexandra Press, 1972.

Roy, Raja Devasish. "Occupations and Economy in Transition: A Case Study of the Chittagong Hill Tracts," in International Labor Organization (ILO), ed. *Traditional Occupations of Indigenous and Tribal Peoples: Emerging Trends.* Geneva: ILO, 2000, pp. 73–122.

Roy, Rajkumari Chandra. *Land Rights of the Indigenous Peoples of the Chittagong Hill Tracts, Bangladesh.* Copenhagen: International Working Group for Indigenous Affairs, 2000.

Syed Mohammad, Maj. Gen. Ibrahim (ret.). *Parbattya Chattagram Shanti Prokria 'O Poribesh Poristhitir Mullayan* (The peace process of CHT and an evaluation of its situation). Dhaka: Mawla Brothers, 2001.

Talukdar, Maniruzzaman. *The Bangladesh Revolution and Its Aftermath.* Dhaka: University Press Ltd., 1988.

Talukdar, S.P. *The Chakmas: Life and Struggle.* New Delhi: Gian Publishing House, 1988.

Tebtebba Foundation. *The Chittagong Hill Tracts: The Road to a Lasting Peace.* Manila: Tebtebba Foundation, 2000.

Timm, Fr. R.W. *The Adivashis of Bangladesh.* London: Minority Rights Group International, 1991.

van Schendel, Willem, Wolfgang Mey, and Aditya Kumar Dewan. *The Chittagong Hill Tracts: Living in a Borderland.* Dhaka: University Press Ltd., 2001.

Ziring, Lawrence. *Bangladesh: From Mujib to Ershad—An Interpretative Study.* Karachi: Oxford University Press, 1992.

Burma

Allott, Anna J. "Language Policy and Language Planning in Burma," in David Bradley, ed. *Language Policy: Language Planning and Sociolinguistics in South-East Asia.* Canberra, Australian Capital Territory: Department of Linguistics, Research School of Pacific Studies, Australian National University, 1985, pp. 131–154.

Allott, Anna, Patricia Herbert, and John Okell. "Burma," in Herbert and Anthony Milner, eds. *South-East Asia Languages and Literatures: A Select Guide.* Honolulu: University of Hawaii Press, 1989.

Aung San Suu Kyi. "Socio-political Currents in Burmese Literature, 1919–1940," in Burma Research Group, ed. *Burma and Japan: Basic Studies on Their Cultural and Social Structure.* Tokyo: Tokyo University of Foreign Studies, 1987, pp. 65–83.

Hla Pe. "The Rise of Popular Literature in Burma," *Journal of the Burmese Research Society,* Vol. 51, No. 2 (1968), pp. 123–144.

Kyaw Thet. "Burma: The Political Integration of Linguistic and Religious Minority Groups," in P.W. Thayer, ed. *Nationalism and Progress in Free Asia.* Baltimore, Md.: Johns Hopkins Press, 1956, pp. 156–168.

Luce, Gordon H. "Burma Languages," *Journal of the Burma Research Society*, Vol. 51, No. 1 (1968), pp. 29–34.

Luce, Gordon H. *Phases of Pre-Pagan Burma: Languages and History.* Oxford: Oxford University Press, 1985.

Minn Latt Yekhaun. *Modernization of Burmese.* Prague: Oriental Institute in Academia, 1966.

Okell, John. *A Reference Grammar of Colloquial Burmese,* 2 vols. London: Oxford University Press, 1969.

Pe Maung Tin. "The Dialect of Tavoy," *Journal of the Burma Research Society*, Vol. 23, No. 1 (April 1933), pp. 31–46.

Taylor, L.F. "Account of the Ethnographical and Linguistic Survey of Burma," *Journal of the Burma Research Society,* Vol. 39, No. 2 (December 1956), pp. 159–175.

Taylor, L.F. "General Structure of Languages Spoken in Burma," *Journal of the Burma Research Society,* Vol. 39, No. 1 (1956), pp. 26–120.

Thein Lwin. "The Teaching of Ethnic Language and the Role of Education in the Context of Mon Ethnic Nationality in Burma: Initial Report of the First Phase of the Study on the Thai-Burma Border, November 1999–February 2000," http://www.students.ncl.ac.uk/thein.lwin/.

Wheatley, Julian. "Burmese," in Bernard Comrie, ed. *The World's Major Languages.* New York: Oxford University Press, 1987, pp. 834–855.

China

Dreyer, June Teufel. *China's Forty Millions: Minority Nationalities and National Integration in the People's Republic of China.* Cambridge, Mass.: Harvard University Press, 1976.

Dreyer, June Teufel. "Language Planning for China's Ethnic Minorities," *Pacific Affairs,* Vol. 51, No. 2 (Fall 1978), pp. 369–383.

Dreyer, June Teufel. "The Potential for Instability in Minority Areas," in David Shambaugh, ed. *Is China Unstable?* Armonk, N.Y.: M.E. Sharpe, 2000, pp. 125–142.

Heberer, Thomas. *China and Its Minority Nationalities: Autonomy or Assimilation?* Armonk, N.Y.: M.E. Sharpe, 1989.

Kaup, Kate Palmer. *Creating the Zhuang: Ethnic Politics in China.* Boulder, Colo.: Lynne Rienner, 2000.

Lee, Chae-Jin. *China's Korean Minority: The Politics of Ethnic Education.* Boulder, Colo.: Westview, 1986.

Lin, Jing. "Policies and Practices of Bilingual Education for the Minorities in China," *Journal of Multilingual and Multicultural Development,* Vol. 18, No. 3 (Fall 1997), pp. 193–205.

MacKerras, Colin. *China's Minority Cultures: Identity and Integration since 1912.* New York: St. Martin's, 1995.

Moser, Leo. *The Chinese Mosaic.* Boulder, Colo.: Westview, 1984.

Ramsey, Robert. *The Languages of China.* Princeton, N.J.: Princeton University Press, 1989.

Zhou Yaowen. "Bilingualism and Bilingual Education in China," *International Journal of the Sociology of Language,* Vol. 97 (1992), pp. 37–45.

India

Basu, D.D. *Introduction to the Constitution of India*. New Delhi: Prentice Hall of India, 1999.

Breton, R.J.L. *Atlas of the Languages and Ethnic Communities of South Asia*. Walnut Creek, Calif.: Altamira, 1997.

Chandra, B. *India after Independence*. New Delhi: Viking, 1999.

Dasgupta, J. *Language Conflict and National Development*. Berkeley: University of California Press, 1970.

Dua, H.R. *Language Planning in India*. Delhi: Harnam, 1985.

Dwivedi, S. *Hindi on Trial*. New Delhi: Vikas, 1981.

Gupta, R.S., et al., eds. *Language and the State*. New Delhi: Creative Books, 1995.

Khubchandani, L.M., ed. *Language in a Plural Society*. Shimla: Indian Institute of Advanced Study, 1988.

King, R.D. *Nehru and the Language Politics of India*. Delhi: Oxford University Press, 1997.

Weinstein, B., ed. *Language Policy and Political Development*. Norwood, N.J.: Ablex, 1990.

Indonesia

Anwar, Khaidir. *Indonesian: The Development and Use of a National Language*. Yogyakarta: Gadjah Mada University Press, 1985.

Errington, James J. *Shifting Languages: Interaction and Identity in Javanese Indonesia*. Cambridge: Cambridge University Press, 1998.

Errington, Joseph S. "Continuity and Change in Indonesian Language Development," *Journal of Asian Studies*, Vol. 45, No. 2 (May 1986).

Heryanto, Ariel. *Language of Development and Development of Language: The Case of Indonesia*. Canberra, Australian Capital Territory: Department of Linguistics, Research School of Pacific and Asian Studies, Australian National University, 1995.

Keane, Webb. "Knowing One's Place: National Language and the Idea of the Local in Eastern Indonesia," *Cultural Anthropology*, Vol. 12, No. 1 (February 1997).

Leigh, Barbara. "Making the Indonesian State: The Role of School Texts," *Review of Indonesian and Malaysian Affairs*, Vol. 25 , No. 1 (Winter 1991).

Mackie, J.A.C. *The Chinese in Indonesia*. Melbourne, Victoria: Nelson, in association with the Australian Institute of International Affairs, 1976.

Moeliono, Anton. "The First Efforts to Promote and Develop Indonesian," in Joshua Fishman, ed. *The Earliest Stage of Language Planning: The "First Congress" Phenomenon*. Berlin: Mouton de Gruyter, 1993.

Nababan, P.W.J. "Language in Education: The Case of Indonesia," *International Review of Education/Internationale Zeitschrift für Erziehungswissenschaft/Revue Internationale de pédagogie*, Vol. 37, No. 1 (1991).

Nababan, P.W.J., Erwina Burhanudin, Tony Rachmadie et al. *Survei Kedwibahasaan Di Indonesia* (Survey on bilingualism in Indonesia). Jakarta: Pusat Pembinaan dan Pengembangan Bahasa, Departemen Pendidikan dan Kebuyaan, 1992.

Van der Veur, Paul. *Education and Social Change in Colonial Indonesia,* Papers in International Studies, Southeast Asia Series No. 12. Athens: Southeast Asia Program, Ohio University Center for International Studies, 1969.

Malaysia

Gladney, Dru C. *Making Majorities: Constituting the Nation in Japan, Korea, China, Malaysia, Fiji, Turkey, and the United States.* Stanford, Calif.: Stanford University Press, 1998.

Harper, Timothy Norman. *The End of Empire and the Making of Modern Malaya.* Cambridge: Cambridge University Press, 1999.

Milne, R.S., and Diane K. Mauzy. *Malaysian Politics under Mahathir.* London: Routledge, 1999.

Nesiah, Devanesan. *Discrimination with Reason? The Policy of Reservations in the United States, India, and Malaysia.* Delhi: Oxford University Press, 1997.

Roff, William R. *The Origins of Malay Nationalism,* 2d ed. Kuala Lumpur: Oxford University Press, 1994.

Vorys, Karl von. *Democracy without Consensus: Communalism and Political Stability in Malaysia.* Kuala Lumpur: Oxford University Press, 1976.

Pakistan

Ahmad, Aijaz. "In the Mirror of Urdu: Recompositions of Nation and Community, 1947–65," in Ahmad, *Lineages of the Present: Political Essays.* Delhi: Tulika Press, 1996 [1993].

Ahmed, Samina. "Centralization, Authoritarianism, and the Mismanagement of Ethnic Relations in Pakistan," in Michael E. Brown and Šumit Ganguly, eds. *Government Policies and Ethnic Relations in Asia and the Pacific,* Cambridge, Mass.: MIT Press, 1997, pp. 83–127.

Geijbels, M., and Joseph S. Addleton. *The Rise and Development of Urdu and the Importance of Regional Languages in Pakistan.* Murree: Christian Study Centre, 198? (year as it appears in the original).

Jahan, Rounaq. *Pakistan: Failure in National Integration.* Dhaka: Oxford University Press, 1973.

Jalibi, Jamil. *Qaumi zaban: yak jihati, nafaz, aur masa'il* (National language: unity, promulgation, and problems). Islamabad: Muqtadirah-yi-Qaumi Zaban, 1989.

Jilani, Kamran. *Qaumiyyat ki tashkil aur Urdu zaban* (The formation of nationality and the Urdu language). Islamabad: Muqtadirah-yi-Qaumi Zaban, 1992.

Oldenburg, Philip. "'A Place Insufficiently Imagined': Language, Belief, and the Pakistan Crisis of 1971," *Journal of Asian Studies,* Vol. 44, No. 4 (August 1985), pp. 711–733.

Rahman, Tariq. *The History of the Urdu-English Controversy.* Series: *Silsilah-yi matbu'at-I Muqtadirah-yi Qaumi Zaban.* Islamabad: National Language Authority, 1996.

Rahman, Tariq. *Language and Politics in Pakistan.* Karachi: Oxford University Press, 1996.

Rahman, Tariq. *Language, Education, and Culture.* Islamabad: Oxford University Press and Sustainable Development Policy Institute, 1999.

Rahman, Tariq. *Language, Ideology, and Power: Language-Learning among the Muslims of Pakistan and North India.* Karachi: Oxford University Press, 2002.

Rahman, Tariq. "Language Policy in Pakistan," *Ethnic Studies Report,* Vol. 14, No. 1 (January 1996).

Rahman, Tariq. "Language, Politics, and Power in Pakistan: The Case of Sindh and Sindhi," *Ethnic Studies Report,* Vol. 17, No. 1 (January 1999).

Rahman, Tariq. "The Pashto Language and Identity-Formation in Pakistan," *Contemporary South Asia,* Vol. 4, No. 2 (Spring 1995), pp. 151–170.

Rahman, Tariq. "The Sindhi Language Movement and the Politics of Sind," *Ethnic Studies Report,* Vol. 14, No. 1 (January 1996).

Rahman, Tariq. "The Siraiki Movement in Pakistan," *Language Problems and Language Planning,* Vol. 19, No. 1 (Spring 1995).

Rashid, Abbas, and Farida Shaheed. *Pakistan: Ethno-Politics and Contending Elites.* United Nations Research Institute on Social Development Discussion Paper No. 45. Geneva: UNRISD, 1993.

Papua New Guinea

Bell, Henry L. "New Guinea Pidgin Teaching: Pidgin and the Army—An Example of Pidgin in a Technically-Oriented Environment," in Steven A. Wurm, ed. *Language, Culture, Society, and the Modern World,* Pacific Linguistics Series C–No. 40, Vol. 3. Canberra, Australian Capital Territory: Department of Linguistics, Research School of Pacific Studies, Australian National University, 1977.

Delpit, L.D., and Graeme Kemelfield. *An Evaluation of the Viles Tok Ples Skul Scheme in the North Solomons Province,* Educational Research Unit Report 51. Port Moresby: University of Papua New Guinea, 1985.

Dutton, Thomas, ed. *Culture Change, Language Change: Case Studies from Melanesia,* Pacific Linguistics Series C–No. 120. Canberra, Australian Capital Territory: Department of Linguistics, Research School of Pacific Studies, Australian National University, 1992.

Dutton, Thomas. *Police Motu: Lena Sivarai.* Port Moresby: University of Papua New Guinea Press, 1985.

Hull, Brian. "The Use of Pidgin in the House of Assembly," *Journal of the Papua and New Guinea Society,* Vol. 2, No. 1 (1968), pp. 22–25.

Johnson, R.K. "Language and Education in Papua New Guinea: Policies and Options," in John Brammall and R.J. May, eds. *Education in Melanesia.* Canberra, Australian Capital Territory: University of Papua New Guinea and Research School of Pacific Studies, Australian National University, 1975, pp. 259–267.

MacDonald, B. *Language and National Development: The Public Debate, 1976,* Occasional Paper No. 11. Port Moresby: Department of Language, University of Papua New Guinea, 1976.

Nekitel, Otto M. "Language Planning in Papua New Guinea: A Nationalist Viewpoint," *Yagl-Ambu,* Vol. 11, No. 1 (1984), pp. 1–24.

Nekitel, Otto M. *Voices of Yesterday, Today, and Tomorrow: Language, Culture, and Identity.* New Delhi: UBS Publishers' Distribution, in association with Nekitelson Pty. Ltd., 1998.

Wurm, Steven A., ed. *Language, Culture, Society, and the Modern World,* Pacific Linguistics Series C–No. 40, Vol. 3. Canberra, Australian Capital Territory: Department of Linguistics, Research School of Pacific Studies, Australian National University, 1977.

Wurm, Steven A., ed. *New Guinea and Neighboring Areas: A Sociolinguistics Laboratory*. The Hague: Mouton, 1979.

Wurm, Steven A., and Peter Muhlhausler, eds., *Handbook of Tok Pisin (New Guinea Pidgin)*, Pacific Linguistics Series C–No. 70, Vol. 3. Canberra, Australian Capital Territory: Department of Linguistics, Research School of Pacific Studies, Australian National University, 1985.

Philippines

Bernabe, Emma J. Fonacier. *Language Policy Formulation, Programming, Implementation, and Evaluation in Philippine Education (1565–1974)*. Manila: Linguistic Society of the Philippines, 1987.

Constantino, Ernesto, Rogelio Cruz, and Pamela D. Cruz, eds. *Filipino o Pilipino?* (Filipino or Pilipino?). Manila: Rex Book Store, 1974.

Constantino, Pamela C. *Pagplaplanong Pangwika tungo sa Modernisasyon: Karanasan ng Malaysia, Indonesia at Pilipinas* (Language planning toward modernization: the Malaysian, Indonesian, and Philippine experiences). Quezon City: Sentro ng Wikang Filipino, Unibersidad ng Pilipinas, 1991.

Gonzalez, Andrew B. *Language and Nationalism: The Philippine Experience Thus Far*. Quezon City: Ateneo de Manila University Press, 1980.

Gonzalez, Andrew B., and Lourdes Bautista. *Language Surveys in the Philippines (1966–1984)*, Vol. 1. Manila: De La Salle University Press, 1986.

Gonzalez, Andrew B., and Bonifacio Sibayan, eds. *Evaluating Bilingual Education in the Philippines (1974–1985)*. Manila: Linguistic Society of the Philippines, 1988.

Paz, Consuelo J. *Ang Wikang Filipino: Atin Ito* (The Filipino language: it's ours). Quezon City: Sentro ng Wikang Pambansa, Sistemang Unibersidad ng Pilipinas, 1995.

Singapore

Chew, Ernest C.T., and Edwin Lee, eds. *A History of Singapore*. Singapore: Oxford University Press, 1991.

Chua, Beng Huat. *Communitarian Ideology and Democracy in Singapore*. London: Routledge, 1995.

Hill, Michael, and Lian Kwen Fee. *The Politics of Nation Building and Citizenship in Singapore*. London: Routledge, 1995.

Quah, J.S.T., Chan Heng Chee, and Seah Chee Meow, eds. *Government and Politics in Singapore*. Singapore: Oxford University Press, 1985.

Tremewan, Christopher. *The Political Economy of Social Control in Singapore*. London: Macmillan, 1994.

Turnbull, C.M. *A History of Singapore, 1819–1988*, 2d ed. Singapore: Oxford University Press, 1999.

Sri Lanka

De Silva, K.M. "Coming Full Circle: The Politics of Language in Sri Lanka, 1943–1996," *Ethnic Studies Report*, Vol. 14, No. 1 (January 1996), pp. 11–48.

DeVotta, Neil. "The Utilisation of Religio-Linguistic Identities by the Sinhalese and Bengalis: Toward a General Explanation," *Journal of Commonwealth and Comparative Politics*, Vol. 39, No. 1 (March 2001), pp. 66–95.

Dharmadasa, K.N.O. *Language, Religion, and Ethnic Assertiveness: The Growth of Sinhalese Nationalism in Sri Lanka*. Ann Arbor: University of Michigan Press, 1992.

Dharmadasa, K.N.O., ed. *National Language Policy in Sri Lanka, 1956–1996: Three Studies in Its Implementation*, Occasional Papers No. 6. Kandy: International Center for Ethnic Studies, 1996.

Kearney, Robert N. *Communalism and Language in the Politics of Ceylon*. Durham, N.C.: Duke University Press, 1967.

Manor, James. *The Expedient Utopian: Bandaranaike and Ceylon*. Cambridge: Cambridge University Press, 1989.

Rajan, A. Theva. *Tamil as Official Language: Retrospect and Prospect*. Colombo: International Center for Ethnic Studies, 1995.

Russell, Jane. *Communal Politics under the Donoughmore Constitution, 1931–47*. Dehiwala: Tisara Prakasakayo Ltd., 1982.

Russell, Jane. "Language, Education, and Nationalism—The Language Debate of 1944," *Ceylon Journal of Historical and Social Studies*, Vol. 8, No. 2 (1982), pp. 38–64.

Tambiah, Stanley J. "The Politics of Language in India and Ceylon," *Modern Asian Studies*, Vol. 1, No. 3 (1967), pp. 215–240.

Weerawardana, I.D.S. *Ceylon General Election, 1956*. Colombo: M.D. Gunasena and Co., 1960.

Wriggins, W. Howard. *Ceylon: Dilemmas of a New Nation*. Princeton, N.J.: Princeton University Press, 1960.

Taiwan

Cheng, Robert Liang-wei. *Tai-wan yen-pien-chung ti Tai-wan she-hui yu-wen: tuo-yu she-hui chi shuang-yu chao-yu* (Taiwan's society and language in transition: a multilingual society and bilingual education). Taipei: Tzu-li wan-pao ch'u-ban-she, 1990.

Copper, John Franklin. *Taiwan: Nation-State or Province?* 3d ed. Boulder, Colo.: Westview, 1999.

Government Information Office. *The Republic of China Yearbook, 2000*. Taipei: Government Information Office, 2000.

Huang, Tung-chiu. *Tai-wan yuan-chu-min yu-yen min-tsu yen-chiu* (A study of Taiwan aborigine customs and language). Taipei: Wen-ho chu-ban-she, 1993.

Hung, Wei-jen. *Tai-wan fang-yen chih lu* (An excursion into the dialects of Taiwan). Taipei: Chien-wei chu-ban-she, 1992.

Kagan, Richard C. *Chen Shui-bian: Building a Community and a Nation*. Taipei: Yeu Chen, 1999.

Lee, Teng-hui. *The Road to Democracy: Taiwan's Pursuit of Identity.* Tokyo: PHP Institute, 1999.

Luo, Chao-chin. *Ke-yu yu-fa* (A Hakka grammar). Taipei: Hsueh-sheng shu-chu, 1991.

Shih, Cheng-feng. "Ethnic Differentiation in Taiwan," *Journal of Law and Political Science*, No. 4 (1995), pp. 89–111.

Thailand

Anuman Rajadhon. *Phya: The Nature and Development of the Thai Language.* Thai Culture, New Series, No. 10. Bangkok: Fine Arts Department, 1963.

Diller, Anthony. "Diglossic Grammaticality in Thai," in William A. Foley, ed. *The Role of Theory in Language Description.* Berlin: Mouton de Gruyter, 1993, pp. 393–420.

Diller, Anthony. "What Makes Central Thai a National Language?" in Craig J. Reynolds, ed. *National Identity and Its Defenders: Thailand, 1939–1989,* Monash Papers on Southeast Asia, No. 25. Melbourne, Victoria, Australia: Centre of Southeast Asian Studies, Monash University, 1991, pp. 87–132.

Gething, Thomas W. "The Thai Language as a Map of Thai Culture," in Robert J. Bickner, Thomas J. Hudak, and Patcharin Pevasantiwong, eds. *Papers from a Conference on Thai Studies in Honor of William J. Gedney,* Michigan Papers on South and Southeast Asia, Center for South and Southeast Asian Studies, No. 25. Ann Arbor: University of Michigan, 1986, pp. 143–148.

Ivarsson, Søren. "Bringing Laos into Existence: Laos between Indochina and Siam, 1860–1945," Ph.D. dissertation. Copenhagen University, 1999.

Keyes, Charles F. "Cultural Diversity and National Identity in Thailand," in Michael E. Brown and Šumit Ganguly, eds. *Government Policies and Ethnic Relations in Asia and the Pacific.* Cambridge, Mass.: MIT Press, 1997, pp. 197–232.

Keyes, Charles F. "The Proposed World of the School: Thai Villagers' Entry into a Bureaucratic State System," in Keyes, ed. *Reshaping Local Worlds: Rural Education and Cultural Change in Southeast Asia.* New Haven, Conn.: Southeast Asian Studies Department, Yale University, 1991, pp. 87–138.

Smalley, William A. *Linguistic Diversity and National Unity: Language Ecology in Thailand.* Chicago: University of Chicago Press, 1994.

Thongchai Winichakul. *Siam Mapped: A History of the Geo-body of a Nation.* Honolulu: University of Hawaii Press, 1994.

Wyatt, David K. *The Politics of Reform in Thailand: Education in the Reign of King Chulalongkorn.* New Haven, Conn.: Yale University Press, 1969.

Vietnam

Cam Cuong. "Thai Writing as a Guarantee of Thai Culture in Vietnam," *Vietnamese Studies*, No. 4 (1999), pp. 32–42.

Diffloth, Gerard. "The Linguistic Treasure of Vietnam," *Vietnamese Studies*, No. 2 (1994), pp. 51–61.

Hoang Van Hanh. "May van de ve giao duc ngon ngu va phat trien van hoa o vung dong bao cac dan toc thieu so cua Viet Nam hien nay" (Some problems in language education and the development of culture in minority areas), *Ngon Ngu*, No. 3 (1994), pp. 1–7.

Le Si Giao. "A Glimpse of the Thai-Tay Speaking Groups in Vietnam," *Vietnamese Studies*, No. 4 (1999), pp. 21–31.

Nguyen Huu Hoanh. "Tinh hinh su dung ngon ngu cua nguoi Hmong" (Use of language by the Hmong), *Ngon Ngu*, No. 1 (1997), pp. 53–61.

Nguyen Tai Can. "12 Centuries of History of the Vietnamese Language: Essay on the Delimitation of Periods," *Vietnamese Studies*, No. 3 (1999), pp. 5–14.

Nguyen Van Loi. "Cac ngon ngu nguy cap va viec bao ton su da dang van hoa, ngon ngu toc nguoi o Vietnam" (Endangered languages and their preservation), *Ngon Ngu*, No. 4 (1999), pp. 47–60.

Nguyen Van Loi. "Mot so van de chinch sach ngon ngu-dan toc" (Some national language policies), *Dan Toc Hoc*, No. 2 (1999), pp. 3–13.

Nguyen Van Loi. "Sinh thai ngon ngu va su phat trien xa hoi" (Linguistic ecology and social development), *Ngon Ngu*, No. 4 (1994), pp. 40–46.

Ta Van Thong. "Chu viet doi voi cac dan toc rat it nguoi" (Writing systems for very small ethnic groups), *Ngon Ngu*, No. 4 (1996), pp. 20–25.

Vien Ngon Ngu Hoc. *Nhung van de chinh sach ngon ngu o Viet Nam* (Issues on language policy in Vietnam). Hanoi: Khoa Hoc Xa Hoi, 1993.

Contributors

Alyssa Ayres is completing her Ph.D. at the University of Chicago. Until November 2001, she was the Assistant Director for South and Central Asia Policy Programs at the Asia Society, a not-for-profit institution dedicated to educating Americans about Asia. At the Asia Society, she was responsible for a wide variety of programs relating to South Asia's international affairs, domestic politics in South Asia, and Indo-U.S. relations. Prior to joining the Asia Society, Ms. Ayres worked for the International Committee of the Red Cross in Kashmir. She is the co-editor, with Philip Oldenburg, of *India Briefing: Quickening the Pace of Change* (M.E. Sharpe, 2002), which analyzes political, economic, social, and cultural developments in India.

Jacques Bertrand is Assistant Professor of Political Science at the University of Toronto, specializing in the politics of Southeast Asia—Indonesia, in particular. His research has focused on issues of ethnic and religious conflict, nationalism, democratization, and peasant resistance. He is currently writing a book on ethnic and religious conflict in Indonesia. He has published articles in *Pacific Affairs, Asian Survey,* and *Comparative Politics.* He received his Ph.D. from Princeton University.

Michael E. Brown is Director of the Center for Peace and Security Studies and Director of the M.A. in Security Studies Program at the Edmund A. Walsh School of Foreign Service, Georgetown University. He is also a co-editor of the journal *International Security.* He is the author of *Flying Blind: The Politics of the U.S. Strategic Bomber Program* (Cornell University Press, 1992), which won the Edgar Furniss Book Award, and the editor of *Ethnic Conflict and International Security* (Princeton University Press, 1993), *The International Dimensions of Internal Conflict* (MIT Press 1996), and *Grave New World: Global Dangers in the 21st Century* (Georgetown University Press, 2003). He is also the co-editor of *Government Policies and Ethnic Relations in Asia and the Pacific* (MIT Press, 1997), *The Costs of Conflict* (Rowman and Littlefield, 1999), and ten *International Security* readers, including *East Asian Security* (MIT Press, 1996), *The Rise of China* (MIT Press, 2000), and *Nationalism and Ethnic Conflict*, rev. ed. (MIT Press, 2001). He is writing a book on the effects of political leaders on the dynamics of ethnic conflicts.

Mary P. Callahan is an Assistant Professor at the Jackson School of International Studies at the University of Washington. She completed her Ph.D. in political science at Cornell University, focusing on Southeast Asian and comparative politics. Her dissertation, "The Origins of Military Rule in Burma," was based on extensive archival and field research in Burma in the early 1990s. She is completing work on a book manuscript (based on her dissertation), entitled "Making Enemies: War and State-Building in Modern Burma." In addition to further research on Burma, she is undertaking comparative research projects, including an interpretive study of military museums in Asia and an analysis of military reforms in Asian democratization processes.

Jyotirindra Dasgupta is Professor Emeritus of Political Science at the University of California, Berkeley, where he also served as Chairman of the Program in Development Studies. His work has focused on development politics, language planning, ethnic mobilization, and socioeconomic development, both in India and in comparative perspective. His publications include *Language Conflict and National Development: Group Politics and National Language Policy in India* (University of California Press, 1970) and *Authority, Priority, and Human Development* (Oxford University Press, 1990).

Neil DeVotta is Visiting Assistant Professor of Political Science at James Madison College, Michigan State University. His research interests include South Asian politics, ethnicity and nationalism, ethnic conflict resolution, globalization and its impact on developing societies, and democratic transitions. He is co-editor of *Understanding Contemporary India* (Lynne Rienner, 2002). He has also published articles on Sri Lanka and other South Asian issues in the *Journal of Commonwealth and Comparative Politics*, the *Journal of Third World Studies*, *Pacific Affairs*, and *Asian Survey*.

June Teufel Dreyer is Professor of Political Science at the University of Miami. She has written on many aspects of China's and Taiwan's domestic politics. She is the author of *China's Forty Millions: Minority Nationalities and National Integration in the People's Republic of China* (Harvard University Press, 1976).

Šumit Ganguly is Professor of Government at the University of Texas at Austin. During the 1999–2000 academic year, he was a visiting scholar at the Center for International Security and Cooperation at Stanford University. He is the author of *The Origins of War in South Asia* (Westview, 1994), *The Crisis in Kashmir: Portents of War, Hopes of Peace* (Cambridge University Press and the Woodrow Wilson Center Press, 1997), and *Conflict Unending: India-Pakistan Tensions since 1947* (Columbia University Press, 2002). He is also the co-editor of *Government Policies and Ethnic Relations in Asia and the Pacific* (MIT Press, 1997).

Caroline S. Hau is an Associate Professor of Southeast Asian Studies at Kyoto University, Japan. She is the author of *Necessary Fictions: Philippine Literature and the Nation, 1946–1980* (Ateneo de Manila University Press, 2001) and editor of *Intsik: An Anthology of Chinese-Filipino Writing* (Anvil Publishing, Philippines, 2000).

Charles F. Keyes is Professor of Anthropology and International Studies at the University of Washington. He is the author of *The Golden Peninsula: Culture and Adaptation in Mainland Southeast Asia* (Macmillan, 1977; University of Hawaii Press, 1995) and *Thailand: Buddhist Kingdom as Modern Nation-State* (Westview, 1987). He is also the editor of *Ethnic Change* (University of Washington Press, 1981), *Asian Visions of Authority: Religion and the Modern State in East and Southeast Asia* (University of Hawaii Press, 1994), and *Social Memory and Crises of Modernity: Politics of Identity in Thailand and Laos* (co-edited with Shigeharu Tanabe, forthcoming). He has been the recipient of fellowships and grants from the National Science Foundation, the Ford Foundation, the Social Science Research Council, the John Simon Guggenheim Memorial Foundation, and the Council for International Exchange of Scholars (Fulbright). In 2001–02 he served as president of the Association for Asian Studies.

R.J. May is a Senior Fellow in the Department of Political and Social Change at the Research School of Pacific and Asian Studies, Australian National University. He was the foundation director of the Papua New Guinea Institute of Applied Social and Economic Research/National Research Institute. He has worked extensively on Papua New Guinea, the Philippines, and comparative ethnicity. He is the author, editor, or co-editor of more than a dozen books on ethnic issues in Southeast Asia, including *Micronationalist Movements in Papua New Guinea* (Australian National University, 1982), *Between Two Nations: The Indonesia–Papua New Guinea Border and West Papua Nationalism* (Robert Brown, 1986), and *The Bougainville Crisis* (Crawford House, 1990).

Amena Mohsin is a Professor in the Department of International Relations at the University of Dhaka. She received her M.S.S. in international relations from the University of Dhaka. She received her M.A. and Ph.D. degrees from the University of Hawaii and Cambridge University, respectively. Her areas of interest include state, nationalism, minority, and gender issues. She is the author of *The Politics of Nationalism: The Case of the Chittagong Hill Tracts, Ban-*

gladesh (University Press, 1997). Other publications include "The Civil and the Military in Bangladesh: An Uneasy Accommodation," in Muthiah Alagappa, ed., *The Soldier and State in Asia* (Stanford University Press, 2000); "Towards a Citizen State: A View from South Asia" (Regional Center for Security Studies, Colombo); and "Governance and Security: A Bangladesh Perspective" (New Delhi). She has also published extensively on the above issues in various national and international journals.

Victoria L. Tinio is completing her master's degree in the Department of Sociology at the University of the Philippines. Her thesis examines the use of English and Filipino in the teaching of algebra and social theory at the tertiary level.

Thaveeporn Vasavakul is Southeast Asia Regional Program Director for the Council Study Center at the Vietnam National University in Hanoi. Between 1994 and 1998, she worked as a researcher at the Department of Political and Social Change, Research School of Pacific and Asian Studies, Australian National University. She also taught Southeast Asian politics at the University of Michigan in 1994, the Australian National University in 1997, and the University of California, Los Angeles, in 2000. Focusing on Southeast Asia, her research interests include transitions from authoritarianism and socialism, the politics of institution building, and nationalism and identity politics. Some of her most recent publications are "Managing the Young Anarchists: Kindergartens and National Culture in Post-Colonial Vietnam" (2000), "Rethinking the Philosophy of Central-Local Relations in Post-Central Planning Vietnam" (1999), and "Viet Nam: Sectors, Classes, and the Transformation of a Leninist State" (1999). She received her Ph.D. from Cornell University.

Index

BCSIA Studies in International Security

Published by The MIT Press

Sean M. Lynn-Jones and Steven E. Miller, series editors
Karen Motley, executive editor
Belfer Center for Science and International Affairs (BCSIA)
John F. Kennedy School of Government, Harvard University

Allison, Graham T., Owen R. Coté, Jr., Richard A. Falkenrath, and Steven E. Miller, *Avoiding Nuclear Anarchy: Containing the Threat of Loose Russian Nuclear Weapons and Fissile Material* (1996)

Allison, Graham T., and Kalypso Nicolaïdis, eds., *The Greek Paradox: Promise vs. Performance* (1996)

Arbatov, Alexei, Abram Chayes, Antonia Handler Chayes, and Lara Olson, eds., *Managing Conflict in the Former Soviet Union: Russian and American Perspectives* (1997)

Bennett, Andrew, *Condemned to Repetition? The Rise, Fall, and Reprise of Soviet-Russian Military Interventionism, 1973–1996* (1999)

Blackwill, Robert D., and Michael Stürmer, eds., *Allies Divided: Transatlantic Policies for the Greater Middle East* (1997)

Blackwill, Robert D., and Paul Dibb, eds., *America's Asian Allies* (2000)

Brom, Shlomo, and Yiftah Shapir, eds., *The Middle East Military Balance 1999–2000* (1999)

Brom, Shlomo, and Yiftah Shapir, eds., *The Middle East Military Balance 2001–2002* (2002)

Brown, Michael E., ed., *The International Dimensions of Internal Conflict* (1996)

Brown, Michael E., and Šumit Ganguly, eds., *Fighting Words: Language Policy and Ethnic Relations in Asia* (2003)

Brown, Michael E., and Šumit Ganguly, eds., *Government Policies and Ethnic Relations in Asia and the Pacific* (1997)

Carter, Ashton B., and John P. White, eds., *Keeping the Edge: Managing Defense for the Future* (2001)

de Nevers, Renée, *Comrades No More: The Seeds of Change in Eastern Europe* (2003)

Elman, Colin, and Miriam Fendius Elman, eds., *Bridges and Boundaries: Historians, Political Scientists, and the Study of International Relations* (2001)

Elman, Colin, and Miriam Fendius Elman, eds., *Progress in International Relations Theory: Appraising the Field* (2003)

Elman, Miriam Fendius, ed., *Paths to Peace: Is Democracy the Answer?* (1997)

Falkenrath, Richard A., *Shaping Europe's Military Order: The Origins and Consequences of the CFE Treaty* (1994)

Falkenrath, Richard A., Robert D. Newman, and Bradley A. Thayer, *America's Achilles' Heel: Nuclear, Biological, and Chemical Terrorism and Covert Attack* (1998)

Feaver, Peter D., and Richard H. Kohn, eds., *Soldiers and Civilians: The Civil-Military Gap and American National Security* (2001)

Feldman, Shai, *Nuclear Weapons and Arms Control in the Middle East* (1996)

Feldman, Shai, and Yiftah Shapir, eds., *The Middle East Military Balance 2000–2001* (2001)

Forsberg, Randall, ed., *The Arms Production Dilemma: Contraction and Restraint in the World Combat Aircraft Industry* (1994)

Hagerty, Devin T., *The Consequences of Nuclear Proliferation: Lessons from South Asia* (1998)

Heymann, Philip B., *Terrorism and America: A Commonsense Strategy for a Democratic Society* (1998)

Kokoshin, Andrei A., *Soviet Strategic Thought, 1917–91* (1998)

Lederberg, Joshua, *Biological Weapons: Limiting the Threat* (1999)

Shaffer, Brenda, *Borders and Brethren: Iran and the Challenge of Azerbaijani Identity* (2002).

Shields, John M., and William C. Potter, eds., *Dismantling the Cold War: U.S. and NIS Perspectives on the Nunn-Lugar Cooperative Threat Reduction Program* (1997)

Tucker, Jonathan B., ed., *Toxic Terror: Assessing Terrorist Use of Chemical and Biological Weapons* (2000)

Utgoff, Victor A., ed., *The Coming Crisis: Nuclear Proliferation, U.S. Interests, and World Order* (2000)

Williams, Cindy, ed., *Holding the Line: U.S. Defense Alternatives for the Early 21st Century* (2001)

The Robert and Renée Belfer Center for Science and International Affairs

Graham T. Allison, Director
John F. Kennedy School of Government
Harvard University
79 JFK Street Cambridge, MA 02138
Tel: (617) 495–1400; Fax: (617) 495–8963;
http://www.ksg.harvard.edu/bcsia   bcsia_ksg@harvard.edu

The Belfer Center for Science and International Affairs (BCSIA) is the hub of research, teaching and training in international security affairs, environmental and resource issues, science and technology policy, human rights, and conflict studies at Harvard's John F. Kennedy School of Government. The Center's mission is to provide leadership in advancing policy-relevant knowledge about the most important challenges of international security and other critical issues where science, technology and international affairs intersect.

BCSIA's leadership begins with the recognition of science and technology as driving forces transforming international affairs. The Center integrates insights of social scientists, natural scientists, technologists, and practitioners with experience in government, diplomacy, the military, and business to address these challenges. The Center pursues its mission in four complementary research programs:

- The **International Security Program** (ISP) addresses the most pressing threats to U.S. national interests and international security.

- The **Environment and Natural Resources Program** (ENRP) is the locus of Harvard's interdisciplinary research on resource and environmental problems and policy responses.

- The **Science, Technology and Public Policy Program** (STPP) analyzes ways in which science and technology policy influence international security, resources, environment, and development, and such cross-cutting issues as technological innovation and information infrastructure.

- The **WPF Program on Intrastate Conflict, Conflict Prevention and Conflict Resolution** analyzes the causes of ethnic, religious, and other conflicts, and seeks to identify practical ways to prevent and limit such conflicts.

The heart of the Center is its resident research community of more than 140 scholars: Harvard faculty, analysts, practitioners, and each year a new, interdisciplinary group of research fellows. BCSIA sponsors frequent seminars, workshops, and conferences, maintains a substantial specialized library, and publishes books, monographs, and discussion papers.

The Center's International Security Program, directed by Steven E. Miller, publishes the BCSIA Studies in International Security, and sponsors and edits the quarterly journal *International Security*.

The Center is supported by an endowment established with funds from Robert and Renée Belfer, the Ford Foundation and Harvard University, by foundation grants, by individual gifts, and by occasional government contracts.